THE OFFICIAL GUIDE

Corel DRAW™ 10

Steve Bain

with
Anthony Celeste
Michael Cervantes
Nick Wilkinson

D1401727

Osborne/**McGraw-Hill**

New York   Chicago   San Francisco
Lisbon   London   Madrid   Mexico City   Milan
New Delhi   San Juan   Seoul   Singapore   Sydney   Toronto

Osborne/**McGraw-Hill**
2600 Tenth Street
Berkeley, California 94710
U.S.A.

For information on translations or book distributors outside the U.S.A., or to arrange bulk purchase discounts for sales promotions, premiums, or fund-raisers, please contact Osborne/**McGraw-Hill** at the above address.

CorelDRAW™ 10: The Official Guide

4567890 DOC DOC 0198765432

Book p/n 0-07-213013-X and CD p/n 0-07-213012-1
parts of
ISBN 0-07-213014-8

Publisher: Brandon A. Nordin
Vice President and Associate Publisher: Scott Rogers
Acquisitions Editor: Megg Bonar
Project Editors: Jenn Tust & Lisa Theobald
Acquisitions Coordinators: Cindy Wathen & Alissa Larson
Technical Editor: Peter Cooper
Copy Editors: Marcia Baker, Judith Brown, Nancy Crumpton
Proofreaders: Linda and Paul Medoff
Indexer: Valerie Robbins
Computer Designers: Lauren McCarthy, Mickey Galicia, Jean Butterfield
Illustrators: Lyssa Sieben-Wald, Michael Mueller, Beth E. Young & Robert Hansen
Series Design: Mickey Galicia & Peter F. Hancik
Cover Illustration: William Voss

This book was composed with Corel VENTURA™ Publisher.

Dedication

This book wouldn't have been possible if it weren't for the endless patience and unwavering support of my wife, Wendy, and son, David, who endured mysterious late-night noises, seven days a week, for months at a time.

This book is also dedicated to you—the reader and CorelDRAW user. Without you, books such as this simply wouldn't exist. It's for you that the high-quality information and creative ideas contained in *CorelDRAW 10: The Official Guide* have been written. I sincerely hope you benefit from the comprehensive information you're about to absorb.

About the Author...

In addition to being an author, Steve Bain is an award-winning illustrator and graphic designer, writer, and software instructor. He has worked in multimedia, print, publication design, media publishing, and related communication fields longer than he cares to admit. Steve's intimate knowledge of CorelDRAW stems from having used the software since early versions and from having worked with Corel engineers and product managers in the development of key software features seen in recent releases.

Over the past dozen years, Steve has written more than 1,000 articles on illustration, Web site design, and publishing techniques. His work has appeared in the *CorelDRAW Journal, Corel* Magazine, *Corel User* Magazine, *Digital Publisher,* and **Designer.com**, as well as *Inside Illustrator* and *Inside QuarkXPress.* Steve is also the author of *Special Edition Using CorelDRAW 9, Special Edition Using CorelDRAW 6, Looking Good Online, Fundamental Adobe Illustrator 7, Fundamental QuarkXPress 4*, and *CorelDRAW 8 Type Techniques.* He can be contacted at **Steve@helix.net**.

About the Contributors...

With CorelDRAW 10's thousands of complexities, few people can be absolute experts in all areas of such sophisticated software. In addition to Steve Bain, three key CorelDRAW gurus from various parts of the world have provided their knowledge in their respective areas of expertise for certain chapters of this book. Let's take a moment to introduce them.

Anthony Celeste is a computer programmer, designer, and writer based in Fort Lauderdale, Florida. Anthony is an expert in the areas of digital color theory, Web design, and bitmap filters. He provides his expertise in Chapter 1, "Installing CorelDRAW 10 and Finding Help," Chapter 24, "Applying Bitmap Filter Effects," Chapter 26, "Import and Export Filters," and Chapter 27, "CorelDRAW 10's Web Resources: Introducing Corel R.A.V.E." Anthony is also the author of the chapters "Filling Objects with Color" (CD-ROM 5), and "CorelDRAW 10's World of Color" (CD-ROM 6), available on the book's companion CD-ROM.

Anthony began his computer career working in the financial industry, designing software to automate word processing, spreadsheet analysis, and database management. He is a regular contributor to numerous Web magazines, including **ulead.com, webutilities.com**, and Corel's **Designer.com**. Anthony owns and manages **acdesigns.com**, a graphic design firm that focuses on illustration and Web and interface design, specializing in animation and interactive multimedia design.

Anthony writes, "The process of writing a book can be extremely trying in just about every way imaginable, and I'm certain that the writers themselves get somewhat trying to those around them during the process. So, I'd like to take this time to thank my family and friends for having mastered the fine art of putting up with me during stressful times. And a special thanks to Liz Fulghum, sometimes a coworker, sometimes a competitor, always a friend, and the person who many years ago convinced me to buy my first copy of CorelDRAW."

Nick Wilkinson is perhaps one of the most knowledgeable CorelDRAW VBA script experts on our planet. He lives in Wales, Great Britain—or rather, the "hills" north of there, as Nick puts it—where he works as a freelance programmer, illustrator, and writer. Nick's unique perspective of CorelDRAW stems from being a manufacturing engineer combined with more than 15 years of hands-on digital design and publishing experience. He's been using computers since he was 6 years old, wrote his first software program at age 10, and has won awards in graphical communication.

Nick provides coverage of text and VBA scripting in Chapter 29, "Adventures with Scripts and VBA," as well as "Mastering Text Properties" (CD-ROM 1), "Linking Text to Objects" (CD-ROM 2), and "Resources for Perfect Writing" (CD-ROM 3), located on the CD-ROM included with this book. Nick has also created IsoCalc, a powerful isometric plug-in for CorelDRAW. Check out Nick's work on his Web site at **www.isocalc.com** or contact him at **nick@isocalc.com**.

Michael Cervantes is a freelance graphic artist, a Corel C-Tech volunteer, and a Corel-certified expert and instructor. Along with Corel's own engineers, Michael is a virtual Corel print engine expert. You'll see why in Chapter 25, "Under the Hood of the Print Engine," which he authored.

Originally from Cuba, Michael is based in Puerto Rico. He is a graduate of the Southern Institute of Business and Technology in Dallas, Texas. You'll occasionally see Michael's feature articles on the use of CorelDRAW and Corel PHOTO-PAINT on Corel's **Designer.com**. Or, if have the opportunity to visit any of Corel's support newsgroups or **I-US.com**, you'll most certainly find him there, sharing his knowledge and providing a valuable service to Corel users.

About the Tech Editor

We each owe a debt of gratitude to Peter Cooper, our extraordinary technical editor. Peter—who affectionately became known as "Mr. Precise"—kept us each in line, exhaustively checking and verifying every technical detail in this immense volume of CorelDRAW 10 reference information. Peter's unbelievable diligence and scrutiny held the information presented here under a microscope, while he checked through possibly thousands of tips, procedures, hot keys, commands, definitions, and shortcuts.

Acknowledgments

Planning, writing, and illustrating the chapters in a book is certainly an enormous undertaking for any individual. During the all-too-short process, we've been helped by several key people who have lent their devotion and support.

Thanks to the publishing team at CorelPRESS (Osborne/McGraw-Hill), with special thanks due to acquisitions editor Megg Bonar, acquisitions coordinators Cindy Wathen and Alissa Larson, project editors Jenn Tust and Lisa Theobald (and their squadron of lightning-fast copy editors and proofreaders), and graphic illustrator Lyssa Sieben-Wald. Also, a big thanks goes out to the production and illustration departments. They spent many, many hours laying out pages, replacing art, and making numerous corrections late in the game. The illustrators also produced the beautiful color insert, which took considerable time and effort and is *much* appreciated. Thanks also goes to Peter Hancik for all his work on the 8-page shortcuts tear-out section. We also want to acknowledge the efforts made by our partners at Corel, including publishing program managers Chip Maxwell and Kristin Divinski, and CorelDRAW 10 product managers Lee Gendreau and Tony Severnuk. And let's not forget the efforts of Corel's largely anonymous software engineers, who put their hearts and souls into the development of CorelDRAW over the past decade or so.

Contents

Foreword

With the availability of CorelDRAW® 10 Graphics Suite, it's now possible for illustrators, designers, and professional artists everywhere to add a new dimension of creative power to their work. Backed by a decade of award-winning creative power, CorelDRAW 10 delivers vector illustration, layout, bitmap creation, image-editing, painting, and animation software all in one package. The enhanced interface, improved customization features, professional output capabilities, and support for text in multiple languages simplify the design process—whether you're creating for print or the Web. Included in the robust new Toolset is Corel R.A.V.E.®, a powerful new animation application that allows you to create live effects over time, generate a time line of edited work, create roll-over graphics, and output images to Macromedia Flash™ SWF format.

And, whether you're an illustrator, designer, engineer, or architectural professional, this CorelDRAW 10 reference delivers expert guidance for mastering a variety of illustration techniques—plus all the support information you'll need to operate every facet of CorelDRAW with confidence. You can learn to produce beautiful graphic images that can be used in print and on the Web. Create in bitmap and vector workspaces. Discover new and refined tools to produce awesome artwork more quickly than ever. Learn from award-winning artist Steve Bain through tutorials designed to help you master universal graphics and illustration skills that will be useful for years to come.

This book is a result of powerful collaboration between Corel and Osborne/McGraw-Hill, and many months of hard work from the authors and writers as well as the product team at Corel. Together, these two teams have worked to make certain that professional designers have the tools they need to explore the depths of their creative imagination. Congratulations to all for producing such fine work!

Derek J. Burney
President and CEO, Corel Corporation
Ottawa, Ontario
December 2000

Introduction

CorelDRAW 10: The Official Guide is a resource for all user levels and has been planned and written with value for the reader in mind. This book is structured as both a reference manual and a learning resource. The concepts and features of the program have been explained using common, everyday language and many of the exercises are easy-to-follow and quick-to-perform. *CorelDRAW 10: The Official Guide* is also supported by a convenient 8-page tear-out section that details application default workspace shortcuts, a special 16-page section providing color-specific examples, and a CD-ROM containing supporting chapter files, evaluation software, and other CorelDRAW-related resources.

Who Should Read This Book?

CorelDRAW 10: The Official Guide is written in nontechnical, everyday language for the intermediate-to-advanced user. A special effort was made to focus on the realistic use of features in the program by the average user, but the book also provides a wealth of information for the concerns of the professional digital publisher.

This book can provide you with a realistic view of the capabilities of tools and functions of the program, which you'll quickly discover are often complex and involved. *CorelDRAW 10: The Official Guide* can serve as a navigator through the hundreds of new features added, as well as provide comprehensive instructions on how to use historical tools and features from previous versions.

CorelDRAW 10: The Official Guide is a necessary part of the CorelDRAW 10 tool kit for the following users:

- **CorelDRAW 10 service bureau operators**, who output native CorelDRAW 10 files using high-resolution image setters and who need to know precisely how to navigate the latest output features built into CorelDRAW 10's print engine.

- **CorelDRAW! upgraders**, who have been using CorelDRAW for years and need a quick reference to the new features.

- **Digital publishers**, who use CorelDRAW in combination with third-party layout, CAD, or rendering applications.

- **Production artists**, whose needs range from simple design for handouts and flyers, to involved full-color publications and brochures.

- **Technical illustrators and engineers**, who demand high precision and illustrative freedom from their software and require the greatest degree of control over their digital drawing tools and drawing objects.

- **Web designers and multimedia creators**, who use digital everything to fill the red-hot graphic needs for such things as Internet, intranet, and extranet Web sites, electronic-multimedia presentations, and interactive electronic documents.

Conventions Used in This Book

As you follow the procedures contained in this book, you're bound to encounter terms specific to manipulating tools, using shortcuts, or applying or accessing commands. The following brief list may help define some of these terms:

- **Click-drag**   This action involves clicking the left mouse button and, subsequently, dragging the tool or cursor while holding down the button. You often find this action described as simply a "drag." Click-dragging is often used for moving objects, manipulating control or object handles, or drawing with tools.

- **CTRL-click**   This term describes the action of holding the CTRL (Control) key in combination with a mouse click.

- **CTRL+SHIFT-drag**   This action describes holding the CTRL (Control) and SHIFT keys together, while dragging an object or Tool cursor.

- **CTRL-drag**   This term describes holding the CTRL (Control) key while dragging, which can have different effects, depending on which tool you are using and the action you are performing.

- **Deselect**   Although this may not be "proper English," this term describes causing an object or interface element to be "not selected." Clicking while holding the SHIFT key deselects most selections. In object-selection terms, you may deselect a specific object within a collection of selected objects or nodes by holding the SHIFT key and clicking the object(s) with the Pick or Shape Tools.

- **Marquee-select**   This term describes the action of click-dragging using the Pick Tool and is often used as a technique for selecting objects within a defined area. As you drag, a dotted marquee-style line appears to indicate the defined area.

- **Menu, Submenu, Submenu**   This commonly found annotation is used to describe the action of accessing application menus and further selecting submenus. The first entry describes the main application menu, while subsequent entries describe further menu access with each menu/submenu name separated by a comma.

■ **Right-click**   This term is used to describe the action of clicking your *right* mouse button—as opposed to the typical left mouse button—and is most often used for accessing context-sensitive commands contained in the pop-up menu. The pop-up menu offers shortcuts to commands or dialogs.

■ **Select**   This action is one of the most basic operations you want to know while using CorelDRAW 10. To select an object, choose the Pick Tool and click once on an unselected object to select it. To select an object node using the Shape Tool, use the same procedure.

■ **Shift-drag**   This term describes the action of holding the SHIFT key while dragging with any Tool cursor. Holding the SHIFT key as a modifier often constrains the action, depending on which tool you are using and which action you are performing.

How This Book Is Organized

CorelDRAW 10: The Official Guide has been organized into 8 parts and 35 chapters. Each chapter is designed to guide you through use of Corel DRAW 10's tools. The parts are structured in a sequence for reference and logical to a typical learning sequence.

Part I: CorelDRAW 10 Quick Start Guide

Whether you're just getting acquainted with CorelDRAW 10 as a first-time user or you're revisiting this latest version, Part I is designed to cover the basics. Chapter 1, "Installing CorelDRAW 10 and Finding Help," covers the installation procedure in both typical and customization scenarios and shows users how they may obtain help using the application from within CorelDRAW 10 and using various Web resources. Chapter 2, "What's New in CorelDRAW 10?" provides brief summaries of the new tools and features available in version 10 in *Reader's Digest* style. If you're new to CorelDRAW, Chapter 3, "A Primer on Using CorelDRAW 10's Interface," helps familiarize you with how to use various application and document window components including docker, Toolbar, status bar, and workspace features. To round off the quick-start reference, Chapter 4, "Opening and Saving Files," covers essential file commands for creating and saving documents and templates, using clipboard commands, and navigating scrapbooks.

Part II: Getting Started with CorelDRAW 10

For somewhat more familiar users, Part II covers getting the most from document-related features. Chapter 5, "Controlling Documents and Pages," details procedures for controlling the size and layout of documents, with tips on controlling individual page options. Chapter 6, "Measuring and Drawing Helpers," offers tips and tricks for using conveniences aimed at making your illustration and drawing operations easier and more productive. Chapter 7, "Zooming and Viewing," explores navigating documents and pages, setting page magnification, and creating custom page views, as well as using the Zoom and Pan Tools and Toolbars critical to making your work accurate. Chapter 8, "Essential Object Commands," details all the ways you can select, move, transform, and arrange your drawing elements.

Part III: Working with Object Tools

Part III is a must-read for users who want to get the most benefit from using CorelDRAW 10's illustration and drawing tools, including rectangle, ellipse, polygon, and spirals, and graph paper. Chapter 9, "Basic Shape Creation," offers techniques for creating and manipulating rectangles, ellipses, polygons, spirals, and graph paper using specific tools. Chapter 10, "Drawing with Line Tools," provides detail on drawing and editing lines and paths, controlling line properties, manipulating Béziers, and applying special line effects. Chapter 11, "Cutting, Shaping, and Reshaping Objects," explores Trim, Weld, and Intersect operations including coverage of Knife and Eraser Tools. Chapter 12, "Managing and Arranging Objects," covers ways to examine and organize graphical objects and to use page layers. Chapter 13, "Object Organization Resources," details object grouping, combining, and locking procedures with explanation of copying, duplicating, and cloning techniques, as well as object align and distribute operations.

Part IV: Organizing Objects and Applying Effects

You'll benefit from Part IV, an invaluable resource about CorelDRAW 10's object distortion and special effects. Version 10 enables you to distort, shape, and reshape objects in near-limitless ways, as explained in detail in Chapter 14, "Envelope and Distortion Effects." Chapter 15, "The Power of Blends and Contours," demonstrates use of CorelDRAW 10's powerful object blend and contour effects applied using interactive tools. For advanced illustrators who employ the use of realistic drawing effects, Chapter 16, "Applying Lens and Transparency Effects," demystifies CorelDRAW 10's powerful object lenses and transparency feature. Chapter 17, "Creating Depth with Shadows," explores use of CorelDRAW's popular Interactive Drop Shadow Tool. Chapter 18, "Drawing and PowerClips," shows how to place objects into other objects.

Part V: Working in 3D

Part V reveals all aspects of 3D illustration with CorelDRAW 10. Chapter 19, "Creating Depth with Perspective Effects," explains how to apply depth to 2D objects. Chapter 20, "Extruding Vector Objects," details depth, fill, lighting, and rotation effects you may apply to vector objects, while Chapter 21, "Applying Bitmap Extrude to Objects," explores CorelDRAW 10's improved bitmap-based 3D extrusion effects. Chapter 22, "Manipulating 3D Models," demonstrates how to incorporate and manipulate 3D models, including controlling camera views and applying 3D depth and lighting options.

Part VI: Working with Digital Images

CorelDRAW 10 includes an enormous range of bitmap-based tools and effects as well as revamped bitmap-image manipulation features. Chapter 23, "Using Bitmap Commands," explains all related techniques for working with bitmaps in your drawing, including techniques for creating, importing, linking, editing, tracing, cropping, sizing, and transforming bitmaps. Chapter 24, "Applying Bitmap Filter Effects," demonstrates special effects available using CorelDRAW 10's new bitmap filters.

Part VII: Beyond the Basics

For the professional extending CorelDRAW beyond beginner levels, Part VII is designed to help you master advanced features. Chapter 25, "Under the Hood of the Print Engine," helps you navigate through CorelDRAW 10's powerful printing features. Chapter 25 also explains advanced-level features and options for correctly producing printed output from your desktop printer or service bureau, and includes troubleshooting strategies if problems occur. Chapter 26, "Import and Export Filters," details use of CorelDRAW 10's importing and exporting filters for getting specific types of data in to and from your CorelDRAW 10 document. Chapter 27, "CorelDRAW 10's Web Resources: Introducing Corel R.A.V.E." explains options for harnessing Web-related features, including techniques for creating animations in Corel R.A.V.E. and using the Web Image Optimizer. Chapter 28, "Take Control Through Customization," shows you how to customize your workspace and application. Chapter 29, "Adventures with Scripts and VBA," guides you through advanced-level programming techniques for creating scripts to automate drawing tasks and control your CorelDRAW 10 application.

Part VIII: Appendix

The Appendix serves as a road map to the many resources available on the CD-ROM. You'll discover where to find electronic document chapters and how to view them; example chapter files; and instructions on how to install certain creative components, such as bitmap frames, clip art, digital photos, animated GIFs, document templates, custom brushes, and spray lists.

The CD-ROM

For beginner or expert-level illustrators and publishers who want to control and manipulate all aspects of text, the chapters CD-ROM 1–3 can be invaluable. CD-ROM 1, "Mastering Text Properties," details text-creation techniques, including high-level text formatting, editing, linking, and style application. CD-ROM 2, "Linking Text to Objects," explores the illustrative aspects of text, detailing text-to-path and text-to-object strategies. CD-ROM 3, "Resources for Perfect Writing," reveals the use of text-composition features, such as working in languages and correcting grammar, as well as using and customizing thesaurus and spell-checking operations.

Illustrators and electronic artists who need to apply accurate color can benefit the most from the information in CD-ROM 4–6. CD-ROM 4, "Mastering Object Outline Properties," explains the various ways CorelDRAW 10 lets you control line properties, such as width, style, pattern, and arrowheads options, as well as advanced line properties such as calligraphic, corner, and end cap shape. For expert coverage of uniform, fountain, pattern, texture, and PostScript fills, CD-ROM 5, "Filling Objects with Color," details all the ways CorelDRAW 10 enables you to apply color fills to objects. CD-ROM 6, "CorelDRAW 10's World of Color," explains all the ways CorelDRAW 10 lets you measure, display, apply, and translate color, including detailed explanation on working with uniform, fixed, and custom palettes, as well as working with color harmonies and using color mixers.

Who Is This Book Written For?

CorelDRAW 10: The Official Guide should be of interest to art and design students, digital artists, illustrators, professional designers, World Wide Web site designers, art directors, and desktop professionals—regardless of the platform on which they work. However, while this book is focused toward creative aspects of CorelDRAW 10's use, it should also be valuable to professionals who aren't entirely familiar with illustration techniques, such as those working in the related industries (technical documentation and commercial publishing) and service-based publishing industries (in-house print shops and service bureaus).

CorelDRAW 10: The Official Guide is a valuable reference and guide for users who are currently using CorelDRAW 10 or are upgrading from a previous version, and who work in one of the following graphic design, illustration, or publishing-related areas:

- Graphic illustrator
- Technical illustrator
- Graphic designer
- Web site designer
- Multimedia designer
- Electronic layout artist
- Publishing specialist
- Digital publishing consultant
- Digital artist
- Desktop instructor
- Service bureau operator

- Media communicator
- Engineering professional
- Drafting technician
- Architectural professional
- CorelDRAW 8 upgrader
- Technical writer
- Magazine publisher
- Prepress specialist

What's So Great About This Book?

Where other CorelDRAW books provide technical information or a program reference, they often lack a degree of reader instruction and learning. And where some how-to graphic books often excel in providing techniques, they often fall short when it comes to a complete program reference. This is where *CorelDRAW 10: The Official Guide* has the advantage.

Not only does this book provide users with a complete CorelDRAW 10 reference and comprehensive feature use, but it also fully reveals drawing tips and illustration techniques used by a master CorelDRAW user. By following the full-color workshops, you'll find that this book serves as a practical guide and teacher for years to come.

While bridging the reference-and-technique gap found in nearly all other CorelDRAW books, *CorelDRAW 10: The Official Guide* also delivers in these areas:

- Explains program operation and feature use without technical jargon
- Covers and addresses both Macintosh and Windows platforms
- Provides loads of tips, tricks, and CorelDRAW 10 shortcuts
- Teaches illustration techniques
- Demystifies complex CorelDRAW 10 features
- Covers print and World Wide Web issues

PART I

CorelDRAW 10 Quick Start Guide

CHAPTER 1

Installing CorelDRAW and Finding Help

Whether you're a new CorelDRAW user or a longtime fan, you're likely to find CorelDRAW 10 to be a powerful, feature-packed graphics suite. The term *graphics suite* has become somewhat overused in the graphics industry; but in the case of CorelDRAW, the term fits perfectly. In addition to the legendary vector editor and page layout program, the CorelDRAW 10 suite also includes Corel PHOTO-PAINT, Corel R.A.V.E., Corel CAPTURE, Corel TEXTURE, Corel TEXTURE BATCHER, Corel TRACE, Corel BARCODE WIZARD, Microsoft Visual Basic for Applications 6.2 (an optional programming tool used to extend and automate features in CorelDRAW), Bitstream Font Navigator 4.0, and Canto Cumulus LE 5.0.

As you proceed through the installation process, you may install the entire suite of programs, or conserve disk space by installing only those programs and features that you require. Should you ever need to update your installation in the future, insert the CD-ROM, and the Setup Wizard will walk you through the process of adding or removing programs and features to suit your individual needs.

Before You Install

If you're new to CorelDRAW, you may find the installation procedure to be a refreshing change from that of typical new programs. Corel's Setup Wizard enables you to have complete control over the entire installation process. You choose which programs you want to install and which features of those programs you want to install, while the Setup Wizard keeps you constantly updated on the amount of disk space that your options will require.

The most important things to consider before you install are whether you'd like to go with a full installation of all programs (definitely the best option if you have the disk space) and whether your system has sufficient resources for a complete installation.

Windows Requirements

Corel recommends the bulleted items in the following list as minimum requirements for installing CorelDRAW 10.

■ *Windows 98, Windows Me, Windows NT 4.0, or Windows 2000* CorelDRAW 10 is also available for the Macintosh OS. The Windows and Macintosh versions are sold in separate packaging.

- *64MB RAM (128MB recommended)*   This may be a somewhat conservative estimate as to the amount of RAM you'll need, depending upon how you plan to use CorelDRAW. If you're going to be making Web graphics in CorelDRAW, or scanning and retouching photographs in Corel PHOTO-PAINT, 64MB of RAM may be fine. As you probably already know, if you plan to do high-resolution print work in CorelDRAW or video editing in Corel PHOTO-PAINT, you'll need 128MB or more RAM.

- *Pentium 200 processor*   When dealing with processors and graphics, the more processor speed you have, the smoother things will run. AMD and Cyrix chip users will be happy to know that there are no known issues of CorelDRAW 10 running improperly on non-Pentium systems.

- *2X CD-ROM drive*   Actually, a 1X CD-ROM drive would probably still work, but the installation process would be slowed down. In general, a 16X (or faster) CD-ROM will make for a smoother installation.

- *Mouse or tablet*   Of course, a drawing tablet is not required, but it can make a nice option.

- *SVGA display*   Although it's not a requirement, a video card with 8MB or more video RAM is always a plus when working with graphics.

- *Minimum 128MB hard disk space*   The hard disk space needed can vary widely, depending upon which programs you plan to install. A typical installation takes up about 300 MB of disk space. If you're installing the entire CorelDRAW suite with all options, you'll need 400MB of disk space. The amount of additional space that you'll need for the Windows swap file will vary depending on how you use CorelDRAW. In general, you'll want *at least* 64MB to 128MB of free space available after installation. The need for additional free space will be lowest for Web imaging and typical desktop publishing, and much higher for high-resolution printing and for video editing.

- *Optional 28.8 or higher modem*   Although a modem isn't an official option, it's one you may want to consider. With the release of CorelDRAW 10, and in particular with the introduction of Corel R.A.V.E. to the CorelDRAW suite, Corel has leapt ahead of the competition in terms of providing a fully Web-capable graphics creation and editing environment.

Registering Your Software

Registering your software is an essential step for receiving technical support and for being kept advised of program upgrades. Should patches or bug fixes be required, Corel will notify you of their availability and make them available via free downloads from the Internet and nominally priced CD-ROMs.

You'll be prompted near the end of the installation process to register your new software. Online registration via the registration Web site is the fastest and easiest registration method. However, if you'd prefer to mail in your registration, you may use the postcard included with CorelDRAW. You may also print your registration form and fax it to Corel.

Slipping in the Disc

To begin installing CorelDRAW 10, just place the CD in your CD-ROM drive. On most systems, the CD will begin running the Setup Wizard automatically. You'll have eight options when the wizard begins (see Figure 1-1).

- *Install CorelDRAW 10, Corel PHOTO-PAINT 10, and Corel R.A.V.E 1.0* The way this is worded implies that it can only be used to install the three listed programs. Actually, this option is the correct one to choose to install CorelDRAW, and any or all of the other Corel programs on the CD. Unless you want to install one of the non-Corel programs (such as the Acrobat reader), this is the option you should select.

- *Adobe Acrobat Reader 4.05 Setup*   This option installs Acrobat, an optional program used to view items such as tutorials or manuals that may be found on the CorelDRAW CDs. Adobe Acrobat files may be identified by the .PDF file extension.

- *Quicktime 4.1.2*   This option installs Apple's Quicktime software for Windows. By default, Corel R.A.V.E. exports animation in the Flash, GIF, and AVI formats; and Corel PHOTO-PAINT exports in the GIF and AVI formats. Installing Quicktime enables the additional option of exporting Quicktime movies from both Corel R.A.V.E. and Corel PHOTO-PAINT.

- *Canto Cumulus Desktop 5 LE*   This option installs Canto Cumulus, an optional program used to catalog your digital media (such as images, page layouts, and videos) into a convenient searchable database.

- *Macromedia Flash Player 5 Plug-in for Netscape Navigator and Microsoft Internet Explorer*   If you use a Web browser, it's very likely that you

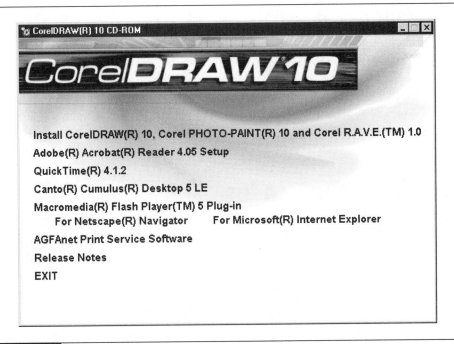

FIGURE 1-1   Main installation screen for CorelDRAW 10

already have the Macromedia Flash plug-in installed. (It's currently installed on over 90 percent of all Web browsers.) If you'd like to ensure that you have the latest version of the Flash plug-in installed, you may select this option. The Flash plug-in may be installed for Microsoft Internet Explorer and Netscape Navigator.

■ *AGFAnet Print Service Software*   You may find this option to be particularly useful if you own a digital camera. The AGFAnet software uses your Internet connection to locate a nearby photo processing bureau, transfer your images to the bureau, arrange payment, and have finished prints delivered to your door.

■ *Release Notes*   This option opens CorelDRAW's release notes in your default Web browser. Since the release notes file is stored on the CD, you do not have to be connected to the Internet to view the release notes.

■ *EXIT*   This option exits the Setup Wizard.

Installation for the Typical User

For a typical installation, begin by selecting the first option. The other options may be installed at any time. Note that if the Setup Wizard does not start automatically, you may use My Computer or Windows Explorer to open the CD-ROM drive and double-click the Intro.EXE file. Alternatively, if you know you only want to install the Corel programs, you may click the Setup32.EXE file. Depending upon how your system is configured, the .EXE portion of the filename may not be visible.

Navigating a Custom Installation

After you accept the Corel licensing agreement, the Setup Wizard will take you to the CorelDRAW 10 Setup Options screen. You'll have three installation options: Typical, Compact, and Custom (see Figure 1-2).

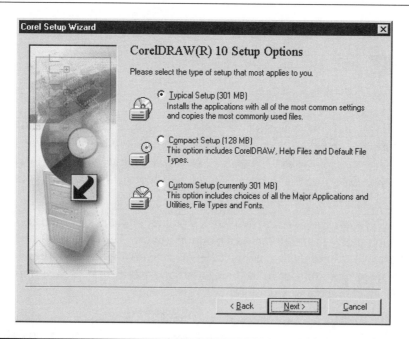

FIGURE 1-2   The CorelDRAW 10 Setup Options screen

The Typical selection is the default selection and is the best choice for most users. This option installs CorelDRAW; Corel PHOTO-PAINT; Corel R.A.V.E.; Corel CAPTURE; Corel TRACE; and commonly used bitmap filters, file import and export filters, writing tools, and fonts.

If you plan to use only CorelDRAW, you may select the Compact option. Expert users may prefer to use the Custom option, since this selection may be used to install additional options, such as device profiles, non-English-language writing tools, and the Microsoft VBA (Visual Basic for Applications) programming interface.

Choosing Utilities

When choosing a custom installation, you'll have complete control over which Corel programs are installed and which are not installed. Since you may not be familiar with every application in the CorelDRAW suite, here are their brief descriptions:

- CorelDRAW is Corel's legendary vector editing and page layout program.

- Corel PHOTO-PAINT is an award-winning bitmap creation and photo-editing program.

- Corel R.A.V.E. is a new and very welcome addition to the CorelDRAW suite. It's used to create vector animation, which may then be exported as Flash movies. It is used to create vector animation, which may then be exported as Flash movies.

- Corel CAPTURE is an advanced screen shot capturing utility.

- Corel TEXTURE is used to create natural-looking bitmap textures such as marble and wood.

- Corel TRACE is a powerful utility for converting bitmap images into vector images.

Installing Bitmap Filter Plug-Ins

Four sets of bitmap filter plug-ins are available for installation. These plug-ins are available in addition to over 80 plug-ins that are installed with CorelDRAW and Corel PHOTO-PAINT by default.

Plug-ins are essentially miniature programs that work within larger programs such as CorelDRAW and Corel PHOTO-PAINT. The following selections are available:

- **DigiMarc**   This plug-in is used to apply a watermark to bitmap images. Watermarks are small, invisible digital signatures that can help identify your images if they're stolen and used without your permission.

- **Corel Fancy Plug-Ins**   This is a set of two plug-ins, the Julia Set Explorer and Terrazzo. The Julia Set Explorer creates fascinating color patterns using fractal geometry, a math process based on naturally occurring energy patterns. Terrazzo is another program based on fractal geometry. It's used to create kaleidoscope-styled patterns and tiles from bitmap images.

- **Squizz**   This plug-in is used for applying effects with a paintbrush tool, and for warping color patterns with a mesh warp.

- **Kai's Power Tools**   This option installs three filters from Kai's Power Tools version 5: Shape Shifter, Smoothie, and FraxFlame. Shape Shifter is used for applying various bevel and bump map effects to images, Smoothie is used for smoothing out rough edges, and FraxFlame is used for creating and exploring mathematically created fractal patterns.

Choosing Fonts

If you'd like to select which fonts to install with CorelDRAW 10, use the custom install option. This will enable access to a font selection dialog during the installation. You may preview the appearance of any font by clicking the font's name. Checking the box to the left of a font's name will tell the Setup Wizard that you want the font installed.

Choosing Additional Features

The CorelDRAW installation program will also enable you to select device profiles, which help match the colors in CorelDRAW and Corel PHOTO-PAINT to the colors available in your hardware devices. By default, generic monitor, scanner, printer, and digital camera profiles will be installed. You may select additional profiles to match your particular hardware by clicking the category name (such as monitor profiles), and then clicking the name and model number of your device. Don't be concerned if your devices aren't listed; the generic profiles are supplied just in case this happens.

Adding and Removing Components

1

You may use the CorelDRAW installation CD to add components at any time. Place the CD in your CD-ROM drive to start the Setup Wizard, or open the drive via My Computer or Windows Explorer and click Intro.EXE.

Select Install CorelDRAW 10, Corel PHOTO-PAINT 10, and Corel R.A.V.E. to add any Corel component. The Setup dialog will open with several selections (see Figure 1-3). Choose the Add New Components option, and click Next. This will take you to the Components dialog, where you may select the components that you'd like to install. Note that a grayed selection box means that only parts of a selected component will be installed. For example, a grayed check box next to Productivity Tools means that at least one tool (such as Visual Basic for Applications) is being installed, while another tool (such as the Barcode Wizard) is not being installed. You may click the grayed check mark to select the component and all of its options, and click the check mark again to deselect the component and all of its options.

To remove components, click Start | Programs | CorelDRAW 10 | Setup and Notes | Corel Uninstaller. Place a check next to any component that you'd like to remove. Please note that you should never attempt to remove a component

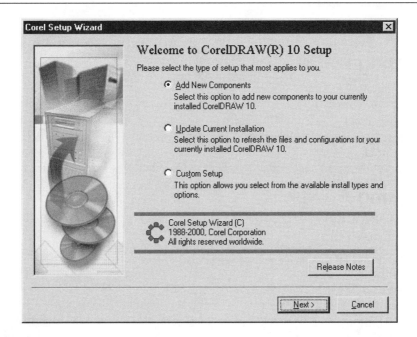

FIGURE 1-3 Adding new components to your CorelDRAW 10 installation

simply by deleting what appears to be its program folder. In order to cut down as much as possible on the amount of disk space needed to install the CorelDRAW suite, many Corel programs share files with other programs. If you accidentally remove one of these shared files, other programs that use the shared file will not work correctly, and may not be able to work at all.

Refreshing Your CorelDRAW 10 Installation

Once you install CorelDRAW 10, you may occasionally need to refresh the installation. Accidentally deleting a CorelDRAW 10 file, problems with the Windows registry, and adding new software that erroneously changes CorelDRAW 10 settings, can all cause CorelDRAW 10 to operate incorrectly (or not at all).

If you need to refresh your current installation (without making any changes such as adding or removing components), select Update Current Installation from the Setup dialog (see Figure 1-3). Your installation will be updated using the same options you selected the last time you installed CorelDRAW.

Using CorelTUTOR

CorelTUTOR contains a series of lessons on learning CorelDRAW. You may follow the lessons from beginning to end, or just select a particular lesson that interests you. The lessons provide hands-on training by both supplying sample images for you to work with and providing instructions to walk you through the entire learning process.

Opening CorelTUTOR

There are two ways to access the CorelTUTOR: When first opening CorelDRAW, select CorelTUTOR from the splash screen; or, once in CorelDRAW, click Help | CorelTUTOR.

Helping Yourself to Help

CorelDRAW ships with several features designed to make learning the application and finding Help a comfortable process. Unlike some competing applications, you'll find Corel's Help tools to be extremely well written, with access to Help only a mouse click away.

Activating ToolTips

ToolTips are brief descriptions of the various parts of the CorelDRAW interface. ToolTips are available for virtually any icon and control in every toolbar, dialog, and docker window. To activate a ToolTip, place your cursor over the item you'd like to find out more about, and hold it there for a second or two. A ToolTip describing the item will automatically be displayed. If you find that ToolTips are not being displayed, click Tools | Options | Display, and make sure that Show ToolTips is checked.

What's This?

Right-clicking virtually anywhere in the CorelDRAW interface will open a pop-up menu with a list of options, including What's This? Help. Clicking on What's This in the pop-up menu opens a small pop-up window that explains the item.

One of the truly unique features of Corel's What's This Help is that you can use it to learn more about how any image you open in CorelDRAW was created. You can try this feature by opening a clip art image from the CorelDRAW clip art CD. Right-click the image and click What's This, as shown here:

CorelDRAW will take a moment to analyze the image to see which features were used to create it, and then provide a pop-up menu with selections for learning more about the features. You may click any of the menu items to learn more about the tool(s) used to create the image, as shown here:

An ellipse is selected.

An ellipse is an oval-shaped, closed-plane curve which is drawn using the Ellipse tool. You can change an ellipse to an arc or a pie shape using the Shape tool. You can also create circles by holding down the CTRL key while drawing with the Ellipse tool.

Using Context-Sensitive Help

Context-sensitive Help is available from the main CorelDRAW screen and for most dialogs as well. To access context-sensitive Help from the main CorelDRAW screen, click the question mark on the right side of the main toolbar, and then click the item in question. To access context-sensitive Help from a dialog, click the question mark icon in the upper-right corner of the dialog, and then click the item in question. Corel's context-sensitive Help then displays an explanation of the item.

Using CorelDRAW Help

Clicking Help and then clicking Help Topics opens the Corel help system (see Figure 1-4). The help system is divided into three categories: Contents, Index, and Find. The Contents menu works like a book's table of contents in that it displays broad subject matter topics that then contain subheadings with more detailed information. The Index tab works like an index at the back of a book, displaying individual words and phrases instead of the broad subject matter that you'll find in the Contents menu. To search for help on a topic, click the Find tab, and enter one or more search words. Results will appear as soon as the search is complete.

You may bookmark items that you've found helpful in order to find them quickly in the future. To bookmark an item, click Bookmark | Define. A default title will be given to the topic, but you may change this title to anything that you feel will assist you in locating the item in the future. When you're comfortable with the title, click OK. The item will then be added to the Bookmark menu, in much the same way that an item is added to the Favorites menu in your Web browser.

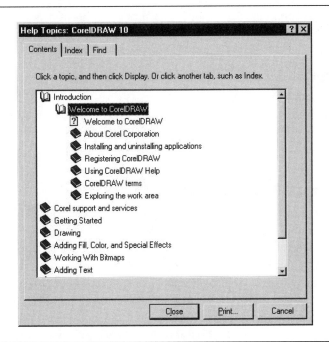

FIGURE 1-4   The CorelDRAW 10 main Help window

To access a previously bookmarked item, click Bookmark, and then click the topic you'd like to view. To delete a bookmarked item, click Bookmark | Define, select the item you'd like to delete (from the lower portion of the dialog), and click Delete. When you're done, click Cancel to close the Bookmark dialog. The help topic itself will not be deleted, only your bookmark will be removed.

Getting Technical Support

Corel provides complimentary and fee-based telephone technical support for the CorelDRAW suite. Classic technical support (free except for long distance charges) is available in the United States and Canada by calling (613) 274-0500, Monday through Friday, from 8:30 A.M. to 7:30 P.M., Eastern Time. This service is available for 30 days from the time you first call for assistance.

Priority support is available on a "pay per incident" basis at (877) 662-6735 and on a "pay as you go" basis at (900) 733-8780. However, in addition to offering Classic technical support, Corel offers a wealth of other free support options, making it unlikely that you'd ever need to use fee-based support.

Using Corel's IVAN Faxback Service

Corel's Interactive Voice Answering Network (IVAN) consists of answers to common support questions that you may listen to on your telephone or have sent to you via fax. The IVAN service is free for U.S. and Canadian users, and is available 24 hours a day, every day of the year, by calling (877) 42-COREL.

Using About CorelDRAW

When contacting technical support, you'll need to provide your CorelDRAW version/build number, serial number, and possibly some additional information regarding your system's resources. To access this information, click Help, and then click About CorelDRAW. The version/build number is located just under the main window, as is your serial number and your PIN number (if one has previously been issued to you by Customer Service).

You may access information regarding your system setup—such as processor type, RAM, and video data—by clicking the System Info button to the right of the main window (see Figure 1-5).

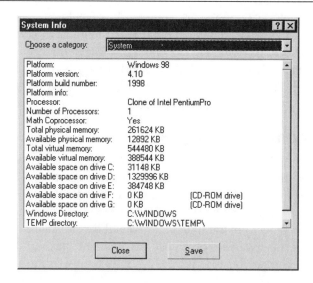

FIGURE 1-5   Accessing your system information from Help | About CorelDRAW

1

Using Hints

Hints that describe the tools in CorelDRAW are provided on the status bar (located on the bottom of your screen). The left side of the status bar contains information on your cursor's current position in your document and information about the tool you're currently using. You'll also find your current fill and outline colors on the right side of the status bar. An X means that no fill or outline is currently selected.

Getting Help on the Web

You'll find a great deal of information about CorelDRAW—including articles, tutorials, patches, and special offers—on Corel's World Wide Web sites. Web-based technical support and FTP file downloads are also available.

Surfing Corel's Various Web Sites

Corel currently has three Web sites that can assist you in answering specific questions and finding general information on just about any CorelDRAW topic.

Designer.com

Designer.com is Corel's community site, where you'll find tips, secrets, articles, tutorials, and free downloads. The authors of *CorelDRAW 10: The Official Guide* are regular contributors to Corel's **Designer.com**.

CorelCity.com

CorelCity.com is a portal site that provides access to online services such as e-mail and instant messaging, along with world news and technology news.

Corel.com

This is Corel's home page. **Corel.com** provides access to Corel news, product information, support, events, and free downloads.

Getting Web-Based Technical Support

You may access Corel Web-based technical support, including the Corel Knowledge Base and Corel e-mail support, via **http://www.corel.com/ support/options/onlineserv.htm**. Corel also has a learning center located at **http://www.corel.com/learning/index.htm**.

About Corel's FTP site

Corel's FTP site provides printer drivers, free patches, and other files via anonymous FTP logon. The address is **ftp.corel.com**. If you don't have an FTP (File Transfer Protocol) program, use your Web browser to access Corel's FTP site by typing the URL **ftp://ftp.corel.com/pub**.

Corel Newsgroups

Newsgroups provide an interactive support environment where you may post questions for Corel's C-Tech volunteers and product users. The Corel newsgroup server is located at **cnews.corel.ca**. Many ISP news servers also carry some Corel newsgroups, such as comp.graphics.apps.corel, and groups in the "corelsupport." hierarchy.

Netscape's and Microsoft's e-mail programs both support newsgroup access. If you're not familiar with how to access newsgroups, try going to **http://www.corel.com/support/options/online_newsgroups.htm** and clicking one of the newsgroup names. After taking a moment to download the information needed to access the news server, the newsgroup should open in your default e-mail viewer. The exact procedure for accessing newsgroups varies from program to program, but you can find the information you need by looking up "usenet" or "news server" in your e-mail program's Help file, or by contacting your Internet Service Provider.

CHAPTER 2

What's New in CorelDRAW 10?

W hether you've recently upgraded to CorelDRAW 10 or you're a brand-new user, it always helps to know what's new and different from past versions. This chapter highlights the most significant features that have been added or changed since version 9 and serves as a divining rod to places where you may find more information in this book.

Onscreen Look and Feel

CorelDRAW 10 now sports a new interface appearance shared throughout the application suite, new streamlined customization controls, enhanced workspace features, and resizable dialogs.

Icon Symbols and Common UI   The most noticeable difference you'll see when first launching CorelDRAW 10 is the graphical interface symbols designed to accompany and visually identify most every option, effect, and object properties in nearly every command menu, docker, and Toolbar. These symbols are common throughout the shared interfaces used by CorelDRAW 10, PHOTO-PAINT 10, and Corel R.A.V.E., and they support the applications CorelTRACE 10, CorelCAPTURE 10, and CorelTEXTURE 10. Unified symbols enable you to recognize quickly the purpose and function of related options and commands that can significantly reduce the time and effort you spend learning individual applications in the CorelDRAW 10 suite. The following illustration shows the applications accessible using CorelDRAW 10's application launcher.

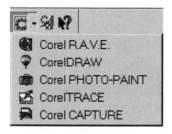

Windows 2000–Compliant Interface Transparency   CorelDRAW 10 takes advantage of the new interface capabilities of Windows 2000, which enables you to individually select the command menus, Toolbars, and docker interface components that you want to be transparent, as shown next. This great new feature allows you to view your drawings without the interface obstructing your view, but it's only available when you use Windows 2000 as your operating system.

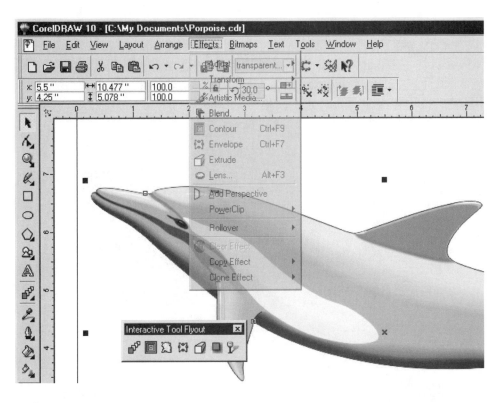

Exchanging Workspaces   Your CorelDRAW 10 workspace may now be more easily shared between other users (and vice versa) by taking advantage of the Import Workspace and Export Workspace commands. This means that you may now control not only the appearance of drawing elements, but also how they are created or edited by other users. With Web access, Workspace features also enable you to e-mail your current workspace quickly to a coworker, client, or service bureau using the Email option (shown next) while exporting a workspace. For information on using Workspace commands, see "Using CorelDRAW 10's Workspace Resources" in Chapter 28.

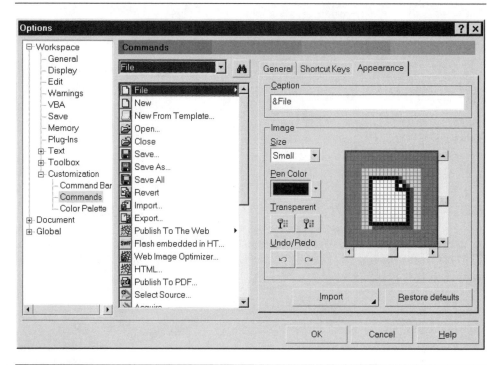

FIGURE 2-1   The revamped Customization page of the Options dialog enables you to
control the appearance of your CorelDRAW 10 interface.

Streamlined Customization Controls   The customization features in CorelDRAW 10
have been significantly streamlined into a single-tabbed dialog page, making them
more straightforward to use. You may now control customization of menus, the
Toolbox, Toolbars, and the Status Bar all at once by using the Customization page
of the Options dialog (see Figure 2-1). You may quickly create and change Toolbars,
edit shortcut keys, and control the appearance of any interface elements. For
information on using these features and steps on performing the most sought-after
customization procedures, see "Top Customization Tips" in Chapter 28.

Resizable Dialogs   In past versions of CorelDRAW, the overwhelming size
of certain dialogs made it difficult, if not impossible, to see even a small portion

2

of your document in the background. Now, many dialogs are resizable, which enables you to refer back to your drawing objects without closing the currently open dialog. Resizable dialogs are recognized by three angled lines in their lower-right corner as shown:

Indicates That Dialog Is Resizable

Productivity and Performance

You'll find CorelDRAW 10 a more efficient drawing workshop now equipped with Real Time Preview, a new Undo Docker, Page Sorter and Navigator View features, common Effect Preset controls for interactive effects, Drag-and-Drop Customization, an up-to-date collection of import and export filters, and significantly expanded VBA scripting abilities.

RealTime Preview   CorelDRAW's new RealTime Preview capabilities enable you to see both the outline and the fill properties applied to objects as they are being moved or positioned on your document page, instead of the typical outline preview in previous versions of CorelDRAW. RealTime Preview also allows you to view formatting options and the results of applying the effects before you actually apply them. When performing certain option-related commands (such as fitting text to a path), you can cycle through Property Bar options, and when you choose specific property variables you get to view the effects onscreen before committing to the change. You may also deactivate RealTime Preview at any time using the General Page of the Options dialog, as shown next:

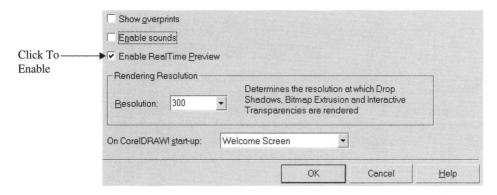

Click To Enable

Undo Docker   The new Undo Docker, shown next, enables you to backtrack—and view the appearance of your drawing to a specific point in your most recent sequence of commands. You may also use the Undo Docker to create and save VBA macros for automating tasks. For more information, see "Using the New Undo Docker" in Chapter 4.

Page Sorter View   When working with multipage documents, the new Page Sorter view, shown next, lets you to view several pages at one time and manage their properties from a bird's-eye perspective. While in Page Sorter View, both your pages and their contents are displayed, enabling you to reorder single or multiple pages in the page sequence and edit page name, size, and orientation. For more information on working in Page Sorter View, see "Specialized View Modes" in Chapter 7.

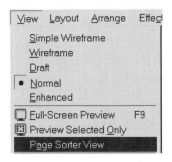

View Navigator   One of the most popular viewing features in PHOTO-PAINT has come to CorelDRAW 10. The View Navigator, shown next, enables you to interactively control the visible screen area of your current document page quickly without having to change tools. The new View Navigator is an integral part of your document window and readily accessible. For more information, see "Using the View Navigator" in Chapter 7.

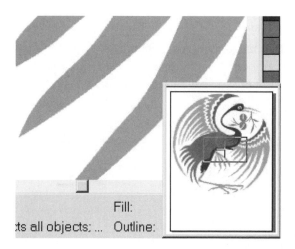

Effect Presets   CorelDRAW 10's Presets feature has been expanded to include all interactive effects, and you may access it from the Property Bar while using interactive tools for Blend, Contour, Distortion, Envelope, Extrude, and Drop Shadows. Presets enable you to quickly apply existing preset effects or create and name your own, as shown:

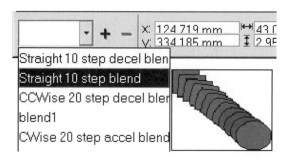

New I/O Filters   With each release of CorelDRAW, the already massive list of input and output filters available to filter objects into and out of your documents gets longer and longer. You may import over 50 different file formats into your CorelDRAW document or choose from nearly 40 filters when exporting. Import or Export native file formats as well as text, vector, bitmap, and specialized file formats when preparing files for Web, animation, or offset printing. For more information on using these filters, see Chapter 26.

Drag-and-Drop Customization   Besides having the ability to control the appearance of your interface, you may now rearrange, assemble, or dismantle the interface interactively and onscreen using drag-and-drop operations, shown next, in combination with modifier keys without having to open dialogs. Move or copy tools, command buttons, options and selectors between menus, Toolbars, and the Toolbox for complete interface flexibility. For more information, see "Moving Toolbar Buttons" in Chapter 28.

Expanded VBA Capabilities   Visual Basic for Applications (VBA) enables you to create macros to control CorelDRAW 10 itself. Corel has hugely extended the range of commands available to the VBA programmer in CorelDRAW 10, greatly expanding on the advancements engineered into CorelDRAW 9. The most notable improvements involve CorelScript Deprecation, VBA Distribution, Command Bars, Object Data and Properties, Document Filename, Exporting, View, ShapeRange, Curve and Node Manipulation, Text, Outline, Fill, Ruler, Grid and Guidelines, and Effects. If this sounds like Greek to you, you can get more information on this incredibly powerful programming tool in Chapter 29 to obtain more on this incredibly powerful programming tool.

Expanded Text Power

When it comes to control over the written word, CorelDRAW 10 now features support for multiple languages in a single document, consolidated writing tools for massaging text content, new text selection and formatting abilities, and new commands for controlling text flow between frames.

Multilanguage Support within Text Boxes   The new multilingual support engineered into CorelDRAW 10 enables you to house different languages within a single text frame. You may also create and correct multilingual documents without the need to change language writing tools, as shown next. For more information on working with multilanguage features, see CD-ROM 3.

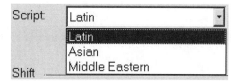

Text Cursor in Text Boxes   While editing text in either Artistic Text strings or Paragraph text frames, the text cursor now flashes, making it significantly easier to locate editing points.

Paragraph Selection   When editing text in Paragraph Text frames, triple-clicking a paragraph with the text cursor now selects the entire paragraph. Holding the mouse button on the final click of the triple-click action and dragging also enables you to select the next or previous complete paragraph as you drag up or down through your text frame, shown next. While editing text in Paragraph Text frames, pressing CTRL+ALT now enables you to select all text in the frame and in any linked frames. For information on working with Paragraph text frames, see "Paragraph Formatting" in CD-ROM 1.

Consolidated Writing Tools   A new and improved Edit Text dialog consolidates all text composition, editing, spell checking, and formatting operations in a single dialog. You may also Import text files from external sources directly into the Edit Text dialog editing window (see Figure 2-2).

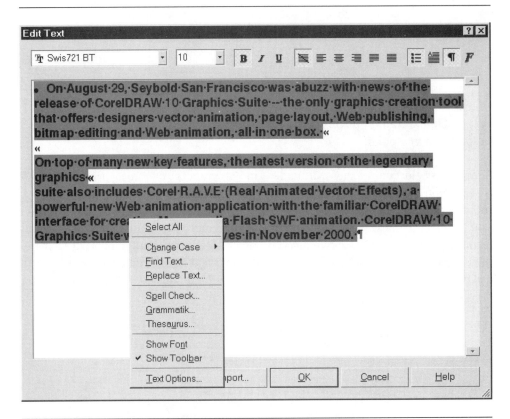

FIGURE 2-2   The Edit Text dialog enables you to control text composition and formatting in a single, resizable dialog.

Revamped Format Text Dialog   While applying text formatting, you'll find that the Format Text dialog structure has been improved to better reflect the differences in available formatting options between Artistic and Paragraph Text. The dialog now also enables you to both change your display and zoom magnification (with Zoom and Hand Tools) and to interactively apply character kerning (using the Shape Tool) to the text in your document without closing the dialog itself. For information on applying text formatting, see "Navigating the Format Text Dialog" in CD-ROM 1.

Linking/Unlinking Text Frames   While working with linked Paragraph Text frames, you may now use the Link and Unlink commands for added control over the direction of text flow. Link and Unlink commands are available from the Text menu when two linked Paragraph Text objects are selected (shown next). Linking and unlinking text frames with menu command avoids the need to choose the Text Tool when controlling text layout between text frames. For further information, see "Linking Blocks of Text" in CD-ROM 2.

Object Handling

CorelDRAW's object handling capabilities now include enhancements to scaling operations, new selection conveniences, a new Micro Nudge feature, Distribute hot keys, automatic tool panning, and improved grid and guideline snapping behavior. When applying object fills and outlines, you'll also discover an improved Outline Pen property editing behavior for multiple object selections, and new Texture and Pattern fill enhancements.

Scale Display   While scaling objects, the Scale Factor value in the Property Bar, shown next, displays the scale factor in progress during object transformation operations. In previous versions, this information was only available as feedback provided by the Status Bar.

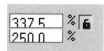

Context-Sensitive Select All   Besides having the ability to quickly select all objects on your document page (CTRL+A), you may now select all by object type, which makes this feature context sensitive. Choose Edit | Select All and choose from Text, Objects, Guidelines, or all Nodes on a compound path and its subpaths.

New Micro Nudge   When an object is selected, pressing your UP, DOWN, LEFT, and RIGHT arrow keys moves objects in typical Nudge fashion by increments of 0.1 inches (by default). Holding SHIFT while nudging applies a Super Nudge that moves objects in larger increments of 0.2 inches (by default). Now, you may also move objects a much smaller distance (0.05 inches by default) with Micro Nudge by holding CTRL as the modifier key. The default of the typical Nudge incremental distance may now be controlled via the Property Bar (shown next) when using the Pick Tool and when no objects are selected. For more information on nudging and controlling Super and Micro nudge increments, see "Using Nudge Keys" in Chapter 8.

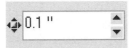

Snapping Controls   Snapping to Guidelines, grid lines, and object points is now much smoother and less jerky, as CorelDRAW 10 uses a more efficient snapping algorithm to control how objects are drawn toward grids and guides.

Distribute   Distribute commands may now be applied as quickly as Align commands and without the need to open the Align and Distribute dialog. New Distribute keys have been implemented that enable you to add even spacing between selected objects. Objects may be distributed using hot keys based on their tops, bottoms, left or right sides, the page, or their vertical or horizontal selection areas. For more information, see "Using Distribute Command Options" in Chapter 13.

Auto Panning with Any Tool   Automatic panning and scrolling now behaves equally for all tools. For example, when drawing a rectangle, you may click-drag to create the shape larger than your visible screen area by dragging off the screen while defining its width or height. As you do so, the page view scrolls to match your drag action.

Edit Only Outline Pen Specifics for Multiple Selections   While multiple objects are selected and different Outline Pen properties are applied, you may now change only a specific property in the Outline Pen dialog. This enables you to leave other Outline Pen properties unaffected. Doing so with previous versions of CorelDRAW caused all objects in the selection to be applied with whichever settings were selected in the dialog. Where Outline Pen properties for the selection differ (for example, Color, Width, and Style), the dialog options appear blank (see Figure 2-3). For more information, see "Applying Outline Pen Properties" in CD-ROM 4.

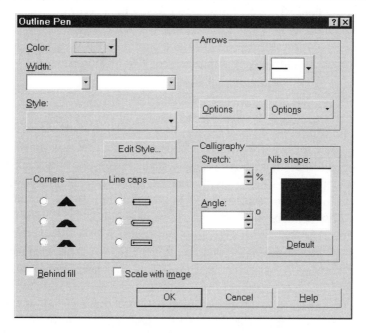

FIGURE 2-3   Properties that differ between objects in a multiobject selection appear blank in the Outline Pen dialog.

Seamless Texture and Pattern Fills Option   While applying Texture or Pattern fills, the Property Bar now features a new Mirror Fill option, shown next, which enables you to use any fill as a seamless tile. For information on controlling Texture and Pattern fill options, see "Applying Pattern Fills" and "Applying Texture Fills" in CD-ROM 5.

Mirror Fill Tiles

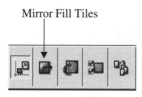

Texture Fill Resolution   The resolution of Texture Fills is now a function of the page resolution used by effects such as Interactive Drop Shadows and Bitmap Extrude. This resolution setting may now also be saved with your document. For information on setting page resolution, see "Controlling Texture Options" in CD-ROM 5.

Tools

What would a new release of CorelDRAW be without a few new tools? You may now create objects that may be dynamically shaped using the new Perfect Shape Tools, which employ use of new glyph nodes. Contour effects may now be applied interactively using the new Interactive Contour Tool. You'll also discover subtle enhancements to the interactive effect tools while applying vector and bitmap extrusions as well as Distortion, Envelope and Drop Shadow effects. New functionality has also been engineered into PowerClip effects, and the abilities for shaping objects with the Knife and Eraser Tools has been improved.

Create Perfect Shapes   The newest addition to CorelDRAW's tool arsenal is a collection of Perfect Shape Tools, shown next, that enable you to quickly create dynamically shaped symbols for diagram creation. Many of these shapes are controlled using *glyph nodes*, which allow you to customize symbol shapes to suit your needs and includes various styles of arrows, flowcharting shapes, stars, and callout shapes. For more information, see "Using Perfect Shape Tools" in Chapter 9.

Interactive Contour Tool   Contour effects may now be applied using the new Interactive Contour Tool, which has been vastly improved to enable you to apply contours to groups of objects (as shown) and use object and color acceleration options that were previously only available for Blend effects. For more information, see "Using the Interactive Contour Tool and Property Bar" in Chapter 15.

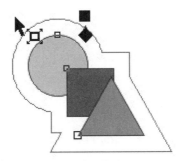

Expanded Knife and Eraser Tool Abilities   Both the Knife and Eraser Tools now enable you to erase portions of bitmaps as well as vector objects. For more information, see the Knife and Eraser Tool sections in Chapter 11.

Pick Tool Marquee Selection   While using Pick Tool marquee-selection techniques, you may select objects without selecting objects which have been locked. This new functionality enables you to quickly select only unlocked objects, avoiding the need to deselect locked objects following a marquee-style object selection.

Applying Interactive Fill Tool Colors   While using the Interactive Fill tool, shown next, to apply custom multicolor linear, radial, square, or conical fills, double-clicking the interactive guide controlling a fill instantly adds a color node, and double-clicking an existing color node immediately deletes it. For information on controlling Interactive Fills, see "Using the Interactive Fill Tool and Property Bar" in CD-ROM 5.

Interactive Extrude Tool   You may now drag-and-drop colors from color palette wells directly onto extruded surfaces or applied bevel effects to quickly control their color. You may also apply Extrude effects to objects within a group. When using the Interactive Extrude Tool, you may now access the visual rotation control from the Property Bar. For information on applying Extrude effects, see Chapter 20.

Sample Envelopes Interactively   The Interactive Envelope Tool Property Bar, shown next, now features an Eyedropper Tool for sampling existing envelope shapes and instantly applying them to selected objects. For information on applying Envelope effects, see "Using the Interactive Envelope Tool and Property Bar" in Chapter 14.

3D Bitmap Extrude   Improvements to the Interactive Extrude Tool in Bitmap mode enable you to quickly transform nearly any two-dimension flat object into a 3D object and fill the extrusion with any type of fill. Plus, Bitmap Extrusion resolution is now controlled by page resolution (as shown). For more information on creating Bitmap Extrude effects, see "Exploring Bitmap Extrude Effects" in Chapter 21.

---Rendering Resolution---------------------------------

Resolution: [150   ▾]   Determines the resolution at which Drop
Shadows, Bitmap Extrusion and Interactive
Transparencies are rendered

Drop Shadows   One of the most favored effects in CorelDRAW, Drop Shadow, has been changed to enable you to CTRL-click to select the shadow applied to an object. For information on controlling Drop Shadow effects using the Interactive Drop Shadow Tool, see "Anatomy of a Drop Shadow Effect" in Chapter 17.

PowerClip   You may quickly enter the editing state of applied PowerClip effects interactively using a CTRL+click. To quickly end a PowerClip editing session,

CTRL+click outside the Powerclip effect. For more information, see "Editing PowerClip Objects" in Chapter 18.

Distortion Effects   When working with Paragraph Text, you may now wildly distort the text frames themselves with the Interactive Distortion Tool. For information, see "Using the Interactive Distortion Tool and Property Bar" in Chapter 14.

Web Features

Web designers will be pleased to learn that one of the most significant areas of new feature development for CorelDRAW 10 has been added Web functionality—not the least of which is the introduction of Corel R.A.V.E. You may also convert any object into a Web button complete with rollover effects, browse the Web from within CorelDRAW itself, analyze your HTML document exports quickly, and optimize Web images before exporting them.

Corel R.A.V.E.   Short for Real Animated Vector Effects, this sophisticated new addition to the CorelDRAW suite enables you to quickly create vector animation based on tweening or from familiar effects, such as Blends and Contours. Create sequences from groups of objects and transformation operations using a Timeline interface. Animations are based on scalable vector object technology geared toward creating memory-efficient files for compelling Web page effects and creation of interactive Web interfaces. For more information, see "Creating Animated Graphics" in Chapter 27.

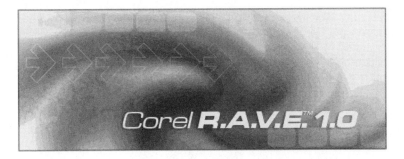

Interactive Web Buttons   Create rollover effects for objects directly within CorelDRAW 10 by creating multiple button states and setting button behavior (as shown next). View the effects of Web buttons directly on your document page and export button designs in Macromedia Flash (SWF) format when creating

Web page designs. For more information, see "Creating Web Objects in CorelDRAW 10 and CorelR.A.V.E." in Chapter 27.

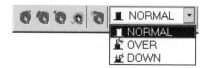

New Web Connector Docker   With online access, browse the Internet directly from with CorelDRAW 10 without leaving your application by using the new Web Connector Docker window, shown next. For information, see "Using the Web Connector Docker" in Chapter 27.

Macromedia Flash Support   Export your drawings in scalable vector format using the new Macromedia Flash (SWF) filter, shown next, for use in Web page design or for editing in Macromedia Flash itself. For information on setting filter options and its capabilities, see Chapter 27.

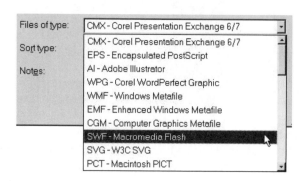

HTML Preflight During Export Quickly evaluate your document for incompatibilities when exporting by using the reengineered Export to HTML dialog's HTML Preflight tab (as shown next). For more information, see "Saving Your Document as a Web Page" in Chapter 27.

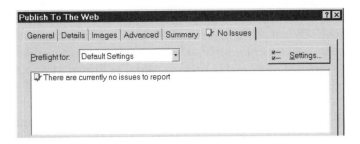

Web Image Optimizer Control and view how images will appear when exported in Web image formats using CorelDRAW 10's new Web Image Optimizer filter. Save images as GIF, JPG, PNG8 or PNG24 file formats and Apply Presets to quickly prepare images or create your own custom presets. For more information, see "Using the Web Image Optimizer" in Chapter 27.

Printing and PDF

CorelDRAW's mighty print engine places even more power at your fingertips with improved Print Merge, In-RIP trapping, and output separation-ordering features. When it comes to creating digital documents, CorelDRAW 10 now supports the latest standards using Adobe's new PDF version 1.3.

Print Merge Wizard CorelDRAW 10's Print Merge Wizard, shown next, has been improved so you can use ODBC database sources. The Print Merge command now features its own Toolbar, which enables you to add, create, load, and edit Print Merge fields and perform Merge functions. Print Merge fields may now be inserted either as text objects, or inline into Artistic or Paragraph Text strings. For more information, see "Print Merge" in Chapter 25.

In-RIP Trapping   CorelDRAW 10's Print Engine now enables you to control In-RIP (raster image processor) trapping by specifying trapping and separation preferences in advance of printing. In-RIP Trapping now supports options for PostScript Level 3 output devices. For information, see "Setting Trapping Options" in Chapter 25.

Print Separations   When printing to imagesetter output devices, you may now specify the order in which color separations are printed and control how printers' marks align to the edge of a graphic or document. For further information, see "Printing Separations" in Chapter 25.

Publish to PDF   The Publish to PDF (portable document format) command now supports PDF 1.3 standards and enables you to embed ICC color profiles, author and keyword information, and export Fountain and Mesh fills as vector-based objects. For more information, see "Setup Options for PDF" in Chapter 25.

CHAPTER 3

A Primer on Using CorelDRAW 10's Interface

When it comes to working with CorelDRAW 10's application and document windows and various feedback and user options, you're faced with all kinds of bells and whistles at your beck and call enabling you to control virtually everything you do. The interface CorelDRAW 10 offers is a complex one, made to appear even more so by the addition of icons and symbols to identify nearly every option and command. In this chapter, you discover how to use these sophisticated resources, ranging from the anatomy of the application and document windows to specifying values and manipulating interface components.

Window Anatomy

As you view an open document in CorelDRAW, you see tools and resources that are available on essentially two levels: Application control and Document control. This theme is underscored several times in CorelDRAW 10. If you're new to working on either of these two levels, the following anatomical look at both of these levels may help.

CorelDRAW 10's Application Window

The Application window is the area you see while CorelDRAW 10 is open, whether or not any document windows are currently open. On this level, you see the basic resources in terms of command menus, toolbars, the Toolbox, Status Bar, and the Color Palette (see Figure 3-1).

While the application window is visible and a document is open, the settings you see in toolbars pertain to the currently active document. For example, the context-sensitive Property Bar displays Paper Type/Size, Orientation, and Unit Measurements, as well as other active option states specifically applied to the current document. Clicking the Close button in the Application window title bar closes CorelDRAW 10, while clicking the Minimize or Maximize/Restore button enables you to hide or change the size of the window itself quickly.

> **TIP** *Even while CorelDRAW 10 is open and all documents are closed, you may still access certain menu commands, including certain File commands, Tool menu functions (such as Customization commands and access to certain dockers), Help Topics, and Corel's online Web resources.*

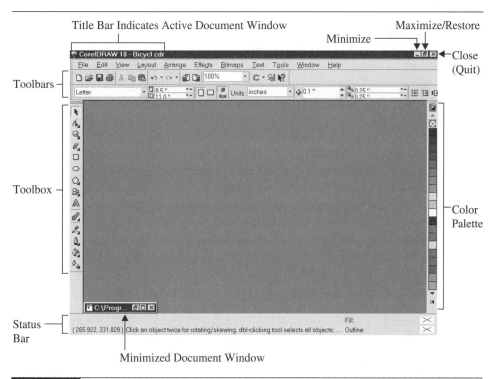

Title Bar Indicates Active Document Window   Maximize/Restore

Minimize

Close (Quit)

Toolbars

Toolbox

Color Palette

Status Bar

Minimized Document Window

FIGURE 3-1   CorelDRAW 10's application window appears the same no matter which document you have open.

Your Document Window Anatomy

Your open Document window displays and enables you to control everything on the document level. Like the Application Window, the Document window also features title bars that identify the document name as well as Minimize, Maximize/Restore, and Close buttons (see Figure 3-2).

One confusing issue for new users is that when a document window is Maximized, the interface may not appear as though more than one level of control exists. This is because while a document window is maximized, it appears as an integral part of the application window. While document window is in this state, you notice the document and application window Minimize, Maximize/Restore, and Close buttons appear together in the upper-right corner of your screen camouflaging the fact that more than one document may currently be open.

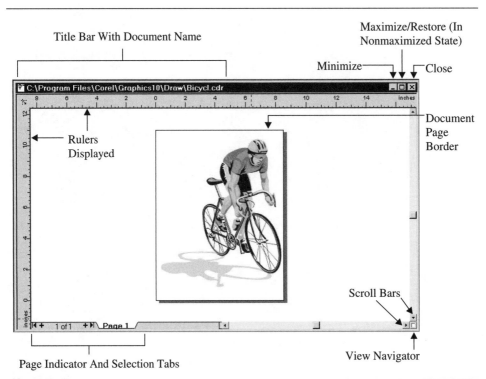

Title Bar With Document Name

Maximize/Restore (In Nonmaximized State)

Minimize

Close

C:\Program Files\Corel\Graphics10\Draw\Bicycl.cdr

Rulers Displayed

Document Page Border

Scroll Bars

Page Indicator And Selection Tabs

View Navigator

FIGURE 3-2   The appearance of the Document Window appears differently, according to which document is active.

CorelDRAW has long offered multidocument support, meaning more than one document may be opened at a time. When more than one document is open, you may quickly change the active document window by clicking the Window menu and selecting a document from the bottom of the list. This enables you to switch between document windows without the need to close one document in order to open another.

3

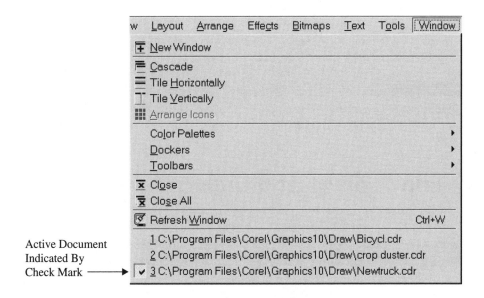

Active Document
Indicated By
Check Mark ————▶

On another level, you may open more than one document window of the same document if you require. This capability enables you to work on a single document in multiple windows. While a document is active, choosing Window | New Window opens a new window view of your active document. Switching between document window views is also done using the Windows menu by making a selection from the bottom of the list. Multiple windows of the same document are indicated by the document name followed by a colon and number.

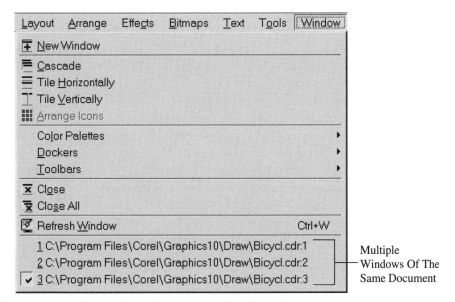

Multiple
Windows Of The
Same Document

You may open as many windows of the same document (or multiple documents) as you wish, enabling you to switch between pages or views of the same document quickly. As you become more familiar with using CorelDRAW 10, you may also do this using the View Manager Docker, which enables you to save and recall views of your document even more quickly. To change the view of your current document page, you may also use scroll bars, the Zoom Tool, or the View Navigator. For information on using any of these features, see Chapter 7.

Specifying Toolbar and Dialog Values

As you control the properties of your document and the objects you create, you're going to encounter various devices for specifying values, setting options and states, and controlling the behavior of interface elements in toolbars, dialogs, and so on. If any of the interface features you're using appear strange or confusing to use, the following quick summary should be of some help.

Num Boxes   Wherever you need to specify numeric values, you find *num* boxes—short for *numeric* boxes. To enter a value, click your cursor in the box or highlight the existing value using a click-drag across the existing value and type your new value. In dialogs, clicking Apply or OK to close the dialog applies the new value. In toolbars, pressing ENTER after typing the value does the same.

Type In Value

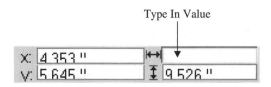

Combo Boxes   The name *combo* is short for *combination* and describes num boxes featuring clickable selection buttons for access to certain preset values. Enter a specific value in a Combo Box by typing or by choosing a value from the accompanying selector. Again, toolbars and dockers often require pressing the ENTER key to apply the new value, while clicking Apply or OK in dialogs does the same.

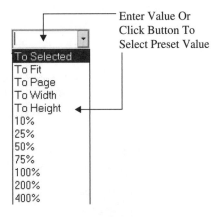

Enter Value Or
Click Button To
Select Preset Value

Flyouts and Popouts   In certain toolbars and dockers, you're likely to encounter flyout and popout menus, which are often accessed by clicking a triangular-shaped button. Popouts are typically selectors where you may choose a non-numeric option while Flyouts often contain ways to change behavior states, apply commands, or access more or less options.

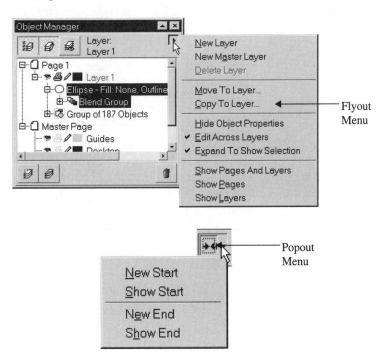

Flyout Menu

Popout Menu

Color Selectors Color selectors are relatively standard, and you often encounter these wherever color options are available with an object property, effect, or tool. You can recognize a typical color selector as a clickable button that has the secondary function of displaying the currently selected color. Clicking on these rectangular-shaped buttons opens the selector to display the current color palette and enables you to click once to specify a color. Most color selectors also include an Other button, which is a shortcut to CorelDRAW 10's full color resources.

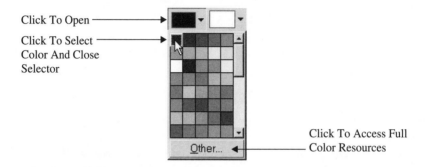

List Selectors A list selector is a button that opens to display a collection of label values. Clicking an associated list selector button once opens the selector enabling you to choose a value, state, or style.

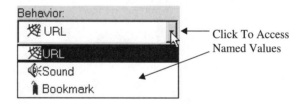

Radio Buttons and Option Boxes These two types of buttons are slightly different not only in shape, but in the choices they offer. Radio buttons are round and come in groups enabling you to choose one option or another—but only one. Option boxes are square shaped and enable you to choose an option or state to be either on (while a check mark appears in the square), or off (while no check mark appears).

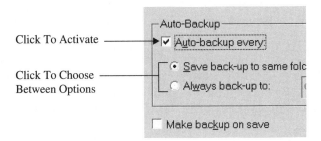

Click To Activate ⟶

Click To Choose
Between Options ⟶

3

Toggle Buttons   Toggle buttons serve to indicate on or off states and appear differently depending on whether they are pressed or not pressed. Generally, a pressed state indicates "on," while the not pressed state indicates "off."

"On" And Activated

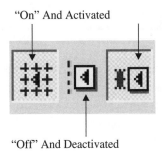

"Off" And Deactivated

Command Buttons   Command buttons appear often with labels indicating an associated command. Clicking one of these either applies a command immediately or opens a dialog offering choices for specifying further options.

Click To Open Dialog

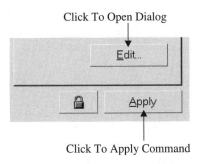

Click To Apply Command

Spinners   Spinners can actually be used in three ways. Similar to combo boxes, they enable you to specify values within a given range by clicking your cursor in the accompanying num box followed by pressing the ENTER key. Or you may use single clicks on the up and down arrow buttons to increase or decrease the values incrementally. You may also use a click-drag action by clicking the separation line between the two arrow buttons by dragging up or down to increase or decrease the accompanying value.

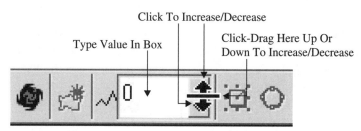

Type Value In Box   Click To Increase/Decrease

Click-Drag Here Up Or
Down To Increase/Decrease

Sliders   Sliders have existed as interface devices in recent releases of CorelDRAW and enable you to set values within a given range—often between 0 and 100 based on percent—by entering values or by dragging a control slider. To manipulate a slider value, use a click-drag action to move the slider "lever" either right (increase) or left (decrease) to change values.

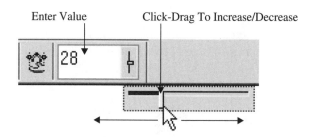

Enter Value   Click-Drag To Increase/Decrease

Pop-Up Menu   The pop-up menu is fully implemented in CorelDRAW 10 for nearly every command function and is completely context-sensitive meaning its available options or commands change depending on the object or interface component clicked. To open the pop-up menu and access most currently available commands and options, click your right mouse button (instead of the typical left-click) on any given point to access the pop-up menu. To close the pop-up menu, click anywhere but the menu itself or click an option or command from the menu as you would any command menu.

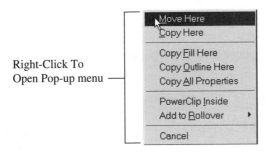

Right-Click To
Open Pop-up menu

3

Working with Dockers

If you've upgraded directly to CorelDRAW 10 from version 7 or 8, you may be wondering to yourself where CorelDRAW's rollups have gone. The quick answer is that they've now all been replaced by *dockers,* or their functions have been wired to the context-sensitive Property Bar. Dockers are interface components that enable you to access application features for nearly everything in CorelDRAW 10. Many of the docker functions are redundant with interactive tools when applying effects or using specialized tools. Regardless of what a specific docker enables you to accomplish, the dockers themselves may be manipulated in various ways to control how they appear.

Opening, Moving, and Closing Dockers

Dockers may be opened in various ways either through the use of shortcut keys or by choosing commands from the Tools or Window menus. For example, to open the Color Docker, choose Window | Dockers | Color. By default, dockers open to their lasted used state, either docked or undocked. While docked, they are attached to the right side of your application window, while the balance of your screen is occupied by your open document window. While undocked, they "float" above the document window and may be positioned anywhere on your screen (see Figures 3-3 and 3-4).

The dockers themselves all feature a common design, whether they are floating or not . Each has a title bar and close button. While undocked, floating dockers may be reproportioned to increase or decrease their size by clicking and dragging at the sides or bottom edges. You may also click the Collapse/Expand button to minimize or maximize them quickly. To move a floating docker, click-drag anywhere on its

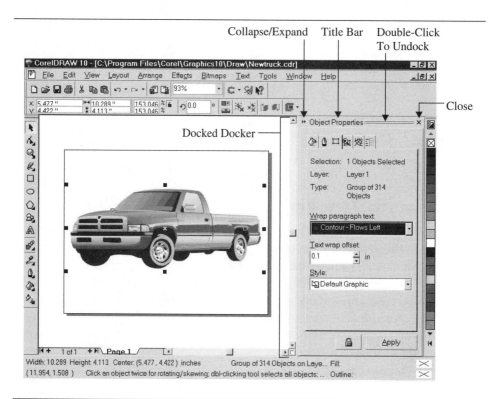

Collapse/Expand   Title Bar   Double-Click To Undock

Close

Docked Docker

FIGURE 3-3   While docked, dockers occupy the right side of your application window.

title bar. Minimized floating dockers appear only as floating title bars (and often with brief command buttons) on your screen. Minimized docked dockers appear as vertical title bars on the right side of your application window.

Click To Expand Minimized Floating Docker

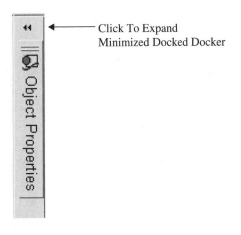

Click To Expand
Minimized Docked Docker

Double-Click To Redock   Collapse/Expand

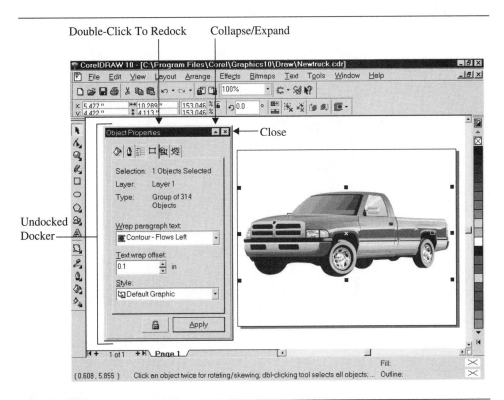

Close

Undocked
Docker

FIGURE 3-4   While undocked, dockers float above your document window.

Nested Dockers

While more than one docker is open, they often appear "nested," meaning that multiple dockers overlay each other on the right side of your application window. While dockers are nested, clicking their individual title bars brings them to the forefront of the interface. Undocked and nested dockers appear with their title bars oriented horizontally, and while docked, they appear oriented vertically (see Figures 3-5 and 3-6).

Although nesting dockers (docked or undocked) is likely the best way of working with multiple dockers, you may quickly separate and "un-nest" them if you prefer. To do this, use a click-drag action by clicking on the name tab identifying the docker and dragging away from the nested docker arrangement. As you do so, you see an outline preview of the frame of your selected docker as you drag indicating its new screen position when the mouse button is released (see

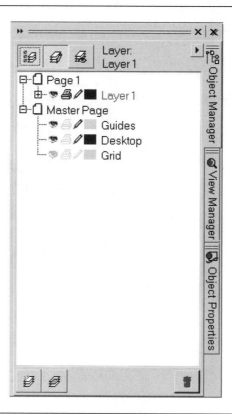

FIGURE 3-5   These three docked dockers are nested.

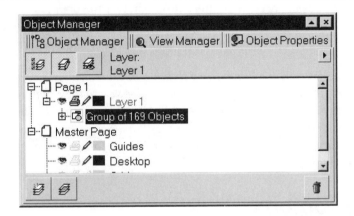

FIGURE 3-6 These three floating dockers are nested.

Figure 3-7). You may also un-nest single dockers to float by dragging them from their docked position using the same action. To nest multiple dockers together

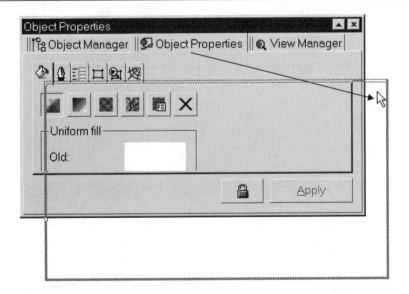

FIGURE 3-7 This floating docker is being detached from its nested position.

essentially requires the reverse of this action whether the dockers are floating or docked. To do so, click-drag on the title bar (while floating) or name tab of the docker and drag it to a position inside the boundaries of another floating docker.

TIP *To control whether title bars of floating dockers are visible, open the Options dialog to the General page, where you find an option called Show Titles On Floating Dockers. To access this option, choose Tools | Options (CTRL+J) and click General under the Workspace heading in the tree directory on the left of the dialog. For more information on customizing your Workspace, see Chapter 28.*

Using the Toolbox

CorelDRAW 10's main Toolbox is where you gain access to each and every tool available. But, like other toolbars, the Toolbox itself may be manipulated to present access to tools in different ways. By default, the Toolbox is attached to the Application window and essentially docked. If you wish though, you may have the Toolbox float over your document window, which can often be more convenient for viewing your document objects. To detach the Toolbox from its docked position, use a click-drag action by clicking on the double line at the top of the docked Toolbox and dragging toward the center of your screen.

Click-Drag Here ⎯⎯⎯⎯⎯▶
To Have Toolbox Float

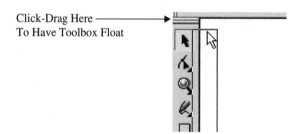

By default, your undocked Toolbox includes a title bar and close box. When floating—and detached from the application window—you may move the Toolbox around your screen by click-dragging on its title bar. Double-clicking the title bar immediately redocks the Toolbox. Clicking the Close box hides the Toolbox from view. Right-clicking anywhere in your document window to open the pop-up menu, and choosing View | Toolbox brings it back again.

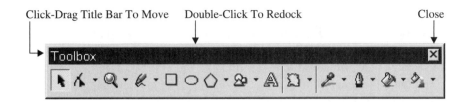

Click-Drag Title Bar To Move   Double-Click To Redock   Close

Whether or not the Toolbox is floating, you may access groups of tools by clicking buttons that appear with flyout buttons. A single click selects a tool, while a click-and-hold action opens the tool flyout. Although this might seem relatively straightforward, what may not be obvious is that you may detach individual flyouts from the main Toolbox and have them float independently. To do so, click-hold to open any group of tools and then use a click-drag action by clicking on the double line of the flyout and dragging away from the main Toolbox. The result is a duplicate of the tool flyout as a floating Toolbox group that may be treated as any floating toolbar, shown next. To hide the duplicate mini-Toolbox group from view, click the Close button.

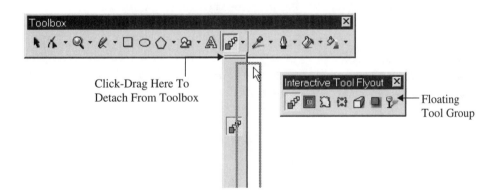

Click-Drag Here To
Detach From Toolbox

Floating
Tool Group

Working with Toolbars

Toolbars are also interface components that may appear docked or floating. This applies to any of the toolbars available in CorelDRAW 10 (such as the Standard Toolbar or Property Bar) or custom toolbars you create yourself. By default, toolbars appear docked, and while in this state, they feature small double-line markings to the left or top of the toolbar contents. To undock any docked toolbar, use a click-drag action by clicking on this double line and dragging away from its docked position in the Application window. As with dockers and the Toolbox, undocked toolbars each feature their own title bar and close button.

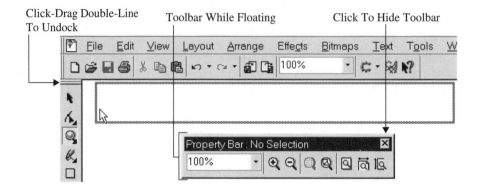

Double-clicking the title bar of a floating toolbar instantly redocks it to the Application window while clicking the Close box hides the toolbar from view. To restore a toolbar to be visible and appear in its lasted docked or undocked state, choose Window | Toolbars and make a selection from the submenu.

For information on customizing toolbars and toolbar item properties, controlling toolbar appearance, and creating your own custom toolbars, see Chapter 28.

Using the Color Palette

The Color Palette has undergone a few changes through past versions of CorelDRAW but remains one of the interface elements that may be docked or undocked. By default, the Color Palette features CorelDRAW's long-standing default CMYK color collection, but typically not all colors may be viewed at any one time when this palette is docked.

3

Viewing Palette Colors

To navigate the color selection visible at any one time, click the Up or Down arrow buttons at the top and bottom of the palette. Single clicks using your left mouse button on these arrow buttons enables you to "scroll" the selection one color well at a time. Single clicks with your right mouse button cause a Page Up and Page Down effect scrolling the visible color selection a complete row up or down (see Figure 3-8).

TIP	*You may reorganize the collection of colors you see in the Color Palette quickly using a click-drag action by clicking on a color well and dragging up or down to change any color well's order in the color palette.*

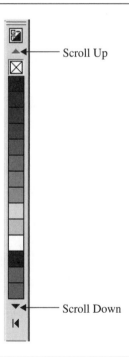

Scroll Up

Scroll Down

FIGURE 3-8   Left-click the arrow buttons to scroll by single colors or right-click the same buttons to scroll by complete rows.

After scrolling your Color Palette, the current selection remains visible. Where this isn't convenient, you may quickly access the full collection temporarily by clicking the Expand button. After making your color selection, the Color Palette automatically returns to its original state.

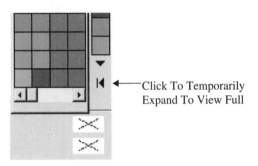

Click To Temporarily Expand To View Full

If you wish, you may also undock the Color palette and have it float. While it's floating, click-drag on its title bar to move it around your screen or click the close button to hide it from view. To retrieve it after doing so, right-click anywhere in your document window to open the pop-up menu, choose View | Color Palettes and select a palette to view. Double-clicking the title bar of a floating Color Palette causes it to be immediately redocked.

Click-Drag To Move;
Double-Click To Redock

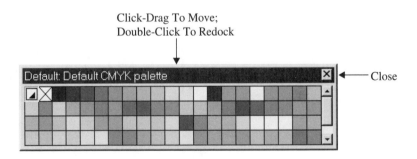

Close

Changing Palette Options

New for CorelDRAW 10's Color Palette is the Options flyout button that gives access to a number of Color Palette commands. This flyout menu enables you to apply Fill and Outline colors by command (as opposed to using left and right mouse button clicks to apply colors to objects) or control how you view the palette itself.

Choose Palette commands from the options flyout to control which palette is currently open, open multiple palettes, or create new color palettes. Choose Edit commands from the options flyout to change a palette color, open the Palette Editor, or locate a specific color. You may also view colors by name only using the Show Color Names option. For more information on working with the Color Palette and editing palettes, see the CD-ROM Chapter 6.

CHAPTER 4

Opening and Saving Files

Using File commands to open and save your drawing files and making use of templates, the Clipboard, and scrapbooks are perhaps among the most basic operations you perform in CorelDRAW 10. Nonetheless, using these commands is an essential part of your work, and you encounter more than a few options and features when doing so. In this chapter, you discover file-saving options such as backward compatibility, working with specialty files such as templates, setting backup options, performing Clipboard operations, and storing and retrieving scrapbook items.

CorelDRAW 10's Welcome Screen

The moment CorelDRAW appears on the screen, a friendly Welcome screen appears, enabling you to choose your very first step into the program (see Figure 4-1). This screen is loosely referred to as the "splash" and invites you to open a new or existing file, your most recently opened or edited file, a template file, or

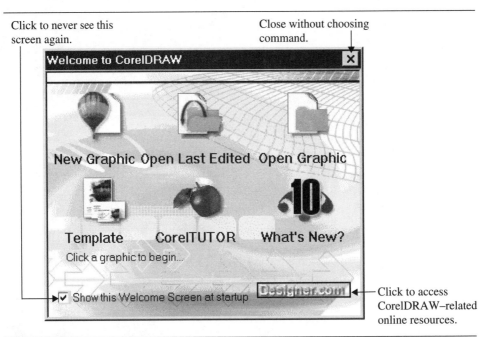

FIGURE 4-1 The Welcome screen offers a convenient way to choose the first task to perform after launching CorelDRAW.

explore CorelTUTOR and What's New for CorelDRAW 10. With Web access, you may also choose to explore Corel's **www.Designer.com** site, where you gain access to topical ways of using CorelDRAW and other Corel resources.

To choose a command, simply click one of the graphic buttons in the Welcome screen or to close the screen without choosing a command, click the Close button. If you're launching CorelDRAW for the first time, chances are the Open Last Edited button will be inactive. To never see the Welcome screen again, click to deactivate the Show This Welcome Screen As Startup button.

Opening Your First New Document File

If you are viewing the Welcome screen, clicking the New Graphic button automatically opens a brand-new document file to display a single blank page formatted to your CorelDRAW 10 default settings. Otherwise, either choosing File | New (CTRL+N) or clicking the New button in the Standard Toolbar, shown next, accomplishes the same result.

Click To Open New Document

Standard Toolbar

When a brand-new CorelDRAW document is created, CorelDRAW opens a new document window in the maximized state and automatically applies the default name [Graphic *X*], where *X* represents the sequence of the newly opened document. For example, opening your first new graphic after launching automatically creates the unsaved file Graphic 1, while opening additional files uses the default name Graphic 2, Graphic 3, and so on (see Figure 4-2). New document default filenames remain until the file is saved, but the sequence remains until CorelDRAW 10 itself is closed. Relaunching the application resets the document default name sequence to the beginning again.

Each open document is listed at the bottom of the Window menu. If you've opened several new files in sequence, you may notice that each document window is maximized to fill the document window area, but only the newest document appears, indicated by the document default name in CorelDRAW's application title bar. This is because while document windows are maximized, only the document in the forefront is visible. Any other opened documents are layered

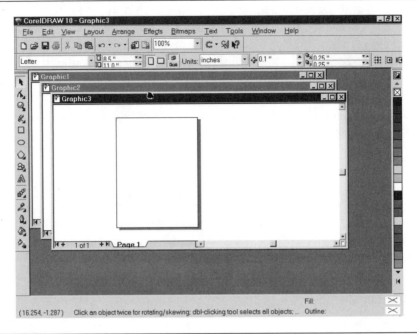

FIGURE 4-2 These three new document files were opened and numbered in sequence and have yet to be saved.

below and hidden from view. To navigate between document windows in the Maximized state, choose Window and then the filename from the bottom of this menu:

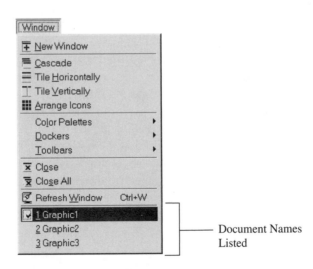

TIP

To see all open document windows and automatically arrange them in your CorelDRAW application window, choose either Cascade, Tile Horizontally, or Tile Vertically from the Window command menu. For example, Figure 4-2 demonstrates the effects of opening three brand-new document files after choosing Window | Cascade.

Opening Document Files

4

If your aim is to open an existing document file, you may do this either by clicking the Open Graphic button from the Welcome screen, clicking the Open button in the Standard Toolbar, or choosing File | Open (CTRL+O). Either way, the Open dialog box appears (see Figure 4-3) to display options for opening various types of files.

When a CorelDRAW, Corel R.A.V.E, or Corel PHOTO-PAINT file is selected—and before being opened—the Open dialog provides various ways of viewing what you have selected by displaying version, application, compression, notes and keywords, date, file type, and language information. You may also extract any embedded ICC (International Color Consortium) profile information, as well as choose to preserve the document's original layering structure. For visual reference, choose to view an optional preview of the file's thumbnail selected off by default.

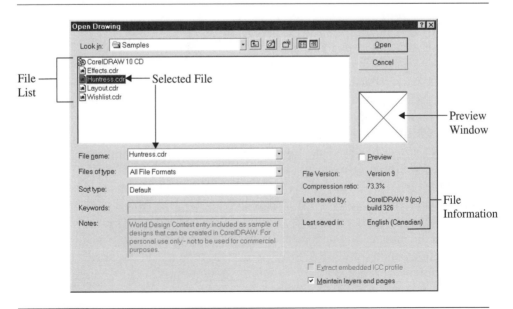

FIGURE 4-3 The Open dialog enables you to choose which file type to open, as well as various other options.

To open your most recent documents, look at the bottom of the File menu, where you find a brief list of your most recently opened documents.

While multiple files are selected, only the filenames of the selected files are displayed.

In the Open dialog, locate and select your document file and click the Open button, or simply double-click the filename, to open a document file. You may also open multiple files in this dialog by holding modifier keys. To open contiguous files in the same folder (meaning files listed in sequence), hold SHIFT while clicking the first and last filenames, or to open noncontiguous files in the same folder (meaning files not in sequence), hold CTRL while clicking to select the filenames, and click the Open button.

Although the Open dialog automatically lists all file formats in your current folder, you may wish to limit the types of files you are viewing to actual CorelDRAW files only, which can be more convenient, given all the file types CorelDRAW 10 is capable of opening. To view only CorelDRAW document files, choose CDR - CorelDRAW from the Files Of Type drop-down menu in the Open dialog.

Opening Files from Other Applications

If you wish, you may open native files from other applications, several of which are listed under the Files Of Type drop-down menu. Typically, CorelDRAW 10 opens the files immediately after its filters have interpreted the content. When CorelDRAW 10 opens a file originally created in a different application, it takes instant ownership of the document by immediately converting it to CorelDRAW format.

In most instances when opening common application files supported by CorelDRAW's Import filters, graphics and text objects are converted to compatible equivalents supported by CorelDRAW. The file remains a native application file until saved as a CorelDRAW version file. Although the Open command is essentially an Import operation, certain file formats may not be opened as documents. In these cases, you may be required to import the files as objects into an open CorelDRAW document. In these instances, an alert dialog (see Figure 4-4) appears to notify you of this requirement.

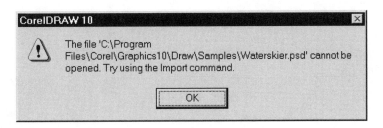

FIGURE 4-4 If the file you are attempting to open can only be imported, CorelDRAW 10 displays this message.

Warning Messages

When opening files—especially older files, or files created on a different system or using a third-party application—warning messages, such as the one below, may appear on your screen before the file actually opens in your CorelDRAW application window. For the most part, these warning messages aren't meant to cause alarm and merely provide information or notifications. Two of the most common messages are the version compatibility and font warnings.

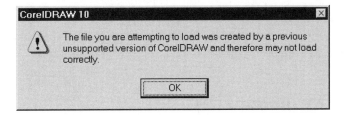

While the version compatibility warning merely serves as a reminder that the file you are opening was created in a substantially older version of CorelDRAW, the Font Matching Results warning dialog enables you to view a list of the fonts used in the document and provides options for substituting new ones (see Figure 4-5). CorelDRAW 10 supports backward compatibility only for versions 5 through 9.

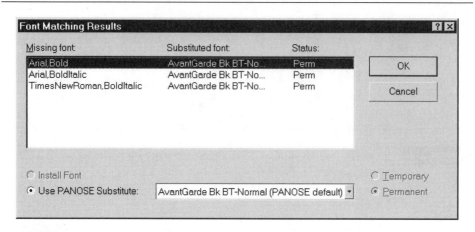

FIGURE 4-5   This dialog warns you that certain fonts used in the document you are opening may not match the available fonts on your current system.

Closing and Saving Documents

Saving files is another of the most basic operations you perform in CorelDRAW 10. Whether you save often (always a good idea), or you're saving your document for the first time, you can control certain properties associated with your document file. When it comes to closing and saving your CorelDRAW 10 files, you have a few key decisions to make, such as setting a location and naming your file, setting thumbnail and version preferences, as well as a few other options.

Closing Document Files

There are several ways to close an open document window: either by clicking the Close button in the upper-right corner of your document window or by choosing File | Close or Window | Close. If you have more than one document file open, you may also choose Window | Close All to automatically close every file.

Regardless of which method you use to close your documents, you automatically are prompted to choose whether or not to save any changes made to the file after it was opened. When closing multiple files, CorelDRAW prompts you separately for each file if changes have been made.

Saving Your First Document

No matter how far along you've progressed in creating a drawing, it may not be wise to wait until it's finished to save your efforts. Saving is a quick operation and is dependent on whether the file is brand-new or has already been saved. Typically, saving an existing document file is done simply by clicking the Save button in the Standard Toolbar or by choosing File | Save (CTRL+S), which causes your most recent changes to be saved immediately and without opening any dialogs.

If you're performing a save on your document file for the first time, it may help to take the following steps.

1. If you've just started a new document and wish to save it, clicking the Save button in the Standard Toolbar using the CTRL+S shortcut or choosing File | Save each results in opening the Save dialog (see Figure 4-6).

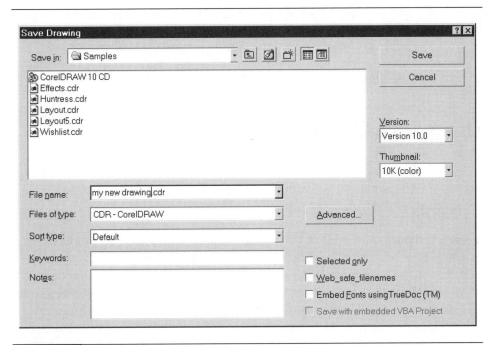

FIGURE 4-6   The Save dialog enables you to save your new document in various ways.

2. With the Save dialog open, use the dialog options to set a location for your document and enter a unique name in the File Name box.

3. If you're saving your document to a format other than CorelDRAW 10, choose a file format from the Files Of Type menu.

4. If saving your document in CorelDRAW or other Corel-supported formats, you may enter Keywords and Notes to include with the file. Keywords and Notes appear only in the Open dialog when the file is reopened.

5. While in the dialog, choose the options you wish to apply to your new document such as version, thumbnail, Web, and font preferences you wish to include.

6. Click the Save button in the dialog to save your efforts immediately using the options you've selected.

TIP   *You can quickly recognize whether a file has been changed in any way by looking at the Save button in the Standard Toolbar. This button automatically becomes available when even the slightest change has been made to the file. If no changes have been made, the Save command is unavailable.*

Using Save Options

If you're new to the available file-saving options in the Save dialog, it may help to browse the following list. Although the purposes of a handful of these options are self-evident, some are not so obvious. The following six items explain the results of choosing typical Save options.

Version   By default, CorelDRAW 10 automatically saves your document to be compatible only with CorelDRAW 10. If you need to, you may save your document to be compatible with previous versions of CorelDRAW as far back as version 5, see the menu, shown next. However, saving your file to be backward compatible may result in the loss of certain dynamic effects introduced through the versions, so you may wish to proceed carefully. Certain effects are rendered as curves or as bitmaps, depending on which version you've used. Attempting to reopen, in CorelDRAW 10, a document saved to a previous version most certainly results in some of these effects being affected.

Thumbnail   Thumbnail is used to describe a miniature representation of your document file. You may control how detailed this is up to a point. Thumbnails are the pictures available as images in the Preview window whenever the file is selected to open in CorelDRAW. The format of your thumbnail is largely determined by the version you have selected. While version 10 is selected, you may choose to save your thumbnail in 1K (mono, meaning black and white), 5K (a limited color representation), or 10K (full color, and the default). You may also choose None to omit the creation of the thumbnail, in which case no image is available in the Preview window of the Open dialog when reopening the file:

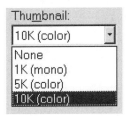

NOTE   *The Thumbnail representation of your drawing includes only the images on the first page of multipage documents, but includes all objects seen on both the document page and the desktop area beyond the page.*

Selected Only   The Selected Only option is incredibly useful for saving only specific objects from a drawing to a new document. However, this option becomes visible only if objects are currently selected in your document before the Save command is selected.

Web_Safe_Filenames   Choosing the Web_Safe_Filenames option is likely useful only if your document will eventually be used to create Web pages. This option automatically places underscore characters in place of spaces when your document file is named.

Embed Fonts Using TrueDoc   Use this option if your document will be moved to a host system where specific fonts you have used are not available. Choosing to embed fonts enables your document to be displayed and rendered, without actually installing the fonts you have used onto the host system. Choosing this option immediately displays a dialog asking you to agree or decline the terms under which you may use this option (see Figure 4-7). Declining the terms closes the dialog but leaves the option disabled.

Save with Embedded VBA Project   If parts (or all) of your document have been created using VBA (Visual Basic for Applications), this option becomes available and enables you to include scripts with your document file. If you wish to preserve your scripts as your own intellectual property, you may want to leave this option unselected. If this option is selected, the VBA Scripts you have saved with your document may be viewed, copied, and used by whoever reopens the document.

> TIP   *For more information on using the power of Visual Basic for Applications, see Chapter 29.*

Save As Command

The Save As command is useful for saving new revisions or copies of a document you have opened and edited, or if you simply need to save an exact copy using a different name or different settings. You may also wish to use the Save As command

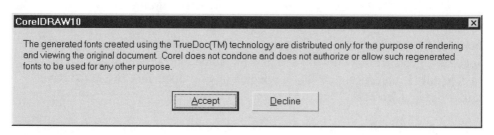

FIGURE 4-7   Before embedding fonts using TrueDoc, you must agree to the terms of their use.

in combination with the Selected Only option, which becomes available while objects in your document are selected and whenever the Save or Save As commands are used. Otherwise, the options available in the Save As command dialog are identical to those in the Save dialog.

For example, let's say you'd like to save a page or portion of your document as a CorelDRAW document file and wish to control the specific Save options. To do so, follow these steps:

1. Using the Pick Tool, select the objects you wish to include as a new document.

2. Choose File | Save As to open the Save As dialog. Notice the Selected Only option is available.

3. Click to select the Selected Only option.

4. Enter a name, choose a file type, and choose any other options you require.

5. Click the Save button to save the objects as a new document. Doing so simply saves the objects as a separate document—without opening or closing your current document file.

| TIP | *Although using the Save As command may seem similar to using the Export command in some ways, the two are quite different, and in some cases it may be more advantageous to use one technique rather than the other. Generally speaking, using the Save As command is the best technique to use when saving native CorelDRAW files, while using the Export command is best for saving your document or selected objects as any other type of file format. For information on using Export commands, see Chapter 26.* |

Advanced Saving Options

While in the Save or Save As dialogs, you may gain access to a series of higher-level file-saving options by clicking the Advanced button. Doing so opens the Options dialog to the Save page, enabling you to set optimization, texture handling, and effect handling options (see Figure 4-8). You may also access this dialog from within your CorelDRAW document before opening the Save or Save As dialogs by choosing Tools | Options (CTRL+J), expanding the tree directory under Document | Guidelines, and clicking Save.

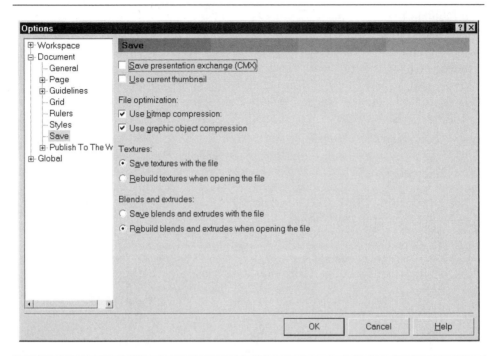

FIGURE 4-8   The Options dialog's Save page enables you to control how bitmaps, textures, graphic objects, and effects are saved with your document.

The following options enable you to control the type of information CorelDRAW 10 includes with your document file.

Save Presentation Exchange (CMX)   Choose this option to save your document to be compatible with Corel's Presentation Exchange file format.

Use Current Thumbnail   Choose this option to preserve the Thumbnail format currently selected for your document.

Use Bitmap/Graphic Object Compression   Choose either or both of these options to enable CorelDRAW 10 to compress bitmaps created for effects (such as Bitmap Extrude, Transparency, and Drop Shadows) and compress information required to describe dynamic graphic objects, such as Perfect Shapes, Polygons, Rectangles, and Ellipses. Compressing files enables you to store your files at a smaller size, but increases the time it takes to Save and Open files because the files are compressed, recompressed, and decompressed.

Save/Rebuild Textures   Choose the Save Textures With The File option (the default) to save the information required to recreate customized texture fills, or choose Rebuild Textures When Opening The File for smaller file sizes, but longer wait times when opening and viewing drawings that include custom texture fills. If you haven't used textures in this file, choosing either option results in the same file size.

Save/Rebuild Blend and Extrude Effects   Choose the Save Blends And Extrudes With The File option to save the information required to recreate the dynamically linked objects involved in Blend and Extrude effects to create smaller file sizes, or choose Rebuild Blends And Extrudes When Opening The File (the default) for smaller file sizes, but longer wait times when opening and viewing drawings that include these effects. If the document you're saving doesn't contain instances of Blend or Extrude effects, choosing either option results in the same file size.

> **TIP**   *Perhaps as a last resort, if you wish to completely discard the work performed in a document file, you may choose File | Revert. Doing so automatically closes and reopens the document without saving any of your changes. Choose this command carefully though because there is no undoing a Revert command.*

Using File Backup Options

When it comes to saving and backing up your document files, take full control over where and how backup files are created or whether they are created at all. Controlling backup options is a function of your CorelDRAW application instead of being document specific, so setting the options once applies to all working files. Backup files enable you to retrieve recent changes made to documents should something unfortunate occur while as you are working, or for those users who haven't yet adopted the habit of routinely saving their files. Backup files created automatically are named AUTOBACKUP_OF_*FILENAME*.CDR where *FILENAME* is the name of your original CorelDRAW document. Backup files may be opened in the same way as any CorelDRAW 10 document file using the File | Open command (CTRL+O).

To access CorelDRAW 10's file backup options, you need to pay a visit to the Save page of the Options dialog (see Figure 4-9), which is opened by choosing Tools | Options (CTRL+J), expanding the tree directory under Workspace, and clicking Save.

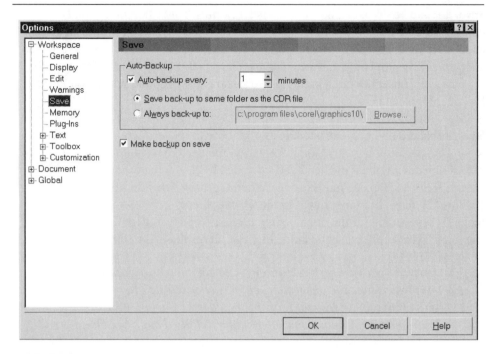

FIGURE 4-9   CorelDRAW 10 enables you to control where and when backup
files are created.

The following define the functions of each of the available backup options.

Auto-Backup   By default, the Auto-Backup option is selected, meaning that your
document files are constantly backed up according to designated time intervals.
Also by default, the time interval is set to ten minutes but may be set anywhere
within a range between one minute and two hours (120 minutes). If the files you
are creating are typically large, short Auto-Backup intervals may do more harm
than good, because your system resources are occupied each time CorelDRAW
saves the backup file.

Backup Locations   While Auto-Backup is activated, you may specify the
location of the backups to be saved in the same folder as your original document
file (the default), or choose Always Back-up To and use the Browse button to
specify a drive and folder location. The default folder for this option is set to
driveletter:\program files\Corel\Graphics10\Draw.

Make Backup on Save   Activating the Make Backup On Save option (selected by default) causes CorelDRAW to update the backup file to match your original document file each time you use the File | Save command (CTRL+S) to save your file. When this option is selected, the backup files created are named Backup_of_*filename*.cdr, where *filename* is the name of the original document. This naming scheme is different from the Auto-Backup feature that saves changes made to your document in time intervals, which saves and names the backup files AUTOBACKUP_OF_*FILENAME*.CDR.

4

Working with Templates

Templates are specialized files that may be saved based on existing settings and/or document content. Template files are slightly different from normal CorelDRAW 10 document files because they may not be accidentally overwritten as document files. Templates are often used as starting points to save repetitive page setup, document defaults, and other document-specific properties. You may recognize template files by their special CDT file extension.

Opening Templates

To open an existing template file with the aim of creating a new document based on the template, choose File | New From Template to open the New From Template dialog (see Figure 4-10). Here you discover one of CorelDRAW 10's new features, which enables you to choose from categories of templates organized into tabs and divided by document type.

Clicking each of the tabbed areas reveals lists of template files included with your CorelDRAW 10 application. While a template is selected, the Preview window displays a thumbnail representation of the first page of the template. To include the template's content as well as its setup formatting when opening a new document based on a template, click the Include Graphics option (selected by default) or deselected the option to open a blank shell. Double-clicking any template file immediately opens a new unsaved document automatically formatted using the template's document properties.

When choosing a template, these preformatted templates are organized into Full Page, Label, Booklet, Side-Fold, and Web templates. To navigate to your own saved template files, click the Browse tab of the New From Template dialog (shown in Figure 4-11) and use the available options to locate, select, and open a new document based on your saved template.

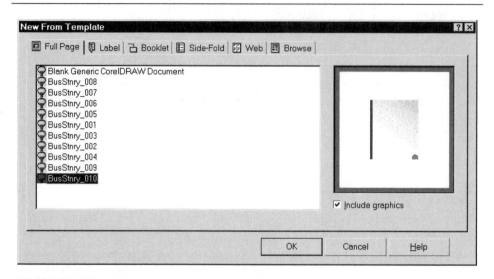

FIGURE 4-10   CorelDRAW 10's new Template feature enables you to choose a Preset template format or open your own saved template.

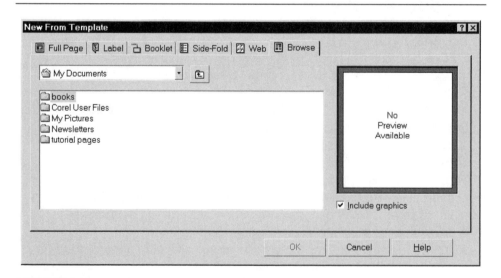

FIGURE 4-11   Click the Browse tab to access dialog options that enable you to open a template you've created yourself.

| TIP | *Preformatted Template files included with your CorelDRAW 10 application are stored in the driveletter:\Program Files\Corel\ Graphics10\Draw\Templates folder.* |

Opening and Saving Templates

To open a template file for editing—meaning you intend to change the actual template format and/or its content—use the File | Open command and choose CorelDRAW Template (CDT) as the file type. Before the template file opens, a convenient dialog appears asking whether you wish to open the template as a new document or for editing. If your aim is to open a new document based on the template content and structure, leave New From Template (shown next) selected (the default) in combination with the With Contents option. If your intention is to actually edit the template file itself, choose Open For Editing.

When saving an edited template file, performing a Save command automatically saves the file as a template without opening any dialogs—and without the need to respecify the file as a CDT template file in the Save dialog.

Clipboard Commands

The Clipboard is essentially a temporary "place" capable of storing the very last objects copied. While an object is stored on this seemingly imaginary area, you may "paste" many duplicate copies of the object into your document. The three most common Clipboard commands you are going to use are Copy, Cut, and Paste—each of which is accessible either from the Edit menu or from the Standard Toolbar:

Copying Versus Cutting

Each time a object is copied to the Clipboard, the previous Clipboard contents are immediately discarded. You can't actually view what is currently on your Clipboard, other than seeing what's available when the contents are pasted back into your document. To copy selected objects onto your Clipboard choose Edit | Copy. Better yet, click the Copy button in the Standard Toolbar or use the standard CTRL+C copy shortcut universal throughout Windows desktop software. You may also use the standard Windows CTRL+INSERT shortcut to achieve the same result. After copying your objects, the objects you copy remain unaltered in your document file.

The Cut command is slightly different. When objects are cut to the Clipboard, the originals are automatically deleted from your document and exist only temporarily on the Clipboard until the next objects are cut or copied. To cut objects to your Clipboard and delete them from your document, click the Cut button in the Standard Toolbar, choose Edit | Cut, or use the standard CTRL+X cut shortcut universal throughout Windows desktop software. You may also use the standard Windows SHIFT+DELETE shortcut to accomplish the same feat.

> **TIP** *To immediately create duplicates of your selected objects, press the + key on your numeric keypad. Copies immediately are placed in front of your selected objects and in the exact same page position. This action works independently of the Clipboard, meaning that your current Clipboard contents remain intact.*

Paste Versus Paste Special

While objects exist on your Clipboard, getting them back into your document requires the Paste command. You may use the Paste command to create as many duplicate copies of the Clipboard contents as you require. When objects are pasted from the Clipboard, they are automatically pasted in the frontmost order of the active layer in the exact same position as they existed when first copied. To paste items from your Clipboard, click the Paste button in the Standard Toolbar, choose Edit | Paste or use the standard CTRL+V shortcut. You may also paste items using the Windows standard SHIFT+INSERT shortcut.

For specialized operations where you wish to place copies of objects from other applications into your CorelDRAW 10 document page, you might consider using the Paste Special command. Paste Special enables you to place Clipboard contents that have been copied from other applications into your document. You may also place the contents into your document and maintain a link to the original third-party application.

These functions are controlled by typical Windows Object Linking and Embedding (OLE) functions. To use the Paste Special command (see Figure 4-12), choose Edit | Paste Special, which opens a dialog enabling you to choose a paste strategy, such as pasting Clipboard contents copied from other applications as a Windows metafile or while maintaining a link to the original application document file.

Depending on which type of object exists on the Clipboard, the Paste Special dialog offers several options for how the objects are placed. For example, copying graphics from other applications may offer options for you to paste the objects as normal or Enhanced Metafile Picture, Device Independent Bitmap, or a typical

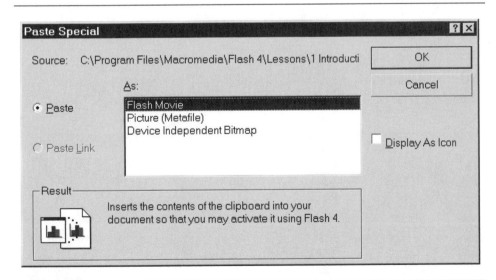

FIGURE 4-12   The Paste Special dialog enables you to paste Clipboard contents different ways.

Bitmap. When text objects are copied, you may have the option of placing the characters in picture format, or as text.

Undo and Redoing Editing Changes

When it comes to backing out of a multistep operation, or accomplishing a task by trial and error, there's nothing better than the Undo command. This little lifesaver enables you to reverse your very last action, regardless of what it was.

Basic Undo Commands

Choose Edit | Undo or use the standard CTRL+Z shortcut. To reverse an Undo command, choose Edit | Redo or use the CTRL+SHIFT+Z shortcut.

CorelDRAW 10 takes both of these commands slightly further by offering Undo and Redo buttons in the Property Bar, which may be used either to Undo or Redo single or multiple commands. The buttons themselves are fashioned into buttons and popouts in which clicking the button applies to the most recent action and clicking the popout reveals a brief listing of recent commands (see Figure 4-13). To reverse either Undo or Redo actions using the popouts, click one of the available commands in the list. Doing so reverses the selected actions back to the point you specified in the popout. Undo and Redo popouts display your most recent actions at the top of the listing.

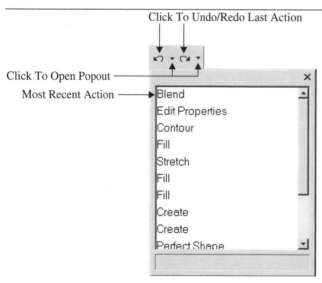

FIGURE 4-13   Use the Undo or Redo buttons, or their corresponding popouts, to reverse multiple commands.

4

TIP	*You may increase or decrease the number of Undo levels CorelDRAW remembers if you wish. By default, CorelDRAW enables you to reverse your most recent 99 actions, but this value may be set within a range between 1 and 99,999 actions. To access these options, open the Options dialog to the General page by choosing Tools	Options (CTRL+J), expanding the tree directory under Workspace and, clicking General.*

Using the New Undo Docker

For a higher level of control over your most recent actions, you may wish to use the new Undo Docker accessed by choosing Tools | Undo Docker. The Undo Docker (see Figure 4-14) enables you to view your drawing as it appeared prior to certain recent actions and/or save your recent actions as a Visual Basic for Applications (VBA) macro.

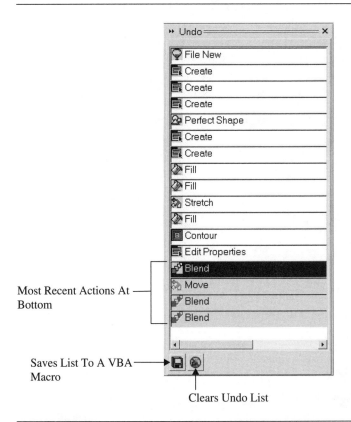

Most Recent Actions At Bottom

Saves List To A VBA Macro

Clears Undo List

FIGURE 4-14   To view the appearance of your drawing before your most recent actions were applied, try the new Undo Docker.

The Undo Docker displays your most recent action in reverse to the Undo and Redo popout menus with recent actions placed at the bottom of the Docker window list. Selecting a command in the list enables you to view your document as it appeared before your most recent actions were performed. Clicking the Clear Undo List icon clears the Docker wi ndow list enabling you to start a fresh session. By default, an alert dialog appears and warns you that this particular action is one that can't be reversed:

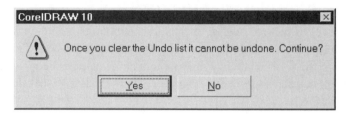

The primary function of the Undo Docker is to enable you to create VBA macros based on your recent actions. Clicking the Save List to a VBA Macro button in the Docker wi ndow opens the Save Macro dialog, shown next, which enables you to provide a name and description for the new macro and store it either with your open document or to CorelDRAW 10's main Global Macros list. When naming macros, spaces are not valid characters, but underscores are.

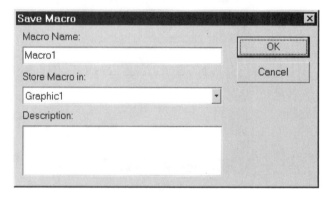

TIP   *For more information on using Visual Basic for Applications with your CorelDRAW 10 documents, see Chapter 29.*

Using Scrapbooks

CorelDRAW's Scrapbook Docker is another feature you may wish to use for quickly storing and retrieving objects. Scrapbooks enable you to permanently store single or multiple objects to be available with any document. You may store virtually anything you can create in CorelDRAW in a Scrapbook, ranging from objects and bitmaps, to complete layouts or drawings. You may also access Clipart, Photos, Favorite Fills, and 3D Models supplied on your CorelDRAW 10 application discs or (with Web access and while online) download items from Corel's Web site. To open the Scrapbook Docker, choose Tools | Scrapbooks | Browse (see Figure 4-15).

4

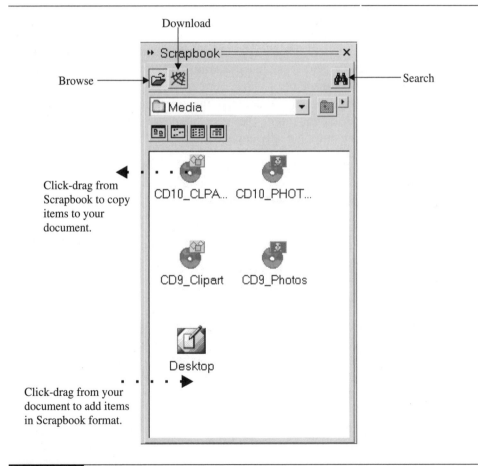

FIGURE 4-15   The Scrapbook Docker enables you to store and retrieve objects of virtually any format to any folder.

To explore Scrapbook features, follow these steps:

1. Using the docker drop-down menu, navigate to a folder containing items you wish to add to your currently open document. The items appear as graphic icons in the Docker wi ndow. To specify a location, click a folder or drive shortcut in the Docker wi ndow. To access the clipart, photos, and 3D models included with CorelDRAW 10, click the CorelDRAW 10 CD shortcut icon while in the Media folder.

2. To add items from the Scrapbook, drag the items from the Docker window onto your document page. The objects are immediately copied with the original Scrapbook item still intact in its folder location.

3. To add selected items from your document page to a folder as a Scrapbook item, use a click-drag action to drag them into the Scrapbook Docker window. New Scrapbook items appear with generic-style Scrapbook icons and are automatically applied with the default name Scrap in sequence. Each time you add a new Scrapbook item, the default names Scrap, Scrap (2), Scrap (3), and so on are automatically applied.

4. To rename a Scrapbook item, click once on the item's name in the Docker wi ndow to select the name, click a second time to highlight the text, enter a new name, and press the ENTER key.

5. To perform a Search, click the Binoculars button in the Docker wi ndow to open change the docker view to Search mode and enter a keyword in the Search For box. Search results are displayed in the docker once the search is complete. To return to the previous view, click the Browse button at the top of the Docker wi ndow.

6. To download items from Corel's Web site, ensure that your Web connection is active, and you have a minimum of 10MB of free storage space on your system, and click the Web button at the top of the Docker wi ndow. Once the download is complete, you may browse and copy the downloaded items from the Scrapbook into your document.

TIP *Items copied directly from your document into the Scrapbook Docker are stored in the current folder in a unique file format using the extension SHS.*

PART II

Getting Started with CorelDRAW 10

CHAPTER 5

Controlling Documents and Pages

While the tools in CorelDRAW provide plenty of ways to actually draw, your document is the quintessential container that holds virtually everything you create. Documents are subdivided into a number of key areas—the most critical of which is the document page. For traditional artists and painters, the page acts as a canvas providing the boundaries and relative dimensions for all visual elements. But in digital terms, your document page is merely one of the "places" where your drawing objects may be positioned. In this chapter, you discover how to control the size, appearance, length, and layout of your document pages in order to tailor them to your drawing or illustration needs.

Evaluate Your Document Needs

Before beginning any drawing project, it helps to take an inventory of your document needs, so you may need to ask yourself a few questions before you begin in order to make decisions about how to set up your CorelDRAW document. In many cases, changing or updating your document setup as your needs change takes just a few moments. However, some changes take longer than others, so the answers to these questions will help you avoid anything drastic down the road. Your question-and-answer session might go something like this:

- What size and length does your document need to be? Will all pages be the same, or will some pages be different from others?

- Does your document require a specialized layout? Will you be printing or exporting typical pages, or does your document need to fit a specific type of format?

- How will your document be reproduced or distributed? Will it be exported to a different application or file format? Is it destined for the Web or for offset reproduction?

- Do you need to create a layout sketch before you begin, or will you be following an existing layout or design?

Not all the answers may be available before you begin your document, but the mental evaluation and preparation may help. Once you do have the answers, CorelDRAW 10 provides all the resources to plug them into your document setup.

Setting Up Your Document Pages

Like any object in CorelDRAW 10, your document page features its own set of properties. Page properties can be narrowed to physical page properties and display preferences. Physical page properties include such things as the size, length, and color of your document, while display preferences include how you would like to view certain page properties. Let's start with the most commonly set options and progress through to the special-purpose features.

Page-Viewing Options

By default, when a new document is created, you see a rectangle on your screen representing your document page proportions. What you won't see, though, are two other page display features: the Printable Area and the Bleed Area. You may control whether any of these Page properties are visible using the Options dialog. To control these options, choose Layout | Page Setup to open the Options dialog to the Size page. Click Page in the tree directory on the left side of the dialog to display your page display options (see Figure 5-1).

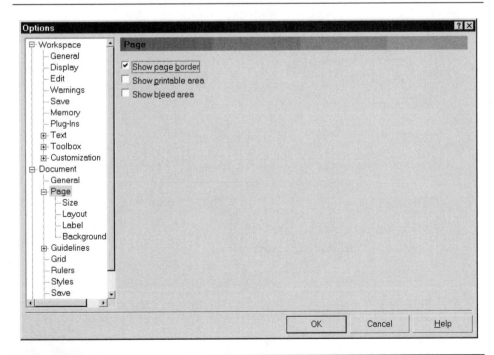

FIGURE 5-1   Although they may be a little tricky to get to, these options control how your actual page is displayed.

Show Page Border

To toggle the display state of the boundaries of your page, click Show Page Border. While this option is straightforward enough, the remaining two options in the dialog are slightly more involved and are both interconnected with other features of CorelDRAW 10.

Show Printable Area

The toggle state of this option enables you to display two key things—the area onto which your currently selected printer is capable of printing, and the size of the printing material your printer is currently set to use for printing the document. Both are represented by dotted lines (see Figure 5-2). These two unique areas may appear inside or outside your document page, depending on whether your current document page size is larger or smaller than what your printer and printing material are capable of reproducing. The physical properties of these two areas are set according to the printer selected in the Print Setup dialog, opened by choosing File | Printer Setup (see Figure 5-3).

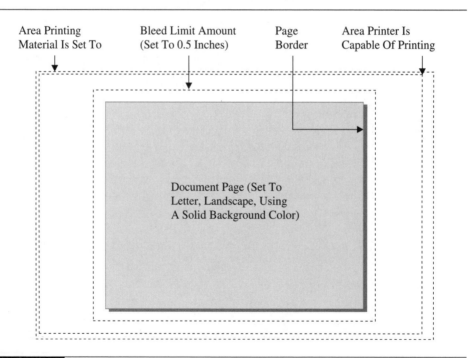

FIGURE 5-2   While the Show Bleed and Show Printable Area viewing options are selected, dotted lines appear when you view your document page.

Click to access your
printer's material size

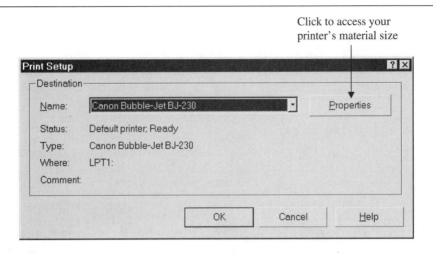

FIGURE 5-3   Printable areas are determined by the printer (and its current printing
material size) set in the Print Setup dialog.

Show Bleed Area

The term "bleed" is related specifically to printing and refers to a specific physical
area surrounding your document page. If the document you are creating is to be
reproduced using offset printing reproduction techniques, this option may be of
interest. Setting a Bleed amount for your document enables you to add an "extra"
portion to the edges of your final printed output. If you have chosen to add a
page background or have objects overlapping the edge of your document page,
increasing the bleed amount enables you to include more of these areas when your
document is printed onto larger output material. To toggle display of the currently
set Bleed amount, click the Show Bleed Area option in this dialog.

However, actually setting the value of the bleed amount is done using a different
dialog. The Bleed amount may be set anywhere within a range between 0 (the exact
edge of your page) and 900 inches. To set the Bleed amount, choose Layout | Page
Setup to open the Options dialog to the Size page and enter a value in the Bleed
option num box.

Controlling Page Size and Orientation

If your document is a single, letter-sized, portrait-oriented page, you'll be pleased
to discover that this is the default size created whenever a new document is created.
If it's not, changing any of these conditions is a quick operation.

Your page size and orientation may be changed a number of ways, the quickest of which is using the Property Bar while the Pick Tool is selected and while no objects are selected. The Property Bar includes a brief set of options for setting your page to standard-sized pages, custom sizes, and orientation, and it provides ways to change all pages at once or only the page being viewed, shown next.

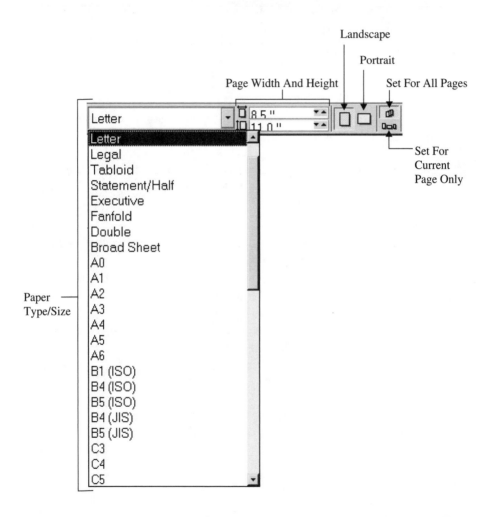

For the most common documents, choosing the Paper Type/Size option and orientation enables you to format your document. When choosing options for specific document formats, the following definitions of CorelDRAW 10's capabilities may help.

Paper Type/Size   To select a standard page size, clicking the Paper Type/Size option in the Property Bar enables you to quickly specify your page size. The list includes typical page sizes such as Slide, Letter, Legal, Tabloid, and so on. Once selected, the sizes are automatically entered as values into the Width and Height boxes in the Property Bar.

Page Width/Height   If you require a custom page size, you may enter specific values based on your current unit measurements directly into the Page Width and Height boxes followed by pressing the ENTER key. Both Width and Height page sizes may be within a range between 0.1 and 1,800 inches. Choosing a nonstandard page size automatically sets your Paper Type/Size to Custom.

Orientation   Choose an orientation for your page by clicking either Portrait or Landscape in the Property Bar while using the Pick Tool and while no objects are selected. If your page width entered is smaller than the page Height entered, your orientation automatically is set to Portrait, and vice versa for Landscape. Changing from Portrait to Landscape (or vice versa) automatically transposes the values in the Width and Height boxes.

Set For Default Page/Current Page Size   CorelDRAW 10 enables you to format your document to be up to 999 pages in length, each of them identical in size and orientation. The Set For Default and Set Current Size Only buttons operate in a toggle state, enabling you to set the page size either for all pages in your document at once (the default) or only for your current page. If you wish to set your current page to be different from the others in your document, click the lower of these two buttons and set your new page size and orientation as needed. Doing so changes only the size and orientation of the current page.

Controlling Page Background Color

To specify a color for the page background for your document choose Layout | Page Background to open the Options dialog (CTRL+J) to the Background page (see Figure 5-4).

The Options dialog Background page features options that allow you to specify the appearance of your page background in the ways that are described next.

Solid   To specify any of the Uniform colors available in CorelDRAW 10, click the Solid option and choose the color selector. Clicking Other in the color selector provides access to all of CorelDRAW 10's various color palettes. Once a color has been specified, your entire page is applied with this color.

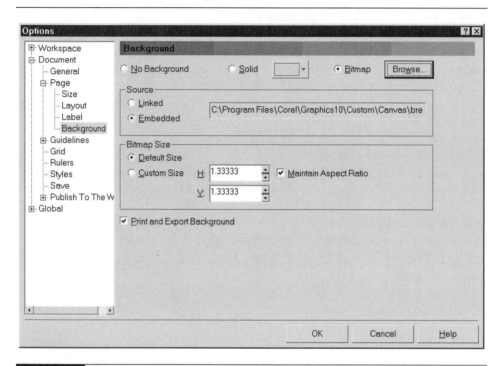

FIGURE 5-4 To control the appearance of your document page, use the Background page of the Options dialog.

Bitmap If you wish, you may specify a tiling bitmap as the page background by clicking the Bitmap option and the Browse button, which opens CorelDRAW's Import dialog. Locate and select the bitmap you wish to use as your page background and click OK to tile the bitmap to the edges of your page background as many times as is required to fill the page.

Source The Source options become available only if you have specified a Bitmap as your page background, and they enable you to either establish an external link to the bitmap file or store a copy of it internally with your CorelDRAW 10 document file. Choose Linked to maintain an external link or Embedded to store the bitmap with your document. While Linked is selected, the file path to the bitmap is displayed, and the bitmap itself must accompany your CorelDRAW document for output.

Bitmap Size The Bitmap Size options also become available if you have specified a Bitmap as your page background, and they enable you either to use the existing size of the bitmap in the tiling operation or specify a new size. Leave Default as the option selected to use the bitmap's original size, or choose Custom to enter new H (horizontal) and/or V (vertical) sizes, each of which may be set independently by deselecting the Maintain Aspect Ratio option.

Print And Export Background

If you wish to control whether or not the page background you have applied to your document page is included when exporting your drawing files or when your document is printed, use the Print And Export Background option. This option becomes available while either Solid or Bitmap is selected for your page background and by default is selected active.

Using Layouts and Labels

Although the setup of your document page includes some of the physical properties set through use of the Property Bar, the Options dialog also provides the only access to specialized page options. Page options are organized into specialized layout and preformatted label options.

Choosing Specialized Layouts

The Layout page of the Options dialog (Figure 5-5) enables you to choose from one of five specialized layouts for your document. Choose Book, Booklet, Tent Card, Side-Fold Card, and Top-Fold Card from the Layout menu.

Choosing one of these layout styles instantly divides your current document page size into horizontal and vertical pages, according to the preview supplied in the dialog.

Full Page   This layout style is the default for all new documents and essentially formats your document in single pages:

  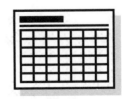

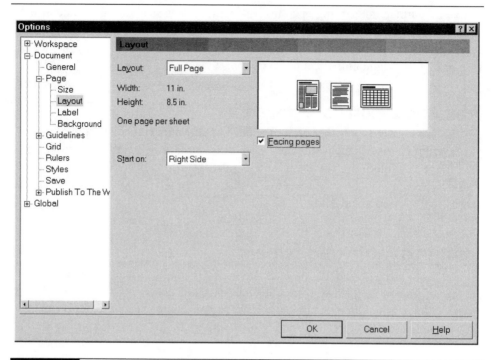

FIGURE 5-5   To choose a specialized layout, use options in the Layout dialog.

Book   The Book layout format, shown next, divides your document page size into two equal vertical portions, while each portion is considered a separate page. When printed, each page is output as a separate page.

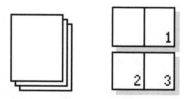

Booklet   In a similar arrangement to the Book layout, the Booklet layout format divides your document page size into two equal vertical portions. Each portion is considered a separate page. But when printed, pages are paired according to typical imposition formatting where pages are matched according to their final position in the booklet layout. In a four-page booklet, this means page 1 is matched with page 4, and page 2 is matched with page 3, as shown:

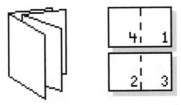

Tent Card   The Tent Card layout format, shown next, divides your document page size into two equal horizontal portions, while each portion is considered a separate page. Since tent card output is folded in the center, each of your document pages is printed in sequence and positioned to appear upright after folding.

Side-Fold Card   The Side-Fold layout format also divides your document page size into four equal parts both vertically and horizontally. When printed, each document page is printed in sequence and positioned and rotated to automatically fit the final folded layout. Folding the output once vertically and then again horizontally results in your pages following in the correct sequence and orientation:

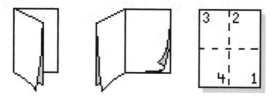

Top-Fold Card   Like the Side-Fold layout, the Top-Fold layout format also divides your document page size into four equal parts both vertically and horizontally. When printed, each document page is printed in sequence and positioned and rotated to automatically fit the final folded layout. Folding the output once horizontally and then again vertically results in your pages following in the correct sequence and orientation:

After choosing a layout style and returning to your document, each subdivision of the layout may be viewed individually. If you wish, you may also view pages in pairs by choosing the Facing Pages option in the Layout page of the Options dialog for certain layout styles. While Facing Pages is selected in the dialog, you may also start your document either on the Left side or Right side for certain layout styles by making a selection from the Start On menu.

Using Preformatted Labels

CorelDRAW has long provided a huge collection of preformatted label layouts from virtually every label manufacturer. But in order to use one of these Label formats, your document page must be formatted to letter-sized portrait; otherwise, the Label option in the Size page of the Options dialog is unavailable. Once the option is available and selected, the Size page transforms into the Label page, offering access to the enormous label collection. Once a label is selected, the preview window shows the general layout of the selected label and indicates the number of rows and columns available (see Figure 5-6).

After choosing a Label layout in the tree directory provided and returning to your document, each of your document pages represents an individual label for the label style you've chosen. You need to specify the exact number of pages to add to accommodate whole pages of labels—CorelDRAW provides no way of automatically adding pages, nor does it feature any options to print to partial label pages.

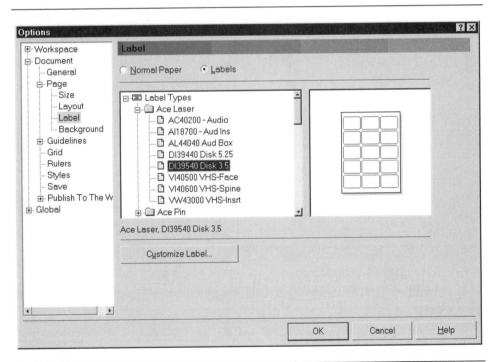

FIGURE 5-6   CorelDRAW likely features the largest selection of label formats available to any graphics application.

In the unlikely event that you don't find the exact manufacturer for a specific type of label you wish to set your document for, the Label feature also enables you to create your own from scratch or based on an existing label format (see Figure 5-7). Choose an existing label from the Label Style menu, customize the number of rows and columns, and set the Label Size, Margins, and Gutters according to your own label sheet. Once created, you may save your label by clicking the plus (+) button in the dialog or delete a selected label from the list by clicking the minus (–) button.

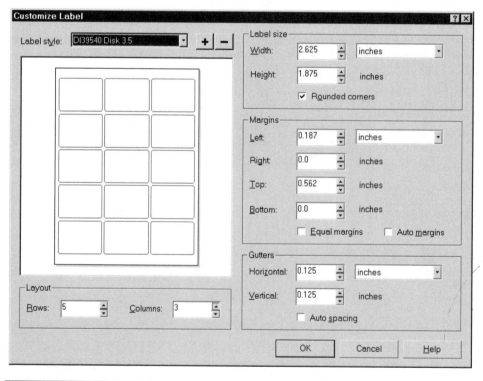

FIGURE 5-7   If you can't locate the label you're looking for, you may adapt an existing label format to suit your own needs using these options.

5

Naming Pages

By default, whenever new pages are added to your document, they are automatically applied with generic names such as Page 1, Page 2, and so on. But these page names are only for reference as you navigate your pages in CorelDRAW. Page names may be customized up to 32 characters in length, if you like, using one of several techniques.

When creating Web page documents—where each document page results in a separate Web page—adding a unique name to the page creates a title for the exported HTML page. When your document is printed, page names may also be set to accompany the output, indicate the contents of the page, or provide other page-specific information.

> **TIP** *To quickly display the previous or next page in your document, press the PAGE UP or PAGE DOWN keys on your keyboard.*

Using the Rename Page Command

The Rename Page command enables you to assign a unique name to your current page. There are two ways to access this command, either using command menus by choosing Layout | Rename Page, or by right-clicking the page tab of your document window and choosing Rename Page from the pop-up menu. Either way, the Rename Page dialog opens, shown next, enabling you to enter a name up to 32 characters in length (including spaces) for your current page and click OK to apply the name.

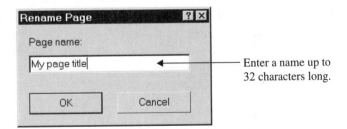

Enter a name up to 32 characters long.

Using the Object Properties Docker

The Page tab of the Object Properties Docker also enables you to name your page. Open this docker by right-clicking a blank space on your page and choosing Properties, or use command menus while no objects are selected by choosing Edit | Properties.

Either way, the Object Properties Docker opens with several tabbed areas available, shown next. Clicking the Page tab displays your page-related options, one of which is the Page Title box.

To quickly open the Go To Page dialog, shown next, double-click between the Next Page and Previous Page buttons at the lower left of your document window. This dialog enables you to move quickly to a specific page in your document.

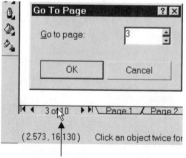

Double-click to open this dialog.

Using the Object Manager

The Object Manager Docker offers advantages when naming pages since it enables you to name any or all pages in your document in a single docker, instead of just your current page. To open the Object Manager, use command menus by choosing Tools | Object Manager. Once the docker is open, click to ensure the docker view is set to display Object Properties by deselecting the Layer Manager view button state (see Figure 5-8).

In this view, all page and object names are displayed. To rename any page (or any object), click once directly on the page title to select the page you wish to name or rename, and click a second time to highlight the page name text and type

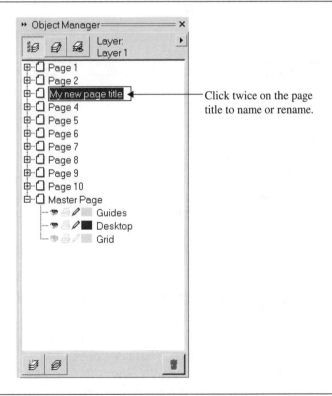

Click twice on the page title to name or rename.

The Object Manager enables you to name any or all pages at once.

a name followed by pressing the ENTER key. Page names appear in the page tabs at the lower left of your document window accompanied by a numeral indicating the page's order in your document:

To see more or less of the pages of your document in the Page tab area of your document window, click-drag on the "seam" between the page tabs and the horizontal scroll bar:

Page Commands

When it comes to adding new pages to your document or deleting existing pages, there's certainly no shortage of methods to use in CorelDRAW 10. Some involve straightforward menu commands, and other methods become available when you use specialized page views. Others come by way of shortcuts while holding modifier keys. In this section, you discover the quickest and most convenient ways.

Inserting Pages and Setting Options

The most straightforward way to add and/or delete pages to control the layout and organization of pages in your document is through use of commands under the Layout menu. To add pages to your document, choose Layout | Insert Page to open the Insert Page dialog (Figure 5-9), which features a host of options for specifying your new page properties and where you would like to add the new page in relation to your existing pages.

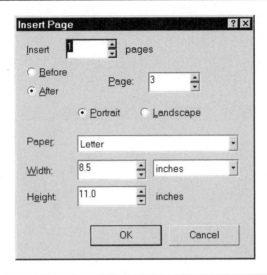

FIGURE 5-9   The Insert Page dialog enables you to choose a format for your new page(s) while adding them to a specific position in your document.

Enter the number of pages you would like to add in the Insert box and select whether you would like them added either Before or After your current page, or a specific point using the Page box. The remaining options enable you to choose Orientation and Paper sizes, or enter custom sizes for all newly added pages.

TIP   *To quickly add a new page to the beginning or end of your document while viewing the first or last page, click the plus (+) symbol, which appears on the left or right of the page buttons at the lower left of your document window. To add a page before or after your current page, right-click the page tab to the right of these buttons and choose either Insert Page Before or Insert Page After from the pop-up menu.*

Deleting Pages

Deleting your unwanted document pages is another layout-related command that's available by choosing Layout | Delete Pages. The Delete Pages dialog enables you to delete one or more of the existing pages in your document. By default, the dialog opens to automatically display your current page as the page in the Delete Page box, shown next, but you may select any page before or after your current page if you wish. To delete an entire sequence of pages, click the Through To Page option, which enables you to delete all pages in a range between the page specified in the Delete Page box through to any page following your current page.

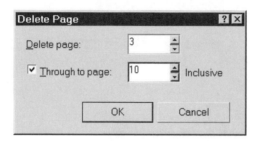

To quickly Move or Copy pages in your document, hold modifier keys while click-dragging the page tabs at the lower left of your document window. To move a page and change its sequential order in your document, use a click-drag action on the page tab to drag it to a new position. To Copy a page—and all its contents— to a specific position in your document, hold CTRL while click-dragging the page tab, dragging the page to a new position:

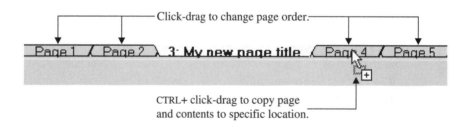

Using the Page Sorter

CorelDRAW 10's new Page Sorter view enables you to take a bird's eye look at your document and all its pages, as well as add, delete, move, or copy pages in a single view. To open your document and all its pages in the Page Sorter view, choose View | Page Sorter (Figure 5-10). The Page Sorter displays all pages in your document.

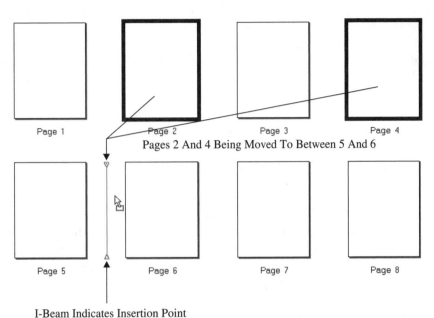

Pages 2 And 4 Being Moved To Between 5 And 6

I-Beam Indicates Insertion Point

FIGURE 5-10   The new Page Sorter view enables you to manage your document pages interactively while viewing all page size, orientation, name, and position information.

TIP   *The Page Sorter enables you to Export either your entire document or single or multiple selected pages quickly. Select the page(s) you wish to Export and choose File | Export, or click the Export button in the Standard Toolbar to open the Export dialog. To export only specific pages, click the option to Export This Page Only, which by default is not selected.*

While in Page Sorter view, a single click selects a page, while holding SHIFT while clicking enables you to select or deselect continuous multiple pages. Holding CTRL while clicking enables you to select or deselect noncontiguous pages. The following actions enable you to apply page commands interactively to single or multiple page selections.

Move Page(s)   To move a page and change its order in your document, click-drag the page to a new location. While dragging, a vertical I-beam appears indicating the insertion point for the page, or the first page of the selected sequence of pages.

Add Page(s)   To add pages to your document, right-click any page and choose Insert Page Before or Insert Page After from the pop-up menu to insert a page relative to the selected page.

Copy Page(s)   To copy pages—and their contents—hold CTRL while click-dragging the page to a specific location. While dragging, a vertical I-beam appears indicating the insertion point for the page copy, or the first page of the selected sequence of pages.

Name or Rename Pages   To add a new name or change an existing page name, click the page name below the page to select it, and click a second time to highlight the page title and enter a new name followed by pressing ENTER. You may also rename a Page by right-clicking a specific page and choosing Rename Page from the pop-up menu to highlight the page name for editing.

Change Page Size/Orientation   In Page Sorter View, the Property Bar displays typical page property options for applying standard or custom page sizes, and changing the orientation between landscape or portrait (see Figure 5-11).

To exit the Page Sorter view, either click the Page Sorter View button in the Property Bar or use menu commands by choosing View | Page Sorter View. After returning to your normal document view, any changes applied while in the Page Sorter are applied to your document. For more information on viewing documents in Page Sorter view, see Chapter 7.

| TIP | *To exit Page Sorter view and simultaneously navigate to a particular page in your document, double-click a specific page.* |

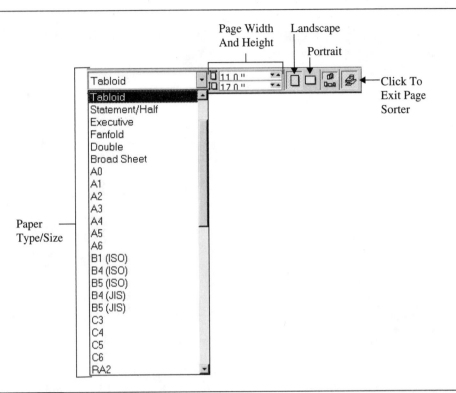

FIGURE 5-11   While in Page Sorter view, the Property Bar offers these typical page-related options.

Examining Drawings and Objects

To get a quick summary of your entire document, use the Document Information dialog (Figure 5-12) opened by choosing File | Document Info. This dialog features options to view all information about your document or view only specific

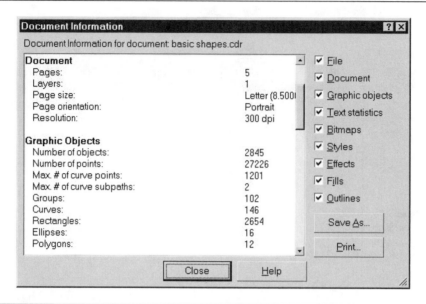

FIGURE 5-12   For a quick and detailed summary of your CorelDRAW file, use the Document Information dialog.

information. Choose from a selection of information types comprised of File, Document, Graphic Objects, Text Statistics, Bitmaps, Styles, Effects, Fills, and Outlines. Using this command is perhaps essential if the document you are preparing is destined for printing at an off-site service bureau, or if you require a quick detailed summary of a document you're unfamiliar with.

This resizable dialog features a viewing window that displays your selected information, and enables you to Save the information listed to a text (TXT) file or Print the information to a connected printer. Clicking the Save As button opens the Save As dialog, enabling you to choose a name and location for the text file. Clicking the Print button opens the Print dialog, featuring access to your connected printer and its related drivers.

CHAPTER 6

Measuring and Drawing Helpers

Having access to resources that help you measure or place your drawing objects used to be something of an innovation in graphics software. These days, the capability to specify infinitesimal amounts, measure gargantuan distances, and place objects virtually anywhere you want instantly has become a significant feature in competing graphics software. Thankfully, Corel leads the way in this race by engineering plenty of resources for measuring and placing objects. In this chapter, you discover just how far CorelDRAW 10 takes these features.

Using the Ruler

Before Property Bars were engineered into CorelDRAW, the Ruler provided one of the few ways to monitor the page position of an object. Back then, precision drawing work was often difficult and time-consuming—perhaps even frustrating. Rulers provided nothing more than a visual reference and a source for "ruler" lines (which also served as nothing more than visual reference). But, like most other features, the Ruler has been developed to be adaptable and an inexhaustible source for *Guidelines*. Guidelines are explored in detail later; for now, let's look more closely at CorelDRAW's Ruler features.

What Do Rulers Measure?

If your Rulers aren't already visible, choose View | Rulers, or right-click a blank space on or off your document page and choose View | Rulers from the pop-up menu.

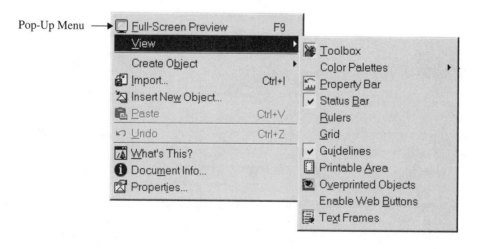

6

Although they're now somewhat redundant with Property Bar and Status Bar display information, Rulers can help when judging spaces on your document page or while positioning objects. Without the use of Rulers, creating virtually any type of drawing with a certain degree of precision involved or when drawing to scale is nearly impossible. When Rulers are visible, they appear as graduated vertical and horizontal indicators at the top and to the left of your document window (see Figure 6-1).

Rulers help predominantly to indicate specific page position of objects or your cursor. As your cursor is dragged across your document window, dotted lines appear on both the Vertical and Horizontal Rulers. Rulers are essentially composed of three basic components: the Vertical Ruler, a Horizontal Ruler, and a Ruler origin. The Vertical Ruler visually shows the vertical page position of your cursor indicating the *Y* value in the Property Bar. This corresponds to *Y* values displayed in certain Property Bar states to indicate vertical page position and measure Height.

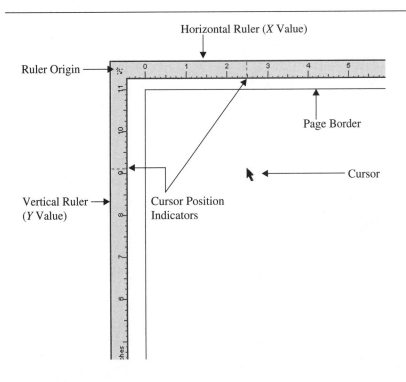

FIGURE 6-1   While visible, CorelDRAW's Rulers provide visual page reference and cursor position.

The Horizontal Ruler visually indicates the horizontal page position of your cursor, displaying an *X* value in the Property Bar and indicating the horizontal page position and Width.

The Ruler origin is the point at which your Vertical and Horizontal Rulers meet; and, essentially, it represents the 0 page position reference where all measurements begin. By default, the bottom-left corner of your page represents the Ruler origin 0 position. The means vertical (*Y*) and horizontal (*X*) page positions above or right of the bottom-left page corner are indicated by positive values, while all values below or left of this point are measured using negative values.

Setting the Ruler Origin

If the default setup of your Ruler origin doesn't suit your needs, you may move the origin point, or undock and move the Rulers themselves to virtually anywhere on or off your document page using a single action. To explore moving your Ruler origin and positioning the Rulers, follow these steps:

1. Using any tool, hold your cursor over the point at which the two Rulers intersect at the upper-left corner of your screen. Notice a small button appears where the intersection symbol is located.

2. Using a click-drag action, click this button and drag toward the lower-right of your screen. Notice as you drag, dashed vertical and horizontal intersection lines appear. This indicates your Ruler's new zero position. Your new zero position will be exactly where these dashed lines intersect when the mouse button is released. To reposition the Ruler origin again, repeat the same operation.

3. Reset the Ruler origin to the default bottom-left page corner position by double-clicking the Ruler origin button. Your Ruler origin is reset.

4. Next, undock the Vertical and Horizontal Rulers from their top and left positions, and then drag them from their current position. To do this, press SHIFT as the modifier key while dragging the Ruler origin in the same direction. As you do this, notice the actual rulers themselves move and are repositioned onto your page (see Figure 6-2).

5. To reposition the Rulers while in their undocked state, press SHIFT again, while using a click-drag action to drag the origin button to a new page position. Using this technique, you may position the Rulers anywhere you want on or off your document page.

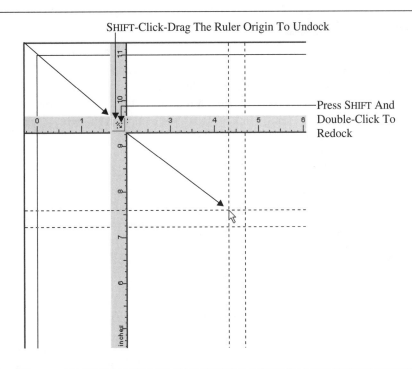

SHIFT-Click-Drag The Ruler Origin To Undock

Press SHIFT And
Double-Click To
Redock

FIGURE 6-2   Holding SHIFT while dragging the Ruler origin enables you to drag the
Rulers away from their docked position and onto your page.

6. For a full experience of the effect of undocked rulers on how your page
   position is indicated, choose the Hand Tool from the main Toolbox
   (pressing *H* selects this tool). You'll find the Hand Tool grouped together
   with the Zoom Tool. Click-drag using the Hand Tool to change your view.
   Notice the Rulers persistently display the current Ruler zero origin.

7. While the Rulers are in this undocked state, you may reposition the Ruler
   zero origin anywhere you want. To do this, click-drag the origin button or
   double-click it to reset it to the bottom-left corner of your page.

8. As a final step, return the Rulers to their original state by pressing SHIFT
   as your modifier key and double-clicking the Ruler origin button. As a
   refresher, this is the point at which the two Rulers intersect. Your Rulers
   are returned to their docked positions.

9. Reset the Rulers to the default page position once again by double-clicking
   the Ruler origin button.

Setting Unit Measure

The markings you see on your Rulers are actually the current unit measures, which increase and decrease in the increments they display, according to changes in your view magnification. By default, Rulers indicate unit measures according to your current Drawing Units selection on the Property Bar. To set the Unit measure, choose the Pick Tool, click a blank space on your page to ensure no objects are selected, and use the Drawing Units option on the Property Bar to make a selection.

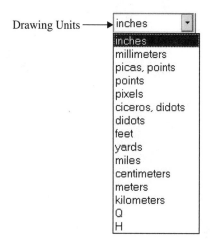

Drawing Units ──▸ inches

inches
millimeters
picas, points
points
pixels
ciceros, didots
didots
feet
yards
miles
centimeters
meters
kilometers
Q
H

Drawing Units control the unit measure displayed not only in Rulers, but also in all other interface areas where dimensions are displayed, including page and object size, and nudge and duplicate offsets. Drawing Units may be set to virtually any type of measurement system used including Standard, Metric, specific printers' measures, and certain specialized measurement systems.

Setting Ruler Options

All the information displayed on your Rulers—including the Ruler origin position and Drawing Units—may be set in the Rulers page of the Options dialog. To access this page quickly, double-click either Ruler using any tool cursor or choose Tools | Options (CTRL+J), click Document, and click Rulers to access the Rulers page (see Figure 6-3).

The options on this page enable you to control the following Ruler (or Ruler-related) characteristics:

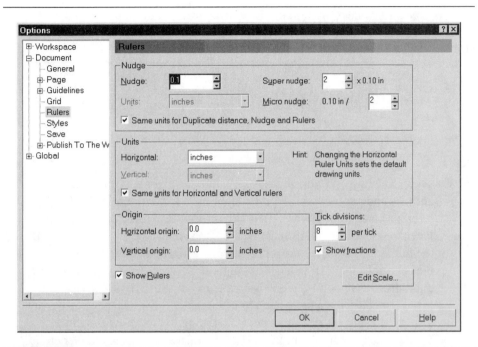

All options controlling Ruler position, units, display, and Tick Divisions
are controlled in the Rulers page of the Options dialog.

■ **Units**   As mentioned earlier, Units are the measurement system currently
selected to be displayed in most areas of CorelDRAW where any Drawing
Units information is either displayed or selected. Choosing a Horizontal
Unit measure enables you to specify unit measures for all Drawing Units
in your document. To specify different Unit measures for Vertical Ruler
and Drawing Units, click to deselect the Same Units for Horizontal and
Vertical Rulers option.

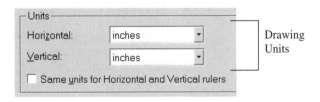

> **TIP** *One of the newcomers to the Unit measures available in CorelDRAW 10 is something named simply Q—a unit measure equivalent to 0.25 millimeters.*

- **Origin** The Origin options essentially enable you to set the Horizontal and Vertical Ruler 0 position—the point from which all reference points, distances, and dimensions are measured—numerically. The Origin point may be set anywhere within a range between −50 and 50 yards in precise increments as small as 0.001 inches.

- **Tick Divisions** If you're thinking a tick is something that usually bites animals and people, you're partly right. In this particular case, the reference is to your Ruler's *Tick Divisions*—the evenly spaced numeric labels seen between the smaller increments displayed by your Ruler. By default, Tick Divisions are automatically set according to the type of unit measure selected. For example, Standard measure displays a default of eight divisions per tick, while Metric measures display ten divisions. Printer-specific measures (such as didots, picas, points, and ciceros) are displayed using six divisions per tick. An option to Show Fractions is also available and set by default while a Unit measure is selected. Generally, fractions are set to display on Rulers while using nonmetric Drawing Units.

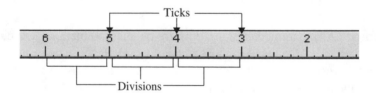

> **TIP** *To set the Spacing and Frequency of your Ruler, see "Controlling Grid Properties," later in this chapter.*

Editing Drawing Scales

Drawing to scale is a method used when the distances involved in drawing to actual size are either too large or too small to be practical when the document is displayed or printed. Drawing using scale representation is often used for drawing work involving trades such as architecture, electronics, or mechanics, or in technical sciences such as engineering, navigation, cartography, oceanography, geography, or astronomy. Setting up a drawing scale for your drawing is done using options in the Drawing Scales dialog, which enables you to apply a quick scale ratio or specify your own custom scale (see Figure 6-4). To open this dialog, choose Tools | Options (CTRL+J), click to expand Document, click Rulers to access the Rulers page, and then click the Edit Scale button.

The Typical Scales drop-down menu includes a selection of the most commonly used drawing ratios ranging between 100:1 to 1:100 with the most common standard measure scales included. When selecting ratios, the first number represents the *object page* distance, while the second number represents the distance in reality (known as *World*) Distance. Typically, smaller objects are illustrated using ratios where the page distance is larger than the World Distance—vice versa for larger objects.

The moment either the Page Distance or the World Distance options are changed, your Typical Scales selection becomes Custom automatically. As mentioned, Page Distance refers to the measured distance on your document page, while World Distance refers to the distances represented by your Ruler and Drawing Units in your CorelDRAW document. Each may be set independently and to different Unit measures within an enormous range between 1,000,000 and 0.00001 inches in increments of 0.1 inches.

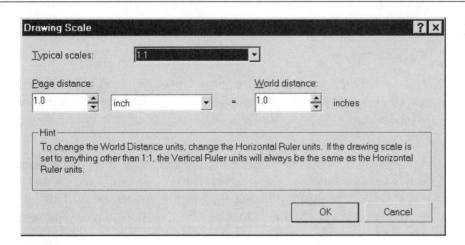

FIGURE 6-4 To change your drawing scale from the default 1:1 scale, use options in the Drawing Scale dialog.

Calibrating Ruler Display

Most users simply take for granted (or simply aren't concerned) that the image they see projected to their screens is accurate, as long as the final printed or exported object dimensions are accurate. If measurement values being displayed by your Ruler don't match real-life measurements and this is a concern, you may adjust the values if required.

To verify whether the display on your screen matches real life, follow these steps:

1. If you haven't already done so, open a document and create an object (such as a rectangle) to a specific width and height.

2. Using Property Bar options, set your view magnification to 100 percent.

3. Using a reliable ruler, measure the object you created as it's being displayed on your screen. If the sizes match those you specified for the object—in almost all cases they will—your Ruler display is accurate. If the measurements don't match, CorelDRAW, nonetheless, enables you to make these adjustments.

To calibrate your Ruler display, keep your reliable ruler handy and follow these steps:

1. Open the Options dialog (CTRL+ J) by choosing Tools | Options.

2. Click to expand the tree directory under Workspace and Toolbox, and then click to select Zoom | Hand Tools. This displays the Zoom, Hand options on the right of the dialog. While in this dialog, click to select the Zoom Relative to 1:1 option.

3. Click Calibrate Rulers to display the Ruler calibration display reference rulers and Resolution options (see Figure 6-5). Notice the vertical and horizontal ruler bars that intersect at the center of your screen. This represents your current Ruler Drawing Units. By default, your Horizontal and Vertical resolution will be set to 72 pixels per inch.

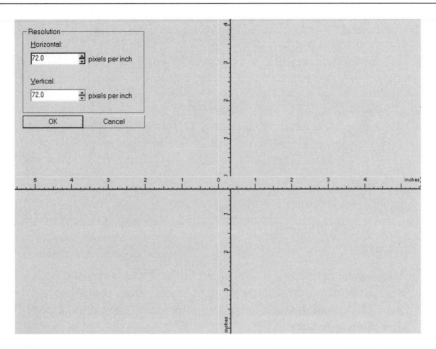

FIGURE 6-5   Match the screen rulers to your real-life ruler using the Horizontal and Vertical Ruler calibration options.

4. Using your real-life ruler, measure both the vertical and horizontal rulers on your screen to see that they match. If they don't, incrementally increase or decrease the Horizontal and/or Vertical options until they match.

5. Click OK to close the calibration dialog, and then click OK again to close the Options dialog. Your rulers are now calibrated.

Using Grids

Grids are rows and columns of nonprinting vertical and horizontal reference lines that appear throughout your document window when visible. The purpose of Grids is twofold. Grids provide a visual reference for aligning objects vertically and/or horizontally to specific page positions according to Ruler increments. They may also be used for quick-alignment methods in combination with CorelDRAW's Snap To Grid option. To control the display of your Grid, choose View | Grid from either the command menus or from the pop-up menu by right-clicking your document page. While the Grid button is depressed, the Grid is selected to display.

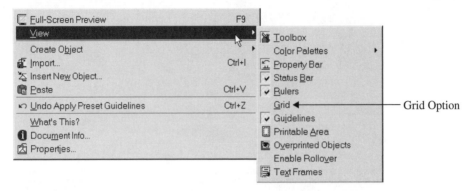

When your Grid is in view, it appears as vertical and horizontal lines of reference across both your document page and your entire pasteboard area (see Figure 6-6). Although you can see these lines on your screen, they will neither print nor export.

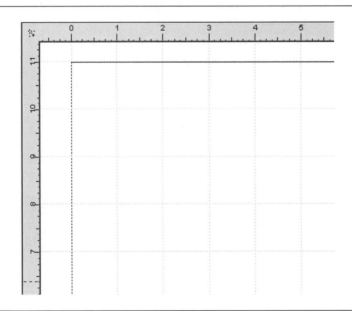

FIGURE 6-6 While the Grid is visible, its vertical and horizontal lines of reference align with your Ruler tick marks.

Controlling Grid Properties

Of course, not all grid setups suit all users or the type of work they do. Because grids may be used for placing drawing objects in industries ranging from technical illustration to publishing layouts, changing the frequency and spacing of the Grid lines of reference is often needed. To set these grid properties, use the Grid page of the Options dialog. To open this dialog, choose View | Grid and Ruler Setup from the command menus or right-click your Ruler and choose Grid Setup.

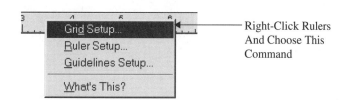

Right-Click Rulers
And Choose This
Command

6

> **TIP** *To control whether your Grids are visible, printable, or editable, use the Object Manager window. Grids are controlled by the Grid layer, located as a layer on the Master Page. To open the Object Manager, choose Window | Dockers | Object Manager. For more information on controlling layer properties, see Chapter 12.*

The Grid page of the Options dialog includes both Frequency and Spacing options that enable you to set the grid appearance (see Figure 6-7). Setting these options is an either-or scenario, meaning you may set your grid by Frequency or by Spacing. As the option names imply, Frequency options enable you to control the grid appearance by specifying the number of lines that appear within a given distance. Or, Spacing options enable you to set the physical space between the lines based on a specific amount of space between the lines. Both options are controlled according to the Drawing Units specified for your Rulers.

> **TIP** *When illustrating or drawing based on a specific unit measure—such as inches—formatting your Grid to match the Ruler unit measure helps. For example, if your Rulers are set to display inches using Tick Division of 8 per inch, setting your Grid to a Frequency value of 8 vertical and 8 horizontal lines per inch causes grid lines to appear every eighth of an inch while using a Drawing Scale ratio of 1:1 (actual size).*

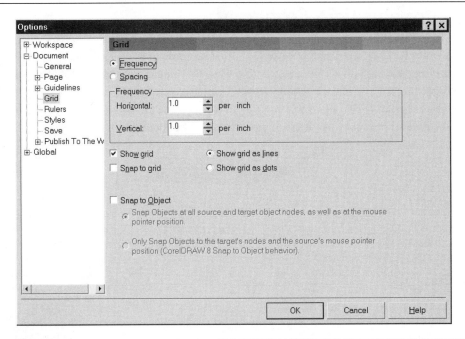

FIGURE 6-7 Set the appearance of your grid lines using either the Frequency or Spacing option in the Grid page of the Options dialog.

Show, Display, and Snap To Options

Four additional options are available in the Grid page of the Options dialog, enabling you to control Grid display. Although the Show Grid and Snap To Grid options are redundant with the View | Grid command and Property Bar options, this area also enables you to control whether the Grid appears as lines or dots.

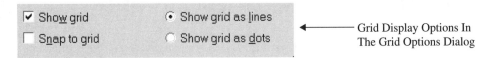

Grid Display Options In The Grid Options Dialog

Again, to open the dialog and access these options, choose View | Grid and Ruler Setup or right-click the Rulers and choose Grid Setup from the pop-up menu. By default, new documents are set to Show Grid as Lines. If you choose, you may set this to Show Grid as Dots. Viewing the Grid as dots instead of lines is useful when working with illustration objects that feature the same outline properties as the grid lines themselves.

Using Snap To Commands

The effects of Snap To commands can save an immense amount of fiddling around when you want to position objects interactively using the Pick or Shape Tools. These *Snap To* commands enable you to specify your drawing objects to "snap" to various drawing helpers, including Grids, Guidelines (discussed in the section to follow), and even other objects.

When activated, *snapping* is similar to a magnet being held near a metallic object, meaning as the magnet (your object) comes close to the object (a grid line, Guideline, or other object), it's seemingly drawn in the corresponding direction. If the magnet comes close enough, it eventually "sticks" slightly to the metal surface (as does your object to the snap point). Snap To effects work exactly the same way. Objects become magnetized and are seemingly pulled closer to specific points.

The characteristics of this particular snapping feature are intriguing and can be extremely useful or quite distracting—depending on the task you are trying to perform. You may control the snapping to Grids, Guidelines, and other objects independently using menu commands, shortcuts, or Property Bar options.

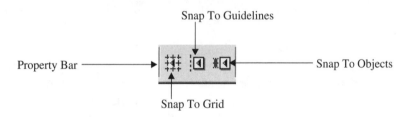

To activate or deactivate Snap To options for each of these elements, use one of the following commands.

Snap To Grid

To have your objects snap to align with a Grid, choose View | Snap To Grid or press the shortcut CTRL+Y to toggle the feature on and off, or click the Snap To Grid button on the Property Bar. When objects snap to a grid, they snap to the grid lines, and they snap even more to grid intersection points.

Snap To Guidelines

To cause your objects to snap to align with vertical, horizontal, or slanted guidelines, choose View | Snap To Guidelines, or click the Snap To Guidelines button in the Property Bar.

Snap To Objects

To cause your objects to snap to and align with other objects, choose View | Snap To Objects or click the Snap To Objects button on the Property Bar. When objects are set to snap to each other, they do so using snap location marks located on either the source or target object. By default, these location marks include path nodes and control points, as well as their corner, top, bottom, left- and right-side surfaces, and center origin, as well as your mouse pointer location—essentially any part of the object or action involved.

To be able to see the points at which your objects are snapping to (known as snapping feedback), activate the Show Snap Location Marks option. To do so, open the Options dialog, expand the tree directory under Workspace, and click Display.

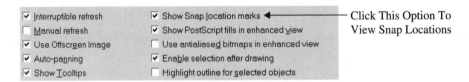

This snap behavior has changed slightly in past versions of CorelDRAW. For example, if you are a recent upgrader from CorelDRAW 8, you may be unaccustomed to both the source and target object locations being involved in the snapping action. If so, you may change this behavior back to that of CorelDRAW 8. Do this by using options in the Grid page of the Options dialog, opened by right-clicking a Ruler and choosing Grid Setup from the pop-up menu, or by choosing View | Grid and Rulers Setup from the command menus (see Figure 6-8).

Working with Guidelines

Guidelines are essentially reference or construction lines that make positioning objects in relation to your page or each other faster and easier for you. With the added capabilities provided by your system and the precision of CorelDRAW 10, placing a Guideline on your page will not only provide you with a visual reference, but also with essential resources for speedy organization. To have Guidelines appear visible on your document page, choose View | Guidelines, which toggles the display state on or off. To have objects snap to the Guidelines you create, choose View | Snap To Guidelines.

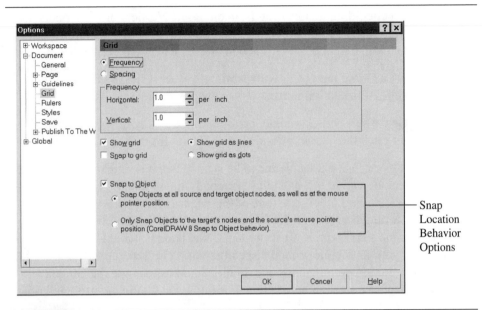

FIGURE 6-8   Click this option to return the snapping behavior to that of CorelDRAW 8, whereby only the source object's location points snap to other objects.

Guidelines placed on your document page extend between the top, bottom, left, and/or right edges of your document window. Typically, Guidelines take the form of vertical or horizontal dashed lines, but Guidelines may also be angled or "slanted." In CorelDRAW 10, Guidelines are considered objects in their own right. Like other objects, Guidelines have certain properties and may be manipulated like other objects in certain ways.

Creating Guidelines

Perhaps the best way to grasp the actions of creating, positioning, and slanting Guidelines is through hands-on experience. To explore placing Horizontal, Vertical, or Slanted Guidelines onto your page, follow these steps:

1. With a document open and your Rulers in view (choose View | Rulers to display), choose the Pick Tool from the main Toolbox (pressing the SPACEBAR quickly selects the Pick Tool).

2. Using a click-drag action, drag from either the Vertical or Horizontal Ruler onto your page and release the mouse button at the point you want your new Guideline to appear. This action creates a new Guideline.

3. Moving a Guideline is relatively straightforward: clicking it once selects it and a click-drag action moves it to a new position.

4. To delete a selected Guideline, press the DELETE key on your keyboard, or right-click the Guideline and choose Delete from the pop-up menu.

5. Moving or causing a Guideline to be slanted is a little trickier. Click once to select the Guideline, and click a second time to display typical object rotation handles. Click-drag one of the rotation handles in view in a circular direction (either clockwise or counterclockwise) to rotate the Guideline (see Figure 6-9). Your Guideline is now slanted. If you want to rotate your Guideline around a specific point, click-drag the center origin to the rotation point and use the rotation handles to angle the Guideline. If you want to move a Slanted Guideline, click the Guideline itself and drag it to the new page position.

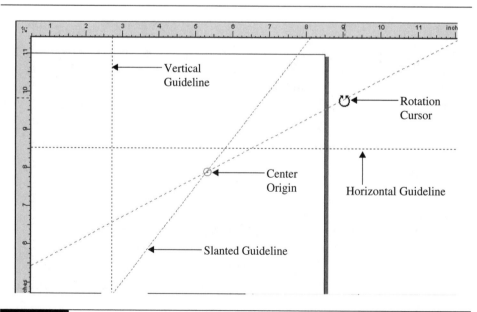

FIGURE 6-9   Rotating a Guideline is done with typical object rotation operations.

> **TIP** *If you want to, you may move and rotate multiple Guidelines at once by pressing SHIFT as the modifier key to select/deselect multiple Guidelines, and then click-drag to move them. To rotate multiple Guidelines while selected, click one of the Guidelines a second time to display typical rotation handles and drag one rotation handle in a circular direction.*

Controlling Guideline Properties

To manage your Guidelines or exactly position single or multiple Guidelines, use the Options dialog. Separate dialog pages are available for controlling the Vertical, Horizontal, and Slanted Guidelines. To access these dialogs, choose View | Guidelines Setup from either the command menus or from the pop-up menu by right-clicking the Rulers. While a Guideline is selected in your document, you may also click the Guidelines Options button on the Property Bar.

Guideline Options Button

The Options dialog lists each of the Guideline types individually on the left side of the dialog. Click one to select it in the tree directory under Guidelines (see Figure 6-10).

Adding, Deleting, and Moving Guidelines

Each of these dialogs is used in a similar way. Each dialog contains a listing of the existing Guidelines on your document page. To explore the use of these options, follow these steps:

1. To create a new Guideline, enter a value in the top-left box according to the position where you want the new Guideline to be created and click the Add button. Your new Guideline is created.

2. To move an existing Guideline, select it in the list, enter a new value in the top-left num box, and click Move. The selected Guideline is moved.

3. To delete a specific Guideline, select it in the list and click the DELETE button. The selected Guideline is deleted.

4. To remove all Guidelines in the list, click the Clear button. All Guidelines are deleted.

Guideline Position

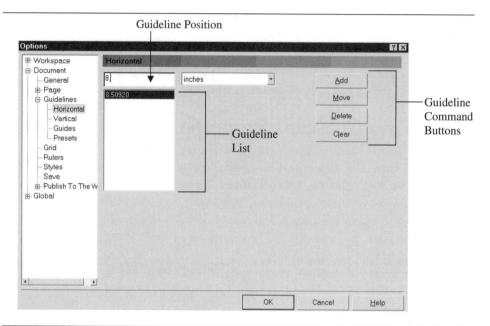

FIGURE 6-10   To control the position of Guidelines precisely, open the Horizontal, Vertical, or Slanted Guideline page in the Options dialog.

Setting Guideline Colors

If you want, you may also control the default color scheme assigned to Guidelines in your document. To do this, use the color selectors available in the Guidelines page of the Options dialog opened by choosing View | Guidelines Setup and choosing Guidelines from the tree directory (see Figure 6-11).

Besides enabling you to Show Guidelines and/or have objects Snap To Guidelines, two color selectors in this dialog enable you to control the Default Guideline Color and the Default Preset Guideline Color. To change one of these default colors, click the corresponding selector, choose a new color, and click OK to close the dialog and save your changes. For more information on using Guideline Presets, see "Using Guideline Presets," later in this chapter.

Locking and Unlocking Guidelines

By default, all Guidelines on your page are editable and moveable, meaning you may click to select them using the Pick Tool and click-drag to move them. If this isn't the behavior you want, you may lock or unlock a selected Guideline using

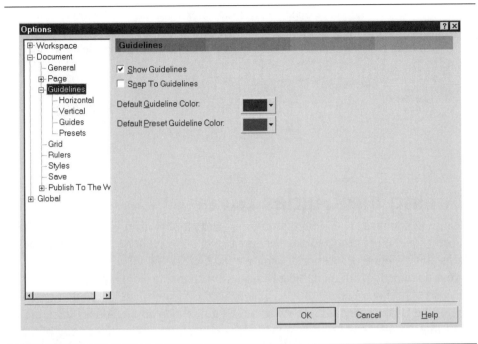

FIGURE 6-11   To control Guideline colors as they appear in your document, use the color selectors in the Guidelines page of the Options dialog.

Property Bar options. While a guide is locked, it may be selected, but it may not be moved or edited in any way. To do so, follow these steps:

1. To Lock an individual Guideline, click the Guideline to select it on your document page using the Pick Tool.

2. Using Property Bar options, shown next, click the Lock button. Your selected guide is locked and the guide-specific Property Bar options become unavailable.

Lock Button

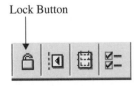

3. To Unlock the guide once again, right-click the guide and choose Unlock Object from the pop-up menu, shown next. Your guide is now unlocked and the guide-specific Property Bar options become available once again.

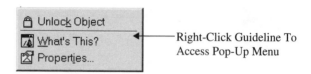

Right-Click Guideline To Access Pop-Up Menu

Controlling the Guides Layer

Because Guidelines are essentially objects—and all objects in your document have properties and must reside somewhere on a layer—CorelDRAW 10 automatically places all Guidelines on a special layer named *Guides*. To view the Layer structure in your document, open the Object Manager by choosing Tools | Object Manager. This particular layer resides only as a layer on the Master Page with other layers controlling Desktop and Grid. By default, all guidelines on the Guides layer are set as Visible, Non-Printable, and Editable. If you want, you may change any of these states by double-clicking the symbols to the left of the Guides layer in the Docker window (see Figure 6-12).

To control all options for a layer at once—including the display color of objects on the Guides layer in the Object Manager Docker, right-click the layer name (Guides) and choose Properties from the pop-up menu. Doing so opens the Guides Properties dialog (essentially a layers property dialog) to reveal further options (see Figure 6-13).

Make an Object a Guideline

In certain cases in which straight or angled Guidelines don't enable you to achieve a task, you may make any drawing object into a Guideline or vice versa. To do this, use features of the Object Manager Docker to move objects between layers. Moving any object to the Guides layer makes it behave as if it were a Guideline and had all the same properties. Once an object becomes a Guideline, objects

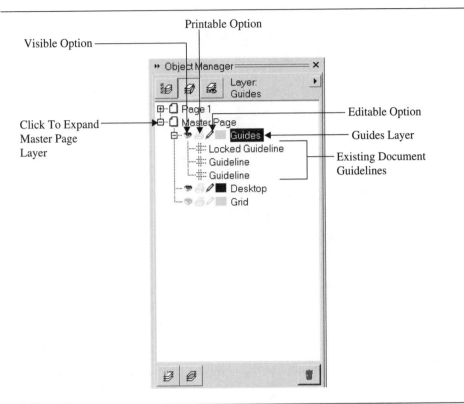

FIGURE 6-12   The Object Manager enables you to view and manage properties of your Guides layer—the default layer for all guidelines in your document.

"snap" to it when the Snap To Guidelines option is activated. In the reverse scenario, moving any Guideline to a different layer automatically makes it a printable object. To move an object to the Guides layer, follow these steps:

1. Open a document and create and/or select at least one object to make it into a Guideline.

2. Open the Object Manager Docker by choosing Tools | Object Manager.

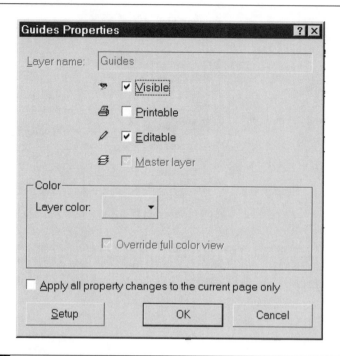

FIGURE 6-13   Right-click the layer name and choose Properties to open this Guides
Properties layer dialog.

3. Expand the tree directories in the Object Manager Docker window to
   locate both your Guides layer on the Master Page and the object you want
   to make into a Guideline so both are in view.

4. Using a click-drag action directly in the Object Manager Docker window,
   click-and-drag your object from its current page and layer to any position
   under the Guides layer on the Master Page. As you drag, notice a
   horizontal I-beam cursor appears, shown next, indicating the object's
   current position as it is dragged.

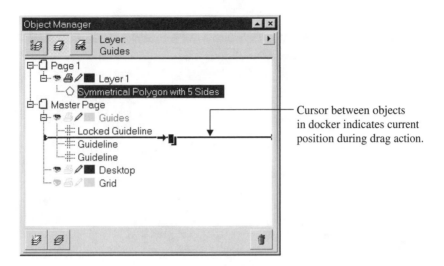

Cursor between objects in docker indicates current position during drag action.

5. Return to your document and notice your object now appears and behaves as if it were a typical guideline.

Using Guideline Presets

As a convenience, CorelDRAW features a collection of Guideline Presets, which may be selected to be displayed on your document page automatically in seconds. To access Guideline Presets, choose Tools | Options to open the Options dialog (CTRL+J), click to expand the tree directory under Documents | Guidelines, and click Presets to display the Presets options page (see Figure 6-14).

Choosing Preset Options

Guideline Presets are organized into Corel Presets and User Defined Presets. In many cases, the Corel Presets perform complex measurements and/or place Guidelines at specific points, depending on the size of your current document and according to your selected printer settings. Although Preset Guidelines behave and appear as other Guidelines, they are toggled on or off by clicking the corresponding dialog options. For example, clicking the One Inch Margins option

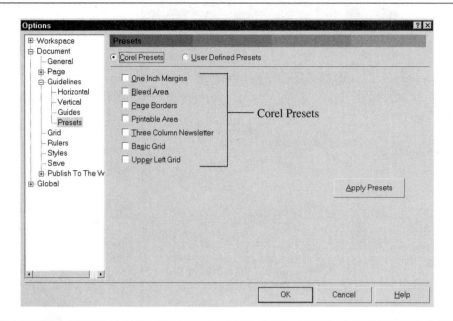

automatically creates margin Guidelines at one-inch inside your page boundaries. Clicking to deselect the option automatically removes these same guidelines.

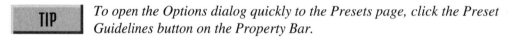

TIP *To open the Options dialog quickly to the Presets page, click the Preset Guidelines button on the Property Bar.*

While choosing other Corel Presets in the dialog, presets perform the following:

- **One Inch Margins** This preset automatically creates vertical and horizontal margin Guidelines within the boundaries of your page borders at a distance of one inch.

- **Bleed Area** This preset creates Vertical and Horizontal Guidelines at the Bleed limits according to your current document setup.

- **Page Borders** Choosing this option creates Vertical and Horizontal Guidelines to the edges of your document page.

- **Printable Area**   Choosing this option automatically positions Guidelines to indicate the areas inside or outside your document page borders where objects will print. This area is defined according to your currently selected printer and the currently selected printing material dimensions.

- **Three Column Newsletter**   Choosing this preset option automatically creates a series of Guidelines geared toward creating a typical three column newsletter. All margin (0.5 inches by default), column, and gutter (1 pica, 2 points by default) Guidelines are created.

- **Basic Grid**   The Basic Grid preset option automatically creates Vertical and Horizontal Grid Guidelines at a basic one-inch spacing by default.

- **Upper Left Grid**   Choosing the Upper Left Grid option creates six Vertical and six Horizontal Guidelines at one-inch intervals at the upper-left corner of your document page.

Saving Your Own Guideline Preset

You may also define your own automated Guidelines by choosing the User-Defined option in the Presets page of the Options. Choosing this option displays a collection of options to create your own custom Margins, Columns, or Grid Guidelines. To activate any or all of these Preset Guideline effects, click the corresponding options and customize the associated preset values (see Figure 6-15).

Preset Guidelines are slightly different than ordinary Guidelines in that they are created automatically and behave as other Guidelines, but attempting to move a Preset generates a warning dialog, shown next. This warning dialog lets you know that moving a Preset automatically converts it to a typical Guideline, which, in turn, eliminates it from the Preset Guideline effect you applied.

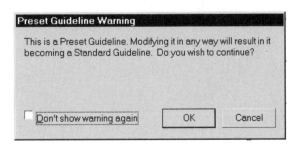

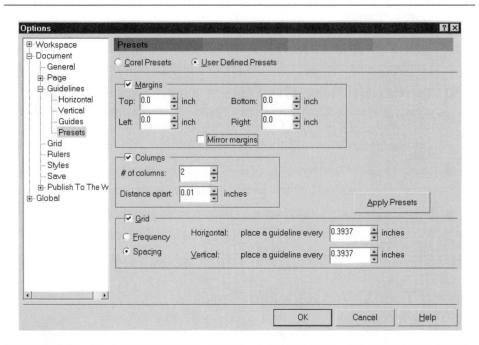

FIGURE 6-15   To apply your own Guidelines according to custom options, click to activate any or all of these User-Defined Presets options in the Presets dialog.

CHAPTER 7

Zooming and Viewing

If you're at all concerned with the appearance of the drawings you create in CorelDRAW—as most people are—this chapter should be of great interest to you—especially if you're a new user. Nothing can be more important than how your objects appear on your screen because the feedback CorelDRAW provides you with visually can enable you to control how your creation displays, prints, or exports. On the other hand, your only function may be to browse or view documents created by someone else. As either the creator or the audience, viewing documents is of the utmost importance, and these operations serve as the first step in any subsequent reproduction processes.

Setting View Mode

Certainly, no shortage of methods exists to view a document in CorelDRAW 10. Some methods are specifically designed for screen redraw speed and these sacrifice display quality, while others are designed to render an image to your screen with the highest quality, regardless of the time displaying the view takes. Thankfully, even the most complex drawings take little time to display, even at the highest view quality setting. The technique you use depends on the task at hand but, in your drawing adventures, you'll certainly want to use more than one.

View modes control how your drawing objects appear onscreen and reflect (with utmost accuracy) how they print or export. Commands for switching between View modes are accessed via the View menu. The View menu indicates the current view using a depressed button state.

When viewing your document, you may choose between Draft, Simple Wireframe, Wireframe, Normal, and Enhanced views. The following section defines how these display conditions render various object types to your screen.

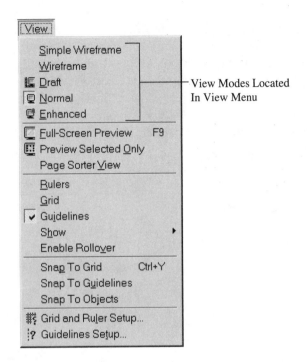

View Modes Located
In View Menu

Wireframe and Simple Wireframe

The term *wireframe* refers to a view state that renders all objects on your screen as black outline paths with essentially invisible fills—regardless of which fill or outline properties you've applied. If you perform detailed path, object-shaping, or drawing tasks, Wireframe views will be invaluable to you because they instantaneously display all object shapes in your drawing. They also enable you to perform node-editing and object-shaping tasks, while seeing only the core object paths of all objects, whether or not they overlap.

The most basic of these View modes is *Simple Wireframe,* which renders only basic object shapes, leaving any dynamically linked objects created by effects such as Blend, Contour, and Extrude essentially invisible. This view is useful if the objects on which you are performing shaping commands are only basic shapes or control objects. For a slightly more detailed View mode, Wireframe also displays all shapes in outlines, but includes the objects created by effects such as Blend, Contour, and Extrude (see Figure 7-1).

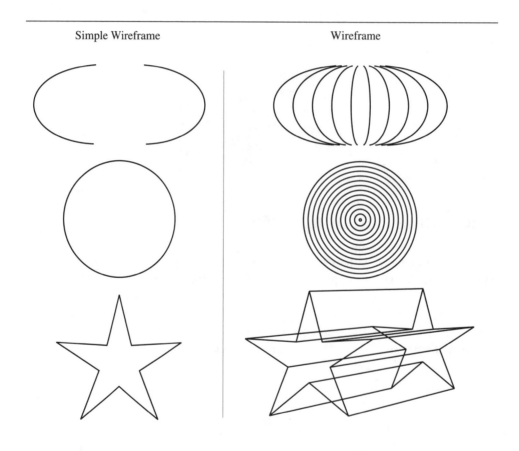

FIGURE 7-1 The Blend, Contour, and Extrude effects applied to these objects are shown here as they would be viewed in Simple Wireframe and Wireframe.

Getting a Draft View

While using the *Draft* view, the objects in your drawing appear as a slightly more detailed version of the actual appearance of objects in your drawing, with slight differences in certain types of properties. For example, in a progression beyond what Wireframe view renders, Draft view displays all outline properties applied to objects and also renders fill types—but only uniform fills.

More complex fill types such as Fountain, Pattern, Two- and Full-Color Pattern, Bitmap Pattern, Texture, and PostScript fill types aren't displayed with any accuracy. Instead, these fill types are displayed using a combination of dithered, checkerboard, symbol, and hatching patterns, which visually indicate their fill types (see Figure 7-2).

Using Normal View

The most common view type you might use more than likely will be Normal view. Choosing Normal renders all outline properties just as you would expect, with no added enhancements to the shape of curves. All fill types you applied to closed-path

7

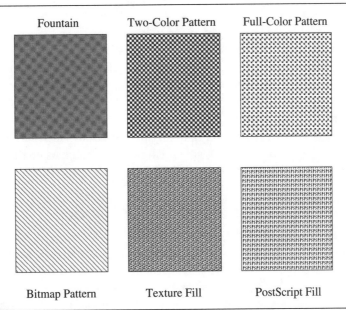

Fountain   Two-Color Pattern   Full-Color Pattern

Bitmap Pattern   Texture Fill   PostScript Fill

FIGURE 7-2   These rectangles have been filled with various fill types and displayed using Draft view.

objects are also rendered accurately—and just as you have created them. In most cases, the rendered effect of the Normal view state shows objects as they would appear when printed to a typical printer or exported using typical default settings.

NOTE *PostScript fills appear in their actual display state only while Enhanced view is in use.*

Using Enhanced View

Using the Enhanced view applies a softening effect to the screen display of both outline shapes and text. This softening effect is referred to as *anti-aliasing,* which has an effect on how adjacent areas of different colors display. With anti-aliasing, the area where two different colors meet is blended to a certain degree, eliminating the hard-edged line where colors meet. Instead, the display pixels are smoothed on either side of this line causing a color progression from one side of the line to the other.

TIP *If you require, you may quickly switch between your current View mode and the last-used View mode by pressing* SHIFT+F9.

Zooming and Panning Pages

Changing the view of a drawing being displayed is one of those commands many experienced users do without too much thought, but if you're new to CorelDRAW, and you're looking for both basic and smarter ways to examine a document, you've come to the right place.

Loyal users who've religiously upgraded their CorelDRAW version with every new release may have noticed only slight changes to viewing features over the years but, with CorelDRAW 10, several significant changes enable new navigation and viewing of documents techniques.

Using the Zoom Tool and Property Bar

To begin, the Zoom Tool is perhaps the most efficient tool either to increase (Zoom In) or decrease (Zoom Out) your document's view magnification. You can use the Zoom Tool in several ways. As you discover in the following section, you'll most likely use all of them at one time or another in your drawing adventures. The Zoom Tool is located in the main Toolbox. By default, the Zoom Tool is located in the third tool position, just below the Pick and Shape Tools, and grouped together with the Hand Tool—another tool for controlling views you learn about later in this chapter.

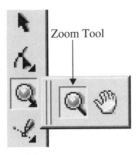

Zoom Tool

While the Zoom Tool *is* the selected tool, the Property Bar includes a series of buttons and menus providing access to Zoom- and view-specific options. These include options for displaying and changing your current magnification, applying Zoom commands, or applying page-specific or selection-specific Zoom commands.

7

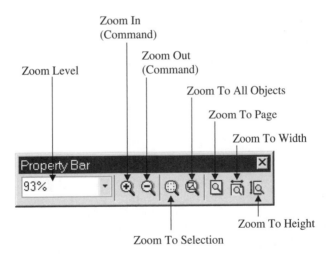

Zoom In
(Command)

Zoom Out
(Command)

Zoom Level

Zoom To All Objects

Zoom To Page

Zoom To Width

Zoom To Height

Zoom To Selection

With the buttons featured in this Toolbar in mind, the following defines the Zoom commands available to you, beginning with the most commonly used and useful, and progressing to Zoom commands, which are very specific.

- **Zoom Levels**   To increase your current view by a specific or preset view magnification, use the Zoom Levels drop-down menu available in the Standard or Zoom Tool Property Bars. This menu contains a listing of preset magnifications ranging from 10 to 400 percent and includes quick views for zooming based on page size. You can also enter a value directly in the Zoom Levels box, followed by pressing the ENTER key. Views saved in the View Manager, which are discussed later in this chapter, are also included in this menu. When a view is chosen from the preset list, the magnification is increase or decreased, but remains centered in your document window.

■ **Zooming In**   Perhaps the first interactive operation you want to use is Zoom In, which is the default state while the Zoom Tool is selected. Clicking the Zoom Tool once at any point on or off your page increases your view magnification by a factor of either 2 or 4, depending on your current view. You can also use the Zoom Tool to perform *marquee* zooming, which involves a click-drag action in a diagonal direction using the Zoom Tool cursor to define either the width or height of the area you want to Zoom In to (see Figure 7-3).

TIP	*CorelDRAW 10 enables you to set your view magnification anywhere within a range between 1 percent and a staggering 405,651 percent.*

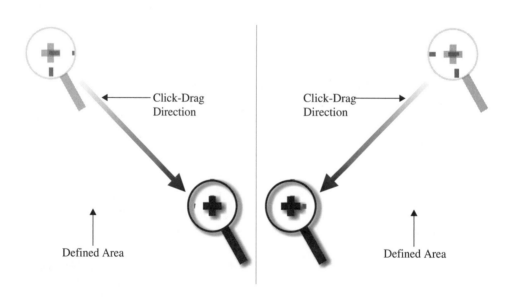

FIGURE 7-3   To marquee Zoom, click-drag the Zoom Tool to define a specific area to Zoom In to.

■ **Zooming Out** To decrease your view magnification using the Zoom
Tool, click the right mouse button anywhere on or off your document page,
or click the Zoom Out button on the Property Bar. Doing so decreases your
view to your last-used magnification or by a factor of 2 or 4. The view on
your screen remains centered around the point at which your cursor was
clicked. To Zoom Out while any tool is selected, press F3.

Zoom Tool (normal
Zoom In state using
left mouse button
click)

Zoom Tool (Zoom
Out state when right
mouse button is
clicked)

7

■ **Zoom One-Shot** The Zoom One-Shot command enables you to select
the Zoom Tool momentarily for a single Zoom In or Zoom Out command
while you are using any tool. Once the Zoom operation is complete, your
previous tool reappears. Press either the F2 or Z shortcut keys to activate
the Zoom One-Shot feature while any tool is selected, or click the
Zoom-One Shot button in the Property Bar while using the Zoom Tool.

■ **Zoom To Selection** If you have objects selected on or off your document
page, choosing this command changes your view magnification to display
the complete object to fill your document window. Choose Zoom To
Selection from either the Zoom Property Bar or the Zoom Levels drop-down
menu. You may also Zoom to a selected object while any tool is selected by
pressing the SHIFT+F2 shortcut.

■ **Zoom To All Objects** Whether or not you have any objects selected on
or off your current document page, choosing Zoom To All Objects changes
your view magnification to display all objects visible in your document
window. Choose Zoom To All Objects from either the Zoom Property Bar
or the Zoom Levels drop-down menu, or use the shortcut F4 while any tool
is selected.

| TIP | *To Zoom To All Objects on or off your document page, double-click the Zoom Tool button in the main Toolbox while any tool is selected.* |

■ **Zoom To Page**   This command essentially changes your view to
whichever magnification is required to fit your current page size
completely within the document window. Choose Zoom To Page from
either the Zoom Property Bar or the Zoom Levels drop-down menu, or
press SHIFT+F4 while any tool is selected.

■ **Zoom To Width/Height Of Page**   Using either of these two commands
accomplishes a similar result as with Zoom To Page, but you may specify
either width or height as the reference point. Choose Zoom To Width (or
Height) Of Page from either the Zoom Property Bar or the Zoom Levels
drop-down menu.

Customizing View Shortcuts

Many of the Zoom and Hand commands in CorelDRAW 10 have preassigned
shortcut keys while using the default workspace, while some do not. These
shortcut keys assigned are based on those existing in previous versions of
CorelDRAW. If you want, you may change or add shortcut keys to your own
favorite or preferred keys using customization tools in CorelDRAW. To access
these View shortcut key commands, follow these steps:

1. Open the Options dialog by pressing CTRL+J or choosing Tools |
   Options.

2. On the left side of the dialog, click Customization | Commands to
   expand the tree directory and display the Commands page.

3. Choose View from the drop-down menu at the top-left corner of the
   dialog and a listing of view-related items appear in the display list.
   In this list, click to select a tool or command.

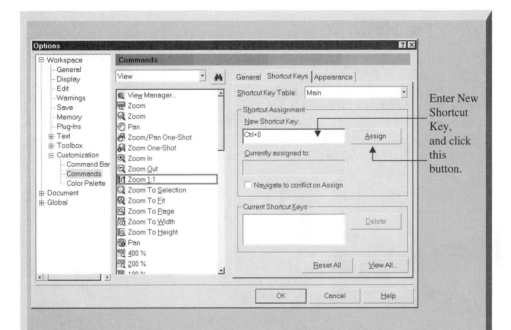

Enter New Shortcut Key, and click this button.

4. Click the Shortcut Keys tab on the right of the page to display the Shortcut Key options, shown above, click your cursor in the New Shortcut Key box, press the new shortcut key (or combination of keys) you want to assign as the new shortcut, and then click the Assign button.

5. To delete a shortcut that is already assigned, click the shortcut in the Current Shortcut Keys box and click the Delete button.

6. Click OK to close the dialog and apply the shortcut key changes.

Using the Hand Tool

The *Hand* Tool (previously called the *Pan* Tool) essentially enables you to "scroll" the view of your drawing as an interactive alternative to using scroll bars (located at the right and bottom of your document window). Panning a document is perhaps less commonly used than Zooming but, nonetheless, offers advantages because it enables you to change the view of your document in any direction without changing the magnification. The Hand Tool is located in the main Toolbox grouped with the Zoom Tool. To select the Hand Tool quickly, press H on your keyboard.

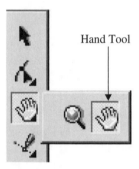

Hand Tool

While the Hand Tool is selected, a hand-style cursor appears on your screen. A click-drag action enables you to scroll your view in any direction. As you scroll, your objects change view position and your scroll bars are immediately updated to reflect the change in page position.

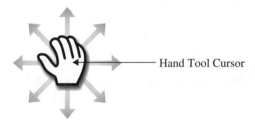

Hand Tool Cursor

TIP	*Double-clicking the Hand Tool button in the main Toolbox instantly centers your page view within your document window, returning the scroll bars to their centered position.*

Several hidden shortcuts are used to change your view while the Hand Tool is selected, which, in most cases, emulate actions of the Zoom Tool. For example, a right mouse button click using the Hand Tool causes a Zoom Out command, while a double-click action causes a Zoom In command to occur. You can also use the keyboard alone to pan the view of your document while any tool is selected. Using the keyboard alone, the following shortcuts are available

- **Pan Left** Press and hold ALT+LEFTARROW
- **Pan Right** Press and hold ALT+RIGHTARROW
- **Pan Up** Press and hold ALT+UPARROW
- **Pan Left** Press and hold ALT+DOWNARROW

Controlling Zoom and Hand Tool Behavior

Under default conditions and while using CorelDRAW 10's default workspace, the behavior resulting from certain actions while pressing the right mouse button and while using the Zoom and Hand Tools is controlled by preference settings in the Options dialog. Right mouse button functionality by default sets right-clicks to Zoom Out for both the Zoom and Hand Tools. With most other tools, however, right-clicking opens the context-sensitive pop-up menu, which offers commands and options based on the item clicked.

If this is your preference instead of the Zoom Out command for right-clicks while Zooming or Panning, you can change it if you want by opening the Options dialog (CTRL+J) and clicking Toolbox | Zoom, Pan (Hand) Tools (see the following illustration). In this dialog, you may set the behavior of right mouse button clicks using either tool to open the pop-up menu instead.

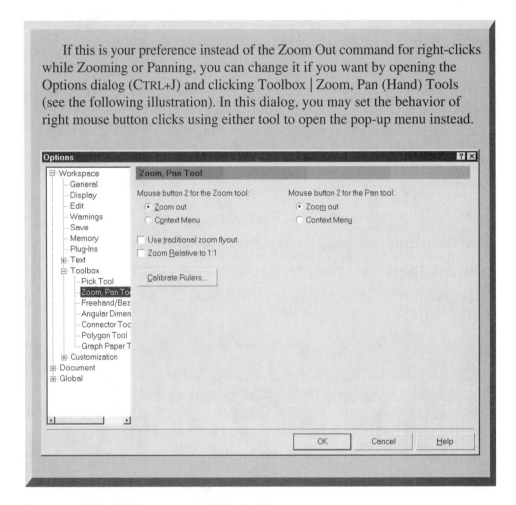

Specialized View Modes

When it comes to special-needs viewing of documents, CorelDRAW 10 features some long-time favorite techniques for displaying your document, as well as some brand-new resources for changing views and sorting document pages.

Page Sorter View

CorelDRAW 10's new *Page Sorter* view is a feature many users have requested for some time. Page Sorter becomes available as a special View mode while your document features multiple pages—at least a minimum of two. To enter Page Sorter View mode, choose View | Page Sorter view.

While viewing your document in Page Sorter view you can view several pages at one time and manage their properties from a bird's-eye perspective. While in Page Sorter View mode, your pages and their contents are displayed. In this view, the Pick Tool also becomes the only available tool, while the Property Bar displays several page options. All other views become unavailable. You can reorder pages by dragging them to different locations in the current order or right-click specific pages to rename, insert, or delete them (see Figure 7-4).

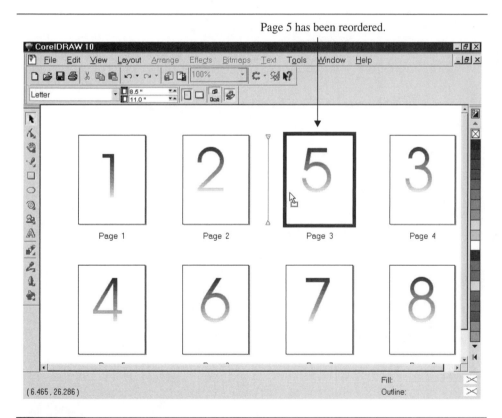

Page 5 has been reordered.

FIGURE 7-4   To illustrate page order, each page includes an Artistic Text object to indicate original order in the Page Sorter view.

While a specific page is selected, use Property Bar options to change its orientation or size to defaults, or to a Preset page size or specific measure by changing values in the page width and height boxes. To exit Page Sorter view and return to your original document View mode, click the Page Sorter View button.

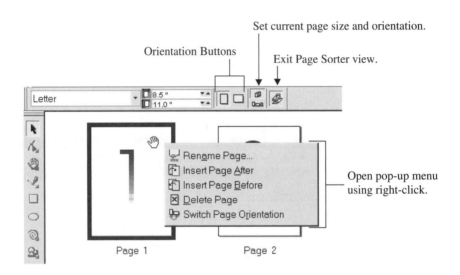

TIP   *To navigate to a specific page in your document, quickly and simultaneously close the Page Sorter view and double-click any page.*

Full-Screen Preview (F9)

If you require a full preview of your document page without seeing any of CorelDRAW's interface components, choose View | Full Screen Preview, or press the F9 shortcut key. Doing so causes CorelDRAW virtually to disappear from view, and previews only your drawing objects and the page border (if enabled). All other elements are hidden from view. To return to your view back to Normal, click anywhere on your page or press the ESC key.

While Full Screen Preview displays your document, the View mode and Page Border View appearance is set according to preferences in the Options dialog. To access these options, choose Tools | Options (CTRL+J) and click Display under the Workspace category on the left side of the dialog to access the Display options. Full Screen Preview options are located in the lower part of the dialog, enabling you to choose either Normal or Enhanced view (the default) as the View mode, and to enable or disable viewing of the page border (see Figure 7-5).

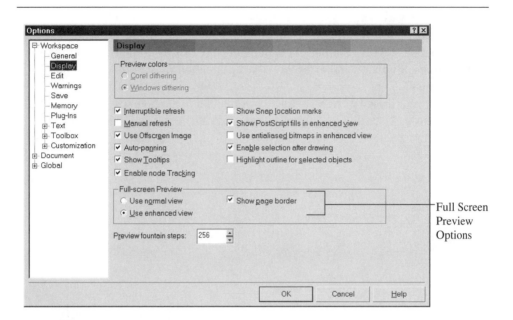

Full Screen
Preview
Options

FIGURE 7-5   Full Screen Preview preferences may be set in the Display page of
the Options dialog.

Previewing Selected Only

The Preview Selected Only command available from the View menu enables you
to preview specific objects selectively as an alternative to viewing your entire
drawing in full color. This option operates in combination with Full Screen
Preview and takes a toggle state either on or off when selected. While selected, it
enables you to view only your selected object after choosing Full Screen Preview.
If no objects are selected, the Full Screen Preview displays exactly that—nothing.

Using the View Navigator

The *View Navigator* has been a feature CorelDRAW users have requested since
it first appeared in Photo-PAINT and is an extremely useful viewing innovation.
Although some might consider this feature slightly redundant with using the Hand
Tool, nonetheless, it has greater advantages because it enables you to see roughly
where you are panning to. The View Navigator is activated by clicking the point
where your vertical and horizontal scroll bars meet at the lower-right corner of
your document window.

To open the View Navigator pop-up, use a click-hold action on the button itself (see Figure 7-6). This causes a pop-up thumbnail color display that represents the objects both on and off your current document page. The preview frame within the View Navigator window indicates the viewing capabilities of your current Zoom settings, enabling you to drag within the View Navigator pop-up display literally to navigate your drawing. As you drag, your document window display is updated simultaneously. Releasing the mouse button ends the navigation.

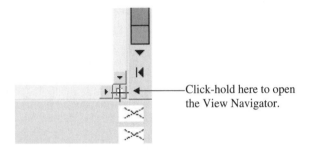

Click-hold here to open the View Navigator.

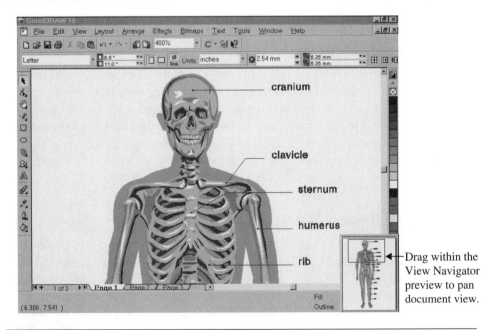

Drag within the View Navigator preview to pan document view.

FIGURE 7-6   The View Navigator enables you to navigate your drawing in the truest sense of the word.

Using the View Manager Docker

Although many users often work extensively in CorelDRAW before taking advantage of the View Manager, it's certainly the most efficient way of managing the views of a complex drawing. The View Manager enables you to save the page and magnification settings of any current view, assign names to the views, and quickly recall views. It also includes a version of Zoom Toolbar for quickly changing view magnification (see Figure 7-7). To open the View Manager, choose Window | Dockers | View Manager or use the CTRL+F2 shortcut.

> **NOTE**   *For an explanation of using buttons in the Zoom Toolbar, see "Using the Zoom Tool and Property Bar" earlier in this chapter.*

7

Page/Magnification Options   Zoom Toolbar   Add Current View

Delete Current View

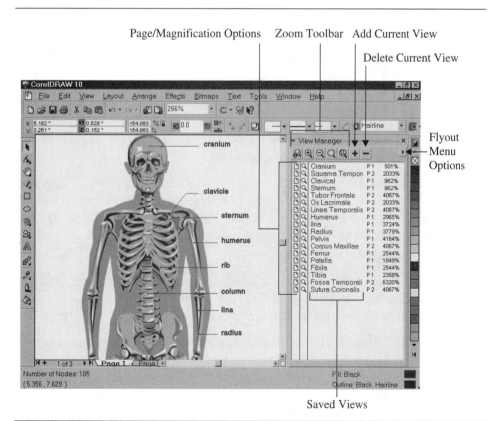

Flyout
Menu
Options

Saved Views

FIGURE 7-7   When working with complex drawings, the View Manager provides a quick way of saving and recalling views.

Exploring View Manager Commands

When a view is saved, the page, position, and view magnification settings are recorded and become a new view in the View Manager Docker window. All but the View mode is saved, meaning if you have selected a specific View mode while saving a view—such as Simple Wireframe, Wireframe, Draft, Normal, or Enhanced—these modes are not saved. To explore saving, naming, and deleting a view, follow these steps:

1. If you haven't already done so, open an existing document of a drawing (either completed or in progress) and open the View Manager Docker window (CTRL+F2).

2. Using page navigation commands and either the Zoom Tool, or the Zoom command buttons in the Zoom Toolbar, and/or the new View Navigator feature, display a specific part of your drawing in the document window.

3. To create and save your current view, click the Add Current View button in the docker. Notice a new item appears in the View Manager Docker. By default, the new view is automatically named View-*XX-XXXX*, where these *X*s represent your new view (numbered sequentially beginning with 1) and appended with the current view magnification setting. Each new view is accompanied by details indicating the page number in your document and the exact view magnification setting.

4. To name the view, click once on the name to select it and type a name to enter the new view name. Your view is now saved. If you want, save more new views using the same procedure by changing the view display in your document window each time and clicking the Add Current View button each time to save each view.

5. To recall a view, double-click either the page number or the view magnification portion of the saved view. Your view is immediately changed to the exact point at which it was saved.

6. To delete a specific view in the docker window, click to select the view and click the Delete Current View button. The view is immediately deleted.

| TIP | *In addition to the interactive methods you can use to save, name, recall, and delete saved views, the same operations can be accomplished by choosing commands in the flyout menu located in the View Manager Docker window.* |

Using Page and Zoom Options

To the left of each saved view in the View Manager, two options appear. These options enable you control how your saved views are recalled. For each view saved, you can toggle display of the Page Only and the Magnification Only to on or off states by clicking the page and zoom options. Single-clicks activate or deactivate these options. While an option appears grayed out, it's in the inactive state.

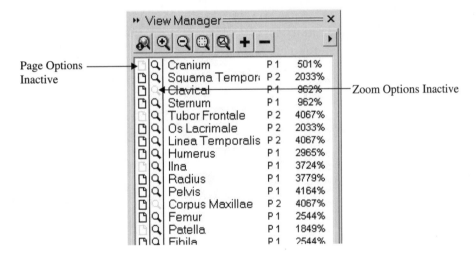

This means while the page symbol is deactivated, recalling the corresponding saved view causes only the magnification to be recalled, or while the zoom symbol is deactivated, only the page display is recalled. While both are deactivated, the saved view is essentially rendered inactive.

CHAPTER 8

Essential Object Commands

If you arrived here in search of how to select, move, transform, or arrange objects using interactive methods, you're at the right place. One of the most critical aspects of learning to use any graphics application is grasping this concept: For a command to be applied to items on or off your document page, you must first have something selected. The action of *selecting* an item can range from clicking a single item, marquee-selecting items within a given area, or using selection commands.

Selecting Objects

Once an item is selected, you notice that many of the display resources in CorelDRAW spring to life, offering information about the item (or items) you selected—their size, position, and so on. Much of this feedback is indicated via the Property Bar (see first illustration), Status Bar (see second illustration), or open docker windows and depends largely on which tool is in use.

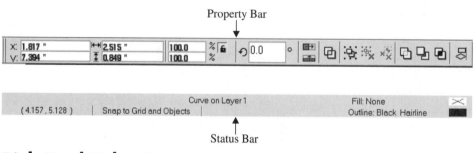

Pick Tool Selections

Although the Pick Tool doesn't enable you to draw or create a single object, it likely is the most significant tool in CorelDRAW. This is underscored because the Pick Tool is listed as the first tool in the main Toolbox. In most instances, straightforward object selection is accomplished with single-click actions using the Pick Tool (shown next).

Pick Tool

Clicking an object selects it and, while selected, the object becomes surrounded by selection *handles*—the eight black markers that surround the object (see Figure 8-1). A small *X* marker also appears at the centermost point of the object.

If you're having difficulty clicking an object that has an outline width applied, but has no fill applied (meaning it has a fill of None), you may want to activate the Treat All Objects As Filled option. To do this, right-click the Pick Tool in the main Toolbox choose Customize | Toolbar Item | Properties from the pop-up menu to open the Options dialog to the Pick Tool options page. Click to select the Treat All Objects As Filled option and click OK to close the dialog (shown on the next page). You may also activate the Fill Open Curves preference using Property Bar options by clicking the Treat As Filled option while the Pick Tool is in use and

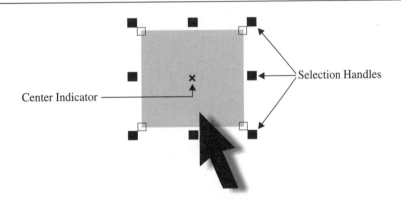

Center Indicator

Selection Handles

FIGURE 8-1   While an object is selected, eight square-shaped selection handles surround the object.

while no objects are selected. This option enables you to select objects by clicking their interior shape, regardless of whether or not they have a fill type specified. This functionality applies to closed-path objects, or to open-path objects while the Fill Open Curves option is selected.

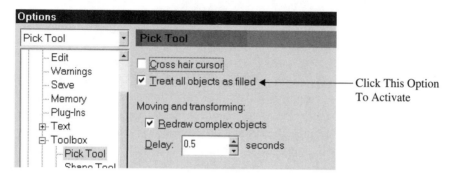
Click This Option
To Activate

Object Selection Techniques

For maneuvering through a selection of objects or for selecting more than one object at a time with the Pick Tool, you can use a number of techniques. Most of these techniques involve holding modifier keys while clicking or click-dragging to select more or fewer objects. Many of these object selection techniques may also be used in combination with each other. As you soon discover, you can define a selection in plenty of interactive ways.

- **Shift-clicking to select**   Holding the SHIFT key while clicking an unselected object adds it to your current selection. This also works in the reverse, where holding SHIFT while clicking a selected object causes it to become unselected.

- **Marquee-selecting objects**   To select all objects in a defined area, click-drag with the Pick Tool diagonally to surround the objects. While doing so, all complete object shapes within the area you define become selected (see Figure 8-2). The key here is that the complete object's shape must be surrounded for it to become selected. Holding SHIFT while using the marquee-selection technique causes unselected objects to be selected, but also causes selected objects to become unselected.

- **Holding ALT while marquee-selecting**   In a twist on typical marquee-selecting, holding the ALT key as the modifier while click-dragging to define a selection area causes all objects within— and contacted by—the selection marquee to become selected. Holding

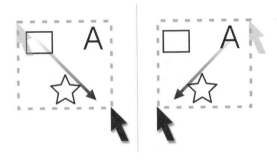

FIGURE 8-2   To marquee-select objects, use a click-drag action to define a specific area.

SHIFT+ALT while marquee-selecting causes the reverse to occur, deselecting any objects already selected in the defined marquee area.

■ **Pressing TAB to select next object**   Pressing the TAB key alone while using the Pick Tool causes the next single object arranged directly in front of your current selection to become selected. Holding SHIFT while pressing the TAB key causes the single object arranged directly behind your current selection to become selected. This action hinges on the basic principle that new each object created is automatically ordered in front of the last created

The Pick Tool's Shape Tool State

If you're thinking the Pick Tool has a whole bunch of hidden functions, you're exactly right. One of the more confusing issues surrounding the use of CorelDRAW's tools is the close relationship shared by the Pick Tool and the Shape Tool. Part of this confusion is because these two tools are relatively close, both in appearance and their interconnected uses. In the next illustration, the Pick Tool doubles as the Shape Tool when only one object is selected:

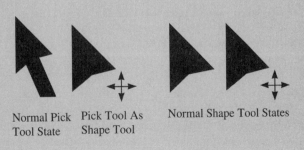

Normal Pick   Pick Tool As   Normal Shape Tool States
Tool State   Shape Tool

For the record, the Pick Tool is used for selecting and transforming objects (under usual circumstances), while the Shape Tool is used for altering or editing shapes and curves. Not only is the Pick Tool used for selecting, moving, and transforming objects, it also enables you to alter the "path shape" of objects. This Shape Tool capability differs depending on the type of object selected, but includes only that—a single object.

When the Pick Tool cursor is held over a node or control point on a shape or polygon, the tool cursor temporarily changes to that of the Shape Tool. Although this functionality may be confusing (even surprising), you quickly realize the convenience it offers—you needn't choose a different tool to alter an object's shape while it is selected. In this state, the node or control point the Pick Tool is held over becomes activate and highlighted, indicated by a highlighting effect on the object while all other handles remain displayed. This applies to virtually any single object selected, including open and closed paths, Ellipse, Star, Polygon as stars, and Graph paper objects. When in its normal state held over an object, the Pick Tool merely selects an object; but, when the cursor is held over an object control point or node, it changes to the Shape Tool state:

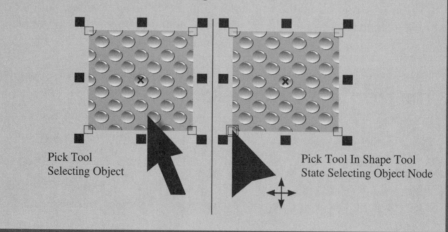

Pick Tool
Selecting Object

Pick Tool In Shape Tool
State Selecting Object Node

object—no matter how the object was created (for example, using various Duplicate, Repeat, Transformation, or object effect creation methods).

Selecting Objects by Type

CorelDRAW 10 enables you instantly to select any objects on or off your current document page in a single command. You may also select all Text objects, Guidelines, or path nodes, however, with a single command by making a command selection from the Select All menu (shown next). Each time you use one of these specific selection commands, a new selection is made with any current selections ignored.

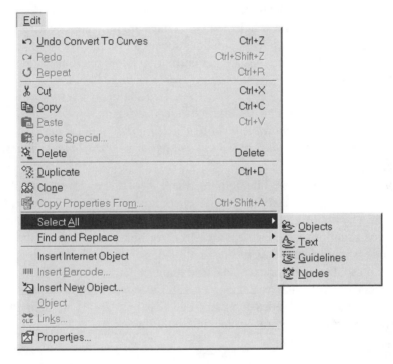

Choosing each of these selection commands has any of the following effects:

■ **Select All Objects**   Choosing Edit | Select All | Objects causes all objects both on and off your current document page to become selected. For a quicker method, use the CTRL+A keyboard shortcut to accomplish the same command. The Select All Objects command selects virtually everything on your document page—including objects grouped using the Group (CTRL+G) command.

TIP   *Double-clicking the Pick Tool selects all objects on and off your current document page.*

■ **Select All Text**   Choosing Edit | Select All | Text instantly selects all text objects both on and off your current document page. Both Artistic and Paragraph Text objects become selected after using this command—unless they have been grouped with other objects, in which case they do not become selected. Text objects applied with effects (such as Contour or Extrude effects) also participate in the selection using this command.

■ **Select All Guidelines**   That's right, guidelines are also considered unique objects. To select all Guidelines on your document page, choose Edit | Select All | Guidelines. Selected Guidelines are indicated by a color change (red by default). To select guidelines successfully, they must be set as visible. If your Guidelines are not currently visible on your page, choose View | Guidelines.

TIP   *Guidelines may be created and positioned using a click-drag action from your Ruler onto your document page. Using the View | Rulers command causes rulers to display at the top and left of your document window.*

■ **Select All Nodes**   While both the Shape Tool and a closed-path object are selected, you may also use the Select command to select all nodes in the object by choosing Edit | Select All | Nodes. For a quicker method in the same situation, use the CTRL+A shortcut, or hold ALT while clicking any node (shown next). This results in all nodes on the path becoming selected. To do so, the object must be a curve (either open or closed). This means special objects, such as Rectangles, Ellipses, and Polygons are not eligible for the Select All Nodes command because their shapes are defined dynamically by "control" points instead of nodes.

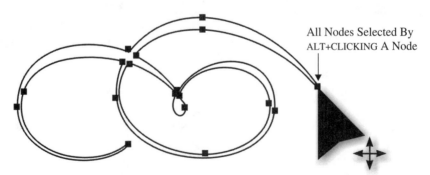

All Nodes Selected By
ALT+CLICKING A Node

TIP   *To select all nodes of an open or closed path instantly, hold CTRL+SHIFT while clicking any node on the path. Using this technique, only nodes on a single path of a compound path become selected. To select all nodes on all paths in a compound path object, double-click the Shape Tool button in the main Toolbox.*

Moving Objects

When objects are selected, changing their position, either on or off your document page, may be done interactively by using the Pick Tool or precise incremental movements.

 For information on moving and transforming objects in precise ways to specific points on your document page, see "Applying Precise Transformation" covered later in this chapter.

Using the Pick Tool

While an object is selected, clicking the Pick Tool on certain areas of the object causes the positioning cursor state to appear—especially in situations where the object you're trying to select is very small. This cursor state enables you to use a click-drag action to move your selected object(s) in any direction. As your object is being dragged, a preview outline of the object appears, indicating the new position. When the mouse button is released, the move is complete (shown next).

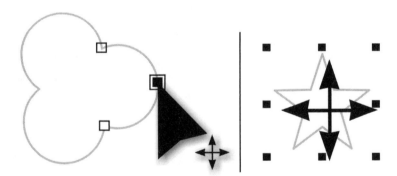

Positioning State Of Pick Tool Cursor

Using Nudge Keys

While an object is selected, you may also move it in any direction using keyboard keys with an action called *nudging,* which refers to moving an object incrementally by a fixed amount. To nudge an object while selected, press the UP, DOWN, LEFT, or RIGHT arrow keys. Your object is moved by the amount specified in the Rulers page of the Options dialog. To access Nudge options, open the Options dialog

(CTRL+J), click to expand the tree directory under Workspace and Document, and click to display the Rulers options page (see Figure 8-3).

Pressing the nudge keys alone performs a single nudge movement, but you may also nudge on larger or smaller nudges, known as *Super* and *Micro nudges*. The fixed amounts applied using either of these nudge types is also controlled according to amounts specified in the Options, Rulers page. Both are applied while holding modifier keys in the following ways:

- **Super Nudge** As the name implies, Super Nudge move your object in larger increments than a typical nudge. To apply a Super Nudge, hold SHIFT while pressing the UP, DOWN, LEFT, or RIGHT arrow keys on your keyboard. By default, this causes your selected object to move by 0.2 inches.

- **Micro Nudge** The smaller version of a typical nudge is the Micro Nudge, which moves your object in smaller increments. To apply a Micro Nudge, hold CTRL while pressing the UP, DOWN, LEFT, or RIGHT arrow keys on your keyboard. By default, Micro nudges cause your selected object to move by 0.05 inches.

Transforming Objects

The term *transformation* may include virtually any type of object change, short of actually shaping the object's path. Object transformation tools and techniques perhaps epitomize the concept of offering multiple ways to perform the same operation. Transformations can range anywhere from changing an object's page position to changing its size, skew, and rotation. Interactive transformations can

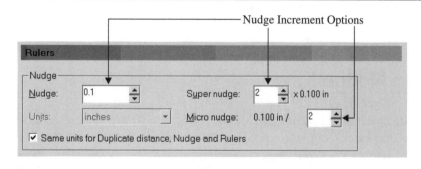

FIGURE 8-3   By default, pressing the UP, DOWN, LEFT, or RIGHT ARROW keys causes a typical nudge movement in increments of 0.1 inches.

often be much more intuitive than precision transformations—each has its own special advantages. In this section, you explore applying transformation using both methods.

Transforming Objects Interactively

As you know, the Pick Tool may be used to transform objects interactively by manipulating one of the eight black square-shaped selection handles that surround one or more selected objects while using the Pick Tool. Generally speaking, dragging any corner selection handle or side handle enables you to *scale* (change an object's size) proportionally, by width only, by height only, or nonproportionally (see Figure 8-4).

During any of these types of interactive transformations, the Property Bar keeps a running tab of the object's current size, position, width height, scale, and rotation angle. But if you've never had the opportunity to perform these operations before, doing so can be an adventure. As you can imagine, mastery of these basic transformation operations is crucial to becoming proficient in CorelDRAW. While transforming objects, you may also constrain the new shape of an object by holding modifier keys.

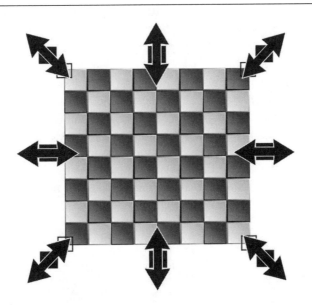

FIGURE 8-4   Selection handles may be used to change an object's size interactively.

> **TIP** *CorelDRAW 10 remembers the original shape of your object from the time it was created, no matter how many transformations have been applied to it. To remove transformations from your object, choose Arrange | Clear Transformations to return your object to its original shape immediately.*

The following actions enable you to apply transformation interactively using the Pick Tool, including the effects of holding modifier keys for constraining:

- **To change object size (scale)**   Click-drag any corner handle to change an object's size *proportionally*, meaning the relative width and height remains in proportion to the original object shape. Hold ALT while dragging any corner selection handle to change an object's shape *nonproportionally*, meaning width and height change, regardless of original proportions.

- **To change width or height only**   Click-dragging any side, top, or bottom selection handle changes the size of the object in the drag direction either horizontally or vertically. Holding SHIFT while doing so changes the width or height concentrically from the center of the object. Holding CTRL while dragging changes the width or height in 200 percent increments from the original size.

> **TIP** *When transforming an object using the Pick Tool, clicking the right mouse button during the transformation causes the active object to be a copy of your original, essentially applying the transformation to a duplicate.*

You may also rotate or skew an object using special Pick Tool states that only become available after clicking a selected object (or objects) a second time. Doing so causes the selection handles to change to rotation and skew handles (see Figure 8-5). When rotating, a movable center marker enables you to set the center around which objects are rotated. As your cursor is pointing to either a rotation or a skew handle, it changes to indicate the condition or state.

To flip an object selection quickly, either vertically or horizontally, use the Mirror Vertical and Mirror Horizontal options available in the Property Bar while using the Pick Tool:

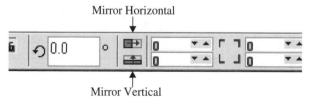

Mirror Horizontal

Mirror Vertical

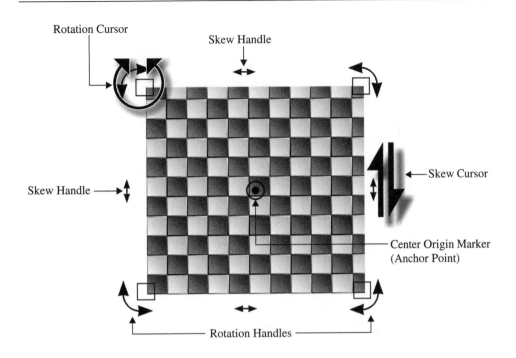

Clicking a selected object a second time displays the rotate and skew handles.

Using the Free Transform Tool

In a twist on the use of the Pick Tool's scale, skew, and rotation states, the Free Transform Tool offers a certain degree of redundancy but, nonetheless, has certain interactive advantages because it offers a live preview of the new shape of the object(s) being transformed. The Free Transform Tool is located in the main Toolbox grouped together with the Shape, Knife, and Eraser Tools (shown next).

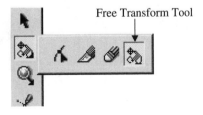

While the Free Transform Tool is selected, the Property Bar offers four basic modes of transformation: Free Rotation, Free Angle Reflection, Free Scale, and

Free Skew (shown next). Each operates in a similar way to using the special state offered by the Pick Tool.

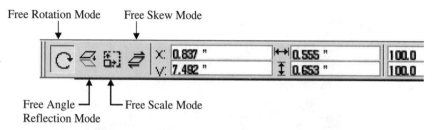

To transform in one of these four modes while an object is selected click to select the mode and then use a click-drag action on your object. As you drag, a live preview of the new object's shape appears. While using Rotation or Angle Reflection modes, a dotted reference line appears as you drag to indicate the object's angle transformation from its original state (see Figure 8-6).

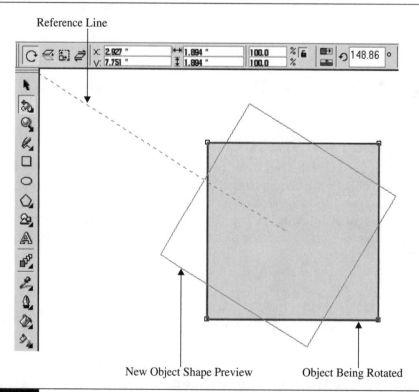

FIGURE 8-6   The Free Transform Tool offers a slightly higher level of interactivity during transformations when compared to Pick Tool transformations.

Applying Precise Transformation

Use the Transformation Docker for combination-style transformations involving multiple transformations of various types applied requiring a controlled and high degree of precision. The Transformation Docker enables you to formulate a combined transformation before applying it. The docker itself is subdivided into five transformation areas: Position (Move), Rotation, Scale and Mirror, Size, and Skew (see Figure 8-7). To open the Transformation Docker window, choose Window | Dockers or Arrange | Transformations, and then choose Position (ALT+F7), Rotate (ALT+F8), Size (ALT+F10), Scale (ALT+F9), or Skew.

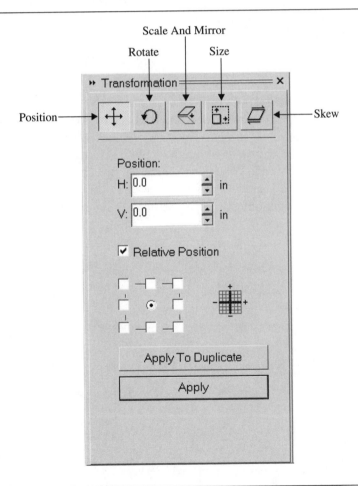

FIGURE 8-7   The Transformation Docker enables you to formulate compound transformations before committing to the settings and options you chose.

Generally speaking, for virtually any type of transformation, click the corresponding Transformation Docker page, enter your desired values, and click the Apply button in the docker window to transform your selected object.

Using the Transformation Docker

When using the Transformation Docker to apply specific transformations to your selected object, the available options vary depending on the type of transformation you require. The following details the use of options available in the Transformation Docker when a specific mode is selected. In each of the visual examples to follow, transformation was applied using only the specific transformation being discussed. However, you may apply several transformations in a single command if multiple transformation values throughout each of the five docker modes have been changed after pressing the Apply button and while the Apply Lock option is inactive.

Positioning (Moving) Objects

The Position page of the Transformation Docker enables you to move your object selection a specified distance *vertically* (*V*), *horizontally* (*H*), or to a specific point on or off your document page (see Figure 8-8). While the Relative Position option is selected, entering new values and clicking the Apply button causes your objects to move by a specified distance. While the Relative Position option is not selected, new values determine your object's page position or move it to a specified point.

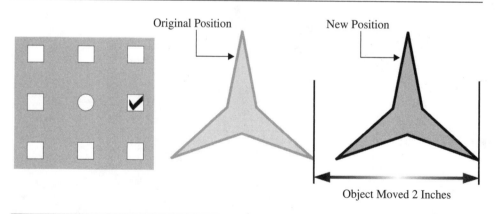

FIGURE 8-8   This Polygon object was moved 2 inches using the Relative Position option and the right-center side as the reference point.

Rotating Objects

Rotating objects with the Transformation Docker enables you to enter exact angles of rotation based on the degrees in a circle to increments of 5 degrees (see Figure 8-9). Negative values cause your object to rotate clockwise, while positive values cause rotation to be applied counterclockwise. Selecting the Relative Center option on this page of the docker enables you to rotate objects either *V* or *H*, according to the object's center marker position, the position of which is specified either *V* or *H*. Changing the existing value in the Horizontal and Vertical boxes allows you to specify a new center origin position for your object's rotation. While Relative Center is not selected, your object is rotated according to a position relative to the page center.

Scale and Mirror Objects

The Scale and Mirror page of the Transformation Docker enables you to enter precise changes in object size based on dimensions of the original object. You may also cause the object to be flipped either *V* or *H*, and simultaneously by clicking one of the two mirror buttons (see Figure 8-10). While the Nonproportional option is selected, your object's new horizontal and vertical scale values are unlinked, meaning you may apply scaling commands to either the width or height, independently of each other. While the Nonproportional option is left unselected, width and

8

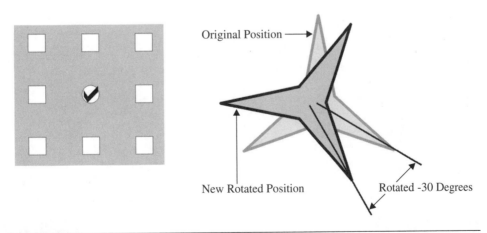

Original Position →

New Rotated Position

Rotated -30 Degrees

FIGURE 8-9 This object has been rotated -30 degrees (clockwise), using the Relative Center option and the object's center as the rotation point.

height scaling operations are locked to each other. This means scaling the width or height by a given percentage value causes the adjacent value to be calculated automatically to preserve your selected object's original proportions.

Sizing Objects

This portion of the docker enables you to alter either the *V* or *H* measure of an object selection, independently or together, based on entered values. For example, entering 2 inches in the Width box and clicking the Apply button causes the selected object to be scaled to a width of 2 inches. While the Nonproportional option is selected, the width and height values may be changed independently. While they're not selected, width and height values are linked and calculated automatically to alter the size of the object proportionally.

Precise Skew

As previously defined, the term "skew" refers to changing the position of two sides in parallel fashion, while leaving the adjacent sides stationary. For example, a vertical or horizontal skew transformation applied to a rectangle shape causes its corners to become nonperpendicular, meaning they are no longer at 90 degrees. The Skew page of the Transformation Docker enables you to apply both vertical and horizontal skew independently or simultaneously by entering degree measures,

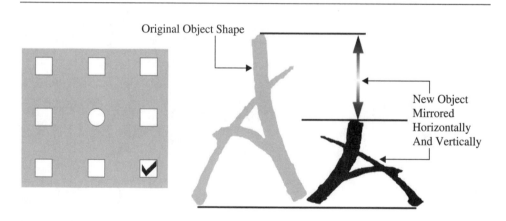

FIGURE 8-10   An Artistic Text object has been scaled by 50 percent using the lower-right corner as the transformation origin.

in turn, transforming the object either *V* or *H*. As with rotation commands, negative degree values cause clockwise skews to be applied, while positive values cause counterclockwise skews. Choosing the Use Anchor Point option enables you to specify left, center, right, top, bottom, sides, or corner points for the point around which your objects are skewed (see Figure 8-11).

Common Transformation Options

In each of the Transformation Docker modes, a set of common options are available, meaning they are available while performing any transformation. These options enable you to apply your transformation according to the relative areas of your selected object(s) or to apply the new transformation to an automatically created duplicate of your object.

Relative Position Grid

During most object transformations, the representative origin grid that is available using each docker mode enables you to transform your object selection based on a specific origin or reference point. Points on the grid essentially represent the top, center, bottom, left, or right sides, and the corner points of your selected object(s). Selecting one of these options causes your applied transformation to originate on any given object point. For example, clicking the center option and,

8

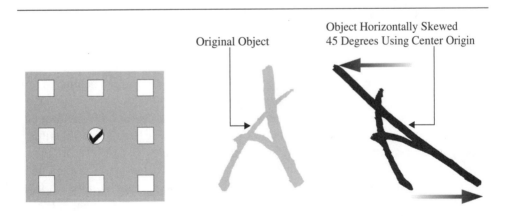

Original Object

Object Horizontally Skewed
45 Degrees Using Center Origin

FIGURE 8-11   This Artistic Text object has been skewed with the Use Anchor Point option selected and the object's center as the transformation origin.

subsequently, scaling an object by 200 percent causes the new object shape to double in size, but to remain centered with its original position. A representative diagram accompanying each docker state indicates the results of positive and negative values.

> | NOTE | *When applying transformation using the Transformation Docker, the default values displayed in the docker represent your object selection's current size, position, rotation, scale, and skew settings. For a transformation to take place, these values must somehow be changed. Otherwise, clicking the Apply button appears to have no effect.*

Applying Transformation to Duplicates

Clicking the Apply to Duplicate button in the Transformation Docker enables you to apply your selected transformation values according to options you selected in the docker, but does so to a newly created copy. This enables you to preserve your original object. By default, in terms of layering the new duplicate object is ordered in front of your original object.

Setting Object Ordering

The term *object ordering* is a key principle to grasp when organizing objects that overlap each other. Ordering objects enables you to control the effect of one object appearing in front—or behind—another. The relative reference points to remember when ordering are your own viewpoint (in this case, your screen) and the page. Your page is always the backmost point, while your screen is always the frontmost point. All objects on or off your document page are positioned in one way or another between these two reference points.

When overlapping objects are ordered, they appear in front of or behind each other, according to how they are ordered. This is a condition you can control after creating your objects. By default, all newly created objects are ordered in front of all other objects. Changing object ordering enables you to rearrange overlapping objects without changing their position and also to control which objects are in front and which are in back. To order objects, CorelDRAW features a selection of order commands. Order commands may be applied using menu commands in the Arrange | Order menu, using shortcut keys, or using buttons available in the Property Bar while your objects are selected. The following brief listing defines how to change the order of your objects in specific ways:

- **To Front**   Applying this command orders your object selection to be in front of all other objects on or off your document page. Pressing SHIFT+PAGEUP or choosing Arrange | Order | To Front applies the command. The To Front command is also available as a Property Bar button when an object is selected.

- **To Back**   Applying this command orders your object selection to be behind all other objects on or off your document page. Pressing SHIFT+PAGEDOWN or choosing Arrange | Order | To Back applies the command. The To Back command is also available as a Property Bar button while an object is selected.

- **Forward One**   Applying this command brings your object selection forward one layer in the current object order. Pressing CTRL+PAGEUP or choosing Arrange | Order | Forward One applies the command.

- **Back One**   Applying this command sends your object selection backward one layer in the current object order. Pressing CTRL+PAGEDOWN or choosing Arrange | Order | Back One applies the command.

- **In Front Of**   Applying this command causes a targeting cursor to appear, enabling you to specify which object you want your object selection to be layered in front of in the current object order. Choosing Arrange | Order | In Front Of applies the command.

- **Behind**   Applying this command also causes a targeting cursor to appear, enabling you to specify which object you want your object selection to be layered behind in the current object order. Choosing Arrange | Order | Behind applies the command.

- **Reversing Object Order**   Applying this command changes the order only of the selected objects relative to each other in reverse of their current order. Front objects become back objects and vice versa (see Figure 8-12). For example, if your objects were numerically ordered 1, 2, 3, and 4, applying this command would cause them to be reordered to 4, 3, 2, and 1. Choosing Arrange | Order | Reverse Order while a selection is in progress applies the command.

8

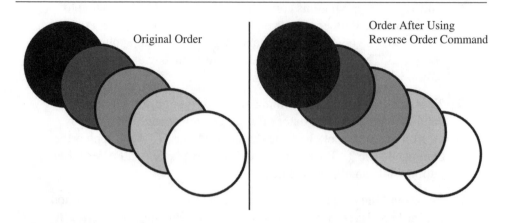

FIGURE 8-12   This series of ungrouped ellipses has been applied with a
Reverse Order command.

PART III

Working with Object Tools

CHAPTER 9

Basic Shape Creation

Mastering basic object creation is something all new CorelDRAW users need to spend time doing. Unfortunately, this particular chapter may be one few users actually read. If you're thinking that creating basic shapes such as rectangles, ellipses, and polygons is among the simplest tasks you can perform, you'd be partly right—the use of these object tools is relatively straightforward. But manipulating the properties associated with these shapes is not as simple as it might first appear. If you've arrived here in a quest to learn all you can about creating basic shapes, you're bound to discover all the weird and wonderful shapes these objects create.

Using the Rectangle Tool and Property Bar

The Rectangle Tool is one of the most straightforward tools you'll use in creating objects—whether the shape you create remains rectangular or you choose to use it for creating something else. Choose the Rectangle Tool, shown in the following illustration, from the main Toolbox or by using the F6 shortcut key.

Besides the usual position, width, and height properties available with all objects, native rectangle shapes offer just one option to be set: corner "roundness," which may be set either interactively or by using the Property Bar Corner Roundness options available while a rectangle is selected. The Property Bar is shown here:

Corner Roundness Values

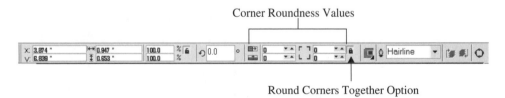

Round Corners Together Option

> **TIP** *Besides choosing the Rectangle Tool from the Toolbox or using the F6 shortcut, you may also choose the Rectangle Tool while any tool is selected by right-clicking a blank space on your document page and choosing Create Object | Rectangle.*

Drawing a Rectangle

Drawing a rectangle may just be one of the simplest actions you'll ever perform in CorelDRAW 10. To do so, choose the rectangle from the main Toolbox, and use a click-drag action in any direction to create the new shape (see Figure 9-1). While the Rectangle Tool is selected, you'll notice that the cursor resembles a crosshair accompanied by a rectangle shape. As you click-drag using the cursor, you'll also notice that the Status and Property Bars show coordinates, width, and height properties detailing the new object's shape.

Each time a new rectangle is created, CorelDRAW automatically applies your default graphic properties for its Outline Pen and Fill properties. If you wish, you may set the Outline Pen Width properties of your rectangle using Property Bar options. But, since a rectangle is not a typical closed curve object, certain Outline Pen options (such as Line Styles) are not available in the Property Bar while one is selected. To change other Outline Pen properties of a rectangle while in its natural Rectangle state, use options in the Pen tab of the Object Properties Docker (select object and choose Windows | Dockers | Object Properties), or use the Outline Pen dialog (F12).

Setting Rectangle Corner Roundness

Corner roundness is based on percentages from 0 to 100 and may be controlled a number of ways, all of which achieve the same result. The Corner Roundness options may be changed any time you wish as long as the shape remains a native rectangle shape, meaning it has not been converted to curves. Corner roundness may be set uniformly for all corners (the default), or independently while the

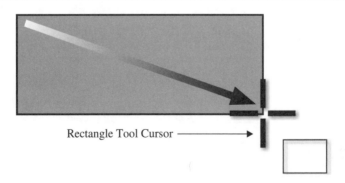

Rectangle Tool Cursor

FIGURE 9-1   Use a click-drag action in any direction to create a new rectangle.

Round Corners Together lock option is selected in the unlocked (not pressed down) state.

TIP *Double-clicking the Rectangle Tool button in the main Toolbox creates an instant rectangle border around your current document page. This quick border is automatically set to outline properties based on your graphic default settings and aligns exactly with the edges of your current document page.*

While a rectangle is selected, use any of the following operations to change corner roundness according to your needs:

■ Use Property Bar Corner Roundness options to enter a percentage value.

■ Set your rectangle's corner roundness interactively using the Shape Tool (F10) by dragging vertically or horizontally at any corner control point to change each corner roundness value individually while the corner options are unlocked, or change all corners equally while locked.

■ Use the Object Properties Docker, opened by right-clicking the rectangle shape and choosing Properties.

The options enabling you to apply corner roundness percentage values to your rectangle appear in each of these interface areas. Corner roundness may be applied for any number of illustration or layout purposes. Figure 9-2 shows a rectangle in various states of corner roundness.

Original: 0 Percent Roundness   25 Percent Roundness   75 Percent Roundness   100 Percent Roundness

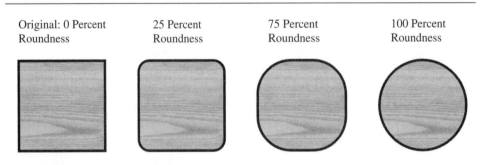

FIGURE 9-2 This rectangle shape demonstrates the effects of rounding corners to various percentage values.

Whenever you create a new object, there are a few rules of thumb to keep in mind. Certain modifier keys may be pressed while you drag various tool cursors, making your drawing experiences much easier and more productive. If you haven't already memorized this short list, you may wish to keep it close to your keyboard as a reminder.

- Hold CTRL while drawing new objects to constrain their shape to equal width and height.

- Hold SHIFT while drawing new objects to constrain their shape from the center origin.

- Hold CTRL+SHIFT together while drawing new objects to constrain their shape from the center origin and to equal width and height simultaneously.

Using the Ellipse Tool and Property Bar

Similar to rectangles, drawing an ellipse is a straightforward operation. But, ellipse shapes are much more dynamic than rectangle shapes, since ellipse shapes can be set to appear (and behave) in several different ways. Typical ellipses most often appear as simple closed-path circular or oval-shaped objects. But they may also quickly be changed into pies or arcs. As the name implies, pie shapes resemble the wedge portions of an oval (either a single slice or a larger pie with a slice removed).

Arc shapes are actually the open-path equivalent of pies. To create a typical ellipse shape, choose the Ellipse Tool, shown next, from the main Toolbox or by pressing the F7 shortcut key, and use a click-drag action in any direction.

While the Ellipse Tool is selected, the Property Bar displays ellipse-specific options, shown next, that enable you to control the state of your new ellipse shape before or after it has been created. Choose Ellipse, Pie, or Arc.

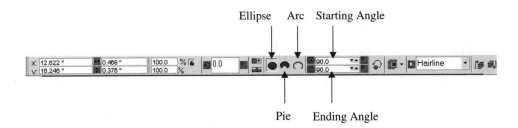

Ellipse Arc Starting Angle

Pie Ending Angle

> **TIP** *Besides choosing the Ellipse Tool from the Toolbox or using the F7 shortcut, you may also choose the Ellipse Tool while any tool is selected by right-clicking in an empty space on your document page and choosing Create Object | Ellipse from the pop-up menu.*

How to Draw an Ellipse

In a few moments, we'll explore controlling pie and arc ellipse shapes; but for now, let's begin by creating a normal elliptical shape. To create an ellipse as a simple circular or oval-shaped object, follow these quick steps:

1. Choose the Ellipse Tool from the main Toolbox, or press F7 to immediately select the tool.

2. Using the Ellipse Tool cursor, shown next, and a click-drag action, drag diagonally in any direction. As you drag the Ellipse Tool cursor, an outline preview of the shape appears.

3. Release the mouse button to complete your ellipse shape creation.

Use Property Bar options to set the outline pen width of a selected ellipse. But, since ellipse shapes are dynamic objects (meaning they have special properties while in the Ellipse state), applying other Outline Pen properties—such as the Line Style—is done using dockers or dialogs instead of typical Property Bar options. To change the Outline Pen properties of an ellipse while in its natural state, use options in the Pen tab of the Object Properties Docker (select object and choose Windows | Dockers | Object Properties), or use the Outline Pen dialog (F12).

Controlling Ellipse States

Although it may not be obvious, each new oval or circular shape you create features two control points that, by default, overlap and are invisible. When these control points are separated, they create either the pie or arc state, and each determines either the *starting* or *ending angle* of the pie or arc.

Separating these control points may be done either by using Property Bar options or by dragging the points using the Shape Tool. Dragging inside the path followed by your ellipse's shape creates the Ellipse Pie state, which has the effect of joining each of the two control points with straight-line segments to the center of the ellipse. Dragging outside the shape creates the Ellipse Arc state, which renders the two straight segments invisible (see Figure 9-3).

9

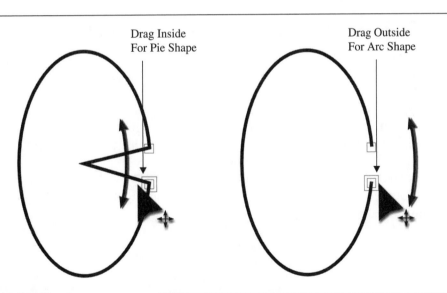

Drag Inside
For Pie Shape

Drag Outside
For Arc Shape

FIGURE 9-3   To change a typical closed-path ellipse shape into a pie or an arc, drag one of the two control points using the Shape Tool.

TIP

Even though pies and arcs appear as if sections or path parts are missing, they remain ellipse shapes. A single click using the Pick Tool on a pie or arc reveals object selection handles that indicate the entire ellipse shape.

If you wish, you may create a new pie or arc as your initial Ellipse state by clicking either the Pie or Arc button in the Property Bar while the Ellipse Tool is selected (and while no other ellipse shapes are selected) before creating the shape. You may also quickly toggle the state of any selected ellipse shape among these three states using the same options. By default, all pies or arcs are applied with a default Starting Angle of 0 degrees and a default Ending Angle of 270 degrees. Starting and Ending Angle values are based on the degrees of rotation around a typical circle and may be set from –360 to 360 degrees.

TIP

If needed, you may set the default properties for all new ellipse shapes by choosing the Ellipse Tool from the main Toolbox and choosing options in the Property Bar before creating any shapes. Each new ellipse shape will then be created according to the options you select, including the state of the new ellipse—Ellipse, Pie, or Arc—and the starting and ending angles for each.

Using Polygons and the Property Bar

Shapes created using the Polygon Tool certainly take dynamic shape physics to a new level, and the capabilities of CorelDRAW's polygon shapes are so far unmatched in any other graphics software. Although its name is slightly esoteric, the Polygon Tool enables you to create perfectly formed shapes with precise accuracy and symmetry. The shapes you create remain fully editable, with a special internal relationship between the number of points and the length of the sides. The shapes you create with the Polygon Tool may be as few as 3, or as many as 500 points and sides. You'll find the Polygon Tool, shown next, in the main Toolbox together with the Spiral and Graph Paper tools. To quickly select the Polygon Tool, press Y.

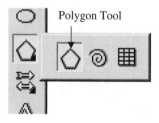

Polygon Tool

While the Polygon Tool is selected, the Property Bar springs to life to display various options, shown next, for controlling the number of sides and points on newly created shapes. You may also set the default properties for all new polygons before creating any shapes by choosing options before creating any shapes, which has the effect of applying your selected options to all new polygons.

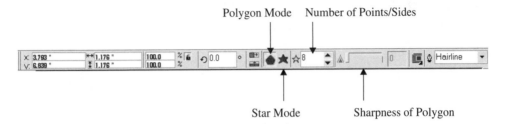

Polygon Mode   Number of Points/Sides

Star Mode   Sharpness of Polygon

Drawing Polygons

Creating a new polygon shape is similar to drawing a rectangle or an ellipse—using a click-drag action in any direction. But this particular tool enables you to create some fascinating shapes that may surprise even the most adept illustrator. All polygon shapes are dynamically editable, meaning you may change the number of points or sides on a selected polygon at any time, or before drawing one (see Figure 9-4).

Polygons may be created in three different states: as Polygons, Stars, or Stars as Polygons. Polygon and Star states are readily accessible using buttons in the Property Bar. *Polygon* refers to the shape in which inner and outer points are

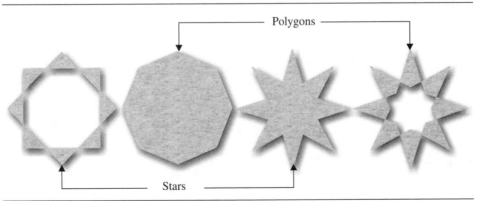

Polygons

Stars

FIGURE 9-4   The Polygon Tool enables you to create various types of polygon shapes, either as polygons or stars.

alternately joined by straight lines. *Star* refers to the points and sides being joined directly between the exterior points, which results in crisscrossing sides. For most users, the technology behind polygons isn't as important as the shapes that result. See Figure 9-5.

Drawing Polygons and Stars

To draw either a polygon or star and explore options, follow these steps:

1. Choose the Polygon Tool from the main Toolbox. Pressing Y quickly selects the Polygon Tool. Notice that the Property Bar now displays polygon options.

2. Use a click-drag action to create the new shape. Your polygon is created according to default values or according to previously set options.

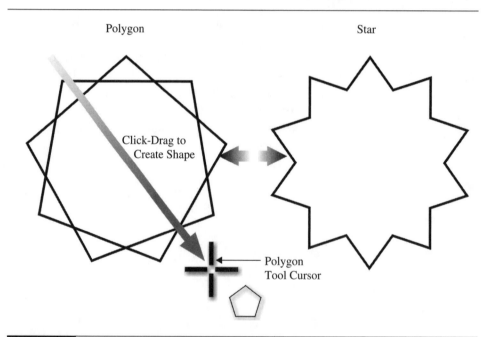

FIGURE 9-5   The Polygon Tool enables you to toggle the state of a selected polygon between Polygon and Star even after the shape has been drawn.

3. Adjust the appearance of your polygon shape by changing the Number of Sides/Points option in the Property Bar. You can use the spinner controls or enter a value followed by pressing ENTER. Notice that each time the points/sides option is changed, the polygon changes in appearance but remains the same dimensions.

4. Toggle the state of your shape by clicking the Polygon and Star buttons in the Property Bar. Notice the difference in the appearance of your shape between polygon and star.

Creating Star-Shaped Polygons

Whether the shape you create is a polygon or a star, another twist exists—the star and/or polygon states may crisscross. A star may emulate a polygon and vice versa, resulting in polygons as stars and stars as polygons.

A third state—Polygon as Star—is available. But choosing this state requires opening the Polygon Tool Properties dialog. To quickly open this dialog, double-click the Polygon Tool button in the main Toolbox; or open the Options dialog (CTRL+J) by choosing Tools | Options, and expand the tree directory under Workspace | Toolbox, clicking Polygon Tool as your tool choice (see Figure 9-6).

Shaping Polygons and Stars

With the Pick Tool active and a polygon or star selected, you may change the width and height of the object in the usual way. However, like rectangles and ellipses, polygons include control points that may be manipulated with the Shape Tool (F10) to control the actual angle of the sides and "sharpness" of the points. Each point on your polygon includes one of these control points, which may be dragged using the Shape Tool in any direction. This has the effect of causing the sides to be angled as they radiate outward from the center of the polygon.

There are two different types of control points to manipulate: interior and exterior. Moving either of these control points causes the points to be positioned at once and performs two essential property changes. Dragging the points enables you to change both the angle and sharpness settings. Holding the CTRL key while dragging any of these points causes them to change position in a constrained effect from the center of the shape, essentially changing the sharpness value only.

Click to make star polygons enclosed shapes.

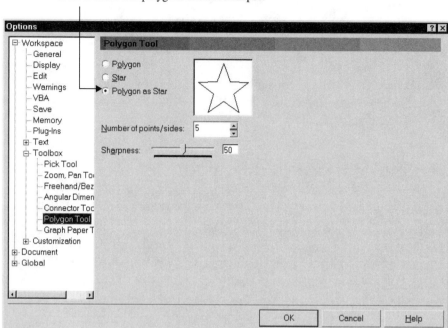

FIGURE 9-6 To set the Polygon Tool to create outline versions of stars, choose Polygon as Star in the Options dialog.

See Figure 9-7. Sharpness may also be changed using the Sharpness Property Bar option. The setting ranges between 0 and 100 percent, the default of which is 50.

Using the Spiral Tool

The Spiral Tool is one of those curious little tools you might find practical for a particular use. It enables you to quickly create symmetrical and progressively circular-shaped paths, which would otherwise be time consuming to draw using other techniques. Spiral objects are composed of a single open path that curves in a clockwise or counterclockwise direction, growing larger toward the exterior of

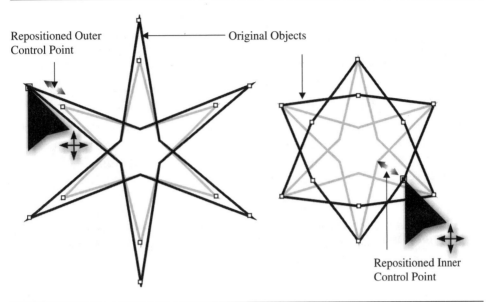

Repositioned Outer Control Point

Original Objects

Repositioned Inner Control Point

FIGURE 9-7 Use the Shape Tool and hold down the CTRL key to reposition the inner or outer control points and edit your star's sharpness.

the object or smaller toward the center. The Spiral Tool, shown next, is located in the main Toolbox, grouped with the Polygon and Graph Paper tools.

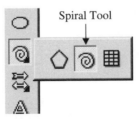

Spiral Tool

While the Spiral Tool is selected, it shares Property Bar options with the Graph Paper Tool and displays options, shown next, for controlling the object you are about to create. These include the Spiral Revolutions, Symmetrical and Logarithmic Spiral modes, and a Spiral Expansion slider control.

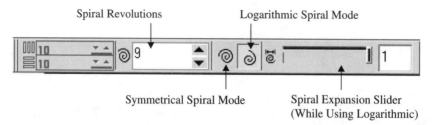

Spiral Revolutions

Logarithmic Spiral Mode

Symmetrical Spiral Mode

Spiral Expansion Slider
(While Using Logarithmic)

Spiral objects may be set to feature as few as 1 revolution or as many as 100. Each spiral revolution is precisely equal to one complete turn around the center point. The direction of the spiral revolutions is controlled according to the click-drag action during creation of the initial shape (see Figures 9-8 and 9-9).

 Spiral objects are not dynamically editable, meaning that you must set their properties before they are created. You may not change the spiral object's properties after it has been created, unless using the Pick or Shape Tool to edit its size or shape.

By default, all new spiral objects are set as Symmetrical types. You may also choose Logarithmic; and while this mode is selected, the Spiral Expansion slider becomes available. These modes and options have the following effects on the spiral objects you are about to create.

FIGURE 9-8   The position of the beginning and end points, and the rotation direction of your spiral objects, depend on how they are created.

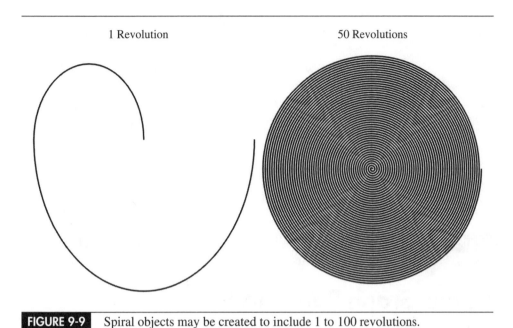

1 Revolution   50 Revolutions

FIGURE 9-9   Spiral objects may be created to include 1 to 100 revolutions.

9

Symmetrical Versus Logarithmic   As the name implies, a symmetrical spiral object appears with its spiral revolutions evenly spaced from the center origin to the outer dimensions of the object. To increase or decrease the rate at which the curves in your spiral become smaller or larger as they reach the object's center, you may wish to use the Logarithmic method. The term *logarithmic* refers to the acceleration (or deceleration) of the spiral revolutions. To choose this option, click the Logarithmic Spiral button in the Property Bar before drawing your shape.

Logarithmic Expansion Option   While the Logarithmic Spiral mode is selected, the Logarithmic Expansion slider becomes available, enabling you to set this rate based on a percentage of the object's dimensions. Logarithmic Expansion may be set from 1 to 100 percent. A Logarithmic Expansion setting of 1 results in a symmetrical spiral setting, while a setting of 100 causes dramatic expansion (see Figure 9-10).

Expansion 1   Expansion 50   Expansion 100

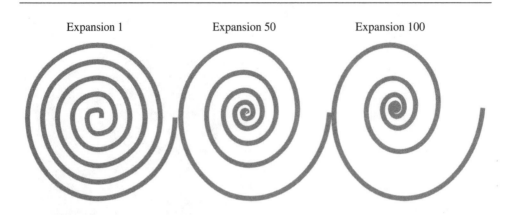

FIGURE 9-10 Three logarithmic spiral objects created using different Logarithmic Spiral Expansion settings.

Using the Graph Paper Tool

Although the Graph Paper Tool creates neither graphs nor paper, it *does* enable you to quickly create hundreds—even thousands—of grouped rectangles in a grid arrangement loosely resembling graph paper. This feature may be of particular interest to technical illustrators, chartists, or engineers, and can significantly reduce the time needed to manually create the same result. The Graph Paper Tool, shown in the following illustration, is located in the main Toolbox grouped with the Polygon and Spiral tools.

Graph Paper Tool

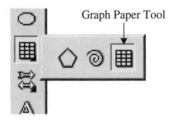

While the Graph Paper Tool is selected, it shares Property Bar space with the Spiral Tool (see the following illustration) and enables you to set the number of rows and columns for your new graph paper object. Like the Spiral Tool, you must set the number of rows and columns you wish your graph paper to feature before drawing your object.

Columns

Rows

To use the Graph Paper Tool to create a series of grouped rectangles and explore using the objects it creates, follow these steps:

1. If you haven't already done so, choose the Graph Paper Tool from the main Toolbox.

2. Using Property Bar options, set the number of rows and columns you wish to have in your new graph paper object.

3. Using a click-drag action, drag to create the new object.

The rectangles in the group are, in fact, native rectangles—meaning each separate object is the same as those created using the Rectangle Tool. Each Row and Column option may be set from 1 to 99, enabling you to create an object with a maximum of 9,801 grouped rectangles (see Figure 9-11).

NOTE   *Graph paper objects are not dynamically editable, meaning that you must set their properties before they are created. You may not change a graph paper object's properties after it has been created, except by using the Pick Tool to edit its size or shape, or by ungrouping the rectangles it creates and editing them together or individually.*

9

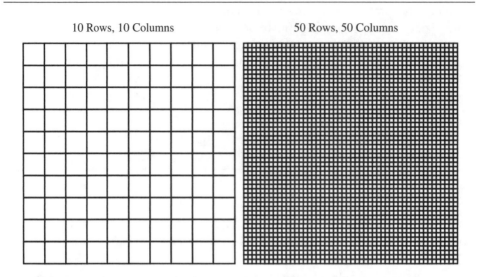

10 Rows, 10 Columns   50 Rows, 50 Columns

FIGURE 9-11   These two objects were created with the Graph Paper Tool using different Row and Column settings.

Using Perfect Shape Tools

The newest tool addition to CorelDRAW 10 is the ability to create objects known as "Perfect Shapes." This is a collection of tools—or rather a single tool with different styles—enabling you to quickly create shapes that would otherwise be difficult to create from scratch. When you first see the various types of shapes that result, you might think of this as a tool that draws basic clip art symbols—and in fact, you'd be partly right.

Perfect Shapes are actually dynamic objects composed of one or more control points called *glyph nodes*. These glyph nodes enable you to dynamically edit these shapes differently, depending on how the symbol has been designed. Instead of simply changing the size of the symbol, a glyph node enables you to change a dynamic portion of the symbol. For example, the symbol representing a donut shape features a single glyph node that enables you to set the diameter of the inner ellipse, leaving the outer diameter unchanged (see Figure 9-12).

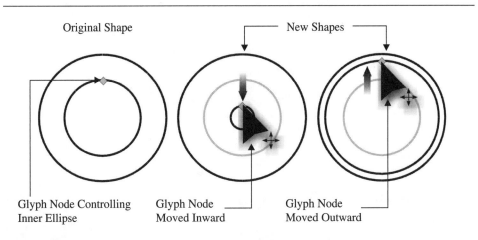

Original Shape — New Shapes

Glyph Node Controlling Inner Ellipse

Glyph Node Moved Inward

Glyph Node Moved Outward

FIGURE 9-12   The glyph node on this donut-shaped symbol enables you to edit the diameter of the inner ellipse independently of the rest of the shape.

Perfect Shape tools are available from the main Toolbox by clicking the flyout to choose a shape category. There are five categorized shape areas to choose from—Basic, Arrow, Flowchart, Star, and Callout shapes, as shown next:

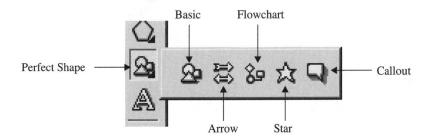

Basic   Flowchart

Perfect Shape   Callout

Arrow   Star

Once a Perfect Shape tool category is selected, the individual shapes are available from the Property Bar while using the tool. You must choose a specific type of shape from the Property Bar Perfect Shape flyout selector, shown next, before creating your new shape, because the shape styles are individual symbols as opposed to being object states.

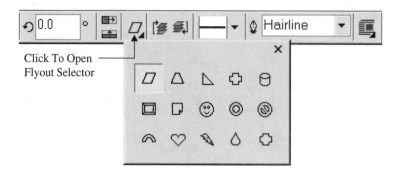

Click To Open
Flyout Selector

Creating Perfect Shapes

Creating a Perfect Shape is relatively straightforward. To do so, follow these steps:

1. Choose a Perfect Shape tool from the main Toolbox by clicking on the flyout and selecting a category.

2. Using Property Bar options, click the Perfect Shape selector and choose the individual symbol you would like to create on your document page by using a click-drag action. For all symbol types except Callout, the direction of your click-drag action will not matter because the symbols are created using a fixed orientation. For Callout shapes, the direction of your click-drag action determines the object orientation.

3. Once your shape has been created, notice that it may contain one or more glyph nodes that control certain shape properties. In cases in which more than one glyph node exists, the nodes themselves are color coded. To position a glyph node, use a click-drag action directly on the node itself.

4. Once your object has been created and any glyph node editing is complete, your other basic shape properties (such as outline and fill) may be changed in the usual way. For example, you can change the width or height of your new shape using the selection handles available.

As the category names imply, Perfect Shapes enable you to create basic symbols, arrows, flowchart, star, and callout shapes, each of which is worth exploring. Figures 9-13 through 9-17 show the various shapes available in each of the categories with a typical radial Fountain fill applied to demonstrate the effects of fills on these shapes.

FIGURE 9-13   Basic Shapes in the Perfect Shape selector

9

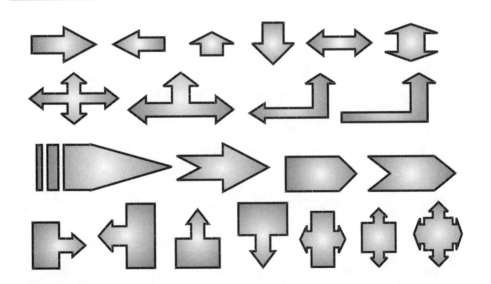

FIGURE 9-14   Arrow Shapes in the Perfect Shape selector

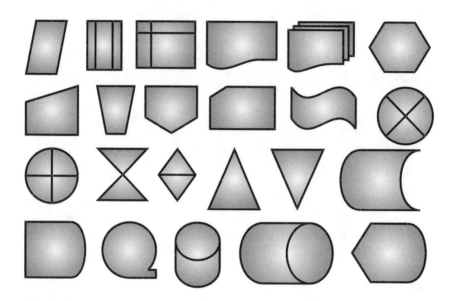

FIGURE 9-15 Flowchart Shapes in the Perfect Shape selector

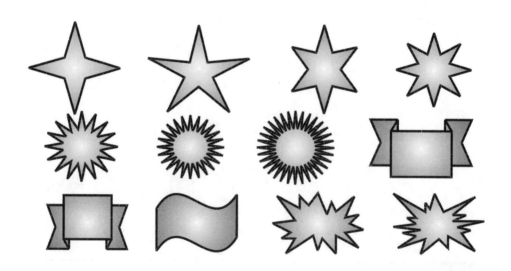

FIGURE 9-16 Star Shapes in the Perfect Shape selector

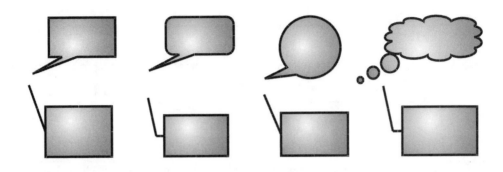

FIGURE 9-17   Callout Shapes in the Perfect Shape selector

Editing Glyph Nodes

The glyph nodes that determine the shape of certain portions of a Perfect Shape behave in many ways similar to the control points on a polygon while being edited. As they are moved, they often have the effect of resizing, reproportioning, or dynamically moving a certain part of an individual symbol. In certain cases in which the symbols themselves are complex, you may discover up to three color-coded glyph nodes available.

To explore the effects of editing glyph nodes, take a moment to follow these steps:

1. Choose the Perfect Shape tool from the main Toolbox and choose Star as the shape style.

2. Using Property Bar options, click the Perfect Shape selector and choose the banner-style shape (middle right in the selector).

3. Using a click-drag action, create a new shape on your page. Notice the shape includes two glyph nodes—one yellow, one red.

4. Click-drag the red glyph node up or down to reposition it several times. Notice its movement is vertically constrained; and as it is moved, the vertical width of each portion of the banner changes.

5. Click-drag the yellow glyph node left or right to reposition it several times. Notice its movement is horizontally constrained; and as it is moved, the horizontal width of each portion of the banner changes to match your movement (see Figure 9-18).

9

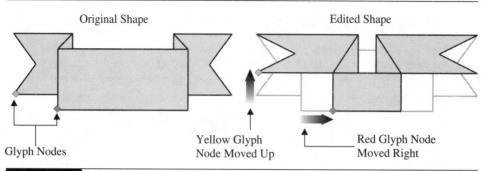

Original Shape   Edited Shape

Glyph Nodes   Yellow Glyph
Node Moved Up   Red Glyph Node
Moved Right

This banner-style symbol features two glyph nodes that enable you to change the symbol's appearance.

Glyph nodes may be edited interactively using the Perfect Shape Tool, the Pick Tool, or the Shape Tool. You may also edit the individual glyph node positions using the Object Properties dialog for a selected Perfect Shape, shown next. To open the Object Properties Docker, right-click the object and choose Properties from the pop-up menu.

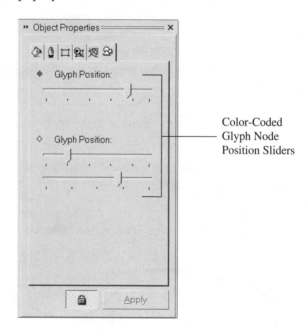

Color-Coded
Glyph Node
Position Sliders

This glyph node editing behavior varies with each of the Perfect Shape symbols available. Some symbols have no glyph nodes, while others feature as many as three. Each available glyph node controls a different portion of the symbol, depending on how the symbol itself has been designed.

You may convert any of the shapes discussed in this chapter to curves, including rectangle, ellipse (and pies and arcs), polygons, and so on, using the Arrange | Convert to Curves command (CTRL+Q). Using this command removes dynamic-editing properties. For example, an ellipse shape may be converted to a pie or arc (and vice versa); but after being converted to curves, you no longer have the option of doing so. The same applies to many types of objects you are able to create in CorelDRAW using object effects. With the exception of the Undo command, once an object is converted to curves, there is no way to return the object to its original dynamic state.

Using the Convert Outline to Object Command

The Convert Outline to Object command enables you to convert your assigned outline width properties to a separate closed-path object. This is a capability many users have been requesting for some time and will be of interest to users wishing to create the appearance of object outlines being applied with special fill types. To apply the command to a selected object, choose Arrange | Convert Outline to Object, or use the shortcut CTRL+SHIFT+Q.

When an object is converted to an outline, CorelDRAW 10 performs a quick calculation of the Outline Pen width applied to the object and creates a new object based on this value. When applying this command to objects that include a fill of any type, a new compound-path object is created based on the outline width. If the object includes a fill of any type, the fill is created as a new and separate object applied with an outline width and color of None (see Figure 9-19). When converting open paths, only the path itself is created as a single outline object of the path according to the Outline Pen width applied. Figure 9-19 shows a filled polygon applied with a black 4-point Outline Pen width that was converted to separate fill and outline objects using the Convert to Outline command. After the conversion was applied, the new outline object was filled with a unique fill of its own.

Original Using 4-Point Outline
Pen Width Bitmap Fill

Using Convert
Outline to Object

Outline Is A Separate
Closed Compound Path

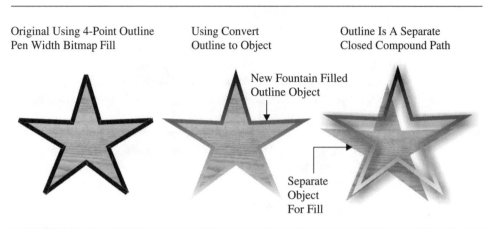

New Fountain Filled
Outline Object

Separate
Object
For Fill

FIGURE 9-19 This polygon was converted to two objects using the Convert Outline to Object command.

CHAPTER 10

Drawing with Line Tools

The ability of vector graphics applications to enable you to create all types of lines easily has long served as the very root of their purpose for existence. When it comes to drawing lines, CorelDRAW 10 is perhaps one of the most intuitive and powerful applications to use. There is certainly no shortage of line-creation tools enabling you to create quite literally all kinds of lines. In this chapter, we explore in detail these backbone features and provide a solid foundation toward mastering their use.

Grasping CorelDRAW 10's Line Tools

The tired old cliché "the quickest path between two points is a straight line" describes only part of the story when it comes to vectors. While the "quickest" path may be a straight line, math and geometry enable lines to be formed into all sorts of shapes. Each of the Line Tools in CorelDRAW 10 enables you to create what are essentially paths between points. These paths are represented by vectors between points. Typically, vectors are referred to as "lines," and the points on the lines are referred to as "nodes" or, in some cases, "control points."

No matter which Line Tool you are drawing with, the basic object you create is simply a line of one type or another. Once lines have been drawn, they may be applied with properties (color, width, pattern, arrowheads, and so on) to alter their appearance. Lines may be straight or curved and composed of two or more nodes. Joining the beginning and endpoints of a path closes the paths, while unjoined, they remain open paths.

CorelDRAW 10's Line Tools are composed of five basic tools (shown next) grouped in the main Toolbox between the Zoom/Pan and Rectangle Tools.

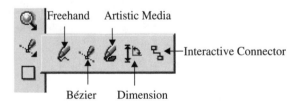

Line Tools include CorelDRAW's standard Freehand and Bézier Drawing Tools, together with the more specialized Artistic Media, Dimension, and Interactive Connector Tools. Some of these tools are closely related, so getting to know their Toolbox locations and the appearance of their tool cursors is a wise strategy (see Figure 10-1).

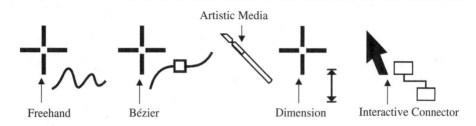

Artistic Media

Freehand   Bézier   Dimension   Interactive Connector

FIGURE 10-1   The quickest way to recognize which tool you currently have selected is
by getting to know their cursor states.

How to Fill an Open Path

Depending on how your CorelDRAW 10 options are currently selected, open-path
objects—in which the beginning and endpoints are not joined—may or may not
enable you to apply a fill color to the interior area of the path. This can be confusing
if you're accustomed to using other applications (such as Adobe Illustrator) that
normally enable open paths to be filled by default. By default, CorelDRAW does not
enable you to apply fill colors to newly created open-ended paths (see Figure 10-2).

To change CorelDRAW 10's drawing behavior to enable all open paths to be
filled—without the need to close the path first—follow these steps:

1. Open the Options dialog by choosing Tools | Options (CTRL+J).

2. Click to expand the tree directory under Document and click General to
display the associated options on the right of the dialog.

10

Unfilled   Filled

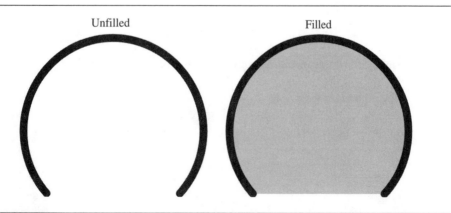

FIGURE 10-2   This open path is shown unfilled and filled.

3. Click the Fill Open Curves option so that it is selected and click OK to close the dialog.

After selecting this option, any open paths you create support the ability for you to apply a fill color to their interior area.

Using the Artistic Media Tool

The Artistic Media Tool is an incredibly powerful tool capable of creating many different types of "line effects." These line effects are unique because they apply dynamically linked effects to lines, rather than changing the line's outline properties. This particular tool enables you either to draw while applying these effects or to apply effects to existing lines. The Artistic Media Tool is located in the main Toolbox grouped together as shown next with CorelDRAW 10's other line-drawing tools.

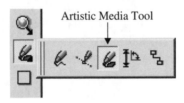

Artistic Media Tool

While selected, the Artistic Media Tool enables you to

- "Paint" brush strokes onto new or existing lines using distorted objects as the painting media

- "Spray" multiple objects onto new or existing lines in a repeating style effect

- Draw with or apply Calligraphic or Pressure-style drawing pen styles

Once the Artistic Media Tool is selected, the Property Bar offers five different line-drawing states to choose from (see Figure 10-3), each of which has its own specific options when chosen.

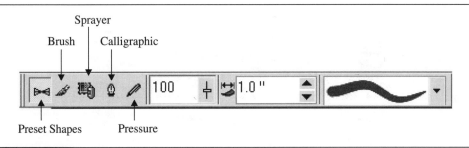

Brush Sprayer Calligraphic

Preset Shapes Pressure

FIGURE 10-3   When the Artistic Media Tool is selected, the Property Bar offers five
different drawing tool states.

Applying Presets to Lines

While Presets is selected in the Property Bar, drawing strokes with the Artistic
Media Tool enables you to draw using specific preset vector shapes, which are
dynamically linked to an underlying path. The smoothness and width of the
applied effect is set according to the Freehand Smoothing and Artistic Media Tool
Width options in the Property Bar (shown next) while the applied shape may be
selected from the existing list of styles in the Preset Stroke List. Smoothing is set
based on percent anywhere within a range between 0 (no smoothing), and 100
(maximum smoothing). Width may be set based on unit measure within a range
between 0.03 and 10 inches.

10

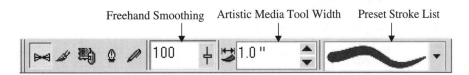

Freehand Smoothing   Artistic Media Tool Width   Preset Stroke List

As you draw, a path is created in freehand style and immediately applied with
your selected preset shape selected from the Preset Stroke List, which features 23
different styles to choose from. Many of these styles vary and alternate the shape
of the middle, beginning, and endpoint shapes of your line. Beginning and endpoints
are varied by rounded and square shapes, while the middle of the path may be thin
or thick, or it may intersect itself at the center point. Figure 10-4 shows these various
Preset styles applied to a simple open curve.

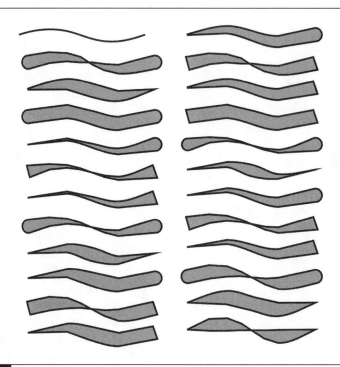

FIGURE 10-4 This simple open-path curve was applied using CorelDRAW 10's available Preset Stroke styles.

TIP *Preset Stroke styles are actually closed-path objects dynamically linked to the path they are applied to. This means they support both Fill and Outline Pen properties once they have been applied.*

To draw a line using a specific Preset Stroke style, follow these steps:

1. If you haven't already done so, choose the Artistic Media Tool from the main Toolbox located (and grouped) with the Freehand, Bézier, Interactive Connector, and Dimension Tools. Your active cursor is now the Artistic Media Tool cursor.

2. Using Property Bar options, choose a width for your new line effect.

3. Click the Preset Stroke List menu to view the selection and choose the style you wish to draw with.

4. Using a click-drag action to draw a line of any shape on your document page. Notice that as you draw, a black outline representing the full width

of your new line effect appears. When you release the mouse button, the path you followed is instantly applied with a line effect.

5. With the object just created still selected, you may use Property Bar options to edit its properties either by adjusting the Freehand Smoothness or Width settings or by choosing a new and different style from the Preset Stroke list. Otherwise, your new line is complete.

Drawing with Brushes

Drawing while Brush is selected as your Artistic Media Tool state, as shown next, enables you to "paint" lines onto your document page in the most interesting way. With each stroke made using the Brush state, the path you create is immediately applied with a saved object distorted to the shape of your path. The Brush used takes the form of various shapes, which have been previously saved specifically as brush strokes. Like Presets, Brushes extend the full length of each stroke you make.

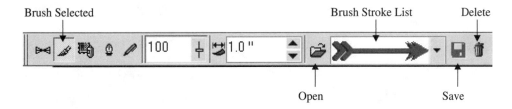

CorelDRAW comes equipped with several Brush Stroke styles, the effects of which are shown in Figures 10-5 and 10-6. (You'll also find a collection of additional custom Brush strokes supplied on the companion CD-ROM.) Choose from one of 20 Brush Stroke styles using the Brush Stroke List selector in the Property Bar. While Brush is your Artistic Media Tool state, both the Freehand Smoothness and the Tool Width options may be used to change the appearance of the graphical object applied to your line.

Just as you can with Presets, you may draw directly onscreen using a specific Brush style or simply apply a Brush style to an existing line. To draw using a brush stroke, choose the Artistic Media Tool and use Property Bar options to choose a Brush style and begin drawing by click-dragging on your page. To apply a new brush stroke to an existing line, select the line using the Artistic Media Tool, choose the Brush state, and use Property Bar options to choose a width and Brush Stroke style. Once a Preset has been drawn or applied to a line, you may use Property Bar options to change its properties at any time.

Open other saved brushes by clicking the Open button in the Property Bar, which opens a Browse dialog enabling you to locate the folder containing the

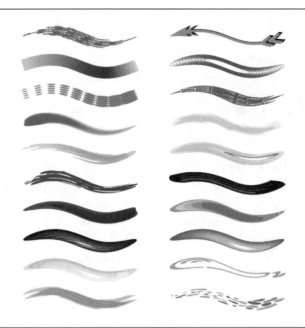

FIGURE 10-5 This line was applied with the available Brush Stroke objects.

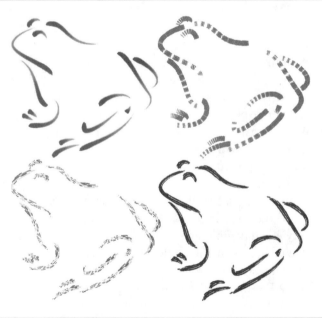

FIGURE 10-6 This line drawing was applied with various Brush styles to demonstrate their practical applications.

brush or list you wish to use. You may also save your own objects as brush strokes and add them to the existing Brush Stroke list by clicking the Save button, which in turn opens the Save As dialog. Brush objects are saved using Corel's standard presentation file format (CMX).

Applying the Sprayer

The Artistic Media Tool's Sprayer state is more complex than other states but is just as straightforward to draw with or apply. While Sprayer is selected, a variety of options become available in the Property Bar, as shown next. The Sprayer state has the effect of repeating a graphical image along a drawn (or existing) path, based on spray options selected in the Property Bar. The Sprayer objects repeat uniformly or randomly the full extent of a path, while the Size/Scale, Spray Order, Dabs, Spacing, Rotation, and Offset options take the form of variables that may be controlled using Property Bar options.

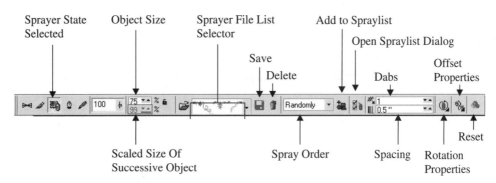

The first use of this feature may be discouraging, since the Sprayer styles appear to be applied in an uncontrolled way—especially if the line you draw or apply these effects to is complex. The truth is, so many variables are at play that it only seems this way. Applying one of these Sprayer styles to a line and experimenting with slight changes to the available options makes their effects become much clearer. With this in mind, the following define the purpose and effect of the options available in the Property Bar when the Artistic Media Tool is set to Sprayer.

Object Spray Size/Scaling   These two options control the initial object size of the Sprayer style based on a scaled percentage of the original spray object selected. While the Size/Scale option is unlocked, you may set the scaling objects of successive objects to be increased or reduced in scale relative to the size of the first object in the Sprayer style.

Spray Order   This drop-down menu (shown next) enables you to set the ordering of the Sprayer objects to Randomly, Sequentially, or By Direction. If the Sprayer style features only one object to vary, changing this option appears to have no effect.

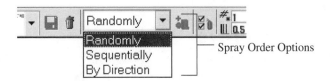

Spray Order Options

Dabs and Spacing   These two values enable you to control the number of objects to be placed along your path and the distance between the centers of each object. Dabs are the individual objects in the Sprayer style, while Spacing controls how many appear within a given distance.

Rotation   The Rotation options (shown next) enable you to set the angle of rotation for the first object of the Sprayer style. Using the Increment option enables you to compound rotation values with each subsequent object. Rotation angles and increment values may be based on the degree measure relative to the page or the path the objects are applied to.

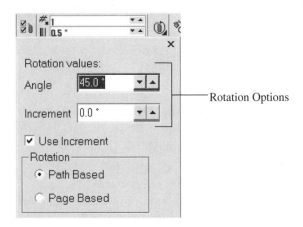

Rotation Options

Offset   The Offset option (shown next) enables you to control the distance between the center origin of the Sprayer objects to the path they are applied to. Offset may be set to be active (the default) at settings between roughly 0.01 and 13 inches. The direction of the offset may also be set to Alternating (the default), Left, Random, or Right. To deactivate the Offset options, uncheck the Use Offset option in the selector which sets the Offset measure to 0.

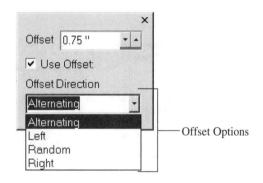

Offset Options

Reset   Clicking Reset enables you to return all Sprayer style settings in the Property Bar to their original default settings.

> **TIP**   *To delete a style from the Sprayer File list, click to select the style in the list and click the Delete button in the Property Bar. Doing so immediately deletes the selected style from the list.*

As with other Artistic Media Tool states, you may draw while applying a line effect using a specific Sprayer style, or apply a style to an existing line. To draw using a Sprayer style, follow these steps:

10

1. If you haven't already done so, choose the Artistic Media Tool from the main Toolbox.

2. Using Property Bar options, choose Sprayer as the tool state, a Tool Width, and a style from the Sprayer File List.

3. Using click-drag action, draw the shape of your path and notice as you draw how the path is defined. When the mouse button is released, the Sprayer style is applied to the path.

4. To apply a Sprayer style to an existing line on your document page, click to select the line using the Artistic Media Tool choose a style from the Sprayer File list in the Property Bar, and the style is applied immediately.

With a Sprayer Style applied and the line selected, you may use Property Bar options to edit the Sprayer style. Doing so edits the style only as it is applied to your line and not the original style in the Sprayer File List selector. Once a Sprayer style has been drawn or applied to a line, you may use Property Bar options to change its properties at any time. Figure 10-7 demonstrates a sampling of the available Sprayer styles applied using default settings. (You'll also find a collection of additional custom Sprayer styles on the CD-ROM.)

FIGURE 10-7 This open path was applied with selected Sprayer File List styles using the Artistic Media Tool.

Calligraphy and Pressure Pens

When the Artistic Media Tool is selected, choosing either Calligraphy or Pressure as your Artistic Media Tool state enables you to create vector objects resembling typical Calligraphic Pen or pressure-based drawing tools.

While Calligraphic is the Artistic Media Tool state, options exist for you to control both the Tool Width and Nib Angle of lines. You may set properties before drawing your lines or to existing lines in your document. Once a calligraphy effect has been drawn or applied to a line, you may use Property Bar options to change its properties at any time.

While drawing with the Artistic Medial Tool Pressure mode, only the width of lines may be set with the Tool Width option in the Property Bar. Pressure mode is meant to mimic the effects of drawing with a pressure-sensitive pen. Perhaps the best results of using this tool are achieved by an electronic stylus or a digital drawing tablet.

Saving Brushes and Spray Styles

As you become more familiar with the use of the Artistic Media Tool, you may wish to create and save your own Brush and Sprayer styles. Both of these tool states enable you to do this and in similar ways. The Brush and Sprayer styles you save will then be available in the Brush or Sprayer File List selectors. To save a Brush or Sprayer style to the selector list using a graphical object you have created yourself, follow these steps:

1. If you haven't already done so, create the graphical object or objects you wish to save as a Brush or Sprayer style. Grouping the objects together (CTRL+G) will make the next step simpler.

2. Choose the Artistic Media Tool from the main Toolbox, choose either Brush or Spray as the tool mode, and click the objects using your tool cursor to select them. The tool mode you choose determines the mode for your selected objects (meaning the Brush or Sprayer Tool states). New Brush objects are saved in Corel Presentation (CMX) format, while new Sprayer objects are saved in CorelDRAW (CDR) format.

3. Select New Spraylist from the Spraylist File list and click the Add To Spraylist button on the Spray Tool property bar. Click the Save button in the Property Bar to open the Save As dialog box (see Figure 10-8).

4. Enter a name for your new Brush or Sprayer style and click OK in the dialog to save it. Your new Brush or Sprayer style is immediately available in Property Bar Brush or Sprayer File List selectors while each tool is selected. By default, all new Brush and Sprayer styles are stored in the folder named CustomMediaStrokes in your Corel/ Graphics10/Draw folder.

5. To delete a Brush or Sprayer style from either selector list, choose the style and click the Delete button.

10

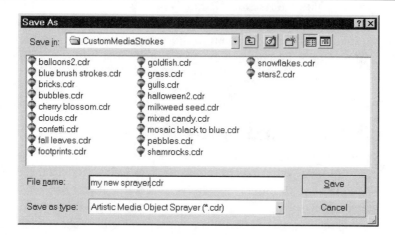

FIGURE 10-8 Clicking the Save button in the Property Bar opens the Save As dialog, which enables you to add your selected objects as Brush or Sprayer styles.

Drawing with the Freehand Tool

The Freehand Tool quite literally enables you to draw as if you were sketching a freehand drawing on a sketch pad with a pencil or pen. In fact, the most intuitive way to draw using the Freehand Tool is likely while equipped with a digital tablet and stylus pen. You may also simply click-drag your mouse button. Either way, sketching a line with the Freehand Tool creates a single open or closed vector path. The Freehand Tool is located in the main Toolbox grouped with CorelDRAW 10's other line-creation tools, as shown next.

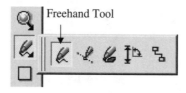

To draw lines with the Freehand Tool, follow these steps:

1. If you haven't already done so, choose the Freehand Tool from the main Toolbox. It is grouped with other line tools for Artistic Media, Bézier, Dimension, and Interactive Connector.

2. To create a continuous line, click-drag using the Freehand Tool to create a path. As soon as the mouse button is released, the line is complete.

3. To draw a straight line between two points on your page, click once to define the start point of the line and a second time at a different page position to define the end point of the line. As soon as your mouse button is released, the line is complete.

4. While your line is selected, use Property Bar options to customize its width, arrowheads, or line style pattern and/or apply a color using a right-click on any of the color wells in the onscreen palette.

At default settings, curves drawn with the Freehand Tool often appear less smooth than when drawn using other drawing tools. You may control this behavior by adjusting the Freehand Smoothing option in the Property Bar *before* drawing your freehand line, meaning adjustments to the slider enable you to draw lines of varying smoothness. Freehand Smoothing may be set within a range between 0 and 100 percent (the default). Lower values apply less smoothing, and higher values apply more smoothing. Figure 10-9 shows the results of adjusting smoothing values.

10

Freehand Smoothing 100

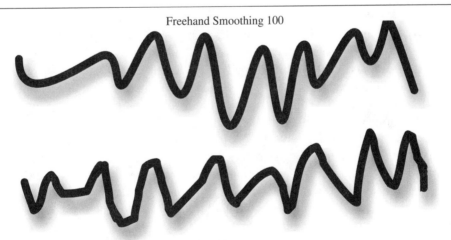

Freehand Smoothing 0

FIGURE 10-9   These two lines drawn with the Freehand Tool were created using different Freehand Smoothing values.

Drawing with the Bézier Tool

The term "Bézier" (bezz-ee-aye) originates from the inventor (Pierre Bézier) who devised a formula for the basic code on which most vector curves are founded. Essentially, the theory asserts that all shapes are composed of lines and nodes. The shape of a Bézier line may be either curved or straight. Line shape is controlled by slope properties of the nodes that comprise them. Two (or more) nodes joined by straight or curved lines are referred to as a "path." In reality, the terms "path" and "line" are essentially interchangeable, while lines may be either curved or straight. Two or more paths combined to form a broken or noncontinuous series of lines and nodes are referred to as a "compound path."

Once a Bézier path exists on your document page, its components may be assigned specific properties. The line portions may be set to specific line widths, styles, arrowheads, calligraphy, and colors, while the node portions may be set to different types (Cusp, Smooth, or Symmetrical), or their shape may be controlled using different Corner and Line Cap styles. Bézier paths may be endlessly manipulated and edited by repositioning nodes between the lines, changing the properties of the nodes, or controlling the position of curve handles controlling the nodes.

Bézier Anatomy

Bézier drawing in CorelDRAW 10 enjoys a high degree of precision and accuracy compared to other graphic applications and is perhaps more intuitive to use. Part of this is due to the fact that while using Bézier Tools, CorelDRAW 10 provides plenty of interface feedback to help you perform your line creation and editing tasks. Information displayed includes selection feedback, preview information, and highlighting effects while nodes and lines are being manipulated.

The shapes of lines are controlled in part by node properties and the position of curve handles. Two lines can have the same number of nodes in the same relative position to each other, but when the node curve properties are changed, theses lines can take completely different shapes. Figure 10-10 shows two identical lines except for the curve properties applied to their nodes. The result is a dramatic difference in the shape of the two paths.

Each node on a line has at least one curve handle controlling the path shape. Nodes at the start or end of a line have only one curve handle. Nodes between line segments feature two (see Figure 10-11). Curve handles of each may be edited to any circular position relative to the node they control.

Nodes may be set either to Cusp, Smooth, or Symmetrical (see Figure 10-12). Cusp nodes enable the path shape to be set independently on either side of a node.

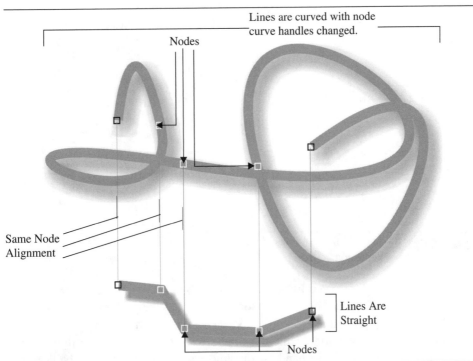

Lines are curved with node curve handles changed.

Nodes

Same Node Alignment

Lines Are Straight

Nodes

FIGURE 10-10 These two lines share the same properties except for the properties of their nodes and lines.

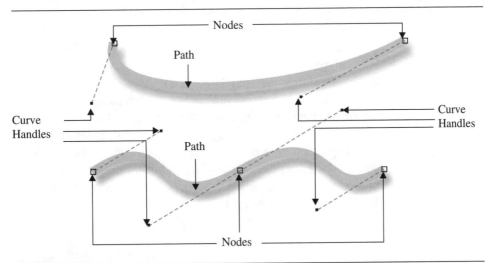

Nodes

Path

Curve Handles

Path

Curve Handles

Nodes

FIGURE 10-11 Line endpoints contain just one node and curve handle, while nodes between lines have two.

10

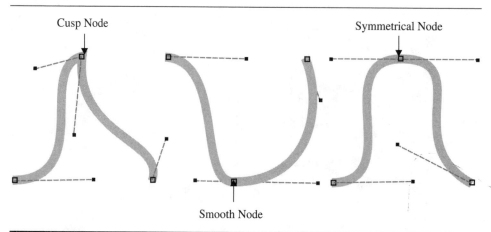

Cusp Node

Symmetrical Node

Smooth Node

FIGURE 10-12   In each of these lines, the center node has been set to different node conditions.

This means straight or curved lines enable the path to change direction abruptly where they meet at a node. For this reason, Cusp nodes are perhaps the most straightforward to manipulate. Smooth nodes cause the path slope and direction to align on either sides of a node, which has the effect of creating a smooth transition at the point of the node. Curve handles surrounding a Smooth node may be unequal distances from the node. Symmetrical nodes cause the line shape on either side to be equal in slope but opposite in angle, meaning they behave similar to Smooth nodes but cause equal curve appearance on either side of a node.

Create a New Bézier

Shaping a path is much easier after it has been drawn, but if you wish, you may draw with the Bézier Tool and manipulate curve shapes as you created them. While drawing with this tool, single clicks define new node positions joined by straight lines. As long as you keep clicking to define new node positions, your line continues to grow. But using a click-drag action has a different effect and essentially does two things: The click-down action defines the node position, while the dragging action defines the shape of the curve. As you drag, your cursor is defining the position of the curve handle controlling the node you just defined. Click-dragging in succession creates a continuous curve shaped by multiple nodes and curve handles.

10

> **TIP**
>
> *When drawing with the Bézier Tool, holding* CTRL *as you click to create new nodes constrains their position to align vertically, horizontally, or within constrained angles relative to the last created node position. Holding* CTRL *while dragging curve handles constrains their angles to 15-degree increments relative to the last node created.*

To explore this drawing action a little further, follow these brief steps:

1. If you haven't already done so, choose the Bézier Tool (F5) from the main Toolbox.

2. Use a single-click action to define the first node position of your line.

3. Click again to define a second point somewhere else on your page. Notice that the two nodes are automatically joined by a straight line.

4. This time using a click-drag action, click to define your third node position in a different location, but continue dragging in any direction. Notice that as you drag, the second and third nodes are automatically joined by a curved line, and two curve handles appear joined by a dotted line. The point you are dragging is one of these handles. The further you drag the curve handle from the node, the more emphasized the curve becomes.

5. Release the mouse button and notice that the curve handles remain in view. You have just created a Bézier curve composed of three nodes.

6. Continue exploring positioning nodes and defining curves by clicking to define new nodes and click-dragging to define new curves.

7. To create a closed path of your new Bézier shape, click your tool cursor directly on the first node you defined. This action closes the path and automatically joins the first and last nodes. To end the session with your path remaining open instead of closing it, press the SPACEBAR to select the Pick Tool.

> **TIP**
>
> *While drawing with the Bézier Tool, holding* ALT *while dragging to define a bézier curve shape enables you to interactively change the position of new nodes as you create your curve shape.*

Béziers and the Property Bar

All path shapes are controlled by properties of the nodes and lines comprising them, each component of which may be edited using the Shape Tool (F10). The Shape Tool can be found in the main Toolbox grouped with the Knife, Eraser, and Freehand Transform Tools.

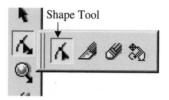

In addition to changing node position and curve shape interactively, a complete range of command buttons is available in the Property Bar when an open or closed curve is selected with the Shape Tool. The command buttons become available depending on which component of a line is selected and offer commands to add or delete nodes, join or unjoin nodes, change lines to curves (or vice versa), toggle

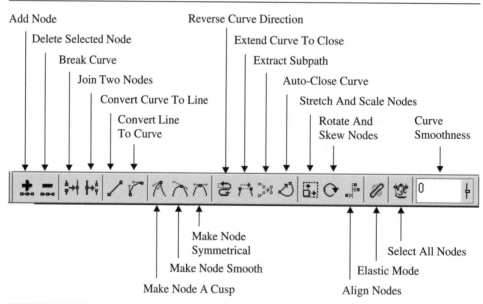

FIGURE 10-13   When editing curves and nodes with the Shape Tool, the Property Bar offers these command buttons.

the condition of lines between straight and curved, and toggle node states between Cusp, Smooth, and Symmetrical. The Property Bar also enables you to change the ordering of nodes and transform selected nodes in various ways using additional options in the Property Bar (see Figure 10-13).

As you perform your curve editing using the Shape Tool, you'll find that you use some of the command buttons available in the Property Bar more often than others because each of the uses performs a specific function ranging from common to highly specialized. Before getting to the practical exploration to follow, it may help to familiarize yourself with their function in the following list:

- **Add/Delete Nodes**   These are very likely the most common buttons you'll use, and they enable you to add new nodes to a curve or delete selected nodes with the Shape Tool. To add a node, click any point on a your line to highlight the new position and click the Add Node button. You may also add a new node to a line simply by selecting one or more nodes and clicking this button to add a node midpoint between the selected node and the next node in the line. Pressing the plus (+) key on your numeric keypad achieves the same result. To delete a node, click to select it with the Shape Tool and click the Delete Node button. Pressing the minus (–) key on your numeric keypad or your DELETE key achieves the same result.

- **Join Nodes/Break Curve**   While two unconnected beginning and end nodes on an open path are selected, pressing the Join Nodes button joins the nodes to result in an unbroken path. On single paths, only the unjoined beginning and ending nodes may be joined. On compound paths, the beginning and ending nodes selected on two existing—but separate—paths may also be joined. While a single node is selected, pressing the Break Curve button results in two nodes becoming unjoined, in turn breaking the path.

- **Line To Curve/Curve To Line**   These two buttons enable you to toggle the state of a selected straight line to a curve state or vice versa. A single click with the Shape Tool selects a line or curve indicated by a round black marker on the line. When curves are converted to lines, the path they follow is automatically changed, but when converting a straight line to a curve, the path remains fixed, but curve handles appear at each end of the segment enabling you to drag the curve handles to manipulate the path shape. When a curve is selected, you may also adjust the shape of the curve using a click-drag action at any point on the curve and dragging to reposition the path followed by the curve.

10

- **Extend Curve To Close** In order for this command to be available, you must have both the beginning and ending nodes of an open path selected using the Shape Tool. Under these conditions, clicking the Extend Curve To Close button joins the two nodes by adding a straight line between them in turn closing the path.

- **Auto-Close Curve** While an open path is selected, clicking this button joins the beginning and end nodes to form a closed path by adding a new straight line between the two nodes. You may also join the endpoints of an open curve automatically by right-clicking an open path, choosing Properties from the popup menu to open the Object Properties Docker, clicking the Curve tab, choosing the Close Curve option, and clicking Apply.

- **Reverse Curve Direction** Using the Shape Tool and while a curve path on a line is selected, clicking this button has the effect of changing the direction of the path. In doing so, the start point of the path becomes the endpoint and vice versa. The results of using this command button are most noticeable when the start or end of the line or path has been applied with an arrowhead, meaning the arrowhead is applied to the opposite end of the line or path. You may also notice subtle changes in the appearance of line styles applied to a path after using this command button.

- **Extract Subpath** This option becomes available only when a compound path is selected. After clicking the Extract Subpath button, the selected path is separated from the compound path, converting it to a separate path. Using this command on a compound path composed of only two different paths is essentially the same as using the Break Apart command. It's more useful when you need to extract a specific path from a compound path comprised of more than two paths.

- **Stretch And Scale Nodes** When at least two nodes on a path are selected, clicking the Stretch And Scale Nodes button enables you to transform their relative distance from each other vertically, horizontally, or from center. Eight selection handles become available enabling you to use a click-drag action from any corner or side selection handle toward or away from the center of the node selection. Holding SHIFT enables you to constrain the stretch or scale operation from the center of the selection.

- **Rotate And Skew Nodes** When at least two nodes on a path are selected, clicking the Rotate And Skew Nodes button enables you to rotate or skew the node selection. Eight selection handles become available, enabling you to use a click-drag action from any corner selection handle to rotate the nodes in a circular direction either clockwise or counterclockwise. Dragging from any side handle enables you to skew the node selection either vertically or horizontally.

■ **Aligning Nodes**   When two or more nodes are selected, clicking this button opens the Node Align dialog, shown next, which enables you to choose from the Align Vertical or Align Horizontal options that automatically align your node selection accordingly. In addition to these options, while only the beginning and ending nodes of an open path are selected, you may also choose to align control points. This has the effect of moving the two endpoints of the line to precisely overlap each other.

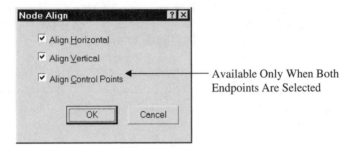

■ **Elastic Mode**   This seldom-used option takes a toggle state either on (while pressed) or off (not pressed and the default) and enables you to move selected nodes according to their relative distance to each other. For example, while a collection of nodes is selected, dragging one of the nodes causes the others to be dragged a shorter distance in relation to the node that is being dragged. While Elastic mode is off, all the selected nodes are moved equal distances.

■ **Curve Smoothness**   The Curve Smoothness slider control enables you to apply local effects to a specific selection of nodes, or to the entire line while the complete line is selected. To apply smoothness, select the nodes controlling the lines you wish to smooth and drag the Curve Smoothness slider control position toward 100. As you drag the slider, the shape of your curves become smoothed. This option is useful for smoothing lines drawn using the Freehand Tool with either the mouse or a tablet stylus.

■ **Select All Nodes**   This button is new in CorelDRAW 10 and enables you to select all the nodes in a path (or compound path) quickly. You may also select all the nodes in a path with the Shape Tool by holding CTRL+SHIFT and clicking any node on the path.

TIP   *To select noncontiguous nodes on a path (meaning nodes that do not follow each other along the path), hold ALT while dragging the Shape Tool cursor to surround the nodes in "lasso" style. Any nodes located within the area you lasso are selected.*

For a practical exploration of using of the most common of these Property Bar options while shaping a line using the Shape Tool, follow these steps:

1. Choose the Ellipse Tool (F7) and create an ellipse of any size. Convert the ellipse shape to curves by right-clicking the object and choosing Convert To Curves from the pop-up menu (CTRL+Q). The result is a closed path with four nodes joined by four curved lines.

2. Choose the Shape Tool from the main Toolbox (F10). Notice that the Property Bar now features all the line and node command buttons. Using Property Bar options, click the Select All Nodes button. All nodes on the path are immediately selected.

3. Using Property Bar options, click the Add Node button (or press the + button on your numeric keypad). Notice that four new nodes are added to each line segment in your path and directly between the four originally selected nodes.

4. Click any of the curved lines on the path once to select it and click the Convert Curve To Line button in the Property Bar. Notice that the curve is now a straight line, and the curve handles have disappeared.

5. Click a node on one of the other existing curves, drag either of the curve handles in any direction, and notice how they change the shape of the path.

6. With a node selected and using a click-drag action, click near the middle of the curve and drag in any direction. Notice that as you drag, the curve handle positions at either end both move and the shape of the curve is changed accordingly.

7. Click any node on the path to select it and click the Make Node Smooth button. Drag the curve handle of this node in any direction. Notice that the curve handle may be dragged only in a single direction. Click the Make Node

A Cusp button and perform the same action. Notice that the lines on either side of the node may be curved in any direction independently of each other.

8. With this node still selected, click the Break Curve button to split the path at this point. Although it may not be obvious, two nodes now exist where the original node used to be. Drag either of these nodes in any direction to separate their positions. The nodes are now control points, since they break the path to form beginning and endpoints.

9. Select one of these nodes, hold SHIFT while clicking the other, and click the Extend Curve To Close button. Notice the curve is now closed again, while the two nodes have been joined by a straight line.

10. Undo your last action (CTRL+Z) to unjoin the nodes and, while they remain selected, click the Align Nodes button to open the Align Nodes dialog. If they aren't already selected, click to select all three options (Align Horizontal, Vertical, and Control Points) in the dialog and click OK to align the points. Notice that they are positioned to overlap precisely. Click to select both nodes and click the Join Two Nodes button in the Property Bar. Your path is now closed, and the nodes are joined.

11. Hold SHIFT and click to select two or more nodes on your path. With your nodes selected, click the Stretch And Scale Node button and notice that eight selection handles appear around your node selection. Hold the SHIFT key (to constrain from center) and drag one of the corner handles toward or away from the center of the selection. All node positions are scaled relative to each other's position, and the lines joining the unselected nodes also change shape.

12. With the nodes still selected, click the Rotate And Skew Nodes button in the Property Bar. Notice that eight rotate and skew handles appear around your selection. Drag any of the corner rotation handles either clockwise or counterclockwise to rotate the nodes. Notice that they are rotated relative to their current position, and the lines joining the unselected nodes also change shape.

While this practical exploration is only a sampling of what can be accomplished while editing at the node level using the Shape Tool, you certainly want to spend much more time practicing your editing skills using all the available node-shaping command buttons in the Property Bar to experience their functions and effects.

Using Draw's Hidden Autotrace Feature

Although no actual autotracing tool exists in CorelDRAW 10's main Toolbox, it is possible to trace bitmaps quickly within CorelDRAW itself and without the use of an external utility. A hidden Autotrace Tool exists, enabling you to trace bitmap shapes using color values. The results are often rough for illustration purposes, but this can be a quick and effective way of tracing around the color areas of bitmap images in an effort to create vector objects based on the bitmap's color values.

Conjuring the Autotrace Tool

Autotrace becomes active only while either the Freehand or Bézier Tool is selected when a bitmap image is selected. To explore use of this somewhat hidden tool, follow these brief steps:

1. For this exercise, you need to have a bitmap image selected on your page. So quickly create a bitmap image based on normal shapes. Using basic shape tools (such as Rectangle, Ellipse, and Polygon), create several objects on your document page. Ideally, these shapes should be relatively small, such as 2 inches in width and height.

2. Position your objects in a cluster, close together but not overlapping. Fill all objects with red and remove any outline colors. To do this quickly, select all the objects, click the Red color well in your onscreen palette with your left mouse button, and click the None color well with your right mouse button.

3. With your objects selected, convert them to a single bitmap by choosing Bitmaps | Convert To Bitmap to open the Convert To Bitmap dialog. Choose RGB Color, set the resolution to 150 dpi, deselect all other options in the dialog, and click OK to create the bitmap.

4. With the bitmap still selected, choose the Freehand or Bézier Tool (F5) from the main Toolbox. When the cursor is held over the bitmap object, notice that it appears with a crosshair accompanied by a dotted line. This is essentially CorelDRAW's Autotrace Tool.

5. Click one of the red shapes on your bitmap. The tracing action of the Autotrace Tool is instant, and the result is a path set to default Fill and

Outline Pen properties. If you wish, click on the other shapes in your bitmap to trace them.

6. To end your tracing session, choose any other tool from the main Toolbox or click anywhere beyond your bitmap object to return your cursor to the Freehand or Bézier Tool states.

> **TIP** *While tracing bitmaps with the Autotrace Tool offers a relatively quick way of tracing a single colored area in a selected bitmap, you may trace all the colors in an entire bitmap at once by using CorelTRACE 10. CorelTRACE 10 may be launched directly from within CorelDRAW 10 when a bitmap is selected by clicking the Trace Bitmap button in the Property Bar or by choosing Bitmaps | Trace Bitmap.*

Controlling Autotrace and Line Tool Behavior

The default settings for Autotrace tracking are controlled in the Freehand/Bézier Tool page of the Options dialog (see Figure 10-14).

To access these options, choose Tools | Options (CTRL+J), expand the tree subdirectory under Toolbox, and click Freehand/Bézier Tool, or you may double-click the Freehand or Bézier Tool buttons in the main Toolbox. Either way, the Options dialog reveals a set of options for controlling line creation settings, and these options are defined as follows:

- **Freehand Smoothing**   The Freehand Smoothing option enables you to set the default value of the Freehand Smoothing option in the Property Bar while drawing with the Freehand Tool. Smoothing may be set based on percent within a range between 0 (minimum smoothing) and 100 (maximum smoothing). This option is largely redundant with the Freehand Smoothing option available in the Property Bar when a curve and the Shape Tool are selected.

- **Autotrace Tracking**   The Autotrace Tracking option controls the how closely the shape of bitmaps are followed while using the Autotrace Tool for tracing. The lower the value, the more closely the area being traced is followed. Autotrace Tracking may be set within a range between 1 and 10, the default of which is 5.

- **Corner Threshold**   The Corner Threshold option enables you to set the default value for corner nodes when drawing with the Freehand or Bézier

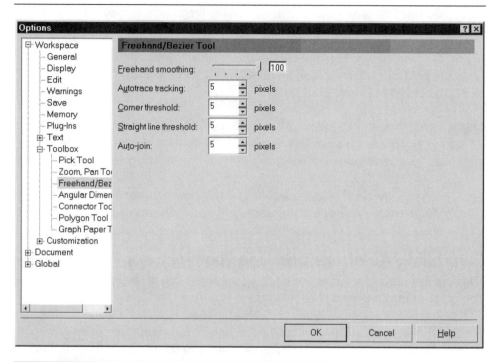

To control the accuracy of the Autotrace Tool while tracing bitmaps, adjust the Autotrace Tracking option.

Tool or while tracing bitmap objects with the Autotrace Tool. Lower values cause nodes to be more likely set to Cusp nodes, and higher values cause them to more likely be Smooth nodes. The range may be set between 1 and 10, the default of which is 5.

- **Straight Line Threshold** Like the Corner Threshold option, using the Straight Line Threshold option enables you to control how the shape of lines or curves are created when drawing with the Freehand Tool or tracing bitmap objects with the Autotrace Tool. Lower values cause nodes to be more likely set to straight lines, while higher values cause them more frequently to be curved. The range may be set between 1 and 10, the default of which is 5.

- **Auto-Join** The Auto-Join option sets the behavior of the Freehand or Bézier Tool while using either tool to draw closed-path objects. This value represents the distance in pixels your cursor must be when clicking near the first node of a newly created path in order to automatically close the path. Auto-Join may be set anywhere within a range between 1 and 10 pixels, the default of which is 5.

Understanding Compound Paths

When working with complex shapes, you undoubtedly encounter compound paths. These are paths that include at least two different paths to compose a single object. These paths may be both open, both closed, or a combination of open and closed. To create a quick example of a compound path, follow these steps:

1. Choose the Text Tool (F8) from the main Toolbox, click to define a point on your page, and type an uppercase letter **O** in Artistic Text format. This is a character whose shape naturally includes two paths: one to represent the "positive" space and one to represent the "negative" space of the character shape (see Figure 10-15).

2. Choose the Pick Tool from the main Toolbox, and with the text objects still selected, use Property Bar options to apply a heavy or bold font—such as Arial Black—and increase the font size to at least 200 points.

3. Select the Pick Tool from the main Toolbox, right-click the text object, and choose Convert To Curves (CTRL+Q) from the pop-up menu. With the object selected, notice that your Status Bar indicates the object is now a Curve on Layer 1 instead of an Artistic Text object.

10

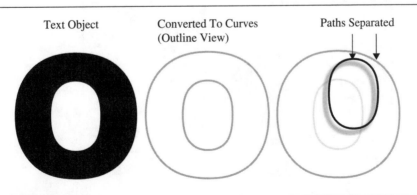

Text Object   Converted To Curves   Paths Separated
(Outline View)

FIGURE 10-15   This text character becomes a compound path after being converted to curves.

4. Change your view to Wireframe by choosing View | Wireframe to easily view the two individual paths composing the shape.

5. Choose the Shape Tool (F10) from the main Toolbox and click to select a node on one of the paths. Using Property Bar options, click the Extract subpath button. Click a blank space on your page to deselect all nodes and click the path once again. Notice the two paths are now separated. You have just converted a compound path featuring two subpaths into two separate paths.

Combining Paths

When two or more paths are combined, they form a compound path, which is essentially a single object composed of more than one open and/or closed path. When paths are combined, changing the Outline Pen properties of the object applies the new properties to all paths in the object. While two or more closed paths are combined, they form positive and negative spaces within the object. Applying a fill to this type of object causes only the positive shapes to be filled, while the negative shapes remain transparent (see Figure 10-16).

A minimum of two separate objects may be combined to form a single object using the Combine command (CTRL+L) by choosing Arrange | Combine while at least two objects are selected. The result is a compound path of all combined

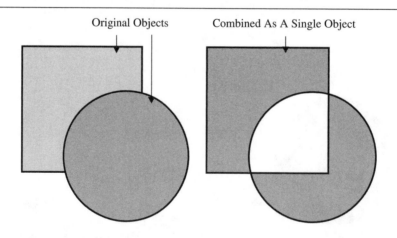

FIGURE 10-16   These two objects have been made into a single compound path using the Combine command (CTRL+L).

shapes. Compound paths are edited the same as any other open- or closed-path object—with the Shape Tool (F10).

Combining objects that normally feature unique properties—such as rectangles, ellipses, polygons, and perfect shapes—permanently converts them to curves, whether the objects are separated using other commands or not.

TIP	*You may also access the Combine command by right-clicking while two or more objects are selected and choosing Combine (CTRL+L) from the pop-up menu, or by clicking the Combine button in the Property Bar while using the Pick Tool.*

Breaking Apart Paths

When a compound path is selected, you may instantly separate all paths from each other using the Break Curve Apart command (CTRL+K). This command becomes available only while a compound path composed of at least two subpaths is selected and is relatively straightforward to use. There are certain advantages to using this command. For example, using the Break Apart command enables you to separate all paths of a compound path in a single command quickly, while using the Extract Subpath command button in the Property Bar when editing a compound path with the Shape Tool enables you to separate only one of the paths (see Figure 10-17).

10

Converting Objects to Curves

Choosing Arrange | Convert To Curves (CTRL+Q) enables you to convert your selected object from a specialized state to a simple or compound path immediately. You may also access the Convert To Curves command by right-clicking an object and choosing Convert To Curves from the pop-up menu. This command is often used to make certain object types compatible with effects or with certain other commands in CorelDRAW. In some cases, objects are automatically converted to curves when applied with certain commands such as Shaping commands (Trim, Weld, or Intersect).

Converting an object to curves removes any relationship it has to its natural state. For example, after a polygon has been converted to curves, you may no longer edit it as a polygon—such as dynamically changing its number of sides or points. Once an object has been converted to curves, it generally remains in the curve state.

A rectangle shape created with the Rectangle Tool may have its corners rounded, but after it is converted to curves, you no longer have the option of doing so. Ellipses, pies, and arcs are all editable as ellipses, but after converting them to

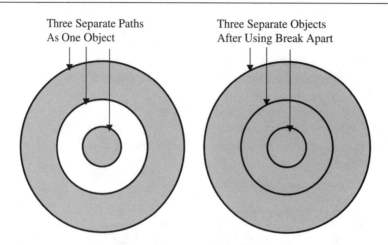

Three Separate Paths
As One Object

Three Separate Objects
After Using Break Apart

FIGURE 10-17   The three unique paths in this compound path were separated quickly by
the Break Apart command.

curves, they become simple open or closed paths. The same applies for many
types of objects you are able to create in CorelDRAW 10. With the exception of
the Undo command, once an object is converted to curves, there exists no way to
return it to its original state.

Generally speaking, any object that is not already a curve may be converted to
curves using the Convert To Curves command. This includes the following types
of objects:

■ Artistic Text objects

■ Effect objects such as Envelopes, Perspective objects, and Extrude objects

■ Frozen Lens objects

■ Natural shape objects such as Rectangles, Ellipses, Perfect Shapes, and
Polygons

Using the Dimension Line Tool

If the document you are creating requires that you indicate linear or angular distances
or degree values, you might consider using dimensioning lines. These are lines that
enable you to automatically indicate sizing of objects or spaces or show angles.

Dimensioning lines are created using the Dimension Tool. This tool may be of interest to users creating technical diagrams such as engineering, architectural, or electrical schematics, which often require accurate display of sizes.

Once a dimensioning line has been drawn, you may edit its line, text, and reference point properties to fine-tune its functions and appearance. Figure 10-18 shows a typical diagram using dimensioning lines to indicate measurements.

Using Dimension Tool States

There are six Dimension Line Tool types to choose from, each of which creates a different type of line with a specific purpose. The Dimension Tool is located in the main Toolbox grouped with the Bézier, Freehand, Artistic Media, and Interactive Connector Line Tools, as shown in the illustration at the top of the next page.

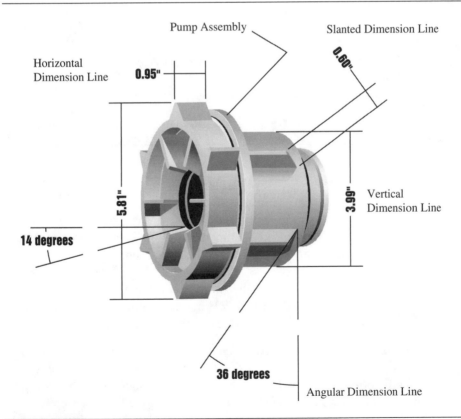

FIGURE 10-18   This diagram shows dimensioning lines in a practical application.

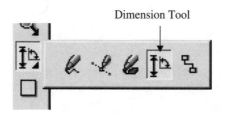

Dimension Tool

When the Dimension Tool is selected, the Property Bar shows six different tool modes that may be selected for specific purposes. These modes, which are shown next, include Vertical, Horizontal, Slanted, Callout, and Angular Dimension Tool states as well as an Auto state. You may also specify the style, precision, and unit values of your displayed dimensions and control the display and appearance of the labeling text.

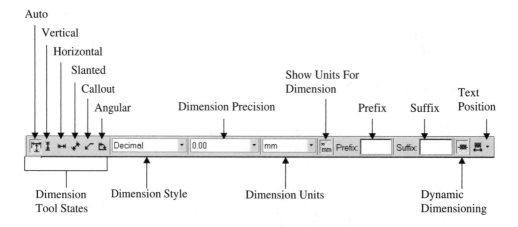

Before choosing which one of these Dimension Tools is best suited for your particular needs, the following briefly defines their function:

- **Auto Dimension Tool** While the Auto Dimension Tool is selected, your dimensions may be either Vertical or Horizontal dimension lines, defined by your initial click-drag action while creating your dimension line.

- **Vertical/Horizontal Dimension Tools** Using the Vertical or Horizontal Dimension Tool states, all dimension lines you create are limited only to a specific orientation. By default, the text labels associated with Vertical dimension lines are oriented at 90 degrees to your page orientation while the Horizontal state creates horizontally oriented labels.

- **Slanted Dimension Tool**   Choose the Slanted Dimension Tool state to create dimension lines that measure distances at an angle. By default, the text labels applied to Slanted dimension lines are oriented to be read upright from left to right.

- **Callout Tool**   This tool is more unique in that it enables you to create lines attached with labels at various positions. As the name implies, the resulting text label merely displays the text you enter and does not measure distances.

- **Angular Dimension Tool**   Choose the Angular Dimension Tool if the object or space you wish to display the measurements of are angles based on degrees, radians, or gradients.

Creating a typical dimension line is usually a three-step operation. During creation of the lines, your first mouse click defines one end or side of the line while the next click defines the other side or end. The third and final click enables you to define the position for the dimensioning text label. To create a typical dimension line, follow these steps:

1. If you haven't already, open a drawing or create an object you wish to apply dimension lines to. Choose the Dimension Tool from the main Toolbox located with the Bézier, Freehand, Artistic Media, and Interactive Connector Line Tools.

2. Using Property Bar options, click to select a Dimension Tool state. Choose the one which best suits your needs.

3. Click to define the first reference point for your dimension line and release the mouse button. Notice as you move your cursor around the screen, the Dimension Tool cursor remains active, and the dimension line changes to reflect the cursor position.

4. Position your cursor at the second side or end of the area you wish to display measurements for and click again to define the point. With this point defined, the area you are measuring has been defined, but your cursor still is active, and it now includes a rectangular-shaped box. This cursor remains active until you complete the next step.

5. Click a point between the first two points you clicked. This position represents where your dimension line text label will be placed. Notice

10

that the measured distance between the first two points is immediately displayed, and the text label is formatted using your default text format properties. At this point, your dimension line is complete.

6. To end your line creation session, press the SPACEBAR to select the Pick Tool.

> **TIP**   *After creating a dimension line, you may format text labels by clicking the text using the Pick Tool and using Property Bar options available when any typical Artistic Text object is selected.*

Dimension Tools and the Property Bar

The Property Bar controls all relevant properties of your selected Dimension Tool state. The Property Bar is organized into various drop-down menus, custom text boxes, and command buttons for controlling the display of angles or distances measured by your dimension lines. The following defines the function of each of these Property Bar options:

- **Dimension Style**   The Dimension Style option enables you to choose among decimal, fractional, or standard measuring conventions, the default of which is decimal. These styles are available only while Auto, Vertical, Horizontal, or Slanted mode is selected.

- **Dimension Precision**   The Dimension Precision option enables you to choose a level of precision. While using Decimal as the measuring style, precision may be specified up to ten decimal places. While using Fractional, precision may be specified using fractions up to 1/1024 of a selected unit measure.

> **TIP**   *Double-clicking the text portion of a dimension line using the Pick Tool automatically displays the Linear Dimensions Docker, which includes options identical to those found in the Property Bar while using the Dimension Tool.*

- **Dimension Units**   Use the Dimension Units option to specify which measurement unit to display your text labels with. You may choose any of the unit measures supported by CorelDRAW 10.

- **Show Units For Dimension**   The Show Units For Dimension option may be toggled on or off to display the units associated with your dimension line.

■ **Prefix/Suffix For Dimension**   The Prefix and Suffix options enable you to enter your own text to appear before and after the text label for your dimension line. Prefix and Suffix text may be any character you wish and applied before or after the dimension line has been drawn.

■ **Dynamic Dimensioning**   The Dynamic Dimensioning option enables you to specify whether your measurement values are updated automatically as the size of the dimension line is changed. By default, this option is selected on for all new dimension lines. If you plan on resizing or changing the drawing scale of your drawing after creating the dimension lines, disabling this option essentially "freezes" the values being displayed so that they remain fixed whether your dimension lines are resized or not.

■ **Text Position Drop Down**   To specify a position for the text labels applied to your dimension line, choose one of the options available from the Text Position option. Choose from either top-centered, middle-centered, bottom-centered for Auto, Vertical, Horizontal, or Callout dimension lines. Text labels applied to Slanted dimension lines may also be oriented upright and/or centered within the line.

> TIP   *The most efficient way of controlling the format of dimensions lines is to do so before you begin your dimension process by setting default properties.*

10

To set the default properties for specific dimension lines, use the Options dialog (see Figure 10-19). To access specific dialog pages controlling dimension lines quickly, double-click your selected Dimension Tool button in the main Toolbox. Once the options are set, your new dimension lines are created according to your preferences, saving you the time required to edit them afterward.

Using the Interactive Connector Tool

Connector lines enable you to draw lines quickly between objects without the need to labor over how they align with the objects or which path they join to the shapes. Connector lines also enable you to reposition the shapes without recreating the lines connecting them. This line drawing feature is powerful enough to create drawings such as planning organizational charts, flow charts, scientific diagrams, teaching aids, or any other style of diagram that requires constant changes. If you're accustomed to drawing lines between objects using the Bézier Tool, this tool may save you an immense amount of time and energy. The Interactive

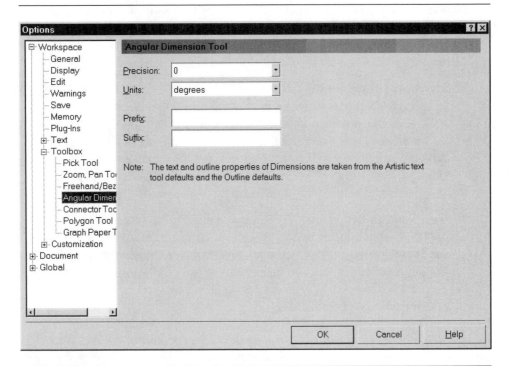

Set the defaults for angled new dimension lines, open in the Angular Dimension Tool page of the Options dialog.

Connector Tool is located in the main Toolbox grouped with other line-drawing tools, as shown here:

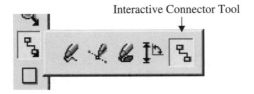

Interactive Connector Tool

Creating connector lines is relatively straightforward as are the options that set the appearance and behavior of these lines. While the Interactive Connector Tool is selected and a connector line drawing session is in progress, the Property Bar includes a few options, most of which apply to most other types of typical open curves. Notice in the illustration shown next that the Interactive Connector Tool has two basic tool states: Angled Connector and Straight Connector.

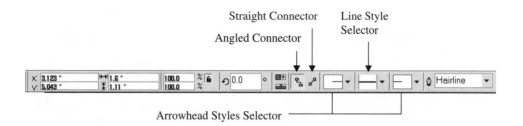

To use the Interactive Connector Tool to connect lines to (or between) objects, follow these brief steps:

1. If you haven't already done so, create at least four objects to connect. If you plan on using connector lines to create flow charts, you may wish to consider using the Perfect Shapes Tool in Flow Chart Shapes mode.

2. Choose the Interactive Connector Tool from the main Toolbox and two of the objects you have created to join using a connector line. Using Property Bar options, ensure that the Angled Connector state is selected.

3. Using a click-drag action, click your Interactive Connector Tool inside (or at the edge of) one of the objects to define the start of the connector line and drag to the object you wish to connect with either in the center or at the edge of the object shape. Your connector line is created. Notice the Angled Connector line is comprised of vertical and horizontal segments.

4. Click inside the second object to define the last point of the connector line and connect the two objects (see Figure 10-20). Your objects are now connected with an Angled connector line.

5. Using Property Bar options, click the Straight Line connector state and locate the remaining two objects on your page. Using the Interactive Connector Tool cursor and a click-drag action, click inside the first object and drag to the second object releasing the mouse button when complete. Your two objects are now joined by a straight connector line.

6. To end your Connector Tool session, choose any other tool from the main Toolbox or press the SPACEBAR to select the Pick Tool.

7. Using the Pick Tool, drag either of the connected objects in any direction to move it. Notice the connector line joining them remains connected to both objects and even changes its connection point on the object in order to maintain the connection.

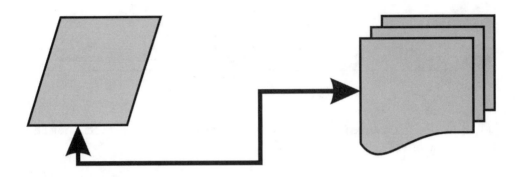

The Interactive Connector Tool enables you to join two objects with a
line quickly and precisely.

8. To set the properties of your connector line, use the Pick Tool to click on
   the connector line to select it and apply the Outline Pen properties such as
   line patterns, line widths, color, arrowhead styles, and so on as you would
   to any other object.

As you likely noticed by following the previous steps, the Interactive
Connector Tool enables you to make dynamically linked connections between
two objects in combinations of vertical and horizontal lines. Once the lines are
connected, the objects they connect may be transformed or moved to any position
on the page without breaking the connection.

Editing Angled Connector Lines

Changing the path followed by an Angled Connector line connecting two objects
is unlike editing any other type of line you encounter in CorelDRAW 10. Angled
Connector lines are composed of both vertical and horizontal lines, but they also
feature control points at the center of the path (see Figure 10-21). These centerline
control points act as "hinge" points enabling you to edit the line, add a vertical
or horizontal segment, and change vertical and horizontal direction between
two objects.

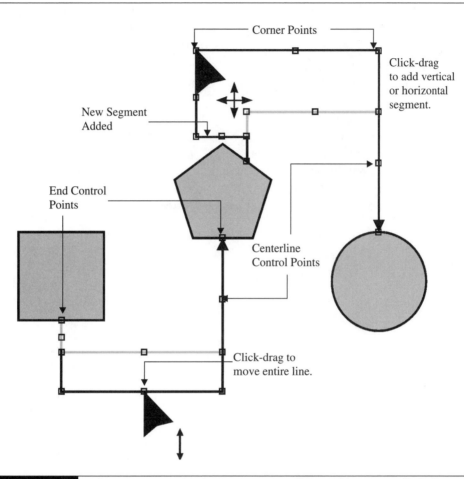

FIGURE 10-21   The center control points on connector lines enable you to edit their paths either vertically or horizontally.

To edit an Angled Connector line, use the Shape Tool (F10) selected from the main Toolbox. To reposition connector line endpoints—where they join to your objects—click to select the point and drag it along the edge of the object. By default, the connector line snaps to the boundaries of the object's edge.

Changing the actual path of the connector line is slightly more complex and is accomplished either by dragging the centerline points of a vertical line segment moves the whole segment either left or right. Perhaps the quickest way to grasp this functionality is through practical experience, but in essence, dragging either the centerline or corner points of an Angled Connector line enables you to manipulate the path.

Dragging the centerline points of a horizontal line segment moves the whole segment either up or down, or you can achieve the same effect by dragging the midpoints of vertical or horizontal segments. Dragging any corner point either vertically or horizontally adds a new segment to the path in order for the line to accommodate the new corner point position. To edit a jagged line to be straight, drag its corner points until they overlap, and the corners are automatically deleted.

CHAPTER 11

Cutting, Shaping, and Reshaping Objects

One of the keys to drawing with any graphic software is realizing that virtually any object you draw in two dimensions is composed of shapes. Virtually any shape you find in an illustration can be dissected into a rectangle, a polygon, a curve, or an oval. Instead of always drawing an object shape from scratch, one of the most efficient ways to create a new object's shape is to take advantage of easily drawn shapes. For example, CorelDRAW 10's collection of basic shape-creation tools—such as the Rectangle, Ellipse, Polygon, and Bézier tools—enable you to create a variety of shapes quickly. Using various techniques to combine these basic shapes, you may create nearly any shape you need. The trick is in knowing which tool to use and how to apply it.

CorelDRAW's Shape Resources

In this chapter, you explore all the various resources and tools CorelDRAW 10 supplies to shape existing objects and to create new ones. Some of the features covered have been in CorelDRAW for years, while others are relatively new or have been vastly improved recently. For example, the Trim, Weld, and Intersect commands have long been the favorites for quickly creating new object shapes based on existing shapes, as shown in Figure 11-1.

In recent years, other tools have also quietly surfaced, enabling you to shape objects interactively by removing or detaching portions. These include the Knife and Eraser Tools. These tools enable you to shape objects manually or to cut them in a number of different ways. The method you choose is determined largely by the task at hand and your own personal preference. Using these tools enables you to create effects quickly on a vector level, which would otherwise seem impossible, as shown in Figure 11-2.

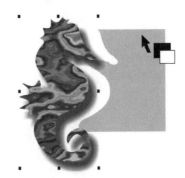

FIGURE 11-1   This seahorse shape was used to trim a portion from the rectangle shape layered beneath it.

Eraser Tool

FIGURE 11-2 The Eraser Tool was used to punch holes in this Artistic Text object.

Trimming, Welding, and Intersecting Object Shapes

11

If you were to take a close look around the room you're in, you'd probably see that each object in the room is composed of basic shapes, including rectangles, polygons, ellipses, and lines. More complex objects may be composed of combinations of these shapes. If you were to examine a complex shape or surface closely, you might even begin to see portions of rough shapes composing it. Drawing these objects from scratch would be tedious and time-consuming, which is where CorelDRAW's Trim, Weld, and Intersection—known as *shaping* commands—make drawing complex objects much easier.

Using the Shaping Docker

Commands for Trim, Weld, and Intersect may be precisely controlled using the Shaping Docker, opened by choosing either the Arrange | Shaping submenu or Window | Dockers | Shaping, and then choosing Trim, Weld, or Intersect. The Shaping Docker is subdivided into three areas controlling each command.

The *Trim* command is perhaps the most commonly used shaping command and has the effect of removing a portion where two (or more) objects overlap each other. The *Weld* command creates a new shape based on the combined shape of two (or more) overlapping objects. The *Intersect* command creates a new object based on the actual overlapping portion of two or more objects.

You must have at least two objects existing in your document (and at least one object selected) for the commands to be available and/or applied (see Figure 11-3). Clicking the corresponding button in the Docker window displays the specific command options, which for the most part are common to each command.

The rudimentary preview window in the docker indicates the typical result of each command, while other options enable you to control how the command is applied. Each shaping command features an apply button, namely Trim, Weld To, and Intersect With. Options take the form of on/off states that enable you to control which original objects remain after the command has been applied. These options fall under the heading Leave Original, which include the following effects:

■ **Source Object(s)**   While this option is selected, the object you selected prior to the shaping operation remains after the command has been applied.

■ **Target Object(s)**   With this option selected, the object you Trim, Weld To, or Intersect With remains after the command has been applied.

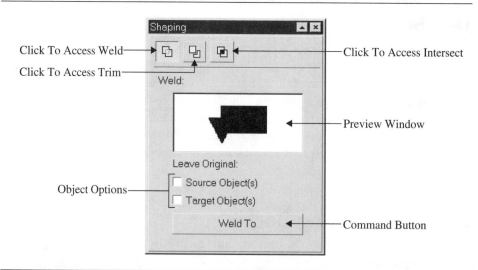

FIGURE 11-3   The Shaping Docker provides access to Trim, Weld, and Intersect commands, including options to control which originals remain.

TIP	*As you'll discover later in this chapter, having the capability to preserve original objects can be an advantage—especially if you need to use the original for other purposes. Otherwise, applying a shape command while both the Source and Target Object(s) options aren't selected simply creates a new shape and automatically deletes the original objects.*

To apply either shaping command, follow these steps:

1. If you haven't already done so, create the objects you want to base your new shape on and position them in such a way that the shape created by their overlapping portions represents your new shape.

2. Select one of these overlapping objects and open the Shaping Docker by choosing Arrange | Shaping | and Weld, Trim, or Intersect.

3. Click the button that represents which shaping command you want to use in the upper portion of the docker.

4. Choose which original object(s) you want to remain after the command has been applied by clicking Source Object(s) and/or Target Object(s), and then click the command button at the bottom of the docker to apply the command. Notice your cursor has changed to one of three targeting cursors, depending on your shaping operation.

Weld Targeting Cursor →   ← Intersect Targeting Cursor

Trim Targeting Cursor

5. Click the object you want your selected object to Trim, Weld To, or Intersect With. Your new shape is immediately created based on the overlapping area of your existing objects.

Shaping Commands and the Property Bar

CorelDRAW 10 also features Property Bar command buttons that enable you to apply Trim, Weld, and Intersect commands instantly to selected objects—without the need to open the Shaping Docker. Advantages certainly exist to using this technique because if offers a speedy way of applying shaping commands. These

Property Bar options only become available while at least two objects are selected—and make shaping commands available, whether or not the objects are positioned to overlap (which may be confusing for newer users unfamiliar with their purpose). Property Bar Shaping buttons are shown here:

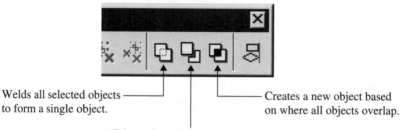

Welds all selected objects to form a single object.

Creates a new object based on where all objects overlap.

Trims selected objects, removing portions where they overlap.

NOTE   *When using Property Bar Shaping buttons, the new shapes are created, but no options exist in the Property Bar to preserve the original source or target objects. If you want to preserve or delete specific original objects during a Shaping command, use the Shaping Docker instead of the Property Bar. The Shaping Docker is the only interface component that enables you to choose specific Leave Original options by selecting the Source Object(s) and Target(s) Object options.*

Using the Leave Original Options

One slightly confusing issue surrounding the use of Shaping commands is the use of the mysterious Leave Original options found in the Shaping Docker when applying Weld, Trim, or Intersect commands to objects. In essence, these options enable you to apply commands while giving you the choice of whether to preserve the original objects with which you start. You may choose either or both of these options to leave the originally selected or target object on your document page unaffected by the results of applying each command.

To clear up some of this confusion, it may help you to take a close look at Figure 11-4, which demonstrates the results achieved using Shaping commands with combinations of the Leave Original options selected.

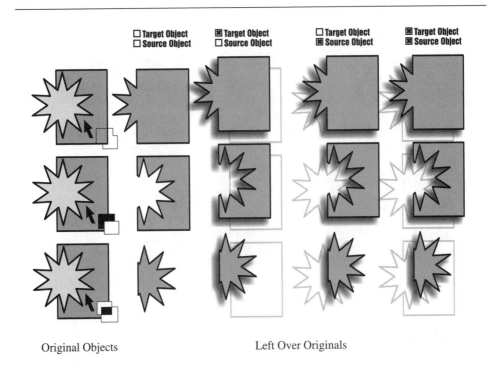

Original Objects   Left Over Originals

FIGURE 11-4   This polygon was Welded, Trimmed, and Intersected with this rectangle using the Leave Original options.

11

Applying Shaping Commands to Objects

The beauty of using Shaping commands to create new object shapes comes into play when you begin to realize the possibilities and apply other effects to the resulting objects. Before applying effects, though, knowing what to expect in terms of the properties of the resulting shapes might help. The outline and fill properties of newly shaped objects are determined by the properties of the target object. Figure 11-5 demonstrates how selecting which object is the target object and which is the source object sets the properties of new objects. In this case, two different polygons have been welded and trimmed with ellipse and rectangle objects. In each case, the resulting object takes on the properties of the target object.

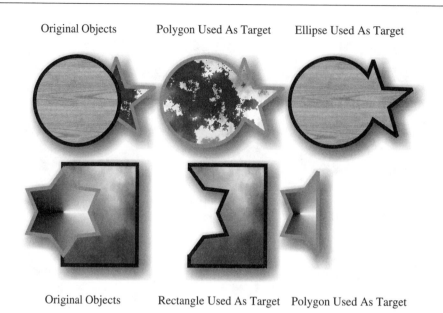

Original Objects   Polygon Used As Target   Ellipse Used As Target

Original Objects   Rectangle Used As Target   Polygon Used As Target

FIGURE 11-5 These polygons were used as source objects in Weld and Trim commands.

Open Paths as Trim Shapes

The previous examples in this chapter demonstrate the effects of applying Trim, Weld, and Intersect commands to closed-path objects containing fills. But, using open paths as trimming shapes can also be an extremely powerful strategy. When an open path is used as the trimming object on a closed-path object, the effect is essentially a controlled cut, completely separating the target object into multiple shapes. Instead of a closed shape being used as the trimming shape, the actual path is used instead. Any outline properties are ignored. This illustration demonstrates how an open path may be used to "slice" a closed-path object into controlled sections.

Bézier Path

Artistic Text

In this example, an open Bézier path was used as the source object and an Artistic Text object as the target while applying the Trim command. Once the text has been trimmed, it becomes uneditable as a text object. The resulting effect is a compound-path object comprised of two closed-paths. By applying the Break Apart command (CTRL+K), you can also detach the paths from each other, meaning they become two separate closed-path objects. In this case, neither the Source nor the Target Object options were selected, leaving only the trimmed text shapes behind.

Real-Life Shaping Strategies

Although many users realize the power behind having the capability to shape objects instantly, what they often lack is engineering this capability into the creative process. Let's take a closer look at a handful of real-life examples where Shaping commands have been used.

Keep in mind that creating the shape of your drawing objects is commonly one of the first steps in any drawing project. Even creating a simple rectangle requires you first define its shape before it can exist. So applying shaping commands to objects is often the first step before finalizing properties for fills or outlines, or applying effects. Figure 11-6 shows another example of an open path used as a trimming object applied to an Artistic Text object.

FIGURE 11-6 This loosely spaced text object was applied with a Contour effect before being trimmed by an open path.

If your intention is to apply effects to object shapes, you may want to apply shaping commands as a way of making the effects more interesting. The shape of objects can significantly affect the results of certain effects being applied, such as Draw's Blend and Contour effects. For example, Figure 11-7 shows a text object applied with an inside contour effect to create a sense of depth. In this case, a series of ellipses were used to trim the text object before the contour was applied, causing the trimmed-away elliptical shapes also to become contoured. During the Shaping operation, the Source Object(s) option was used to cause the original ellipses to remain.

In the next example (see Figure 11-8), several shaping commands were applied in succession before applying a Vector Extrude effect. In this case, a gear arrangement was created using a 40-point star polygon trimmed with an open arc. The trimmed portions were then deleted and the resulting object was shaped again by Welding an ellipse. The hole in the center was trimmed out using a third Trim command, and a custom linear fountain fill was applied. The object was then copied, and an Extrude effect applied using a Shared Vanishing Point.

As a final shaping example, Figure 11-9 demonstrates the creation of a thread arrangement. In this case, a rectangle is transformed using a Skew command and two triangles are welded to its ends. The resulting object was precisely applied

FIGURE 11-7   The inside contour effect creates a sense of depth

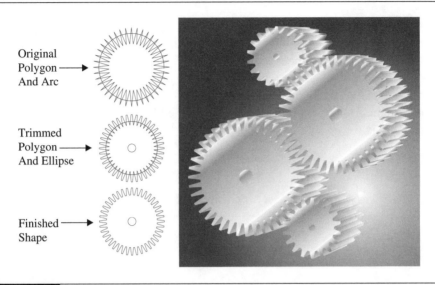

Original Polygon And Arc →

Trimmed Polygon And Ellipse →

Finished Shape →

FIGURE 11-8 The cogs in this gear assembly were created using a succession of Shaping commands before an Extrude effect was applied.

with a linear fountain fill to provide a simulated depth effect. The filled shape was then copied and a custom linear fountain-filled rectangle was arranged behind to create a mechanical thread arrangement.

11

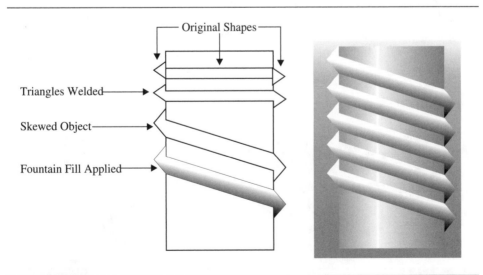

Original Shapes

Triangles Welded →

Skewed Object →

Fountain Fill Applied →

FIGURE 11-9 This threaded-bold effect was created by welding three objects together.

Knife Tool

For an interactive freehand-style method of dividing objects into portions, the Knife Tool is perhaps your best choice. The Knife Tool enables you to use a click-dragging action to define a freestyle cutting path, which results in areas on either side of the cutting path being separated. You can find the Knife Tool in Draw's main Toolbox grouped together with the Shape, Eraser, and Free Transform tools.

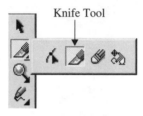

Knife Tool

Cutting Objects with the Knife Tool

Using the Knife Tool can be a tricky exercise if you're unfamiliar with its use. The Knife Tool can be used to perform a cut whether or not the object is selected. However, the start and end points of the cut must be defined at the very edges of the object you want to cut. After a Knife Tool operation has been performed, each of the resulting portions takes on the fill and outline properties of the original object before the cutting operation was performed. You can create either perfectly straight cuts or freehand-style cuts depending on the action used. Performing a straight cut (see Figure 11-10) is less complex than a freehand cut, but both operations use similar techniques.

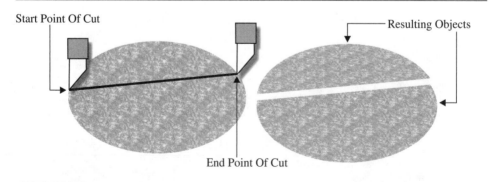

Start Point Of Cut

Resulting Objects

End Point Of Cut

FIGURE 11-10   This ellipse has been cut using the Knife Tool in a straight cut technique.

To perform a straight cut using the Knife Tool, follow these steps:

1. If you haven't already done so, create the object you want to cut and choose the Knife Tool from the main Toolbox nestled in with the Shape, Eraser, and Free Transform tools. While the Knife Tool is selected, your cursor changes to resemble the point of a cutting tool.

2. Begin your cut by holding the Knife Tool cursor over one edge of your object. Notice the cursor changes angle slightly and perpendicular to the object's edge. Click the object edge once to define the starting point of the cut.

3. Define the end point of the cut by clicking any other point on the object's edge. Your straight cut is complete and the object is now divided into separate shapes.

A freehand path—referred to as a *slice path cut*—may be created by dragging the Knife Tool during a cut. Behind the scenes, this operation is based on Bézier principles, meaning it enables you to perform freehand cuts and emulate the exact path of the cut. To perform a freehand cut using the Knife Tool, follow these steps:

1. If you haven't already done so, create the object you want to cut and choose the Knife Tool from the main Toolbox.

2. As with a straight cut, define the starting point of your cut, and hold the Knife Tool cursor over the edge of your object.

3. At this precise point, click-and-hold while dragging along the path you want to cut toward the inside of the object's shape. Continue holding-and-dragging through the object interior toward a different point on the edge of the object. Notice that as you hold-and-drag the cursor inside the object's shape, the Knife Tool cursor changes angle again and a preview of the cutting path appears.

4. When you reach the end of your cutting path at a different point on the object's outer edge, the cursor changes once again to its perpendicular state. At this point, release your mouse button. Your cutting operation is complete.

5. Once your Knife cut is complete, notice the object has been divided into at least two portions. To verify this, choose the Pick tool from the main Toolbox, click each of the cut portions once, and notice each includes its own selection handles, indicating they are separate objects.

11

While using the Knife Tool to define the endpoint of a cutting operation, your mouse button must be released at a point on the object's outer edge. Otherwise, your cut won't be successful.

To clarify the action a little further, Figure 11-11 demonstrates various stages of a Knife Tool cutting operation used to freehand cut a closed-path object into two portions.

Setting Knife Tool Behavior

In most instances, using the Knife Tool to cut an object results in just what you'd expect—divided objects. But it is comforting to know you can control limited behavioral characteristics using two Property Bar options while the Knife Tool is selected. Each of these options features an on or off state, depending on your specific cutting requirements.

Leave As One Object ———⌐ ⌐——— Auto-Close On Cut Mode

- **Using Auto-Close On Cut Mode**   This option (active while depressed) is the default state and sets the Knife Tool behavior to create closed-path objects following a freehand cutting operation, which is just what you'd expect. While this option is not selected, the Knife Tool may be used only to break paths at specific points, in essence, adding a pair of unjoined nodes to the path. While in this state, the Knife Tool may not be used to create freehand cuts using click-dragging actions.

- **Using Leave As One Object Mode**   While this option is not selected (the default), the Knife Tool cuts objects and breaks apart (separates) the two divided portions into individual objects. While this option is selected, the cutting operation results in compound paths that are not separated, even though a straight or freehand cut has been performed.

TIP   *Improvements to both the Eraser and Knife Tools now enable you to perform erase and cutting operations on both bitmap and vector objects—which previously only included vector objects. The types of objects that prevent you from applying these tools are externally linked files or images, or objects applied with dynamically linked effects.*

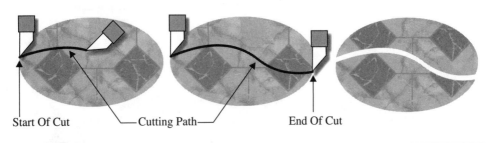

Start Of Cut   —Cutting Path—   End Of Cut

FIGURE 11-11 This ellipse featuring a bitmap pattern fill was cut in two portions using the Knife Tool.

Using the Eraser Tool

If Draw's Shaping commands or the Knife Tool don't do the trick when attempting to alter an object's shape, you may want to consider using the Eraser Tool as an object-shaping strategy. The Eraser Tool enables you to remove specified portions or paths interactively from objects—just like a real art eraser, but minus the elbow work. You can find the Eraser Tool located in the main Toolbox grouped together with the Shape, Knife, and Free Transform tools.

Eraser Tool

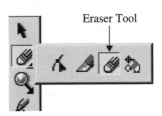

Exploring Eraser Operations

The Eraser Tool enables you to remove portions of objects in three ways: using a double-click action, a single-click action, or a click-drag action. Double-clicks remove portions of an object where the cursor is clicked to match the Eraser Tool's shape and width. Single-clicks enable you to define the start and end points of straight eraser paths. Click-drag actions enable you to remove large portions of an object continuously, as shown in Figure 11-12. You may also erase multipoint paths if you require.

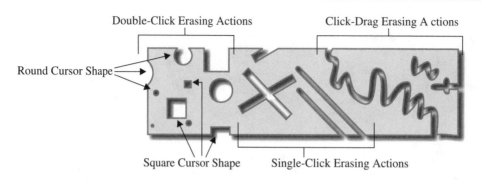

Round Cursor Shape

Square Cursor Shape   Single-Click Erasing Actions

FIGURE 11-12   Single Eraser Tool cursor clicks erase specific points only, while click-dragging the cursor continuously erases.

To explore the Eraser Tool and remove portions of an object, follow these steps:

1. Create the object you want to shape and select it using the Pick tool.

2. Choose the Eraser Tool from the main Toolbox and determine the area you want to erase. If necessary, adjust the width and/or shape of the Eraser Tool cursor using Property Bar options.

3. To erase a specific point on your object to match the size and shape of the current cursor, place your cursor above the specific point and double-click the spot. Notice a portion was removed.

4. Next, erase another portion using a continuous freehand-style action and a click-drag action. To do this, click-and-hold while dragging the Eraser Tool over your object and release the mouse when complete. Notice all areas your cursor touched during the continuous erase as you click-dragged.

5. Erase yet another portion (hopefully, you aren't running out of objects at this point), using single-click erase actions to erase between two points. Using this technique, your first click defines the start point, and your second click defines the endpoint. Single-click any two different points with at least one point within the shape of your object. Notice the erase path is straight between the two points and matches the width of your tool cursor. After defining the first point, a path preview followed the cursor until the second point was defined.

The final technique is slightly more complex, and it involves erasing continuously in straight paths between multiple points. For this, you need to press the TAB modifier key after each single-click to define the erase points. To create a multipoint erase path, follow these steps:

1. To begin, single-click anywhere on your object to define the first point and move your cursor over the next point you want to define without clicking. Notice as you move the Eraser Tool now, a path preview follows the cursor.

2. Press the TAB key on your keyboard—but don't click your mouse button. Notice a new erase path appears between the first single-click point and the exact point where your cursor was located when the TAB key was pressed.

3. To define a third point, hold your cursor over a specific point (without clicking the mouse button) and press the TAB key again. A third point is defined, and the path between the second and third points is erased.

4. Define a fourth point by moving the cursor to a new position and press the TAB key again. An erase path is created between the third and fourth points, as shown in Figure 11-13.

5. To define a fifth point, and this time simultaneously end the Erase session, move your cursor to a new position over the object and use a single-click. Your erase session is complete.

11

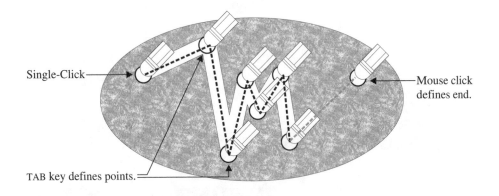

Single-Click

Mouse click
defines end.

TAB key defines points.

FIGURE 11-13   The TAB key enables you to define multiple intermediate points between your first and last erase path points.

NOTE   *Each time the Eraser Tool cursor is clicked to erase portions of an object, CorelDRAW considers the action a unique and separate erase session. This means Eraser Tool actions may be reversed using the Undo command in steps, depending on which erase technique was used. While using the single-click technique, an Undo command is needed to reverse each erase point. During a continuous erase using the click-drag action, a single Undo command reverses each continuous erasing session.*

Setting Eraser Tool Properties

Both the width and shape of the Eraser Tool are set using Property Bar options while the tool is actively selected. The complexity of the removal shape created during an erase session may also be controlled. These properties may significantly affect the shape of the removal areas of erased objects.

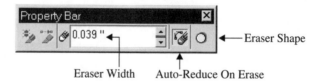

Erase Width

The Eraser Tool width may be set within a range between 0.001 and 100.0 inches either by entering values in the Property Bar num box while the Eraser Tool is selected or by pressing the Up and Down arrow keys on your standard keyboard to increase or decrease the size (respectively). Each keypress changes the Eraser Width by 0.025 inches.

TIP   *Use the keyboard to change the cursor size during an erase session. Press the Up and Down arrow keys on your standard keyboard keys while using a click-drag action to erase continuously.*

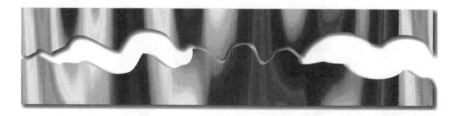

Eraser Tool Shape

Your Eraser Tool shape can be set to Square or Round, and it can be set using the shape toggle button in the Property Bar while the tool is selected. While depressed, the Eraser shape is Square. While not depressed, the Eraser Tool shape is Round.

Auto-Reduce Mode

When erasing continuous paths, the removed portions of vector objects are created at the Bézier level, meaning an actual shape or path contains straight and curved lines joined by nodes. How closely the new line shapes follow your erase path is determined by the number and properties of the nodes representing the shape. The more nodes, the more complex and accurate the shape. While active, the Auto-reduce on Erase mode affects the complexity of the resulting erase shape while erasing in continuous freehand-style paths.

Adding nodes to an already complex object, however, can possibly create an overly complex object when it comes to controlling its shape in other operations, or when applying vector-based effects such as Contour, Blend, or Extrude effects. The Auto-reduce on Erase option enables you to reduce the complexity of erased area shapes. To activate the Auto-reduce on Erase option, click the button to the depressed position (the default), or deactivate it by clicking it to the undepressed state.

| TIP | *Eraser Tool Auto Reduce on Erase settings are controlled according to the Freehand Smoothing default setting used by the Freehand and Bézier tools, which may be set within a range between 0 and 100 percent (the default for this is 100 percent). To set this option, open the Options dialog by choosing Tools | Options (CTRL+J) and choose Freehand/Bézier from the Toolbox group.* |

11

CHAPTER 12

Managing and Arranging Objects

If the concept of managing objects from the top down sounds slightly esoteric from your perspective, you may be right. The need to manage objects often stems from the need to arrange, structure, or change large collections of objects. If the drawings you create are relatively uncomplicated, you likely don't need these management resources.

On the other hand, where your documents involve hundreds—even thousands—of different types of objects, you have specific resources in CorelDRAW to navigate, select, control, or change object properties quickly. In this chapter, we'll demystify the use of the Object Manager, learn to find and replace object properties quickly, and create and apply graphic styles.

Viewing and Changing Object Properties

Before plunging too far into higher-level concepts of object management, let's look at how CorelDRAW sees the drawing objects you create. If you browsed through the menu commands, dialogs, or dockers to any extent, you likely already know object *properties* apply to all things in CorelDRAW. In fact, without any properties, an object simply couldn't exist.

If you need to find out any detail about an object selection, this is certainly the place to do it. The advantage of using the Object Properties Docker over information provided by the Property Bar is you essentially have one stop for your information shopping. Each type of object you create in CorelDRAW features a collection of properties set by you. These can be defaults, which are applied during object creation, or specific properties you decide on yourself.

The sheer number of variables involved makes this inventory of properties so complex. Object types may include anything from text to bitmaps, while their properties include page, position, dimension, outline, and fill—including all combined variations. With all these variables, expecting anyone to remember every detail would be inhuman—which is why CorelDRAW does this for you by way of the Object Properties Docker (see Figure 12-1). To open the Object Properties Docker, right-click any object and choose Properties from the pop-up menu, or choose Edit | Properties.

Once opened, notice the Object Properties Docker is subdivided into tabbed pages that appear according to which type of object you selected. Generally, anything you can click to select features a set of property variables, each of which

Tabbed Property Areas

Manual Apply

Apply Lock

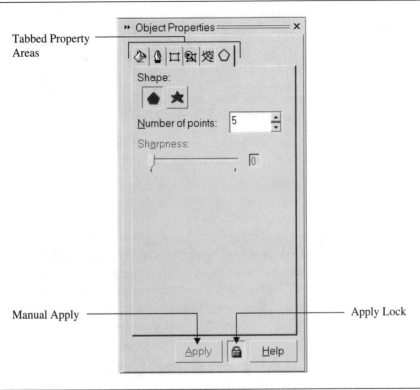

FIGURE 12-1   The Object Properties Docker enables you to view or edit any of the properties applied to your selected objects.

12

has its own tabbed page in the Object Properties Docker. The list of different tab types that may appear includes the following:

■ Your selected object's Fill properties, with complete options for editing any applied or selected fill type

■ Your object's Outline Pen properties, including complete access to any options or dialogs for editing the object's current outline properties

■ General information about your selection, including the number of objects selected, the layer they are on, the type(s) of object selected, and any graphic styles or text wrapping applied

- Object details, such as the width, height, center origin of selection, and center origin of rotation

- Your document page properties (while nothing is selected), such as the Page Title, HTML Filename, and Page information

- Any object created with specific tools such as Rectangle, Ellipse, Perfect Shapes, Polygons, Text, Dimension Lines, Curves, and Bitmaps

- Internet properties, such as Rollover states, behavior, assigned URLs, Target Frames, ALT Comments, Hotspot options, and Internet Objects

- Text properties, including full access to font, size, scripts, frame, and formatting options

Whenever an object is selected, the tab featuring properties associated with the specific object type are selected by default to display in the docker. Click any available tab to navigate between them. Any property editing changes made in the docker are applied immediately while the Apply Lock button is pressed. Or, you may apply all editing changes made at once by unlocking this feature, editing the properties or options, and clicking the manual Apply button.

Grasping CorelDRAW's Layer Concept

You might be surprised to discover that using Layers to organize and structure a drawing is a feature you use depending on your own character and how you think. Some people can easily adapt to using Layers, while others simply either can't or won't. These people often have trouble grasping the purpose of Layers, no matter how hard they try to understand. If using Layers is a new experience for you, let us clarify the concept before you take the plunge.

If you've ever had the experience of creating artwork in which portions of the visual elements have been separated onto individual see-through overlays, you already have a perfect understanding of how Layers operate. In this real-life analogy, the multiple artwork overlays are taped or pinned into position on a firm base board. Adding or removing the overlays causes the picture appearance to change, while the picture's actual composition remains the same, meaning the overlay art is unchanged. The picture's appearance changes depending on which overlays are laid in place.

CorelDRAW's Layer concept works much the same way, if not exactly. Your drawing objects may be moved to specific layers. This feature also enables you to create multiple layers, name them, and control their order in respect to your page surface. You may also order objects within the layers, group objects, and use available resources to obtain object information, such as the type of objects and their properties. You needn't be an organized person to capitalize on the use of layers, but you do need to plan out a strategy for layer structure, depending on the type of document you're creating.

Exploring the Object Manager

All Layer functions are controlled by one interface component—the Object Manager Docker (see Figure 12-2). This docker enables you to navigate between document pages, create and name your layers, select and move objects between layers, and control whether layers are editable, whether they print, and/or

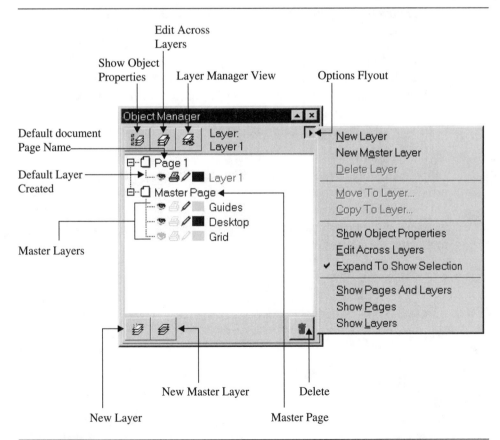

FIGURE 12-2 The Object Manager Docker is where all Layer functions are controlled.

whether they're visible. To open the Object Manager Docker window choose Tools | Object Manager.

If you've never used Layers for structuring a drawing before and you're opening it for the first time, the previous figure is likely similar to what you first see. Each page in your document contains a listing of its layers, while each layer is accompanied by options. A Master Page also appears by default and, by default, includes layers controlling your Guides, Desktop, and Grid objects.

Navigating Pages, Objects, and Layers

To begin, let's concentrate on getting to know how document pages and their layers in the Object Manager can be used for navigating your document, selecting layers, and controlling Layer options. Figure 12-3 shows a typical default layer structure for a new document, identifying the various parts.

To explore how these controls may be used, follow these steps:

1. If you haven't already done so, open a new or existing document and open the Object Manager Docker by choosing Tools | Object Manager. By default, the Object Manager appears docked to the right side of your application window. Notice the docker lists each page in your document. For each page, a default layer named Layer 1 exists and is accompanied by three symbols and a black color indicator.

2. If your document is new and contains no objects, create a Rectangle, Ellipse, and Polygon on your document page and then fill them with different fills. By default, as you create your objects, they appear as objects belonging to Layer 1 on Page 1, and are accompanied by symbols and brief descriptions of each. This is because the active layer—and the only layer that exists so far—is Layer 1.

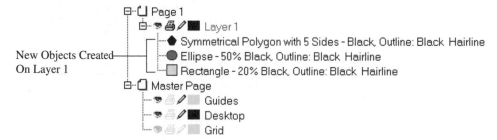

3. Add a new layer by clicking the New Layer button in the lower-left corner of the docker. Notice a new layer appears in the Docker window using the default name Layer 2 and is listed above your active Layer 1. If you want,

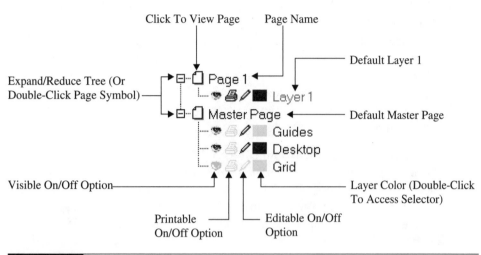

FIGURE 12-3   Under typical defaults, this is how your document's layer structure will
appear in the Object Manager.

you may enter a name for the new layer simply by typing now. Otherwise,
press ENTER to accept the layer name as is. Notice Layer 2 is now your
active layer and highlighted in red in the docker list.

4. In the Object Manager Docker window, click your Rectangle object to
select it. Notice the Rectangle also becomes selected in your document.
Using a click-drag action, click-and-drag the Rectangle *within the Object
Manager Docker* window onto the new Layer 2 and release the mouse
button. Notice the Rectangle in your document hasn't changed position,
but in the Docker window, it now appears under Layer 2. You have just
moved the Rectangle object from one layer to another.

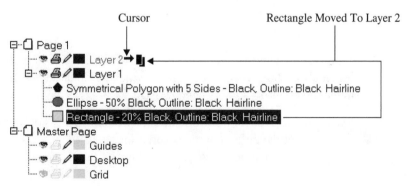

5. Click the Eye symbol beside Layer 2 once, so it becomes grayed out. Notice the Rectangle you just moved to Layer 2 disappears from view, although it still appears in the Docker window listing. Notice also the information describing the Rectangle on Layer 2 now appears grayed out also. This action toggles the display of all objects on a specific layer. The same applies for Printable and Editable options, which means clicking the corresponding symbols enables or disables printing and/or editing of a specific layer.

6. Add a new page to your document by right-clicking the page symbol beside Page 1 and choose Insert Page After from the pop-up menu. Also, notice you may choose Insert Page Before, or Rename, Delete, Resize The Page, or Switch The Current Page's Orientation. After doing so, notice the page now appears in the Docker window, and your view is automatically changed to Page 2.

7. Click to expand the view of Page 2 to view its contents. Notice Page 2 also includes the same two layers as Page 1, although neither layer includes any objects. This is a key characteristic—the layers for your document remain constant across pages, but layer contents are unique to each page.

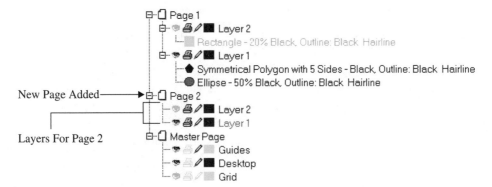

8. In the Docker window, click the page symbol beside Page 1. Notice your view immediately changes to Page 1, which demonstrates another key characteristic of the Object Manager Docker—page navigation.

9. Create a third layer for your document by clicking the Add Layer button again. Accept the default name by pressing ENTER. Notice again, the layer is added to all document pages. Click the new layer once to ensure it's

selected and create a new object anywhere on your document page. Notice the new object is automatically created on the new layer. This demonstrates another key behavior of the Object Manager Docker—new (or imported) objects are created on the currently selected layer on your current page.

10. Click the Eye symbol beside Layer 2 to make it visible again. All three objects should now be visible on Page 1. Using the Pick Tool, drag the Rectangle, Ellipse, and Polygon objects on your document page to overlap each other while leaving them on their current layers. Notice the Ellipse and Polygon objects on Layer 1 appear behind the Rectangle on Layer 2. This is because the objects on Layer 2 are ordered above the objects on Layer 1.

11. Using a click-drag action in the Object Manager Docker window, click the text label of Layer 1 on Page 1, drag it vertically upward and just above the position of Layer 2, and then release the mouse button. Notice the Ellipse and Polygon objects now appear in front of the Rectangle. You just changed the order of your layers. As you dragged, you may have noticed the cursor changing to indicate that compatible areas the layer may be positioned and a horizontal insertion-point indicator appear just above Layer 2 and before you released the mouse button. This is yet another key function of the Object Manager Docker—reordering layers.

> **TIP** *If you want, you may assign unique names to pages, layers, and even to objects in the Object Manager Docker. To name any of these elements within the docker, click the text label of the page, layer, or object name once to select it and a second time to highlight the text for editing. Enter the text for the new name, and then press ENTER.*

12

Using Object Manager Editing and View States

As you work in the Object Manager, three view state buttons appear at the top of the Docker window enabling you to control the information the Object Manager shows and how objects on layers may be edited. Each button may be clicked to toggle its state on or off.

> **TIP** *You may use Combine, Group, or Convert to Curves commands on objects in the Object Manager Docker by selecting the objects, right-clicking them, and choosing any of these commands from the pop-up menu.*

The purpose and function of these buttons enables you to change the Object Manager Docker display and editing behavior in the following ways:

- **Show Object Properties**   The Show Object Properties button may be toggled on or off to control whether the fill and outline of each of your drawing objects on each page and layer appear visible. In certain instances in which object details are lengthy, you may prefer to see only the object type listed and omit the display of these details.

- **Edit Across Layers**   Clicking the Edit Across Layers button enables or disables your capability to select, move, or copy objects on layers. While not depressed and inactive, objects listed under layers in the Object Manager Docker appear grayed out. In this state, only objects on your current page layer or the Desktop may be selected or edited. While the Edit Across Layers button is depressed and active, you may select, move, or edit any object on an unlocked layer.

> **TIP**   *You may PowerClip, change object order, copy fill, and/or outline properties between objects. You may also create or add an object to an existing group in the Object Manager, right-click-drag one object onto another, and choose a command from the pop-up menu. Grouping and PowerClip commands apply only when right-click-dragging objects within the same layer.*

- **Layer Manager View**   The Layer Manager View button offers a specialized view of your layers, and while it is depressed, only your document's layer information is displayed. When working with complex documents that feature multiple pages, layers, and objects, using this view can be significantly easier to manage Layer properties. In this state, all page and object information is omitted. The Layer Manager View also provides a way of moving objects between layers within a multilayer document. You may also find this view useful if you want to import or create new objects onto a specific layer. While Layer Manager View is not depressed and inactive, the Object Manager displays all your document's pages, layers, and objects normally.

> **TIP**   *To delete a layer in your document, right-click the layer and choose Delete. Keep in mind, however, any objects on the layer you delete are also immediately deleted.*

Controlling Layer Properties

Figure 12-4 shows the document window view of an aircraft illustration in which the various parts have been grouped and assigned to specific layers. Notice the layer names reflect the structure of this specific drawing, while certain layers have been assigned specific layering and view states, making the objects on these layers either visible, printable, or editable.

If you created layers in your document and saw how they're presented in the Object Manager Docker, you likely already have some idea that you may control the visible, printable, and editing properties of Layers. But, a few additional layer properties available aren't seen in this docker and they're controlled by selecting options in the Layer Properties dialog (see Figure 12-5). To open this dialog,

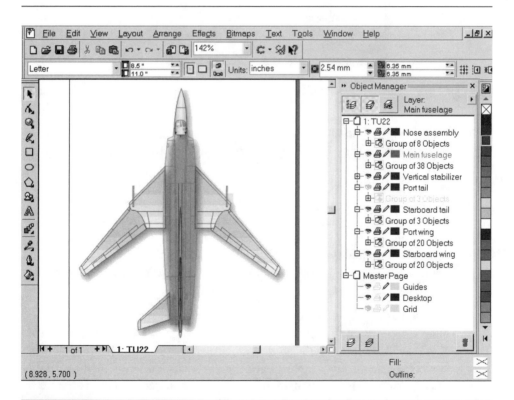

12

FIGURE 12-4   This aircraft drawing has been structured using layer functions of the Object Manager Docker, while the layers themselves have been set with specific properties.

FIGURE 12-5   The Layer Properties dialog provides all options for controlling a layer.

right-click the layer in the Object Manager Docker and choose Properties from the pop-up menu. Choosing options in this dialog has the following effect on your selected layer.

- **Naming a Layer**   The Name option enters a unique name in the Layer Name box in the dialog. You may also name or rename a layer without use of this dialog by clicking once to select it, clicking a second time to highlight its name, typing a new name, and then pressing ENTER. Ideally, the name you apply to your new layer should provide you with an idea of its contents.

- **Visible Layer**   The Visible option in this dialog enables you to control whether objects on the selected layer appear visible or are hidden from view. You may also control the visibility of objects on a layer by clicking the Eye symbol beside the layer in the Object Manager Docker to toggle the visibility of objects on the layer. By default, all new layers are created as visible.

- **Printable Layer**   The Printable option enables you to control whether objects on a specific layer are printed along with other document objects. Objects on nonprinting layers appear the same as objects on printable layers, so you may want to keep a close eye on which layers you make nonprinting. You may also control whether layer objects are printable by clicking the Printer symbol beside the layer in the Object Manager Docker to toggle the printing state of objects on the layer. By default, all newly created layers are printable unless specified otherwise using this option.

> **TIP** *When a layer is specified as nonprinting by deselecting the Printable option in the Object Manager, the objects are neither printable nor exportable. This means that if objects selected on a nonprinting layer are to be included in the export process using the Export command, the layer they reside on must first be set as Printable.*

- **Editable Layer**   Toggling the state of the Editable option enables you to lock or unlock all objects on a layer. While a layer is noneditable (locked), the objects may not be edited or even selected. You may also control whether layer objects are editable by clicking the Pencil symbol beside the layer in the Object Manager Docker to toggle the editing state of objects on the layer. By default, all newly created layers are editable.

- **Setting Layer Colors**   Clicking the button labeled Layer Color opens a color selector that enables you to choose a layer color. The Layer Color option provides you with a method of color-coding the layers you create in your document to make it easier to recognize them as they appear in the docker. Setting the Layer Color also determines object colors when viewed using nonwireframe views while the Override Full Color View option is selected. You may also set the color-coding for a layer by double-clicking the color indicator next to a layer name to open a typical color selector menu and clicking any color.

- **Override Full Color View**   Choosing the Override Full Color View option enables you to control how the objects on the layer appear in your document when viewed either using Normal or Enhanced views. By default, this option is left deselected. When selected, it has the effect of displaying all objects in wireframe using the color you specified using the Layer Color option.

- **Applying Layer options for a specific page**   If you want, you may change the Visible, Printable, Editable, and Color options for a specific layer to apply only to a specific page by clicking the Apply All Property Changes to the Current Page Only option. As the name implies, any option

12

changes made in the dialog applies only to the layer on the page for which you are changing options.

Working with Master Page Layers

Whenever a new document is created, it is automatically applied with a Master Page, actually named Master Page by default. The default Master Page isn't a physical page in your document, so much as an invisible place where repeating document objects may be placed. Placing any object onto the Master Page causes the object to be visible and printable on every page in your document, making this an extremely powerful resource to control.

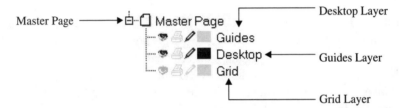

Master Pages are extremely useful to create repeating page elements, such as page or document identifiers (headers and/or footers), company logos, and so on, throughout your document. Moving any object onto a layer on the Master Page makes it a Master Page element and, subsequently, causes the object to appear on each document page. To do so, follow these steps:

1. If you haven't already done so, open the Object Manager Docker window.

2. Create the object(s) you want to appear on every page on any layer.

3. Click the New Master Layer button at the lower-left corner of the Docker window to create a new layer on the Master Page. A new layer is automatically added to the Master Page only. If you want, enter a name and/or press ENTER. By default, your Master Page is prefixed with the name Master. This new Master Layer serves as the "container" or placeholder for your repeating page elements.

4. Using a click-drag action, click to select the objects you want to have appear on each page either in the Object Manager Docker window or on your document page, and then drag them onto the color indicator beside your newly created Master Layer. After you release your mouse button, two key things happen: the objects now appear grayed out on your document page, and both objects now appear on the new Master Page layer.

5. Click to select the new Master Page object(s) on your document page. Notice you may still select, move, and edit it as you want. Once you finish positioning objects on a Master Page, it may also be a wise strategy to change the Master Page layer to be noneditable. To do this, click the Pencil symbol beside your Master Page layer to deactivate it. This enables you to avoid any accidental editing of the objects.

As you may have already noticed, several default layers already exist on your document's Master Page. These layers are permanent fixtures and enable control of specialized items that appear on your document such as Guides, Grids, Desktop, and Internet Objects.

■ **Guides Layer**   Whenever a new guide is placed onto any document page, it is automatically placed on the Guides Layer of your Master Page. This includes guides dragged from your onscreen rulers or created manually using the Grids and Guides Setup dialog. This means, by default, that placing a guide on any page makes the guide available to all pages. Also, by default, all guides are set as Visible and Editable, but not Printable. If you want, you may change the guides properties by using options in the Guides Properties dialog, opened by right-clicking the Guides Layer and choosing Properties from the pop-up menu.

You may move selected guides from the Guides Layer to any other layer in your document by dragging the guide within the Object Manager Docker window to a layer on one of your document pages. Doing so causes the guide to be available only on the page layer to which you move it. This action also makes the guide visible—a characteristic unlike typical guides you create. The action also causes a warning dialog to display (as shown), which lets you know the guide is about to become printable and recommends that you create a new nonprinting layer just for guides available to specific pages.

12

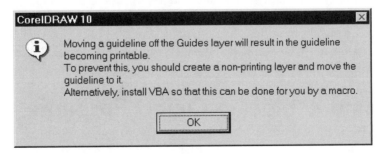

> **TIP** *If needed, you may make any object behave as if it were a page guide by placing it onto the Guides Layer. Any objects placed on the Guides Layer may be used as Guide snap points while the Snap To Guides option is selected active. To make any object into a Guide, drag it within the Object Manager Docker window (or directly from your document page) onto the Guides Layer of the Master Page. All objects set as guides appear grayed out on your document page according to options in the Guides Layer Properties dialog.*

- **Grid Layer** By default, the Grid Layer controls the appearance of grids throughout your document when they are selected visible. You may control the Grid color and visibility, but you may not set the Grid Layer to be printable, and you can't change whether it's editable or add objects to that layer. Options in the Grid Layer Properties dialog enable you to control the Grid display color or to gain quick access to the Grid dialog page of the Options dialog by clicking the Setup button in the dialog. To open the Grid Layer Properties dialog, right-click the Grid Layer under the Master Page in the Object Manager Docker and choose Properties from the pop-up menu.

> **TIP** *The Grid Layer visibility may also be toggled on or off by choosing View | Grid in the command menus.*

- **Desktop Layer** The Desktop Layer is where all objects not positioned on any specific page are automatically listed in the Object Manager Docker, meaning the area surrounding your document page border. By default, objects placed on the Desktop Layer are Visible and Editable, but not Printable, unless specified otherwise. This means that objects placed on the Desktop may not be exported using the Export command unless the Desktop Layer is first made printable.

- **Internet Layer** The Internet Layer appears as your topmost layer only if you have placed an Internet Object on a page in your document using the Edit | Insert Internet Object command. Internet objects include specialized objects such as Java applets, buttons, check boxes, text fields, text boxes, pop-up menus, or options lists available from the Insert Internet Objects submenu and Web-compatible text. By default, the Internet Layer is set to Visible, Printable, and Editable.

Finding and Replacing Object Properties

CorelDRAW 10 enables you to search for objects according to fill and/or outline properties, scaling, or overprinting properties. You may also perform highly specific search and/or replace commands using specialized wizards. Wizards are specifically designed to be user friendly and guide you through a task using a simple question-and-answer sequence in a series of progressive dialogs.

In this regard, CorelDRAW 10 includes two separate wizards: one for finding and selecting objects and one for replacing object properties. As these wizards are used, if all questions are addressed, each wizard enables you to find exactly what you want and/or replace or change specific object property. Wizards may also be navigated forward or in reverse, enabling you to back out of your selections and/or make changes to your search. Once a search or replace script is created, you may save it as a unique script and reuse it from the Find menu any time you want.

Finding Objects with Specific Properties

The Find Wizard enables you to specify exactly what type of object properties you want to locate in your document—no matter how specific. The Find Wizard enables you to choose an nonspecific object property or to specify the exact object and property you want to find. To use the Find Wizard, follow these steps:

1. If you haven't already done so, open an existing document and choose Edit | Find and Replace | Find Objects. This launches the Find Wizard and the first dialog appears (see Figure 12-6). Choose either Begin a New Search or Load a Search from Disk, and then click the Next button. If you

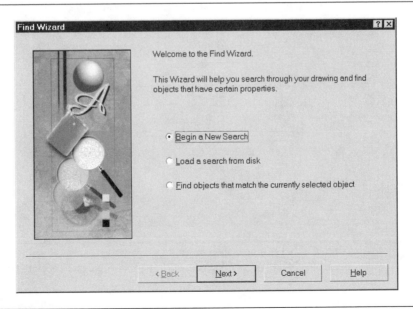

FIGURE 12-6   When you start a search, the Find Wizard presents three options for selecting how to begin the search.

12

currently have an object selected, you may also search for similar objects by choosing the Find Objects That Match the Currently Selected Object option. Choosing Load a search from Disk opens the Open dialog box and enables you to select a saved search. Click OK to proceed to the next wizard page. The selected variables from previously saved searches are automatically specified as the selected Wizard options.

2. In the second page of the wizard (see Figure 12-7), choose either the Object Type, Fill Type, Outline, or any applied Special Effects by clicking each of the dialog tabs and selecting the Variable options. Leaving the variables unchecked leaves them out of the current search. Selecting options within each of the tabbed areas of this dialog causes the Find Wizard to display additional editing dialogs for each object type, fill type, outline, and Special effect, and enables you to narrow the parameters further. After confirming or further specifying your choices, proceed to the next dialog by clicking Next. Choose Find Any Type of Object if the

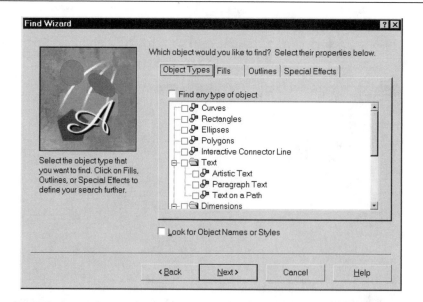

FIGURE 12-7   When you begin a new search, the Find Wizard presents all of the available object types, fill types, outline properties, and special effects.

object type is unimportant, or choose Look for Object Names or Styles to proceed to a dialog that enables you to enter the exact style or object name. After specifying object properties, proceed by clicking Next.

3. The final page of the wizard (see Figure 12-8) displays a summary of the object properties you selected for your search. To change a selection, simply click the Back button to confirm or change your search selections. This final dialog enables you to save the parameters you selected using a unique name, so you may load or retrieve the search any time you choose. When a search is saved, it's available for searching any of your CorelDRAW documents. To continue your search operation and exit the wizard, click Finish.

4. Click Finish to open the Find dialog (see the next illustration) and select the first search object. If more objects are located in your document, the Find dialog offers several command buttons: Find Previous to return to the previous object (if any), Find Next to proceed to the next object

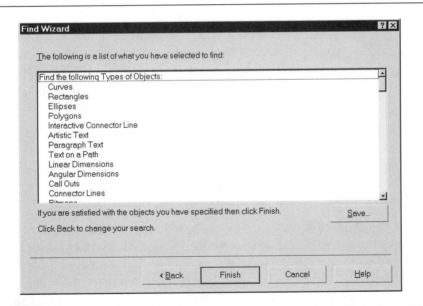

FIGURE 12-8   After you complete the Find Wizard dialogs, a final page presents a summary of your search.

(if any), Find All to select all search objects on your document page instantly, and Edit Search to return to the Find Wizard.

Replacing Object Properties

Using the Replace Wizard to edit or make changes to the objects in an existing document can be extremely efficient. The Replace Wizard enables you to find an unlimited number of objects with specific properties and to change them. The wizard interface provides the most logical sequence for this task, and the Replace Wizards guides you through the process using a series of questions and answers, beginning with a selection of choices for selecting which properties to replace. You may choose from replacing a Color, a Model or Palette, an Outline Pen property, or a Text property.

To explore using the Replace Wizard, follow these steps:

1. If you haven't already done so, open an existing document containing objects in which you want to change the properties. Launch the Replace Wizard by choosing Edit | Find and Replace | Replace Objects. The Replace Wizard opens to reveal the first set of options (see Figure 12-9).

2. Select a property to replace. Choose from Color, Color Model or Palette, Outline Pen Properties, or Text Properties. By default, the replacement properties you specify apply to all objects in the document. However, you may choose the Apply to Currently Selected Objects Only option to limit the range. The next dialog to appear depends on which option you select here. Click the Next button to proceed.

3. If you chose to replace a Color, the next dialog presents choices for specifying a color and options for specifying which types of color fills or outlines to apply as the replacement. If your choice was Color Model or Palette, the next dialog presents options for specifying a color model or palette, specifying a replacement model or palette, or replacing outline or fill colors. If your choice was Outline Pen Properties, the next dialog offers choices for specifying which pen properties to find and which to use

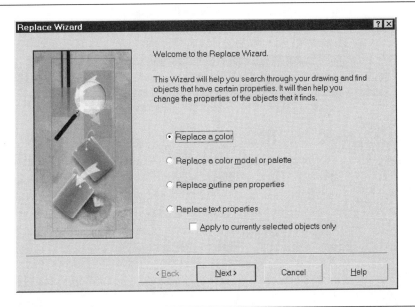

FIGURE 12-9   The Replace Wizard begins by offering you choices for selecting the type of properties you want to change.

as replacements, including the outline width, scale with image, and overprinting options. If your choice was to replace Text Properties, the next dialog provides Find and Replace options for specifying the Font, Weight, and Size of text. Click Finish to close the wizard and proceed to the Find and Replace dialog.

4. Regardless of which property you chose to replace, the Find and Replace dialog subsequently appears (see the next illustration). If the Replace command locates multiple objects having the properties you specified, the Find and Replace dialog features several active buttons: Find Previous, Find Next, Find All, Replace, and Replace All. Clicking Find Previous Find Next simply selects the previous or the Next detected object. Clicking the Find All button selects all the relevant objects in the document without performing the replacement operation. Clicking Replace or Replace All replaces the selected objects with the specified replacement properties or

12

simply replaces all relevant objects in the document with the replacement properties without any further prompting.

Using Graphic Styles

If you use styles to format text in your document, you may already realize what a huge time saver styles are. In CorelDRAW, styles may be created, saved, and applied not only to text, but also to objects. These styles are known as *graphic* styles. Once a graphic style has been created, the style itself may be edited to affect all the objects to which the style has been applied. Graphic styles are essentially collections of fill and outline properties.

 For more detailed information on creating, saving, and applying text styles, see CD-ROM 1.

Using Graphic Style Commands

The most convenient application of commands for creating, saving, and applying graphic styles in CorelDRAW 10 is through the pop-up menu accessed by right-clicking any object and navigating a series of submenus. The pop-up menu features the Styles submenu, which enables you to Save and/or Apply graphic styles.

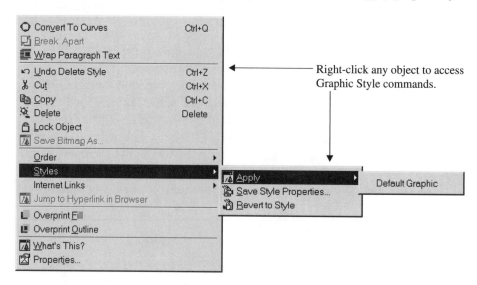

Right-click any object to access Graphic Style commands.

If your immediate need is to familiarize yourself with their location and effects, follow these brief steps:

1. If you haven't already done so, create several objects on your document page and apply different fill and outline properties to them.

2. Right-click one of the objects and choose Styles | Save Style Properties to open the Save Style As dialog to begin saving your style. Enter a name for the style, accept the fill and outline properties as they appear, and then click OK to save the style and close the dialog.

3. Right-click a different object on your document page and access the Style, Apply submenu. Notice the new style you just saved now appears in the list. Choose this new style as your style for the second object by selecting it from the list. The same object fill and outline color applied to your first object and its saved style is now applied to the second object.

4. With the second object still selected, change either its fill or outline properties to something different from what was applied by the new style. With the object properties now changed, right-click the object again and choose Styles | Revert to Style. The style properties are once again applied and the property changes you just made are changed.

5. Right-click the same object and choose Properties from the pop-up menu to open the Object Properties Docker. By default, the docker opens to describe the properties specific to the type of object.

6. Click the General tab in the docker to show information about the selected object. Notice the Style drop-down menu in the docker shows that the new style you saved earlier is applied to the object. These are the most convenient graphic styles commands available, barring the opening of any further dockers or dialogs.

If you just followed the previous steps, you may already know Graphic Styles may be saved any time you like by right-clicking an object and choosing Styles | Save Style Properties from the pop-up menu. This opens the Save Style As dialog (see Figure 12-10), which enables you to provide a style name and/or change the style's Fill and Outline Pen properties. Once a graphic style has been saved, it's stored with your document.

12

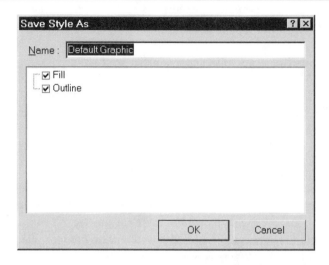

To save any graphic style and open the Save Style As dialog, right-click any object and choose Styles | Save Style Properties.

Using the Graphics and Text Docker

For a complete inventory of the graphic styles saved with your document, open the Graphics and Text Docker by choosing Tools | Graphic and Text Styles (CTRL+F5). By default, the Graphics and Text Docker window lists all the Graphic, Artistic, and Paragraph Text styles available in your document, including default styles (see Figure 12-11). Thumbnails in the Docker window depict the graphic styles in the Docker window, visually mimicking their Fill and Outline Pen properties accompanied by the name of the style.

To explore features of the Graphic and Text docker, follow these steps:

1. If you haven't already done so, create any type of object on your document page and apply unique fill and outline properties to it.

2. Open the Graphic and Text Styles Docker by choosing Tools | Graphic and Text Styles (CTRL+F5). By default, the Docker window opens to show all styles available in your document.

3. To hide the view of nongraphic styles, click the Graphic and Text options flyout menu and choose Show | Artistic Text Styles and then click it again to select Show | Paragraph Text Styles to deactivate their view state. If

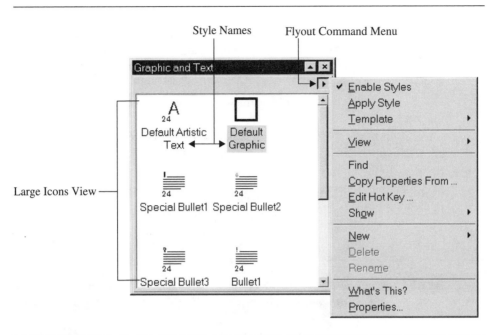

FIGURE 12-11   The Graphic and Text Docker window enables you to view and manage all styles stored with your open document.

your document includes only Graphic Styles, choosing Show | Auto-View while an object is selected enables you to do this quickly.

4. Click the flyout menu in the docker again and choose New | Graphic Style. A new default graphic style is added to the Docker window automatically named New Graphic. Rename this style by clicking the style name twice to highlight the name and enter a unique name.

5. Change your Thumbnail view in the Docker window to enable the docker to reflect the applied Graphic Styles properties visually by clicking the flyout menu in the docker and choosing View | Large Icon so a check mark appears beside the menu item.

6. On your document page and using a click-drag action, drag the object you created onto your new Graphic Style in the Docker window. Notice that the style in the docker is automatically updated with the object's assigned fill and outline properties with these properties indicated in the thumbnail representation.

7. To change the properties associated with your new graphic style using
dialogs, right-click your new graphic style in the Docker window and
choose Properties from the pop-up menu to open the Options dialog to the
Styles page. Doing so automatically selects the new graphic style in the
styles list (see Figure 12-12). Expanding the tree directory under the style
in the list reveals the Fill and Outline options, enabled by default. To edit
these properties, click the Edit button adjacent to either property at the
lower right of the dialog. Doing so opens the respective dialog boxes
controlling these properties. Click OK in any dialogs that remain open
to return to the Options dialog and then click again to return to your
document page. Any changes you make to the style are immediately
updated in both the style and any document objects applied with the style.

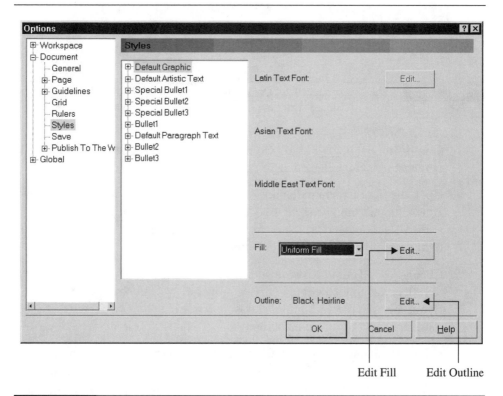

FIGURE 12-12   To view and/or edit the properties of a graphic style, right-click the
graphic style and choose Properties to open the Options dialog.

8. Return to the object on your document page and change either of its fill or outline properties. Using a right-click-drag action, right-click the object and drag it over the new Graphic Style in the Docker window. Doing so causes the pop-up menu to appear, offering command options to modify the Style, Style Fill, Style Outline, Style Element, or Cancel. Choose whichever one you want and notice how your new graphic style thumbnail changes to reflect the new graphic style properties.

Right-click-drag your object onto the graphic
style to access these pop-up menu commands.

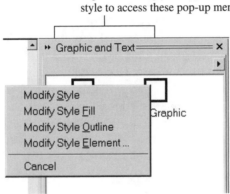

9. Create a second object on your document page using default fill and outline properties and then drag the newly created style from the Docker window onto your new object. Your Graphic Style fill and outline properties are applied to the object.

10. To locate objects in your document that were applied with a specific graphic style, right-click any style in the Graphic and Text Docker window, and choose Find from the pop-up menu. Doing so locates and selects the first found object applied with the graphic style. To find and select more objects applied with the same style, right-click the style again and choose Find Next.

Using Graphic and Text Docker Options

While using the Graphic and Text Docker, further options are available, including viewing and copying graphic styles, template commands, and hot key assignments. The following defines the use of these commands and options available from the Graphic and Text Docker pop-up menu or options flyout menu.

12

Loading Styles from Saved Templates

The Graphic and Text docker flyout menu includes a Template submenu enabling you to choose from one of three commands: Load, Save As, and Save As Default for New Documents. Choosing the Load command from the flyout menu opens the Load Styles from Template dialog (see Figure 12-13), which enables you to select and load styles from any templates you saved.

Choosing Save As from the flyout menu opens the Save Template dialog (see Figure 12-14) and enables you to save all the styles in your current document to a new template document, including Artistic and Paragraph Text styles. Your styles are saved to a separate template document with or without the content of the document. Once the template has been saved, you may use the Load command from this same flyout menu to load your styles into a new document.

Choosing Save As Default for New Documents takes this one step further by automatically saving all currently saved styles to be available to all newly created CorelDRAW 10 documents. Doing so adds your document's styles to the default Coreldrw.cdt file, which includes default styles available whenever a new document is created.

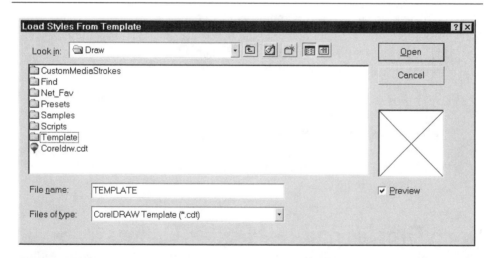

FIGURE 12-13 The Load Styles dialog enables you to import styles from saved templates for use in your current document.

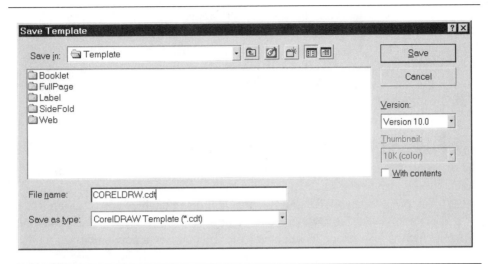

FIGURE 12-14   The Save As command enables you to save your document's saved styles to a new template file.

Controlling Docker Views

Use the View submenu to control style views in your Graphic and Text Docker window. Choose between Large or Small icons, List (strictly a text-based view), or Details to view both the style names and a brief description of each style's properties. Using either the List or Details views is useful if the document you're working with contains a large collection of styles.

Copying Properties from Objects

Choosing the Copy Properties From command from the Graphic and Text Docker flyout menu enables you to update a selected style using the fill and outline properties applied to a specific object in your document or from another existing graphic style. After choosing this command, your active cursor becomes a targeting cursor used to click the object or style from which you want to copy properties.

Assigning and Editing Hot Keys

To apply your most favorite saved styles quickly, assign hot keys to them. *Hot keys* are keyboard shortcuts that instantly apply a style. To assign or edit a hot key,

12

click to select a graphic style and choose Edit Hot Key from the flyout menu. Doing so opens the Options dialog to the Shortcut Keys dialog (see Figure 12-15). To assign a hot key after choosing this command, click your cursor in the Press New Shortcut Key box, press the actual keyboard shortcut you want to apply as the new hot key assignment (instead of typing it), click the Assign button, and then click OK to close the dialog.

Deleting and Renaming Graphic Styles

Choosing the Delete command from the Graphic and Text Docker flyout menu enables you to delete any selected styles, which is redundant with pressing the DELETE key on your keyboard. The Rename command enables you to highlight the text name of a selected style and enter a new name quickly, which is redundant with clicking the text label of a selected style and entering a new name.

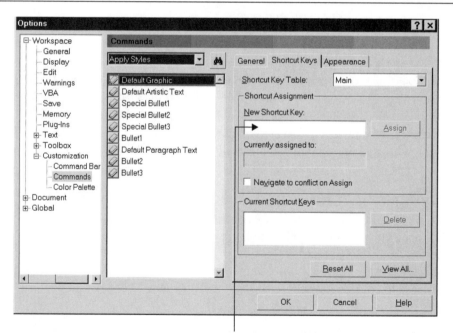

Click here and press the keyboard keys you wish to use.

FIGURE 12-15   Assigning hot keys to Graphic Styles is perhaps one of the most efficient ways to apply your most commonly used styles.

TIP	*If the document you're working in contains a large collection of styles, you may reorder the styles as they appear in the docker using a click-drag action. To do this, click directly on the style thumbnails to give them a new order location within the Graphic and Text Docker window. Ideally, you want your most commonly applied styles to appear near the top of the list.*

Using the Object Data Docker

Although this next feature is used only by a select few, CorelDRAW 10 enables you to associate data—such as text names and/or comments, numerical and/or capital values, or measurements—with your drawing objects. The capability to do this is useful for engineering, architecture, or other related industries or professions that involve planning or tracking of objects using numerical data. All functions of this are done using the Object Data Manager Docker (see Figure 12-16), opened by choosing Tools | Object Data Manager.

The purpose of this Docker window is to enable you to assign data to each individual object in your drawing and to obtain quick summaries of the data in spreadsheet presentation format. For example, if your drawing depicts the various parts of an industrial product, assigning dollar values to each part and then obtaining a quick summary of the total cost of all parts may be useful. The Object Data Docker enables you to do exactly that. You may also associate other data,

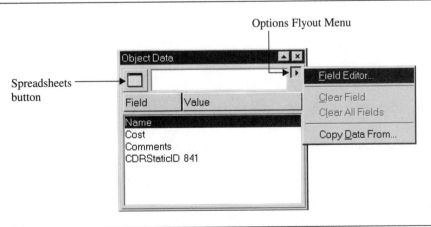

12

FIGURE 12-16   The Object Data Manager Docker window enables you to associate values with your document objects.

such as text comments and add summaries. Although the functions of this feature are limited, it provides you with a method of applying unique values to your drawing objects.

Briefly, to explore applying values to objects using the Object Data Manager Docker window, follow these steps:

1. If you haven't already done so, create several drawing objects on your document page (at least three).

2. Open the Object Data Docker by choosing Tools | Object Data Manager.

3. Select one of the objects and notice (by default) each new object includes four values for Name, Cost, Comments, and the CDRStaticID number, the latter being the numeric ID CorelDRAW 10 assigns to all objects, regardless of the feature-assigned data values.

4. Click the Cost item under the Field column in the Docker window to select it and click your cursor in the field at the top of the docker.

5. Enter a dollar value such as 20 and press the ENTER key on your numeric keypad. Your new value is added to the Cost row of the Value field in the Docker window and formatted to read "$20.00" according to the default field format.

6. Repeat this same operation for all three of your objects, assigning dollar values such as 40 and 60. Each time you do so, the dollar value will read "$40.00" and "$60.00" using these example values.

7. Select all three of the objects on your page and click the Spreadsheet button at the top of the Docker window to open the Object Data Manager spreadsheets dialog (see Figure 12-17).

8. With all three objects selected, the Spreadsheets dialog instantly calculates the total of all three objects and displays this value in the Total row below the Cost column—in this case, $120.00.

By following these steps, you'll have only the most basic understanding of how the Object Data Manager is used to assign values to your drawing objects and obtain summary calculations of selected objects. This example uses Cost to track dollar values, but you may customize the specific fields to support any variable

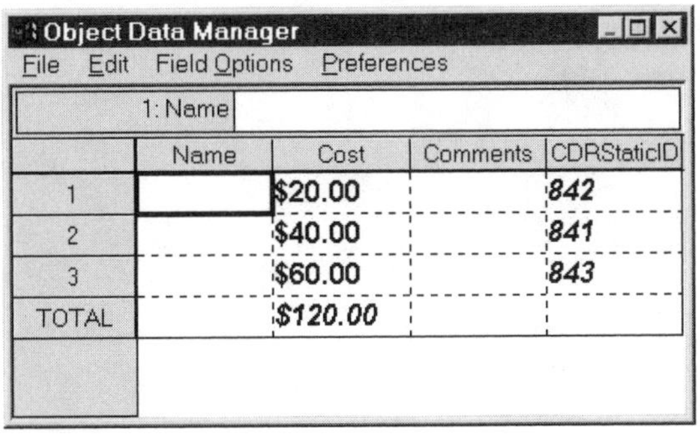

	Name	Cost	Comments	CDRStaticID
1		$20.00		842
2		$40.00		841
3		$60.00		843
TOTAL		$120.00		

FIGURE 12-17   Clicking the Spreadsheets button opens the Object Data Manager, which enables you to perform calculations based on the values assigned to your objects.

you require and/or display measurement data in any format you choose. To edit a specific variable or field, double-click it to open the Object Data Field Editor (see Figure 12-18) and choose the options you require.

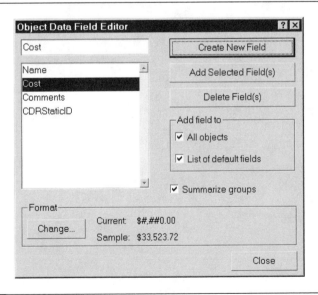

FIGURE 12-18   The Object Data Field Editor provides you with ways to create, edit, or customize each of the fields in your Data Manager spreadsheet.

CHAPTER 13

Object Organization Resources

As everyone knows, a gathering of birds is called a flock, and several cattle huddled together make a herd. But a selection of graphical objects in CorelDRAW (or virtually any other graphics application) is simply that—a *selection.*

Grouping and Ungrouping Selections

However, when more than one object in your document is selected, the Group command becomes available. Grouping objects together is perhaps one of the most basic of object relationships you can establish between a selection of objects. While a selection of objects is in a group state, they behave as a single object, and their relative position to each other is fixed for the most part. Any position changes, transformations, or other types of property changes made to a selected group of objects affects each object in the group in the same way.

For example, selecting a group of objects and applying a green fill color changes all object fills in the group to green. With all the various elements that can often compose a drawing, the capability to group objects provides a way to assemble multiple objects into a single unit, offering a simple way to organize and simplify your drawing elements at the lowest level.

The group relationship concept is emphasized by the fact that each object in a group is a child object. A *child object* is merely one selected element of a group. Groups of objects may also include lower-level groups, meaning you may group several objects together with other groups. This condition is loosely referred to as *nesting.* This simple concept offers excellent convenience and control over how your objects are arranged and organized.

Group Commands

Grouping a selection of two or more objects together is a straightforward operation. To do so, simply select the objects using the Pick Tool and choose Arrange | Group or use the CTRL+G shortcut. Clicking the Group button in the Standard Property Bar achieves the same result.

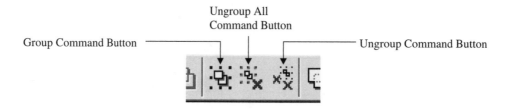
Ungroup All
Command Button

Group Command Button

Ungroup Command Button

Using either command on a selection of objects creates the group and causes the objects to behave as a single element. Your selected group is also indicated as a group by your Status Bar display. While your Status Bar is set to display Object Information, properties about your selected group include the number of objects it contains (even if one of those objects happens to already be a group). The Status Bar is your best source for information when it comes to object selections.

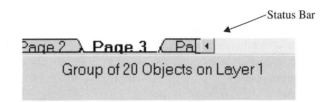
Status Bar

Ungroup Commands

Reversing the action of grouping several object together involves using the *Ungroup* command, which has the effect of returning the group of objects to their original condition before being grouped. Ungrouping merely undoes the group relationship between the objects and doesn't undo any transformations or property changes made to the objects while they were part of the group.

To Ungroup a selected group of objects, choose Arrange | Ungroup or press CTRL+U. Clicking the Ungroup command button in the Standard Toolbar achieves the same result. You may also choose Ungroup from the pop-up menu after right-clicking a selected group of objects. Ungroup works with a single group of objects or a selection including multiple groups.

13

TIP *Several of the effects you may apply to your drawing objects automatically create "effect groups," which are dynamically linked to the control object(s) involved in the effect. To ungroup these types of groups, they must first be separated using the Break [effect] Group Apart command available from the pop-up menu while right-clicking the effect portion before they may be Ungrouped.*

If you want to Ungroup a group and suspect it *already* contains more groups, choosing Ungroup All has the effect of completely ungrouping all groups in the selection. The significant difference between simply using the Ungroup command and using Ungroup All is that choosing to Ungroup a group undoes the Group command to only the first level. If the group contains nested groups, these are preserved. To ungroup each selected individual group further, simply choose Arrange | Ungroup (CTRL+U) a second time.

Choosing Ungroup All undoes the group relationship for *all* grouped items in the group—whether the items are nested groups or not. This means that if the grouped objects have been carefully arranged in a logically organized structure, this is lost completely.

Editing Grouped Objects

Because it's not only possible—but likely—that you'll find yourself grouping your drawing objects, it's good to know ways exist to edit individual child objects without separating them from their group arrangement. This means even though a selection of objects has been grouped, you needn't Ungroup the objects before you can make a change to the properties of a single—or child—object in the group.

Hold down the CTRL key as a modifier and click a specific object in a group while using the Pick Tool, and the object becomes the only selected object. Taking this concept a little further, if the selected child object is actually a group (read this slowly), hold down the CTRL key and click a second time to select a child in the group. This selection action is loosely referred to as *drilling* down through groups.

While a child object is selected, the selection handles surrounding the object (or child group) are round instead of the usual square handles of ordinary objects or groups (see Figure 13-1). Although they appear different, object selection

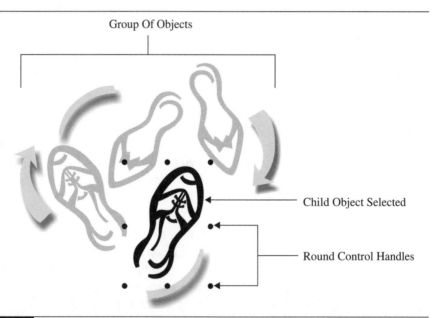

Group Of Objects

Child Object Selected

Round Control Handles

FIGURE 13-1   The child object in this group was selected using a CTRL-click action. While selected, round control handles appear around the object.

handles perform the same function as normal selection handles, enabling you to scale, skew, rotate, or otherwise transform the object as you require.

| TIP | *When selecting child objects within a group, only one child object may be selected at a time. This means you can't marquee-select or SHIFT-select multiple objects while selecting child objects.* |

While a child object is selected, the Status Bar also indicates the status of the selected child object. Individual objects within a group are referred to as Child objects, such as Child Curve, Child Rectangle, Child Ellipse, and Child Artistic Text. Groups that are themselves objects within a group are referred to as Child Groups. Within a group, items that are dynamically linked with an effect are referred to as Child Control objects, such as Child Control Curves, Child Control Rectangles, Child Control Ellipses, and Child Control Artistic Text. Child objects for which an actual effect portion is linked to a Child Control object are referred to as Child Effect Groups, such as Child Blend Group, Child Contour Group, and Child Extrude Group. To select a child object, follow these steps:

1. Using the Pick Tool, hold CTRL while clicking any part of the object.

2. After doing so, if the resulting object is still a selected group, repeat the operation until the child object you're attempting to select is the only object selected.

3. Perform your editing or property changes to the object.

4. Click a blank space on your page to deselect the object. Your child object has been changed without separating it from its group.

Locking and Unlocking Objects

So far, you've seen how the relative size and position of objects become fixed while they are grouped. Grouping objects together essentially locks them to each other. If you want, you may lock objects to a page using the Lock command. While objects are locked, they may be displayed, viewed, printed, or selected, but they cannot be moved, edited, or have their properties changed in any way.

Locking objects enables you to preserve them either temporarily or permanently, and is useful for any situation where you require drawing elements to be unaffected by commands applied to surrounding objects. No limit exists to the

13

number of objects you may Lock in your drawing or the number of objects you may lock at one time.

Similar to object Group commands, Lock commands are threefold, comprising Lock, Unlock, and Unlock All. To Lock an object selection, choose Arrange | Lock Object, or right-click the object and choose Lock Object from the pop-up menu. This results in your object becoming uneditable until it is unlocked. CorelDRAW indicates that an object is currently locked in two ways. The first (and most visually obvious), is the display of object selection handles that feature lock symbols (see Figure 13-2).

Next, the Status Bar precedes identification of locked objects by the term *Locked.* For example, while a simple curve is locked and selected, the Status Bar identifies it as a Locked Curve on Layer *X* (where *X* represents the layer name).

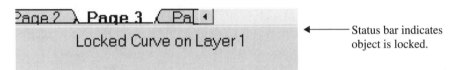
Status bar indicates object is locked.

To Unlock a locked object, choose Arrange | Unlock object. You may also use the Unlock option available from the pop-up menu by right-clicking a locked

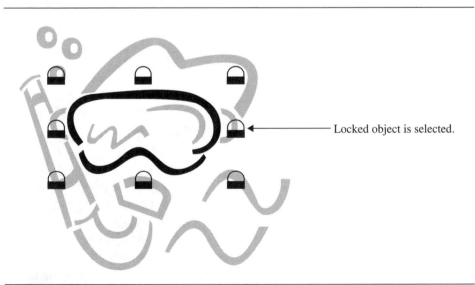
Locked object is selected.

FIGURE 13-2   The control handles surrounding this object indicate it is selected, but locked.

object using any tool. To unlock all locked objects in a drawing, choose Arrange | Unlock All, which results in unlocking all locked objects.

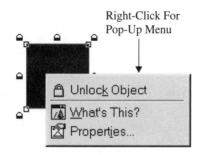

Right-Click For
Pop-Up Menu

1. Using the Pick Tool, select the object(s) you want to lock.

2. Choose Arrange | Lock Object. Notice the selection handles now resemble miniature locks.

3. Try dragging the object in any direction. Notice it remains stationary regardless of your efforts. Besides the presence of display handles and the Status bar indication, CorelDRAW 10 ignores an object even if it's selected.

4. While the objects is selected, choose Arrange | Unlock Object. Notice the selection handles return to typical square black selection handles. Your object is once again available for editing.

13

> **TIP** *While an object is locked, it may not be selected as part of a multiple selection. So if you are attempting to select a number of objects on your document page in which only one is locked, the locked object won't be selected. Instead, all unlocked objects will be selected.*

Copying, Duplicating, and Cloning Objects

The capability to make copies of objects is one of the most basic operations you perform, and this enables you to harness the drawing power of your CorelDRAW (and your computer). Copies may be created in different ways, by either simply creating a separate copy, duplicating a copy to a specific page location, or creating a copy that maintains a relationship to the original. These three different operations are referred to as copying, duplicating, and cloning, each of which have their own unique strengths.

Creating Quick Object Copies

CorelDRAW has long provided innovative and incredibly powerful ways to create copies of objects, either on the fly, while holding modifier keys, or single keystrokes. Each technique has different advantages, and once you make use of these methods, you'll likely want to use all three in specific situations and to accomplish different tasks.

- ■ **Using the right-mouse-click method** The first and most intuitive way of making a quick copy of an object involves using a drag-click operation—the click being a right-mouse-button click. As you drag, rotate, or transform an object using the Pick Tool, a single-click of your right mouse button causes the object currently being dragged to become a copy, leaving the original object in its original position (see Figure 13-3). The a small + symbol accompanying the active cursor indicates that a copy is being dragged by it. Once the mouse button is released, the copy is created in position. However, additional right-clicks while dragging the object do not create additional copies.

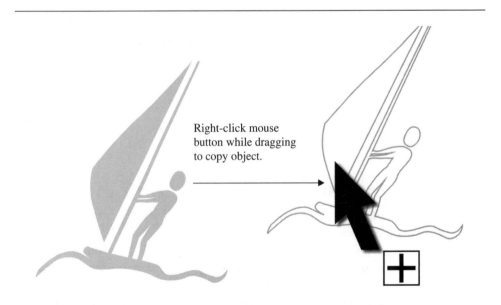

Right-click mouse button while dragging to copy object.

FIGURE 13-3   The object being dragged using the Pick Tool is a copy of the original.

TIP | *Using the right-click method to make a copy of your selected object as you transform it applies to moving, scaling, rotating, and skewing of objects—all basic transformations using the Pick Tool. However, shape transformations don't apply with this copy technique. For example, while reshaping an object using the Shape Tool, right-clicking during the Shaping operation has no effect and a copy is not created.*

■ **Using the SPACEBAR method**   Pressing the SPACEBAR while dragging, rotating, or transforming an object using the Pick Tool also makes a copy of the object—but in a slightly different way than the right-click method. While dragging, rotating, or transforming an object, pressing the SPACEBAR during the action causes a copy to be created *in situ*, meaning the copy is created—and remains—in the position your active object was when the SPACEBAR was pressed. This technique enables you to create multiple copies of an object interactively while it's being dragged, while still leaving your original object as the one you are dragging (see Figure 13-4). In a twist on this method, pressing and *holding* the SPACEBAR causes your key-repeat action to create multiple copies for as long as the SPACEBAR is held. Key repeat rate and settings are a function of your operating system.

■ **Press + on numeric keypad method**   While an object is selected, pressing the + key on your numeric keypad instantly manufactures a copy of the selected object in exactly the same position and arranged in front of the

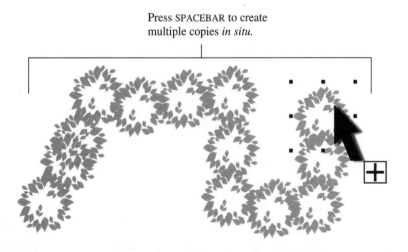

Press SPACEBAR to create
multiple copies *in situ*.

FIGURE 13-4   This arrangement of copies was created by pressing the SPACEBAR repeatedly to create multiple copies while dragging the original object.

13

original object. After pressing the + key, the selected object becomes the copy, which is extremely important because objects that are identical in shape and size can be problematic to select individually. You may create as many copies as you want using this method but, remember, each additional copy is arranged in front of the last and in the exact same position.

Using the Duplicate Command

The Duplicate command is one that's been available since the early days of graphics software. It enables you to create a copy simultaneously, but also to position the copy to a specific offset measure. To apply the Duplicate command on a selected object, choose Edit | Duplicate or use the CTRL+D shortcut. The duplicate object has no relationship to the original object, other than the fact that it's an exact copy.

The horizontal and vertical offset measures to which all copies created using the Property Bar while no objects are selected. By default, duplicates are placed 0.25 inches above and to the right of the selected original (see Figure 13-5). Both vertical and horizontal offsets may be set within a range between -600 and 600

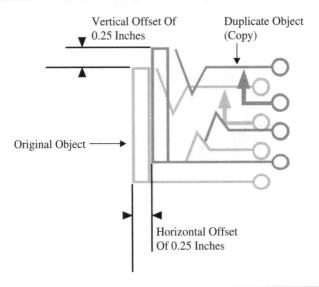

Vertical Offset Of 0.25 Inches

Duplicate Object (Copy)

Original Object

Horizontal Offset Of 0.25 Inches

FIGURE 13-5   The Duplicate command enables you to create a copy of a selected object to an exact offset measure (the default is 0.25 inches above and to the right of your original object).

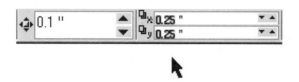

FIGURE 13-6 To change your Duplicate offset placement, use the Vertical and Horizontal Duplicate Distance options in the Property Bar.

inches (in increments of 0.05 inches), where negative values place duplicates below or to the right of your original.

To change these offset measures, use the Duplicate Distance options in the Property Bar while the Pick Tool is selected and no object is selected (see Figure 13-6). Change the values using either the spinner controls or by entering specific values in the Property Bar num boxes.

Cloning Objects

Contrary to recent scientific trends, creating a clone in CorelDRAW 10 neither requires a laboratory nor does it contravene the natural laws of physics. In fact, cloning objects is a powerful feature of which few users take advantage. Although the concept of cloning may seem somewhat heady and confusing at first, object cloning can significantly increase your productivity if the drawings you create include multiple objects with similar properties.

Copies, duplicates, and clones of objects are created in similar ways in CorelDRAW 10, but each has a different object behavior. The name *clone* describes object copies that feature a relationship to their original "master." Once an object has been cloned, the clone imitates any property changes made to the master object from which it was cloned. Cloning enables you to create drawing elements destined for duplication in your document and provides the capability for you to change specific properties of all clones instantly, simply by editing the properties of the master. These properties are the object's Position, Fill, Outline, Path Shape, Transformations, and Bitmap Color Mask.

Making a Clone

To create a clone of a selected object, choose Edit | Clone and your original will become the master object controlling the clone. The clone is initially placed into

13

your document using the same offset measures as copies created using the Duplicate command.

To explore creating a clone, follow these steps:

1. Using the Pick Tool, click an object to select it and choose Edit | Clone, which, in turn, creates a "copy" of your object to the duplicate offset placement position. Reposition the new clone copy to another position on your page, so the entire object is visible.

2. Select your original control object and change its fill or outline color using the onscreen color palette. Notice the clone also changes color. Perform any other object commands—such as transformations—on the master and notice that the commands are repeated on the clone.

3. Select your master object and choose Edit | Clone a second time. Another clone is created. Drag this second clone away from the original, so the complete object is visible.

4. Select the master control object and change one or more of its properties. Notice the master and the properties of both clones also change.

> **TIP** *Once your first clone has been created, a hierarchy is created. You may create additional clones from the master control object, but you may not create clones from clones.*

Locating Clones and Their Master Objects

Creating a clone is a simple feat, but locating clones and/or their masters takes a few extra steps. Because clones and masters have the same appearance, it's difficult to identify which is which visually. One simple way of identifying a clone or master is to monitor the Status Bar while the objects are each selected. Unfortunately, the Status Bar doesn't specify which clone goes with which master when multiple masters and clones exist in your document. To locate or select a clone or its master quickly, right-click your object to open the pop-up menu. If a selected object is a master or a clone, the following commands are available

■ **Select Clones** If your selected object is a master control object, choosing Select Clones from the pop-up menu, shown next, selects all clones. Only the clones on your current page become selected.

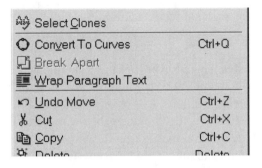

- **Select Master**   If your selected object is a clone, choosing this command causes the master control object associated with the selected clone to be selected. If the master is situated on a different page, CorelDRAW 10 automatically changes your page view to the specific document page.

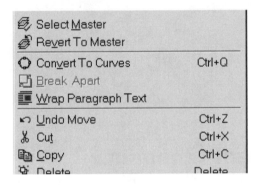

Working with Clones and Master Links

The link between a master and its clone creates a relationship based on shared properties. Changing the properties of a master changes its clone, but changing the properties of the clone breaks the link between the master and the clone for only that altered property. All other properties remain unaffected. For example, changing the outline color of a clone breaks only the outline color link with the master and, subsequently, changing the outline color of the master has no effect on the clone's altered outline color. However, changing a different property on the master—such as the fill color—still cause the clone to reflect this new property.

If the properties of a clone have been changed to be different from the master control object, right-clicking the clone object and choosing Revert to Master from the pop-up menu enables you to restore certain master object properties. The following command, which is available while working with masters and clones, is

■ **Revert to Master**   The Revert to Master command becomes available from the pop-up menu (by right-clicking the clone) only if the clone has been edited somehow after it was created. Choosing this command opens the Revert to Master dialog, which enables you to restore specific properties of the original master object. Only those properties that are different become available; these comprise Clone Fill, Clone Outline, Clone Path Shape, Clone Transformations, and Clone Bitmap Color Mask.

Using the Repeat Command

Having the capability to repeat your last performed command enables you to perform a number of different object-related operations quite quickly. This is perhaps another of those commands you might want to be aware of while doing virtually any type of drawing work. The Repeat command enables you to repeat your most recent command or action on the same object—or a completely different object—but with certain restrictions.

To apply the Repeat command, choose Edit | Repeat *command*, where *command* specifies the last operation performed. Or, use the shortcut CTRL+R. The Repeat command is available for basic object-editing commands such as copying, scaling, skewing, or rotating objects. For example, if your last command was to copy an object while transforming it, the Repeat command enables you to perform the identical operation again using exactly the same transformations and relative positioning as you did originally. But, because the Repeat command repeats only commands, you may also apply it to the same object or a *different* object—provided you have performed no other commands since then.

Menu specifies last
command performed.

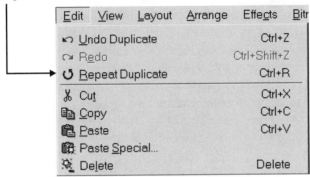

This functionality also extends to editing object properties. For example, if
your most recent operation was to fill a selected object with a specific fill type,
you may select a different object and apply the identical fill using the Repeat
command—saving you the effort of opening dialogs or using tools to repeat
the command. Unfortunately, the Repeat command is restricted only to single
editing commands. For example, if your last transformation involved scaling
and then, subsequently, rotating an object, the Repeat command only repeats
the rotation.

To explore using the Repeat command on any selected object, follow these
brief steps:

1. If you haven't already done so, select an object and perform a basic
   transformation or property-editing command.

2. With the same object (or a different object) selected, choose Edit | Repeat
   command or press CTRL+R. Your most recent command is automatically
   performed again.

3. Select the same or another object and apply the Repeat command again.
   Notice that the same operation may be performed repeatedly and endlessly
   on the same or different selected objects, so long as no other command was
   used since then.

TIP	*The Repeat command capabilities include object transformations, such as Copy Properties From, Layer Ordering, Duplicate, Clone, Arrange, Align, and Distribute commands; however, most other complex operations, such as bitmap commands, effects commands, and text property commands, aren't included as part of the Repeat command's capabilities.*

Aligning and Distributing Objects

When it comes to organizing your objects in relation to your page or to each other, CorelDRAW has always offered complete and precise controls via the Align and Distribute dialog. If perfection comes through trial and error, these tools are perhaps as perfect as they come because they have been well-refined through past versions. Align commands enable you to align object shapes in various and relative ways, while Distribute commands provide ways to distribute objects evenly within a given space. Both commands are located in a single dialog opened by choosing Arrange | Align and Distribute or by clicking the Align and Distribute button in the Property Bar while at least two objects are selected.

Click to open align and
distribute dialog.

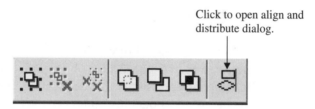

Aligning Hot Keys

If you need to align objects quickly, you may do so without the need to open dialog boxes by using shortcut keys while at least two objects are selected and while using the Pick Tool. The following shortcut keys apply to align objects:

Align Tops	T
Align Left Sides	L
Align Right Sides	R
Align Bottom	B
Align Horizontal Center	E
Align Vertical Center	C
Center to Page	P

Using Align Command Options

The Align command enables you to move and line up objects physically, based on their shape outline shape. While the Align and Distribute dialog is open and the Align tab is clicked, alignment options appear with the effect of options accompanied by representative symbols, which hint at their effects. To have your selected objects align in a specific way, simply select an option. Once an option is selected, you may click the Preview button to check that your selection suits your purpose or click the OK button to apply the alignment and close the dialog.

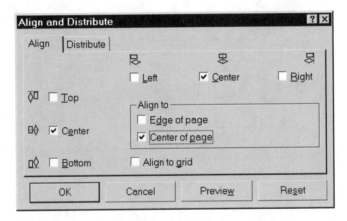

Options are organized into essentially three areas of alignment, including Vertical (at the upper-right of the dialog), Horizontal (at the left side of the dialog), and Page options. You may choose one vertical and/or one horizontal alignment option for each Align operation. Choosing these options has the following effects on how your objects are aligned:

- **Vertical alignment**   Choose Left, Center, or Right to align your objects accordingly. Figure 13-7 shows the results of a typical vertical alignment of a selection of objects. In the Left or Right alignment operations, the object farthest from the center of your selection determines the point at which the objects align.

- **Horizontal alignment**   While aligning objects horizontally, you have the option of using the Top, Center, or Bottom portions of your selected objects. Only one of these three may be selected at any one time. Again,

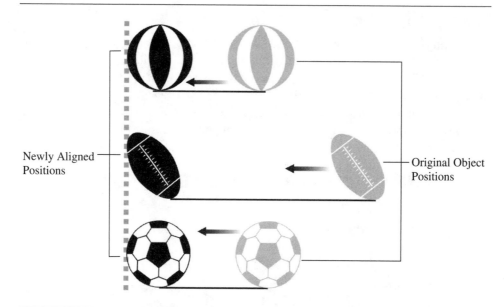

Newly Aligned Positions

Original Object Positions

FIGURE 13-7   This selection of objects has been aligned using the Left alignment option.

the alignment symbols accompanying the options may help when choosing which to use. Figure 13-8 shows the results of a typical horizontal alignment of a selection of objects. While using either the Top or Bottom alignment options, the furthest object from the center of your selection determines the point at which the objects align.

- **Edge of Page alignment**   Three options exist for aligning objects in relation to your page borders in combination with—or independently of—choosing either vertical and/or horizontal alignment options. If you want to use the edge of your page as the point of alignment, choose the Edge of Page option together with either the vertical Left or Right options and/or the horizontal Top or Bottom options. For example, to align your selected object(s) to the upper-right corner of your current document page, choose Top and Right in combination with Edge of Page. To align your object(s) only with the upper edge of your document page without changing their horizontal position, choose Top together with Edge of Page. Choosing this option by itself won't change your selected object's position. Edge of Page alignments may be used with one or more objects selected.

- **Center of Page alignment**   Choosing this option causes your object(s) to be centered on your page based on their width and height measures. If Left,

Newly Aligned Positions

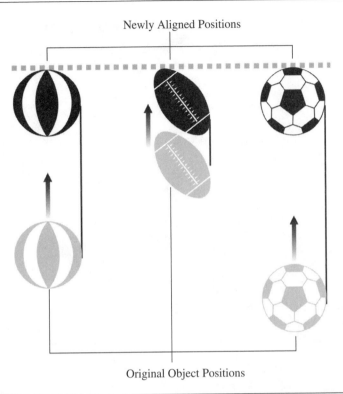

Original Object Positions

FIGURE 13-8   This selection of objects has been aligned using the Top alignment option.

13

Right, Top, or Bottom are selected as the vertical or horizontal align options, they are both immediately changed to Center. Center of Page alignments may be used with one or more objects selected.

- **Grid Alignment option**   If you need to have your selected object(s) align with the closest grid line on your page, choose the Align to Grid in combination with a vertical and/or horizontal align option. Choosing this option causes your selected objects to align to the closest grid based on your selection. For example, choosing Align to Grid in combination with the Bottom alignment option causes the bottom of your object to align to the closest grid line. Align to Grid may be used with one or more objects selected. To view your page grid, choose View | Grid. To change your Grid Frequency and Spacing, open Options dialog (CTRL+J) to the Grid page by choosing View | Grid, and Ruler Setup (see Figure 13-9).

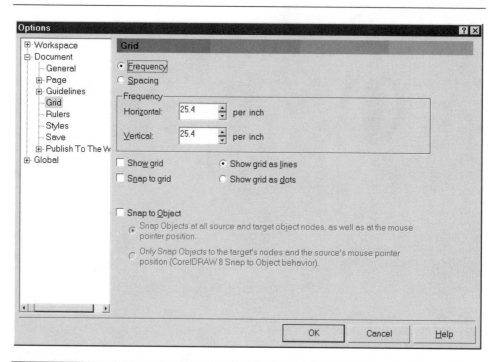

FIGURE 13-9 To change Grid Frequency or Spacing, use options in the Grid page of the Options dialog.

 Choosing the Center of Page as your align option automatically selects both vertical Center and horizontal Center options in the Align tab. To select both vertical and horizontal center options quickly at the same time without centering your objects in relation to the page, double-click the Center of Page option on first opening the dialog box.

Using Distribute Command Options

Although its name may be a little misleading, Distribute commands function in a similar way to Align commands—by repositioning your objects automatically in a specific way. The real strengths of this feature are perhaps more accurately referred to as *automated spacing* commands. To access these commands while two or more objects are selected, click the Align and Distribute button in the Property Bar or choose Arrange | Align and Distribute, and then click the Distribute tab.

Distribute options enable you to apply even spacing between objects based on their width and height. They also enable you to apply even spacing to their centers with representative pictures that visually indicate their effects beside the options.

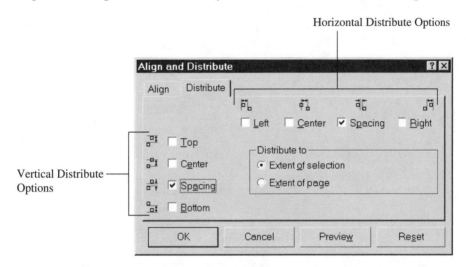

Distribute commands add even spacing between your selection of objects in one of two ways, using either the outermost objects from the center of the selection to determine the extent, or using your current page width or height. The remaining options enable you to specify the object reference points when the space is evenly divided. Several variables are at play here, which often cause Distribute options to be confusing to grasp at first.

Distribute Using Extent of Selection

While the Extent of Selection option is selected, your objects are evenly spaced vertically and/or horizontally according to their Top, Center, Left, Right, or Bottom edges, or by adding equal spacing *between* their width or height, regardless of their size. You must select at least one of these options for the distribution to affect the spacing of your objects. You may also choose both a vertical option together with a horizontal option to space your objects evenly within the width and height simultaneously.

Figure 13-10 demonstrates an example of objects evenly spaced (distributed) vertically. The most difficult aspect to grasp when using the Extent of Selection option is you can't actually see the defined area within which your objects will

Distributing Hot Keys

If you need to align objects quickly, you may do so without the need to open dialog boxes by using shortcut keys while at least two objects are selected and while using the Pick Tool. The following shortcut keys apply to align objects:

Distribute Tops	SHIFT+T
Distribute Left Sides	SHIFT+L
Distribute Right Sides	SHIFT+R
Distribute Bottom	SHIFT+B
Distribute Horizontal Center	SHIFT+E
Distribute Horizontal Spacing	SHIFT+P
Distribute Vertical Center	SHIFT+C
Distribute Vertical Spacing	SHIFT+A
Center to Page	SHIFT+P

FIGURE 13-10   These objects have been vertically spaced using Spacing and Extent Of Selection options.

be distributed. Nonetheless, your outermost objects define the width or height of this area.

Distribute Using Extent of Page

Using the Extent of Page option is slightly less confusing to use than Extent of Selection because your objects are evenly spaced within a defined area you can actually see—your physical page borders. Choose a Vertical and/or Horizontal spacing option together with Extent of Page to apply even spacing between the selected reference point on your objects. Figure 13-11 shows an example of a horizontal Distribute command using Left and Extent of Page.

Even Horizontal Spacing Applied To Page Extent

FIGURE 13-11   The same objects have been vertically spaced using Center and Extent Of Selection options.

PART IV

Organizing Objects and Applying Effects

CHAPTER 14

Envelope and Distortion Effects

For some time now, CorelDRAW users have enjoyed the ability to apply envelope effects to objects. In software terms, envelopes are relational-type mapping shapes applied to an object's outline path shape. Once an envelope has been applied to an object, changing the envelope shape changes the object it's applied to—but in different ways, depending on the kind of envelope applied. In simple terms, this means you may push or prod virtually any shape in your document until it resembles a completely different shape, and alter or change the envelope properties at any time without destroying the inherent shape of your original object.

The beauty of using envelopes is that different types of envelopes can create different effects. For example, on a simple level, an ellipse may be shaped to resemble a flower, or a rectangle may be shaped to resemble a balloon. On a slightly more complex level, an Artistic Text headline may be shaped to imply a sense of depth or perspective to add visual impact, or the frame of a Paragraph Text object may be changed to fit a specific space or shape as shown in Figures 14-1, 14-2, and 14-3.

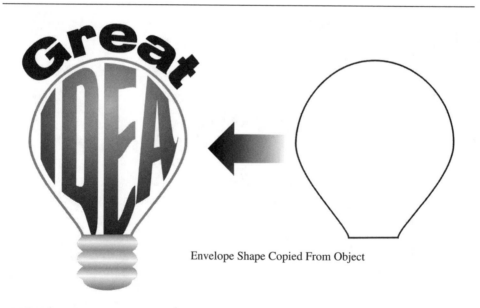

Envelope Shape Copied From Object

FIGURE 14-1   This Artistic Text object was applied with an elliptical-shaped envelope.

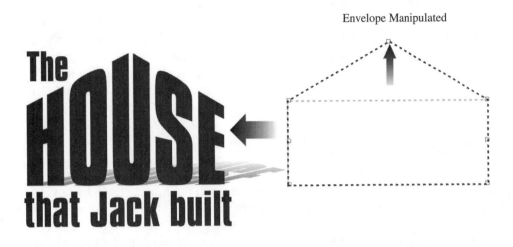

FIGURE 14-2   The simple envelope effect applied to this Artistic Text object was shaped to resemble a house structure.

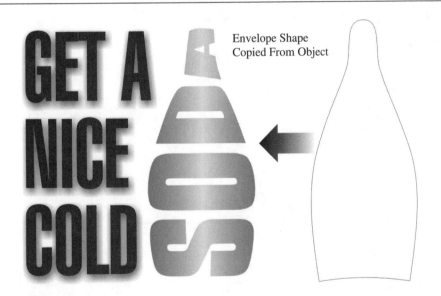

FIGURE 14-3   The Artistic Text seen here was applied with an envelope effect by sampling the path of a bottle-shaped object.

From a practical view, applying envelopes to objects causes them to change shape without altering their original properties. For your drawing objects, this means once an envelope has been created and applied, its properties may be edited or removed at any time and copied or cloned to other objects using single commands. For example, the properties applied to an envelope that molds a rectangle into a balloon shape may be copied to an Artistic Text headline to apply a similar effect.

Creating Envelope Effects

One of the keys to using CorelDRAW's Envelope feature is in finding or creating an appropriate shape. When applying envelopes, you have three strategies at your disposal. New envelopes may be simply applied to objects and their inherent shape manipulated in a number of ways until the shape is satisfactory before being "applied" to an object, where your desired shape already exists in the form of an object on your page, you may simply *copy* its outline shape to use as your new envelope's shape. You may also apply preset envelope shapes to objects, based on the saved shapes stored in the Envelope Preset collection.

Using the Interactive Envelope Tool and Property Bar

The first technique we explore involves using the Interactive Envelope Tool in combination with Property Bar command buttons and options. The Interactive Envelope Tool is located in CorelDRAW's main Toolbox (shown next) grouped with other interactive tools for Extrude, Drop Shadow, Distortion, Blend, and Contour.

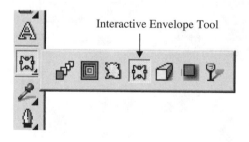

Interactive Envelope Tool

When the Interactive Envelope Tool is selected and an object is selected on your document page, the Property Bar displays a series of specific Envelope buttons and options, as shown next. The Property Bar contains all the resources necessary to apply manual or preset envelope shapes to any selected object.

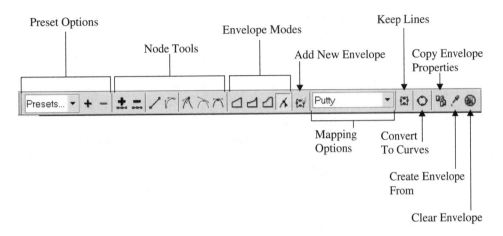

If you've never used the Interactive Envelope Tool before, grasping the technique may not be entirely obvious. There's a sequence you must follow in order to be successful. To apply a typical default envelope effect, follow these brief exploration steps:

1. If you haven't already done so, create and/or select an object to apply your new envelope effect to and choose the Interactive Envelope Tool from the main Toolbox. (Ideally, choose an object that is not rectangular, such as a polygon or ellipse, to see the full effects of the final result.) Notice that the Property Bar displays a collection of envelope options.

2. In the Envelope Mode buttons area, locate and click on the mode resembling a square with one corner higher than the other. This is the default Envelope mode known as Straight Line. Notice that your object is now surrounded by a series of nodes and dotted lines.

3. Using the Interactive Envelope Tool cursor, drag one of the nodes on your object in any direction. Notice that the direction is constrained to either vertical or horizontal movement and the shape of your object instantly changes to match the envelope shape once the mouse button is released.

14

Continue exploring by dragging two or three other nodes in any direction. Each time you release the mouse button, your object shape changes to match the new envelope shape.

4. Explore a little further by clicking the next Envelope mode button in the Property Bar resembling a square with one curved side (known as Single Arc). Drag any node in any direction and notice that the object shape is updated instantly, but this time in a different way.

By following this exploration, you've applied a basic envelope effect to your object, but the inherent shape of the object remains intact. For example, if the object you were working with was a polygon, selecting the object with the Pick Tool and viewing the available Property Bar options indicate that the object remains a polygon, with all the polygon-specific options still available. The same holds true if your object was created with the Rectangle or Ellipse Tools.

Using the Envelope Docker

If you're a recent upgrader to CorelDRAW 10, you may be accustomed to applying effects using a Docker window. The Envelope Docker offers options identical to and redundant with the Interactive Envelope Tool and Property Bar and provides an alternative technique. The advantage to using the Envelope Docker is that it enables you to select options before they are actually applied to your object. To open the Envelope Docker window (see Figure 14-4), choose Effects | Envelope or press CTRL+F7.

The most significant difference between using the Interactive Envelope Tool with Property Bar options and applying an envelope effect using the Envelope Docker window is that the envelope shape must be *manually* applied before it causes your object to change shape. Any other commands related to envelopes, such as copying, cloning, or clearing an envelope effect are available from the Effects menu while an envelope is selected on your document page.

To apply the effect in the Envelope Docker, follow these quick steps:

1. Create and/or select the object you wish to shape using the Pick Tool and open the Envelope Docker (CTRL+F7).

2. Click the Add New button in the Docker window. Notice your tool cursor automatically changes to the Interactive Envelope Tool, and your object is

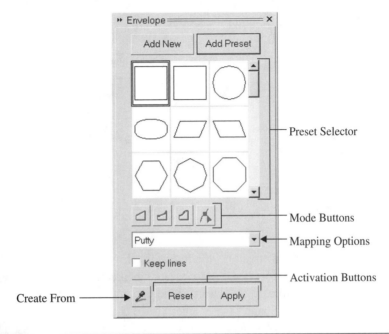

Preset Selector

Mode Buttons

Mapping Options

Activation Buttons

Create From

FIGURE 14-4   The Envelope Docker options are similar to those found in the Property
Bar when using the Interactive Envelope Tool and are supplemented by
commands available from the Effects menu.

now surrounded by a series of nodes and dotted lines. Click one of the
Envelope mode buttons such as the Straight Line or Single Arc mode buttons.

3. Using the tool cursor, drag one of the nodes in any direction and notice that
    the dotted line shape changes to reflect the new envelope shape, but your
    original object shape remains unchanged.

4. Click the Apply button in the Docker window. Notice that your object
    shape is mapped to resemble the envelope shape.

Envelope Tool Cursor States

If you've followed either of the previous step sequences to apply an envelope shape
to an object, you may already have noticed the two different cursor states available
(shown next) while using the Interactive Envelope Tool. These two cursor states

14

enable you to change the shape of your envelope in different ways, depending on the mode you have selected in either the Docker window or Property Bar.

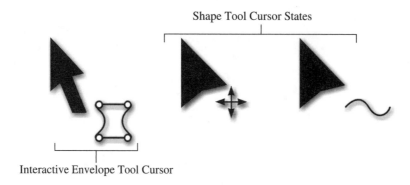

Shape Tool Cursor States

Interactive Envelope Tool Cursor

When shaping an applied envelope, the Interactive Envelope Tool cursor merely indicates that an envelope effect is in progress. But when your cursor is held over nodes or envelope guides (the dotted lines surrounding your envelope shape), the Shape Tool takes over. The Shape Tool enables you to change the states of the nodes and guidelines representing your new envelope shape interactively and is used in the same manner as when shaping any path (see Figure 14-5).

> **TIP** *For more information on using the Shape Tool to change the shape of objects by moving and changing nodes states and working with straight and curve line states, see Chapter 10.*

While shaping the Envelope nodes, the Shape Tool is accompanied by a reposition symbol, which signifies that the node may be moved using a click-drag action. When held over an envelope guideline, the Shape Tool is accompanied by a curved line symbol, signifying that the curve representing the envelope guideline may be moved. Using either cursor state alters your envelope's shape, but shaping envelope curves may be done only while the Unconstrained Envelope mode is selected. The section to follow details differences between applying each of the four types of Envelope modes.

> **TIP** *To enter the envelope editing state quickly for an object that has already been applied with an envelope effect, double-click the object. Your active tool automatically becomes the Interactive Envelope Tool with the Envelope nodes and guides displayed around your object.*

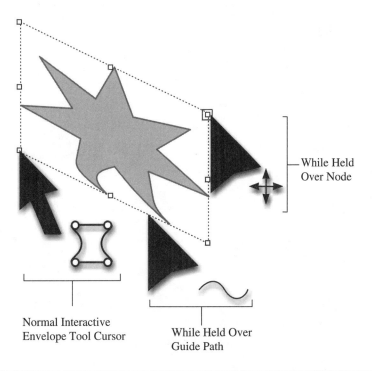

While Held
Over Node

Normal Interactive
Envelope Tool Cursor

While Held Over
Guide Path

FIGURE 14-5   The Interactive Envelope Tool includes three functional cursor states,
shown here, when held over various parts of an envelope effect in progress.

Choosing an Envelope Mode

As mentioned earlier in this chapter, the type of Envelope mode you choose has a
profound effect on the resulting shape of your envelope and subsequently on how
the envelope shapes your object. The key to using these modes is in understanding
the difference in behavior between the corner nodes and side nodes composing your
envelope shape. Depending on which mode is selected, corner and side nodes take
on different properties resulting in different envelope shapes as seen in Figure 14-6.

In technical terms, these modes have the following effects during
envelope-shaping operations:

- **Straight Line**   While this mode is selected (the default), the shape of
envelope guidelines are represented as straight lines. This means that dragging
either corner or side nodes causes the adjoining envelop guidelines to connect
in straight paths. In this case, all node positioning is constrained to either

14

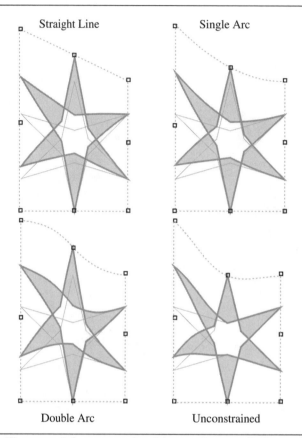

Straight Line   Single Arc

Double Arc   Unconstrained

FIGURE 14-6   The upper-left corner node of the envelope applied to each of these identical polygons was dragged directly upward using each of the four Envelope modes.

vertical or horizontal position changes. As corner nodes are dragged, side node movement is updated to match the guideline path, while side nodes may be moved independently of corner nodes.

■ **Single Arc**   This mode behaves in a similar way to the Straight Line mode, with the resulting guideline paths being set to curves, with side nodes to Smooth nodes and corner nodes to Cusp nodes. Using this mode, dragging corner nodes creates a curved side on the envelope, while side nodes (and their curve handle positions) align with the path of the resulting curve. Node movement is constrained to vertical or horizontal movement, while side nodes may be moved independently of corner nodes.

- **Double Arc**   As the name implies, this mode creates the effect of sine-wave-shaped sides. Behind the scenes, corner points become Cusp nodes, while side nodes become Smooth nodes. However, the curve handles of side nodes remain stationary in relation to the nodes, causing the guidelines to take on a double-arc shape. The same vertical and horizontal constraint restrictions as with the previous modes apply. Side nodes may be moved independently of corner nodes but apply a similar curve effect as with the Single Arc mode.

- **Unconstrained**   For complete freedom when shaping an envelope, the Unconstrained mode enables you to position either side or corner nodes as if they were ordinary shaped nodes. In this mode, the Shape Tool enables you complete control, and nodes may be dragged in any direction to shape the envelope to virtually any shape. Unconstrained also enables you to add or delete nodes, change any line segment states to straight or curved, or change the properties of nodes to Cusp, Smooth, or Symmetrical using Property Bar options.

Choosing an Envelope Preset Shape

Since envelopes may take the form of virtually any shape, a convenient collection of Presets is available in both the Envelope Docker and the Property Bar when using the Interactive Envelope Tool. These Presets take the form of the most common shape styles, such as squares, rectangles, polygons, and ellipses with a few other hybrid shapes thrown in for good measure. By using a preset shape, you avoid the need to create your own object from scratch, and it offers some time savings.

The procedure for applying a preset envelope shape differs only slightly between using the Property Bar options or Envelope Docker. Choosing a Preset from the Property Bar instantly applies the shape, while Presets selected in the Envelope Docker are applied only after pressing the Apply button. To apply a Preset quickly, select your object using the Pick Tool, choose the Interactive Envelope Tool from the main Toolbox, click the Add Preset button (+) in the Property Bar, and choose a shape from the Preset selector.

To apply a Preset using the Envelope Docker window, follow these quick steps:

1. With your object selected, open the Envelope Docker (CTRL+F7).

2. Click the Add Preset button in the Docker window. Notice that the Envelope nodes and guidelines appear on your object and the Preset collection becomes available.

14

3. Click a preset shape in the preview list. Notice that a new envelope shape automatically surrounds your object.

4. Click the Apply button in the Docker window to apply the new envelope shape to your selected object.

Saving and Applying Envelope Presets

One key new feature in CorelDRAW 10 regarding envelopes is the addition of the Preset List selector to the Property Bar available when using the Interactive Envelope Tool. The Preset List selector (shown next) contains any presets you have saved (in this case Envelope Presets) and comprises three basic components that enable you to apply, add, or delete your own preset envelope shapes as you require quickly.

Preset List   Click to add new
                                                       envelope shape.

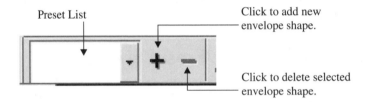

                                                       Click to delete selected
                                                       envelope shape.

Choosing a Preset from the list immediately applies the new envelope shape to a selected object. When an object shape in your document is selected, you may add it as an new envelope shape with the Add button. While saved envelope shapes exist in the Preset List selector, selecting an envelope shape enables you to delete it with the Delete button (–). As a practical exercise in creating, applying, or deleting preset envelope shapes, follow this brief exploration:

1. If you haven't already done so, create and/or select a simple shape object in your document. Ideally this shape is composed of a single noncompound path type object.

2. Choose the Interactive Envelope Tool from the main Toolbox. Notice that the Property Bar now features Envelope options—including the Preset List selector, as well as the Add and Delete preset buttons.

3. To add the shape of your object to the Preset List selector, click the Add button in the Property Bar. The Save As dialog opens with the Save As Type drop-down menu automatically listing preset files. In this dialog

(see Figure 14-7), enter a unique filename for your new Envelope Preset and click Save. Your preset envelope shape is saved.

4. To verify that your new Envelope Preset is available, create and select a new and different object in your document. Choose the Interactive Envelope Tool again and click to view the Preset List selector. Notice that a small thumbnail representation of your new envelope exists in the list. To apply your new envelope shape, choose it from the list. The new envelope is applied.

5. To delete an envelope shape from the Preset List selector, click a blank space on your document page to ensure that no objects are selected. Still using the Interactive Envelope Tool, choose your newly saved envelope shape from the Preset List selector.

6. With the new preset envelope shape selected, click the Delete preset button. Confirm your deletion in the prompt that follows and your preset envelope shape is now deleted.

NOTE   *Saved Envelope Presets available in the Presets List selector are not saved in the Preset collection available in the Envelope Docker (CTRL+F7). This means that saved Envelop Presets are accessible only from the Presets List selector in the Property Bar when using the Interactive Envelope Tool.*

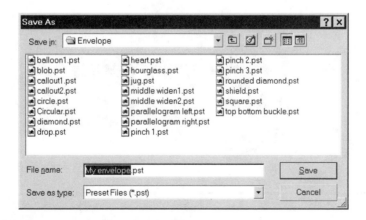

FIGURE 14-7   Clicking the Add preset button in the Property Bar opens the Save As dialog, which enables you to name and save your new preset envelope shape.

14

Choosing Envelope Mapping Options

With all this discussion about how to apply envelope shapes to objects, one key aspect remaining to be explored is how mapping is employed when envelope shapes are applied. Mapping options exist in both the Envelope Docker and when using the Interactive Envelope Tool and Property Bar options, and they enable you to control precisely how the shape of an envelope distorts or contorts you object's shape (see Figure 14-8).

Mapping options enable you to apply envelope shapes in different ways, by giving preference to the shape of your original object's node positions and path shapes. To select a Mapping option, choose Putty (the default), Horizontal, Vertical, or Original (shown in the following illustration) when applying an envelope shape to an object.

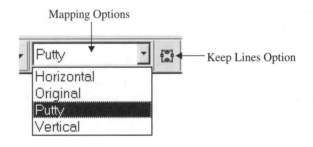

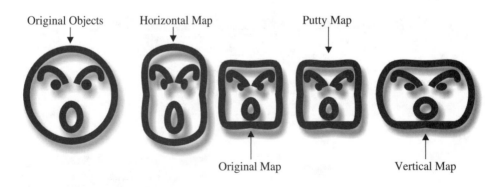

FIGURE 14-8 This simple group of objects was applied with a circular-shaped Envelope Preset using the different Mapping options.

While using these options with envelopes, the following effects apply:

- **Putty**   This option is CorelDRAW's default and has the effect of distorting the overall shape of your object to match the shape of the applied envelope as closely as possible. The Putty option maps the envelope shape to your object, including all interior and exterior node positions and line shapes, which results in a relatively accurate and smoothly mapped effect.

- **Horizontal**   Choosing the Horizontal option has the effect of mapping the lines and node positions in your original object to match the horizontal shape of the envelope. The Horizontal option alters your object's horizontal shape to match the envelope's horizontal shape, without significantly altering the vertical shape of the original object.

- **Vertical**   Using the Vertical option has a similar effect to using the Horizontal option, but in the opposing direction. Choosing Vertical as your envelope Mapping option results in the lines and node positions in your original object being mapped to the vertical shape of the envelope, with the horizontal shape largely ignored.

- **Original**   The term "original" refers to CorelDRAW's own original Mapping option, way back when there was only one (in version 3). Original is largely similar to Putty, in that the mapping applies both vertical and horizontal envelope shapes to the selected object. However, the difference is that Original maps only the outer shape of your original object to the envelope shape. More specifically, the corner nodes (represented by the corner handles when selected) of your envelope shape are mapped to the corner nodes of your original object's shape, while interior node positions and line shapes are mapped using an averaging value.

- **Text**   The Text option becomes available only while a Paragraph Text object frame is selected. In fact, while this type of object is selected, text mapping is the only option available. This option enables you to apply envelopes to a unique type of object: the frame properties of a Paragraph Text. It also opens a completely different avenue of text effects. Since Paragraph Text objects are simply text fit into rectangular-shaped frame objects, envelopes may be applied to reshape the frames themselves (see Figure 14-9).

14

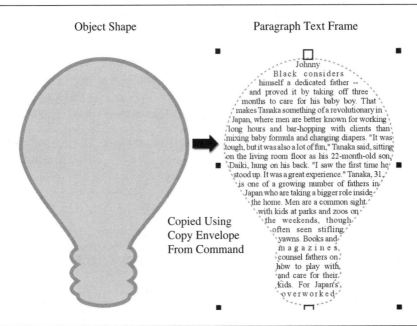

Object Shape   Paragraph Text Frame

Johnny Black considers himself a dedicated father -- and proved it by taking off three months to care for his baby boy. That makes Tanaka something of a revolutionary in Japan, where men are better known for working long hours and bar-hopping with clients than mixing baby formula and changing diapers. "It was tough, but it was also a lot of fun," Tanaka said, sitting on the living room floor as his 22-month-old son, Daiki, hung on his back. "I saw the first time he stood up. It was a great experience." Tanaka, 31, is one of a growing number of fathers in Japan who are taking a bigger role inside the home. Men are a common sight with kids at parks and zoos on the weekends, though often seen stifling yawns. Books and magazines counsel fathers on how to play with, and care for their kids. For Japan's overworked

Copied Using
Copy Envelope
From Command

FIGURE 14-9 The frame of this Paragraph Text object was reshaped using an envelope resembling a light bulb shape.

- **Keep Lines**   This final option affecting mapping applies while any of the Mapping options are chosen. When left unselected (the default), all node positions and lines in your original object are reshaped to match the envelope shape—even if this means changing straight lines to curved lines. When selected, the Keep Lines option has the effect of shaping only the node positions in your object to match the envelope shape being applied, leaving any existing straight lines unaffected. If your object is composed only of curved lines already, choosing Keep Lines has no effect (see Figure 14-10).

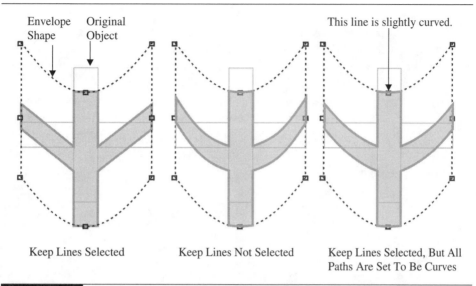

FIGURE 14-10 Notice that when the object's shape is composed only of curves, there is no visible difference when using the Keep Lines option.

Breaking a Dynamic Envelope Effect Link

While an envelope effect is applied to any object, the envelope shape remains dynamically linked to the object's original shape, meaning that the shape of the envelope may be edited at any time without affecting the inherent properties of the object to which it's applying a shape.

In certain instances though, you may wish to "break" the link between the envelope shape and the original object—without losing the applied shape. Let's say, for example, you wish to apply a Vector Extrude effect to the

14

shape created by your envelope effect. Unfortunately, in the case of Vector
Extrude, CorelDRAW won't allow you to extrude objects applied with
envelopes. Clearing the envelope effect returns your object to its original
shape, so that's not really an option. The solution is to turn your current
envelope effect into an ordinary object so that the new effect may be applied.
To do this, use the Convert To Curves command either using the CTRL+Q
shortcut or by pressing the Convert To Curves button in the Property Bar
(shown next) available while both your object and the Interactive Envelope
Tool are selected.

Convert To Curves Button

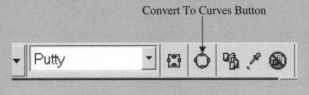

Constraining Envelope Shapes

As discussed previously in this chapter, you may shape an applied envelope effect
to virtually any shape you wish using the Interactive Envelope Tool in its Shape
Tool mode. Both the nodes and lines surrounding your envelope effect may be
poked and prodded until the shape is just the way you require.

However, you may wish to use certain invaluable shortcuts when shaping an
envelope around your object. These shortcuts come in the form of constraining
keys held as modifiers during the shaping process and have long existed as useful
tricks for CorelDRAW users to take advantage of. Each may be used in combination
with shaping operations, and each applies when using Straight Line, Single Arc,
or Double Arc Envelope modes.

Shaping Two Sides Concentrically

If you require, you may alter two sides of the shape simultaneously—and
concentrically—in opposite directions by holding the SHIFT key while dragging
any node. This technique enables you to create a perfectly concentric envelope
shape around the center origin of your original object (see Figure 14-11) using a
single click-drag action. While the SHIFT modifier is held, dragging any side or

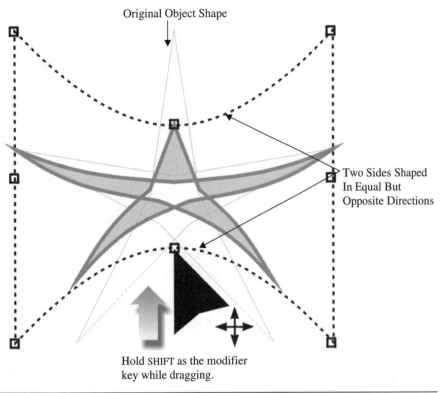

Original Object Shape

Two Sides Shaped
In Equal But
Opposite Directions

Hold SHIFT as the modifier
key while dragging.

FIGURE 14-11   Two sides of this polygon are being shaped simultaneously and
concentrically using the SHIFT key as a modifier to constrain
the new envelope shape.

corner node causes the corresponding node on the opposite side to move in the
opposite direction as your drag movement.

Shaping Two Sides Simultaneously

In a slightly different twist on constraining, you may also distort the shape of an
envelope by dragging two sides in the same direction by equal values when holding
the CTRL key as a modifier. This enables you to shape two sides simultaneously
and to identical distortions, in a single mouse action. While the CTRL key modifier
is held, dragging any node causes the corresponding node on the opposite side to
move in the same direction and by an equal distance as the node being dragged
(see Figure 14-12).

14

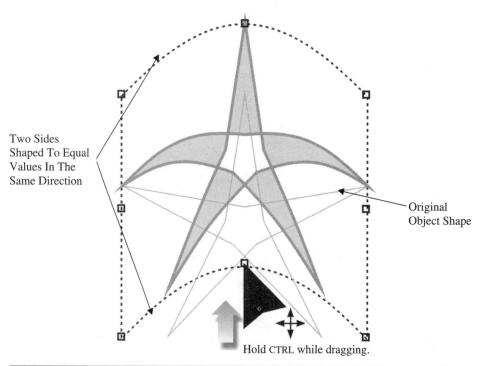

Two Sides Shaped To Equal Values In The Same Direction

Original Object Shape

Hold CTRL while dragging.

FIGURE 14-12 Two sides of this polygon are being shaped simultaneously in the same direction and by equal values while holding the CTRL key as a modifier while dragging a single node.

Using Envelope Shapes Between Objects

When deciding where to get your new envelope shape, you have a number of avenues to pursue, including manual shaping and/or applying Presets. One of the more common strategies is to copy envelope shapes from other objects—or even other envelopes—that already exist in your drawing. You might also decide to abandon the envelop strategy altogether, in which case you need to remove the effect from your object. In any case, the commands for these operations are available from the Effects menu or by using the shortcut buttons in the Property Bar when the Interactive Envelope Tool is selected shown in the following illustration.

Create Envelope From

Copy Envelope Properties   Clear Envelope

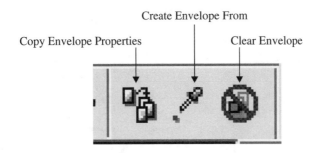

Copying Envelope Properties from Other Envelopes

Suppose you've gone to the effort of specifically shaping an envelope effect around an object on your document page and you wish apply the same shape to a different object. In such situations, you need to copy the envelope properties, including mode, mapping, and shaping properties, and apply them to the new object using the Copy Envelope Properties command and a special targeting cursor. To use this command, follow these brief steps:

1. Select the object you wish to apply the existing envelope shape to and choose the Interactive Envelope Tool from the main Toolbox.

2. Using Property Bar options, click the Copy Envelope Properties button. Notice that your cursor changes to a Targeting cursor.

3. Using the Targeting cursor, click on the object with the applied envelope effect you wish to copy from. The envelope effect is immediately copied and applied to your currently selected object (see Figure 14-13).

14

> **NOTE** *The Copy Envelope Properties option becomes available only if an object applied with an envelope effect currently exists on your document page— or on the pasteboard area surrounding your page. If the envelope effect you wish to copy is located on a different page of a multipage document, try placing a temporary copy of the object on your pasteboard or on the page you are currently working on.*

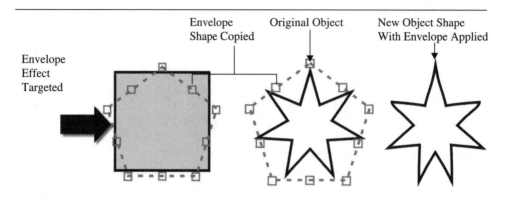

FIGURE 14-13   The five-pointed polygon envelope effect applied to this rectangle is copied to this seven-pointed polygon using the Copy Envelope Properties command.

Creating Envelopes from Objects

The concept of creating envelope shapes from the shape of existing objects in your document is much less difficult to grasp and more commonly used than copying actual envelopes between objects. The create operation enables you to instantly create and apply new envelope shapes based on the targeted object's shape (see Figure 14-14).

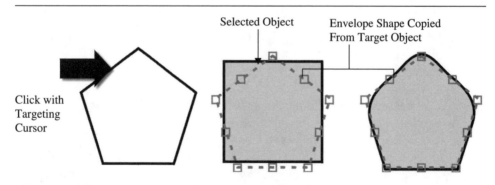

FIGURE 14-14   A new envelope shape is created from the existing shape of this polygon and applied to this rectangle.

To copy the shape of an object as your new envelope shape, follow these quick steps:

1. With the object you wish to apply the new envelope shape selected and the object shape you wish to copy from in view, choose the Interactive Envelope Tool from the main Toolbox.

2. Using Property Bar options, click the Create Envelope From button. Notice that your cursor changes to a Targeting cursor.

3. Using the Targeting cursor, click the object you wish to create a new envelope shape from. Your new envelope is immediately applied to your selected object.

> **TIP** *You may also use the Envelope Docker window (CTRL+F7) to sample the shapes of existing objects for use as new envelope shapes. To do this, select the object you wish to apply an envelope effect to, click the button featuring the eyedropper symbol in the Docker window, and click the Apply button to create the effect.*

Targeting Objects for New Envelopes

To target the shape of an existing object as a new envelope shape and apply it to your current object, the target object must exist on your current document page (or the pasteboard surrounding your page) and must not be grouped. Before attempting to target an object's shape as a new envelope, ungroup the target object with the Ungroup (CTRL+U) command before attempting to target it by pressing the Ungroup button in the Property Bar while the grouped objects are selected.

When targeting other objects using the Targeting cursor, click directly on the object to sample its shape or envelope effect. For objects without fills applied, click the outline path of the object. If you don't successfully target

14

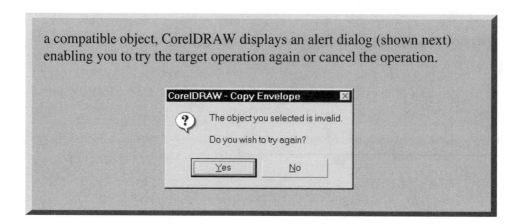

a compatible object, CorelDRAW displays an alert dialog (shown next) enabling you to try the target operation again or cancel the operation.

Clearing an Envelope Shape

Removing an envelope effect from an object is a quick operation. When an envelope effect is removed, the effect is completely removed. This means that if you shaped an envelope effect using several different and separate shaping operations, all shaping is removed at once. To remove an envelope effect and return your object to its original shape just prior to the effect being applied, follow these brief steps:

1. Select the object applied with the envelope effect and choose the Interactive Envelope Tool from the main Toolbox.

2. Using Property Bar options, click the Clear Envelope button. All envelope effects are removed, and your object is returned to its original condition before the envelope effect was applied.

The preceding commands are also available from the Effects menu and may be applied while an object is selected and without the need to choose the Interactive Envelope Tool. To access these commands, select the object applied with an envelope effect and choose Effects | Copy Effect | Envelope From or Effects | Clear Envelope.

Grasping Distortion Effects

CorelDRAW's distortion effects enable you to create controlled or seemingly uncontrolled changes to your objects' shape. Several different methods and variations to applying distortion effects are available in CorelDRAW—most are relatively straightforward to apply, while a few are quite complex. The principles behind these distortion effects stem from the application of mathematical algorithms applied to the curve paths comprising your object.

As with other effects in CorelDRAW, applied distortion effects are dynamic, meaning that they merely apply Distortion properties—without altering the inherent properties of objects. The values representing the Distortion properties may be changed or edited at any time, saved as custom Distortion Presets, or cleared from your object altogether.

For the most part, distortion effects cause the paths of objects to be transformed, leaving the Interior Fill properties unchanged. When a distortion effect is applied to a path, the curve values and node properties may be affected in highly dramatic ways. The more complex your original object is—and the more nodes and lines it includes—the more dramatic the distortion effect. Because distortion effects have the appearance of applying controlled or somewhat random path distortions, they may be useful in simulating natural or organic-style path effects as shown in the examples depicted in Figure 14-15.

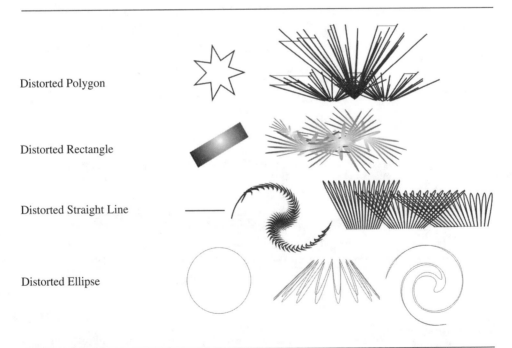

Distorted Polygon

Distorted Rectangle

14

Distorted Straight Line

Distorted Ellipse

FIGURE 14-15   These basic shapes were distorted with various settings and options available when using the Interactive Distortion Tool, resulting in interesting effects.

Using the Interactive Distortion Tool and Property Bar

Distortions may be applied to objects using the Interactive Distortion Tool, located in the main Toolbox and grouped with other interactive tools for Blend, Contour, Envelope, Drop Shadow, Extrude, and Transparency. When the Interactive Distortion Tool is selected, the Property Bar displays all options and variable settings available when applying distortions. Unlike many other interactive tools though, distortions may only be applied with this tool, meaning that no other docker or interface component controls this effect.

When browsing the Property Bar in this state, you may notice that distortions are subdivided into three basic Distortion modes: Push and Pull, Zipper, and Twister. When each of these modes is selected, a different set of variables to control the applied distortion becomes available. For the most part, these variables include Amplitude and Frequency values that may be varied in combination with certain other options and settings discussed later in this chapter. Variables may be controlled by manipulating Interactive Markers or by entering exact values in num boxes on the Property Bar. For the moment though, knowing that these three basic modes exist is a precursor to understanding how this effect is organized (see Figure 14-16).

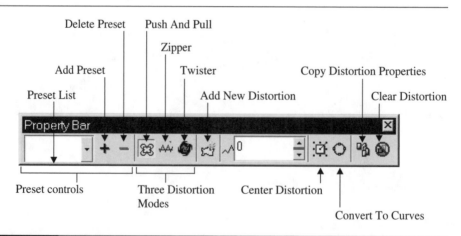

FIGURE 14-16   During a distortion operation, the Property Bar displays all relevant values and options for applying and controlling a distortion effect.

Choosing Distortion Modes

If you've ever had the opportunity to explore distortion effects, you may already realize how esoteric this feature can appear. For the most part, creating a desirable effect with these tools can be by trial and error at the best of times. In many instances, it may not even seem possible to anticipate the results of the applied distortion. However, with a little exploration, you may discover that even subtle distortions can often create practical effects for use for even the most complex drawing needs. However strange the names of the three available modes and their related values sound to you, their effects may become more evident in the discussion to follow.

Generally speaking, a distortion effect may be applied using either the Interactive Distortion Tool cursor or by dragging the Interactive Markers that surround your selected object while a distortion is in progress. When entering values directly in Property Bar num boxes, pressing ENTER on your keyboard causes the entered values to be applied. Interactive Marker states vary by the Distortion mode selected and are identified in the sections to follow.

Push and Pull Distortion

As the name vaguely implies, a Push and Pull distortion has the effect of inflating or deflating the slope of curves created during a distortion. While a Push and Pull distortion is in progress, Amplitude is the single variable available in the Property Bar. Amplitude may also be manipulated interactively by dragging the Amplitude marker. The applied Amplitude value determines the magnitude of the effect, essentially sloping the curves of paths away from or toward an object's original path.

Amplitude values may be set within a range between 200 and –200 percent. Negative amplitude values cause the effect to distort the path away from the center origin of the object, which creates the "push" condition of the distortion. Positive amplitude values cause the effect to be distorted toward the object's center origin, hence the "pull" condition. A zero Amplitude value sets the distortion to none. Figure 14-17 shows the effects of positive and negative Amplitude values.

14

Zipper Distortion

When Zipper is selected as your current distortion effect, paths in your object are applied with a unique distortion generally resembling the zig-zag effect seen in the shapes composing a zipper. The paths in your object are set to distort away from

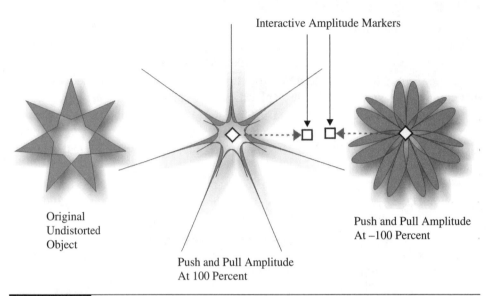

FIGURE 14-17 This seven-point star polygon has been applied with Push and Pull distortion using numeric values entered directly in the Property Bar Amplitude num box.

the original path based on the amount of amplitude applied. When the Zipper Distortion mode is selected, the Property Bar provides an Amplitude option that may be set within a range between 0 and 100 percent. In addition to this option, more options are available including a Frequency variable and options for Random, Smooth, or Local distortion (shown next).

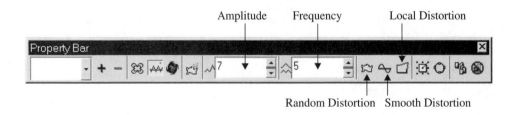

While manipulating interactively, the outer marker represents the Amplitude value, while the slider control sets the Frequency, which enables you to set the number of zig-zags within a given distance. Both may be set within a range of 0 and 100

percent. The effects of various Amplitude and Frequency values while applying a Zipper distortion to a straight line path are demonstrated in Figure 14-18.

Zipper distortions are likely the most complex to apply and control, due to the sheer volume of variables that may be set. Besides using varying settings for Amplitude and Frequency, you may also control the distortion using one of three additional options for controlling the shape and size variation of the zig-zag shapes in a Zipper distortion. Each of these options may be selected to be on or off, meaning that you may mix and match their applications. Zipper shaping and sizing options have the following effects:

- **Random**   Choosing the Random option to be active causes the zig-zag Zipper distortion on your object's path to vary randomly between your selected Amplitude values and zero. This creates the appearance of nonrepeating frequency and varied wave size, creating an uncontrolled distortion appearance (see Figure 14-19).

- **Smooth**   While the Smooth option is selected, the curves in your zig-zag Zipper distortion become rounded, instead of the default sharp corners normally seen. Figure 14-20 shows constant Amplitude and variations in Frequency when the Smooth option is applied.

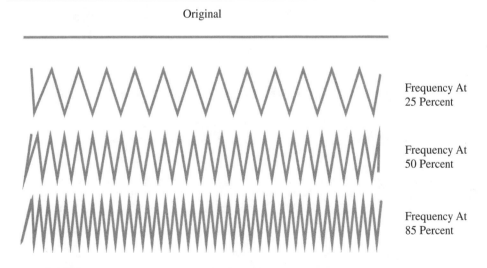

Original

Frequency At 25 Percent

Frequency At 50 Percent

Frequency At 85 Percent

14

FIGURE·14-18   This straight line composed of just two end nodes was applied with various Zipper distortion effects.

364 CorelDRAW 10: The Official Guide

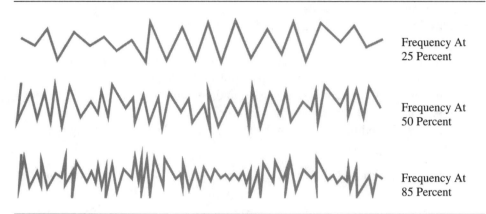

Frequency At
25 Percent

Frequency At
50 Percent

Frequency At
85 Percent

FIGURE 14-19 This straight line has been applied with a constant Amplitude value of 50 percent, while the Frequency values have been varied using a Zipper distortion.

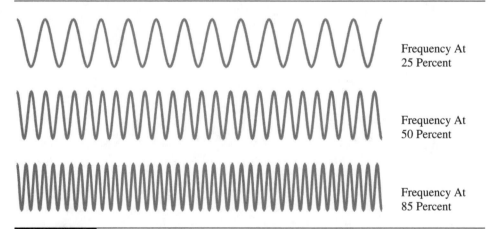

Frequency At
25 Percent

Frequency At
50 Percent

Frequency At
85 Percent

FIGURE 14-20 The Smooth option is selected when a Zipper distortion has been applied to the same straight line with Amplitude at 50 percent and Frequency values varied.

■ **Local**   Using the Local Distortion option has the effect of varying the Amplitude value of your distortion effect around the center origin. At the center of the distortion effect, Amplitude is at its maximum value. Amplitude then tapers to 0 as the distortion emanates from the center origin of the effect. The results of applying the Local Distortion option while the Frequency is varied are shown in Figure 14-21.

TIP	*As with other interactive effects, distortions may be cleared from your object completely, which returns your object back to its original state before any distortion was applied. To clear distortion effects from your object, click Clear Distortion Effect in the Property Bar or choose Effects	Clear Distortion in the command menus. If you've applied multiple distortions to the object, each distortion step is cleared individually, enabling you to step out of the effect incrementally.*

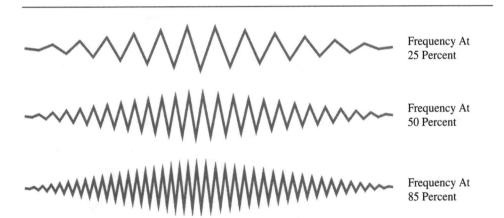

Frequency At 25 Percent

Frequency At 50 Percent

Frequency At 85 Percent

FIGURE 14-21   The Local option has been used in distortions to the same straight line. Amplitude is again fixed at 50 percent while Frequency values vary.

14

Twister Distortions

Twister Distortion effects cause the paths and nodes representing the outer shape of objects to be rotated in either clockwise or counterclockwise directions, while the curves joining the interior nodes of the shape remain stationary. The variation in the outer curves causes the effect of distorting an object's shape to appear to "spin" or twist concentrically around its center origin. Options controlling the Twister distortion are available in the Property Bar when Twister is selected as the Distortion mode and include rotation direction, rotation amount, and degree of additional rotation.

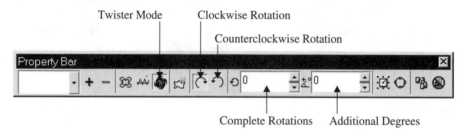

Applying and controlling Twister distortions is likely the least complex of all Distortion modes to work with on an object. While a Twister distortion is in progress, you may set its rotation to be clockwise or counterclockwise, but the appearance of the rotation is most dramatically affected by the amount of rotation applied. Rotation may be set in whole rotations to a maximum of 9, while additional rotation amounts added to the complete rotation may be set up to 359 degrees, or nearly another complete rotation. Figure 14-22 demonstrates the typical effects of rotation on circular and rectangular objects.

TIP   *If an object has been applied with distortion effects, you may no longer edit its paths or nodes using the Shape Tool. To edit the object's nodes or paths, remove the distortion with the Clear Distortion button in the Property Bar. Double-clicking an object with a distortion effect applied quickly launches an editing session.*

Using Interactive Distortion Tool Markers

Although you may apply distortion values numerically when creating distortion effects, you may also control many of the variables interactively by moving, rotating, or dragging the small Interactive Distortion Tool markers that surround

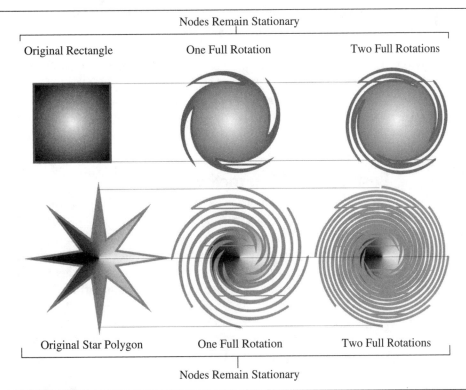

Nodes Remain Stationary

Original Rectangle   One Full Rotation   Two Full Rotations

Original Star Polygon   One Full Rotation   Two Full Rotations

Nodes Remain Stationary

FIGURE 14-22   These polygon- and square-shaped rectangles were each applied with the same Twister distortions; in each case, only the outside path of each object is distorted, while the nodes controlling them remain stationary.

your object while a distortion effect is in progress. Depending on which Distortion mode you are using, these Interactive Markers have differing purposes.

Generally speaking, Interactive Markers are composed of a center marker and at least one other variable marker, with the two being joined by a directional guide. Regarding distortions, the center marker indicates the center origin of the distortion, which by default aligns with the center origin of your original object before any distortion effect is applied. The adjoining marker represents amplitude while applying Push and Pull and Zipper distortions. When Zipper distortion is being applied, a small extra slider appears between these two markers and controls the amount of frequency applied. In the case of Twister distortions, the outer marker merely serves as a handle for determining the degree angle and amount of rotation you wish to create around your object.

14

> **TIP** *While applying distortion effects to objects, dragging the center most interactive handles enables you to offset the center origin of the distortion—which can have dramatic distortion effects. However, once you drag this marker away from center, recentering it manually is strictly visual unless you use the Property Bar. To realign the center marker with the center of the distortion, click the Center Distortion button in the Property Bar while the Interactive Distortion Tool and the distorted objects are selected.*

Changing Push and Pull Interactively

While a Push and Pull distortion is in progress, two Interactive Markers are associated with the distortion. The diamond-shape marker indicates the center of the distortion and is joined by a dotted line to a square-shaped marker controlling the Amplitude value. Either marker may be repositioned causing immediate changes to the distortion. The center marker in this case may be positioned anywhere around the object, but the Amplitude marker movement is constrained to left or right movement. Dragging the Amplitude marker left of center increases or decreases the negative Amplitude values, causing the push effect. Dragging the Amplitude marker right of the center marker increases or decreases the positive Amplitude values, causing the pull effect. Figure 14-23 shows the effects of typical Interactive Marker positions.

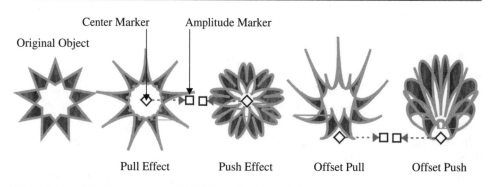

FIGURE 14-23 This nine-pointed polygon has been applied with various Push and Pull distortions using the available Interactive Markers.

Changing Zipper Interactively

The interactive handles surrounding a Zipper distortion are similar to Push and Pull. A diamond-shaped center marker indicates and controls the center origin while a square-shaped marker to the right side controls the Amplitude value. Between these two markers is a small rectangular slider, which may be dragged left or right between the center and Amplitude markers and controls the Frequency value. Moving the Frequency slider right increases the frequency, adding more zig-zag shapes to your object's path, while dragging it left has the opposite effect. Typical Interactive Marker positions and effects are depicted in Figure 14-24.

Changing Twister Interactively

Controlling Twister distortions interactively is likely the most effective way to apply this Distortion mode since one motion enables you to set two key variables at once, both of which have a dramatic effect on the distortion. Interactive Markers during a Twister distortion are comprised of a diamond-shaped center marker and a circular-shaped rotation handle. Dragging the rotation handle around the center marker causes distortion based on the angle of the guide between the center and rotation markers and the number of times the rotation marker is dragged completely around the center marker. Figure 14-25 shows examples of Twister distortions and positions of Interactive Markers.

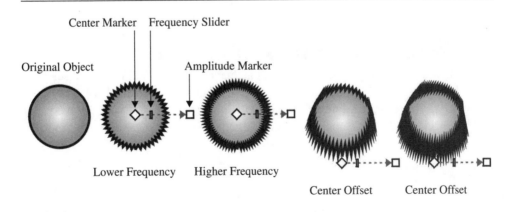

FIGURE 14-24   This ellipse is applied to a Zipper distortion with varying degrees of frequency, amplitude, and center offsets using Interactive Markers.

14

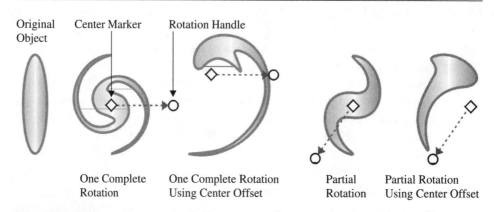

Original Object   Center Marker   Rotation Handle

One Complete Rotation   One Complete Rotation Using Center Offset   Partial Rotation   Partial Rotation Using Center Offset

FIGURE 14-25   This transformed ellipse is applied with Twister distortion and shows the relative positions of the interactive rotation handle and the center markers.

TIP   *As with other effects, distortion effects are a collection of applied properties. These distortions recipes may be copied between objects. To copy the Distortion properties of an existing distortion to your selected object, click the Copy Distortion Properties button in the Property Bar or choose Effects | Copy Effect | Distortion From. Use the Targeting cursor, which appears, to click the object you wish to copy the Distortion properties from.*

Using Distortion Preset Commands

A new feature regarding distortion effects is the addition of the Preset List selector to the Property Bar available when using the Interactive Distortion Tool. The Preset List selector (shown next) contains any Distortion Presets you've saved and comprises three basic components that enable you to quickly apply, add, or delete your own Distortion Preset as you require.

Preset List   Click To Add Distortion As Preset

Click To Delete Selected Preset From List

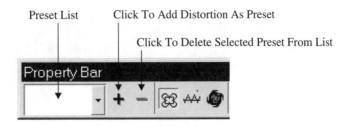

Exploring Distortion Preset Commands

Choosing a Preset from the list immediately applies a new distortion effect to a selected object. While an object shape in your document is selected, you may add it as an new Distortion Preset using the Add button. If you've already saved a distortion effect, using the Delete button enables you to delete a selected Distortion Preset. As a practical exercise in creating, applying or deleting Distortion Presets, follow these steps:

1. If you haven't already done so, create and/or select an object in your document and apply a distortion to it using the Interactive Distortion Tool and Property Bar options.

2. In the Property Bar, notice the Preset List selector, as well as the Add and Delete Preset buttons at the far left side.

3. To add your Distortion properties as a saved Preset to the Preset List selector, click the Add button in the Property Bar. The Save As dialog opens with the Save as Type drop-down menu automatically lists the preset files. In this dialog (see Figure 14-26), enter a unique filename for your new Distortion Preset and click Save. Your new Distortion Preset is saved.

14

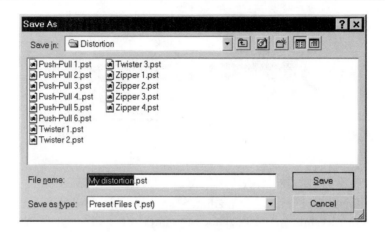

FIGURE 14-26 Clicking the Add preset button in the Property Bar opens the Save As dialog, which enables you to name and save your new Distortion Preset shape.

4. To verify that your new Distortion Preset is available, create and/or select a new and different object in your document. Choose the Interactive Distortion Tool again and click to view the Preset List selector. Notice that a small thumbnail representation of your new distortion now appears in the list. To apply your new distortion shape, simply choose it from the list, and the new distortion is applied.

5. To delete a saved distortion effect from the Preset List selector, click a blank space on your document page to ensure that no objects are selected and, while still using the Interactive Distortion Tool, click to select your newly saved distortion effect from the Preset List selector.

6. With the new Preset Distortion selected, click the Delete preset button. Confirm your deletion in the prompt that follows, and your distortion Preset is now deleted.

CHAPTER 15

The Power of Blends and Contours

There are both similarities and differences between the results of applying CorelDRAW 10's Blends and Contours you may want to consider before choosing between these two effects. *Blend* effects enable you to create a collection of intermediate shapes between two or more objects, while *Contour* effects create concentric shapes around an object's outline path and involve a single object only.

Comparing Blend and Contour Effects

Blend effects create a series of new objects with the properties of the intermediate steps influenced by both original objects. Contour effect shapes are influenced by the properties of only the one original object to which they are applied. Grasping the differences between these two powerful effects will help you decide which is the best effect to use when formulating an illustration strategy. But before you can decide which effect is best suited to your specific drawing purpose, exploring both may be worthwhile to some degree—especially if you've never before used one or the other. This chapter explores in detail both Blend and Contour effects, and demonstrates the results of choosing options available with each. As you're about to discover, both effects may be applied and controlled with relative ease, enabling you to create dozens, or even hundreds, of complex objects instantly just as you require, with a single command. When it comes to illustration power, few other effects come close.

Using CorelDraw's Blend Effect

The basic principles behind a Blend effect are relatively straightforward. Blending enables you to create a series of dynamically linked objects whose properties are based on a transition between two or more control objects. The term *Blend* may create some initial confusion for users migrating from other applications because it's often used to refer to blending color within the interior of an object (as is the case with QuarkXPress's Color Blend feature). To clarify, CorelDRAW 10's Blend effect involves blending between separate objects and the effect includes not only color, but *all* objects' properties.

While a typical two-object blend is applied, the intermediate blend steps change in shape, color, fill, outline, size, and position in a calculated progression between the two objects. In an extension of this power, you may also edit the condition of a blend by altering its properties at any time—without the need to start from scratch. You may control the number of objects created by the blend or set the rate at which the blend progression occurs. The entire arrangement may be set to follow a specific object path or the blend itself may be divided into several subblends or dismantled altogether.

Real World Blending

The number of applications for Blend effects is virtually unlimited. Typically, Blend effects are used in high-end illustration for creating realistic depth. Figures 15-1 and 15-2 demonstrate two instances in which Blend effects are used to create depth effects. In both cases, two similar objects were blended to simulate a highlight or shadow area in a drawing. In both drawings, object copies arranged in front were shaped and colored similar to the originals. The applied Blend effects simply created a smooth transition of color. This has long been the typical use for blends.

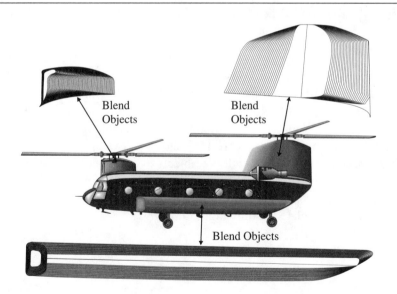

FIGURE 15-1   This technical-type drawing of a Chinook helicopter uses blends to create highlights in an effort to simulate a 3D drawing effect.

15

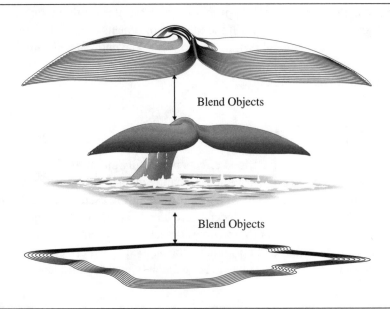

Blend Objects

Blend Objects

FIGURE 15-2 The shape of the tail objects uses multiple blends for a nonuniform 3D shape, while depth in the water portion uses a simple two-object blend.

But the practical uses extend to include nearly any drawing scenario when instant creation of multiple objects is needed. Almost any two (or more) types of objects in CorelDRAW may be involved in a Blend, including identical objects or completely different objects. Figure 15-3 shows an example of identical objects blended to create a collection of multiple objects to create a quick technical chart. In this instance, the bars of the chart and the horizontal reference lines were blended to create a specific number of evenly spaced objects. The blended objects were then used to complete the drawing.

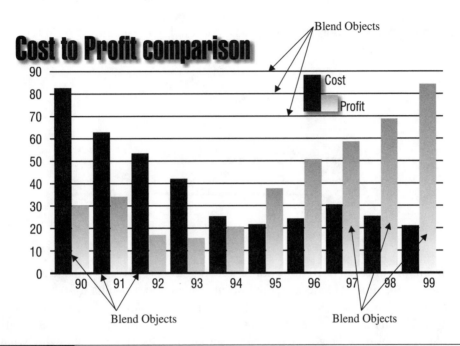

FIGURE 15-3   Almost all the objects in this technical chart were created using Blend effects. The Blend Groups were then dismantled and edited into the shapes needed.

The Interactive Blend Tool and Property Bar

In CorelDRAW 10, Blend effects are created solely based on the use of the Interactive Blend Tool in combination with Property Bar options. If you've used the Blend Docker in the past, this interface element is also available for applying

15

blends and is largely redundant with the Interactive Blend Tool Property Bar options. The Interactive Blend Tool is located in the main Toolbox, grouped with other interactive tools for Contour, Distortion, Envelope, Drop Shadow, and Transparency.

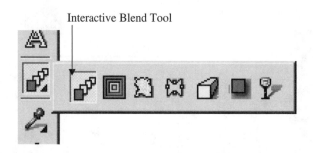

Interactive Blend Tool

While the Interactive Blend Tool is selected, the Property Bar features a complex collection of blend-specific options, shown next, which may be set once a blend has been created. By default, whenever a blend is first created, a series of 20 intermediate objects appear between the two objects. From that point, all other options must be adjusted to suit your needs. The trick is in knowing what these options do and successfully adjusting the effect to suit your needs. In many cases, all that's required is a quick adjustment to the number of steps, while CorelDRAW 10 does the rest.

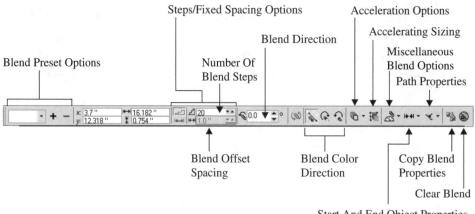

Steps/Fixed Spacing Options

Blend Direction

Acceleration Options

Accelerating Sizing

Miscellaneous Blend Options

Path Properties

Blend Preset Options

Number Of Blend Steps

Blend Offset Spacing

Blend Color Direction

Copy Blend Properties

Clear Blend

Start And End Object Properties

Creating a Typical Blend Effect

You're probably eager to start creating Blend effects yourself, so let's first create a blend and examine the results. To create a typical Blend effect between two objects, follow these steps:

1. If you haven't already done so, create two objects using any tool you want. Apply any fill or outline properties and arrange them on your page.

2. Choose the Interactive Blend Tool from the main Toolbox. Notice that your cursor changes conditions and the Property Bar features a selection of grayed-out options. These will become available once your blend has been applied.

3. Using the Interactive Blend Tool cursor and a click-drag action, click on or inside one of the objects and drag until your cursor is on or inside the other object. Notice once your mouse button is released a series of new objects appears between them, and the Property Bar comes to life with all options available now. You've just created a default blend between your objects.

TIP	*To remove a Blend effect completely from your objects, click the Blend portion of the effect to select it and choose Effects	Clear Blend; or while using the Interactive Blend Tool, click the Blend effect portion and click the Clear Blend button in the Property Bar. The effect is immediately removed and your objects are returned to their usual state.*

Anatomy of a Blend

To understand which parts of a blend control what, let's examine a Blend effect in progress. The makeup of a typical two-object blend includes several key components. Your original objects have now become control objects—any changes made to either of these has an effect on the appearance of the effect itself. The effect portion— referred to as a *Blend Group*—and the control objects maintain a relationship as long as the blend remains intact.

Along with these, several interactive markers appear around your Blend effect, each of which have a corresponding Blend option in the Property Bar. Before exploring what these interactive markers do and how they affect your blend, examining the markers and location, and getting to know what parts of the blend they represent might help. Figure 15-4 shows the basic anatomical parts of a typical two-object blend.

15

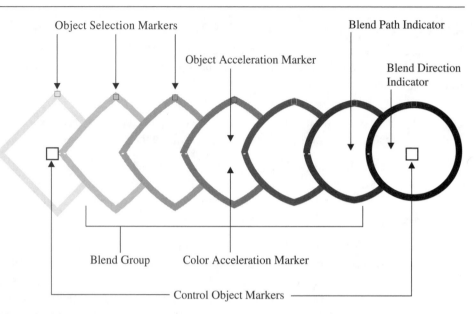

FIGURE 15-4 This direct blend between two basic shapes shows the interactive markers that appear around your objects while a Blend effect is in progress.

Selecting the various parts of a blend for editing can be tricky the first time. To select a complete Blend effect using the Pick Tool, click the Blend Group itself. Doing so selects the blend, together with its control objects. To select a control object, click only the control object itself. To recognize which objects are selected, keep in mind that selecting a blend causes the object selection markers of all objects in the blend to appear, while selecting an individual control object causes only its selection handles to appear. Selection markers appear as single node-like indicators, while selection handles appear as a collection of eight black markers surrounding an object.

TIP *To enter the editing state of a Blend effect quickly while the Pick Tool is selected, double-click the Blend Group portion of your effect. Doing this immediately causes your cursor to change to the Interactive Blend Tool and the associated Property Bar options to become available.*

As you apply a Blend effect, you notice the Interactive Blend Tool features several different cursor states. While the cursor is held over a compatible Blend effect object, it appears with the Blend cursor; or, if the object is incompatible, the cursor also indicates this. While the actual effect is being applied and your cursor is clicked onto a compatible object, a Start Blend indicator appears. While the cursor is dragged to a second compatible object, an End Blend indicator appears.

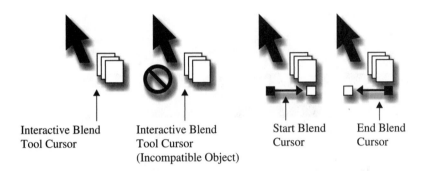

| Interactive Blend Tool Cursor | Interactive Blend Tool Cursor (Incompatible Object) | Start Blend Cursor | End Blend Cursor |

Editing Blend Effects

You can do plenty of things to change the appearance of a Blend effect. In fact, you can do so many things, your first visit to the available Property Bar options can seem overwhelming. This is object blending taken to a perfect science. Let's explore Blend effect options starting with the most common—such as blend steps, rotation, color, and acceleration, and then progress through the most complex options, covering blend paths, multipoint blends, and multiple-object blends.

Setting Blend Options

The options you may set to control your Blend effect significantly affect the appearance of the blend itself. These include options to change the steps value, rotation, color, and acceleration of the Blend objects, as well as saving the final effect as a preset.

Controlling Blend Steps

One of the first Blend effect properties you want to change is the number of steps in the Blend Group composing your effect. Steps may be set to a finite number within a range between 1 and 999. To specify the number of steps, enter a value in

15

the Property Bar Blend Steps num box and press ENTER (the fastest technique), or change the value using the spinner controls.

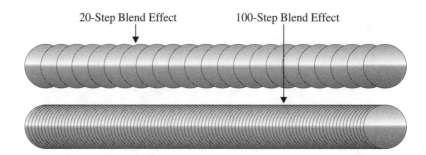

20-Step Blend Effect   100-Step Blend Effect

Specifying Blend Spacing

If you require applying a specific spacing value between your blend steps, it may help to know this option only becomes available while your Blend effect has been applied to a path. The reason for this that is the distance between your blend control objects must be fixed by the given length of the path. While your blend is applied to a path, you may choose the Fixed Spacing option in the Property Bar and enter the value to a specific unit measure. CorelDRAW, in turn, automatically calculates the number of objects required to fit the path's length. The Fixed Spacing value may be set within a range between 0.010 inches and 10.00 inches, in increments of 0.010 inches. For information on applying a blend to a path, see "Assigning a Blend Path," later in this section.

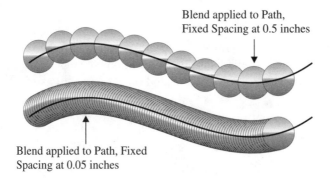

Blend applied to Path, Fixed Spacing at 0.5 inches

Blend applied to Path, Fixed Spacing at 0.05 inches

Rotating a Blend

If the need arises, you may rotate the objects in your Blend Group by fixed degree measures using the Blend Direction option. Enter an angle value based on degrees of rotation where positive values rotate the objects counterclockwise and negative values rotate them clockwise. While rotation is applied, the last object in the Blend Group is rotated the full angle, with the intermediate steps rotated in even increments starting at 0 degrees rotation—the rotation value of your Start Blend control object.

Last object in Blend Group rotated –45 degrees

When the Blend Direction option has been set differently from 0 degrees in the Property Bar, the Loop Blend option becomes available. Choosing the Loop Blend option has the effect of applying both rotation and path Offset effects to the Blend Group. Looping a blend works in combination with the Blend Direction value offsetting the objects from their original direction and rotating them simultaneously.

Blend Direction set to 360 degrees with Loop Blend selected

15

Changing Color Rotation

While a default Blend is applied, the colors between your Blend objects are blended directly from one color to the next in a smooth transition of colors. If you want to, however, you may change this using one of the two Color Blend variations. Using either variation causes the colors of your Blend effect to be rotated around the standard color wheel. Choose either Blend Clockwise or Blend Counterclockwise to have your Blend Group colors create variations of rainbow color effects during the blend.

Acceleration Options

Acceleration options have the effect of either increasing or decreasing the rate at which your Blend Group objects change shape as they progress between the Start and End control objects of the effect. You can choose from two different aspects of acceleration: Object Acceleration or Color Acceleration. While a default Blend effect is applied, both these settings are set to neutral, meaning the Blend Group objects change in color and size evenly between the two control objects. If you want, you may alter these two Acceleration rates simultaneously (the default) while the two options are linked or individually by clicking the Unlink Acceleration option.

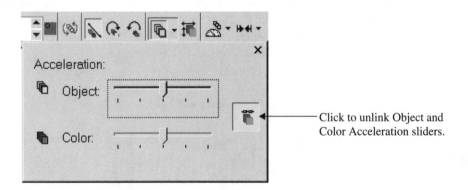

Click to unlink Object and Color Acceleration sliders.

To change acceleration while a Blend effect is applied, click the Object and Color Acceleration buttons in the Property Bar to access a pop-out menu and adjust the corresponding slider controls. The Unlink Accelerations button is also located in this pop-out menu. Moving either slider to the left of the center position reduces (or slows) the acceleration from the Start object toward the End object of the Blend effect. Moving either of the sliders to the right increases the acceleration of your Blend Group objects from the Start object toward the End object of the Blend effect. Interactive acceleration markers may also be used to adjust these values. While the two rates are unlinked, changing the Object Acceleration affects only the progression of shapes in the Blend Group. Figure 15-5 shows the effects of increasing and decreasing the Object Acceleration of a typical Blend effect.

While the Object Acceleration sliders are unlinked, changing the Color Acceleration affects only the change in progression of the fill and outline colors between the two objects, leaving the object shape unchanged. Moving the sliders (or interactive markers) left or right increases or decreases acceleration. Changing the Color Acceleration also affects the width properties applied to outline paths of objects. Figure 15-6 shows the results of changing the Object Acceleration while unlinked from the Object Acceleration values.

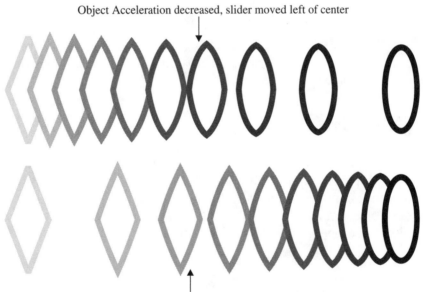

Object Acceleration decreased, slider moved left of center

Object Acceleration increased, slider moved right of center

15

FIGURE 15-5   The Object Acceleration of the Blend effect between these two objects has been unlinked to demonstrate the effects of increased or decreased Object Acceleration.

Color Acceleration decreased, slider moved left of center

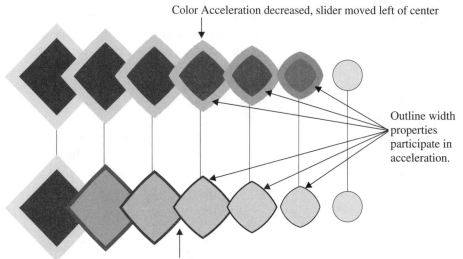

Outline width
properties
participate in
acceleration.

Color Acceleration increased, slider moved right of center

FIGURE 15-6   The Blend effect Acceleration rates between these two objects has been
unlinked. Notice that the rate at which the Blend Group objects are
shaped remains constant.

Using Blend Presets

Up to this point, the effects of changing blend steps, rotation, color, and Acceleration
rates of applied Blend effects have been explored. These values constitute the basic
properties that apply to virtually any Blend effect. Next, let's look at saving these
Blend properties as presets for applying to other existing blends because other
options available with Blends—such as Blend paths, multipoint blends, or multi-
object blends—are applied manually and may not be saved with presets.

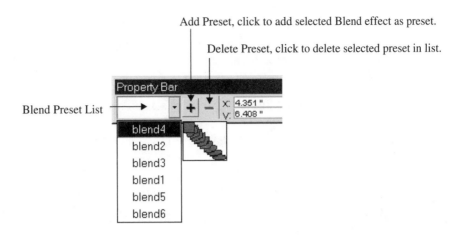

Add Preset, click to add selected Blend effect as preset.

Delete Preset, click to delete selected preset in list.

Blend Preset List

The Blend Presets are used in the same manner as other preset controls associated with other interactive effects such as Envelopes, Drop Shadows, Distortion, Contour, Extrude, and Transparency. Blend Presets may be saved and reapplied to two or more selected shapes in your document. To apply a saved Blend Preset to selected objects and explore adding or deleting Blend Presets, follow these quick steps:

1. If you haven't already done so, create and select at least two objects on your document page using the Pick Tool.

2. Choose the Interactive Blend Tool from the main Toolbox.

3. Using Property Bar options, choose a saved Blend effect from the Preset List. The properties of the blend are immediately applied and its current effect properties are displayed in the Property Bar.

15

4. To save an existing Blend effect as a preset while using the Interactive Blend Tool and Property Bar, click to select the Blend Group of the effect and click the Add Preset (+) button. The Save As dialog opens. Enter a new name for your new Blend preset in the File Name box and click Save. Your Blend Preset is added to the Preset List.

5. To delete a saved Blend Preset, deselect all objects by clicking a blank space on your page. Choose the preset from the Preset List selector to select it, and then click the Delete Preset button (–) in the Property Bar. The saved preset is immediately deleted.

 By default, saved Blend Presets are stored in the Program Files/Corel/ Graphics 10/Draw/Presets/Blend folder as typical default installation directory names.

Advanced Blend Effects

If you're comfortable with applying typical Blend effects and you have a good grasp on manipulating interactive marker to control a Blend Group, you may want to progress to more advanced blending techniques. Advanced blending techniques can solve difficult and specific illustration challenges when a typical direct blend can't. These operations include creating multipoint blends, mapping blend control object nodes, and applying blends to paths. If you've never had the opportunity to experiment with these technique in the past, you definitely want your thinking cap firmly attached to grasp these advanced blend issues.

Creating Multipoint Blends

CorelDRAW's Blend effect feature enables you to blend between two or more objects, while the blend itself is composed of two control objects and a single Blend Group—typically in a linear direction between the objects with no path applied. If necessary, however, you may designate individual objects in the Blend Group as Child objects of the blend, which, in turn, has the effect of causing them to behave as control objects of sorts. The properties of these Child Blend objects may be edited in the same way as control objects, which, in turn, affects the appearance and condition of the Blend effect applied between control objects and/or other Child Blend objects.

This operation is referred to as *splitting* a blend. While a blend is split, the Blend objects between the Child objects and the control objects become Child Blend Groups. Repositioning the Child objects of a split blend enables you to cause blends to follow indirect paths between control objects. Changing the properties of Child objects affects the appearance of the Child Blend Groups between the child and control objects. If this sounds confusing to you, you may be relieved to know this is as complex as blending gets (although knowing this may be little consolation for the mental acrobatics required).

The Child objects controlling a split blend may also be returned to their original condition as Blend Group objects, essentially eliminating the split. This operation is referred to as *fusing* and is accomplished by using the Fuse End command. You'll soon begin to explore using these commands; but before diving in, familiarize yourself with what can be achieved by splitting and fusing a Blend effect. Figure 15-7 details the anatomy of the before and after effects of a split blend. In this case, two Blend objects within a Blend Group have been specified as Child Blend objects and repositioned, resulting in a multipoint Blend effect. Notice each time the blend is split, a new set of interactive markers appears between the control and Child Blend objects on the path of the Child Blend Groups.

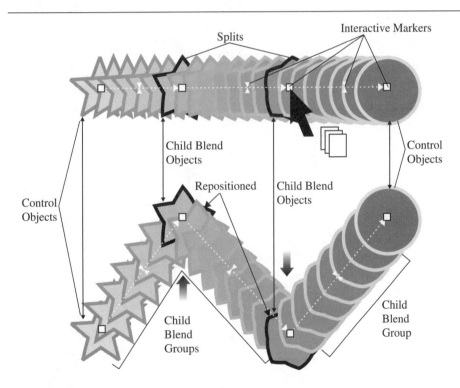

FIGURE 15-7   A default 20-step Blend effect between this star and ellipse was applied, while two of the original Blend Group objects were split and moved to create a multipoint Blend effect.

15

Splitting and Fusing a Blend

Splitting an existing Blend effect may be accomplished using the Interactive Blend Tool and Property Bar options, or solely by using the Interactive Blend Tool. Fusing a split blend is done the same way using the Fuse End command. To split an existing Blend effect, follow these quick steps:

1. If you haven't already done so, apply a Blend effect and have the Interactive Blend Tool selected as your current tool. Notice the interactive markers surrounding your effect.

2. Pick the Blend Group object where you want the blend to be split and double-click this object. Your Blend effect is now split. Drag this object away from the original blend path by click-dragging directly on the new marker it includes. Notice it now moves independently of other Blend Group objects.

You may also use Property Bar options to split a blend, which can be useful if the object you want to split from the blend is difficult to select. To do this, click the Miscellaneous Blend Options button in the Property Bar and click the Split button (as in the following). Your cursor immediately changes to a targeting cursor, enabling you to click the object on your Blend Group where you want the split to occur.

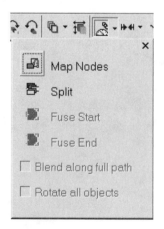

Take a close look at your blend. Notice the object you double-clicked now includes its own object marker identical to a control marker. This marker indicates it's now a Child Blend object. Notice also the Blend path between your new Child object and the control objects at the start and the end of your blend now includes Acceleration markers.

Returning a Child Blend object to its original state is also a quick operation using the Fuse Start or Fuse End commands. This operation is accomplished using the Interactive Blend Tool (the quickest method). To fuse a Child object back to the Blend Group it belongs to, follow these quick steps:

1. Using the Interactive Blend Tool, click to select an existing blend that already includes a split at some point along the Blend Group.

2. Locate the split you want to fuse and double-click directly on its interactive control marker. The Child object is immediately returned to the Blend Group.

> **TIP** *While a blend has been split at one or more points, you may also use the Pick Tool to select the Child objects—just like the control objects. To select a Child Blend object, click directly on the object itself.*

Mapping Control Object Nodes

When a Blend effect is applied, the shape of objects in the Blend Group is created in a progression between the control objects of the blend. Behind the scenes, CorelDRAW is actually calculating the position of each node on the control objects and creating the outline paths of the new shapes of the blend steps to match, in addition to all the other properties being blended. The appearance of each step in the resulting Blend Group is calculated based on node mapping. By default, your control object nodes are mapped according to their relative position. In abstract cases, where the two objects being mapped are completely different, this default node mapping might not be exactly what you had in mind.

Fortunately, CorelDRAW enables you to match the nodes of your control objects manually to each other to achieve your desired blend. When blending complex objects or when trying to achieve a particular Blend effect, this is actually quite a common practice. To map nodes while using the Interactive Blend Tool and Property Bar options, click the Miscellaneous Blend Options button and click the Map Nodes button. Your active cursor immediately becomes a targeting cursor of sorts. In this state, use the cursor to click the pairs of nodes you want to map to each other. Node Mapping is a two-step operation, whereby the cursor reappears after clicking the node on the Start Blend control object, enabling you to click a corresponding node on the End Blend control object (see Figure 15-8).

15

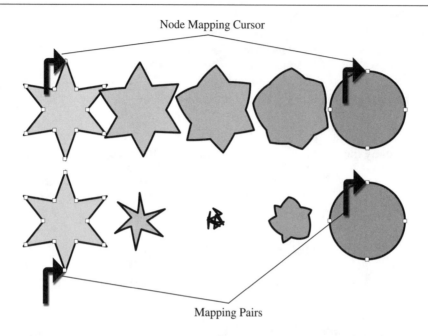

Node Mapping Cursor

Mapping Pairs

FIGURE 15-8   The Blend effect between this star and ellipse was mapped using two different control object node pairs.

NOTE   *Node mapping is unavailable if a Blend effect has been split into a multipoint blend.*

Assigning a Blend Path

Assigning Blend objects to follow a path enables you to create extraordinary Blend effects. In these instances, you can precisely position and/or evenly space a specified number of objects along an object's path—an operation that would otherwise be extremely time-consuming (if not impossible in certain cases) using manual methods. While a blend is applied to a path, a host of options is also available for you to control the blended objects. You also should be aware of a few tricks and techniques. Blend objects on a path may be rotated or offset from the path, or they can be set to fill the path completely using relatively quick procedures. Blend effects are applied to paths using commands in the Path Properties button, which opens a pop-out menu while the Interactive Blend Tool and an existing blend are selected.

Path Properties Button

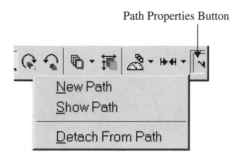

To apply an existing Blend effect to a path, follow these steps:

1. With a Blend effect already created on your document page, and an open or closed path nearby, choose the Interactive Blend Tool from the main Toolbox and click the Blend Group portion of your effect to select it.

2. Using Property Bar options, click the Path Properties button and choose New Path. Notice your cursor changes to a targeting cursor.

3. Click the open or closed path object you want to have your Blend effect follow. The result is immediate and your Blend effect now follows the path of the object targeted. Notice also that the blend has changed position to align with the path exactly where it's positioned. Figure 15-9 shows a simple Blend effect applied to a path.

While a Blend effect is applied to a path, you may also make use of a few other commands as nifty conveniences. Choosing New Path while a Blend effect is already applied to a path enables you to assign a new and different object as the blend path. To remove your Blend effect from the path, use the Detach From Path command. If the Blend effect you applied to the path includes so many steps that the path layered below it is hidden—or if the path itself is not visible because it has no outline color applied—the Show Path command enables you to select and highlight the path object for editing.

15

> **TIP** *If you want the open or closed path object to which you apply your Blend effect not to appear in the final effect, set its fill and outline colors to None. This enables you to edit the path at any time without the need to deconstruct the effect or delete the original path object to hide it from view.*

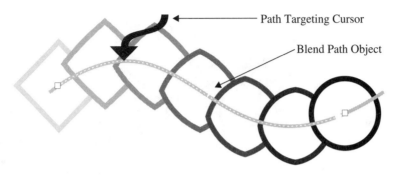

Path Targeting Cursor

Blend Path Object

| **FIGURE 15-9** | These two objects were set to follow this open Bézier path using the New Path command. |

Rotating Blend Objects

By default, whenever objects are set to follow a path, they do so using their original unaltered orientation. For example, a blend involving vertical lines when blended to a path results in the centers of objects aligning with the path, but their orientation will be vertical. In certain instances, you may need your Blend Group objects actually to *align* with the orientation of the path itself to create a realistic effect of the objects influenced by the path direction.

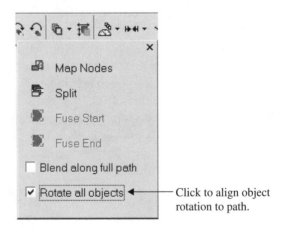

Click to align object rotation to path.

In these cases, choose the Rotate All Objects option available in the Miscellaneous Blend Options button pop-up menu in the Property Bar while a Blend effect is selected to follow a path. Doing this applies rotation values to each of the objects in your Blend Group to align with the direction of the path (see Figure 15-10).

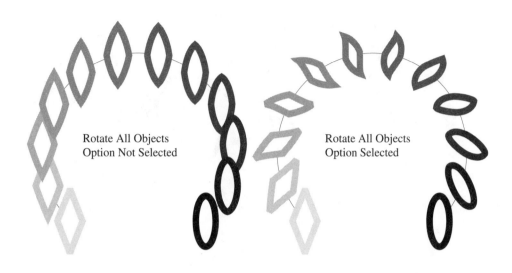

Rotate All Objects
Option Not Selected

Rotate All Objects
Option Selected

FIGURE 15-10   These two path Blend effects are identical while one uses the
Rotate All Objects option.

Blend Along Full Path

If the path to which you applied your Blend effect is the right size and length to
cover your Blend effect completely, you may automatically have the Blend Group
and control objects cover the entire path by choosing the Blend Along Full Path
option in the Miscellaneous Blend options pop-up menu. When this option is
selected, the center origins of the control objects in your Blend effect align with
the first and last nodes of the Blend path object. Figure 15-11 shows the effects
of using this option while a blend is applied to an open path.

Controlling Blend Object Path Alignment

As mentioned previously, when a Blend effect is applied to a path, the default
point at which all objects align with the path is determined by their center origin.
The *center origin* is the point at which all objects are rotated during any rotation
transformation. For the most part, controlling how a blend aligns to a path is one
of those hidden features you won't find in any dialog or Property Bar option.
Instead, the center origin must be moved manually using object rotation and skew
handles. By moving the center origin of the control objects of a Blend effect, you
may manipulate how control objects—and the blends they control—align with the
path to which the Blend effect is applied.

15

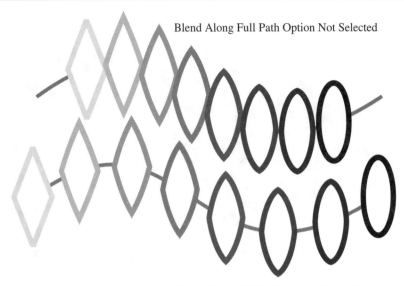

Blend Along Full Path Option Not Selected

Blend Along Full Path Option Selected

FIGURE 15-11   These two Blend effects are identical with one applied using the
Blend Along Full Path option.

For example, Figure 15-12 shows two objects blended and applied to a path.
In the default condition, the blend centers all objects on the default object center.
If you reposition the center origin of a control object, however, the Blend effect
offsets how the control object is aligned with the path, in turn affecting how the
Blend Group aligns with the path. To move an object's center origin, select the
object with the Pick Tool and drag the center origin marker to move it. Once the
center origin is moved, the Blend effect is updated immediately.

Managing Multi-Object Blends

Blending between multiple objects is a relatively simple operation made easier
by implementation of the Interactive Blend Tool several versions back. Using this
tool, you need only to click-drag between different objects on your document
page. Each time you do so, a new Blend effect is created between the objects. The
dynamic link is maintained between all objects in a multi-object blend, meaning
you may edit the properties of control objects or reposition them anywhere on your
screen and the linked Blend effects are instantly updated. Figure 15-13 shows two
Blend effects applied to three different objects with the blend sequence varied.
At the left, a rectangle was blended to a star and then to an ellipse; on the right,
a rectangle-ellipse-star blend was created using the same objects.

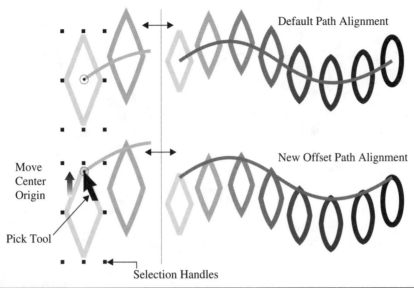

The center origin of these control objects was offset to control how the Blend objects align with the applied path.

When a multi-object blend is applied, each Blend Group is considered an individual Blend effect, meaning each has its own control objects with defined Start and End Blend objects. If you want, you may change the start and end objects at any time using the Start and End Properties pop-out menu commands available in the Property Bar while a blend is selected. This is where the Start and End objects of your Blend effect play a key role.

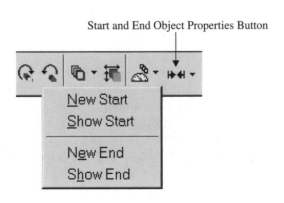

15

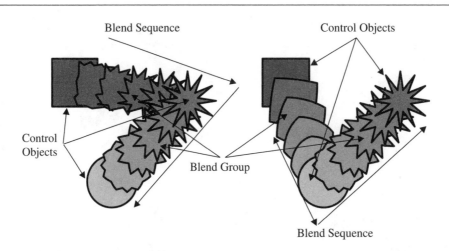

Blend Sequence   Control Objects

Control
Objects

Blend Group

Blend Sequence

FIGURE 15-13   These three objects were blended using different sequences.

If you're unsure which of your objects is the Start or End object, choose the Show Start or Show End commands from this menu to have the corresponding object automatically highlighted and selected. Choosing New Start from this menu causes your cursor to become a targeting cursor, which enables you to unlink the Blend effect from one object and to target another. Doing so creates a new effect each time a different object is targeted. Choosing New End operates the same way.

TIP   *When working with multi-object blends, clicking any Blend Group in the entire effect selects all control objects and all Blend Groups. To select a specific Blend Group, hold CTRL while clicking a Blend Group. Blend effect properties across multiple objects may only be edited individually and only while selected.*

After a Blend is complete, you may need to take the effect apart for other purposes and break the link between the control objects, the Blend objects, a Blend path, or all objects involved. Dismantling is a quick operation, but once it's done, the effect cannot be reassembled without re-creating the effect from scratch or by applying a saved Blend Preset. To dismantle a Blend effect and convert all control, path, and Blend Group objects to their original state as ordinary objects, right-click the Blend effect and choose Break Blend Apart from the pop-up menu. The control objects then become separate objects while the Blend portion of the effect remains a group. To dismantle the effect completely, select only the Blend Group using the Pick Tool and choose Ungroup (CTRL+U) from the Arrange menu.

Copying and Cloning Blends

As is the case with other effects available in CorelDRAW, you may copy or clone from existing Blend effects in your document. Neither command requires you to have the Interactive Blend Tool selected to do so, and both operations are accomplished by using command menus.

Copying Blends

When you copy a Blend effect, at least one Blend effect must be in view and at least two objects must be selected on your screen. To copy a Blend effect, choose Effects | Copy Effect | Blend From. Your active cursor then immediately becomes a targeting cursor. Use this cursor to target the Blend portion of an existing Blend effect to copy all Blend properties. This command is also accomplished while using the Interactive Blend Tool by clicking the Copy Blend Properties button.

Cloning Blends

Cloning a Blend effect achieves a slightly different result. When an effect is applied through cloning, the master clone effect object controls the new effect. Any changes made to the master are immediately applied to the clone, hence, the term. Any changes made to the clone properties essentially override the properties applied by the master, with any unchanged effect properties maintaining a perpetual link to the master clone effect. To clone a Blend effect, you must have created at least one other Blend effect and have this in view. You must also have at least two objects selected on your screen.

To clone a Blend effect, choose Effects | Clone Effect | Blend From. Your cursor then immediately becomes a targeting cursor. Use this cursor to target the existing Blend effect you want to clone by clicking directly on the Blend Group portion of the effect.

15

Using the Blend Docker

Up to this point, you've seen all the various aspects of creating blends and their associated options using the Interactive Blend Tool and Property Bar options, which is the most efficient way to apply Blend effects. Before the interactive tool existed, all Blend effects were applied using the Blend Docker. If you're a long-time CorelDRAW user, you may have grown accustomed to applying Blend effects using this docker, although it's now redundant with the Interactive Blend Tool. CorelDRAW version 9 users may have been surprised to discover the Blend Docker was virtually unavailable and inaccessible while using CorelDRAW 9's default workspace. Users were required to load the CorelDRAW 8 workspace to access it.

Thankfully, access to the Blend Docker has been made available in CorelDRAW 10's command menus, so you needn't dig up an older workspace to open it. To open the old Blend Docker, choose Effects | Blend or choose Window | Dockers | Blend. The Blend option in this docker are organized into four tabbed docker pages comprised of Steps, Acceleration, Color, and Miscellaneous Options Blend (see Figure 15-14). Although options in this docker are organized a little differently, the same properties may be applied as when using the Interactive Blend Tool. The Blend Docker, however, enables you to choose many Blend options before manually applying them by using the Apply button.

Understanding Contour Effects

CorelDRAW 10's Contour effect is slightly less complex than the Blend effect, but it's just as effective when it comes to illustration techniques. Contour effects may be used for an enormous number of purposes. They enable you to create perfect outlines of open or closed paths, letting you create a single Contour object, or hundreds of them—all in an instant. The results of a Contour effect are much the same as when viewing a topographical map, where indicator lines are drawn to join physical areas of equal elevation. This effect enables you to create evenly spaced lines, however, with large or minuscule spacing.

When a Contour effect is applied to an object, dynamically linked shapes are created. The shapes themselves are created concentrically aligned with the center origin of the selected object based on its outline shape. Contours may be created outside or within an object to a specific collection of contouring properties. Behind the scenes, CorelDRAW 10 performs mathematical calculations for each contour step in the effect. It applies progressive outline and fill colors based on the original object's properties and those chosen to apply to the contours.

While a Contour effect is linked to an object, the object itself becomes a control object, and the objects created by the effect become a Contour Group. Any changes made to the properties of the original are immediately reflected in the linked Contour Group; and while the Contour Group is selected, properties of the effect may be edited at any time—without having to begin the effect from scratch.

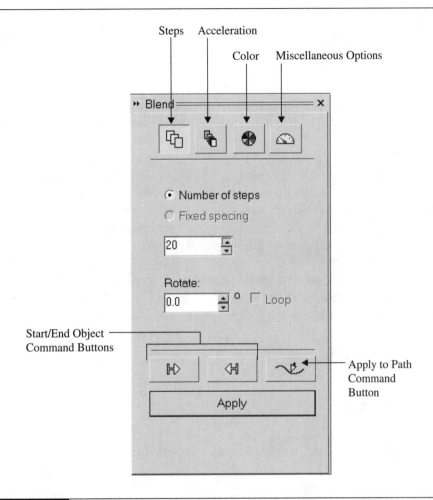

Steps   Acceleration

Color   Miscellaneous Options

Start/End Object
Command Buttons

Apply to Path
Command
Button

FIGURE 15-14   The Blend Docker (formerly the Blend rollup) makes its return to the CorelDRAW 10 workspace.

15

Exploring Draw's Contour Effect

Before diving into all the bells and whistles available while applying a Contour effect, let's explore a few examples of what this effect enables you to do. In illustration, one of the most practical uses for Contour effects is to simulate depth, similar to Draw's Blend effect. The advantage here is you needn't create a second object, as long as you want your final effect to be created.

Figure 15-15 shows two versions of a map graphic. One version of the map uses simple uniform color to differentiate and highlight specific geographic areas, while the other uses Contour effects (as well as a few other embellishments) to create a more graphically compelling sense of depth to the same graphic. In this example, the control objects still use uniform color, but the Contour effect uses a slightly different color with the spacing between the objects set so small it creates a smooth color transition between the original object and the final Contour object of the effect.

Figure 15-16 shows a text effect created using a Contour effect. In this case, the characters were converted to curves before a Contour effect was applied to the inside of the shapes. The original character shapes serve as the control objects and are filled with linear Fountain fills from black to white using the Interactive Fill Tool at an angle of roughly 30 degrees. Each step in the applied Contour effect also uses the same linear Fountain fill, which has the effect of creating an interesting sense of depth and lighting on the character shapes. Similar to the map example, the step spacing has been set so small, the individual steps are virtually invisible, creating a smooth transition of color between the control and Contour objects. A shadow was added to emphasize the sense of depth, using the Interactive Drop Shadow Tool.

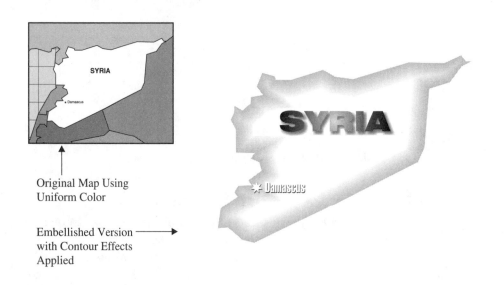

Original Map Using
Uniform Color

Embellished Version ⟶
with Contour Effects
Applied

FIGURE 15-15   The graphic appeal of this map was vastly improved by using
Contour effects.

FIGURE 15-16   The soft depth effect on this text was created using a Contour effect and linear Fountain fills.

In a slight variation from the previous example, Figure 15-17 shows another text effect, while the original character shapes were filled using a custom radial Fountain fill created by using the Interactive Fill Tool. The Contour effect applied also uses the same fill type, with a small step value applied to the inside of the shapes. A white shadow was applied to the final effect using the Interactive Drop Shadow to create the glow effect around the characters.

FIGURE 15-17   The hard-edged bevel shape on these text characters was created using a Contour effect and custom, radial Fountain fills.

15

Using the Interactive Contour Tool and Property Bar

The quickest method to use when applying Contour effects is through the use of the Interactive Contour Tool in combination with the Property Bar. The Interactive Contour Tool is located in the main Toolbox, grouped together with other interactive tools for Blend, Drop Shadows, Envelope, Distortion, Extrude, and Transparency.

Interactive Contour Tool

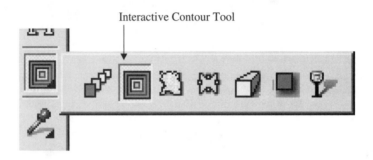

When any effect is applied to an object, the object itself becomes the control object for the effect. Any property changes made to the control object affect the linked effect. But, the control object always retains its original properties, regardless of which effect is applied. For example, a rectangle remains a rectangle and its corners may still be rounded. A star polygon may still have its number of sides/points changed and its shape may still be edited using the Shape Tool. Ellipses may still be converted to pies or arcs, and so on.

While the Interactive Contour Tool is selected and an object is selected, the Property Bar displays all options associated with applying Contour effects. Options controlling Contours include Contour preset options; Contour Direction; steps and offset spacing; color rotation; outline and fill color; and a collection of effect conveniences, such as copying and clearing applied Contour effects.

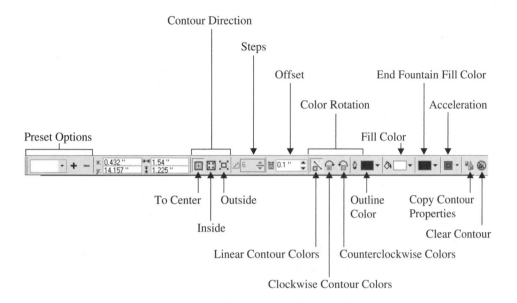

Contour Direction
Steps
Offset
Color Rotation
End Fountain Fill Color
Acceleration
Preset Options
Fill Color
To Center   Outside
Inside
Outline Color
Copy Contour Properties
Clear Contour
Linear Contour Colors
Counterclockwise Colors
Clockwise Contour Colors

Applying a Contour Effect

If you've arrived here looking for a quick way to apply a typical Contour effect to an object in your drawing, you're probably eager to start Contouring right away. First, let's create a typical contour and examine the results. To apply a typical Contour effect, follow these steps:

1. If you haven't already done so, create and select the object to which you want to apply the Contour effect. Apply any fill or outline properties before moving on.

2. Choose the Interactive Contour Tool from the main Toolbox. Notice your cursor changes condition and the Property Bar features a selection of Contour options.

15

3. Using the Interactive Contour Tool cursor and a click-drag action, click your object and drag in the direction to which you want the contour to be applied. Dragging from the inside to the outside creates an Outside Contour effect, while dragging in the opposite direction creates an inside Contour effect. The angle of the drag action has no effect on the contours themselves–only the direction relative to the center origin of your object. Notice as you drag, an outline preview of the final object in the effect appears.

4. Release your mouse button to have CorelDRAW perform the calculations for your contours. Your effect is complete.

You just created a typical Contour effect, but adjusting the effect to suit your current needs may require a little more work. Notice once your mouse button is released, a series of new objects appears outside or inside your object's outline path, and the Property Bar Contour Direction option displays your Contour Direction. The object applied with the Contour effect is also surrounded by a series of interactive markers. The next section identifies these markers and explains their purposes and how to manipulate them.

> **TIP** *To remove a Contour effect completely from your object, click the Contour portion of the effect using either the Interactive Contour Tool or Pick Tool to select it and choose Effects | Clear Contour. The effect is immediately removed and your object is returned to its usual state.*

Editing Contours Interactively

Once a Contour effect has been applied, you may alter or edit it any time you want using the Interactive Contour Tool in combination with interactive markers and/or Property Bar options. While the tool is selected and an applied contour is in progress, a collection of interactive markers surround the control object. Many of these markers enable you to adjust the properties of your Contour effect interactively using click-drag actions without the use of the Property Bar.

These markers may be used to adjust the direction, spacing, and Offset values of the effect. The black diamond-shaped marker indicates which object is the control object of the effect. A white rectangle indicates the last object in the Contour Group, and its position sets the distance between the control object and the last object in the effect. A slider between these two enables you to adjust the spacing between the Contour steps interactively, which, in turn, sets the number of steps by dividing the difference. Figure 15-18 shows the basic anatomy of a Contour effect and identifies the interactive markers used to manipulate it.

TIP *Different types of objects are eligible for Contour effects in CorelDRAW 10. If you require, you may apply Contour effects to closed-path, compound-path, or grouped objects. Applying Contour effects to a group of objects applies the effect to all objects in the group. An object applied with the Contour effect is not eligible for other effects (such as Extrude, Drop Shadow, and Blend) unless it's first grouped with its linked Contour effect object.*

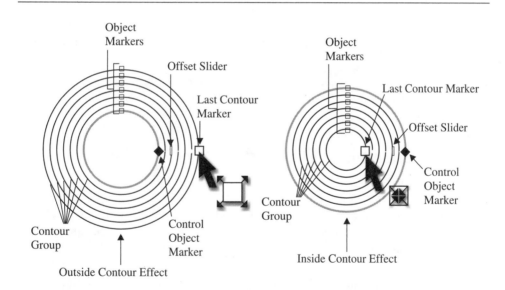

FIGURE 15-18 These two circular ellipses have identical Contour effects applied in opposite directions. Notice the interactive markers that surround the objects.

15

Also notice, while using the Interactive Contour Tool, the cursor state changes, depending on certain conditions. Different cursors appear when dragging outside, inside, or to the centermost point of your selected object. While held over specific objects, the cursor also indicates whether an object is eligible for a Contour effect.

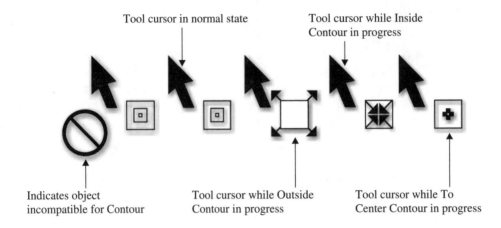

Tool cursor in normal state

Tool cursor while Inside Contour in progress

Indicates object incompatible for Contour

Tool cursor while Outside Contour in progress

Tool cursor while To Center Contour in progress

> **TIP**   *To enter an editing state immediately when a Contour effect has been applied to an object, double-click the effect portion of the Contour effect using the Pick Tool.*

Choosing Contour Direction

In addition to click-dragging your Contour effect to set the direction, you may also use Property Bar options to change direction instantly—a method that may be much faster than click-dragging because no interactive preview outline is required. Choosing from To Center, Inside, or Outside causes the contours to be applied in the corresponding direction in relation to your object's outline path. While Inside or Outside are selected, you may set the number of steps or offset spacing between the steps by entering values in the Steps or Offset boxes in the Property Bar, followed by pressing the ENTER key.

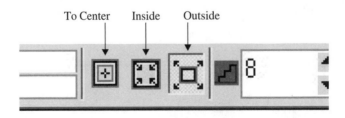

To Center   Inside   Outside

> **TIP**
>
> *If needed, you may detach the Contour Group created and break the dynamic link to your original object by right-clicking directly on the effect portion and choosing Break Contour Group Apart from the pop-up menu. Once a control object has been separated from its linked effect, the control object becomes an ordinary object and the effect portion becomes an ordinary group of objects.*

Contour Direction, Contour spacing, and the Offset value are interconnected, meaning the direction and Step or Offset values often affect one another. In the examples to follow, the figures indicate control objects using slightly larger outline-width values. During an actual Contour effect, outline-width values remain constant across all objects in the effect.

Contour Inside

Choosing Inside as the Contour Direction causes the objects created by the Contour effect to be within the outline path of your object. When applying an Inside Contour effect to an object, if the Offset spacing value entered in the Offset box in the Property Bar exceeds the number of steps the distance allows, the Step value automatically is reduced to fit. Figure 15-19 shows typical results of applying inside contours to different objects. Notice in these examples that open paths are not eligible for Inside Contour effects.

Contour Outside

Choosing Contour Outside has the opposite effect of choosing Contour Inside. It creates the new contours outside your object's outline path. The number of steps may be set to a maximum value of 999, while the Offset values applied may be set within a range between 0.001 and 300 inches. Figure 15-20 shows a typical Contour effect applied using the Outside option. Notice open paths are eligible for Outside Contour effects.

15

Contour To Center

Using To Center as the Contour Direction enables you to create contours to fill your object completely between its outline path and its center origin. While To Center is selected, the Offset value is the only variable you may set because the number of steps are calculated automatically. Figure 15-21 shows typical Contour effects applied using the To Center option. Notice open paths are not eligible to use this option.

FIGURE 15-19 These different objects have been applied with an identical Contour effect using the Inside option, a Step value of 4, and an Offset value of 0.05 inches.

Setting Contour Colors

In addition to controlling the actual contour shapes, controlling the progression of color between your original object and the colors of the Contour effect is perhaps the most important aspect of achieving a successful effect. You can control color in several ways, some of which you use constantly with this effect, and others you probably won't ever need. During the progression of a Contour effect, you may specify a nonlinear color rotation, control Pen and Fill colors for basic color schemes, or control Fountain fill colors for complex applications.

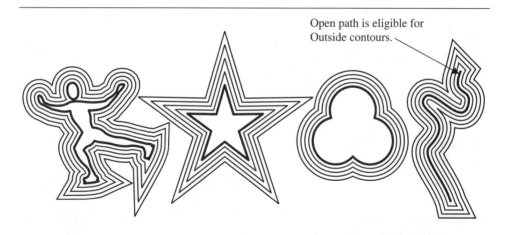

Open path is eligible for
Outside contours.

FIGURE 15-20 The same objects in this case each feature identical Outside Contour effects using a Step value of 4 and an Offset value of 0.05 inches.

FIGURE 15-21   The To Center option creates contours to the exact center, while the number of steps is calculated automatically and determined by the Offset value and your object's width and height.

Color Rotation Options

As with Blend effect color options in CorelDRAW 10, a typical Contour effect blends the colors of fills and outlines in a steady progression between your original object and the last Contour object in the effect. This is the default condition for all Contour effects. For special color effects, you may choose to rotate the progression of outline and fill. To do so, choose either Clockwise or Counterclockwise Color, which has the effect of applying fill and outline colors based on color positions located around the standard color wheel.

Linear   Clockwise   Counterclockwise

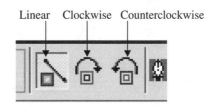

Pen Color

The Pen color option actually controls the outline colors of your Contour effect, causing the colors to progress steadily between your original object and the last Contour object in the effect. By default, if your object doesn't have an outline color applied, this option still displays Black as the default color, but no color will be applied to your contours. To set the outline color, click the Pen color selector and choose a color. Color changes are applied immediately.

Pen Color   Fill Color

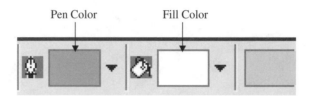

Fill Color

Setting the Fill color has the most dramatic effect on the appearance of your Contour colors. By default, if your object doesn't have a Fill color applied, this option still displays Black as the default color, but no Fill color will be applied to your contours. To set the fill color, click the Fill color selector and choose a color. Color changes are applied immediately.

Smooth Contour Effects

One of the most sought-after techniques when applying contours to an object is to achieve a smooth transition between your original object's color and the Contour colors. Achieving a smooth progression of color for your Contour effect requires a few steps to be taken to "hide" the individual contour steps. Begin by assigning an Offset value small enough to hide the steps. The smallest value available is 0.001 inches. You may enter this value directly in the Offset box in the Property Bar while a Contour effect is in progress, or use the spinner controls available to decrease the value gradually.

The second step is to eliminate any outline colors. Select your original object using the Pick Tool and set the Outline Pen color to None. To do this while your object is selected, right-click the None color well. The result is a smooth progression of color based on the Contour Direction you selected.

The example in the following illustration shows objects applied with no outline color and an Offset value of 0.001 inches. The original objects are filled with Black and the Contour Fill color has been set to White using Property Bar options. The objects feature a Contour effect direction of To Center, with a smooth transition of color. The individual Contour steps are virtually invisible.

Fountain Fill Color

As you may have noticed in the contour examples at the beginning of this section, Contour effects support the use of special fill types, such as Fountain fills. While a Fountain fill is applied to your original object, the color fill properties of the Contour Group are also applied with the same fill type by default. In these instances, the Property Bar enables you to set the last color in the Contour Fountain fill. If your object doesn't include a Fountain fill, this color selector remains unavailable.

Contour effects may be copied or cloned to other objects. To perform either operation, the effect you want to copy or clone must be in view on your screen the same time as the object to which you want to copy or clone the effect. To copy an existing Contour effect to your selected object while using the Interactive Contour Tool, click the Copy Contour button in the Property Bar and use the targeting cursor to click an existing Contour effect. While using the Pick Tool, choose Effects | Copy Effect | Contour From, and use the same targeting operation. To clone a Contour effect to a selected object, use the Pick Tool and choose Effects | Clone Effect | Contour From, and target the existing effect.

15

Controlling Contour Acceleration

Contour Acceleration options are a new feature of CorelDRAW 10. They have the effect of either increasing or decreasing the rate at which your Contour Group objects change shape as they progress between the control object and the final object in the Contour effect. You can choose from two different aspects of acceleration: Object Acceleration and Color Acceleration. While a default Contour effect is applied, both these settings are set to neutral, meaning the Contour Group objects change in color and size evenly between the two control objects. If you want, you may alter these two Acceleration rates simultaneously (the default) while the two options are linked, or individually by clicking the Unlink Acceleration option.

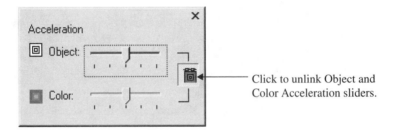

Click to unlink Object and Color Acceleration sliders.

To change acceleration while a Contour effect is applied, click the Object and Color Acceleration button in the Property Bar to access a pop-out menu and adjust the corresponding slider controls. The Unlink Accelerations button in also located in this pop-out menu. Moving either slider to the left of the center position reduces (or slows) the acceleration rate between the control object and the final contour in the effect. Moving either slider to the right increases the acceleration of your Contour Group objects between the control object and the final contour in the effect. While the two Acceleration options are unlinked, changing the Object Acceleration affects only the progression of shapes in the Contour Group. Figure 15-22 shows the effects of increasing and decreasing the Object Acceleration of a typical Contour effect.

While the Object Acceleration sliders are unlinked, changing the Color Acceleration affects only the change in progression of the fill and outline colors between the control object and the final contour in the effect, leaving the change in object shape unchanged. Moving the sliders (or interactive markers) left or right increases or decreases acceleration between the control object and the final contour in the effect. Changing the Color Acceleration also affects the width properties applied to outline paths of objects. Figure 15-23 shows the results of changing the Object Acceleration rates while unlinked from the Object Acceleration values. Notice that the rate at which the Contour Group objects are shaped remains constant.

Object Acceleration increased,
slider moved right of center

Object Acceleration decreased,
slider moved left of center

FIGURE 15-22   The Object Acceleration of the Contour effect between these two
objects has been unlinked to demonstrate increased or decreased
Object Acceleration.

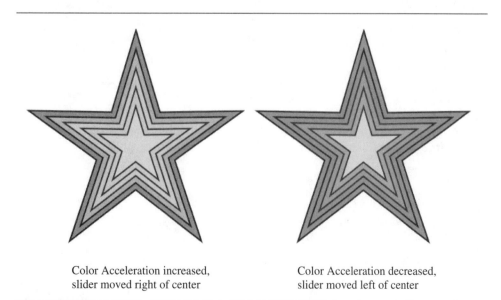

Color Acceleration increased,
slider moved right of center

Color Acceleration decreased,
slider moved left of center

FIGURE 15-23   This object's Contour effect Acceleration rates have been unlinked to
demonstrate of increased or decreased Color Acceleration.

15

Using Contour Presets

Up to this point, you've learned about the effects of changing Contour Direction, steps, offsets, color rotation, and Pen and Fill colors of applied Contour effects. These values constitute the basic properties that apply to virtually any Contour effect. Next, you learn about saving these Contour properties as presets to apply to other existing Contours using Property Bar options.

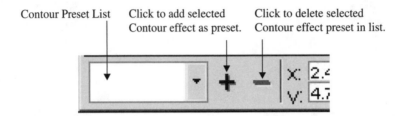

Contour Preset List   Click to add selected   Click to delete selected
Contour effect as preset.   Contour effect preset in list.

Contour Presets are used in the same manner as other preset controls associated with other interactive effects, such as Envelopes, Drop Shadows, Distortion, Blend, Extrude, and Transparency. Contour Presets may be saved and reapplied to a selected object in your document. To apply a saved Contour Preset to selected objects and explore adding or deleting Contour Presets, follow these quick steps:

1. If you haven't already done so, create and select an object on your document page using the Pick Tool.

2. Choose the Interactive Contour Tool from the main Toolbox.

3. Using Property Bar options, choose a saved Contour effect from the Preset List. The properties of the Contour are immediately applied and its current effect properties are displayed in the Property Bar.

4. To save an existing Contour effect as a preset while using the Interactive Contour Tool and Property Bar, click to select the Contour portion of the effect and click the Add Preset (+) button. The Save As dialog opens. Enter a new name for your new Contour preset in the File Name box and click Save. Your Contour preset is added to the Preset List.

5. To delete a saved Contour Preset, choose the preset from the Preset List selector to select it and click the Delete Preset button (–) in the Property Bar. The saved preset is immediately deleted.

TIP   *By default, saved Contour Presets are stored in the Program Files/Corel/Graphics 10/Draw/Presets/Contour folder using typical default installation directory names.*

Using the Contour Docker

So far, you've learned about creating Contours using the Interactive Contour Tool in combination with Property Bar options. Although this is perhaps the most efficient way of applying Contour effects, you may be more accustomed to applying these effects using the old Contour Docker (redundant with the Interactive Contour Tool).

To open the Contour Docker, choose Effects | Contour, or choose Window | Dockers | Contour (CTRL+F9). Contour options in this docker are organized into three separate docker pages accessed by clicking buttons for Steps, Color, and Acceleration (see Figure 15-24). Options in this docker are organized a little differently than in the Property Bar, but the same properties may be applied— although the Contour Docker enables you to choose all Contour options before you manually apply them using the Apply button.

15

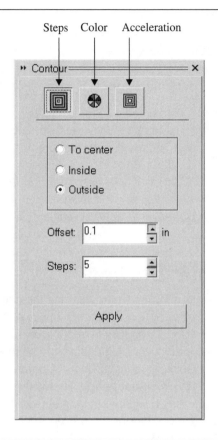

FIGURE 15-24 If you're unaccustomed to using interactive tools or if you prefer to apply your Contour effects manually, you may still do so using the Contour Docker.

CHAPTER 16

Applying Lens and Transparency Effects

If the distorted reality seen in *Alice in Wonderland* holds appeal for you, then CorelDRAW's Lens effects should be of interest. Lens effects enable you to create weird and wonderful abstractions of your drawing objects in practical ways that are useful whether your purpose is creative or technical. If you've never had the opportunity to apply these effects before, you're in for a treat. If you're already familiar with their use, you may discover a few valuable tips here to use certain lenses for illustration or distortion purposes.

Understanding Lens Effects

Lens effects may be applied to virtually any type of vector object in CorelDRAW 10, which opens both creative and design avenues, as well as enabling you to solve technical illustration challenges. Unfortunately, many new or unfamiliar users often abandon the use of Lens effects strategies due to a lack of understanding. To clarify their operation a little, imagine for a moment that this type of effect is like looking through a window or porthole. The view seen through the opening may be controlled by varying the properties of the glass. For example, a tinted window is essentially a Lens effect where the colored glass itself alters the color of objects seen though it. But also keep in mind that the shape of the tinted glass itself also plays a part.

While using CorelDRAW 10's Lens effects, the same basic principles apply. In order to achieve a successful effect, at least two overlapping objects must be involved—one arranged in front to represent the window or porthole, and the other arranged behind it to comprise the window view. While applied with a Lens effect, the object in front changes the appearance of the object (or portions of the object) seen through it. Lens effects may apply color, magnification, or distortion to the underlying objects to varying degrees, and only where the two objects overlap does the effect take place. Any color fill properties already applied to the new lens object are essentially discarded.

Using the Lens Docker

Unlike other effects that employ use of interactive tools and Property Bar options, the only way to apply a Lens effect in CorelDRAW is through use of the Lens Docker, opened by choosing Effects | Lens or using the ALT+F3 shortcut. The Lens Docker (see Figure 16-1) is relatively straightforward to use, featuring a drop-down menu to select lens type and a manual Apply button to apply your chosen lens properties to a selected object, which in turn causes underlying objects to appear differently.

While an object is selected in your document, the Lens Docker preview window displays a representation of the selected lens effect, while other options specific

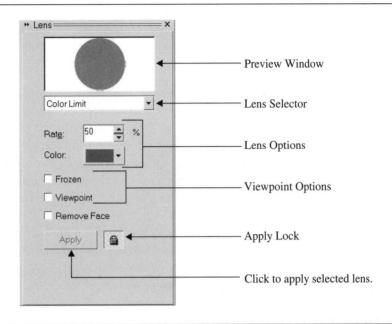

Preview Window

Lens Selector

Lens Options

Viewpoint Options

Apply Lock

Click to apply selected lens.

FIGURE 16-1   Lens effects are applied only using the Lens Docker—there aren't any other tools to apply these effects.

to the lens appear beneath it. Keep in mind that the effect appears only when two objects have been arranged to overlap. You may apply virtually any Lens effect using these quick steps:

1. If you haven't already done so, arrange your objects to overlap and apply any desired fill or outline colors to both objects. Using the Pick Tool, click the object arranged in front and open the Lens Docker (ALT+F3).

2. In the Lens Docker window, choose a Lens effect from the drop-down list. Notice the preview window displays a representation of your object with a generic representation of the selected lens. Below the drop-down menu, you may also notice certain options specific to the selected lens.

3. Choose any variable options you wish or accept the default values and click the Apply button in the docker. Notice the appearance of your underlying object changes to reflect the type of lens applied where the two objects overlap.

4. If you wish to alter the view seen through the lens, choose different option settings and click the Apply button to manually update the changes.

> **TIP**   *CorelDRAW 10 now includes an Apply Lock button in the Lens Docker. While this option is selected (the depressed button state), any lens type or option changes made in the Lens Docker window are applied immediately to the selected object.*

Exploring Lens Effects

Over the years, the collection of lenses included with CorelDRAW has remained largely unchanged. In total, there are 11 different lens types to choose from. Each lens features its own set of options, which may be changed to create variations on each effect depending on your needs. The following section defines each of these lenses and features examples of the applied effects using typical options. For a closer examination of these effects, open the specified CorelDRAW file, included on the companion CD-ROM, in the directory folder CorelDRAW 10: The Official Guide/Tutorial/Chapter 16. Since many of the effects seen here control color, certain of these examples appear in the color section of this book as indicated by references similar to this: see *topic* in the color section and open the file Tutorial/Chapter 16/Color *filename*.

In each example to follow, a graphic illustration of an old-fashioned looking glass demonstrates the effects. While the looking glass itself is an illustration composed of grouped objects, only the actual ellipse representing the bezel holding the lens has been applied with Lens effects. In each case, the lens type and specific options have been varied to demonstrate typical results as they affect a vector graphic drawing example.

> **TIP**   *While applying a Lens effect and choosing lens options, you may update the effect each time options are changed by clicking the Apply Lock button in the Lens Docker. Doing so causes the new properties to immediately be applied to your selected lens object.*

Brighten Lens

While the name may at first appear simple, the Brighten lens has powerful capabilities. Colors applied to objects viewed through the Brighten lens may appear either brighter or darker, depending on the Brighten Rate percent value selected. The Brighten Rate value may be set within a range between 100 and −100. Choosing positive values causes the colors of underlying objects to brighten, while choosing negative values causes them to darken, as shown in Figure 16-2. A Brighten Rate

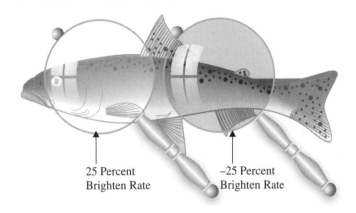

25 Percent
Brighten Rate

−25 Percent
Brighten Rate

FIGURE 16-2   The lens of our looking glass has been applied with a Brighten Lens effect.

value of 25 percent, which brightens the underlying objects, has been applied to the left example; while a Brighten Rate value of –25 (a negative value), which affects all colors seen through the lens, has been applied to the right. (See Brighten Lens Effect in the color section of this book and open the file Tutorial/Chapter 16/brighten.cdr.)

Color Add Lens

Colors seen through objects applied with the Color Add Lens effect are achieved by adding a selected color by a specified value. The color you select to add may be virtually any of the colors available in CorelDRAW 10 using the color selector, while the rate at which the color is added may be set within a range between 0 and 100 percent in increments of 5 percent. Higher values add more color, while 0 adds no color at all. Figure 16-3 shows examples in which instances of our looking glass have been applied with two different colors using the same Rate value. In this illustration, the left example adds red, while the right example adds Cyan to the underlying objects using the Color Add Lens. In both instances, the Rate value has been set to 80 percent (see Color Add in the color section of this book and open the file Tutorial/Chapter 16/Color add.cdr).

Color Limit Lens

Although you may have already guessed it, the Color Limit Lens effect has the opposite effect of Color Add, instead removing a specified color at a specified

16

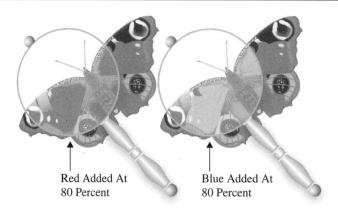

Red Added At
80 Percent

Blue Added At
80 Percent

FIGURE 16-3   In these instances of our looking glass, a Color Add Lens effect is applied.

rate. As with Color Add, the color you are limiting is selected using the color
selector and may be any of those available in CorelDRAW 10. The rate at which
colors may be limited is set within a range between 0 and 100 percent. A setting
of 100 decreases the color to black, while a setting of 0 removes no color at all.
Figure 16-4 shows the results of limiting two different colors at identical rates
using the same image examples as with the Color Add Lens effect. The looking
glass on the left limits a red color at a rate of 50 percent, while the one on the

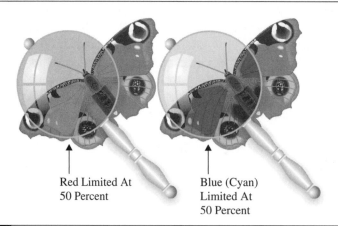

Red Limited At
50 Percent

Blue (Cyan)
Limited At
50 Percent

FIGURE 16-4   Color Limit Lens effect applied.

right limits a 100 percent cyan (blue) color by 50 percent. (See Color Limit in the color section of this book and open the file Tutorial/Chapter 16/Color limit.cdr.)

Custom Color Map Lens Effects

This next Lens effect operates on similar principles to the previous two discussed, but features more control over color mapping options. The Custom Color Map effect enables you to transform the colors seen through the lens object to fall within a specific color range. Colors may be mapped directly between two colors by choosing From and To colors using the color selectors available. Colors are then mapped between these two around the standard color wheel using either direct or rotational mapping. If you're familiar with color wheel positions, you have an advantage when it comes to anticipating the results of a specific color and palette type selection. If not, certain palette rotation options may require a little exploration. Figure 16-5 shows four examples of Custom Color Map effects using various options. (See Custom Color Map in the color section of this book and open the file Tutorial/Chapter 16/Custom Color map.cdr.)

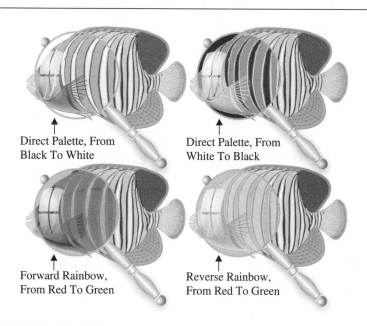

Direct Palette, From
Black To White

Direct Palette, From
White To Black

Forward Rainbow,
From Red To Green

Reverse Rainbow,
From Red To Green

FIGURE 16-5   The Custom Color Map Lens effects here use three basic palette rotation options.

16

The most puzzling aspect of the Custom Color Map lens is understanding the background calculations CorelDRAW is performing while colors are being mapped and predicting the results. Color mapping is accomplished by mapping the RGB grayscale values of your object colors to grayscale values of colors found around the standard color wheel. Mapping options consist of three palette-mapping choices.

Direct Palette   Choosing this option enables you to select two colors (From and To) and maps the colors found in your objects evenly between the grayscale values of colors found directly between these two around the standard color wheel.

Forward Rainbow   This option has the same effect as Direct Palette, but in this case, each of your object colors is mapped to all colors located around the standard color wheel in a clockwise rotation between your two chosen colors.

Reverse Rainbow   The Reverse Rainbow option has the effect of mapping the colors in your object to the RGB grayscale values of all colors found on the standard color wheel between your two chosen colors in a counterclockwise direction.

    To quickly swap your selected From and To colors in the Lens Docker while applying Custom Color Map Lens effects, click the small button labeled with the symbols < > located between the From and To Color selectors.

Fish Eye Lens Effect

The Fish Eye lens is perhaps one of the more popular Lens effects used, since it enables you to distort the appearance of underlying objects in a way similar to that of a common wide-angle camera lens. This effect offers useful applications for a wide variety of drawing uses, ranging from illustrative to technical. Fish Eye is controlled by setting the rate of distortion in an effect similar to magnification but with an added degree of concentric distortion. Rate may be set within a range between 1,000 and –1,000 percent. The effect is so dramatic at maximum settings, the object shapes seen through this lens become unrecognizable. At more subtle rates, the effect is much more tangible, as shown in Figure 16-6. The left instance features a positive value and has the effect of convex distortion, while the right instance features a negative value and renders a concave distortion (see Fish Eye in the color section of this book and open the file Tutorial/Chapter 16/Fish eye.cdr).

Fish Eye Rate
At 100 Percent

Fish Eye Rate
At −100 Percent

FIGURE 16-6   The looking glass in this example has been applied with two different
Fish Eye Lens effects.

Heat Map Lens Effect

Just as you might expect, applying the Heat Map Lens effect causes the colors
of your objects to become warmer. Underlying objects seen through it appear
roughly as though being viewed through an infrared lens. Colors in the objects
are mapped to a limited number of predetermined palette colors, comprising white,
yellow, orange, red, blue, purple, and light blue. This lens causes colors on the
warm side of the standard color wheel to appear typically as either red or orange,
and colors on the cool side to appear as white, yellow, purple, blue, or light blue.
Generally, colors found in your object are mapped to the warmer side, as shown
in Figure 16-7 (see Heat Map in the color section of this book and open the file
Tutorial/Chapter 16/Heat map.cdr).

The appearance of object colors viewed through the Heat Map lens are controlled
by entering palette rotation values in the Lens Docker. Palette rotations map the
colors of your object to the closest color in the limited color selection used by this
Lens effect. The Palette Rotation value may be set within a range between 0 and
100. Values between 0 and 49 cause colors to appear warmer, whereas values
between 50 and 100 cause colors to become cooler.

16

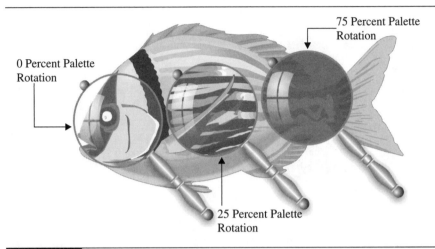

75 Percent Palette
Rotation

0 Percent Palette
Rotation

25 Percent Palette
Rotation

| FIGURE 16-7 | Applying variations of Heat Map lenses to these looking glasses increases the intensity of colors. |

Invert Lens

The Invert lens simply applies a color inversion effect to the colors of underlying objects. In this case, the original colors in your object are directly mapped to colors found on the opposite side of the standard color wheel. If you've ever examined the colors found in color negative film, you already have some idea of the results of using this lens. During color inversions, blacks change to whites, light grays turn to dark grays, reds turn to greens, yellows turn to blues, and so on, as shown in Figure 16-8 (see Invert in the color section of this book and open the file Tutorial/Chapter 16/invert.cdr).

Magnify Lens Effect

Another of the more practical and commonly used Lens effects is Magnify. This lens causes the appearance of objects layered below to be uniformly enlarged or reduced, depending on the settings entered in the single Rate option. The effect of the Magnify lens shouldn't be confused with the Fish Eye lens, with which convex and concave distortions are applied. The magnification rate may be set within a range between 0.1 and 100, where values between 1 and 100 cause increased magnification and values less than 1 cause reduced magnification. Figure 16-9 shows a typical magnification Lens effect (see Magnify Lens effect in the color section of this book and open the file Tutorial/Chapter 16/magnify.cdr).

FIGURE 16-8   The looking glass shows the color inversion effect created while the Invert Lens effect is applied.

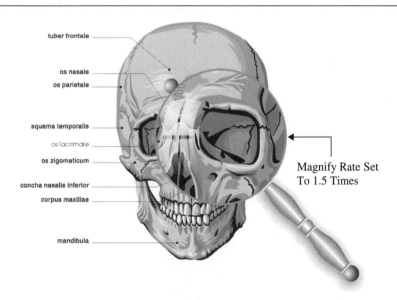

tuber frontale

os nasale
os parietale

squama temporalis
os lacrimale
os zigomaticum

concha nasalis inferior
corpus maxillae

mandibula

Magnify Rate Set
To 1.5 Times

FIGURE 16-9   A Magnify Lens effect of just 1.5 times is enough to enlarge this object without causing it to be unrecognizable.

16

Tinted Grayscale Lens Effect

The term *grayscale* is slightly misleading in the name of this particular lens effect. The Tinted Grayscale lens has the effect of converting the colors of underlying objects seen through objects applied with this effect to grayscale values, but the actual colors may be any color you choose. Simply select a color using the single color selector option available to convert the color in underlying objects to grayscale values of your chosen color plus white, as shown in Figure 16-10. In this illustration, the instance on the left uses an orange color, while the other is applied with a purple color (see Tinted Grayscale in the color section of this book and open the file Tutorial/Chapter 16/Tinted grayscale.cdr).

Transparency Lens Effect

The Transparency Lens effect is a highly simplified version of the effects that can be achieved using CorelDRAW's Interactive Transparency Tool with one slight difference. With this Lens effect applied to an object, the object itself becomes transparent to varying degrees, based on the Rate value applied. The Transparency Rate may be set within a range between 0 and 100 percent. A rate value of 0

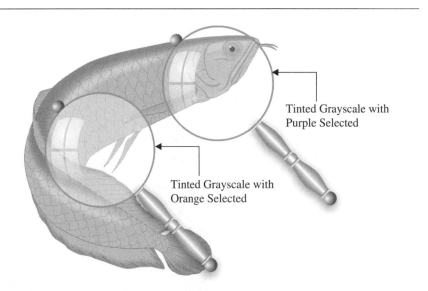

Tinted Grayscale with
Purple Selected

Tinted Grayscale with
Orange Selected

FIGURE 16-10   These two looking glasses have been applied with different colors using the Tinted Grayscale lens.

applies no transparency, leaving the object essentially opaque; while a value of 100 percent applies the full transparency, leaving the object fully transparent—meaning it becomes invisible, as shown in Figure 16-11. While a Transparency lens is applied, you may also specify a color to apply to the lens object using the color selector available. The far left instance is applied with 50 percent white, the middle instance with 50 percent black, and the far right instance with 100 percent cyan (see Transparency Lens effect in the color section of this book and open the file Tutorial/Chapter 16/transparency.cdr).

Wireframe Lens Effect

The last effect in the Lens Docker is the Wireframe lens, which has the effect of converting the color and outline properties of underlying objects to specific color selections. While selected, the Wireframe lens enables you to set the outline and fill colors of objects viewed through it to any uniform color you choose using the available color selectors, as shown in Figure 16-12. In essence, the fill and outline colors of your objects are replaced with the selected colors, while outline properties—such as applied widths and line styles—are discarded. In Figure 16-12, the left

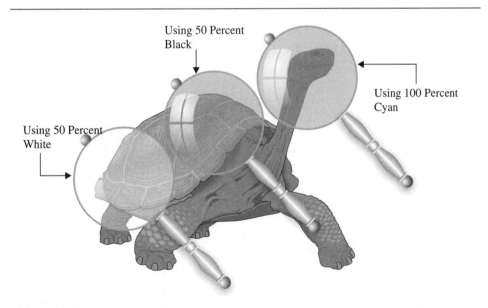

16

These three looking glasses each feature a Transparency Lens Rate value of 50 percent.

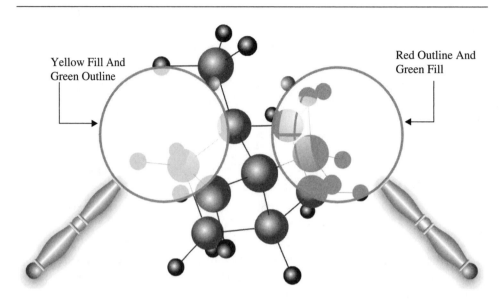

Yellow Fill And
Green Outline

Red Outline And
Green Fill

 FIGURE 16-12   These two looking glasses use the Wireframe lens effect and their fill
and outline colors are controlled using the available lens options.

instance uses a yellow fill and green outline, while the right uses a red outline and
green fill (see Wireframe Lens effect in the color section of this book and open the
file Tutorial/Chapter 16/wireframe.cdr).

> **NOTE**   *While using the Wireframe lens, the fill and outline colors of underlying
> objects are changed to your specified Wireframe Outline and Fill colors,
> wherever the lens object overlaps the underlying objects. However, the
> colors of outlines appear through the lens only where a width value and
> color have been applied already. This means that if the underlying objects
> do not have outline colors applied, the appearance of the underlying
> object outlines remain invisible.*

Using Lens Options

Up to this point, you've explored the options available while each Lens effect is
applied to an object and how they affect the appearance of underlying objects.
However, with each Lens effect selected, three key options exist and are common
to all lenses. These options provide even more control over how Lens effects are
applied by enabling you to temporarily lock the effect, alter viewpoints, or control
whether the page background is involved in the effect.

Using the Frozen Option

While the Frozen option is selected with any chosen Lens effect, the appearance of the view seen through the lens remains consistent—even if the lens object itself is moved or transformed. This capability provides the flexibility to apply and freeze the lens object view and use it for other illustration purposes. Behind the scenes, something quite interesting occurs. A Frozen Lens effect may actually be dismantled to create a new set of objects based on the Lens effect you've applied.

After the Frozen option is selected, the actual lens object may be ungrouped (CTRL+U). This action breaks the dynamic link between the lens object and the view of objects seen through it, and converts the effect to a collection of ungrouped vector objects. Each of the objects representing the complete effect becomes a separate object, including the lens object, the page background, and the objects within the Lens view. Figure 16-13 shows an example of an Artistic Text object viewed through our looking glass object with a Magnify Lens effect applied. In this illustration, the Frozen option was selected, and the resulting effect ungrouped using the Ungroup command. The Frozen option was selected and applied, and the resulting effect ungrouped to create a series of vector objects representing the complete effect.

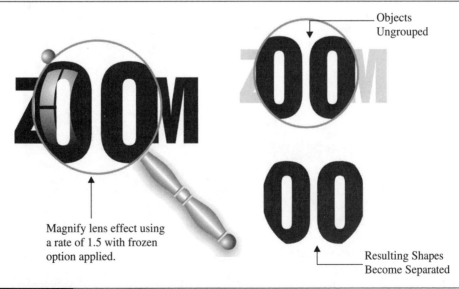

Objects
Ungrouped

Magnify lens effect using
a rate of 1.5 with frozen
option applied.

Resulting Shapes
Become Separated

16

FIGURE 16-13   This Magnify Lens effect was applied to our looking glass with Artistic Text as the underlying object.

Changing a Lens Viewpoint

This next option enables you to control the view of your Lens effect, underscoring the fact that what you are seeing through your lens objects is essentially a view of the underlying objects distorted in some way. Choosing the Viewpoint option in the Lens Docker while a lens object is selected causes a hidden Edit button to appear to the right of the Viewpoint option. Clicking the Edit option enables you to interactively click-drag to reposition the viewpoint of the Lens effect either using your cursor (indicated onscreen by an "X" marker) or by entering numeric values in the X and Y page position boxes. Figure 16-14 shows the viewpoint of a Magnify Lens effect in the process of being edited.

Lens Object With Magnify Applied

Numeric Entry Boxes For Viewpoint Page Position

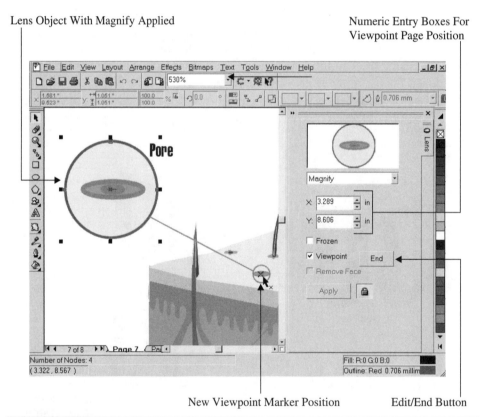

New Viewpoint Marker Position

Edit/End Button

FIGURE 16-14   The Viewpoint of this Lens effect has been repositioned to alter the view seen through the lens object.

NOTE   *The view seen through a lens object is a function of object layering, meaning all objects layered below the lens object appear in the lens. While the viewpoint is repositioned, you may find an object either does or doesn't appear visible. Arranging objects in back of the lens object causes them to participate in the effect; arranging them in front of the lens object omits them from the view.*

The default viewpoint position of a Lens effect is always the center of your object, but you may reposition the viewpoint anywhere on or off your document page. When finished positioning a viewpoint, clicking the End button and then the Apply button in the Lens Docker applies the new viewpoint position. Figure 16-15 shows a finished illustration in which lens objects illustrate callouts of a diagram with their viewpoints repositioned to enlarge specific drawing areas.

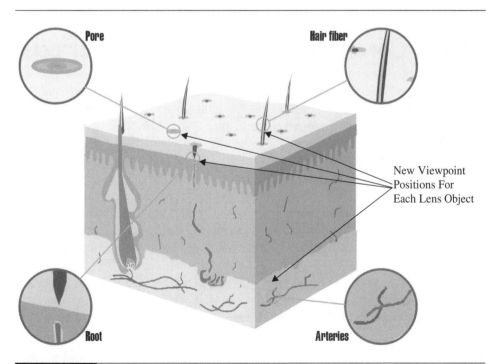

Pore   Hair fiber

New Viewpoint
Positions For
Each Lens Object

Root   Arteries

16

FIGURE 16-15   This illustration shows a typical use for edited viewpoints.

Using the Remove Face Option

The Remove Face option is available for certain types of Lens effects and enables you to control whether or not the color of your original objects participate in your Lens effect. By default, whenever a Lens effect is applied, is always involved in the effect.

However, if the lens you are using alters colors by its nature and you don't wish your original object color to be changed within the view seen through the lens object, choosing this option leaves the object color unaltered.

> **TIP** *If you've gone to the effort of formulating a specific Lens effect using the Lens Docker, you may copy the lens properties between objects without the need to define them from scratch. To do this, choose the new object you wish to copy an existing Lens effect from and choose Effects | Copy Effect | Lens From. Using the Targeting cursor that appears, click the object that has the Lens effect already applied to copy its properties. When Lens effects are copied, even altered viewpoints are copied along with the effect.*

Grasping CorelDRAW's Transparency Effects

For quite some time now, CorelDRAW users have been able to apply levels of transparency to either vector or bitmap drawing objects, whereas other mainstream graphic applications have lacked this ability. Unfortunately, this is another of those higher-level drawing tool features new users often abandon in frustration after trying to unsuccessfully apply it. Transparency requires a certain degree of understanding in order to fully understand—and capitalize on—the capabilities it provides.

Transparency is essentially a Lens effect engineered to the next higher level. Transparency effects enable you to cause a selected object to appear "see-through" to varying degrees. While an object is not transparent, it is referred to as "opaque," meaning it blocks all view of the underlying objects. When an object is at least partially transparent, you're able to see the color and details of underlying objects through it.

The ability to apply varying degrees of transparency to objects in your document enables you to elevate your drawing realism to the next higher level. Transparency enables you to mimic real-life effects. It can simulate the appearance of gases, such as smoke, fog, mist, and steam, or simulate the appearance of nearly any type of translucent liquid. Transparency effects also enable you to simulate light effects, such as light reflections or highlighting.

The degree to which an object is transparent depends on its color. The key lies in its grayscale values, which are measured and translated into varying degrees of transparency. In terms of grayscale, black colors become completely transparent while white colors remain opaque. This principle applies whether the object you are applying with transparency is filled with uniform color, or whether it features a Fountain or Pattern fill.

Using the Interactive Transparency Tool and Property Bar

Transparency effects are applied using the Interactive Transparency Tool located in the main Toolbox and grouped with other interactive tools for Distortion, Extrude, Contour, Blend, Drop Shadow, and Envelope effects; shown here:

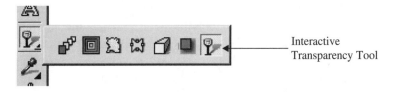

Interactive
Transparency Tool

TIP	*CorelDRAW 10 now enables you to control whether the fill and outline properties of objects participate in a transparency effect. Choose All, Fill, or Outline using Property Bar options while the Interactive Transparency Tool is selected and while a transparency effect is in progress.*

While the Interactive Transparency Tool is selected, the Property Bar displays all options to control your Transparency effect. These options are used together with any Interactive Markers specific to the type of transparency being applied. Although the available Transparency options vary significantly depending on which type of

16

Transparency effect is being applied, the options generally common with each effect type are identified in the following illustration.

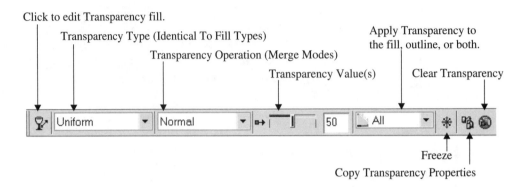

Click to edit Transparency fill.

Transparency Type (Identical To Fill Types)

Transparency Operation (Merge Modes)

Transparency Value(s)

Apply Transparency to the fill, outline, or both.

Clear Transparency

Freeze

Copy Transparency Properties

To apply a Transparency effect to an object and grasp the results of doing so, follow this brief exploration:

1. If you haven't already done so, create at least two objects: one arranged in front to act as the object to apply the Transparency effect to, and at least one other to view through the Transparency effect. Arrange these objects to partially overlap. For this exploration, set the object layered in front to have a uniform fill of light gray and the object layered behind to have a detailed fill type, such as a bitmap Pattern or Texture fill.

2. With your setup complete and your objects positioned, choose the Interactive Transparency Tool from the main Toolbox and click to select the object arranged in front. Notice the Property Bar displays a series of Transparency options, with the transparency type drop-down menu set to None.

3. Using Property Bar options, change the transparency type to Uniform. Notice your object becomes partially transparent, based on the default Transparency value in the Property Bar, which is set at 50 percent. Uniform transparency applies even transparency to your object.

4. With your transparent object still selected and using Property Bar options, change the transparency type to Fountain. By default, a horizontal linear white-to-black Fountain fill is immediately applied to your object and represents your current Transparency effect. Notice the area near the white marker is less transparent than the area near the black marker. This

demonstrates an essential aspect of controlling Transparency effects—white remains opaque, while black becomes transparent.

5. To explore transparency slightly further, experiment by changing your transparency type to other Fountain fill types, or to the various styles associated with pattern and texture. Notice each time the transparency fill type is changed, the white areas remain opaque, while the black areas become transparent. Notice also that the same Interactive Markers used to manipulate corresponding fill types appear around your object and may be used to manipulate the transparency properties.

NOTE	*Changing the transparency type affects only how transparency is applied, leaving the actual fill colors of your object unchanged. Complex fill types, such as Pattern or Texture fills, combined with complex transparency types may produce overly complicated Transparency effects that can often be confusing to control.*

Setting Transparency Properties

When applying Transparency effects to your drawing objects, a host of options and properties are at your disposal. Options may be changed either through dragging the Interactive Markers surrounding the effect or by using Property Bar options (or both). You may apply a specific type of transparency and control the transparency value of the colors and patterns selected. You may also make use of one of 19 available Transparency operations (also referred to as "merge modes"). The section to follow demonstrates the most common of Transparency effects and defines each of the merge modes available.

Setting Transparency Types

If you've followed the previous exploration of the functional application of Transparency effects, you may have noticed that the functional controls are nearly identical to CorelDRAW's Interactive Fill Tool resources. If you already have a good grasp of how the Interactive Fill Tool is used to apply and manipulate various fill types, you should recognize the specific transparency types immediately and be able to manipulate them using the same interactive and Property Bar techniques. With respect to transparency, Property Bar options deviate only slightly from the Fill type options.

16

Uniform Transparency

While Uniform is selected as your effect from the transparency type drop-down, your selected object features an even transparency value throughout the object's fill. Using the Property Bar options, Uniform transparency may be set using a slider control within a range between 0 and 100 percent, while 50 percent is the default value applied, shown here.

Uniform Selected

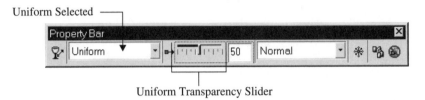

Uniform Transparency Slider

Figure 16-16 shows the word "INVISIBLE," which originally featured a 40 percent black fill applied with a Uniform Transparency effect. The text applied with the default 50 percent transparency value has been arranged in front of a rectangle filled with a Bitmap Pattern fill to demonstrate visual results. Notice the Uniform transparency does not include Interactive Markers—just like a regular Uniform fill.

Fountain Fill Transparencies

If you've had experience with applying Fountain fills to objects using the Interactive Fill Tool, you should recognize many of these next Transparency options. While Linear is selected as the transparency type in the Property Bar,

FIGURE 16-16   This text object has been applied with a default Uniform Transparency effect.

your object's transparency mimics the properties of a Linear Fountain fill. The Property Bar Transparency Type drop-down menu also includes options to select Radial, Conical, or Square transparency types; a slider control for setting the midpoint position of each of these types; and Edge Pad and Angle options (shown next) for a typical fountain-style transparency. Clicking the Edit Transparency button opens the Fountain Transparency dialog box, which contains options specific to the Fountain fill type selected.

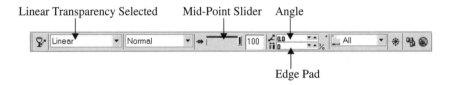

Figure 16-17 shows our text and object arrangement with the word "INVISIBLE" applied with 100 percent black fill and a default white to black linear Transparency effect. In this case, the midpoint of the transparency has been adjusted to roughly 90 percent in order to emphasize the effect. Notice that the Interactive Markers surrounding the Fountain transparency are identical to that of a linear transparency fill. If you wish, you may also customize the Fountain transparency to include multiple "colors" of transparency, keeping in mind that only the corresponding grayscale values to any colors you add are applied as transparency.

Pattern and Texture Transparency

Pattern and Texture transparencies are perhaps among the most complex conditions of any Transparency effect you may apply in CorelDRAW 10. With either selected as the transparency type, each employs use of identical options to their corresponding fill types. The Transparency Type drop-down menu includes Two-Color Pattern, Full-Color Pattern, and Bitmap Pattern transparency types. With each of these selected, a Starting Transparency slider controls the percentage of transparency applied to the lightest grayscale pattern colors, while an Ending Transparency slider controls the percentage of transparency applied to the darkest grayscale colors in the selected pattern, as shown here.

16

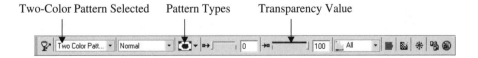

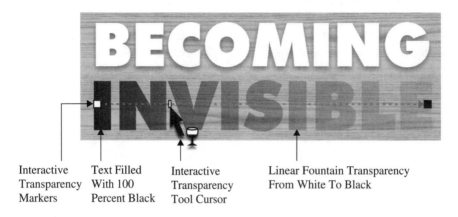

Interactive Transparency Markers

Text Filled With 100 Percent Black

Interactive Transparency Tool Cursor

Linear Fountain Transparency From White To Black

FIGURE 16-17 In this case, the arrangement with the word "INVISIBLE" set to 100 percent black shows the results of applying a default Linear transparency from white to black.

The Texture transparency type includes selectors to access CorelDRAW's saved Texture Libraries and a Texture List selector to access individual texture lists. As with the Pattern transparency type, Texture transparency may also be controlled using the Starting and Ending Transparency sliders, which enable you to apply varying levels of transparency to the lightest and darkest areas of the selected textures, as shown here.

Texture Selected   Texture Library Selector   Ending Transparency Slider

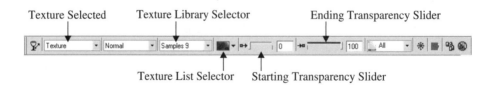

Texture List Selector   Starting Transparency Slider

To demonstrate the complexity of applying either Pattern or Texture transparency to an object, Figure 16-18 shows our text object applied with a Pattern Transparency effect using a bitmap pattern for the effect. In this case, the original text object has been filled with a 100 percent black fill with the transparency properties applied at default settings. Notice the interactive Pattern fill markers appear around the object to indicate the dimensions, rotation, and center orientation of the applied bitmap tile.

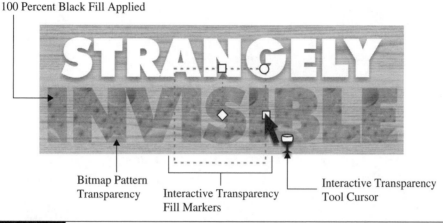

100 Percent Black Fill Applied

Bitmap Pattern Transparency

Interactive Transparency Fill Markers

Interactive Transparency Tool Cursor

FIGURE 16-18   This example has been filled with 100 percent black and uses a bitmap Pattern Transparency set to default transparency values.

> **TIP**
>
> *To edit the specific fill properties of a selected Transparency effect, click the Edit Transparency button in the Property Bar while the Interactive Transparency Tool is selected. This opens the Edit Transparency dialog, which enables you to edit the applied properties based on the corresponding fill type. For more information on setting fill properties, see CD-ROM 5.*

Using Transparency Operations (Merge Modes)

While the Interactive Transparency Tool is selected and a Transparency effect is applied to a selected object, the Property Bar features a mysterious little option to control how your transparency colors react with the colors of underlying objects. These Transparency operations are sometimes referred to as "merge modes" because of the way they cause the grayscale values of your original object to react with colors of underlying objects or your page background (or both).

Merge modes apply values and set conditions based on mathematical calculations using the difference in grayscale values detected between your applied transparency and underlying objects. Merge modes are sometimes useful for creating more or less dramatic variations in the intensity or color of a Transparency effect. Figure 16-19 shows a series of star polygons filled with white, 50 percent black (gray), and black and applied with Uniform transparency arranged over a rectangle filled with a typical

16

bitmap Pattern fill. A black outline was applied to the shapes to identify their position even while appearing fully transparent (see Merge Modes in the color section of this book and open the file Tutorial/Chapter 16/Merge modes.cdr).

When applying a transparency merge mode, the following definitions describe the resulting effects of using each merge mode type.

Normal   Under typical situations, where a regular Transparency effect is all that is required, the Normal merge mode may be used and is the default whenever a new Transparency effect is applied to an object. Choosing Normal causes white-colored areas to remain opaque, black-colored areas to become transparent, and the grayscale values between to be divided evenly based on a percent division between 0 and 100. Normal also serves as the benchmark merge mode for all other transparency merge modes.

Add   The name "Add" is actually short for "Additive" and applies transparency based on the combined grayscale values of both the original and underlying objects. Choosing Add often has the result of causing the transparency object to brighten where it overlaps other objects.

Subtract   The name is short for "Subtractive" and creates transparency by adding all color values and then subtracting 255 (the grayscale equivalent of white).

Difference   Choosing Difference creates transparency by subtracting your object's grayscale equivalent color from the color of underlying objects and multiplying by 255 (white). If your object's transparency grayscale value is 0, the transparency color becomes 255 (white).

Multiply   Choosing Multiply creates transparency grayscale by multiplying the original object's grayscale color by the Normal transparency grayscale value and dividing that value by 255. This most often results in a darker transparency value than you would get by choosing Normal.

Divide   Choosing this option applies transparency by dividing your object's grayscale color value by the Normal transparency grayscale color. If your object is lighter than the Normal transparency grayscale color, the division operation is reversed.

If Lighter   As the name implies, choosing If Lighter has the effect of making your object transparent where the underlying colors are lighter and opaque where the they are darker.

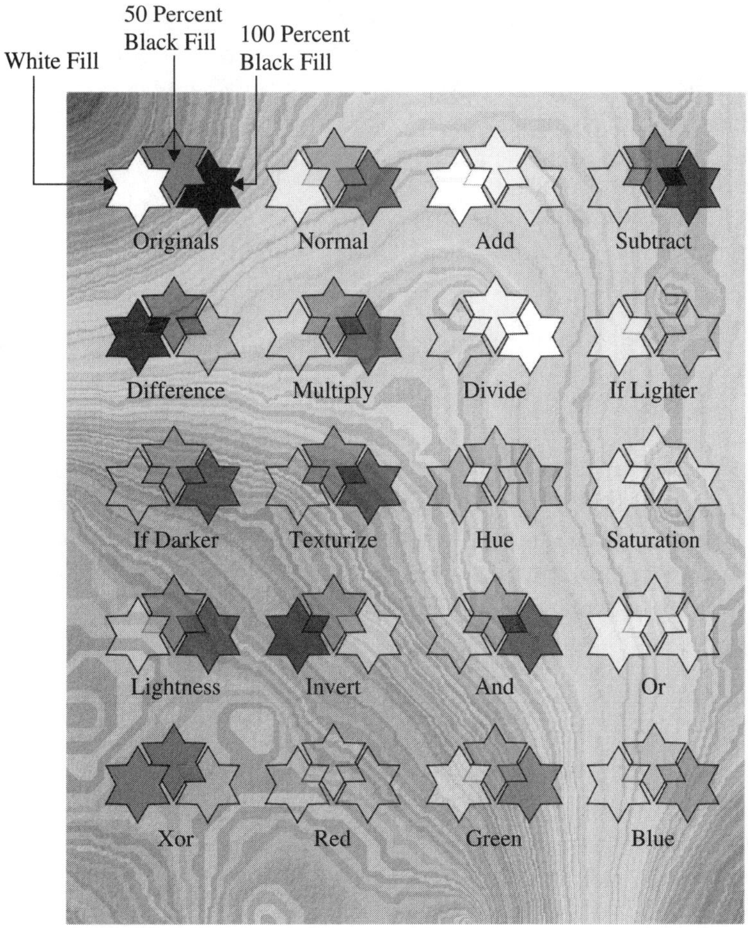

FIGURE 16-19   These groups of star polygons are filled with white, gray, and black and applied with Uniform transparency using the various merge modes available.

If Darker   As an opposite to the If Lighter merge mode, choosing If Darker creates a transparency by making your object opaque where the underlying colors are lighter and transparent where the underlying colors are darker.

Texturize   Choosing Texturize creates transparency by multiplying the grayscale value of your original object's color by the grayscale value of the colors of underlying objects.

Hue   The Hue merge mode creates transparency by comparing the grayscale value of the hue color of your original object to the saturation and lightness of underlying object colors. If the underlying objects are already gray, there is no change, since the underlying grayscale color contains no actual hue color. The resulting transparent object changes color accordingly.

Saturation   The Saturation merge mode results in a transparency color based on both the lightness and hue of the object's color, and the saturation value of the transparency color based on the Normal merge mode.

Lightness   The Lightness merge mode causes a Transparency effect by comparing the hue and saturation of the original object's grayscale color value to the lightness of the original object.

Invert   If you're familiar with numeric positions on the standard grayscale color wheel, the effects of using the Invert merge mode will make sense to you. The resulting transparency color is based on the Normal merge mode transparency color but uses the grayscale value on the opposite side of the wheel. In cases in which the transparency grayscale color value is equal to 127 (dead center on the color wheel), your object remains opaque.

And, Or, and Xor   The three modes are inter-related while their functions seem more geared toward mathematicians than average users. The term "And" means "Logical AND," which creates transparency by converting the transparency grayscale values to binary values and applying the Boolean formula AND. Choosing Or, short for "Logical OR," creates transparency in the same way but applies the Boolean formula OR to these values. Choosing Xor creates transparency in the same way but applies the Boolean formula XOR.

Red, Green, and Blue   Grasping the Transparency effects resulting from use of these three merge modes is also an exercise in mathematics. Each of these merge modes filters out a respective (RGB) channel to arrive at a transparency grayscale color value. The resulting transparent object changes color accordingly.

Using Transparency Freeze

The ability to lock the viewpoint of a transparent object isn't unique to Transparency effects—CorelDRAW's Lens effects feature something similar using the Frozen option. What is unique, though, is what occurs behind the scenes. While a Transparency effect is in progress, you may lock the current condition of the view of underlying objects by pressing the Freeze option in the Property Bar. By selecting the Freeze option (active while the button is depressed), the object applied with transparency may be repositioned or transformed any way you choose, without changing the relative composure of the view, meaning the Freeze option enables you to use CorelDRAW's Transparency resources to take a "snapshot" of sorts.

———— Freeze Option

While active, the Freeze option converts your Transparency effect to a series of shapes that include both vector and bitmap objects. Ungrouping a Transparency effect applied with the Freeze option using the Ungroup All command (in the Property Bar) reveals that the objects are comprised of vector objects representing the outline—possibly a page background object—as well as a bitmap object applied with a softmask effect representing the actual transparency portion (see Figure 16-20). Notice the ungrouped arrangement of objects in this case is actually composed of a vector object and a bitmap object representing the two portions of the effect.

TIP	*Deactivating the Freeze option (without ungrouping it) returns a transparent object to its usual condition.*

Copying Transparency Effects

If you've made a special effort to apply a specific Transparency effect, or if you have multiple objects requiring the same Transparency effect to be applied, you may copy the transparency properties from existing effects using the Copy Transparency Properties button (shown next). This command is accessible while an object is selected and while any tool is in use using command menus. You may also copy existing Transparency effects to your selected object while the Interactive Transparency tool is selected.

16

_____ Copy Transparency
Properties Button

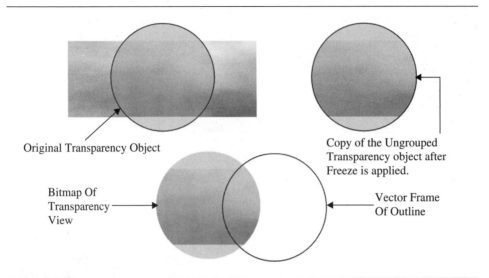

Original Transparency Object

Copy of the Ungrouped
Transparency object after
Freeze is applied.

Bitmap Of
Transparency
View

Vector Frame
Of Outline

FIGURE 16-20   The view through this transparent object was locked using the Freeze
option after the transparency properties were applied.

To copy transparency to an object using either of these techniques, follow
these steps:

1. If you haven't already done so, select the object you wish to apply
   transparency to and move it into position. Apply any required fill or
   outline properties. Be sure the object you wish to copy the transparency
   properties from is on the same page as your current object, or on the
   pasteboard area surrounding your document page.

2. To use command menus with any tool selected, choose Effects | Copy
   Effect | Lens From. Notice your cursor immediately changes to a Targeting
   cursor. Using the Targeting cursor, click the transparent object you wish to
   copy transparency properties from. The effects are immediately copied,
   and your selected object becomes transparent.

3. To accomplish the same effect while an object is selected with the
   Interactive Transparency Tool, click the Copy Transparency Properties
   button. Notice your active cursor changes to a Targeting cursor. Using
   this cursor, click the transparent object you wish to copy transparency
   properties from. Again, the effects are immediate.

Brighten Lens Effect

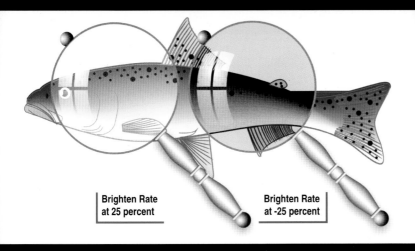

Brighten Rate at 25 percent

Brighten Rate at -25 percent

The lens of our looking glass has been applied with a Brighten Lens effect. The left example has been applied with a Rate value of 25 percent that brightens the underlying objects, while the right example uses a Rate value of -25 (a negative value) affecting all colors seen through the lens. See Brighten Lens in Chapter 16 and open the file Tutorial/Chapter 16/c16-01.tif. on the CD-ROM.

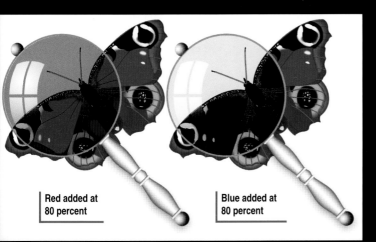

Red added at 80 percent

Blue added at 80 percent

Color Add Lens Effect

The left example is adding red, while the right example is adding blue to the underlying objects using the Color Add Lens. The Rate value has been set to 80 percent. See Color Add in Chapter 16 and open the file Tutorial/Chapter 16/c16-02.tif on the CD-ROM.

Color Limit Lens Effect

The looking glass on the left is limiting a red color at 50 percent, while the looking glass on the right is limiting a 100 percent cyan (blue) color by 50 percent. See Color Limit in Chapter 16 and open the file Tutorial/Chapter 16/c16-03.tif on the CD-ROM.

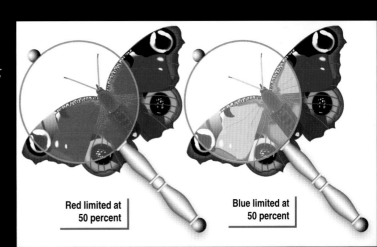

Red limited at 50 percent

Blue limited at 50 percent

Custom Color Map Lens Effect

These four instances of Custom Color Map Lens effects use the three basic palette rotation options as indicated. See Custom Color Map in Chapter 16 and open the file Tutorial/Chapter 16/c16-04.tif on the CD-ROM.

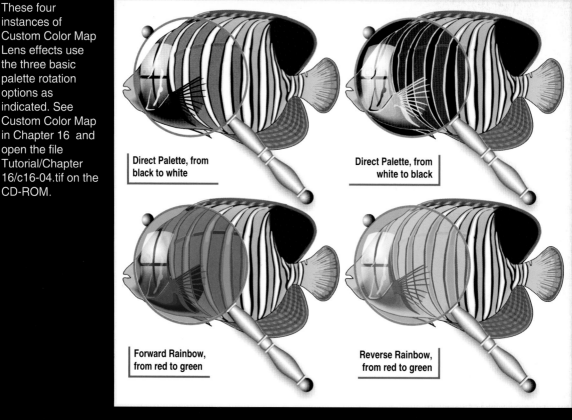

Direct Palette, from black to white

Direct Palette, from white to black

Forward Rainbow, from red to green

Reverse Rainbow, from red to green

Fish Eye Lens Effect

The looking glass has been applied with two different Fish Eye Lens effects. The left features a positive value and has a convex distortion, while the right features a negative value and renders a concave distortion. See Fish Eye in Chapter 16 and open the file Tutorial/Chapter 16/c16-05.tif on the CD-ROM.

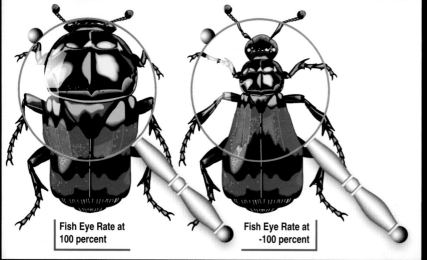

Fish Eye Rate at 100 percent

Fish Eye Rate at -100 percent

This illustration already features a warm color scheme. Applying variations of Heat Map Lenses to the looking glasses increases the intensity of the colors. See Heat Map in Chapter 16 and open the file Tutorial/Chapter 16/c16-06.tif on the CD-ROM.

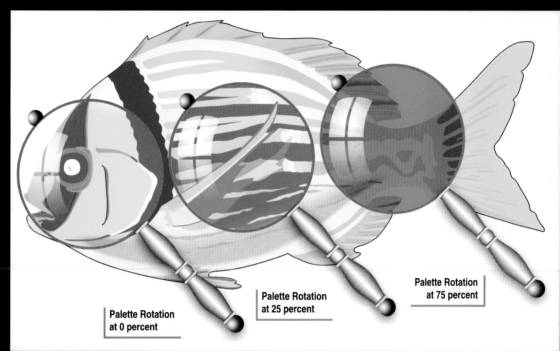

Palette Rotation at 0 percent

Palette Rotation at 25 percent

Palette Rotation at 75 percent

Invert Lens Effect

In this example, our looking glass demonstrates the color inversion effect created while the Invert Lens effect is applied. See Invert Lens Effect in Chapter 16 and open the file Tutorial/Chapter 16/c16-07.tif on the CD-ROM.

A Magnify Lens effect of 1.5 times enlargement is enough to enlarge this object without making it unrecognizable. See Magnify in Chapter 16 and open the file Tutorial/ Chapter 16/c16-08.tif on the CD-ROM.

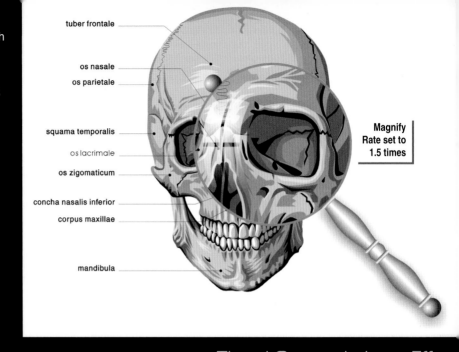

tuber frontale

os nasale

os parietale

squama temporalis

os lacrimale

os zigomaticum

concha nasalis inferior

corpus maxillae

mandibula

Magnify Rate set to 1.5 times

Tinted Grayscale Lens Effect

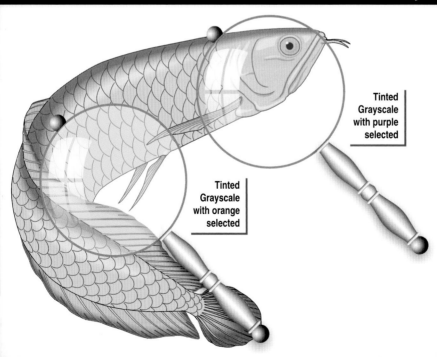

Tinted Grayscale with purple selected

Tinted Grayscale with orange selected

These two looking glasses have been applied with different colors using the Tinted Grayscale Lens: the left uses an orange color, while the right uses a purple color. See Tinted Grayscale in Chapter 16 and open the file Tutorial/Chapter 16/c16-09.tif on the CD-ROM.

Transparency Lens Effect

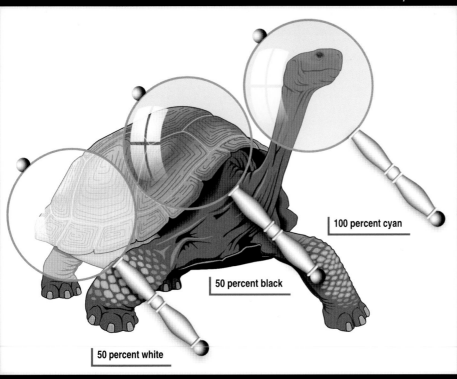

These looking glasses each feature a Transparency Lens Rate value of 50 percent. The far left is applied with 50 percent white, the middle with 50 percent black, and the far right with 100 percent cyan. See Transparency in Chapter 16 and open the file Tutorial/Chapter 16/c16-10.tif on the CD-ROM.

100 percent cyan

50 percent black

50 percent white

Wireframe Lens Effect

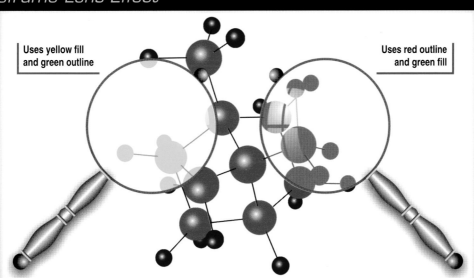

Uses yellow fill and green outline

Uses red outline and green fill

These looking glasses use the Wireframe Lens effect and both have their fill and outline colors controlled using the available lens options. The left uses a yellow fill and green outline, while the right uses a red outline and green fill. See Wireframe in Chapter 16 and open the file Tutorial/Chapter 16/c16-11.tif on the CD-ROM.

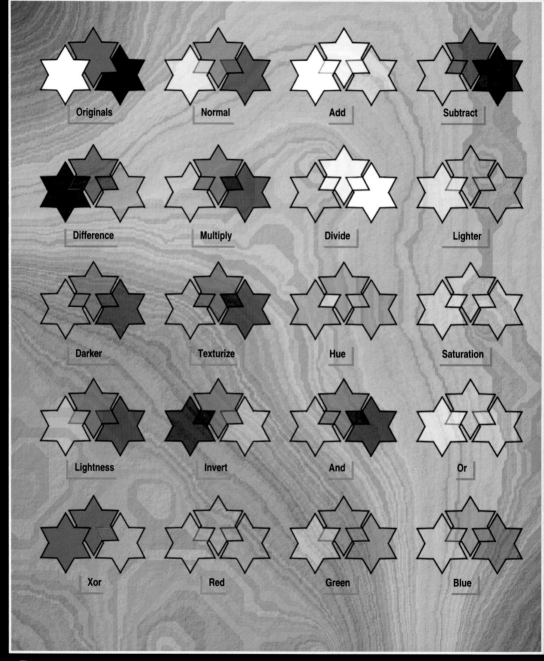

These groups of star polygons are filled with white, gray, and black and applied with Uniform Transparency using the various merge modes available. See Merge Modes in Chapter 16 and open the file Tutorial/Chapter 16/c16-12 on the CD-ROM.

Original

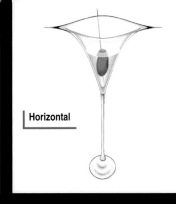

Horizontal

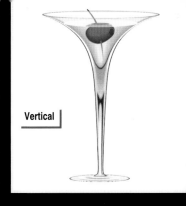

Vertical

Page Curl Effect

Page Curl may be applied with an opaque or transparent effect

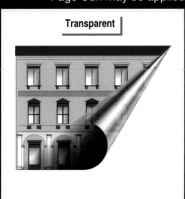

Original

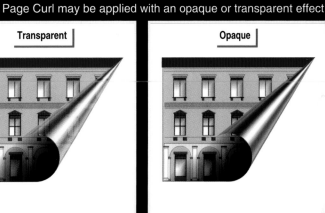

Transparent

Opaque

The Sphere effect spreads an image's center pixels toward the edges and squeezes the edge pixels into a smaller area, creating a curved look.

Sphere Effect

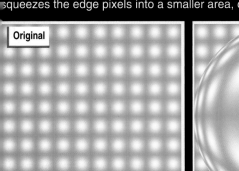

Original

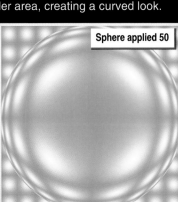

Sphere applied 50

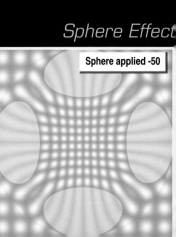

Sphere applied -50

Original

Conte Crayon

Crayon

Cubist

Impressionist

Palette Knife

Pointillist

Sketch Pad

Watercolor

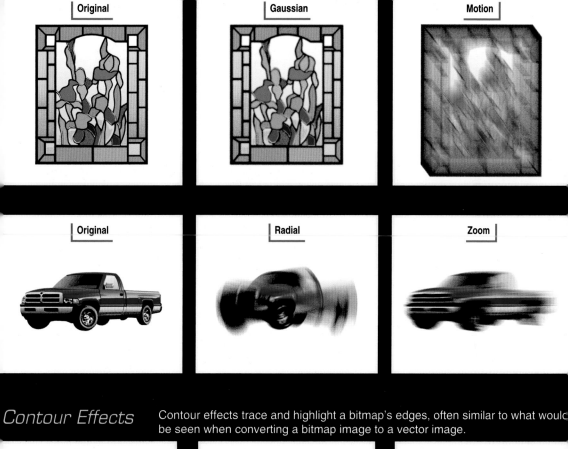

Original | **Gaussian** | **Motion**

Original | **Radial** | **Zoom**

Contour Effects

Contour effects trace and highlight a bitmap's edges, often similar to what would be seen when converting a bitmap image to a vector image.

Original

Edge Detect

Trace Contour

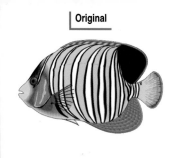

Original

Bit Planes

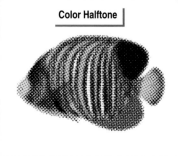

Color Halftone

The Psychedelic effect alters image colors on a sliding scale from 1 to 255, with the most intense color changes occurring at the 255 setting. The Solarize effect converts an image's colors to their negative counterparts. A setting of 0 produces a completely black negative, while higher values introduce additional color and brightness.

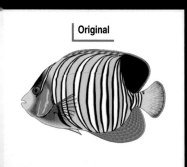

Original

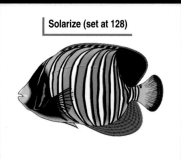

Solarize (set at 128)

Solarize (set at 255)

Psychedelic (set at 128)

Psychedelic (set at 255)

The Crafts filter is capable of simulating six crafts, including Puzzles, Ceramic Tile, and Poker Chips.

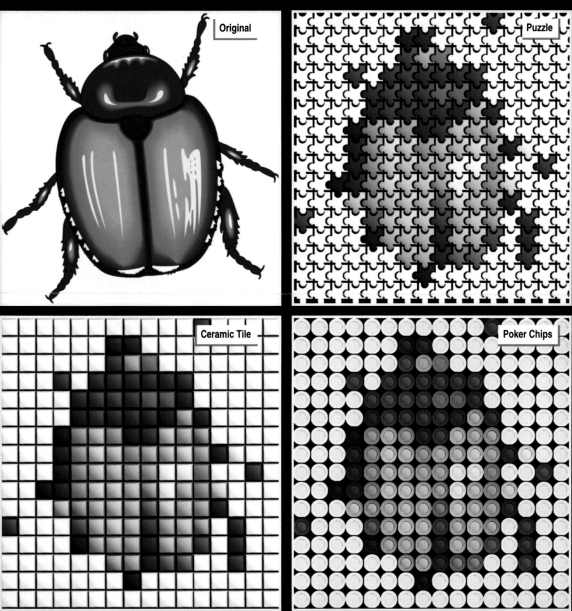

Original

Puzzle

Ceramic Tile

Poker Chips

Crafts Filters

Original

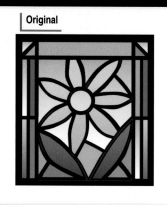

Crystlalize

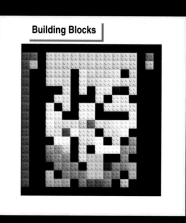

The Crystallize effect turns your image into blocks of color in irregular crystal shapes.

Glass Block

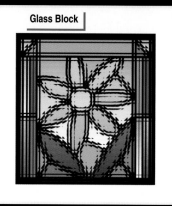

The Glass Block effect simulates looking at your image through a translucent block of glass.

Lite Pegs

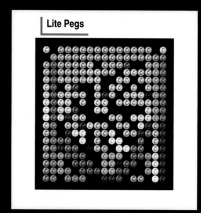

Building Blocks

Kids Play Filters

The Kids Play filters mimic the lite pegs or building blocks found in children's toys. Kids Play may also be used to create a Finger Paint or Paint By Numbers effect.

Finger Paint

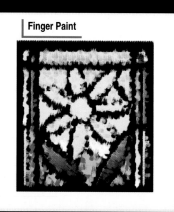

Paint by Numbers

The Scatter filter disperses the pixels in your image, which is similar to a Blur filter, but the pixels retain greater detail than they would when using a blur. The Stained Glass filter converts your image into stained glass; the size and color of the "solder" that holds your glass pieces together may be adjusted when applying the filter.

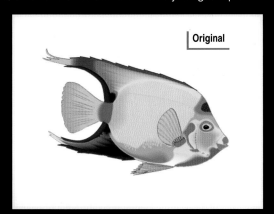

Original

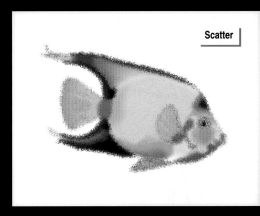

Scatter

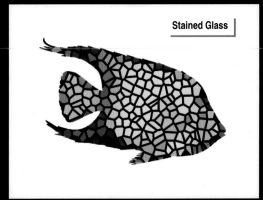

Stained Glass

Vortex Filters

The Vortex filters work by increasing the selected effect as it emerges outward from a central point.

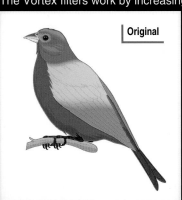

Original

Brushed

Layered

Weather Effects

Weather effects are a relatively new addition to the CorelDRAW Bitmap effects collection. The filter may be used to create Snow, Rain, and Fog. Snow is adjusted on a scale ranging from flurry to storm, Rain is adjusted on a scale ranging from drizzle to downpour, and Fog is adjusted on a scale ranging from mist to pea soup.

Original

Snow

Rain

Fog

CorelDRAW 10 has a wide range of distort tools for applying unique effects to your images. The Blocks filter cuts your image into blocks and offsets them against a background color. Pixelate creates an effect similar to what would be seen if you intentionally resampled an image at too high a setting. Ripple and Swirl both work by applying geometric curves to your image. The Tile filter slices your image into a series of repetitive tiles.

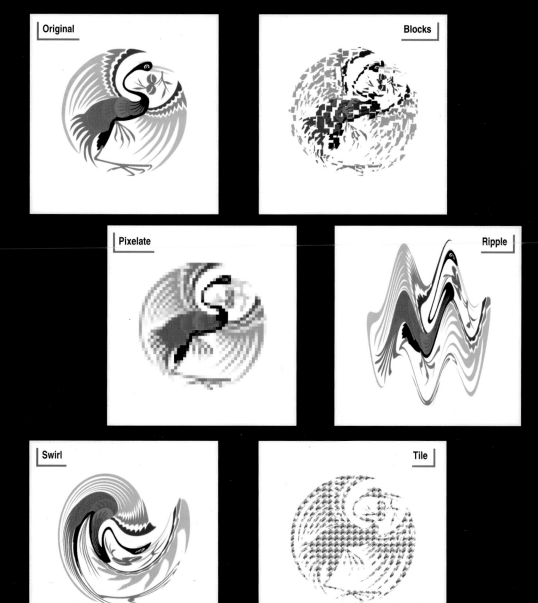

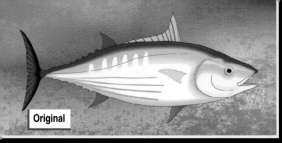

Original

Whirlpool

Strength and opacity applied at 100 (applied twice) create the "windy" illusion.

Wind Effect

Original

Wind

Sharpen Filters

The Sharpen filters work by enhancing fine detail already present in your image. In this example, the Unsharp Mask filter is applied to enhance the image's edges and brighten its colors.

Original

Unsharp Mask

Copying Transparency Effects

Copying transparency from an object to other multiple objects can often save considerable time. But in certain situations, you may not be able to target the transparent object you wish to copy properties from using the Targeting cursor. This can happen if the object is hidden due to the arrangement of objects or if the object is grouped with other objects. In these instances, you might consider placing a separate copy of the target in a convenient and accessible location. To make a quick copy of any object, drag the object while clicking the right mouse button. The actively selected object immediately becomes the new copy. Since the new copy has all the same transparency properties as the original, you may now use it as the target for your transparency.

16

CHAPTER 17

Creating Depth with Shadows

451

CorelDRAW's Drop Shadow has become one of its users' favorite effects since it was first introduced several versions ago. The Drop Shadow feature enables you to create soft, transparent shadows in seconds, and to adjust or edit the effect at any time. This is a far cry from the hard-edged shadows users have historically applied manually using copies of vector objects, and it's an efficient alternative to the laborious task of converting vector copies to bitmaps and applying blur effects.

How CorelDRAW 10's Drop Shadow Effect Works

When CorelDRAW creates a shadow effect, it uses the shape of your object to manufacture a transparent bitmap layered behind your original (see Figure 17-1). Your original object remains unchanged while the shadow is applied. But, like other effects, this bitmap shadow is dynamically linked to your object, meaning any property changes made to the original object are automatically reflected in the shadow effect. Because the shadow maintains a "live link" to the original, its position, color, opacity (transparency), and a host of other properties may be customized to suit a specific illustration purpose. Shadows also incorporate all properties of your original object, including both the object fill and outline values.

Using the Interactive Drop Shadow Tool and Property Bar

The ease of use of this effect is because Drop Shadows are applied solely using the Interactive Drop Shadow Tool in combination with Property Bar options. The tool itself is located in the main Toolbox grouped together with other interactive tools for Transparency, Blend, Distortion, Envelope, Contour, and Extrude.

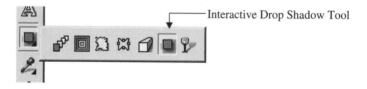
Interactive Drop Shadow Tool

While the Interactive Drop Shadow Tool is selected and a Drop Shadow effect is in progress, the Property Bar displays all options controlling the shadow effect. Drop

Fast and Elegant
Shadows

FIGURE 17-1   A basic Flat-Style Drop Shadow has been applied to this Artistic Text object at default settings, as many of the visual examples in this book do.

---

shadows can be applied in two basic states: Flat or Perspective. The availability of options in the Property Bar changes, depending on which state is in use. *Flat shadows* appear as roughly the same shape, but offset from the original position of your object. *Perspective shadows* take a different, somewhat distorted shape from your original and are oriented to emanate from the top, bottom, left, or right sides of your object. This difference is key to manipulating shadow properties because perspective shadows feature additional options, which can be adjusted. Before we get too far into applying shadow effects, let's look closely at the Property Bar while applying a basic Flat-Style shadow (see Figure 17-2).

If you arrived here looking for the technique to apply a basic Drop Shadow effect to an object, how these options affect your shadow is discussed later. But, for now, follow these next steps and explore the capabilities of the effect:

1. If you haven't already done so, create and select the object you want to apply a shadow to. Apply a fill color to the object and any Outline properties you want.

2. Choose the Interactive Drop Shadow Tool from the main Toolbox. You'll find it grouped together with other interactive tools. Notice your cursor

17

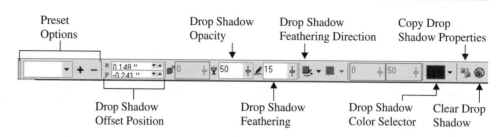

FIGURE 17-2   While a typical Flat-Style shadow is in progress using the Interactive Drop Shadow Tool, the Property Bar displays these options.

changes to something that resembles the Pick Tool accompanied by a rectangle. Notice also the Property Bar now features various Interactive Drop Shadow Tool options.

3. Using a click-drag action, drag from roughly the center of your selected object and continue holding down the mouse button. Notice a preview outline appears that matches your selected object's shape. This preview indicates the position of the new shadow. Notice a white marker has appeared in the center of your object, another marker has appeared under your cursor (as you drag it), and a slider control has appeared at the mid-point of a dotted guideline joining the two markers.

4. With the outline preview of your new shadow roughly in the position you require, release the mouse button. Notice that a gray-colored shadow appears beneath your object. This is a default shadow, colored using black, and it's applied with other default Drop Shadow properties for opacity and feathering.

5. Drag the slider control on the guideline between the two square-shaped markers toward the center of your original object. Notice the shadow appears to become lighter while, in fact, you have only reduced its Opacity value, allowing the page background color (and any underlying objects) to become more visible.

6. To change the color of the shadow, click the color selector on the Property Bar and select a color. Notice the color is applied but still matches your current Opacity value.

7. Drag the White marker to the edges of one side of the original object. Notice the shadow changes shape and the marker snaps to the edge. This action changes the perspective position of the shadow.

8. Using Property Bar options, change the default Feathering value from 15 to 4, and then press the ENTER key. Notice the edges of the shadow become more defined. Change this value to 35 using the same operation. Notice the shadow edges become more blurred.

9. Using Property Bar options, click the Fade slider control and increase it to a setting of 80. Notice the shadow now features a graduated color effect, with the darkest point closest to the original object becoming a lighter color as the effect progresses further away from your object.

10. Using Property Bar options again, click the Drop Shadow Stretch slider and increase it to a value of 80 percent. Notice the shadow becomes physically greater in length in the direction it has been applied toward the furthest interactive marker.

11. To end your Drop Shadow session, click a blank space on your page to deselect the effect or choose the Pick Tool from the main Toolbox.

> **TIP** *To launch quickly into the editing state of an existing Drop Shadow effect applied to an object, double-click the effect portion of an applied Drop Shadow effect using the Interactive Drop Shadow or CTRL-click the effect portion using the Pick Tool.*

Anatomy of a Drop Shadow Effect

While a basic Flat-Style Drop Shadow effect is in progress, several interactive markers appear around your object. The markers themselves include an offset position and color marker and an Opacity slider. If you're unaccustomed to using interactive controls, Figure 17-3 identifies these markers and demonstrates their effects.

In Figure 17-3, the position of the shadow has been changed by moving the combination Offset/Color marker. The shadow effect on the left uses a black shadow set to an Opacity value of 50 percent, while the example on the right uses a 40 percent black shadow set to an Opacity value of 80. The Feathering value (which may only be changed using Property Bar options) remains at the default of 15 percent. The Offset/Color marker can be set to virtually any position on or off your document page, with the corresponding offset values in the Property Bar measuring the offset from your original object's position. You may apply any color you want to your Drop Shadow effect either by choosing a color from the Color selector in the Property Bar or simply by clicking to select the Drop Shadow color marker and clicking a color well.

17

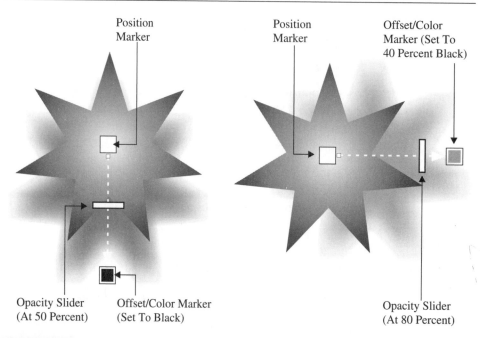

Position Marker

Position Marker

Offset/Color Marker (Set To 40 Percent Black)

Opacity Slider (At 50 Percent)

Offset/Color Marker (Set To Black)

Opacity Slider (At 80 Percent)

FIGURE 17-3 These two identical polygons feature slightly different Flat-Style Drop Shadow effects adjusted using the interactive markers.

Using Flat Drop Shadow Options

As mentioned, while a Flat-Style shadow is applied, you can control its opacity and feathering—both of which dramatically affect the appearance of the shadow, no matter which color you select for it. Opacity can be set interactively, while both options can be controlled using the slider controls available in the Property Bar while the shadow is selected.

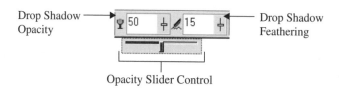

Drop Shadow Opacity

Drop Shadow Feathering

Opacity Slider Control

If these two terms remain a mystery to you, the following definitions may help.

- **Controlling Shadow Opacity**   The Opacity slider essentially applies a transparency value to your Drop Shadow effect, meaning the bitmap that represents the shadow is set to a uniform transparency based on percent. Opacity can be set within a range between 0 and 100 percent, in which lower values cause the shadow to be less opaque (or more transparent), while higher values cause the opposite effect. A value of 0 renders the shadow invisible, while 100 percent causes it to be almost completely opaque, with the default value applied to all new shadows of 50 percent. You can adjust the opacity using either Property Bar options or the interactive slider control. Both achieve the same result.

- **Adjusting Shadow Feathering**   The term *feathering* refers to the effects caused by softening the edges of the bitmap representing the shadow effect, much the same as the effect achieved while applying a Gaussian blur bitmap filter effect to a bitmap object. By default, new shadow effects are applied with a Feathering value of 15 percent, but can be set within a range between 0 and 100 percent, where lower values result in less feathering and higher values increase the effect. Increasing the Feathering value automatically increases the size of the pixel-spreading effect and results in a larger bitmap representing your shadow effect. Feathering can be adjusted only by using the Property Bar Feathering slider.

Copying and Cloning Drop Shadow Effects

As is the case with other effects available in CorelDRAW, you may copy or clone from existing Drop Shadow effects in your document. Both operations are accomplished by using command menus, and they require at least one Drop Shadow effect to be in view and one object must be selected. To copy a drop shadow, choose Effects | Copy Effect | Drop Shadow From. Your active cursor immediately becomes a targeting cursor. Use this cursor to target the Drop Shadow portion of an existing Drop Shadow effect to copy all Drop Shadow properties. Cloning a Drop Shadow effect achieves a slightly different result. When an effect is applied through cloning, the master clone effect object controls the new effect. Property changes made to the master effect are immediately applied to the clone. To clone a Drop Shadow effect, choose Effects | Clone Effect | Drop Shadow From. Again, use the targeting cursor that appears to target the existing Drop Shadow effect you want to clone by clicking directly on the Drop Shadow Group portion of the effect.

17

Opacity 50,
Feathering 15
(The Default)

Opacity 50,
Feathering 5

Opacity 50,
Feathering 50

Opacity 25,
Feathering 5

Opacity 75,
Feathering 5

Opacity 100,
Feathering 5

FIGURE 17-4   The Drop Shadows applied to this graphic symbol demonstrate
differences in Opacity and Feathering values.

To illustrate the effects of varying Opacity and Feathering values visually,
Figure 17-4 shows a graphical symbol applied with various values using identical
offset values.

Feathering Direction

The remaining option available while a Flat-Style Drop Shadow effect is applied is
the Feathering Direction option, which enables you to fine-tune how the feathering
effect applied to your shadow is created. This particular shadow property can be

selected by choosing Average (the default), Outside, Middle, or Inside from the Feathering Direction selector on the Property Bar. Choosing any of these options has an immediate—but, perhaps, more subtle—effect on your shadow, compared to adjusting Feathering or Opacity values.

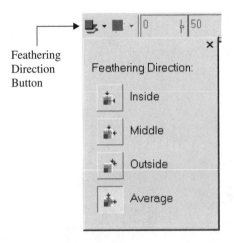

Feathering
Direction
Button

As the name implies, this option enables you to control where the feathering is centralized, in relation to the edges of your shadow. The shape of Feathering edges corresponds to your original object's shape. The following definitions clarify the effects of choosing these options.

- **Average**   By default, Average is used whenever a new Drop Shadow is created. Average has the effect of feathering your shadow to an even shape, centered over the corresponding outline shape of your original object.

- **Inside, Outside**   Each of these two options has the opposite effect of the other. Essentially, each one limits the feathering effect applied to your shadow to the inner or outer edges as those edges correspond to the shape of your original object. If the Inside option is applied to a shadow layered directly behind your original (meaning 0 offset values), however, the shadow is then completely hidden from view.

- **Middle**   Choosing the Middle option has the effect of applying the feathering equally to either side of the corresponding original object's shape.

As you can imagine, the resulting effects of choosing Inside, Outside, or Middle feathering make slight differences in the appearance of your shadows but, nonetheless, offer an additional level of control over their visual appearance. Figure 17-5 illustrates these differences in Feathering Direction while a shadow effect is applied to an object.

17

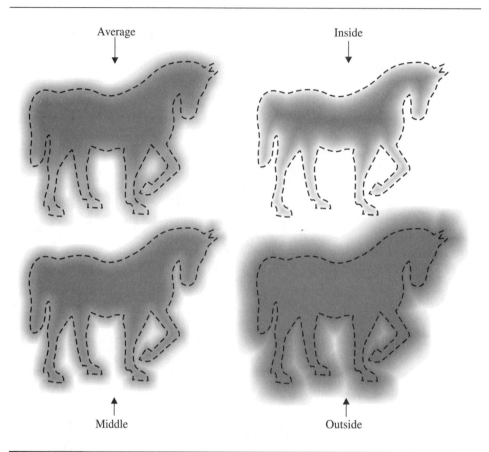

FIGURE 17-5 This symbol was applied with a default shadow using the four available feathering options.

Feathering Edges

To add yet another level of fine-tuning to the appearance of Drop Shadows, while the Inside, Middle, or Outside feathering option is selected, you can control the appearance of the actual edges of your feathering. By default, when a new Drop Shadow is applied to an object, the feathering is applied using an Average Feathering Direction. The feathering is created concentrically as pixels are spread beyond the corresponding outline shape of your original object.

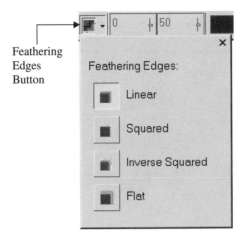

Feathering
Edges
Button

With different Feathering Edge options, you can choose a style that is slightly different from normal concentric—or Linear—pixel spreading. These additional options include Squared, Inverse Squared, and Flat edge feathering, and are defined as follows:

- **Linear**   This setting (the default) creates an even-edge effect for the feathering style applied.

- **Squared, Inverse Squared**   When using either of these options, the most noticeable difference appears when using Outside as the Feathering Direction and when viewing convex shapes. Squared feathering edges spread pixels perpendicular to and away from the original object path shape, while Inverse Squared has the opposite effect.

- **Flat**   As the name implies, while Flat is selected as the edge feathering option, edges aren't exactly feathered but instead appear as uniform flat color, much the same as a uniform fill color and perhaps defeating the purpose of applying any feathering at all. Figure 17-6 shows the effects of using Flat, Squared, and Inverse Squared edge feathering options.

Controlling Shadow Perspective

17

Until recently, Drop Shadow effects were restricted to Flat-Style shadows layered and offset behind your original—providing the effect of light being cast from somewhere in front of the object. Perspective effects now enable you to create

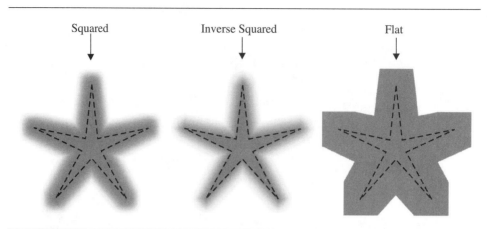

Squared   Inverse Squared   Flat

FIGURE 17-6 This polygon was applied with the same default Drop Shadow effect with various Outside Feathering Directions.

the effect of shadows being cast from the top, bottom, left, or right sides of your object. As many photographers realize, this side-lighting often provides the most dramatic visual effects because of the long distorted shadows created. Although

Clearing and Separating Drop Shadow Effects

To remove a Drop Shadow effect permanently, click the bitmap representing the Drop Shadow portion with the Interactive Drop Shadow Tool and click the Clear Drop Shadow button in the Property Bar. While the shadow portion is selected using the Pick Tool, choosing Effects | Clear Drop Shadow achieves the same result. To separate a Drop Shadow from your object without deleting the bitmap object representing the shadow portion, right-click the shadow bitmap and choose Break Control Drop Shadow Group Apart from the pop-up menu. Doing this permanently breaks the dynamic link between the two objects and enables you to apply other effects to the object. Once separated, the shadow becomes a typical bitmap.

these effects are applied with the Interactive Drop Shadow Tool, these shadow types are no longer "drop" shadows but, instead, are "cast" shadows.

Perspective shadows can also be set to mimic characteristics of real-life shadows. While a Perspective shadow is in progress, you can set the angle (from the Angle option) at which the shadow is cast in relation to your object. You can also control the rate—with the Fade option—at which the shadow intensity fades as it progresses away from your original object, and a Stretch option enables you to set the length of the shadow. These three options are available on the Property Bar while a drop shadow is in progress, but *only* while the shadow applied is a Perspective-style shadow.

Drop Shadow Angle   Drop Shadow Feathering   Drop Shadow Stretch

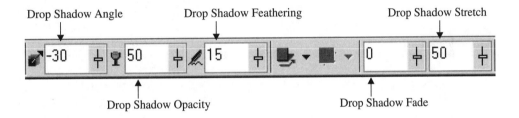

Drop Shadow Opacity   Drop Shadow Fade

To create a Perspective-style shadow, the center marker (which determines the shadow Offset position) of an existing Drop Shadow effect must be dragged to one side of your original object until it snaps to the side of the object using the Interactive Drop Shadow Tool. Or, to create a new Perspective shadow initially, and while no shadow is applied, begin dragging the Interactive Drop Shadow Tool cursor from the side of the original object away from the object, as shown in Figure 17-7. Changing a Perspective shadow from one side of your object involves simply dragging this same marker from one side of your original object to another.

■ **Controlling Drop Shadow Angle**   The most intuitive way of controlling the angle of a Perspective-style shadow is by dragging the Offset/Color marker around the side at which your shadow is attached. Angle values are measured in degrees of rotation around the object's side. To adjust the Angle value, enter the degree value in the Property Bar Angle num box, or click to move the slider control. Different Angle values have no effect on other shadow properties.

17

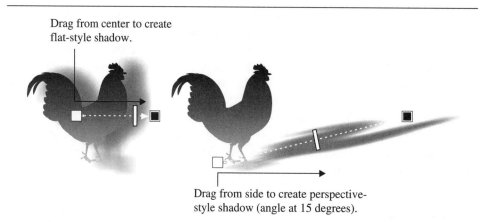

Drag from center to create flat-style shadow.

Drag from side to create perspective-style shadow (angle at 15 degrees).

FIGURE 17-7 This symbol has been applied with a shadow using two different techniques: one creates a Flat shadow, while the other creates a Perspective shadow.

■ **Setting Shadow Fade**   The Fade value of your shadow emulates the effect of decreasing intensity of the shadow's color as it progresses away from your object and is measured in percent values between 0 (the default) and 100. Increasing the Fade value has the effect of reducing the color intensity of the shadow at its furthest point by a specific value. This, in turn, creates a smooth, even (and linear) shadow fountain-style color between the center marker and the Offset/Color marker.

No Fade Applied
(Fade 0)

Fade Applied
(Fade 80)

■ **Applying Shadow Stretch**   The Stretch value essentially applies a distortion command to the bitmap representing the shadow—without stretching the pixels that it comprises. As with Fade, Shadow Stretch can be applied in a percentage between 0 and 100, where 50 represents the default. Values below 50 have the effect of shrinking the length of the shadow, while values above 50 have the opposite effect. Because the Stretch value applies a command (instead of acting as a setting), however, the value you apply has a permanent effect on the shadow. This means that applying repeated shrink and/or stretch values compounds the Stretch effect.

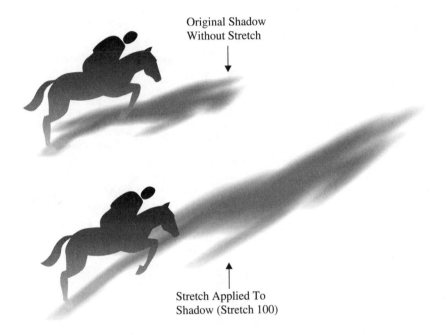

Original Shadow
Without Stretch

Stretch Applied To
Shadow (Stretch 100)

17

About Drop Shadow Color and Resolution

Because the inherent properties of all Drop Shadow effects are based on bitmap characteristics, two questions many users often ask are the following: "What color model is my shadow based on?" and "What is the resolution of the bitmap representing my Shadow effect?"

Regarding Drop Shadow color, you can choose any uniform color supported by CorelDRAW 10—including spot ink colors in fixed palettes. By default, the shadow applied to objects is Black and automatically layered behind the original object. The default color applied to all shadows is based on four-color process inks used in process color printing (CMYK). If you're printing spot colors, however, and you want your Drop Shadow to print in a specific spot color ink, you have some work ahead. The shadow bitmap must be separated from your original object and converted to a duotone composed of a single spot color ink. To convert the Drop Shadow to a fixed-palette ink color, follow these steps:

1. If you haven't already done so, finishing applying your Drop Shadow effect using the required options and ensure the shadow is the way you need it to appear before proceeding.

2. With your Drop Shadow effect in place, right-click the shadow portion itself and choose the Break Drop Shadow Group Apart command from the pop-up menu. Doing so permanently breaks the dynamic link between your original object and the Drop Shadow effect.

3. Using the Pick Tool, click to select only the shadow bitmap and choose Bitmaps | Mode | Duotone (8-bit). The message "Bitmap Has Color Mask" appears, warning that you are about to eliminate the transparency mask applied to the bitmap. Click OK to proceed.

4. The Duotone dialog opens to the Curves tab, where exact color values can be specified. To change from the current color, double-click the ink color name to open the Select Color dialog.

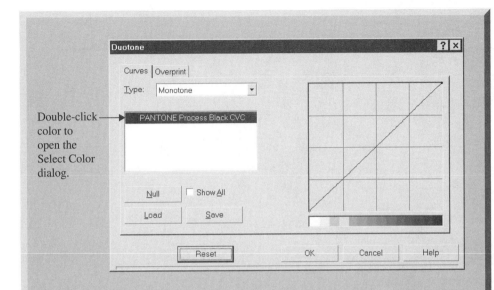

Double-click color to open the Select Color dialog.

5. In the Color Select dialog, choose the ink color you want to use—such as a spot color of ink from one of CorelDRAW's Fixed Palette collections. To access these colors, click the Fixed Palette tab in the dialog.

6. After choosing your ink color, click OK to close the Select Color dialog, and then click OK to close the Duotone dialog and the new spot ink color is applied.

7. Controlling the shadow resolution is slightly less involved. By default, all drop shadows are rendered using a resolution setting of 300 dpi (dots per inch); but, if you require, you can change this value anywhere within a range between 60 and 1,000 dpi, using settings in the Options dialog by choosing Workspace General page. To access this option, open the Options dialog by choosing Tools | Options (CTRL+J), click General under the Workspace heading on the left side of the dialog, and then change the value in the Resolution box shown next.

17

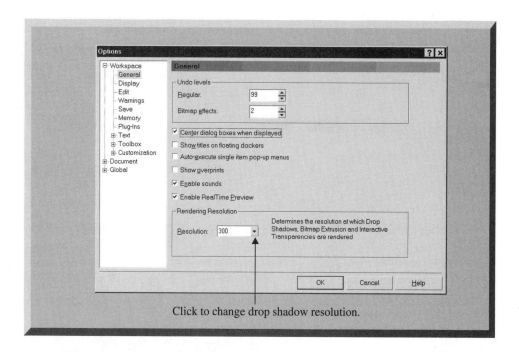

Click to change drop shadow resolution.

Using Drop Shadow Presets

Up to this point, you've learned about the effects of applying specific Flat and Perspective Drop Shadow effects, Opacity and Feathering options, and applying colors to shadow effects. These values constitute the basic properties that apply to virtually any Drop Shadow effect. Next, you learn about saving the Drop Shadow properties you applied as saved presets for use with other objects.

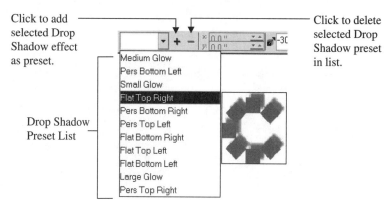

Click to add selected Drop Shadow effect as preset.

Click to delete selected Drop Shadow preset in list.

Drop Shadow Preset List

Medium Glow
Pers Bottom Left
Small Glow
Flat Top Right
Pers Bottom Right
Pers Top Left
Flat Bottom Right
Flat Top Left
Flat Bottom Left
Large Glow
Pers Top Right

Drop Shadow Presets are used in the same manner as with other interactive effects, such as Envelopes, Contours, Distortion, Blend, Extrude, and Transparency. Drop Shadow Presets can be saved and reapplied to a selected object in your document. To apply a saved Drop Shadow Preset to selected objects and explore adding or deleting Drop Shadow Presets, follow these quick steps:

1. Look at applying an existing Preset, several sample versions of which are included with CorelDRAW. If you haven't already done so, create and select an object on your document page using the Pick Tool.

2. Choose the Interactive Drop Shadow Tool from the main Toolbox.

3. Using Property Bar options, choose a saved Drop Shadow effect from the Preset List. The properties of the Drop Shadow are immediately applied, and its current effect properties are displayed on the Property Bar.

4. To save an existing Drop Shadow effect as a preset while using the Interactive Drop Shadow Tool and Property Bar, click to select the Drop Shadow portion of the effect and click the Add Preset (+) button. The Save As dialog opens. Enter a new name for your new Drop Shadow Preset in the File Name box and click Save. Your Drop Shadow Preset is added to the Preset List.

5. To delete a saved Drop Shadow Preset, choose the preset from the Preset List selector to select it and click the Delete Preset button (–) in the Property Bar. The saved preset is immediately deleted.

TIP	*By default, saved Drop Shadow Presets are stored in the Program Files/Corel/Graphics 10/Draw/Presets/DropShadow folder using typical default installation directory names.*

Adopting Smart Drop Shadow Strategies

The Drop Shadow effect is certainly one of the most compelling and dynamic effects you can apply to objects. And, if you've used this effect substantially in your illustration or design tasks, you probably appreciate its ease of use, as many other users have. Even experienced users might consider a few tricks that result in more efficient and/or creative applications of this effect.

17

Shadows as Glow Effects

In case you hadn't already considered this yourself, CorelDRAW's Drop Shadow effect needn't always be restricted to shadows. The effect is easily adapted to create the converse appearance—Glow effects.

By default, whenever a new shadow is created, Black is automatically the applied color. But this color can be any you choose. Under typical conditions, in which your goal is to simulate light being cast from somewhere in front of your object, the shadow typically applies. You can reverse this effect by applying light-colored shadows to dark-colored objects arranged on a dark page background or in front of a darker-colored object. Figure 17-8 shows a Black-filled Artistic Text object layered over a dark background with a light-colored shadow effect applied, resulting is a realistic Glow effect.

Avoiding Overlapping Shadow Bitmaps

The result of using Drop Shadow effects in your document results is that a bitmap is being created and, unfortunately, bitmaps can dramatically increase document file sizes. As a general rule, the more bitmaps you create in your document, the larger and more cumbersome to open, save, and print your document becomes. Although this is an unfortunate side effect of using Drop Shadows, you can use something to minimize this: Grouping.

Switching to Wireframe view reveals the outlines of any bitmap bounding boxes associated with objects to which you have applied Drop Shadows in your document. If you notice multiple overlapping Drop Shadow effects applied to objects that are in close proximity to each other, it might be more efficient to clear the individual shadows, Group (CTRL+G) the objects, and apply your Drop Shadows to the objects as a Group. Doing this eliminates the overlap effect and

FIGURE 17-8   This Artistic Text object demonstrates the two visual effects a Drop Shadow creates.

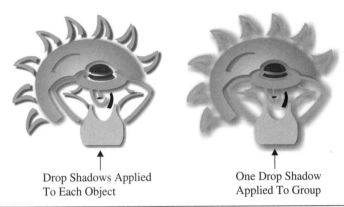

Drop Shadows Applied   One Drop Shadow
To Each Object   Applied To Group

FIGURE 17-9   These closely arranged objects were applied with Drop Shadow effects
individually (left) and white grouped (right).

creates a single Drop Shadow for all objects in the group. Figures 17-9 and 17-10
show the different results that occur when applying Drop Shadow effects to
individual versus groups of objects.

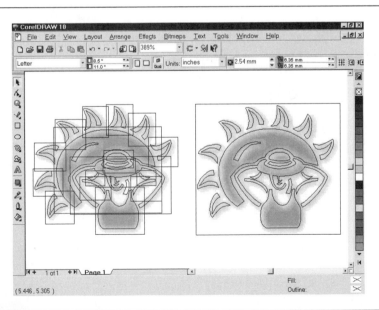

FIGURE 17-10   In Wireframe view, you can see the difference in the number of bitmaps
created to achieve the effect in each case.

17

CHAPTER 18

Drawing and PowerClips

Mastering Draw's PowerClip Feature

CorelDRAW 10's PowerClip feature is one of the least complex to use and enables you to perform tasks no other feature can. The name PowerClip stems from the action of one object "clipping" the boundaries of another where the two objects overlap. Other applications, such as Adobe Illustrator, refer to this effect as masking. With CorelDRAW's PowerClip effect, each object plays a specific role. One object serves as the container, while the other(s) become contents.

The colors of all objects involved remain visible where no other object obscures the view, meaning that the properties of PowerClip objects remain unchanged after the contents have been placed. In typical PowerClip effects, there may be several content objects clipped by a container object. In a literal depiction, Figure 18-1 shows a text object PowerClipped into a rectangle container. The edges of the text are clipped where they overlap the rectangle. Although this example shows the areas being clipped in a lighter shade, in reality they remain hidden from view.

For more complex needs, you may create multilevel PowerClip effects, in which several containers exist. In these cases, the PowerClip containers are essentially nested—one container is PowerClipped into another container already containing a PowerClipped object(s). Each PowerClip container may have its

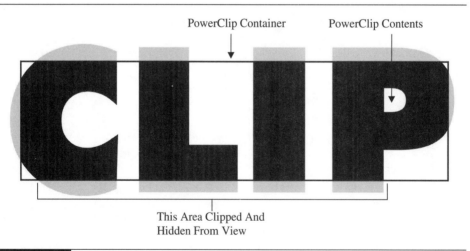

PowerClip Container   PowerClip Contents

This Area Clipped And
Hidden From View

FIGURE 18-1   This text has been PowerClipped into this rectangle.

Text PowerClipped
Inside Rectangle

Stars PowerClipped
Inside Text Object

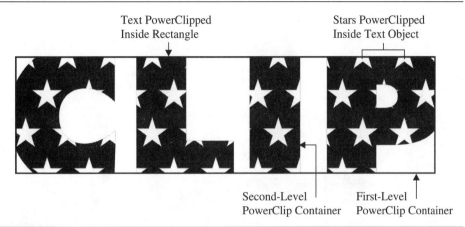

Second-Level
PowerClip Container

First-Level
PowerClip Container

FIGURE 18-2 The first-level container object in this PowerClip effect contains a series of star polygons that were previously PowerClipped into the text.

own contents, creating a hierarchy of sorts (see Figure 18-2). The most beneficial aspect of PowerClips is that they remain editable. Each of the containers and their contents remain intact, with their shape altered by the PowerClip effect, so they may be edited at any time or returned to their normal state as ordinary objects.

For certain applications, the ability to PowerClip objects into other objects can be considered invaluable. The PowerClip feature enables you to perform operations such as placing a digital image (a photograph, for example) into an unevenly shaped object and applying a decorative border to an image, without the need to trim the PowerClip content objects.

PowerClipping an Object

PowerClip has been available since very early versions of CorelDRAW and is applied or edited either interactively or by using submenu commands available when you choose Effects | PowerClip (see Figure 18-3).

The procedures used for placing and editing PowerClip objects differ between using menu commands and interactive actions. PowerClipping by using menu commands is a typical exercise, while interactive PowerClip commands are applied using right mouse button click-and-drag actions. We'll begin with the

18

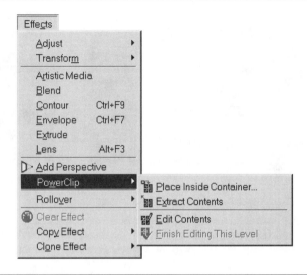

FIGURE 18-3 The submenu accessed by choosing Effects | PowerClip lists all commands for PowerClipping.

menu command technique, since it is the least tricky to perform. To PowerClip any object inside another separate object using command menus, follow these quick steps:

1. If you haven't already done so, create all objects to be involved in the PowerClip effect—one to represent the container object and one (or more) to act as the content object(s).

2. If your intention is to use multiple objects as your PowerClip contents, position the objects relative to each other in the same way you'd like them to appear inside the container object. Using the Pick Tool, select the object(s) you wish to act as the contents.

3. With the objects selected, choose Effects | PowerClip | Place Inside Container. Notice that your cursor changes to a targeting cursor.

4. Using this cursor, click to target and specify your container object (see Figure 18-4). The content objects are moved into the container and centered within its width and depth (the default behavior). If you have selected multiple objects to be placed inside the PowerClip container, they will maintain their relative position to each other.

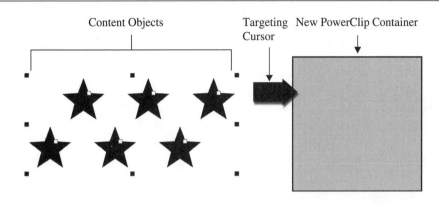

Content Objects   Targeting   New PowerClip Container
                   Cursor

FIGURE 18-4 This arrangement of polygons is being PowerClipped into a rectangle using the targeting cursor to target the new container object.

Using interactive methods is a slightly different operation and involves a right mouse button click-and-drag action—a deviation from the typical left-click method you may be accustomed to. To PowerClip using the interactive method, follow these quick steps:

1. Create and position the object(s) you wish to place inside a container object.

2. Using the Pick Tool, select the object(s) and use a right-click and drag action to drag the object(s), holding your mouse button down until your cursor is inside the new container object. Notice that once your cursor enters the inner boundaries of the new container object, a crosshair cursor appears.

3. Release the mouse button and notice that a pop-up menu appears containing a collection of context-sensitive commands. Choose PowerClip Inside from the pop-up menu to complete the operation. Your objects are now PowerClipped into the container.

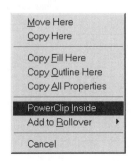

18

To remove all content objects from a selected PowerClip container and return the container and contents to their usual state, right-click the container object and choose Extract Contents from the pop-up menu.

Controlling PowerClip Behavior

Under default workspace settings, new PowerClip contents are automatically centered when placed into new containers. The option controlling this behavior is located in the Options dialog and enables you to choose whether or not new PowerClip objects are centered (see Figure 18-5). In fact, this is an option that is changed more often than not if you use this feature frequently.

Click To Activate Or Deactivate

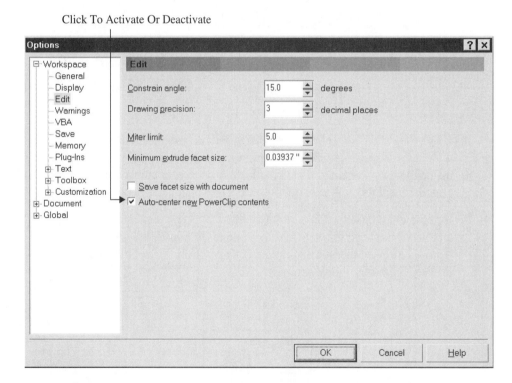

FIGURE 18-5   PowerClip centering behavior is controlled by an option found at the bottom of the Edit page of your Workspace Options dialog.

To access this option and change it to the state you prefer, follow these steps:

1. Open the Options dialog by choosing Tools | Options (CTRL+J) and click the (+) symbol beside Workspace on the left side of the dialog to expand the tree directory.

2. Click on Edit to display the Edit page on the right side of the dialog.

3. Click Auto-Center New PowerClip Contents to reflect the condition you prefer. When selected, all new PowerClip contents will be centered within the container dimension. When PowerClipping multiple objects, these will remain in position relative to each other at the time they are PowerClipped.

4. Click OK to accept the change and close the Options dialog.

If you've never performed a PowerClip operation before or you happen to be unfamiliar with your current workspace settings, it is entirely possible that your PowerClip contents may seem to vanish after they are placed into a new container. The reason for this is likely due to the current setting of the PowerClip option controlling how new PowerClip contents are placed. This option may be set to place all new PowerClip content objects *in situ*, meaning they are placed into the PowerClip container without moving from their current page position.

Editing PowerClip Objects

While objects have been placed into a PowerClip container, you needn't remove them to change their properties or to manipulate them. PowerClip contents may be edited by selecting the container itself and choosing Effects | PowerClip Edit Contents. This action places you temporarily in the PowerClip editing state.

 To instantly select a container object while editing its PowerClip contents, ALT-*click any of the content objects it contains.*

Launching PowerClip Editing State

Since all objects within a PowerClip are preserved and retain all their original properties, they may be edited at any time without removing them from their PowerClip container. While in this state, your container objects are displayed only

18

as outlines, similar to viewing the objects in Wireframe view, while the unclipped content objects become fully visible and editable. In this state, you may edit the properties of container objects, but their position remains fixed. During PowerClip editing state, an editing level indicator button appears at the lower-left corner of your document window to indicate that editing is under way (see Figure 18-6).

Once your editing is complete, there are several ways to exit the editing state. Choose Effects | PowerClip and choose Finish Editing This Level, right-click the content object(s) and choose Finish Editing This Level from the pop-up menu, or click the editing state indicator button at the lower-left corner of your document window. Any of these actions will return you to your usual working state.

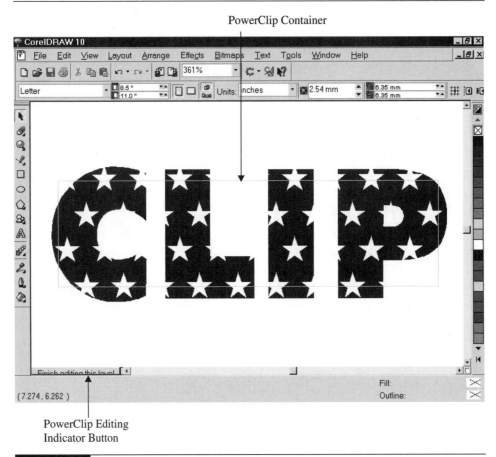

FIGURE 18-6 The PowerClip editing state

TIP	*To quickly enter the PowerClip editing state for single-level PowerClip objects, CorelDRAW 10 now lets you CTRL-click the PowerClip container object, after which its contents become fully visible for editing. To quickly exit the PowerClip editing state, CTRL-click outside the PowerClip container.*

Navigating a Multilevel PowerClip

This PowerClip extraction process becomes slightly more complex if the container from which you are extracting contents contains further—or lower-level—PowerClipped objects. When faced with a multilevel extraction situation, the Extract Contents command must be performed on each lower-level container object individually. In other words, the Extract Contents command must be performed at each level, no matter how many PowerClip levels exist.

Navigating in and out of multilevel PowerClip effects requires more steps than those with only single layers. Editing this type of effect requires drilling down through the PowerClip levels, selecting each of the subsequent PowerClip containers, and editing them individually. To drill down through the editing states of a typical multilevel PowerClip effect, follow these generic steps:

1. Using the Pick Tool, select the PowerClip container that contains all content and PowerClip content objects and choose Effects | PowerClip | Edit Contents. Notice that the top-level container object is displayed as an outline, while its content objects (including any additional PowerClip container objects) become fully visible. Perform any editing you require on the content objects.

2. Locate another PowerClip container among your current content objects and click to select it.

3. Again, choose Effects | PowerClip | Edit Contents. The second-level container is displayed as an outline, and its contents become fully visible. You may continue this same procedure to gain access to contents of any further container objects.

4. Once your editing is complete, begin backing out of your multilevel editing operation by choosing Effects | PowerClip | Finish Editing This Level.

18

> **5.** Repeat the previous step for each level until you have reached the top-level object. Your editing operation is complete.
>
> When editing a multilevel PowerClip, only the current PowerClip container and its contents become visible on your screen for editing. After editing of a specific level is complete, you will need to navigate back up through each individual level in order to completely exit the editing state.

The Object Manager Docker enables you to examine all the levels of a PowerClip effect and obtain information on each individual object, the object type, the level on which it resides, and all properties. To access the Object Manager Docker, choose Window | Dockers | Object Manager.

TIP *When viewing PowerClip container objects in the Object Manager Docker, you may also extract or edit a PowerClip effect by right-clicking the object name and choosing Extract Contents or Edit Contents from the pop-up menu.*

To fully grasp this concept, let's examine a simple multilevel PowerClip effect. The following illustration reveals the structure of a two-level PowerClip indicated in the Object Manager Docker window. In this case, an arrangement of 40 polygons has been PowerClipped into an Artistic Text object, which has in turn been PowerClipped into a rectangle. The Object Manager Docker displays the structure of each level and lists the individual objects for each, enabling you to obtain a quick structure of a multilevel PowerClip effect before entering the editing state.

Structure
of Multilevel
PowerClip
Effect

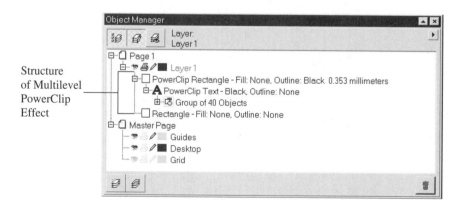

To back out of editing states of a multilevel PowerClip effect quickly, click the Finish Editing This Level button at the lower left of your document window while editing any level, until the indicator button disappears.

PowerClip Lock Options

By default, all new PowerClip contents are "locked" to their container object, meaning that under default conditions and with a typical PowerClip effect, any transformations made to the PowerClip container object also automatically transform its contents. However, after an object becomes a PowerClip content object, you may change its relationship to the container any time you wish through locking and unlocking options.

Depressed Button Indicates Contents Are Locked ———→

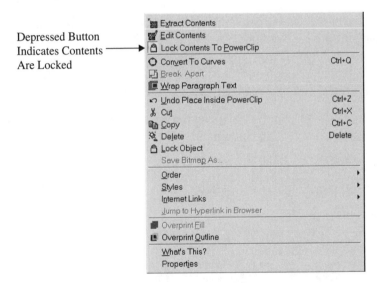

PowerClip locking options are different from normal object-locking commands. When an ordinary object is locked using CorelDRAW's Lock command, the object itself remains locked to your document page. When a PowerClip content object is locked, it may be manipulated and moved freely around your document page as long as it remains inside the container.

PowerClip content-locking options are available only through right mouse button functionality by changing the Lock Contents to PowerClip option, which may be toggled on or off. This particular option is available only from the pop-up

18

menu when right-clicking an existing PowerClip object on your document page. In the depressed state, this option indicates that your PowerClip contents are locked to their container. To unlock your PowerClip content objects so that they remain unchanged while the container object is being manipulated, choose the option again to deselect it.

PowerClip Limitations

Although virtually any simple vector object can be specified as a PowerClip container object, there are some object types that may not be used as containers. Before attempting to use a specific object as a PowerClip container, you may wish to keep this brief list of invalid PowerClip container types in mind:

■ Imported or created bitmap objects are invalid as PowerClip containers, including Portable Network Graphic (PNG), JPEG, Compuserve GIF, Windows Bitmap (BMP), Tagged Image File Format (TIF), Targa bitmap (TGA), Scitex CT bitmap, OS/2 Bitmap (BMP), CALS Compressed bitmap, and CALS Wavelet Compressed Bitmap.

■ Objects that have been locked using the Arrange | Lock Object command are invalid as PowerClip containers.

■ All Paragraph Text objects are invalid.

■ Inserted Internet objects are invalid.

■ Rollovers are invalid.

Real-World PowerClip Effects

If the practical application of CorelDRAW's PowerClip effect is eluding you, the following examples may provide food for thought when approaching use of a PowerClip effect. To begin, Figure 18-7 shows an Artistic Text object used as a PowerClip container.

When specifying Artistic Text objects as your PowerClip container objects, using the interactive method is slightly problematic, since CorelDRAW's default behavior tries to place the object you are right-dragging between your Artistic Text object's characters. To eliminate this hazard when specifying Artistic Text objects as containers, use command menus and the targeting cursor instead.

Hidden Portion Of Image

FIGURE 18-7   Artistic Text serves as the PowerClip container for this digital image imported into CorelDRAW.

In the figure, an imported and embedded digital image has been PowerClipped into a text object. The character spacing of the Artistic Text was manually reduced so that the characters actually overlap and provide a clearer view of the image through the character shapes. For illustration purposes, the hidden area of the digital image is indicated as a ghosted image.

For graphic design or illustration tasks, PowerClipping can be an excellent and less permanent alternative to trimming objects to fit a specific shape. For example, Figure 18-8 shows an eye that uses a PowerClip effect to hide a portion of the inside eyeball. In this case, the actual ball portion of the eye was grouped with the other eyeball objects and placed into an object representing the outline shape of the eye opening. For demonstration purposes, the shape of the hidden clipped portion is indicated by a dotted line above and below the eyeball shape.

Figure 18-9 shows an advertising flash headline using a PowerClip effect as a technique for creating a backdrop for the text. The bubble shapes were created using simple ellipses filled with offset radial fountain fills and applied with Uniform Transparency effects. The bubble shapes were copied and transformed to various sizes, and the entire arrangement was PowerClipped into a polygon-shaped object, which already included a uniform fill. For demonstration purposes, the clipped portions of some of the shapes are visible as lighter portions.

18

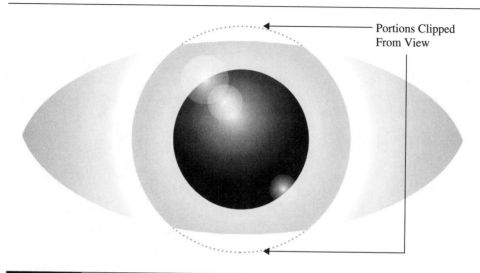

Portions Clipped
From View

FIGURE 18-8 This graphic illustration uses a PowerClip effect to create a nonpermanent trimmed shape for the shape of an eyeball.

Clipped Portions

FIGURE 18-9   This advertising graphic uses a PowerClip effect to place a backdrop graphic inside a polygon shape.

PART V

Working in 3D

CHAPTER 19

Creating Depth with Perspective Effects

489

Everything we see in the real world has at least some degree of perspective distortion, no matter how slight. If you want the shapes in your drawing objects to look realistic, adding a sense of perspective is certainly going to accomplish this. Perspective enables you to simulate the effect of things appearing smaller as the distance between your eyes and the objects increases.

How Perspective Effects Work

Perspective is an optical effect caused by the distance between reference points appearing to diminish as the distance between our plane of vision and points along an object's surface increases. Things that are closer appear larger, while things that are farther away appear smaller. The relationship between objects sharing the same perspective is fixed and is influenced by their relationship to several reference points—the horizon line (line of sight), the depth of the objects, and the plane of vision. These perspective effects often create a sense of depth and volume, which enables you to simulate a third dimension while drawing on only two dimensions. If your intention is to create realistic-looking 3D effects in your drawing or illustration, adding perspective to your object shapes should be your first strategy.

How Perspective Creates Depth

Manually creating object shapes to appear in perspective is an acquired skill—not a mysterious talent as some people often view it. As long as you understand the relationships between the points of reference involved in a perspective effect, you can always apply your own sense of depth and volume to individual objects or throughout an entire illustration. These points of reference include your plane of view (essentially, your eyes), a "horizon" line (to provide horizontal and vertical reference), and vanishing points.

Vanishing points in particular create the effect of diminishing volume, no matter where they are positioned in a setting. Most often, vanishing points align with the horizon line, and all surfaces diminish as they progress toward these points. Figure 19-1 shows two objects drawn in perspective, each with its own pair of vanishing points. Notice that the vanishing points align with the horizon line, and the guidelines show how all straight-line surfaces point toward them. Notice also that, depending on the shape of your object, certain portions of your object may (or may not) be visible while the object exists above or below this line.

As mentioned, a true perspective effect involves vanishing points, which may be above, below, or to one side or the other in relation to an object or scene.

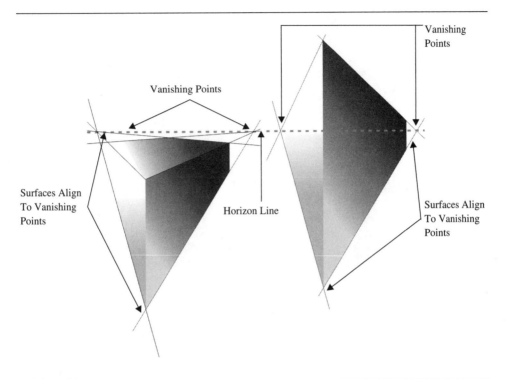

FIGURE 19-1   These two objects have their own vanishing points but share the same horizon line.

If you have previous experience drawing with perspective effects, the concept will likely come much easier to you. As you work with CorelDRAW's Perspective effect, you'll begin to realize that achieving a true perspective effect involves a little more than simply *applying* this effect. For now, we'll leave these limitations for later discussion and concentrate on what applying a Perspective effect enables you to do.

CorelDRAW's Simulated Perspective

Compared to other dynamic effects in CorelDRAW 10, Perspective is relatively uncomplicated and straightforward. Draw's Perspective effect enables you to apply perspective to single objects or groups of objects in an intuitive way by manipulating a set of four corner nodes or one of two vanishing points automatically placed around your object. While an object is being manipulated using the Perspective effect, the Shape Tool provides all manipulation functionality, enabling you to move these nodes and points the same way you would move any other object. Figure 19-2 shows our previous example shapes applied with CorelDRAW's Perspective effect.

19

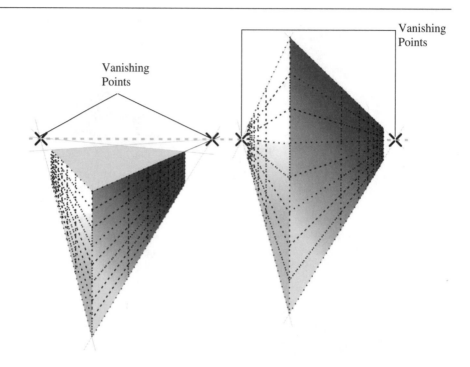

FIGURE 19-2 Our two example objects are created using CorelDRAW's Perspective effect.

As an object is being manipulated in Perspective, CorelDRAW automatically subdivides the shape into eight horizontal rows and eight vertical columns (see Figure 19-2) to align with your page and provide visual reference for the effect. Since this type of applied perspective effect is a manipulation (rather than a created 3D effect), portions of objects that are often hidden (such as the top surface of the right object) are not created by CorelDRAW.

For example, all objects applied with perspective are manipulated as two-dimensional objects—as if they were paper thin. This means no additional surfaces are created and no third dimension is applied. Any distortion applied during a Perspective effect occurs only to the outline shape of the object, while all other properties—including any applied fill types—are left unaltered. For example, if your object has been applied with Fountain, Pattern, or Texture fill, or includes an outline width and/or line pattern, so will your Perspective effect.

Applying Perspective

Depending on the complexity of your perspective effect, you may wish to do a little preparation work ahead of the effect. For example, if you're preparing to create a scene containing multiple objects using a shared set of vanishing points and horizon line, you may want to create guides for reference as you apply the perspective effects. Try using guidelines (angled or not), or draw actual Bézier lines to represent the horizon and vanishing points.

Beginning the Perspective process requires that only one command be applied to your selected object: Effects | Add Perspective (shown next). The rest is up to you. The key to the success of this effect lies in your manipulation of your object's shape. If you have never applied a Perspective effect before, you may find the process tricky the first time out.

Let's begin by exploring the application and manipulation of the effect:

1. Create an object to apply your Perspective effect to, and choose the Pick Tool.

2. Select your object and choose Effects | Add Perspective. As soon as you apply the command, your object's shape is immediately subdivided into a series of horizontal and vertical grid lines. Notice also that your cursor has changed to the Shape Tool.

19

3. Using the Shape Tool cursor, drag any of the Perspective grid control handles to begin distorting the object. Notice that each time you move a handle, the representative perspective grid is mapped to the newly distorted shape. If your initial distortions are dramatic enough, you may see one or both of the vanishing points come into view. If not, decrease your zoom magnification by pressing F3 until at least one of the vanishing points becomes visible. Vanishing points resemble an X symbol where you would expect two sides to converge.

4. To make adjustments to a vanishing point, drag the X marker itself and position it at the point toward which you wish your object to diminish. Rough perspective effects may not require precision; but if your effect will be applied across multiple objects for illustration purposes, precision may be more important. Notice that when you move the horizontal vanishing point toward the object, the top and bottom of the bounding box continue to point toward it, while the farthest side becomes smaller and the size of the closest side remains constant. The closer the vanishing point is to the object, the smaller the farthest side will become.

5. Once your object's Perspective has been completed, click your page background or any other tool or object to deselect your distorted object and end your Perspective session.

Editing a Perspective Effect

Once a Perspective effect has been applied to an object, it essentially becomes a "perspective" type object, meaning that the Perspective distorting its shape may be edited at any time. Editing involves moving either the vanishing points or the Perspective control handles to reshape the effect.

Relaunching Perspective Controls

While the object in your document is applied with a Perspective effect, the applied distortion is dynamic as long as the effect is applied. This means that you may edit your object in Perspective any time you wish in one of two ways:

- While using the Shape Tool, click the object once to select it.

- While using the Pick Tool, single clicks simply select the object, enabling you to manipulate it as any ordinary object. Double-clicking the object using the Pick Tool automatically selects the Shape Tool and makes the object available for Perspective editing.

In either situation, your object will feature the Perspective effect distortion grid and any vanishing points, enabling you to continue refining the effect.

Moving Vanishing Points and Control Handles

While a Perspective distortion is applied, vanishing points will appear around your object as visual indicators of where lines of perspective converge. This happens automatically, meaning you can't "create" vanishing points. They simply appear during the course of the effect. However, you can manipulate the Perspective effect by dragging the vanishing points into position, which is much easier than trying to position them by dragging control handles. Using control handles enables you to quickly bring the vanishing points into view; but once these points are in close proximity to your object, using the control point to position them becomes cumbersome due to the amount of distortion applied.

Depending on how you've manipulated your Perspective effect, one or two vanishing points may appear around your object. Typical Perspective effects often include just one vanishing point that appears above or below your object (the vertical vanishing point), or to the left or right (the horizontal vanishing point). Figure 19-3 shows a rectangle applied with a Perspective distortion where a single vanishing point appears.

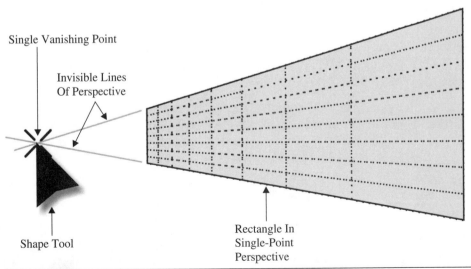

FIGURE 19-3 During a Perspective distortion, vanishing points show perspective direction and act as interactive control handles.

19

In complex Perspective effects (depending on your illustration needs), both the vertical and horizontal vanishing points may come into play. Two visible vanishing points indicate that your object's Perspective is being distorted both horizontally and vertically, as shown in Figure 19-4.

> **TIP** *Perspective vanishing points may be positioned anywhere on or off your document page.*

While manipulating a Perspective effect, the four control handles that appear at the corners of the imaginary bounding box surrounding your object may also be used to make adjustments to the distortion. These markers may be dragged in any

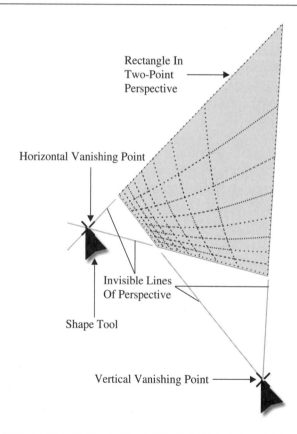

Rectangle In Two-Point Perspective

Horizontal Vanishing Point

Invisible Lines Of Perspective

Shape Tool

Vertical Vanishing Point

FIGURE 19-4   The dramatic Perspective distortion being applied to this rectangle features both vertical and horizontal vanishing points.

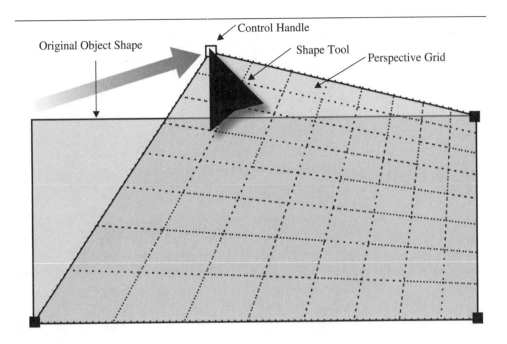

Original Object Shape

Control Handle

Shape Tool

Perspective Grid

FIGURE 19-5 The upper-left corner control handle of this rectangle is being dragged as a technique for manipulating the object's perspective based on object shape.

direction, enabling you to shape the Perspective effect based on object shape rather than a perspective vanishing point location. Moving these corner handles may seem similar to manipulating the nodes on an Envelope effect, although the resulting distortion is much different from an envelope. Figure 19-5 shows a Perspective effect being applied by dragging a control handle to apply distortion.

Constraining Perspective

When shaping a Perspective effect, pressing CTRL enables you to constrain the angular movement of Perspective effect corner control handles to align with the angles of the existing Perspective bounding box shape. This in turn enables you to manipulate the Perspective of each side of your object without distorting it vertically or horizontally. Pressing CTRL+SHIFT while moving a control handle constrains the same movement, but enables you to move two control handles at once and applies a centering distortion to the Perspective effect. No movement-constraining key exists when dragging vanishing points though. So, moving control handles may be a preferred method when

19

constraining the shape of your object's Perspective. The following illustration shows the results of pressing constraining keys when manipulating Perspective control handles. Two rectangles are undergoing Perspective shaping while pressing constraining keys to preserve shape and movement. The left example shows the effect of pressing CTRL while dragging, while the right shows the result of pressing CTRL+SHIFT.

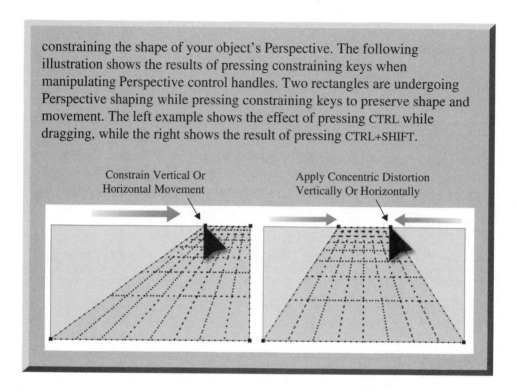

Constrain Vertical Or Horizontal Movement

Apply Concentric Distortion Vertically Or Horizontally

Enhancing a Perspective Effect

The appearance of Perspective effects applied to objects can often be significantly enhanced by adding a sense of realism in the form of linear Fountain fills. While applying Fountain fills, keep in mind that as object surfaces appear farther away, the color saturation changes. If you're working with simple color schemes, creating shading is relatively straightforward using the Interactive Fill Tool. Figure 19-6 shows several examples of how you can increase the visual impact of the applied Perspective effect by adding Fountain fills to the Artistic Text objects.

Color may be quickly applied to the Perspective effects of most objects by using the following steps:

1. After applying a Perspective effect to an object, choose the Interactive Fill Tool from the main Toolbox. You'll find it grouped with other tool button resources for applying object fills.

2. Apply a base fill color by clicking a color well in your onscreen palette. This will serve as the basis for the darkest area of your perspective fill.

3. Using the Interactive Fill Tool, drag across your object beginning at the farthest side and ending at roughly the edge of the nearest side. This will create a default linear Fountain fill using your object's current fill color at the darkest point and applying white as the highlight color. If you wish, you may update the color for the highlight of the linear fill by dragging other colors onto either of the markers.

4. To further customize your Perspective effect fill, increase or decrease the rate at which the two colors progress toward each other by dragging the edge pad slider located between the two interactive color markers.

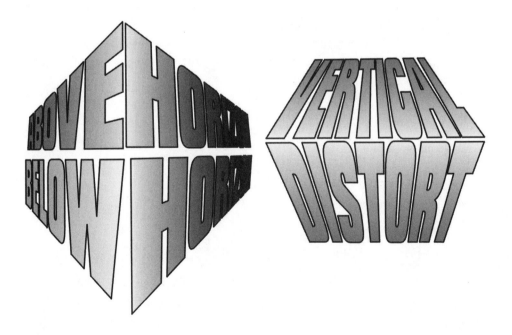

FIGURE 19-6   These Artistic Text objects have had various Perspective effects applied, with linear fills used to emphasize depth.

19

Limitations of Draw's Perspective Effects

Perspective effects may be applied to nearly any single object in your CorelDRAW document. But you may not apply the effect while multiple objects are selected. Instead of applying perspective to individual objects, create a group by using the Group command (CTRL+G) while the objects are selected, and apply the Perspective effect to the entire group. Use the same technique to apply perspective to grouped objects as to single objects; and after the objects are ungrouped once again, the Perspective effect remains intact.

Experienced illustrators may already have realized some of the key limitations of CorelDRAW's Perspective effect. Although this effect enables you to distort objects using single vertical and/or horizontal vanishing points, you may *not* apply multiple vanishing points on a single plane. As mentioned earlier, only one vanishing point controls the horizontal perspective, while the other controls the vertical perspective—meaning that if the perspective effect you're attempting to create involves more than one vertical and/or horizontal vanishing point, you'll have some extra drawing work ahead.

There are several other limitations to keep in mind as you use this effect. For example, you may not apply Perspective effects to the following types of objects:

- Bitmap objects

- Blend groups

- Contour groups

- Drop shadow effects

- Extrude groups

- Inserted Internet objects

- Objects applied with Envelope effects

- Objects reshaped using Interactive Distortion Tools, such as Push and Pull, Zipper, and Twister

- Paragraph text objects

With all of these limitations, however, you *may* apply perspective effects to the control objects applied with these effects. For example, choosing the objects in a Blend effect constitutes a multiple-object selection, which is ineligible for the

Perspective effect. Instead of trying to apply perspective to all objects, try either applying perspective to a single control object, or deconstructing the Blend effect using the Break Blend Group Apart and Ungroup (CTRL+U) commands, regrouping all objects together and then applying the Perspective effect. The same solution holds true for Extrude and Contour effects.

Converting any of the objects in these effects to curves using the Convert to Curves command (CTRL+Q) often enables you to apply perspective to virtually any eligible object type. When working with text objects, only Artistic Text is eligible for the Perspective effect. If your selected text has been created as Paragraph Text, the Add Perspective command will be unavailable in the Effects menu.

Copying and Clearing Perspective

Copying a Perspective effect from one object to another merely copies the distortion of the effect, without causing the objects to share vanishing points. Sharing vanishing points creates the illusion that the objects share the same physical space. When Perspective effects are copied from one object to another, vanishing points remain stationary relative to the distortion. This means that to have two or more objects share the same vanishing point, you must copy an existing Perspective effect from one object to another and then edit the new object's vanishing point so that it shares the same coordinates as the first. This technique may sound complex, but doing so takes only moments and the results can often be rewarding.

To copy perspective from one object to another, follow these steps:

1. If you haven't already done so, apply a Perspective effect to an object by choosing Effects | Add Perspective and manipulating the control handles and/or vanishing points as needed. Creating reference points for yourself using small rectangles or guidelines at the vanishing point positions of this object will make the next step much easier.

2. Using the Pick Tool, select the object you wish to copy the Perspective *to*, and move it roughly into position on your page. Choose Effects | Copy Effect | Perspective From, and target the object you wish to copy the existing Perspective *from* by clicking it using the targeting cursor (shown next). The effect is copied to the new object.

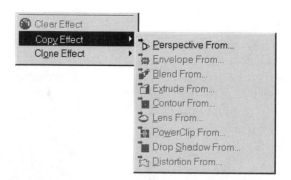

3. As mentioned, the vanishing point of your newly distorted object may not be in the right position. With the newly applied perspective control handles and vanishing point still visible, drag the corresponding vanishing point to the reference points you created earlier. Your Perspective effect is copied, and your two objects now share a common vanishing point.

Perspective effects may be applied, edited, and re-edited as many times as you wish. But unlike other effects in CorelDRAW (such as Envelope effects), Perspective effects are not compounded as they are edited—meaning that once a Perspective effect is applied and subsequently edited, the previous perspective distortion is overwritten by the new distortion shape.

Removing a Perspective effect is a one-step operation. To remove a Perspective effect, select the perspective object and choose Effects | Clear Perspective. Doing so immediately deletes all perspective properties from the object and returns it to the shape before any perspective was applied.

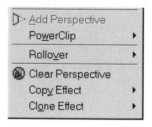

CHAPTER 20

Extruding Vector Objects

Although its name does this sophisticated feature little justice, *extrude* perhaps accurately describes its effects on objects. Defined literally, extrude means to protrude or bulge. Although several real-life positive and negative instances of this immediately come to mind, when it comes to making 2D objects appear in 3D there is no quicker effect to use. Extrude has existed in CorelDRAW since early versions and has long been one of the most powerful drawing features of the program. Uses of Extrude effects range from simple nuances added to objects to create quick depth effects (see Figure 20-1) to complete and realistic-looking drawings involving shared vanishing points.

How Vector Extrude Works

To begin understanding how this feature works, you'll need to be aware of the fact that CorelDRAW 10 actually features two different types of Extrude. The first, which we'll explore in this chapter, involves Vector Extrude, whereby a series of vector paths and objects are created and dynamically linked to your original object to create the illusion of three dimensions. The second—Bitmap Extrude (discussed in Chapter 21)—creates a 3D bitmap object from your original vector object, which may be manipulated in various ways in 3D space. Both features create 3D objects, but in completely different ways that employ different 3D properties.

When a Vector Extrude effect is applied to an object, the original object becomes a control object, and its dynamically linked Extrude effect becomes the Extrude Group. Any changes in shape, position, and/or object properties made to the control object are immediately reflected in the appearance of the extruded

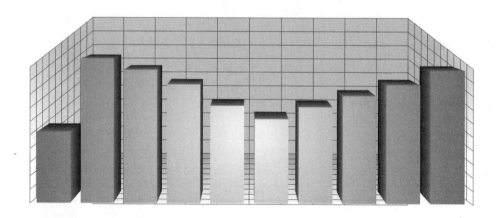

FIGURE 20-1   An Extrude effect applied to the bars in this chart provides depth in this box-shaped 3D graph.

portion of the effect. As you'll soon discover, the Extrude Group may be controlled and manipulated in a number of ways, enabling you to create quickly simulated 3D objects complete with 3D depth, color, lighting, and rotation effects. All this is accomplished while maintaining all objects as a collection of vector objects. Figure 20-2 shows the collection of vector objects applied to a simple extrusion to demonstrate a behind-the-scenes look at an Extrude effect. Figure 20-3 shows how a vector object may be both extruded and rotated in 3D space.

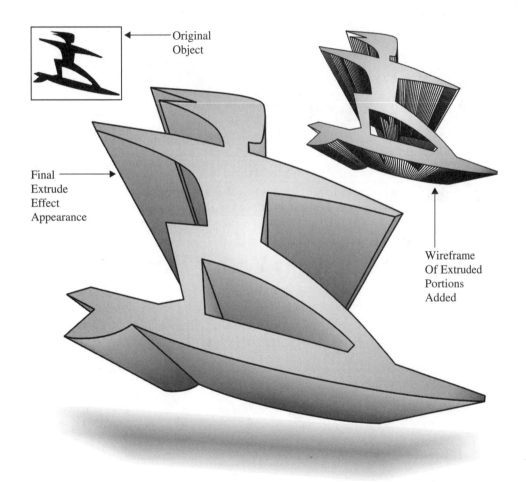

Original Object

Final Extrude Effect Appearance

Wireframe Of Extruded Portions Added

FIGURE 20-2   This simple graphical object shows the results of applying an Extrude effect. Notice the complex series of vectors that CorelDRAW creates in order to extrude each portion.

FIGURE 20-3 As a basic example of what is possible with Extrude effects, this Artistic Text object features both depth and rotation applied with Extrude Tools.

Choosing and Applying Vector Extrude

As with other drawing resources in CorelDRAW 10, Vector Extrude may be applied interactively with the Interactive Extrude Tool located in the main Toolbox and grouped with other interactive tools for Drop Shadow, Envelope, Distortion, Blend, Transparency, and Contour effects.

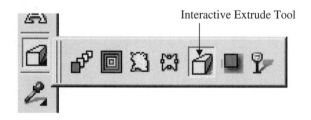

Interactive Extrude Tool

When the Interactive Extrude Tool is selected, the Property Bar provides access to all options for controlling the appearance and properties of the effect applied to your selected object. Browsing Property Bar options will give you some idea of how complex an Extrude effect can be. Options are grouped into areas for saving your applied extrusions as Presets and controlling the shape, depth, vanishing point position, rotation, lighting, color, and bevel effects (see Figure 20-4).

Applying an Extrude effect is a relatively straightforward operation, and if you've arrived here looking for a way to do it quickly, let's get started. If your immediate need is to apply a default Extrude effect to an object, follow these basic steps:

1. If you haven't already done so, create and select the object you wish to Extrude. Although you can change them later if you wish, apply fill and/or outline properties to the object before going any further.

2. Choose the Interactive Extrude Tool from the main Toolbox. Notice that your cursor changes shape and now sports an Extrude cursor. When held over your object, the cursor includes a Start symbol.

3. Using the Extrude cursor, drag from the center of your selected object outward in any direction. Notice that your object is now surrounded by a series of interactive markers, including a preview outline and an X symbol. This preview indicates the shape and direction of your new Extrude effect, while the X symbol you are currently dragging represents the Extrude vanishing point position. Notice also that the preview changes shape and position as the vanishing point is repositioned.

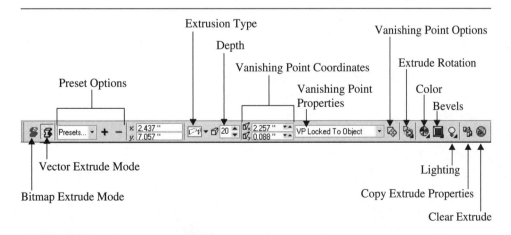

FIGURE 20-4 When the Interactive Extrude Tool is selected and an Extrude effect is in progress, the Property Bar displays these options.

4. Drag this vanishing point until your extrusion is roughly the shape you want, and release the mouse button to complete the operation. Notice that as soon as you release the mouse the Extrude Group linked to your object appears automatically. You have just applied an Extrude effect using CorelDRAW's default extrusion settings.

> **NOTE**   *By default, whenever a new Extrude effect is created with the Interactive Extrude Tool, the mode selected is always Vector Extrude. If you wish to apply a Bitmap Extrude effect, you must choose Bitmap Extrude mode in the Property Bar as the first step and before creating any initial extrusion. If you've chosen the Bitmap Extrude mode in error, you'll need to Undo (CTRL+Z) the command, since an initial Bitmap Extrude effect begins by converting your selected object into a bitmap.*

Anatomy of a Vector Extrusion

At this point, let's examine what the Extrude effect creates for you and the available controls for manipulating the attached shapes. Notice that the new extrusion includes outline and fill properties similar to your original object. If needed, you may change these properties any time by using the Pick Tool to select the control object and then altering its properties. This in turn causes the linked effect to be updated immediately. In the sections to follow, you'll discover all the Extrude properties you may apply to your object. In the meantime, though, let's take a look at the various parts of an Extrude effect in progress.

Figure 20-5 shows an Extrude effect being applied to an Artistic Text object. When the Extrude effect is in progress, interactive markers enable you to control the position, depth, and vanishing point position and enable you to change the shape of the extrusion in combination with the preview indicators.

Using the Interactive Extrude Tool and Property Bar

As mentioned, any property that may be applied to an Extrude effect can be found in the Property Bar when the Interactive Extrude Tool is selected and an Extrude effect is in progress. You may find yourself changing some of these options often, while others will remain virtually untouched, depending on the type of drawing work you're performing. Regardless, we'll be exploring each option as it affects the appearance of your extrusion.

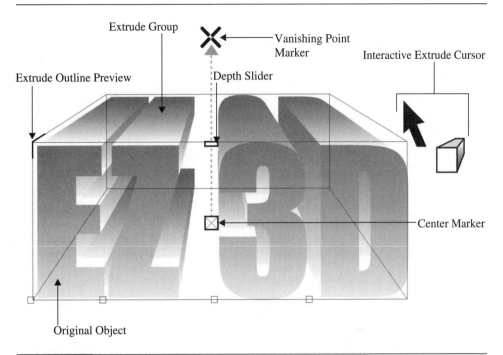

Extrude Group

Vanishing Point Marker

Interactive Extrude Cursor

Extrude Outline Preview

Depth Slider

Center Marker

Original Object

FIGURE 20-5   A Small Back Extrude effect set to a default depth of roughly 40 percent is being applied to this Artistic Text object.

Interactive Extrude Tool States

The Interactive Extrude Tool appears differently among cursor states, shown next. This is a subtle new addition to CorelDRAW 10. When selected and held over your document page, the cursor takes its usual state; but when held over an object eligible for an Extrude Effect, it appears with a Start symbol. If an object is ineligible for an Extrude effect, the cursor will indicate this visually.

Interactive Extrude Tool Cursors

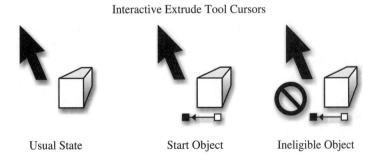

Usual State   Start Object   Ineligible Object

20

Setting Extrusion Shape

The shape of the Extrude Group protruding from your object will no doubt be of critical concern. The shape of your extrusion is not set interactively, but instead by using the Extrusion Type selector, shown next, in the Property Bar, which features six types to choose from. While a specific type is selected, the extruded portion of the effect can be set to protrude in a direction relative to your object. Choosing a Front style causes the vanishing point to be layered in front of your object, and for Back styles, vanishing points are layered behind your object. The representative symbols in the selector indicate their effects, with the darkened line indicating your original object.

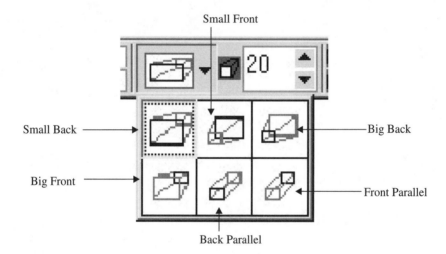

Small Front

Small Back

Big Back

Big Front

Front Parallel

Back Parallel

Choosing an Extrusion Shape

Although the names are slightly confusing, at first some of these styles may seem the same. But in fact, the opposite is true. Choosing an extrusion type enables you to control how the extruded portion protrudes from your object. Imagine for a moment that the extruded portion needs three key questions answered before it may be created: Which direction is the vanishing point, to what depth, and is it in front of or behind the original object?

Choosing the extrusion shape enables you to determine at least two of these variables: vanishing point direction and relative direction to the object (front/back). Figure 20-6 shows the results of applying each of these six extrusion styles to the

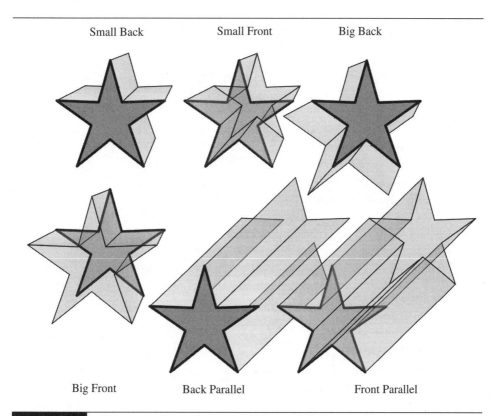

Small Back   Small Front   Big Back

Big Front   Back Parallel   Front Parallel

FIGURE 20-6   This star polygon features a different default extrusion type in each case.

same polygon using default options. Styles have been applied in an arrangement identical to the Property Bar option arrangements to clarify their effects. Only the extrusion types have been changed. Notice in each case that the extruded portion varies by relative position and direction.

Small Back   Choosing this option (the default setting) causes the extrusion and vanishing point to be layered behind your original object. Small Back is perhaps the most commonly applied extrusion type.

Small Front   Choosing this option causes the extrusion and vanishing point to be layered in front of your original object.

20

Big Back   Choosing this option causes the extrusion to be layered behind your original object, while the vanishing point is positioned in front.

Big Front   Choosing this option causes the extrusion to be layered in front of your original object, while the vanishing point is positioned in back.

Back Parallel   Choosing this option causes the extrusion to be layered behind your original object so that the extruded surfaces appear parallel to the original surfaces. When this option is selected, the vanishing point sets the depth of the extrusion, while the actual depth option in the docker is unavailable. No vanishing point accompanies this extrusion style.

Front Parallel   This option causes the extrusion to be layered in front of your original object so that the extruded surfaces appear parallel to the original surfaces. While this option is selected, the vanishing point sets the depth of the extrusion, while the actual depth option in the docker is unavailable. No vanishing point accompanies this extrusion style.

Setting Extrude Depth

The Depth value for your Extrude effect is likely one of the properties you'll find yourself adjusting most often. It may be set one of two ways: interactively, by dragging the Depth slider control, or by entering a value in the Depth box in the Property Bar while an Extrude effect is in progress. The Depth value may be set between 1 and 99 and is based roughly on the percentage of width and depth of your original object. Figure 20-7 shows two extreme Depth values on a typical Extrude effect.

Setting Vanishing Point Properties

The vanishing point position determines the point toward which all lines of perspective in your Extrude effect appear to diminish. The vanishing point may be set anywhere on or off your document page and is set relative to the center origin of your original object. It's rather important to keep in mind that the direction of the vanishing point determines only the point toward which objects diminish, and does not control whether the extruded portion protrudes from the front or back of the object.

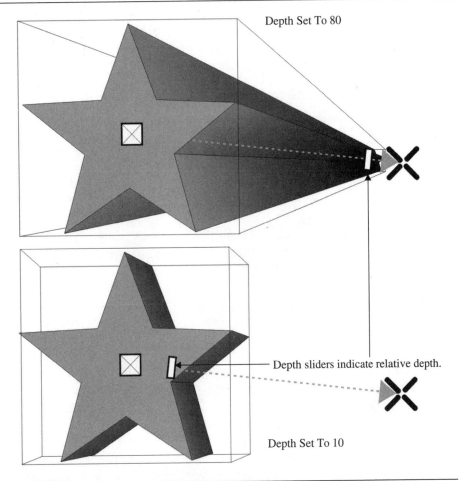

Depth Set To 80

Depth Set To 10

Depth sliders indicate relative depth.

FIGURE 20-7   This star polygon has had two different Depth values applied, while all other Extrude properties remain identical.

TIP   *Vanishing points may be set on four of the six available extrusion types: Small Back, Big Back, Small Front, and Big Front. The sides of the extruded portions created in the Front Parallel or Back Parallel types never converge, so no vanishing point is involved.*

20

Setting the position of the Extrude vanishing point enables you to specify a point on (or off) your document page toward which your extruded object portions appear to diminish. The Vanishing Point Properties selector enables you to access this brief selection of commands.

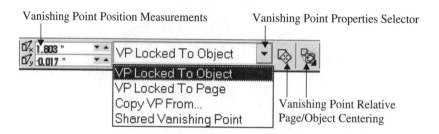

Vanishing Point controls enable you to lock your extrusion's vanishing point, copy vanishing points from an existing extrusion, or share vanishing points between extruded objects in the following ways:

Locking to the Object   Choosing the VP Locked To Object option (the default setting) "locks" the vanishing point in a position relative to the object, no matter where the original extruded object is positioned.

Locking to the Page   As the term implies, VP Locked Tto Page enables you to fix the vanishing point to your page, forcing the extrusion to diminish toward a fixed page position, no matter where the original object is moved. To experience the effects of this condition, reposition your object after the extrusion has been applied.

Copying Vanishing Points   This is more of a command than an option and enables you to copy a vanishing point position from any other object that features an Extrude effect. Immediately after choosing Copy VP From, your cursor changes to a vanishing point targeting cursor, which enables you to target any other extruded object on your document page with the aim of copying its vanishing point position. In order for this to be successful, you must have at least one other Extrude effect applied to an object and in view. After the vanishing point has been copied, the Property Bar will indicate the object's vanishing point as VP Locked To Page, meaning that the vanishing point may not be repositioned.

Sharing Vanishing Points   Choosing Shared Vanishing Point enables you to have multiple objects share the *same* vanishing point, but you must have applied at least an initial Extrude effect to your objects before attempting to use this command.

Immediately after choosing this option, your cursor changes to a vanishing point targeting cursor, enabling you to target any other extruded object with the aim of creating a common vanishing point position for multiple objects. This may be repeated for as many objects as you wish. When multiple objects share a vanishing point, they may be repositioned anywhere on your document page, but the extrusion shape is immediately updated to realign toward the shared vanishing point position. This option is most useful when creating the effect to appear in perspective in the same simulated 3D space. Figure 20-8 may help clarify the results of setting up a shared vanishing point arrangement.

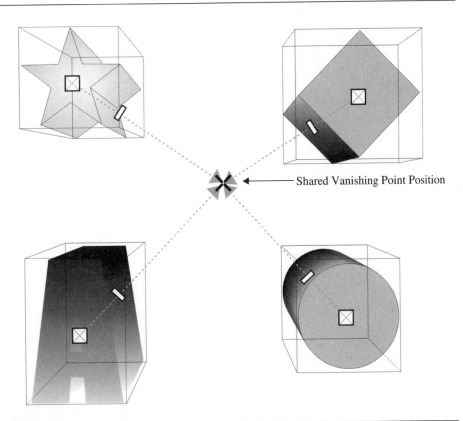

Shared Vanishing Point Position

FIGURE 20-8   These four simple objects share the same vanishing point, applied with the Shared Vanishing Point command.

20

Setting a Relative Position for Vanishing Points   Two buttons in the Property Bar also enable you to toggle the measurement state of vanishing points of objects. When the Position Vanishing Point Relative to Page Origin is selected, the vanishing point position boxes enable you to specify the vanishing point relative to your page origin—a value determined either by the lower-left corner by default, or by the zero markers on your ruler origin. When the Position Vanishing Point Relative to Object Center is selected, the center of your currently selected object is used as the measurement value, which changes according to the object's page position.

Setting 3D Rotation

The ability to rotate an applied Extrude effect throws a whole new twist (excuse the pun) on creating depth effects with this feature. Rotation involves using a different set of cursor tools to rotate both your original object and the applied extrusion shape. Although these tools and the results of using them may at first seem complicated or confusing, the key to grasping and manipulating a rotated extrusion comes from familiarity with cursor states and rotation effects in a simulated 3D space.

Extrusions may be rotated vertically, horizontally, clockwise, and/or counterclockwise around the center origin of your original object with either the Interactive Tool cursor or the Rotation options in the Property Bar. However, you must have already applied at least a default extrusion effect in order for these tools and options to be available. Property Bar rotation controls may take one of two states: using either a representational-style rotation option or numeric entry boxes measuring rotation on X, Y, and X axes. You may toggle between the two display states by clicking the button located to the lower right of the selector.

Using the representational-style rotation option, a hand cursor appears within the selector, enabling you to click-drag to manipulate the rotation of the representative Corel logo, which in turn applies corresponding rotation to your selected Extrude effect objects. As you apply rotation in the selector, a yellow arc-style path appears, providing a visual representation of the applied rotation. Clicking the X button in the lower left of the selector returns rotation values to zero.

Extrude Rotation Button

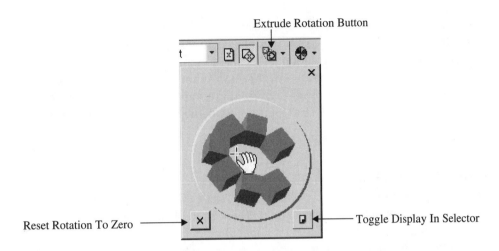

Reset Rotation To Zero ——————→

Toggle Display In Selector

When using the numeric rotation boxes, you may enter positive or negative values to rotate your Extrude effect. If you require a more precisely controlled rotation, you may choose to enter the values using numeric boxes. These are accessed by clicking the numeric switch button to the lower right of the symbol, which displays three Rotation Value boxes labeled X, Y, and Z. All three of the rotational values found here are based on units of percentage and may be set between 100 and −100 (a negative value).

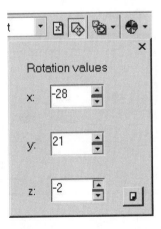

When entering numeric values, Y represents vertical rotation on the standard *Y* axis. Positive Y values represent rotation about the vertical (*Y*-axis), resulting in the left edge of the object moving toward you. Negative Y values have the opposite effect. The X represents horizontal rotation on the standard *X* axis. Positive X values represent rotation about the horizontal (*X*-axis), resulting in the top edge of the object moving toward you. Again, negative X values have the opposite effect. The Z value represents circular rotation on the *Z* axis. Positive values represent counterclockwise rotation, while negative values represent clockwise rotation.

Using the Interactive Rotation Tools

Perhaps a more intuitive way of rotating an Extrude effect is through use of interactive cursors, but these appear only when manually activated and only after an initial Extrude effect has been applied to your selected object. Before attempting to use these cursor states to rotate your extrusion, it may be worthwhile to examine Figure 20-9, which identifies the various interactive markers and controls that appear around your object in this state.

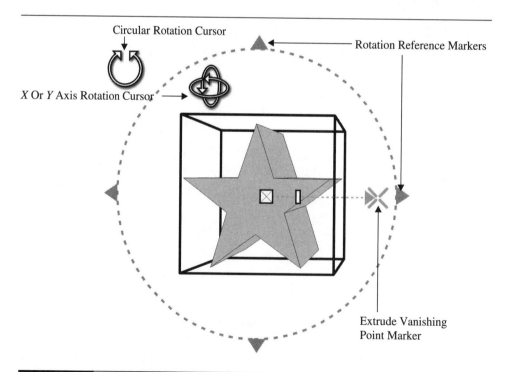

FIGURE 20-9   This polygon is surrounded by CorelDRAW's Extrude Rotation cursors and controls.

| NOTE | *While either Back Parallel or Front Parallel are selected, Extrude Rotation controls will be unavailable to you, since parallel extrusions must remain fixed in order to remain parallel. When the vanishing point is locked to the page, Extrude Rotation is also unavailable.* |

Rotating a Vector Extrude Effect

Entering the interactive rotation state for an Extrude effect may be slightly tricky your first time out. Launching these controls requires a series of precise click operations on a specific area of your applied effect. To launch the controls, follow these steps:

1. If you haven't already done so, create an object and apply at least a default Extrude effect to the object using the Interactive Extrude Tool and Property Bar options. If your object already has an Extrude effect applied, double-clicking the extruded portion of the effect will immediately launch you into the editing mode of the effect with the Interactive Extrude Tool and Property Bar in view.

2. With an Extrude effect applied and the interactive Extrude markers now surrounding your object, single-click the *extruded* portion. If you successfully double-clicked the actual Extrude effect portion, your interactive rotation tools will now be in view. Notice the circular guides surrounding the effect. The inside and outside areas of this circular area determine your tool cursor state.

3. Hold your tool cursor outside the circular area and notice that it resembles the cursor while outside the area. This cursor controls the clockwise and counterclockwise Extrude rotation. Keeping the cursor held outside the circular shape, click-drag in either a clockwise or counterclockwise direction. Notice that your entire Extrude effect rotates in the direction you dragged.

4. Next, hold your tool cursor inside the circular area and notice that it resembles the cursor while inside the circular area. This cursor controls the clockwise and counterclockwise Extrude rotation. While keeping your cursor held inside this area, click-drag either up, down, left, or right slightly. Notice how your entire effect now rotates in both X and Y rotational directions as you drag.

5. To end the rotation session, click a blank space on your document page well beyond the interactive rotational cursor area to deselect the effect.

Your cursor returns to the normal Extrude cursor state. You've just completed rotating your Extrude effect.

If you've just worked through the above steps, it may help to know certain modifier keys that are available while rotating your Extrude effect on the X and Y axes and while the interactive rotation cursor is held inside the circular guide area. Holding CTRL has the effect of constraining the rotation of your extrusion on either the vertical or horizontal planes, which can provide more control over the rotation of your effect.

> **NOTE** *After an Extrude effect has been rotated, you may adjust the Extrude Depth of the effect, but the vanishing point position may not be adjusted unless the rotation is cleared by using the Reset button in the Extrude Rotation selector.*

Adding Lights

For truly realistic 3D effects, adding lights to your extrusion (whether it has been rotated or not) opens new opportunities for a heightened sense of realism. CorelDRAW's Extrude effect has featured these lighting options since early versions, and little has changed since their introduction. To access the lighting controls for your Extrude effect, click the Extrude Lighting button in the Property Bar when an Extrude effect is in progress.

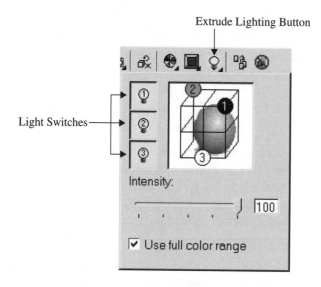

Anatomy of the Lighting Controls

The Extrude lighting features take a degree of familiarity to use. There are essentially three light sources available for you to use, each of which may be activated, positioned, and customized independently of the other two lights. Lights are also omnidirectional, meaning that they may not be aimed at a specific point, but simply positioned. Their intensity may be set between 0 and 100 percent by using the slider control when a specific light is selected.

When you first access the Extrude Lighting feature, all lights are deactivated—the default state. To activate a light, you must click one of the three Light Source buttons in the selector (see Figure 20-10). Once a light is activated, it is positioned on a representative grid arrangement around your object, indicated by a representative sphere in the selector preview. The light does not actually appear in your drawing

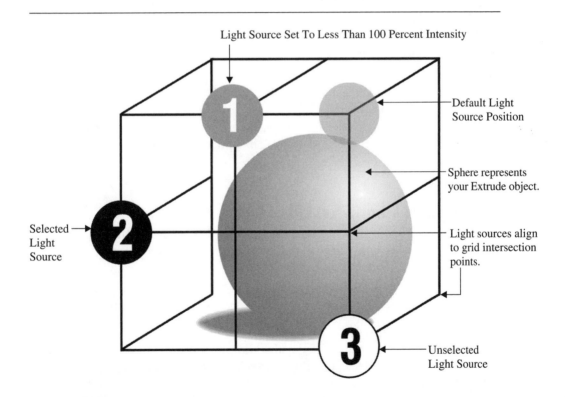

Light Source Set To Less Than 100 Percent Intensity

Default Light Source Position

Sphere represents your Extrude object.

Selected Light Source

Light sources align to grid intersection points.

Unselected Light Source

FIGURE 20-10   A grid arrangement surrounds a preview in the Extrude Light selector, enabling you to activate and manipulate lighting for your extrusion.

around your object, but remains invisible with only the light cast visible. When a light source is activated, a numeral identifies which light source it is. Light sources may be selected with single clicks or repositioned on the 3D grid with a dragging action.

When adding multiple light sources in succession, keep in mind that all newly activated lights are positioned in the same default position. When a light is activated, it's automatically set to appear at the upper-right front corner of the grid. This means if two or more light sources are activated in succession without being moved, the unfortunate result may be three light sources piled one on top of another. If this happens during your lighting operation, simply drag the lights off the default corner position one at a time and reposition them around the grid.

A *selected* Light Source is indicated by a black circle on the preview selector, while unselected light sources are indicated by white circles. Light Sources that have been set to brightness levels less than 100 percent appear in various gray colors relative to their brightness setting. As these light sources are dragged around the 3D grid, they automatically snap to points on the grid where lines intersect. You may not position lights at the back-mid-center or back-center-bottom positions.

| NOTE | *Engineering light sources into your Extrude effect certainly opens avenues for drama and creativity for objects. However, the lights you apply to your objects may only be white and ambient in their nature, meaning that using colored lights or spotlighting isn't an option. Lights may not be colored, nor may they be directed.* |

Adding and Editing Extrude Lights

Now that you have a firm understanding of how lights are activated and positioned, the following steps will guide you through the process of adding a new light source to your Extrude effect:

1. If you haven't already done so, create an object and use the Interactive Extrude Tool to apply an Extrude effect.

2. With the object still selected and while still using the Interactive Extrude Tool, click the Extrude Lighting selector in the Property Bar to access the light sources and options.

3. Click the Light Switch 1 button to depress it. Notice that a light source symbol appears at the default position in the upper-right front corner of the grid, represented by a black circle containing the numeral 1. A representative sphere also appears within the grid. Notice also that the Intensity slider becomes available. This indicates light source 1 is currently selected. Notice that the colors of your Extrude effect are altered to reflect the new light source being cast.

4. Drag the symbol representing light source 1 to a different position on the representative 3D grid, and notice how the coloring of your effect changes to reflect the new lighting position.

5. With Light Source 1 still selected, drag the Intensity slider to the left to roughly the 50 percent position and notice how the brightness of the affected areas is lowered.

6. Click the Light Switch 2 button to activate it. Notice that it appears in the same default position as the first Light Source, and the symbol representing light source 1 appears gray, indicating that it is no longer selected. Drag Light Source 2 to a different grid position and observe the results.

7. Finally, click both Light Switches 1 and 2 to deactivate them, and notice how the lighting effect is removed and the coloring of your Extrude effect is returned to its original state. To end the session, click anywhere outside the Extrude Lighting selector.

TIP	*You can remove an Extrude effect from your original object at any time by clicking on the extruded portion of the effect and choosing Effects	Clear Extrude, or you can use the Interactive Extrude Tool by clicking the Clear Extrude button in the Property Bar.*

Controlling Light Properties

Besides the fact that you may activate up to three Light Sources and customize the position of each, two additional options are available when using lighting. They have the following effects on your extrusion:

Lighting Intensity As mentioned, the Intensity slider determines the brightness of each light. While a light is selected, the range may be set between 0 and 100 percent, where higher values cause brighter lighting.

Lighting Color   Below the Intensity slider is the Use Full Color Range option, which is often misunderstood when using Extrude lighting. By default, this option is selected and enables CorelDRAW to use the a full gamut of colors when coloring the surfaces of your original object and its extruded portion. The term *gamut* refers to the use of the complete range of colors available to CorelDRAW, depending on the color mode of your original object and the extrusion. When working in CMYK process or RGB color, this won't necessarily affect the color composition of your objects, and in these cases you'll definitely want to leave it selected to get the maximum benefit of color when light sources are applied. While objects are filled with CMYK or RGB color, the resulting variations also use these respective color modes.

However, if your original object and/or the extruded portion use spot colors, this option may be of interest. Deselecting it has the effect of limiting the color variations caused by light sources to only those percentages of the spot colors specified in both your original object and its extruded portion. Unfortunately, deselecting this option limits color depth and diminishes the effects of the lighting you apply, but results in a valid spot color tint, as opposed to RGB. This means that if your objects are filled with spot color, you may wish to deactivate this option.

Setting Extrude Color

After applying an Extrude effect, you'll likely want to take full advantage of the simulated 3D illusion of depth by varying the colors on either your original object or its attached extrusion. However, this doesn't occur entirely automatically and requires that you do a little work. For example, if your object is filled with a flat uniform color, a default extrusion will also appear flat, since the default color fill for your extrusion uses the original object's fill. However, there are certain defaults in place that make it easier to create the illusion of depth—such as when using fountain fills to fill your original object. You'll notice that the extrusion color (created at defaults) automatically creates the extruded portion of the effect to be filled with a fountain fill color from your object's color to a Black default color.

Your Extrude effect's color may be adjusted instantly by selecting options available in the Extrude Color button on the Property Bar (see Figure 20-11). Color options include using your object's fill color, specifying a solid fill color, and creating color shading effects. In each case, further different options become available, depending on your selection.

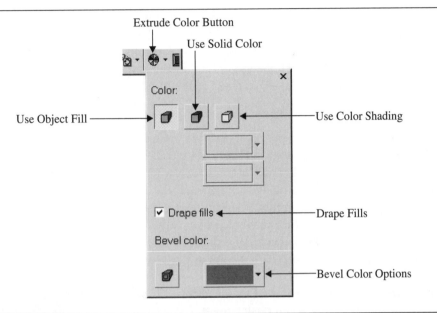

Extrude Color Button

Use Solid Color

Color:

Use Object Fill ────── Use Color Shading

☑ Drape fills ◄────── Drape Fills

Bevel color:

Bevel Color Options

FIGURE 20-11 The Extrude Color selector, which is subdivided into three color areas here, is available in the Property Bar while an Extrude effect is in progress.

The effects of choosing these options for your Extrude effect color are as follows:

Using Your Object's Fill The Use Object Fill option is the most straightforward to use, but does not automatically create a realistic depth effect. If your original object is filled with a uniform color, a pattern fill, or a texture fill, this option becomes the default for your new Extrude effect and has the effect of filling the extruded portion with your original object's color. When this option is selected, the Drape Fill option also becomes available (and selected by default). Drape Fill is discussed later in this section.

TIP *If your original object has no outline applied, it may be difficult to see the edges between the original and extruded portions. Applying an outline in many instances will help create definition between the edges of the two portions.*

20

Choosing Your Own Solid Fill   To select a different uniform color for your Extrude effect, choose the Use Solid Color option, which enables you to specify any other uniform color with a color selector. This results in the extruded portion of your effect being filled with the specified uniform color, regardless of the fill type currently applied to your object (see Figure 20-12). The secondary color option becomes available only while Use Color Shading is selected.

Using Color Shading   The Use Color Shading option creates a depth effect by using your object's own color as the From color and Black as the To color. If the object you've applied your Extrude effect to is already filled with fountain fill color, Use Color Shading automatically becomes the default. If not, you're free to apply it to any extrusion simply by selecting it. Choosing Use Color Shading enables you to specify two different colors, labeled From and To, which enable you to specify the fountain fill colors used for the shading effect. Most often, depth effects are improved by using a darker color as the To color (see Figure 20-12).

Draping Your Object's Fill over the Extrude Effect   The term *drape* refers to the effect of covering your original object and its extruded portion with the color specified for the original object. While Drape Fill is selected (the default) your original object's fill color is automatically set to fill the full extent of the extrusion. If your object uses uniform fill color, the effects of using this option won't be

Extrude Color Applied With Use Object Fill Option

Extrude Color Applied With Use Color Shading Option

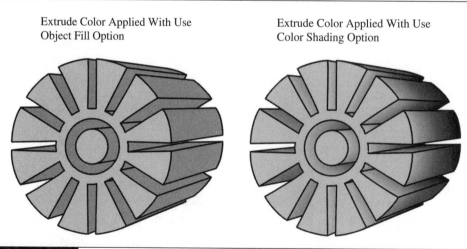

FIGURE 20-12   This object has a typical Extrude effect applied. Each original object features the same color fill with a different Extrude Color.

apparent. However, if your original object is filled with a tiling pattern or texture fill, you'll notice that the fill seams extend across both the original object and its extrusion. When the Drape Fills option is not selected, tiling fills are set to repeat for the original and for each Extrude effect surface—an effect that is often more complex, but more realistic looking than the effect you get when this option is selected. Figure 20-13 shows the different results (selected and not selected) of the Drape Fills option.

Using Bevel Color   This option becomes available only when your Extrude effect has been applied with a Bevel effect. Bevel options are located in the Bevels selector in the Property Bar (discussed in the next section). If your Extrude effect includes bevels, selecting this option (the default) has the effect of draping whichever extruded portion is currently selected across the bevel surface. When not selected, the accompanying color selector enables you to specify a uniform color fill of your choice for the Bevel effect. If your Extrude effect has a Pattern or Texture fill applied, you may wish to leave this option selected, since the effects are often more visually appealing.

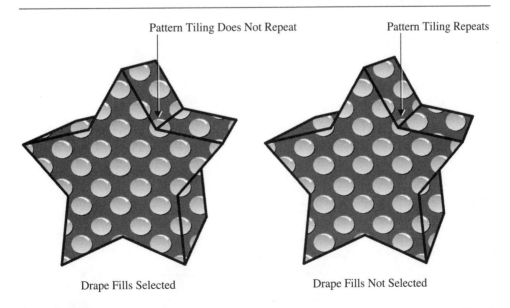

FIGURE 20-13   This star polygon has been filled with a full-color bitmap pattern and has a typical Extrude effect

TIP *You may dismantle an Extrude effect any time you wish by right-clicking the extruded portion of the effect and choosing Break Extrude Group Apart from the pop-up menu. Doing so breaks the dynamic link between the extruded portion and your original object. What remains will be your original object unchanged by the effect and the group of objects that originally made up the effect.*

Applying Extrusion Bevels

In real-life objects, the term *bevel* refers to the flattening of the corner or edge surfaces of an object, which gives it a refined or carved appearance. For Extrude effects, bevels mimic this real-life scenario. They have the effect of applying flat angled surfaces to your object, and are added concentrically within the interior of your original object's shape. Bevels are in fact a hybrid of CorelDRAW's Extrude effect and may be used in combination with Extrude effects or set to appear as the only portion of the effect.

When a Bevel effect is applied to an object, it is built in the opposite direction relative to the extruded portion. In other words, if your Extrude effect protrudes from the *back* of your object, the bevel will be created to appear at the *front,* which is perhaps the biggest difference between the two effects. The opposite is true for Extrude effects applied to the front of your object. Bevel shape is based on the angle and depth specified in the Bevel selector.

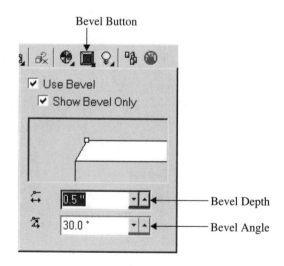

Bevel Button

Bevel Depth

Bevel Angle

Using Only Bevels

The first time you use these Bevel options, you may notice that only the Use Bevel option appears and is not selected (the default state). Selecting Use Bevel causes the remaining options in the selector to become active. Bevel effects may only be applied after an initial Extrude effect has been applied, so if you choose to apply bevels and wish only the Bevel effect to be visible, select the Show Bevel Only option. This renders any applied Extrude effect inactive, with no extruded portion being created.

Setting Bevel Shape

As mentioned earlier, bevels are applied in the opposite direction of the extruded portion, but the shape of the bevel itself is determined by the Bevel Depth and Bevel Angle options in the Bevel selector of the Property Bar while an Extrude effect is in progress. Your new Bevel Depth may be set between 0.001 inches and 1,980 inches.

Bevel Angle may be set to a maximum of 89 degrees. Shallow angles of less than 30 percent often provide the best visual results. The preview window in the Bevels selector roughly indicates a cross-sectional representation of the depth and angle settings entered. Figure 20-14 shows the results of applying a typical Bevel effect with and without an Extrude effect involved.

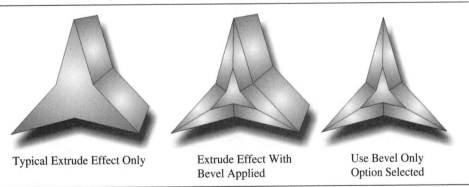

Typical Extrude Effect Only   Extrude Effect With   Use Bevel Only
                                      Bevel Applied   Option Selected

FIGURE 20-14 This three-pointed polygon includes a Bevel effect with and without the extruded portion included.

20

Using Vector Extrude Presets

So far, we've explored the results of creating Extrude effects; manipulating vanishing points; applying lighting; and setting color, rotation, and bevels. These are the basic properties that you may select with any Extrude effect. Next we'll look at saving these Extrude properties as Presets for applying to other existing Extrude effects by using Property Bar options.

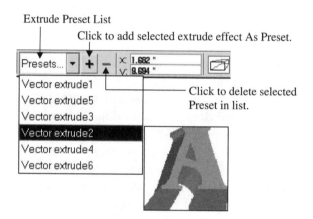

Extrude effect Presets are used in the same manner as other Preset controls associated with interactive effects such as Envelopes, Drop Shadows, Distortion, Blend, Contour, and Transparency. Extrude effect Presets may be saved and reapplied to a selected object in your document. To apply a saved Extrude effect Preset to selected objects and explore adding or deleting Extrude effect Presets, follow these quick steps:

1. If you haven't already done so, create and select an object on your document page using the Pick Tool.

2. Choose the Interactive Extrude Tool from the main Toolbox.

3. Using Property Bar options, choose a saved Extrude effect from the Preset List. The properties of the Extrude effect are immediately applied, and its current effect properties are displayed in the Property Bar.

4. To save an existing Extrude effect as a preset while using the Interactive Extrude Tool and Property Bar, click to select the extruded portion of the effect and click the Add Preset (+) button. The Save As dialog opens. Enter

a new name for your new Extrude effect Preset in the File Name box and click Save. Your Extrude effect Preset is added to the Preset List.

5. To delete a saved Extrude effect Preset, select the Preset from the Preset List and click the Delete Preset button (–) in the Property Bar. The saved Preset is immediately deleted.

By default, saved Extrude effect Presets are stored in the Program Files/ Corel/Graphics 10/Draw/Presets/VectorExtrude folder using typical default installation directory names.

Using the Extrude Docker

Up to this point, we've explored all the various aspects of applying Extrude effects and using associated options by using the Interactive Extrude Tool and Property Bar. Although this is perhaps the most intuitive way of applying Extrude effects, there's always the Extrude Docker, which still exists. If you're a longtime CorelDRAW user, you may have grown accustomed to applying Extrude effects with this docker, although it is now redundant with the Interactive Extrude Tool.

To access the Extrude Docker, choose Effects | Extrude or choose Window | Dockers | Extrude. The Extrude options in this docker are organized into five tabbed docker pages: Camera (referring to shape), Rotation, Light, Color, and Bevels (see Figure 20-15). Although options in this docker are organized slightly differently, you may apply the same properties as when using the Interactive Extrude Tool. Note however, that the Extrude Docker enables you to choose your Extrude settings before manually applying them with the Apply button.

Controlling Extrude Complexity with Facet Size

When applying your Extrude effects, you may have noticed how the curves and shading are applied with the Use Color Shading option. Smooth curves and shading involve complex calculations and produce greater or fewer Extrude effect portions to maintain a smooth effect. Curves and shading that are less smooth are much less complex. However, the smoother the curve and shading, the better the display and print quality will be.

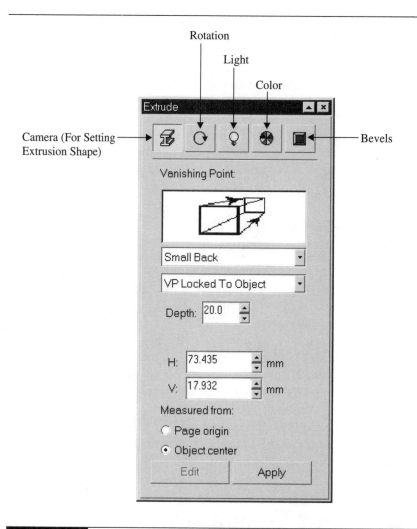

FIGURE 20-15 The Extrude Docker is organized into these five tabbed areas.

When CorelDRAW creates an Extrude effect, the smoothness of curves and the number of objects used to create shaded extrusion fills are controlled by something called *facet*. The facet size is a factor of the smoothness of curves and shading. Facet size is a value that may be controlled, but few users realize it exists.

You may set the facet size at any time by choosing Tools | Options or by pressing the shortcut (CTRL+J) and clicking Edit in the left-hand listing of the

Copying and Cloning Extrude Effects

As is the case with other effects available in CorelDRAW, you may copy or clone from existing Extrude effects in your document. Neither command requires that you have the Interactive Extrude Tool selected to do so, and both operations are accomplished by using command menus.

When copying an Extrude effect, at least one Extrude effect must be in view, and at least one object must be selected on your screen. To copy an Extrude effect, choose Effects | Copy Effect | Extrude From. Your active cursor will immediately become a targeting cursor. Use this cursor to target the extruded portion of an existing Extrude effect to copy all applied Extrude properties.

Cloning an Extrude effect achieves a slightly different result. When an effect is applied through cloning, the master clone effect object controls the new effect. Any changes made to the master will immediately be applied to the clone. Any changes made to the clone properties will override the properties applied by the master, with any unchanged effect properties maintaining a perpetual link to the master clone effect. In order to clone an Extrude effect, you must have created at least one other Extrude effect and have this in view. You must also have at least one object selected on your screen.

To clone an Extrude effect, choose Effects | Clone Effect | Extrude From. Your cursor will immediately become a targeting cursor. Use this cursor to target the existing Extrude effect you wish to clone by clicking directly on the Extrude Group portion of the effect.

Options dialog (see Figure 20-16). The option itself is named Minimum Extrude Facet Size and may be set between 0.001 inches and 36 inches—the default is 0.05 inches. Higher values cause Extrude effect curves to display and print less smoothly, while lower values increase the smoothness of extruded curves and significantly increase display and printing times (see Figure 20-17). Notice the difference in complexity of the shading applied to curves. If you wish, you may also use the Save Facet Size with Document option in this dialog to avoid the need to change the facet size each time your document is reopened.

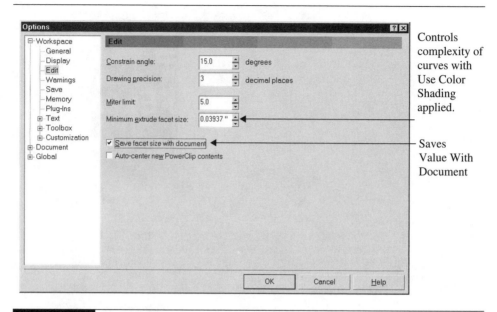

Controls
complexity of
curves with
Use Color
Shading
applied.

Saves
Value With
Document

FIGURE 20-16 Adjustments to the Facet size setting enable you to control the complexity of your Extrude effects in relation to the curves and shading created.

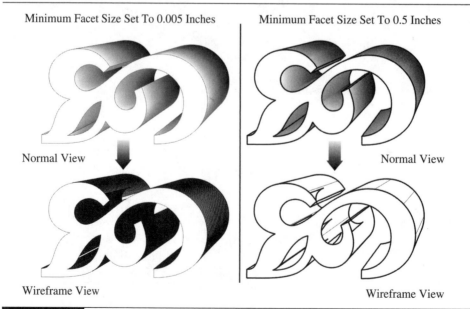

Minimum Facet Size Set To 0.005 Inches

Minimum Facet Size Set To 0.5 Inches

Normal View

Normal View

Wireframe View

Wireframe View

FIGURE 20-17 These two Extrude effects (shown in both Normal and Wireframe views) applied to identical objects were applied using different Facet sizes.

CHAPTER 21

Applying Bitmap Extrude to Objects

If you long to have the ability to create smooth 3D effects to drawing objects, you're in luck—CorelDRAW 10 features a significantly improved Bitmap Extrude effect. The capabilities of this effect have been extended to include more object types and their functionality has been made vastly more efficient with CorelDRAW 10's new Live Preview capabilities. In this chapter, you explore how to apply bitmap extrude effects to objects and control the options that affect how they appear.

How Bitmap Extrude Works

Bitmap Extrude effects are applied using the Interactive Extrude Tool in Bitmap Extrude mode. CorelDRAW 10's Bitmap Extrude effects may be vaguely similar in appearance to vector extrusions, but they're actually quite different. As the name implies, Bitmap Extrude operates on bitmap principles. This means that although the effects are created using vector objects, the object producing the visual effect is actually a bitmap rendering of the properties applied. Bitmap-rendered effects are often more elegant looking than vector-based extrusions because they use anti-aliasing display methods to render the effects.

Certain differences exist between the techniques and available options when applying each of these two effects. In addition to the tool differences covered in this chapter, you'll notice that vanishing points, fills, and lighting capabilities are each used in different ways and produce different results in the following ways:

- **Vanishing Points**   Bitmap Extrude effects have no vanishing points— their perspective effects are applied to each individual object separately, meaning Bitmap Extrude objects may not easily share vanishing points.

- **Fill Properties**   The fills applied to the extrude portions of a Bitmap Extrude effect are automatically shaded (using black) and draped (using the object fill), meaning you may not apply a different fill type to the original versus its extrude portion.

- **Lighting**   Bitmap Extrude effects may be illuminated using both Ambient Light and/or multiple Point Lights, each of which may be set to its own color and position.

One of the most significant issues to remember when applying Bitmap Extrude effects to your drawing objects is this: Once your object has been applied with this type of effect, there's no turning back. Once your object(s) have been applied with this effect, they permanently become bitmap-based objects. Short of using the Undo commands to reverse application of this effect, you may not Clear Bitmap Extrude effects from objects.

Before diving too quickly into applying Bitmap Extrude effects, keep in mind that Bitmap Extrude and Vector Extrude are completely different types of effects applied in two different modes—even though they're both applied using the same tool. You may not toggle the state of your effect between these two modes.

Bitmap Extrude and the Property Bar

Bitmap extrusions are applied using the Interactive Extrude Tool selected from the main Toolbox. You find it grouped with other interactive tools for Blend, Drop Shadow, Contour, Distortion, Envelopes, and Transparency.

Interactive Extrude Tool

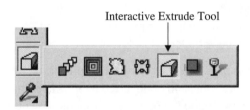

By default, whenever the Interactive Extrude Tool is selected from the main Toolbox, it is automatically set to Vector Extrude mode. This means that to apply a bitmap extrusion to your selected object, you must first choose the Bitmap Extrude mode using the Property Bar. Once selected, the Property Bar comes alive to display the available options.

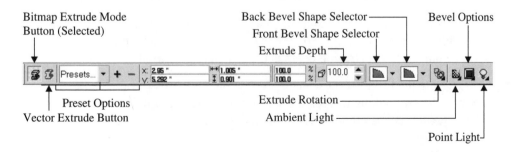

Bitmap Extrude Mode Button (Selected)
Back Bevel Shape Selector
Bevel Options
Front Bevel Shape Selector
Extrude Depth
Preset Options
Vector Extrude Button
Extrude Rotation
Ambient Light
Point Light

Exploring Bitmap Extrude Effects

If your immediate need is to apply a bitmap extrusion and you have some familiarity with the Interactive Extrude Tool and Property Bar options, follow these steps:

1. If you haven't already done so, open a new or existing document and create an object shape to which you can apply a bitmap extrusion. For this example, use a simple object such as a Rectangle, Ellipse, Artistic Text, or Symbol object.

2. Apply a Fill property to your object in the usual way using either the Interactive Fill Tool for special fill types or the onscreen palette for quick access to Uniform fill colors.

3. With your object selected, choose the Interactive Extrude Tool from the main Toolbox. Notice that the Property Bar features two buttons on the far left that control the mode of your extrusion. By default, the Vector Extrusion button is selected. To switch the extrusion mode to apply a bitmap extrusion, click the Bitmap Extrude mode button.

4. Double-click the object to launch the Bitmap Extrude rotation controls. Notice your object is instantly converted to a bitmap object and a "bounding box" now appears around the object accompanied by circular, horizontal and vertical rotation guides. Your cursor also changes, depending on which guide it's held over.

5. Using a click-drag action directly on each of the guides, explore rotating your object from its original state using the three available rotation cursors. Your object appears wafer-thin as it's rotated. This is because of the depth value applied, which, by default, is set to 100 percent.

6. Using Property Bar options, increase the extrusion depth by entering a higher value (such as 500) in the Depth box followed by pressing ENTER. Your object's extrusion depth is immediately increased.

7. Using the Front Bevel selector, choose one of the five available Bevel styles by clicking to open the selector and clicking a style. Your new Bevel shape is immediately applied to the front surface of the object.

8. With a Bevel applied, click the Ambient Light button in the Property Bar to open the selector and display a representative preview (sphere) of your current Ambient lighting. By default, your Ambient Light is activated (On) and set to a White color using a Brightness value of 50. If you want, change the color and/or Brightness of the Ambient Light and click the Apply button in the selector. Notice how if affects the overall color of your object. Typically, increasing the Brightness lightens your object's color, while decreasing it has the opposite effect.

9. With a Bevel applied to your object, the Bevels option becomes available. Using Property Bar options, click the Bevels button to open the Bevel selector. By default, your Bevel is set to a Bevel Width of 10 and a Bevel Height of 20. If you want, enter new values and press ENTER. Notice the Bevel effect applied to your object is changed accordingly.

10. Finally, click the Point Lights button in the Property Bar to open the selector. Notice that a representative preview (sphere) shows your current Point Lights, but, by default, none exist yet. To add a new Point light, click the + button in the selector. A new Point Light is added and Color and Brightness options become available. Notice how the new Point Light affects the appearance of your Bitmap Extrude effect.

11. To end the session, click a blank space on your document page to deselect the object. Your Bitmap Extrude session is complete and the final effect is applied to your object.

If you recently upgraded to CorelDRAW 10 from version 8 or 9, you might notice a few subtle changes to the available options when applying Bitmap Extrude effects. To begin, the Fill options have been removed

Anatomy of a Bitmap Extrude Effect

If you just completed the previous exploration of applying a Bitmap Extrude effect to an object, you likely already have some idea of how the effect is used. If you're accustomed to manipulating the 3D interactive controls that appear to surround your object while the effect is in progress, you'll discover they're relatively straightforward to operate. Figure 21-1 shows a typical Bitmap Extrude effect in progress and depicts the various interactive cursors used to manipulate your object on three dimensions.

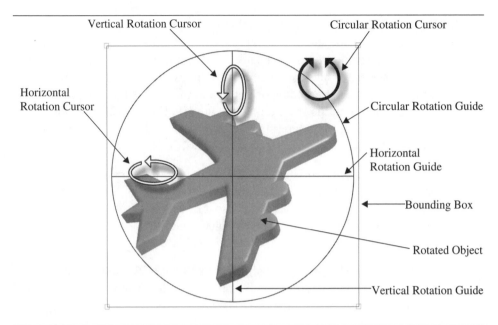

Vertical Rotation Cursor

Circular Rotation Cursor

Horizontal
Rotation Cursor

Circular Rotation Guide

Horizontal
Rotation Guide

Bounding Box

Rotated Object

Vertical Rotation Guide

FIGURE 21-1   The interactive cursors that appear while applying a Bitmap Extrude effect enable you to rotate your object in any direction.

Rotating a Bitmap Extrude effect interactively is a much more intuitive process than might first appear, and it involves rotating on one of three planes. While your cursor is positioned over the vertical guide, your object may be rotated to any orientation around the vertical (X) plane (indicated by the cursor shape). While positioned over the horizontal guide, the object may be rotated on the horizontal (Y) plane. Both operations involve click-drag actions. To rotate the object clockwise or counterclockwise around the circular (Z) plane, hold the cursor over the circular guide and use a click-drag action in either direction.

For highly precise or controlled rotation, you may want to use the Extrude Rotation options available in the Property Bar while a Bitmap Extrude effect is in progress. Rotation controls may be used in one of two states: either interactively using a click-drag action to rotate a representation (Corel logo) or by entering values in XYZ num boxes based on degrees of rotation.

By default, clicking the Extrude Rotation selector in the Property Bar displays the representative version of these controls. Using a click-drag action directly on this representative preview, you may apply rotation in a similar way to rotating a Vector Extrude effect. Clicking the *X* button in the selector resets your applied rotation to zero.

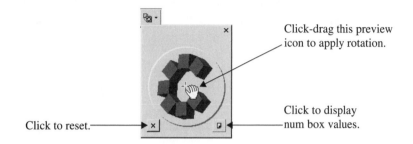

Click-drag this preview icon to apply rotation.

Click to display num box values.

Click to reset.

Clicking the page icon in the interactive version of the selector changes to reveal the XYZ num boxes, where you may enter values based on degrees of rotation. The *X* value controls vertical rotation, the *Y* value controls horizontal rotation, and the *Z* value controls circular rotation. Each rotation value may be set within a range between 180 and –180 degrees. Negative values rotate objects upward on the vertical (*X*) plane, to the left on the horizontal (*Y*) plane, and clockwise on the circular (*Z*) plane, while positive rotation values have the opposite effect. These three numeric boxes are also accompanied by spinner controls, which enable live rotation as they are held. Pressing ENTER after changing any value applies the rotation to your Bitmap Extrude effect.

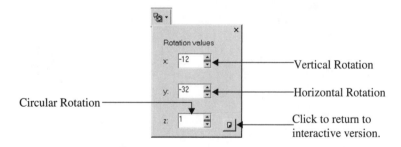

Circular Rotation

Vertical Rotation

Horizontal Rotation

Click to return to interactive version.

TIP   *There's no need to spend too much time on the Outline Pen properties of the objects you intend to apply with Bitmap Extrude effects—they're eliminated as soon as the effect is applied to your object.*

Controlling Extrude Depth

Setting the Depth of your Bitmap Extrude effect is the key to enhancing the appearance of volume and dimension for your object. Changing the extrusion depth may be done using the Property Bar either by entering a value and pressing ENTER, or by using the spinner controls accompanying the Depth option, shown here:

Depth Option

By default, all bitmap extrusions are applied at a depth of 100, which is relatively small. But the depth of your effect may be set anywhere within a range between 0 and 999. Figure 21-2 shows the same object applied with two different depth settings.

Depth Set To 50   Depth Set To 500

FIGURE 21-2   Changing depth can dramatically affect the appearance of your Bitmap Extrude effect.

Using Bevels

CorelDRAW offers five different Bevel styles for you to choose and apply to either the front and/or back of your bitmap Extrude effect. Applied Bevels become part of the bitmap's own shape, meaning they use the same fill, rotation, and lighting properties applied to the rest of the effect. By default, no Bevel is applied when a Bitmap Extrude effect is first created, meaning you must first select a style to create the Bevel.

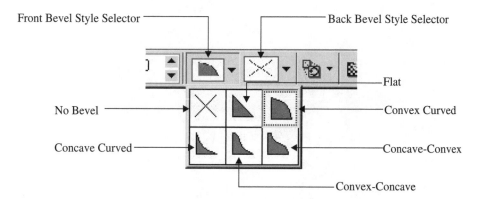

Choosing any of the available styles automatically applies the Bevel using a default Bevel Height of 20 and a default Bevel Width of 10 to the top, side, and bottom surfaces of your object. Bevel styles comprise flat, convex curved, and concave curved, as well as two additional variations that combine convex- and concave-shaped Bevel styles. Figure 21-3 demonstrates the shape of applying each of these five Bevel styles, including the original object set to defaults with no Bevel style applied.

To apply (or change) your effect's Bevel style while a bitmap extrude effect is in progress, use Property Bar options to choose one of the five Bevel styles

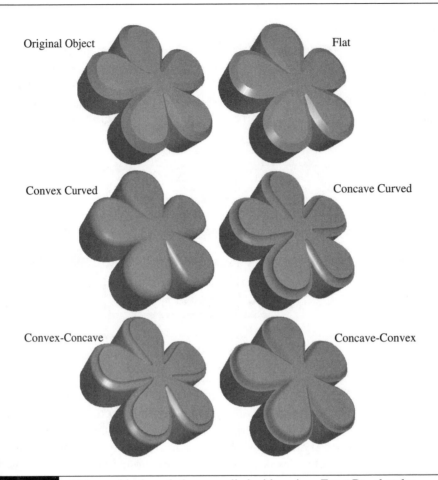

Original Object

Flat

Convex Curved

Concave Curved

Convex-Concave

Concave-Convex

FIGURE 21-3 This graphical symbol was applied with various Front Bevel styles.

using either (or both) the Front Bevel or Back Bevel flyout selectors. To clear a Bevel that has already been applied, choose No Bevel from the selector.

Two Bevel option variables are available in the Property Bar for you to control the shape of your applied Bevel style: Bevel Width and Bevel Height. By default, the Width value is set to 10, while the Height value is set to 20.

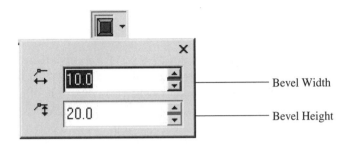

Bevel Width

Bevel Height

Each of the Bevel options may be set independently within a range between 1 and 999. Width and Height settings work in combination with each other to create the effect of the Bevel angle. This means that to create a shallow Bevel angle, specify the Width to be less than the Height. To create a steep angle, set the Height to be less than the Width (see Figure 21-4).

TIP *When Bevels are applied during a Bitmap Extrude effect, the actual Bevel shape is built on top of the surfaces of the bitmap, meaning the surfaces may become larger in size, depending on the width and height values you choose.*

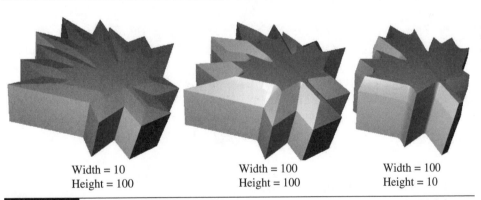

Width = 10
Height = 100

Width = 100
Height = 100

Width = 100
Height = 10

FIGURE 21-4 Create a shallow Bevel angle using a Width value less than the Height, or vice versa for steeper angles.

21

Lighting Your Extrusion

As any photographer will attest, lighting is everything when it comes to controlling the appearance of models within any scene. The same holds true when creating 3D objects. CorelDRAW 10 enables you to apply two types of lighting to Bitmap Extrude objects in sharp contrast to what can be achieved using Vector Extrude effects. Choose either Ambient Light and/or Point Lights for your effect.

Ambient Light Button ———————  ——————— Point Lights Button

Ambient Versus Point Light

You may choose either (or both) Ambient or Point Lights, depending on your illustration needs. As the name implies, Ambient Light enables you to cast an overall lighting onto your extruded object from an indirect source. Point Lights are more focused and localized, meaning they tend to cast light on a specific area of your object. The most significant difference between the two is that you may have only one Ambient Light source, while you may create multiple Point Lights at different positions around your object.

The resolution of the display and printing of your Bitmap Extrude effects are controlled by your document's Render Resolution, which, by default, is set to 96 dpi. To access and/or change this setting requires that you open the Options dialog to the General page. To do so, choose Options | Tools (CTRL+J) and click General under the Workspace category. You'll find the Render Resolution setting in the lower left of the dialog. Render Resolution may be set within a range between 60 and 1,000 dpi.

Ambient Lighting Settings

The overall light cast on your Bitmap Extrude effect is controlled using the Ambient Light option in the Property Bar while a Bitmap Extrude effect is in progress. To access this option and control the lighting applied to an existing effect, click the Ambient Light button in the Property Bar to open the selector.

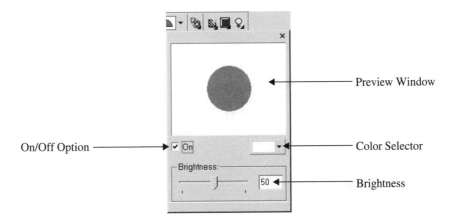

On/Off Option

Preview Window

Color Selector

Brightness

By default, whenever a new Bitmap Extrude effect is applied, the Ambient Light is automatically selected On, using a White light color set to a Brightness of 50. You may choose any color you want using the Color selector; or you can set the Brightness anywhere within a range between 0 and 100 percent by entering a value in the num box or using the slider control, to apply the new properties immediately. Generally speaking, changing the color of your ambient lighting equally affects the color appearance of both the object and the extrude surfaces of your Bitmap Extrude effect, without affecting the visual definition of the shapes (see Figure 21-5).

Creating Point Lights

As mentioned earlier, Bitmap Extrude effect Point Lights may be applied to illuminate your effect in special ways. Point Lights have a tendency to enhance the shape definition of the effect and enable you to add drama and enhance the volume of your new 3D shape. But, before this can happen, you need to create at least one

Brightness Set To 50
(The Default)

Brightness Set To 75

FIGURE 21-5 The Bitmap Extrude effect applied to this object features two different Ambient Light Brightness settings.

Point Light, using options in the Point Light selector on the Property Bar while a Bitmap Extrude effect is in progress.

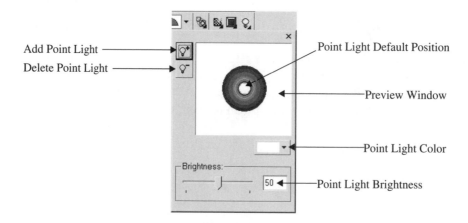

By default, no Point Lights are applied to your Bitmap Extrude effect when it's first created. To add a Point Light to your selected bitmap extrusion, follow these steps:

1. If you haven't already done so, apply a bitmap extrude effect to an object.

2. With the effect selected, click the Point Light button in the Property Bar to access the Point Light flyout selector.

3. Click the Add Point Light button (+). A new Point Light is added and appears in the Preview window. By default, this new light appears front and center of your effect, and is set to a White color using a Brightness setting of 50. Notice the red ellipse around the light in the Preview window indicating this is the currently selected (and only) Point Light. Notice also the light effect cast on the representative sphere in the Preview window.

4. If you want, change the Point Light's color using the Color selector or adjust its intensity using the Brightness slider.

5. To position the Point Light away from its default position, use a click-drag action by clicking directly on the light in the Preview window and dragging it to a different position around your object. Notice as you drag, the light is cast on a different point on your object indicated in the Preview.

6. Moving your new Point Light away from the default position makes it easier to add a second Point Light. To do so, click the Add Point Light button again. Notice a new Point Light appears front and center in the Preview window, and is automatically the selected light set to White with a Brightness of 50. Change either of these properties now if you choose.

7. If you want, you may move this new light to a different position also using a click-drag action. As you move the new light, the Preview indicates the resulting effect. To delete a selected Point Light, click the Delete Point Light (–) button in the selector. Your new Point Lighting is applied.

Adding Point Lights to a Bitmap Extrude effect enables you to create dramatic lighting to emphasize your object's new shape. For high-contrast dramatic lighting, try deactivating the Ambient Light using only multiple Point Lights to illuminate the effect. The result is often much more appealing than using both light sources in combination with each other (see Figure 21-6).

Ambient Light Only   Point Lights Only

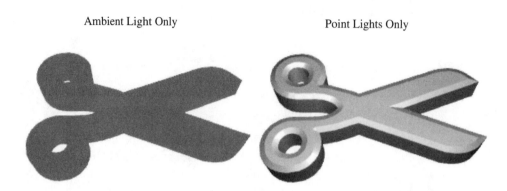

FIGURE 21-6   This object has been applied with two different lighting effects. One uses only Ambient Light, while the other uses only multiple Point Lights.

> **TIP** *To edit the properties of an existing Bitmap Extrude effect, click to select the object using the Pick Tool. Once the object is selected, the Property Bar automatically displays Bitmap Extrude options. To enter rotation mode quickly, double-clicking the object automatically selects the Interactive Extrude Tool and displays the rotation guides and associated cursor states.*

Using Bitmap Extrude Presets

So far, you explored the effects of applying various types of properties to a bitmap extrusion, including depth, Bevel, rotation, lighting properties, and so on. These properties comprise the make up of virtually any Bitmap Extrude effect. Next, you learn about saving the Bitmap Extrude properties you applied as Presets for use with other objects.

Click to add selected Bitmap
Extrude effect as preset.

Click to delete selected Bitmap
Extrude preset.

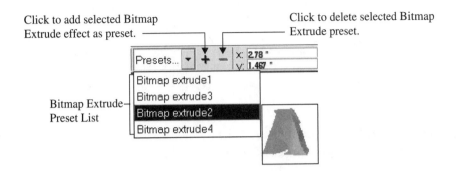

Bitmap Extrude—
Preset List

Bitmap Extrude Presets are used in the same manner as with other interactive effects such as Envelopes, Contours, Distortion, Blend, Extrude, and Transparency. Bitmap Extrude Presets may be saved and reapplied to a selected object in your document. To apply a saved Bitmap Extrude Preset to selected objects and explore adding or deleting Bitmap Extrude presets, follow these quick steps:

1. Let's look at applying an existing Preset, several sample versions of which are included with CorelDRAW 10. If you haven't already done so, create and select an object on your document page using the Pick Tool.

2. Choose the Interactive Extrude Tool from the main Toolbox.

3. Using Property Bar options, click the Bitmap Extrude button to specify the bitmap mode. Your property bar changes to display bitmap extrude options, including the Presets specific to bitmap extrusions.

4. Choose a saved Bitmap Extrude effect from the Preset List. The properties of the Bitmap Extrude are immediately applied and its current effect properties are displayed in the Property Bar.

5. To save an existing Bitmap Extrude effect as a Preset while using the Interactive Bitmap Extrude Tool and Property Bar, click to select the Bitmap Extrude portion of the effect and click the Add Preset (+) button. The Save As dialog

opens. Enter a name for your new Bitmap Extrude Preset in the File Name box and click Save. Your Bitmap Extrude Preset is added to the Preset List.

6. To delete a saved Bitmap Extrude Preset, choose the Preset from the Preset List selector to select it and click the Delete Preset button (–) in the Property Bar. The saved Preset is immediately deleted.

TIP   *By default, saved Bitmap Extrude Presets are stored in the Program Files/Corel/Graphics10/Draw/Presets/BitmapExtrude folder using installation directory names as typical defaults.*

CHAPTER 22

Manipulating 3D Models

If you've recently upgraded to CorelDRAW 10 from version 9 or 8, you're about to discover that the tools available for manipulating imported 3D models have undergone significant streamlining and have generally been made much more efficient and easier to use. In this brief chapter, we'll explore how to import and manipulate 3D models, create and control lighting, and set display resolution of the resulting bitmap objects as they appear on your document page.

Using Draw's 3D Model Tools

CorelDREAM hasn't been a component of the CorelDRAW suite of applications for some time now, but CorelDRAW 10 itself still includes ways for handling 3D objects. Although you can't actually *create* 3D models or edit the composition of 3D objects, you may still control how these specialized objects appear on your document page.

In past versions, 3D models were controlled directly on your document page using a specialized Toolset that appeared during the manipulation. This is no longer the case. Instead, manipulation is done entirely within a 3D Import dialog before the objects ever reach your page surface. Tools that existed for manipulation have been streamlined into a brief collection of tool mode buttons, tabbed lighting, and resolution option dialogs. This new dialog-based Toolkit is more efficient, while the streamlined tools are much less complex than in the past.

Accessing 3D Models

The first step to exploring the 3D models feature is to locate and import an existing 3DMF file—the 3D model format compatible with CorelDRAW 10. Corel provides a collection of sample files on Disc 3 (CD10_Photos) in the 3D folder. You'll recognize these files by their three-letter 3DM extension.

Although you may use drag-and-drop or scrapbook methods to import a 3D model into your document, the Import command is perhaps the ideal technique to use.

22

To import a 3D object using the Import command, follow these brief steps:

1. With your document open, choose File | Import (CTRL+I) or click the Import button in the Standard Toolbar. The Import dialog opens.

2. With the Import dialog open (the illustration below), select 3DMF - 3D Model from the Files of Type drop-down menu. Locate and select your 3D model file and click the Import button to proceed to the next dialog, the Import 3D Model dialog (the illustration on the next page).

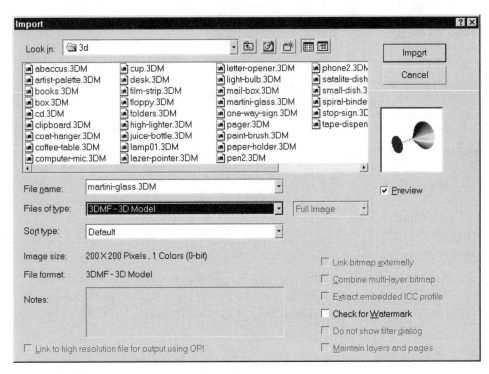

3D View Window

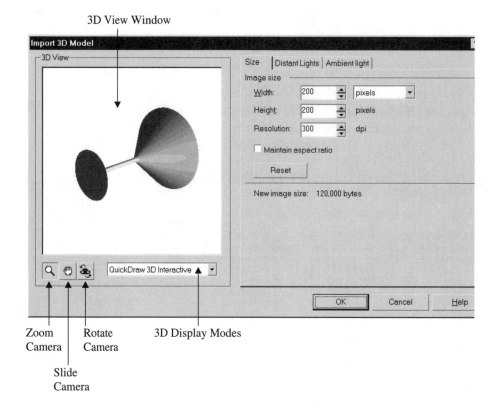

Zoom
Camera

Slide
Camera

Rotate
Camera

3D Display Modes

3. In the Import 3D Model dialog, a 3D View preview window appears on the left, while tabbed options appear on the right. If the 3D model appears just as you would like it to, click OK to close the dialog and return to your document.

4. Your active cursor is now a typical import cursor accompanied by the name of the file being imported—in this case your 3D model. Define a page position for the image using a single click to define the upper-left corner position, or a click-drag action to define the dimensions and simultaneously scale the image to complete the import operation.

With these steps complete, your 3D model will automatically be the selected object on your document page and will appear roughly as it did in the 3D View preview window. Once a 3D model exists on your document page, it is rendered as a bitmap object, but retains its properties as a 3D model.

> **TIP** *After your 3D model has been imported, you may quickly return to the manipulation state and open the Import 3D Model dialog by double-clicking the 3D model on your document page.*

Changing Camera Viewpoints and Display

In the majority of cases, you'll likely want to change the appearance of your 3D model before it even reaches your CorelDRAW document page. There are three essential tools to enable you to do this, and they exist solely in the Import 3D Model dialog. They enable you to change the view magnification, view position, and rotation of the model itself using the Zoom Camera, Slide Camera, and Rotate Camera Tools.

All three of these tools enable you to control the *camera*, meaning the distance to the 3D model and the angle at which it is viewed—just like controlling the view of a real camera. Each tool is selected by clicking the associated button in the dialog. Once selected, all manipulation is done using click or click-drag actions directly on the 3D model in the 3D View preview window. When each tool is selected, cursor states change to emulate the action being performed.

Zoom Camera

Using the Zoom Camera enables you to change the view magnification of your 3D model. But, its use is slightly different from what you might be accustomed to. First, the Zoom Camera enables you to control how much, or how little, of your 3D model is visible in the 3D View preview window, and eventually within the 3D bounding box on your document page. Using the Zoom Camera does not actually change the width and height measures of your 3D model as it will appear on your page.

To change the Zoom Camera, do one of the following:

- **Zooming In**   To increase the view magnification and bring the camera "closer" to your 3D model, click the Zoom Camera button and use a click-drag action *upward* in the 3D View preview window of the Import 3D Model dialog.

- **Zooming Out**   To decrease the view magnification and move the camera "farther" away from your 3D model, click the Zoom Camera button and use a click-drag action *downward* in the Import 3D Model dialog's 3D View window.

The results of click-dragging the Zoom Camera Tool in the Preview window are shown next. Click-drag upward to increase zoom; click-drag downward to decrease zoom.

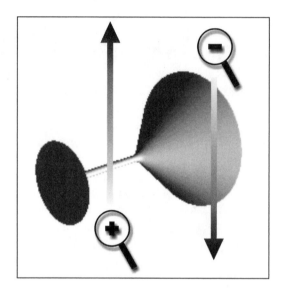

The borders of the 3D View preview window represent the bounding box surrounding your 3D model as it will appear on your document page. Since changing the view magnification of your 3D model with the Zoom Camera Tool controls only the camera zoom, the actual size of the bounding box remains fixed. This means that increasing or decreasing the zoom magnification changes *only* the portion of the 3D model visible within its bounding box. Extreme close-ups may cause the bounding box to clip the edges of your 3D model, while reduced zoom views may cause your 3D model to appear minuscule in relation to its bounding box.

Slide Camera

Using the Slide Camera Tool enables you to move your 3D model up, down, left, or right in any direction within the Import 3D Model preview window, which in turn causes the view in the 3D model bounding box on your document page to change once the dialog is closed. The Slide Camera resembles the hand-style cursor of the Pan Tool and is used in exactly the same way. Click-dragging in any direction directly in the 3D View preview window moves the camera position. Holding CTRL prior to click-dragging in any direction enables you to constrain the slide movement to either vertical or horizontal slides, shown next:

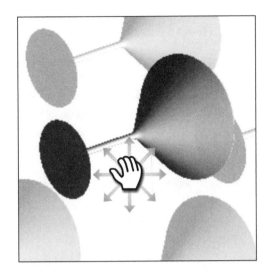

Rotate Camera

The Rotate Camera Tool is slightly more involved than the other two Import 3D Model
dialog tools. When selected, this tool enables you to rotate the camera around your 3D
model while all other states remain fixed—including any relative lighting points. While
in the rotate mode, a circular guide appears around your 3D model, and the cursor changes
to a typical rotate cursor in the 3D View preview window.

This cursor has two different states, depending on where it is positioned in relation
to the rotate guides. While within the guides, the Rotate Camera Tool cursor enables
you to apply both vertical and horizontal rotation simultaneously. While positioned
on the outside of the guides in the 3D View preview window, it enables you to rotate
your 3D model in a circular motion, shown next:

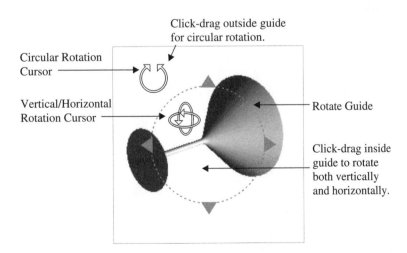

Choosing QuickDRAW 3D Display

You can control how your 3D model is previewed and displayed by choosing
between QuickDRAW 3D Interactive or QuickDRAW 3D Wireframe from the
drop-down menu in the Import 3D Model dialog. The QuickDRAW 3D Wireframe
mode enables you to display your 3D model quickly in typical wireframe view
with all objects rendered in only their outline shapes. Any lighting, advanced color
depth, shading, shadows, and surfaces are omitted from this display, making this
method the faster of the two, shown next. For the full display of all lighting,
shading, surface textures, and shadowing, choose QuickDRAW 3D Interactive
mode (the default).

QuickDRAW 3D Interactive   QuickDRAW 3D Wireframe

Controlling Size and Lighting

Lighting your 3D model is the key to controlling how it appears on your document
page after the Import dialog is closed. Controlling the size and lighting of your
imported 3D model is done with options in the three tabbed areas of the Import
3D Model dialog. These options are subdivided into Size, Distant Lights, and
Ambient Light.

Setting Size Options

The Size tab of the dialog, shown next, includes options for controlling the Width, Height, and Resolution of your 3D model. Width and Height values may be set either independently (the default) or together (while the Maintain Aspect Ratio option is selected) to whichever unit measure you choose. By default, the dimensions are set using pixels. Regardless of the Width and Height values you've entered, clicking the Reset button in this dialog returns your image size to its original values.

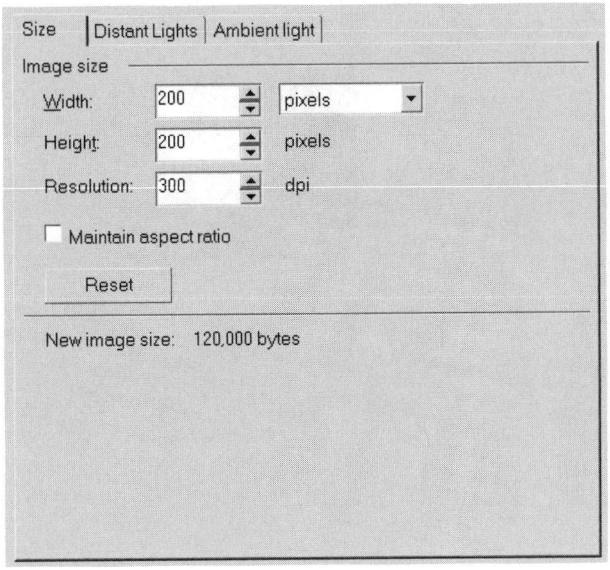

The Resolution option in this dialog tab controls the final rendered quality of your 3D model. Resolution is measured in dpi (dots per inch) and may be set between 10 and 600 dpi. Higher values render more detail in the final 3D model image, while lower values have the opposite effect. By default, Resolution is set to 72 dpi, typical of screen resolution display.

Distant Lights

Clicking the Distant Lights tab of the Import 3D Model dialog displays lighting features that include a lighting representation of your 3D model, a drop-down menu for selecting a lighting style, and Add and Delete Light buttons:

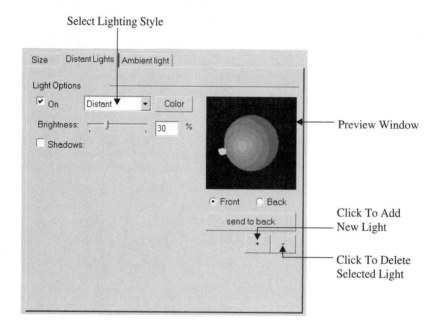

By default, no lights are created when a 3D model is first imported. In order to shed light on your 3D model, you must first create a new light source. To do so, follow these steps:

1. Click the Add Light button located below the preview representation in the Distant Lights tab, following which a light will be displayed and automatically selected. By default, the light is set to a white color at a Brightness value of 30 percent and positioned in front of your 3D model to the lower-left area indicated by the preview. Although the light itself appears yellow, this color merely indicates it is a light source and does not affect the light color.

2. Using a click-drag action in the preview window of the Distant Lights tab, move the light in relation to the representative sphere. Notice that the focal

point of the light being cast on your 3D model changes as the light is moved, and the lighting effects on your 3D model on the 3D View preview window of the dialog immediately reflect this.

3. Experiment by changing the lighting color of your Distant Light by clicking the Color selector button and choosing various colors and making adjustments to the Brightness slider. Notice as you do that both the Distant Lights preview window and the 3D View preview window reflect the changes.

4. Click-drag to position your light at the front and center of the representative sphere, and click the Back button. Notice that the representation of your lighting in the preview window has been changed to show the view of your3D object from behind your 3D model. This provides a way for you to obtain a view of and lights the opposite side of the model, since lights may only be interactively positioned around the front portion of the object under typical circumstances. Click the Front option below the preview to return your view to the front side of your 3D model.

5. Click the Add Light button a second time to create a new light source. By default, a new light is added in the same position as your current light in the preview and is automatically selected. Use a click-drag action to reposition this light to a different location, and notice how both lights affect the lighting of your 3D model. With this light selected, click the Delete Light button. The light is immediately deleted.

The Distant Lights tab features a set of lighting options that vary depending on the type of light selected. When choosing a light style from the drop-down menu, you may specify either Distant, Spot, or Point. Each of these lighting types casts a different type of light on your 3D model, but only one type may be selected and in use at a time. Although you may specify multiple Distant Lights, you may only specify one Spot or one Point Light at a time.

TIP *In order for either Point or Spot Lights to exist, you must first add a Distant Light source by clicking the Add Light button in the Distant Lights tab of the Import 3D Model dialog. If no light sources have been created as Distant Lights, both the Spot and Point Light styles will be unavailable.*

Specifying your Distant Lights as either Spot or Point Lights enables you to control Light Color and Brightness, but also features an additional control for the Distance Falloff in the form of a drop-down. This option includes two lighting variables enabling you to control how quickly the light being cast is diminished before illuminating a point on your 3D model. Choose from either None (meaning no distance falloff is applied), Distance^-1 (least falloff), or Distance^-2 (most falloff):

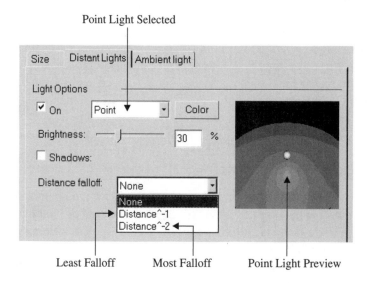

Point Light Selected

Least Falloff Most Falloff Point Light Preview

> **TIP** *Activating the Shadows option in the Distant Lights tab of the Import 3D Model dialog creates shadows where multiple objects exist in your 3D model.*

As with Point Lights, specifying your Distant Lights as Spot Lights in the drop-down menu, shown next, also offers Color, Brightness, and Distance Falloff options, but includes three more options for controlling the falloff and angle properties of Spot lighting.

22

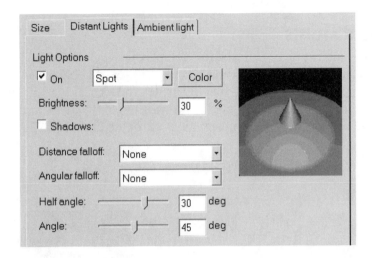

Changing these variables has the following effect on your Spot Lighting:

Angular Falloff   This value represents the rate at which the angular light being cast by a directional Spot Light object fades. the Angular Falloff drop-down menu features four options: None and Preset values for Linear, Exponential, and Cosine.

Half Angle/Angle   Angular Falloff of your Spot Lighting also includes further options for setting the disbursement of the light using Half Angle and Angle slider controls. Given the complexity of this feature and the nearly unlimited variables that can be achieved, you may wish to experiment with the Angle Falloff options before applying them to your Spot Light objects.

TIP   *With your Distant Lights added and created as Distant, Point, or Spot Lights, clicking the On option to be inactive turns all Distant Lights off, while leaving their settings intact. If you're using Distant Lights in combination with Ambient Lights and experimenting with applied settings, this option certainly offers some convenience.*

Ambient Lights

Controlling Ambient Lights is much less complex than creating and controlling specialized Distant Lights. Ambient is an indirect style of lighting and applies an even lighting value to all areas of your 3D model. In fact, this type of lighting has virtually the same effect as changing the intensity of color bitmap images. To access these options, click the Ambient Light tab of the Import 3D Model dialog:

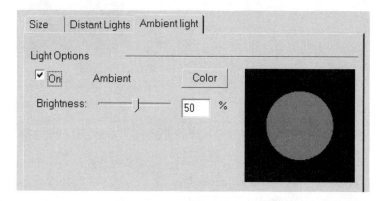

By default, when a new 3D model appears in the Import 3D Model dialog, the Ambient Light is set to On, using a light color of white at a Brightness setting of 20 percent. The accompanying preview window roughly indicates the lighting level applied using a representative sphere as the object. In most instances, the default Ambient Lighting properties provide the bare minimum necessary to illuminate your 3D model. When using Ambient Lighting alone (and without Distant Lights set to On), you may find that increasing this value to at least 50 percent illuminates more of the shape detail of your 3D model.

PART VI

Working with Digital Images

CHAPTER 23

Using Bitmap Commands

When it comes to producing printed or Web documents, you have three essential ingredients to convey ideas: text, graphics, and digital images and pictures. More often than not you'll be using all three. Even though the CorelDRAW 10 suite includes PHOTO-PAINT 10 for manipulating a bitmap's pixels, you'll likely want to incorporate bitmap images directly into your CorelDRAW 10 documents. With the increased demand to provide digital agility for illustrators and layout artists, CorelDRAW 10 includes several property-altering options and image-control features to deal specifically with bitmaps. In this chapter, you'll discover exactly how to use them.

A Bitmap Is Not a Vector Object

Even though your CorelDRAW 10 application suite includes PHOTO-PAINT 10, you'll no doubt want to incorporate digital images directly into your documents. CorelDRAW 10 includes an array of options and image-control features for manipulating and adjusting digital images directly in the vector illustrations you create. Bitmaps may be manipulated, shaped, transformed, and enhanced with bitmap effects.

The properties of digital images—or bitmaps, as they are often called—are different from those of text or vector objects. Bitmaps include properties such as dimension or physical size, resolution, type of color, and number of colors, just like vector objects, but their composition is based on pixels. Pixels are essentially bits of information arranged in a fixed gridlike pattern. These bits of information are (for the most part) rectangular shaped. Their color and frequency properties render and determine the depth and quality of the "pictures" you see when they are displayed or printed.

CorelDRAW 10's Bitmap Resources

Although you can't actually edit bitmap images pixel by pixel directly in CorelDRAW 10, you *can* do just about anything else. Besides having the ability to apply a huge assortment of effects to your bitmap images, you may also perform object-related commands, such as scaling, skewing, and transformations or work in the bitmap's appearance by applying color, mask, and cropping commands. Ideally, any pixel editing of bitmaps coming from external sources should be done before the bitmap reaches your CorelDRAW document page. For this, there's PHOTO-PAINT 10.

TIP	*To edit a selected bitmap image at the pixel level while it resides on your document page, launch in PHOTO-PAINT 10 using Property Bar options by clicking the Edit Bitmap button. Once your editing is complete, closing PHOTO-PAINT 10 will return you to your document page and to your newly edited bitmap.*

Importing Bitmaps into Your Document

CorelDRAW 10 includes a huge range of importable bitmap filters. Although detailed Import commands are discussed in Chapter 26, there are a handful of import options that apply specifically to bitmaps, and you might find them useful if you handle bitmaps often. Table 23-1 lists a basic inventory of the most common bitmap formats you may import into your CorelDRAW 10 document.

Bitmap Type	File Extension
WordPerfect graphic bitmap	WPG
Windows bitmap	DIB/RLE
Windows bitmap	BMP
Wavelet compressed bitmap	WVL
TIFF bitmap	TIF
Targa bitmap	TGA
Scitex CT bitmap	SCT, CT
RIFF - Corel Painter 5/6	RIF
Portable Network Graphic	PNG
PC Paintbrush bitmap	PCX
OS/2 bitmap	BMP
MACPaint bitmap	MAC
Macintosh PICT	PCT
Lotus Pic	PIC
Kodak PhotoCD bitmap	PCD
Kodak FlashPix Image	FPX
JPEG bitmap	JPG (plus JFF and JFT)
GEM paint file	IMG
Corel PHOTO-PAINT	CPT
Computer graphics metafile	CGM
CompuServe bitmap	GIF
CALS compressed bitmap	CAL
Adobe Portable Document File	PDF
Adobe PhotoShop	PSD

TABLE 23-1   CorelDRAW 10 Importable Bitmap Types

Importing a bitmap from an external source onto your document page is a relatively straightforward operation. To do so, follow these steps:

1. Choose File | Import (CTRL+I) or click the Import button in the Standard Toolbar to open the Import dialog box (see Figure 23-1).

2. Choose the bitmap format of your image from the Files of Type menu or leave the menu selection at All Files (*.*). By default, the Import dialog is set to import the Full Image. If the cropping and resolution of the image you're importing are correct for your purposes, click the Import button to proceed with the operation. If not, proceed to the next step.

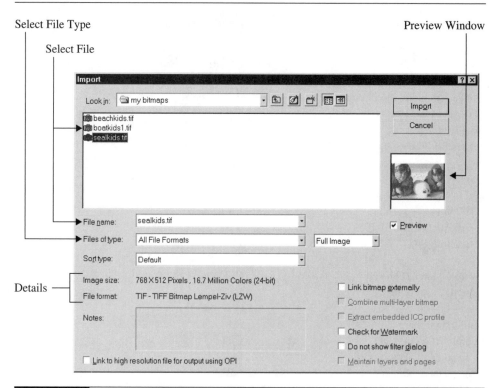

FIGURE 23-1 Import dialog options enable you to locate and select your bitmap image for importing onto your document page.

23

3. To alter the image before it reaches your document, choose Crop or Resample from the drop-down menu. Choosing either option will open an additional dialog offering further options. After choosing your Crop or Resample options, click the Import button to close the dialog and return to your CorelDRAW 10 document.

After the Import dialog closes, your cursor will automatically change to a specialized positioning and sizing cursor. This particular cursor has two significant functions. It enables you to specify the upper-left corner of your new bitmap using a single-click action, which in turn imports the image on your document page as it was originally prepared. It also enables you to specify a new width and depth for the imported image using a click-drag action as if you were drawing a typical rectangle. After specifying the width and depth with a click-drag action, the bitmap is imported to closely fit the defined area with the original proportions of the bitmap preserved. As you drag, the cursor inverts and a preview of the image's bounding box appears indicating the size and placement of the image (see Figure 23-2). While importing during either operation, the original filename is displayed beside the cursor before the position is defined.

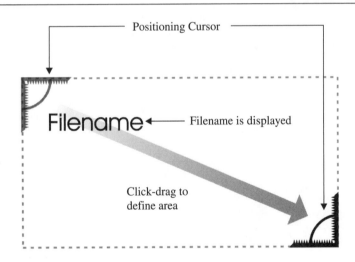

Positioning Cursor

Filename ◀— Filename is displayed

Click-drag to
define area

FIGURE 23-2   Using a click-drag action while positioning an imported image enables you to specify a new width and height for your bitmap.

During import, choosing either the Crop or Resample option causes other dialogs to appear before your file is imported. Each dialog offers its own set of additional options. Choosing Crop enables you to specify part of the image for import using cropping handles (Figure 23-3). Choosing Resample enables you to change your imported bitmap's size or resolution (see Figure 23-4). In either case, your original bitmap image remains unaffected, meaning that the bitmap you are importing is actually a copy.

NOTE *Choosing the Link Bitmap Externally option in the Import dialog causes the Crop and Resample options to be unavailable.*

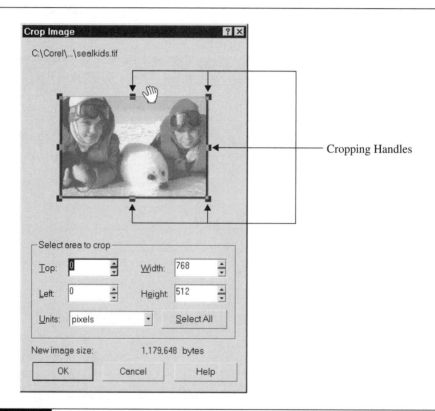

FIGURE 23-3 Choosing Crop in the Import dialog causes this additional dialog to appear, enabling you to specify which part of your bitmap you wish to import.

23

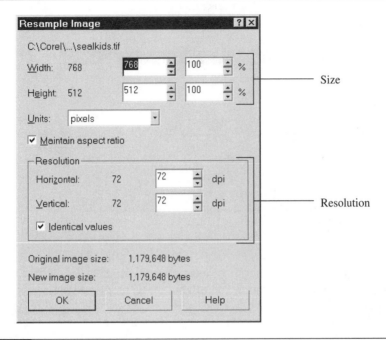

Size

Resolution

FIGURE 23-4   Choosing Resample during import opens this dialog, enabling you
to change the dimensions and resolution of the imported bitmap.

TIP   *To import more than one digital image at a time, hold* SHIFT *while clicking
to select contiguous files or* CTRL *while clicking to select noncontiguous
files in the Import dialog. For different file types, set the Files of Type
option to All Files. As multiple files are imported, your cursor will
indicate the name of the file currently being imported.*

Converting Vectors to Bitmaps

Besides being able to import images directly into your CorelDRAW 10 document
from external sources, you may convert existing vector images into bitmaps with
the Convert to Bitmap command. This command eliminates all vector properties
from your objects and converts them to pixel-based objects, from which point the
new object may be manipulated as a bitmap. To apply this command with one or

more objects selected, choose Bitmaps | Convert to Bitmap to open the Convert to Bitmap dialog, shown here:

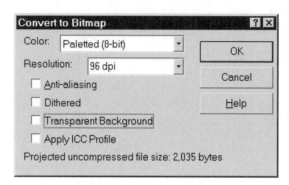

When this dialog is open, you'll be faced with a number of choices to make, depending on how you'd like your new bitmap to appear. The Convert to Bitmap dialog lets you choose color depth, resolution, anti-aliasing, and color masking properties during the conversion. The effects of each of these settings or options are described next.

> **TIP** *For more information on importing bitmaps, see Chapter 26.*

Color Model During your bitmap conversion, you may choose which color model you would like your bitmap to be based on. Choose from any of CorelDRAW 10's supported color models: Black and White (1-bit), 16 Colors (4-bit), Grayscale (8-bit), Paletted (8-bit), RGB (24-bit), or CMYK Color (32-bit).

Dithered The Dithered option becomes available only while your chosen color model is Black and White (1-bit), 16 Colors (4-bit), Grayscale (8-bit), or Paletted (8-bit). Choosing this option applies a pattern like a checkerboard or cross-hatching to any shades or color in the resulting bitmap.

> **TIP** *To quickly save a selected bitmap in your document as a separate file and store it externally, right-click the bitmap, and choose Save Bitmap As from the pop-up menu to open the Export dialog, enter a filename, set the location, and click the Export button to save the file.*

Resolution Choose one of the convenient preset resolutions for your new bitmap, ranging from 72 dpi to 300 dpi. You may also use a value of your own choosing by entering a custom resolution value in the numeric box. Resolution values may be set between 60 and 10,000 dpi. Typically, bitmaps prepared for the Web require

23

| Original | Converted At 72 DPI | Converted At 300 DPI |

FIGURE 23-5   These identical objects were converted to bitmaps with different resolutions selected during the bitmap conversion.

a resolution of 72 dpi, while bitmaps prepared for offset printing require as high as 266 dpi or higher (see Figure 23-5).

Transparent Background   Choose Transparent Background only if the object(s) you're converting to a bitmap will create a nonrectangular shape and only if you wish the uneven shape surrounding the objects to be transparent. Choosing this option has the effect of applying a "soft mask" to the resulting bitmap, which enables objects layered below to be visible through the uneven edges. Leaving this option unselected creates a typical rectangular bounding box frame around your converted objects (see Figure 23-6).

Anti-Aliasing   Choosing the Anti-aliasing option enables you to create your bitmap with a "smoothing" effect. Anti-aliasing typically causes areas where

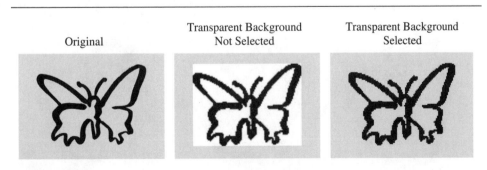

| Original | Transparent Background Not Selected | Transparent Background Selected |

FIGURE 23-6   This unevenly shaped object layered in front of a colored background was converted to a bitmap at a low resolution with Transparent Background selected and not selected.

adjacent colors in your objects contact each other to appear smoothed, meaning that the transition between two or more colors is less harsh. When this option is not selected, the edges of resulting bitmaps appear serrated on curved or angled edges—particularly at lower resolutions (see Figure 23-7).

Apply ICC Profile   Choosing this option incorporates the capabilities or limitations of your currently loaded ICC (International Color Consortium standard compatible) Color Profile to be embedded in the newly created bitmap.

CorelDRAW 10 enables you to obtain a quick summary of any bitmap object on your document page using the Object Properties dialog. To open the dialog quickly, right-click your bitmap and choose Properties from the pop-up menu. If it isn't already selected, click the Bitmap tab (shown next) to examine your bitmap's size, color, and resolution information.

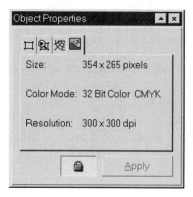

Original

Converted With
Anti-Aliasing Not Selected

Converted With
Anti-Aliasing Selected

FIGURE 23-7   These objects were converted to a bitmap at 72 dpi resolution and enlarged roughly 200 percent with Anti-aliasing selected and not selected.

23

Transforming Bitmaps

All bitmaps on your CorelDRAW document page may be manipulated in the same way as other objects. You may scale and skew a bitmap object interactively using the Pick Tool or alter its physical shape using the Shape Tool.

Scaling and Skewing Bitmaps

To scale a bitmap quickly, click it once with the Pick Tool and use a click-drag action to drag one of the bitmap's corner selection handles to apply proportional scaling, or drag its side handles to scale the image nonproportionately (see Figure 23-8). You may also enter specific unit measures directly into the Property

FIGURE 23-8   The Pick Tool enables you to scale your bitmap proportionally or nonproportionally.

Bar Width and/or Height numeric boxes to apply scaling to exact measures or enter percentage values in the Vertical and/or Horizontal scale boxes. When using Property Bar options, press ENTER to apply your selected transformation.

To rotate or skew a selected bitmap using the Pick Tool, click the bitmap a second time after selecting it to activate the rotate and skew handles. Use a click-drag action on corner handles to rotate the bitmap or a click-drag action on the top, bottom, or side handles to skew the bitmap (see Figure 23-9).

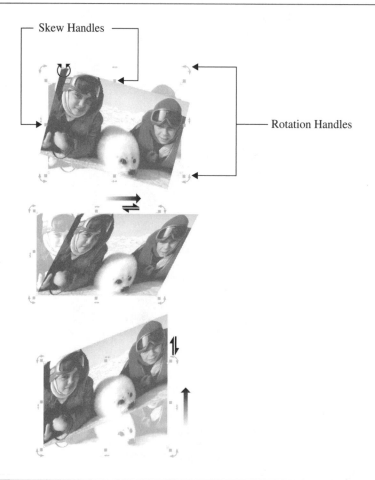

FIGURE 23-9 Clicking your selected bitmap a second time causes the rotate and skew handles to become available for applying transformations interactively.

Cropping a Bitmap

Cropping bitmaps in CorelDRAW 10 is performed using the Shape Tool (F10) to drag the corner nodes of the clipping path bitmap. Dragging these points causes the clipping path shape to change, which enables you to hide portions of the bitmap from view without deleting the pixels.

To crop a bitmap by changing the clipping path shape, follow these steps:

1. If you haven't already done so, create a bitmap on your document page through conversion or importing.

2. Choose the Shape Tool (F10) from the main Toolbox and click to select the bitmap. Notice that four corner nodes appear around the outline path of the image.

3. Using the Shape Tool cursor, click one of these nodes and drag it toward the center origin of the image. Notice that after you release the mouse, a portion of the image is hidden.

4. Drag the same corner node back to roughly its original position and notice that the hidden portion of the image is visible again. You have just performed the most basic of cropping operations.

Typically, bitmaps are often cropped either vertically or horizontally to fit square or rectangular spaces. This requires that corner nodes are moved while constrained to be in alignment with each other. To perform a side, top, or bottom cropping operation on a bitmap, you need to have at least two corner nodes selected at once, and they must be moved while being constrained. This is a little trickier than you might think, since it involves selecting and moving two corner nodes while holding a modifier key to constrain the drag movement. To crop a bitmap in this way, follow these steps:

1. Using the Shape Tool, click to select the bitmap. Determine which side you wish to crop, and select both corner nodes on the side by holding SHIFT while clicking once on each node, or select them with the marquee.

2. Once the nodes are selected, hold CTRL as the modifier key while dragging both nodes toward the center of your bitmap. Holding CTRL constrains your dragging movement, which keeps the sides in vertical and horizontal alignment.

3. Continue cropping any of the sides using this same procedure until the cropping operation is complete. Figure 23-10 shows a typical cropping operation in progress.

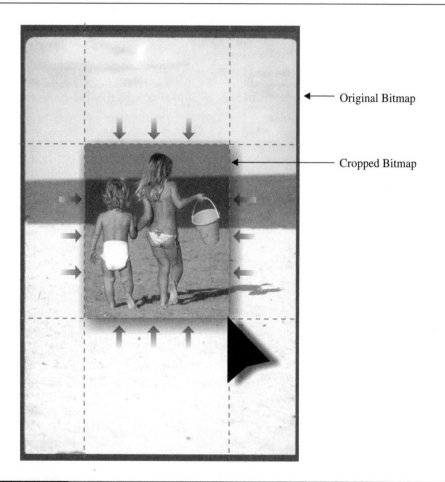

Original Bitmap

Cropped Bitmap

FIGURE 23-10 This bitmap is being cropped horizontally and vertically to isolate a specific portion of the image.

Essential Bitmap commands

When a bitmap is selected on your document page, the Property Bar springs to life to display a unique collection of bitmap-related command buttons, as shown next. These include shortcuts to dialogs, dockers, and related bitmap commands.

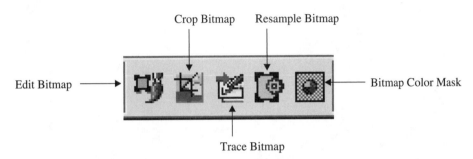

Edit Bitmap

Clicking the Edit Bitmap button in the Property Bar while a bitmap is selected automatically launches Corel PHOTO-PAINT 10 (provided you have it installed on your system). Your bitmap is opened into PHOTO-PAINT temporarily while being edited in the PHOTO-PAINT native CPT file format (see Figure 23-11).

Once your bitmap editing is complete, closing PHOTO-PAINT returns you to CorelDRAW 10 and to your newly edited bitmap. If you must edit your bitmap on a pixel-by-pixel basis, or if you wish to apply a bitmap filter or command available only in PHOTO-PAINT 10, choose this command button. This command is also available by choosing Bitmaps | Edit Bitmap from the command menus or by right-clicking the bitmap and choosing Edit Bitmap from the pop-up menu.

Crop Bitmap

The Crop Bitmap button in the Property Bar becomes available only if you have cropped your bitmap differently than when it was first created or imported. If you've just completed converting one or more vector objects to bitmaps and nothing else, this command button will be unavailable. For directions on cropping a bitmap, see "Cropping a Bitmap" earlier in this chapter.

The Crop Bitmap command has the effect of permanently eliminating the hidden and unneeded portion of a cropped bitmap in an effort to reduce your document file size if necessary. This command is also available by choosing

FIGURE 23-11 Clicking the Edit Bitmap button in the Property Bar temporarily opens your bitmap for editing in PHOTO-PAINT 10.

Bitmaps | Crop Bitmap from the command menus or right-clicking your selected bitmap and choosing Crop Bitmap from the pop-up menu.

Trace Bitmap

Tracing operations have been integrated with CorelDRAW so that you don't need to start a separate application to trace an image. When a bitmap is selected in your CorelDRAW document, choosing Bitmaps | Trace Bitmap automatically launches CorelTRACE 10 with your image as the open document ready for tracing (see Figure 23-12). CorelTRACE lets you automatically create a group of vector objects to resemble your bitmap image by using various tracing styles and effects. You may also launch your selected bitmap for editing in CorelTRACE 10 by right-clicking the bitmap and choosing Trace Bitmap from the pop-up menu.

23

Preview Of Original   Preview Of Traced Bitmap

FIGURE 23-12   This bitmap is in the process of being traced into a series of vector
objects using CorelTRACE 10.

With CorelTRACE 10 open, a few control and interface improvements become
obvious. CorelTRACE 10 uses its own unique set of command menus, Toolbars,
Toolbox choices, View, and Image controls with the familiar-looking Status Bar
display and Property Bar options. Clicking the Apply button immediately initiates
the tracing operation based on the tracing mode and options selected. Once the
tracing operation is complete, closing the application returns you to your
CorelTRACE document and your newly traced image. By default, the traced
image remains a copy of your original bitmap, and the vector objects created
by the tracing operation are automatically grouped.

TIP   *For more detailed information on using CorelTRACE 10, see "Tracing
Bitmaps into Vectors" later in this chapter.*

Resample Command

When a bitmap is selected, choosing Bitmaps | Resample opens the Resample bitmap dialog, which enables you to change the Image Size and/or Resolution of your bitmap (see Figure 23-13).

The Resample command is used often to increase or decrease the size or resolution of your bitmap for a specific purpose. Bitmaps are often reduced in resolution to *downsample*, or eliminate excess resolution. Increasing bitmap resolution is often done to increase the amount of potential detail the bitmap is capable of displaying for purposes such as applying bitmap effects. Typically, increasing the resolution does not render a clearer or more detailed appearance of your bitmap.

Avoid situations where you have "oversampled" a bitmap destined for importing into your CorelDRAW 10 document. This often happens when scanning an image. If your document is destined for offset reproduction, prepare your images at twice the line screen specified for printing. For example, if your document is destined for printing at a line screen of 133 lpi, prepare your scanned images with a resolution of 266 dpi while at their final size. Oversampled images can often unnecessarily increase Save and Print times and increase required file storage space.

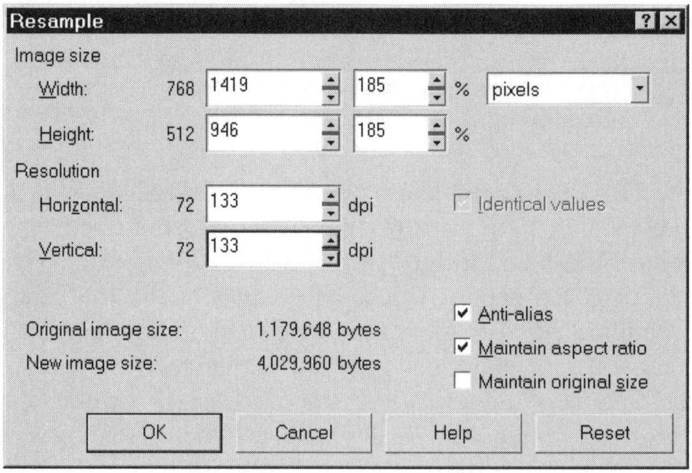

FIGURE 23-13 The Resample dialog enables you to choose settings for increasing or decreasing the size and resolution of your selected bitmap.

When choosing command options in the Resample dialog, the available options have the following effects.

Image Size   The Width and Height values of your resampled bitmap may be entered as specific unit measures in this area. Width and Height may be specified in pixels (the default) or in any drawing unit you wish. You may also alter the size based on the percentage of the original within a range between 1 and 30,000 percent.

Resolution   Enter the new resolution for your resampled bitmap in the Horizontal and Vertical numeric boxes, which are available only when the Identical Values option is left unselected. Deselecting the Maintain Aspect Ratio option enables you to set Horizontal and Vertical values independently of each other while the Identical Values option is unselected. Resolution values may be set between 10 and 10,000 dpi.

Anti-Alias   Choosing this option has the identical effect as when converting objects to bitmaps. Anti-alias (selected by default) causes adjoining colors in your resampled bitmap to be smoothed where they meet, reducing the effect of hard-edged color transition.

Maintain Aspect Ratio   Choosing this option preserves the original proportions of your bitmap and locks the Horizontal and Vertical resolution values to be identical. When Maintain Aspect Ratio is selected, the Identical Values option becomes unavailable.

Maintain Original Size   Choosing Maintain Original Size causes your new resampled bitmap to remain the same in required memory size as the original and leaves only the Resolution values available.

Bitmap Brightness, Contrast, and Intensity

With a bitmap selected in your document, choosing Effects | Adjust | Brightness-Contrast-Intensity opens the Brightness-Contrast-Intensity dialog, which enables you to broadly adjust the overall tonal appearance of your bitmap (see Figure 23-14), such as the appearance of imported bitmaps. You can adjust these values to compensate for poor photographic exposure, incorrect scanning, or for other creative purposes. You may also open this dialog while virtually any object type is selected by choosing Effects | Adjust | Brightness-Contrast-Intensity.

Shortcut To Other Bitmap Effects

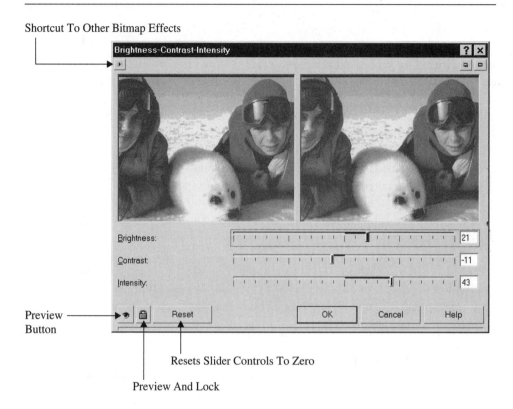

Preview Button

Resets Slider Controls To Zero

Preview And Lock

FIGURE 23-14   Changing the brightness, contrast, and intensity of a bitmap is commonly needed for correcting poorly prepared imported images.

Brightness, Contrast, and Intensity sliders may be set between 100 and -100 percent. Positive values increase the effect of each, while negative settings have the opposite effects. Clicking the Preview button causes the bitmap preview in the dialog to be updated according to your selected settings while clicking OK applies the settings and closes the dialog. Clicking the Lock button provides a perpetual preview as each setting is changed. To set all of the sliders back to their 0 positions, click the Reset button.

Balancing Bitmap Color

To make broad adjustments to the overall color of a selected bitmap, choose Effects | Color Balance to open the Color Balance dialog (see Figure 23-15). Options in the Color Balance dialog enable you to balance broadly color values in

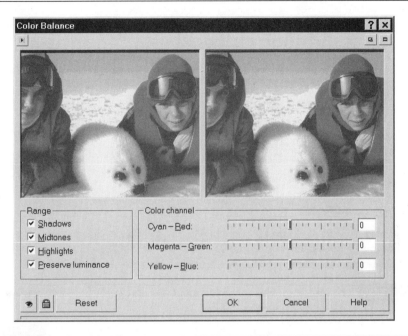

FIGURE 23-15   Color Balance options in this dialog enable you to broadly correct for poor color balance.

your digital image between CMY (cyan, magenta, yellow) and RGB (red, green, blue) colors. Colors are represented in pairs, enabling you to shift between Cyan-Red, Magenta-Green, and Yellow-Blue. Moving the slider controls in the direction of the colors increases the amount of that specific color, while reducing the value of the adjacent color in your bitmap.

Range options in the dialog are divided into Shadows, Midtones, and Highlights areas representing the dark, medium, and light areas of color in your bitmap. Each of these Range options may be enabled or disabled, causing that area of your image either to be affected or disregarded by changes in color balance. A Preserve Luminance option also enables you to change color ranges in your bitmap without altering any ICC Color Profile that may have been previously embedded in the bitmap. This enables you to make color balance changes while maintaining the bitmap's original color correction.

Adjusting Bitmap Gamma

Choosing Effects | Gamma while a bitmap is selected opens the Gamma dialog (see Figure 23-16). The term *gamma* describes the range of color or tones that may

FIGURE 23-16   Gamma adjustments enable you to increase or decrease the contrast of the midtones in your bitmap.

be measured and/or reproduced by a given technique or device. Gamma is defined by the amount of color or tonal contrast displayed in the midtones of your bitmap. Typically, gamma is measured by the difference between the lighter and darker areas in your bitmap—essentially, contrast.

Your bitmap's Gamma may be set between 0.10 and 10.0, where a value of 1.00 applies no change. Lower Gamma values result in less contrast to the midtones of your bitmap, causing it to appear darker. Higher Gamma values result in higher contrast to your bitmap's midtones, causing it to appear lighter.

Adjusting Hue, Saturation, and Lightness

Choosing Effects | Hue/Saturation/Lightness while a bitmap is selected opens the Hue/Saturation/Lightness filter dialog (see Figure 23-17). This filter enables you to adjust the appearance of your bitmap color based on the HLS color model.

The terms hue, saturation, and lightness are referred to often when measuring the color values in a bitmap. *Hue* refers to the dominant color of your bitmap (red, green, blue, yellow, and so on), while *saturation* is the amount of this color. For example, green grass and green leaves are colored with hues of green. *Lightness* is the amount of black in the color. The less black in a hue, the lighter it becomes.

23

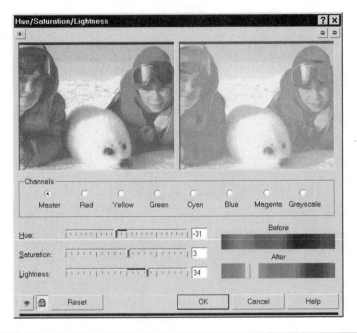

FIGURE 23-17   Adjust the appearance of your bitmap color based on HLS color model principles.

For example, new grass is often lighter in color than mature grass. The actual color has less black in it, but the "new grass" color green is still considered a less saturated hue of green.

Hue, Saturation, and Lightness sliders enable you to set each value between 100 and –100 percent. Adjust these values based on all color Channels or individually by choosing master, red, yellow, green, cyan, blue, magenta, or grayscale. While grayscale is selected, Saturation may only be set between 180 (very saturated) and –180 (not saturated).

Using the Bitmap Color Mask Docker

To apply a transparent color mask manually, use the Bitmap Color Mask Docker (see Figure 23-18). Using the Pick Tool, click the Bitmap Color Mask button in the Property Bar while a bitmap is selected, or choose Bitmaps | Bitmap Color Mask. This feature has changed little over past versions of CorelDRAW and enables you to specify up to ten different colors for your color mask.

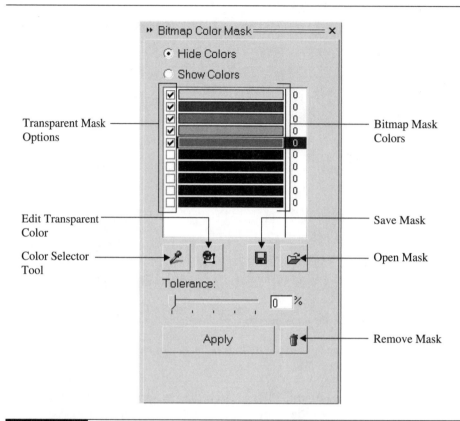

Transparent Mask Options

Bitmap Mask Colors

Edit Transparent Color

Save Mask

Color Selector Tool

Open Mask

Remove Mask

FIGURE 23-18   The Bitmap Color Mask Docker enables you to specify mask colors and apply and save color masks.

Color masks have the effect of making the selected colors transparent, meaning the entire object becomes visible or invisible to varying degrees based on the transparency values and options set in the Color Mask Docker.

Creating a Color Mask

To use the Color Mask Docker to manually apply a new bitmap color mask to your selected bitmap, follow these steps:

1. If you haven't already done so, use the Pick Tool to select the bitmap you wish to apply a color mask to, and open the Bitmap Color Mask Docker by choosing Bitmaps | Bitmap Color Mask.

2. Click the button for the Color Selector Tool, resembling an eyedropper tool, in the docker window and click the area and color in your bitmap that you wish to be transparent. By default, the first color in the docker is set to the color you initially specify.

3. Click the check box beside the new mask color you have specified in the list to make it active.

4. Click Apply to create the new color mask. The colors in your bitmap are immediately masked according to the color specified using the Color Selector Tool.

5. To expand the masking effect, you may fine-tune the mask color if needed. To do this, change the Tolerance slider control roughly five percent to the right and click the Apply button. The color mask area is updated.

6. To mask any additional colors in your bitmap, click the second color in the docker list to select it, click the Color Selector Tool again and click a new and different color in your selected bitmap. The Color Selector Tool samples the new color, automatically displaying it in the selected color mask in the docker list. To apply this additional mask color, click the check box beside it in the docker list and click the Apply button. The new color is applied to the mask in addition to the first color. If needed, adjust the Tolerance of the selected mask color and click the Apply button again. You may repeat these same steps for each of the remaining available color selectors in the docker list if needed.

Using Bitmap Color Mask Docker Options

If you've just followed the previous steps to apply a color mask manually to a bitmap, you likely have a solid understanding of how this feature may be used. As you apply color masks manually to your selected bitmap, you have at your disposal several additional options for controlling either mask display or behavior. Choosing these options has the following effects on the docker display, the color mask behavior, or when opening or saving color masks:

Edit Color   Clicking the Edit Color button in the docker opens the Edit Color dialog of CorelDRAW 10's color dialog. Using typical color selection methods, you may specify each color for a selected mask.

Hide/Show Colors   The Show Colors and Hide Colors buttons at the top of the Bitmap Color Mask Docker window toggle the state of an applied bitmap color mask. When the Hide Colors option is selected (the default), the colors you have selected for your mask are hidden. Choosing the Show Colors option has the reverse effect, instead displaying all but the masked colors in your bitmap image.

Remove Mask   Clicking this button clears the mask properties completely from your selected bitmap and returns it to its normal state.

Save/Open Mask   Clicking either of these two buttons causes the Save Mask or Open dialogs to open, enabling you either to save the color mask you've created for applying to other bitmaps or open a previously saved color mask. Bitmap color mask file formats use INI file extensions.

Tolerance   The Tolerance slider and num box enable you to adjust how closely a selected color masks a specific color, based on percentage values between 0 and 100. A setting of 0 applies the mask using the exact color specified. Higher Tolerance values expand this color within a given range and include color pixels close to the pixels of the specified color mask to varying degrees.

Using the Link Manager

If the image that you wish to appear on your document page comes from an external source, you'll need to use the Import command (CTRL+I) to bring it into your open document. To do so, click the Import button in the Standard Toolbar (shown in the following illustration) or choose File | Import.

Import Button In Standard Toolbar

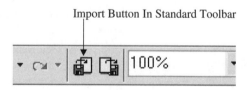

After choosing this command, the Import dialog will open, offering resources to locate and specify your file and its type (see Figure 23-19). If you do not wish to store a copy of the image within your CorelDRAW 10 document page, there's an option you'll have to select before clicking the Import button: Link Bitmap Externally.

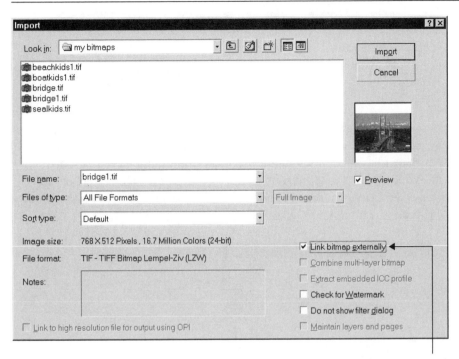

Click This Option To Establish
The External Link

FIGURE 23-19   Establishing an external link to a saved bitmap must be done prior to importing the bitmap into your document.

  For more information on importing bitmap images into your document and choosing options in the Import dialog, see "How to Import a File" in Chapter 26.

Establishing an External Link

To establish an external link during import, follow these steps:

With your document open, choose File | Import (CTRL+I) or click the Import button in the Standard Toolbar to open the Import dialog. Locate the folder containing the bitmap you wish to establish a link to, and select it by clicking on it.

1. Choose Link Bitmap Externally and any other options you require for the Import operation. If the Link Bitmap Externally option doesn't appear in the dialog, your file type may not be compatible for an external link.

2. Click Import to close the dialog and import the file. Your cursor takes the form of the import cursor, accompanied by the filename of your selected bitmap.

3. Click or click-drag to define a position for your bitmap on your document page. Your bitmap is now imported with an external link established.

Once a bitmap has been imported and externally linked, the image you see on your document page is merely a placeholder and a visual representation of the original bitmap, not the original image itself. Externally linked bitmaps are indicated by information displayed in the Object Properties Docker when the object is selected. To open this docker (shown next), right-click the bitmap and choose Properties from the pop-up menu.

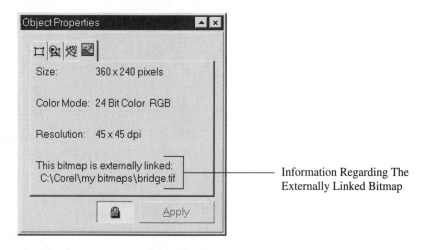

Information Regarding The Externally Linked Bitmap

> **NOTE** *When a bitmap is externally linked, you will not be able to apply certain commands to it. These include Color Balance, Brightness, Contrast, Intensity, Gamma, Hue, Saturation, and Lightness. These options are only available when a bitmap image is embedded, meaning that a copy has been stored in your CorelDRAW 10 document.*

Using Link Manager Commands

As soon as a bitmap has been imported with the Link Bitmap Externally option during the Import process, it may be tracked and controlled through use of the Link Manager Docker window. To open this docker, choose Tools | Link Manager. Once opened, the Link Manager Docker lists all files that have been

23

Thumbnail   Path Link   Page

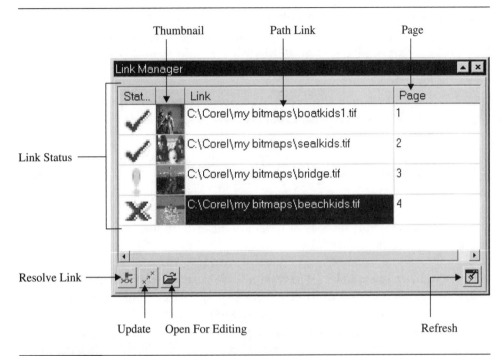

Link Status

Resolve Link

Update   Open For Editing   Refresh

FIGURE 23-20 The Link Manager enables you to obtain a quick inventory of any externally linked bitmaps.

imported and externally linked (see Figure 23-20) and provides an array of options for managing linked files.

The options in the Link Manager Docker window may be used to manage and apply commands to externally linked bitmaps in the following ways.

Link Status And Path Information This information is displayed in the file list of the docker. A green check mark under Status indicates that the link has been verified. A red X in the listing indicates that the path to the associated file is not valid and the file may be moved or missing. A yellow exclamation mark indicates that the image has changed or has been modified since being imported. The information displayed in the Link column details the last verified path of the linked file.

Page The Page information shows which page of your CorelDRAW 10 document the linked file has been imported onto. If the file has been placed on the desktop and outside of the document page, this will be indicated by the word "All," meaning that it is available while all pages are viewed.

Select Linked Image To immediately select an externally linked file in your document, right-click the file where it appears in the Link Manager list and choose Select. CorelDRAW 10 will immediately select and display the file on the page on which it exists.

> TIP: *To instantly locate, display, and select a specific linked image, double-click the file's name in the Link Manager list.*

Verifying Link Information To verify that the path to an externally linked file listed in the Link Manager Docker is correct, right-click the file where it appears in the docker window and choose Verify from the pop-up menu. To verify all files listed in the docker at once, click the Refresh button at the lower-right corner of the docker window. Any missing or modified files will immediately be indicated in the Status column of the docker.

Resolving and Updating Links The term *resolve* means to embed a copy of the image as it exists in your document and eliminate the external link to the original file. Click the Resolve Link button to *embed* a selected externally linked file in the docker window immediately, after which the file will no longer appear in the Link Manager inventory list. The Update button becomes available only when the Link Manager detects that a selected file in the list has changed in some way. Clicking Update immediately updates the thumbnail representation of the selected image. You may also update the screen representation of an externally linked bitmap independently of the Link Manager Docker by selecting the object on your document page and choosing Bitmaps | Update From Link.

Fixing Broken Links If the file you've imported with an external link has been renamed, moved, modified, or is missing, this will be indicated by a red X beside it in the Link Manager Docker. To relink to the file or establish a link to a different file, right-click the image name in the Link Manager Docker window and choose Fix Broken Link from the pop-up menu. This will cause a version of the Import dialog to open, offering you a way of locating, selecting, and reestablishing another external link to either the same file or a different one.

Thumbnail Display Options Between the Status and Link columns in the docker, either a small or large thumbnail image of the linked file appears. Thumbnail size may be set to either small or large by right-clicking anywhere within the Link Manager Docker window and choosing Display Small or Display Large Thumbnails.

Inflating Bitmaps

Inflating a bitmap simultaneously increases the size of its clipping path and the actual dimensions of the bitmap image itself. In CorelDRAW 10, all bitmaps must reside inside a clipping path, which in turn defines their shape. The two Inflate commands—Manually Inflate Bitmap and Auto Inflate Bitmap—are found under command menus by clicking Bitmaps | Inflate Bitmap. Each command has a different purpose and function. Choose between these two Inflate methods for the following effects:

Auto Inflation   The Auto Inflate Bitmap state may be toggled on (the default) or off and comes into effect whenever effects are applied to bitmaps. When in the on state, Auto Inflate Bitmap causes the width and depth of your bitmaps to increase automatically—physically increasing the number of pixels whenever effects are applied. For example, applying a bitmap filter effect (such as a blur effect) to your bitmap often causes the existing pixels to be "spread" to achieve the effect. While Auto Inflate Bitmap is off, effects applied to bitmaps may sometimes result in flattened edges where effects spread pixels (see Figure 23-21).

Manual Inflation   As the name implies, Manually Inflate Bitmap is a command, rather than a state. Choosing this command opens the Inflate Bitmap dialog box (see Figure 23-22), providing you with options to physically expand your selected bitmap by a specific pixel measure or inflate it by percentage values.

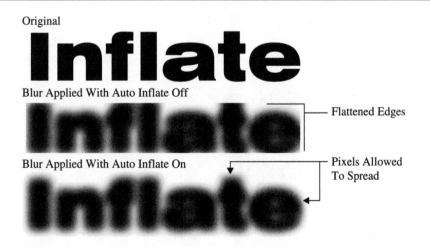

FIGURE 23-21   This text has been converted to a bitmap and had a Gaussian blur effect applied with Auto Inflate Bitmap on and off.

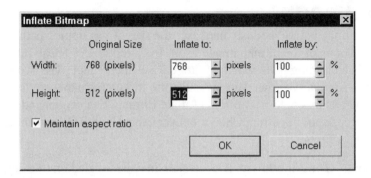

FIGURE 23-22   These options enable you to specify a new size for your bitmap manually.

One efficient strategy you might consider when converting objects to bitmaps is to create a rectangular-shaped invisible frame around your objects manually before converting them into bitmaps. To do this quickly, create a frame to your required dimensions and set the Outline Pen and Fill properties to None using the X color well in your onscreen color palette. Scale your vector drawing to fit within the frame, and include this frame as part of your selection when converting (or exporting) the objects to a bitmap. By doing this, you can manually control the physical dimensions of the resulting bitmap and prevent color pixels from contacting its edges.

Tracing Bitmaps into Vectors

Although it may only be a support utility, you may be surprised to discover just how powerful and efficient CorelTRACE 10 is. Tracing operations have been integrated with CorelDRAW 10, so you don't need to launch a separate application to trace a bitmap image. When a bitmap is selected in your CorelDRAW document, clicking the Trace Bitmap button in the Property Bar or choosing Bitmaps | Trace Bitmap automatically launches CorelTRACE 10 with your image as the open document to be traced. Behind the scenes, CorelTRACE 10 opens the selected bitmap as a PHOTO-PAINT (CPT) document.

With CorelTRACE 10 open, you'll notice that the controls and interface features are quite familiar. CorelTRACE 10 is actually a stand-alone application, complete with its own set of command menus, Toolbars, Toolbox choices, View and Image controls, Status Bar display, and Property Bar options. Your selected bitmap is the open document ready for tracing.

Clicking the Apply button initiates the trace operation based on your tracing mode and options selected. While this is in progress, CorelTRACE displays two separate windows: one containing the original image, the other containing your traced objects (see Figure 23-23). Tracing modes each feature their own Property Bar, which displays a set of options controlling the trace operation. Each time the Do Trace button is clicked, your original image is "scanned," and the tracing operation is repeated using the currently selected settings. Once the tracing is finished, closing CorelTRACE 10 automatically returns you to your CorelDRAW document. The resulting traced objects are placed as a separate group of objects on your document page, layered directly in front of your unaltered original bitmap.

The group of traced shapes that CorelTRACE creates are vector objects, meaning that they are made up of either open or closed paths as opposed to being pixel based. All CorelTRACE sessions create a collection of automatically grouped objects, meaning that they may be handled as a single drawing object when you return to your CorelDRAW drawing. Unlike the original bitmap, however, their shape may be altered or edited at the node level. You may also apply any Outline Pen properties or fill colors you wish.

FIGURE 23-23   During the tracing operation, two windows indicate the original (on the left side) and the tracing progress and final results (on the right side).

Choosing a Tracing Method

CorelTRACE 10 offers eight tracing methods to choose from, which may be narrowed down to five primary tracing modes. Choose from Outline, Centerline, Sketch, Mosaic, and Woodcut. Each mode is available from the CorelTRACE Toolbox (shown here), while the Property Bar features the associated options.

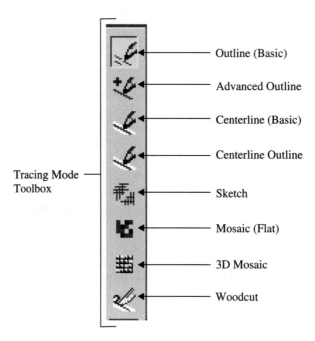

Creating Outline Traces

The Outline tracing method traces your bitmap by searching for similar-colored pixels and creating a closed path object filled with uniform color to represent them. Choose from two similar tracing methods: Outline or Advanced Outline. Outline (the default) serves as the simplified version of the two, offering a single Accuracy slider control. Adjusting the Accuracy slider enables you to determine how closely your image is traced. Increasing the Accuracy setting creates traced vector drawing shapes that more closely resemble color areas in your original image, but also increase the complexity of these objects (see Figure 23-24).

Choosing the Advanced Outline method offers several more variables to control. Advanced Outline traces the color areas of an image using one of several

Accuracy At 30 Percent
(152 Objects)

Accuracy At 70 Percent
(1,416 Objects)

Original

FIGURE 23-24   This bitmap (left) was traced using Outline at two different
Accuracy settings. The center uses roughly 150 objects, while
the other uses nearly 1,500.

preset tracing styles. Choose between Accurate, Clip Art, Photo Low Res, Photo
High Res, and Silhouette. You may also save your own style based on selected
variables, such as Noise, Complexity, Maximum Number of Colors (2 to 256),
Node Reduction, Node Type (Cusp or Smooth), and Minimum Object Size, which
you can change using the Advanced Outline Property Bar (shown next). Figure 23-25
shows a bitmap traced using an Advanced Outline preset.

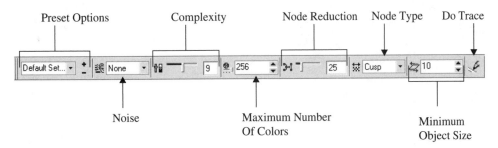

Photo Low Res
(114 Objects)

Photo High Res
(7,088 Objects)

Original

FIGURE 23-25 This bitmap was traced using two Advanced Outline Presets. In the center, 114 objects result from the tracing operation, while on the right 7,088 objects are the result.

Centerline Tracing

The Centerline tracing method traces your bitmap quite differently than other tracing methods and converts your selected bitmap into a vector drawing composed mostly of open paths. The path shapes are based on defined black-and-white areas in the image, instead of color. Centerline is ideal for creating highly accurate vector drawings from scanned maps, high-contrast photographs, text, or similar tracing work where open paths are preferred over closed paths (see Figure 23-26). You may also use a more advanced version of this mode by choosing Centerline Outline mode. This particular mode enables you to combine the effects of Centerline together with Outline, creating both open outline

23

Centerline (2,207 Objects)

Original

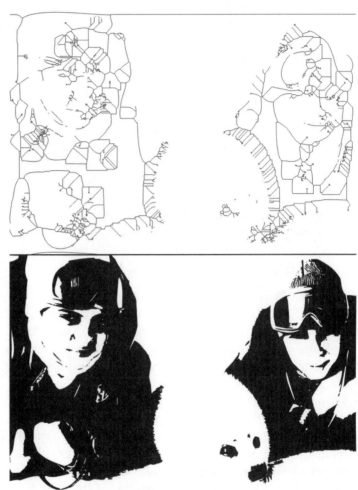

Centerline Outline (2,430 Objects)

This bitmap was traced using the default Centerline and Centerline Outline trace modes.

paths and closed filled paths. Centerline Outline includes an Accuracy slider for controlling how closely the shapes created by your bitmap's colors are followed.

Your bitmap needs to be black and white in order to be compatible for a Centerline trace. To quickly change color modes directly in CorelTRACE, choose Image | Mode | Black and White, and choose a Threshold setting to complete the conversion. Choosing a Threshold setting enables you to define which image colors convert to black and which convert to white. Once converted, the black-and-white version provides CorelTRACE with the reduced color definition it requires to determine the Centerline paths.

When Centerline is selected as your tracing method, the Property Bar includes options for choosing saved preset styles: Map, Smooth and Accurate, Text, and Silhouette. You may also customize and save your own styles. The tracing variables for the Centerline method include a Node Reduction setting that enables you to control loosely how many nodes paths are composed of and their complexity. An Iterations option also enables you to control how closely the new vector paths follow changes in tone based on black and white.

Turning Bitmaps into Sketches

Unlike the sketch-emulating effect applied by bitmap filters, the Sketch option available in CorelTRACE 10 enables you to trace by creating a series of black hairlines in a hatching/cross-hatching arrangement. The Detailed Shadows preset of the Sketch method is ideal for creating standalone line-drawing versions of bitmaps or for simply creating a sketched effect (see Figure 23-27).

The Sketch tracing method also features specific variables in the Property Bar when selected. The lines created by a Sketch trace are evenly spaced and may be created in several layers, each of which may be set to a specific angle and threshold value. You may add up to 32 layers for each Sketch trace and control the spacing, angle, and threshold of each layer individually. Varying the Threshold and Line Frequency values enables you to control the amount of highlight and shadow detail rendered by the Sketch trace. Controlling the angle determines the appearance of hatching or cross-hatching.

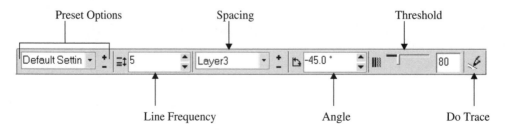

23

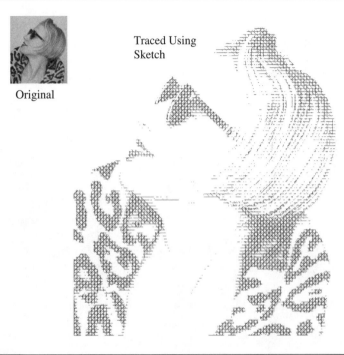

Original

Traced Using
Sketch

FIGURE 23-27   This Detailed Shadows preset features a line spacing of five pixels and
five individual sketch layers set to varying threshold values and angles.

Creating Flat or 3D Mosaics

The next two tracing methods create similar results, in that they create an effect
resembling pixelation. Using either the Flat or 3D Mosaic style creates a series of
vector polygons based on the color of your bitmap. Use the Flat method to create a
typical pixelation effect using shapes filled with uniform color. Using 3D Mosaic
automatically applies a depth effect, with the individual shapes containing preset
highlights and shading (see Figure 23-28).

Both Mosaic methods include a collection of Presets and options to create
your own Presets using Property Bar options. Both the Flat and Mosaic feature
options enable you to trace using Rectangle, Circle, or Diamond shapes. When
using 3D Mosaic, you may also choose from Pyramids, Bricks, or Fans. Each
method includes tiling options to set the number of horizontal and/or vertical tiles
for your trace operation.

Mosaic (Flat)   3D Mosaic (Set To Pyramids)

Original

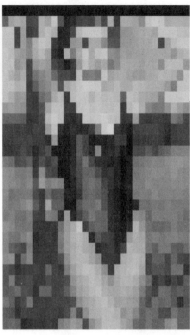
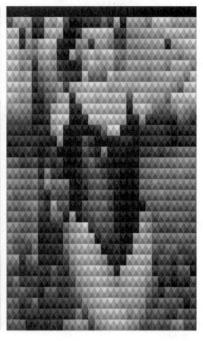

FIGURE 23-28   This image was traced using the Flat and 3D Mosaic modes, both using 30 vertical and horizontal tiles.

Tracing with Woodcut

The Woodcut tracing method is perhaps the most complex of all, due to the enormous number of variables that may be selected. This method creates a series of closed-path sliver-shaped objects for a chiseled-out version of your bitmap (see Figure 23-29). Sliver thickness and endpoint shapes emulate the wood-carved effect. This technique has long been used for converting digital photographs to high-contrast line graphics.

Using the Woodcut method, choose from a preset list (Basic, Continuous Color, Detailed Color, Fine Grained, and Shadows) or create your own Presets based on current settings using options in the Property Bar (shown next). The basic variables include Node Reduction, Threshold, Angle, and Width, which have effects similar to the other available tracing methods. You may also choose

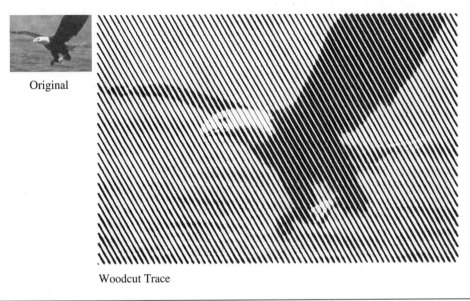

Original

Woodcut Trace

FIGURE 23-29   This Woodcut method uses a Node Reduction of 10, a Threshold of 255, an Angle of 120 degrees, a Width of 10, and Continuous Cut property.

options from the Properties flyout to control the color, shape, and length of the Woodcut strokes, offering nearly endless opportunities for experimentation.

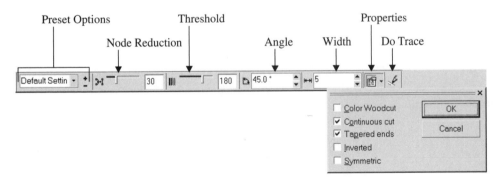

CHAPTER 24

Applying Bitmap Filter Effects

Vector imaging offers unparalleled power and flexibility for everything from the most basic of images to the most complex. At times, however, you'll still want to convert your vector images to bitmaps to apply finishing touches, create special effects, and enhance productivity, since some results can be achieved in seconds with bitmaps that would require more time if working with a vector image.

You may ask the question, "Why not just export the image to Corel PHOTO-PAINT?" There are two answers to this question: One is convenience. If you can edit a bitmap from within CorelDRAW, without having to take the time to export the image, open Corel PHOTO-PAINT, and then import the image, taking the route that causes less interruption in your workflow makes sense. The second answer is vector power. CorelDRAW enables you to convert any selected object to a bitmap, while keeping all other objects in their original vector format. This unique combination of vector and bitmap editing from within the same program is a feature you'll likely find quite useful.

Anatomy of CorelDRAW's Bitmap Filter Dialog

CorelDRAW's Bitmap Filter dialogs are built around a central theme of giving you complete control over the creative process. Each Bitmap Filter dialog features a set of controls for manipulating the effect, three different preview modes, and quick access to all other bitmap effects, as this illustration shows.

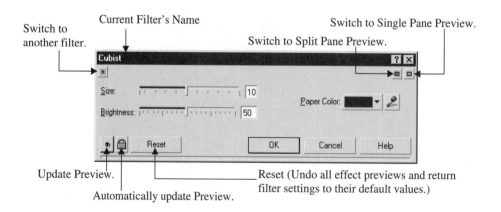

Choosing Filter Preview Modes

The three Preview modes are Full Screen (no pane), Split Pane, and Single Pane. Switching from mode to mode is controlled by two small buttons on the upper-right side of the dialog (they're located just to the left of the Help and Cancel buttons).

In Full Screen mode, you can hide a filter's dialog if you press and hold the F2 key while previewing the filter's effect. This can be particularly helpful when working with large images.

Single Pane

The Single Pane Preview mode opens a single, large preview window over the filter's controls. When you're in either Full Screen or Single Pane mode, clicking the second of the two preview buttons switches you to Single Pane Preview mode, as shown in Figure 24-1.

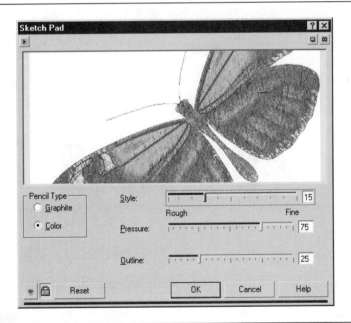

FIGURE 24-1   Choose Art Strokes | Sketch Pad to apply this effect to a bitmap in Single Pane mode.

Split Pane

The Split Pane Preview mode opens two windows above the filter's controls. The window on the left contains the original image, and the window on the right contains a preview of the image with the filter applied. When you're in Full Screen mode, clicking the first of the two preview buttons switches you to Split Pane mode. When you're in Single Pane mode, clicking the second of the two preview buttons switches you to Split Pane mode, as shown in Figure 24-2.

Note that you can set the Default Preview mode by accessing the Options dialog. Click Tools | Options, or press CTRL+J. Click the Global heading | Bitmap Effects subheading. You can choose between Full Screen (No Pane), Before and After (Split Pane), and Result Only (Single Pane). The Last Used option is also available, which automatically opens a filter's dialog to whatever view you used the last time you applied the filter. You can set the dialogs to the last settings you applied (instead of their default effect settings) by checking Prefill Dialogs with Last Used Values.

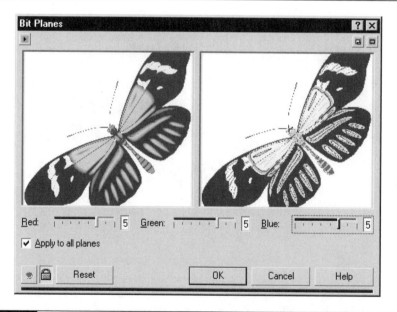

FIGURE 24-2   Split Pane mode displays the original bitmap on the left and a preview of the bitmap with the effect applied on the right.

No Pane

The No Pane Preview mode turns off the dialog preview windows and enables you to preview the image in the drawing area. This can be useful when you work with large images and you need to compare the image to its surroundings in your document. If the Filter dialog is in the way, it can be moved by dragging-and-dropping it or minimized by pressing and holding the F2 key. In Split Pane or Single Pane mode, you can switch to No Pane mode by clicking the first preview button.

Using Filter Zoom and Hand Tools

When using Split Pane or Single Pane mode, you can zoom in by clicking the left mouse button and zoom out by clicking the right mouse button. Also, in both Single Pane and Split Pane modes, you can pan the preview by clicking-and-dragging in the preview window.

You may switch from the effect you're currently using to any other effect, by clicking the arrow button in the upper-left corner of any Bitmap Filter dialog.

3D Effects Filters

CorelDRAW 10 ships with a set of powerful *3D Effects* filters that enable you to quickly add depth and dimension to your images (see 3D Effects Filters in the color section of this book). The 3D Effects menu (see the following illustration) contains seven filters:

3D Rotate

The *3D Rotate* filter enables you to rotate your image in 3D by dragging-and-dropping a 3D model (located on the left side of the filter's dialog). You may also enter rotation values in the Vertical and/or Horizontal text boxes. Rotation values can range from –75 degrees to +75 degrees.

Cylinder

The *Cylinder* filter creates an illusion of wrapping your image around a cylinder. When you apply settings with positive numbers, colors in the middle of the image are stretched out toward the edges, while edge colors are squeezed into a smaller space. When you apply settings with negative numbers, edge colors are stretched toward the center, and center colors are squeezed into a smaller space. Settings may be adjusted from –100 percent to +100 percent on either a horizontal or vertical plane.

Emboss

The *Emboss* filter is used to create a raised or sunken effect on an object. Emboss accomplishes this by applying lighting changes to an image. To visualize the effect, imagine a circle surrounding the image. The light shone on the image can be placed anywhere on this 360-degree circle.

> **TIP** *Light shone on an image from the upper left of the circle (at about the 135-degree point) tends to apply a raised effect, while light shone from the lower right (at about the 315-degree point) tends to apply a sunken effect. The effect may be emphasized by adding a drop shadow to the image on the side opposite where the light originated (so, if the light is in the upper left, place a drop shadow in the lower right).*

Page Curl

The *Page Curl* filter creates the effect of the corner of an object being lifted up and pulled toward the object. The icons in the Page Curl dialog are used to determine which corner of the object should be used for the Page Curl. The height, width, direction, transparency, and color of the Page Curl are all adjustable.

24

Perspective

The *Perspective* filter adds depth to an image. A square model in the dialog with four handles (one on each corner) is used to apply perspective, by dragging-and-dropping the handles. This causes the top, bottom, left, or right side of the object to appear closer to the viewer (if the side is enlarged by the Perspective filter) or further away (if the side is shrunk by the Perspective filter). The *Perspective* option works by pulling two adjacent squares closer together or further apart. A *Shear* option is also available, which pulls two adjacent squares in the same direction, instead of moving them closer together or further apart.

Pinch Punch

Th *Pinch Punch* filter is used to warp the center of an image so the image appears closer to the viewer or further away from the viewer. Imagine holding a printed image in front of you and pinching its back near the center—the center would appear pulled slightly further away from you than the rest of the image. This demonstrates the *Pinch* effect, as shown in Figure 24-3. On the other hand, if

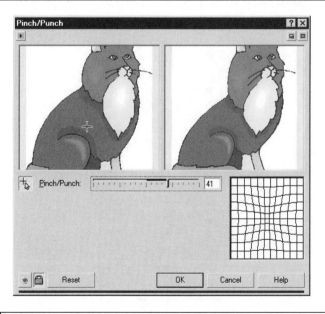

FIGURE 24-3   Creating a slimmer cat with the Pinch filter

you were to punch the paper in the middle from the back, the middle would bulge out and appear slightly closer to you. This demonstrates the *Punch* effect. The Pinch effect is applied on a scale of +1 to +100, while the Punch effect is applied on a scale of –1 to –100.

Sphere

The *Sphere* filter is used to give images a rounded appearance. Pixels near the center of the object are pulled out toward the edges in all directions, while pixels near the edge are pushed slightly closer together. While this may sound similar to the Cylinder filter, the Cylinder filter only displaces the image's pixels in a vertical or horizontal line, while the Sphere filter displaces pixels in a 360-degree circle.

Art Strokes Filters

The *Art Strokes* filters transform your drawings into images that look as if they were created by a variety of natural drawing methods, such as charcoal, and natural drawing styles, such as Impressionist (see Art Strokes Filters in the color section of this book). The Art Strokes menu (see the following illustration) contains 14 filters:

Charcoal

The *Charcoal* filter applies changes to your image to make it look as though it were sketched with charcoal sticks. The good news is that you can use this filter without having your fingertips turn black. Both the size of the charcoal stick and the strength of the edge contouring are adjusted on a scale of 1 to 10. Of course, because natural charcoal sticks are always black, the resulting image contains only grayscale colors. Note that the image's color model won't be changed, just the colors in the image.

Conté Crayon

A *Conté Crayon* is a hard drawing pencil made of a mixture of graphite and clay. Given the chemical makeup of the pencil, sketches made by a Conté Crayon contain quite a bit of black, brown, and off-red shades. You may select from five colors you want highlighted in your image: white, black, sanguine, sepia, and bistre. The Pressure control is used to control color intensity, and the Texture control is used to control the granularity of the texture.

Crayon

The *Crayon* filter makes your image appear as though it were drawn with a wax crayon. The basic colors of your image aren't changed, but the colors are scattered throughout the image, in a manner similar to what a wax crayon creates. The Size controls set the size of the tip of the crayon, and the Outline control sets the strength of the crayon along hard edges.

Cubist

Cubist painting is a somewhat abstract style created by Parisian painters, including Pablo Picasso and Georges Braque, in the early 1900s. The term *Cubist* was originally meant to scorn the style of creating art based on cubes and angular shapes, instead of more naturally occurring shapes (see Figure 24-4). The Size control of the *Cubist* filter enables adjustment of the size of the cubes and angles, and the Brightness control determines the amount of light in your image. The paper color selector may be used to add additional color to the image.

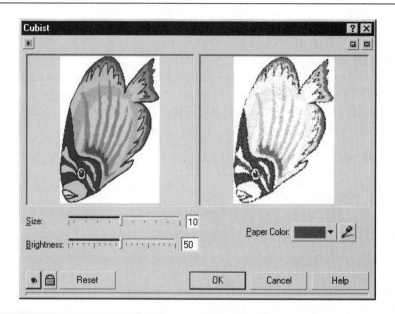

FIGURE 24-4   The Cubist filter applies cube and angular brush strokes to an image.

Impressionist

Impressionist painting is one of the original art forms that eventually became known as *modern art.* The *Impressionist* filter simulates this appearance by applying an oil painting–like effect to your image. The Style area of the dialog is used to choose between large strokes of paint versus small dabs of paint. The technique area of the dialog enables you to set the strength of the stroke or dab, the amount of colorization, and the amount of brightness.

Palette Knife

Palette knife painting uses an artist's palette knife (usually a flexible knife with no cutting blade) instead of a brush to apply paint to an image. The *Palette Knife* filter creates the look of an image painted with a palette knife, right down to the thick ridges you would expect when painting with a knife instead of a brush. The blade size setting is used to control the length of the strokes, with lower settings

24

creating hard, beveled edges and higher settings creating longer, smoother edges. The soft edge setting controls the strength of the effect along raised edges. The angle setting is used to define the angle at which the strokes are created.

Pastels

The *Pastels* filter is used to create a pastel-colored image. In the Pastel Type area of the dialog, use the Soft option to create a pastel drawing look or the Oil option to create a pastel painting look. Stroke size sets the length of the brushstrokes, and Hue Variation enables you to enter color variation into the image with pastel "pencils" or pastel "oil paints."

Pen & Ink

The *Pen & Ink* filter changes your image's appearance to that of a grayscale pen and ink drawing. The Style section of the dialog is used to choose between the Stippling style (which uses dots of ink) and the Crosshatch style (which uses intersecting, angled strokes of ink). The density setting controls the strength of the ink dots or strokes, and the ink pools setting controls the collection of ink along the edges.

Pointillist

The Pointillist style of painting (or *Pointillism*) uses dots of ink to create images. In the *Pointillist* filter, the size of the paint dots are set via the Size control and the amount of light in the image is set via the Brightness control.

Scraperboard

Scraperboard is a term for an image with two layers of paint. The bottom layer contains either colors or white, and the top layer is black. Paint is then scratched away from the top layer to reveal the paint on the bottom layer. In the Scraperboard filter, the Scrape section of the dialog controls whether the bottom layer consists of colors or white. The Density control determines how close together scrapes are placed, and the Size control determines the size of the scrapes.

Sketch Pad

The *Sketch Pad* filter is used to simulate a graphite or color pencil sketch. The pencil type area of the dialog sets whether the image is to be "sketched" using a graphite pencil (which results in a grayscale look) or colored pencils. The style setting controls the width of the pencil strokes: Lower settings somewhat resemble an oil painting and higher settings resemble pencil sketch. When in *Graphite* mode, you may select rougher or finer lead; when in *Color* mode, this control changes to a pressure selector. The outline settings adjust the thickness of borders in the image.

Watercolor

The *Watercolor* filter is used to make your image resemble a watercolor painting. As with real watercolor, the colors produced are mainly pastel shades, with significant bleeding from color to color. The brush size setting is used to control the size of the watercolor dabs. Granulation is used to control the texture of the paper and also affects color strength (lower settings allow stronger shades, while higher settings tend to create pastel shades). The water amount setting controls how much of a water effect is applied to the paint: Lower settings create the look of a more concentrated paint; higher settings create a look of heavily diluted paint. The bleed setting controls how much colors bleed into each other, and the brightness setting controls the amount of light in your image.

Water Marker

The *Water Marker* filter creates an illusion of an image painted with a water soluble marker. The Variation section of the dialog controls the basic style of the effect. Three variations are available: default, order, and random. The default setting provides a mildly wet look to the image, the order setting creates a pattern of large and small color dabs, and the random setting simulates larger dabs created at various random angles. The size setting controls the overall size of the strokes, and the color variation setting controls the contrast and sharpness between colors.

Wave Paper

The *Wave Paper* filter creates the look of an image painted on rough or textured paper. The Brush Color control is used to choose color or grayscale, and the Brush Pressure control is used to set the intensity of the color dots.

Blur Filters

CorelDRAW 10 ships with one of the largest assortments of *Blur filters* you can find in any graphics editor. Blur filters are widely used for both editing imported bitmaps (such as photographs) and creating special effects. Blur filters all work on the same general principle of smoothing sharp changes in color, but each filter has a unique set of capabilities that set it apart from the other available Blur filters (see Blur Filters in the color section of this book). Nine blur filters are available, as shown here:

Directional Smooth

The *Directional Smooth* blur filter provides one of the most subtle blur effects found in CorelDRAW's blur filter collection. You may find it particularly useful for smoothing rough, aliased edges that sometimes form in vector drawings.

Gaussian Blur

This is one of the more traditional and popular blur effects. The *Gaussian* blur filter is often used in lower amounts in photo touch up, with higher amounts frequently used for creating a blurred special effect. Gaussian blurs tend to have a slightly more random effect than traditional smoothing blurs.

Jaggy Despeckle

The *Jaggy Despeckle* blur filter does exactly what its name implies: removes speckled and noisy areas of images. Jaggy Despeckle can also be used for removing aliasing (Figure 24-5), particularly in images that don't respond sufficiently to the Directional Smooth filter. Jaggy Despeckle can also be useful on scanned images that contain a screen or moiré pattern.

 The best cure for moiré patterns is to avoid them in the first place. Scanning at two or three times the required resolution, and then resampling the image to the appropriate resolution is often a convenient way to avoid moiré problems.

Low Pass

The *Low Pass* blur filter can be thought of as a particularly smart filter because it targets only certain pixels in an image. When using this filter, you set a pixel radius value, which tells CorelDRAW what areas it should smooth when the Low Pass filter is applied. Lower pixel radius settings affect only extremely noisy areas of an

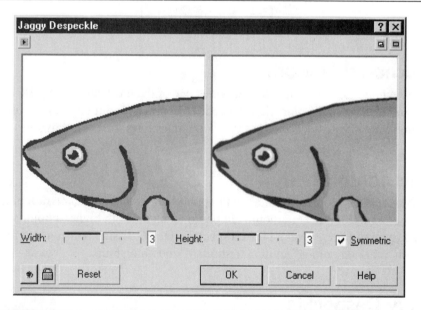

FIGURE 24-5   Smoothing rough, aliased edges with the Jaggy Despeckle filter

24

image, while higher settings affect a broader area of pixels. The percentage setting controls the strength of the blur applied to the pixels within the pixel radius range.

Motion

The *Motion* blur filter is another popular filter and, as its name implies, is generally used for creating an illusion of motion. The Motion blur filter creates this effect by focusing its blurring effect at an angle, which you define in the filter's dialog.

Radial

The *Radial* blur filter applies a blurring effect that radiates outward from a central point. The blurring effect is highest in areas furthest away from the center point. By default, the center point is the center of your bitmap. You may change the location of the center point by clicking the Crosshair Tool in the filter's dialog, and then clicking the image (Full Screen Preview), the left window pane (Split Pane Preview), or the preview image (Single Pane Preview).

Smooth

Th *Smooth* blur filter applies one of the most subtle blur effects. Smooth is most often used for minor photo touch up and can also be used for removing the artifacts caused by overcompressing JPEG images.

Soften

The *Soften* blur filter is virtually identical to the smooth filter. When images need a very mild blur effect, it's often a good idea to try both of these filters and see which produces the best result.

Zoom

The *Zoom* blur filter is similar to the Radial blur in that the effect is applied beginning at a center point, with the effect getting more and more intense as it moves away from that point. As with the Radial blur filter, the center point is set by default at the center of your bitmap. You may change the location of the center point by clicking the Crosshairs Tool in the filter's dialog, and clicking the image (Full Screen preview), the left window pane (Split Pane preview), or the preview image (Single Pane preview). The Zoom filter creates an effect of blurred edges that gradually zoom into a focused center point.

Color Transform Filters

Vector editing isn't traditionally thought of as a design field in which color transformation is available. When working with vector images, you must change fill and outline color properties to change the image's color. Conversely, bitmap editing allows for a wide range of color transformations. Art is often said to imitate nature; but when using color transformations, you may find yourself creating completely unique color patterns that couldn't realistically be created by any other artistic method (see Color Transform in the color section of this book). The Color Transform menu contains five filters, as the following illustration shows:

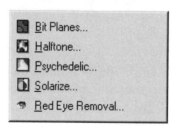

Bit Planes

The *Bit Planes* color filter breaks your image down into the three basic planes of red, green, and blue. Changes in the strength of the Bit Planes filter may be adjusted one color channel at a time or adjusted all at the same time, by disabling or enabling the Apply to All Planes check box. This filter may be used both for creating a colorful special effect and for analyzing the flow of color in your image.

Halftone

One of the more common commercial methods of printing, called *process color,* breaks colors down into the primary print color channels of cyan, magenta, yellow, and black. Each of these colors is then printed on its own screen, and the screens are lined up at appropriate angles to produce a continuous flow of color in the final image. The *Halftone* color filter is the onscreen equivalent of the halftone process. It breaks colors down into CMYK color channels, and it enables you to select the size of the halftone dots and the angle at which each color halftone is displayed.

Psychedelic

As its name suggests, the Psychedelic filter is used to create wildly colorful variations on your image's original color. Lower values tend simply to replace your image's colors with brighter colors. Higher values apply brighter colors and also rotate colors similar to the way color can be rotated with a Hue control, but with less predictable, more random results.

Solarize

The *Solarize* color filter converts your image into what it could look like as a photographic negative. Lower values lead to darker images. Higher values create more colorful images that more closely resemble color film negatives.

Red Eye Removal

The *Red Eye Removal* color filter is new to CorelDRAW 10, and it's used to remove red eye from imported photographic bitmaps. The *Eye Picker* is used to tell CorelDRAW where you would like the filter applied, and the *Color Picker* is used to define a replacement color.

Contour Filters

Contour filters identify edges and contours in your image, and they apply effects only to these parts of your image. The remainder of your image is converted to a neutral color (see Contour Filters in the color section of this book). The three Contour filters are shown here:

Edge Detect

The *Edge Detect* filter finds the edges in your image and replaces them with lines and curves, as shown in Figure 24-6. This filter generally produces a more subtle result than the other Contour filters. You can use the Background Color Picker in the dialog to set a background color for your image.

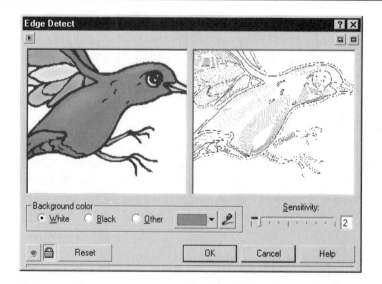

| FIGURE 24-6 | The Edge Detect filter highlights edges and converts fills to the background color. |

24

Find Edges

The *Find Edges* filter is similar to the Edge Detect filter, but it has more options. The Find Edges filter enables the selection of a soft edge or a harder, "solid" edge detection. The Level control is used to set the intensity of the effect.

Trace Contour

The *Trace Contour* filter traces the colors in your image, creating a sort of outline inside your image's outline. The colors for the images are replaced with selections from the Window's 16-color palette. The Level control is used to set a threshold for applying the effect. The Lower and Upper buttons are used to determine what range of colors will be affected by the filter (those below or above the threshold).

Creative Filters

Exploring CorelDRAW 10's Creative filters is a journey into the more unusual and bizarre aspects of bitmap filter design. Although you probably won't find much in the *Creative* filters for traditional filter use such as photo editing, you will find a collection of imaginative filters for sparking your creativity and creating special effects (see Creative Filters in the color section of this book). The Creative menu contains 14 filters, as shown here:

Crafts

The *Crafts* filter is actually six unique filters built into one interface. The drop-down list box (see the following illustration) contains six different Crafts options: Puzzle, Gears, Marbles, Candy, Ceramic Tile, and Poker Chips. The Size control is used to set the size of the Crafts items created (such as Gears or Marbles), the Complete control determines how much of the image is to be converted to Crafts items, and the Brightness control defines the brightness of the Crafts items. You may rotate the angle at which light is applied by dragging the rotation arrow or setting a value in the rotation text box.

Crystallize

The *Crystallize* filter makes your image look as though it's being viewed through semiopaque crystal. The Size control is used to determine the size of the crystals.

Fabric

The *Fabric* filter is similar in construction to the Crafts filter. It contains Size, Complete, Brightness, and Rotation controls, as well as a drop-down list box with six unique options: Needlepoint, Rug Hooking, Quilt, Strings, Ribbons, and Tissue Collage. You may find this filter particularly useful for creating textile-like fills for objects and image backgrounds.

Frame

The *Frame* filter is used to place a creative frame around your bitmap (see Figure 24-7). The dialog has two tabs: Select and Modify. The *Select* tab is used to choose a frame and to add new frames to the selection list. New frames may be added by clicking the open folder icon.

Once you select a frame, the *Modify* tab adds options for customizing the frame's appearance. The Color box is used to change the color of your frame.

The Opacity control affects the frame's overall transparency, while the Blur/Feather control determines application of semitransparent areas along the frame's inside edges. The Scale controls are used to control the horizontal and vertical size of the frame, you may click the Lock button to force identical horizontal and vertical values. The frame may also be flipped horizontally or vertically, or rotated along a 360-degree curve. You may also change the center point of the frame by clicking the Align button and then clicking the preview image. To recenter the frame, click the Recenter button. You may save your settings for future use by clicking the plus (+) sign on the bottom right of the screen and typing a name for your preset.

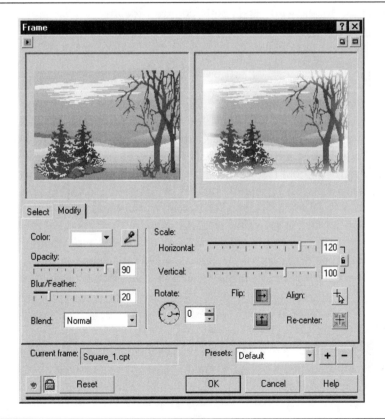

FIGURE 24-7   Adding a Feathered picture frame with the Frame filter

NOTE
You can create new frames in Corel PHOTO-PAINT. Create a new blank white image, 2,000 pixels by 2,000 pixels in size. Add a mask, which is then used as your frame. Invert the mask and color the outside of the mask black. Semitransparent areas may be added by using shades of gray. Darker shades of gray are almost opaque, and light shades are nearly transparent. Convert the image to grayscale and save it as a CPT file.

Glass Block

The *Glass Block* filter applies a semitransparent, patterned effect to your image. The effect is similar to what you would see if you were to look at an image through a glass partition, such as a shower door. The width and height of the Glass Blocks are adjustable with the width and height controls. Identical values may be locked into place by clicking the lock button.

Kid's Play

The *Kid's Play* filter is a fairly new addition to CorelDRAW—it was introduced in version 9. Kid's Play is actually four filters in one. You choose which of the four filters you want to use by clicking the Game drop-down list box, and selecting from Lite Pegs, Building Blocks, Finger Paint, and Paint by Numbers. Light Pegs and Building Blocks both resemble popular childhood games, as you may recognize when viewing the sample images in this book's color section. Finger Paint and Paint by Numbers both offer a creative combination of blur and color transformation applied at the same time. As with the Crafts and Fabric filters, Size, Brightness, Rotation, and Completeness are all adjustable. Note that in Paint by Numbers mode, the Size control is replaced with a Detail control, and the Rotation and Complete controls are unavailable because the filter doesn't require them.

Mosaic

The *Mosaic* filter applies a pattern of Mosaic tiles to your image. Size and Background can both be adjusted, and a fading Vignette pattern may be added by checking the Vignette box.

Particles

The *Particles* filter is also relatively new and was introduced in CorelDRAW 9. You may choose from two types of particles: stars and bubbles. The Size control determines the size of the particles, the Density control determines the number of particles added, the Coloration control adds color to the particles, and the Transparency control adjusts the transparency of the particles against your image. The Angle indicator adjusts the angle of the light that strikes the particles.

Scatter

The *Scatter* filter rearranges the location of pixels in your image so they appear scattered. Both Horizontal and Vertical controls are provided, along with a Lock button for forcing matching horizontal and vertical values. When just a touch of scattering is used, your image looks as if it were being viewed through a wet, translucent surface, such as a rain-covered window. More intense scatter settings remove detail from your image and replace it with a more intense scatter pattern.

Smoked Glass

As its name implies, the *Smoked Glass* filter creates the appearance that your image is being viewed through colored glass. Color, Tint, and Blurring are all adjustable.

> **TIP**   *You may find the Smoked Glass filter useful for adding clouds to your image. Use low to moderate Tint and Blurring settings and apply a light blue, light gray, or white color.*

Stained Glass

The *Stained Glass* filter makes your image look as though it's being viewed through stained glass. You may adjust the color and width of the solder that holds the glass pieces together and apply a slightly beveled edge to the glass pieces by checking 3D Lighting. The size of the glass pieces and intensity of the background light are also adjustable.

Vignette

The *Vignette* filter applies a fading vignette pattern to the center of your image. Four vignette shapes (circle, ellipse, square, and rectangle) are available, as is a color selector. The Offset control sets the size of the Vignette in relation to the image size, and the Fade control sets how gradually or quickly the inner portion of the image fades into the Vignette's background.

Vortex

The *Vortex* filter is a popular special effects filter that applies a swirling pattern to your image, making it look as though the outside areas of the image are being drawn into the center of the image. The center point of the image is adjustable with the Crosshair Tool.

Four types of vortex patterns are available: Brushed (in which the pattern looks as though it were applied with a paint brush), Layered (which creates the look of several layers of vortex patterns being applied), Thick (which makes the image look as though the vortex pattern was applied using a thick brush), and Thin (which allows quite a bit of the underlying image to show though). The size of the vortex and its inner and outer directions are all adjustable.

Weather

The *Weather* filter is another relatively new addition to the CorelDRAW package, first appearing in version 9. Weather is used to apply Snow, Rain, or Fog to your image. The Size control adjusts the size of the weather particles (the snow, rain, or fog), while the Strength control adjusts the intensity of the effect (for example, a higher strength setting creates a more intense snowstorm). You may click the Randomize button to change the location of the weather particles randomly. Note that the Rain control has an Angle control used to adjust the angle of the rainfall.

Distort Filters

Many of the Bitmap filters discussed thus far are intended to repair or augment images, sometimes leaving significant parts of the image intact. The Distort filters differ in this regard because all of them are designed to apply some type of distortion to most or all of the image. The selection of Distort filters runs from the traditional, such as Swirl and Ripple, to the unique, such as Blocks and Wet paint (see Distort Filters in the color section of this book). Ten Distort filters are available, as shown here:

Blocks

Applying the *Blocks* filter is a bit like carefully tearing up an image into a collection of neat square blocks. The Blocks filter does just that, creating a series of squares or rectangles based on your original image.

Displace

Using the *Displace* filter is similar to applying a reflection map to your image. A Displace pattern is selected from the drop-down list box, and the image is then mapped to include both its original data and the data in the displacement pattern.

Offset

The *Offset* filter has the effect of cutting your image into pieces and then putting it back together in a different order. For example, the top left of your image may be relocated to the bottom right of your image.

Pixelate

The *Pixelate* filter combines and averages the values of neighboring pixels to create an image that looks pixelated, a process that often occurs after enlarging a bitmap image. The square and rectangle modes are similar to the effect created by using the Glass Blocks filter, while the Radial mode creates the effect of pixelation radiating out from the center point of the image. The center point is adjustable with the Crosshairs Tool.

Ripple

The *Ripple* filter applies an up and down wave distortion pattern to your image. The default wave is parallel to the top and bottom of the image, and a perpendicular wave may also be added. The direction of the waves may be adjusted using the angle setting.

Swirl

The *Swirl* filter is similar to the Ripple filter in that it applies a distortion pattern to your image. In the case of swirl, the pattern is applied in a clockwise or counter clockwise circular motion.

Tile

The *Tile* filter creates a smaller version of your image, and then repeats that image over and over until your original image is completely filled with repetitions of the smaller image.

Wet Paint

The *Wet Paint* filter simulates the effect of too much paint being used on a canvas. As you can see in Figure 24-8, this filter rearranges pixels to make it look as though your image is dripping paint.

Whirlpool

The *Whirlpool* filter maps your image to a series of swirling vortexes. The mapping is performed mathematically (as opposed to being performed with an

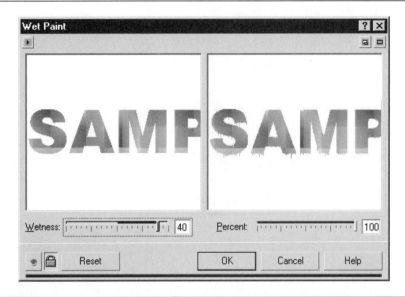

FIGURE 24-8   Applying the Wet Paint filter rearranges pixels to simulate a dripping effect.

image), so a virtually infinite amount of whirlpool distortion may be added to your image.

Wind

The *Wind* filter is similar to the Motion blur filter, in that it creates an illusion of movement in your image. Wind is generally less destructive to your image than Motion blur and may be used when a more subtle motion blur effect is desired.

Noise Filters

Noise is the graphics term for pixels in an image that appear to be unnecessary or out of place. A classic example of a noisy image is a television set tuned to a station where only snow is coming in, instead of a station. The randomly appearing snow is the television equivalent of noise.

Noise is often added to an image before applying other bitmap filters. The addition of *Noise* can give another filter more color to work with when generating its effect. In addition to adding noise, some of the Noise filters are used to reduce noise in an image. Eight Noise filters are available, as shown here:

Add Noise

The *Add Noise* filter is a powerful tool for adding noise to your image and customizing the way in which the noise is added. Three noise types are available: Gaussian, Spike, and Uniform. The *Gaussian* noise type adds noise along a *Gaussian Curve,* a bell-shaped curve used to apply effects to an image in a slightly random appearing pattern. The *Spike* noise type adds less noise than the Gaussian type and often produces brighter areas of noise as well. The *Uniform* noise type applies noise in a fairly even distribution across your image.

The Add Noise dialog also has three color modes: Intensity, Random, and Single. Intensity adds a high level of grayscale noise to an image, similar to what you would see on an old black-and-white television. The Random color mode randomly adds color noise to your image, similar (but sometimes more colorfully) to the noise seen on a color television. The Single Color mode enables selection of a single noise color that's distributed across the entire image.

The Level control is used to set the intensity of the noise effect. The Density control defines how close together neighboring noise pixels may be placed.

Diffuse

The *Diffuse* filter diffuses or spreads out concentrated points of light in your image, as shown in Figure 24-9. In smooth images, the Diffuse filter's action may barely be noticeable. In noisy images, this filter may also be used as a mild blur filter.

24

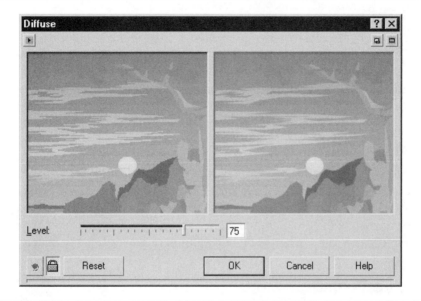

FIGURE 24-9   The Diffuse filter applies a mild blurring effect that smoothes out noisy edges.

Dust and Scratch

The *Dust and Scratch* filter is used to remove noise instead of adding noise. This filter can be particularly useful in removing dust and scratches from scanned photographs, thus, its name.

Maximum

Maximum is one of three noise removal filters that work by changing the color value of a noisy pixel to match the average color value of surrounding pixels. When using the Maximum filter, color values are averaged based on the maximum color value of surrounding pixels.

Median

Median is another filter that removes noise by averaging color values. In this case, the median color value of surrounding pixels is used to replace noise in the image.

Minimum

As you've likely realized by now, the *Minimum* filter removes noise by averaging the minimum color value of pixels surrounding the noise in an image. No hard and fast rules exist to assist in deciding which filter—Maximum, Median, or Minimum—to try first when removing noise from an image. Trial and error is generally the only way to determine which filter will work best on your image.

Remove Moiré

The *Remove Moiré* filter helps to remove moiré patterns on scanned images. As you increase the amount of the Remove Moiré value, more of the pattern is removed, but more blurring also occurs. You may also downsize your images dimensions from within the Remove Moiré dialog. This action, even when used without a Remove Moiré filter, is often helpful in removing a moiré pattern.

Remove Noise

The *Remove Noise* filter is similar to the Maximum, Median, and Minimum filters. It attempts to remove noise and, at the same time, do so with as little blurring as possible. The Threshold control is used to define a brightness threshold. Pixels with a value higher than the threshold value are removed and replaced based on the average color value of surrounding pixels.

Sharpen Filters

The *Sharpen* filters are used to sharpen images and bring out detail. Although they are most commonly used as Photo Editing tools, Sharpen filters may also be used to add brightness and detail to vector images that were converted to bitmaps (see Sharpen Filters in the color section of this book and/or open the file Tutorial Examples/Chapter 24/). As shown in the following illustration, the Sharpen menu contains five Sharpen filters:

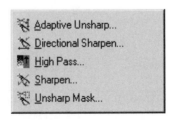

Adaptive Unsharp

The *Adaptive Unsharp* filter is one of the more mild Sharpen filters. It works by highlighting edge details in an image.

Directional Sharpen

This filter works similarly to the Adaptive Unsharpen filter. The *Directional Sharpen* filter takes the added step of determining in which direction it can apply the sharpen effect to do the least amount of damage to the underlying image.

High Pass

The *High Pass* filter removes shaded areas of an image and highlights brighter areas. The additional brightness creates a sharpened effect.

Sharpen

This traditional filter is seen in virtually every image editor. The *Sharpen* filter works mainly by increasing contrast in blurred areas. This is one of the stronger Sharpen filters, so be certain to check your preview image when using it for signs of oversharpening. Oversharpening an image can create color artifacts and a pixellated effect.

Unsharp Mask

Along with Adaptive Unsharp, this is one of the more gentle Sharpen effects. The *Unsharp Mask* filter helps increase detail, much like the High Pass filter, but Unsharp Mask does so without damaging or replacing the less-detailed areas of an image. Unsharp Mask can also have a brightening effect on an image.

Working with Plug-Ins

One of the many strengths of CorelDRAW is its compatibility with third-party plug-ins, sometimes referred to as *Photoshop Plug-Ins*. CorelDRAW 10 ships with several third-party plug-ins, and thousands more are available on the Internet.

Installing a Plug-In

To make a plug-in available in CorelDRAW, open the Options dialog by clicking Tools | Options (see Figure 24-10). In the tree view on the left side of the dialog, click Plug-Ins. Click the Add button on the right side of the dialog, add the folder containing your new plug-in(s), and click OK. Unlike most of its competition, you needn't close and reopen CorelDRAW for the plug-ins to be available—CorelDRAW is one of the few graphics programs that makes new added filters available immediately.

Keep in mind that you must have an object selected and the object must either have been imported as a bitmap or converted to a bitmap to use a plug-in. Many plug-ins are designed only to work in RGB Color mode; so if you find some plug-ins are unavailable in other Color modes, try switching to RGB by clicking Bitmaps | Mode | RGB Color (24-bit). Once the plug-in is applied, you can switch back to your original color model.

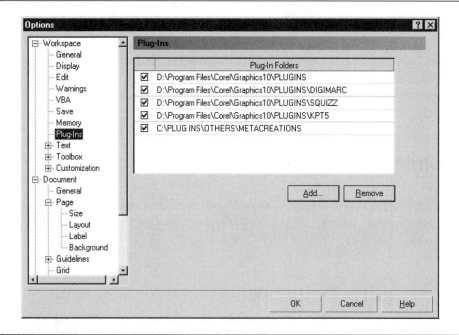

FIGURE 24-10   CorelDRAW's Plug-Ins dialog

CorelDRAW 10's Plug-In Collection

In addition to the default plug-ins previously described, CorelDRAW 10 ships with third-party plug-ins, including Human Software's Squizz, Digimarc's watermarking plug-ins, Corel's Terrazzo and Julia Set Explorer, and three filters from the Kai's Power Tools (KPT) collection (Smoothie, FraxFlame, and Shape Shifter).

A Tour of the Plug-Ins Available

The *Squizz* plug-in offers two main options: Brush and Grid. In Brush mode, you use a Paint Brush Tool to brush on special effects, such as pixelization. In Grid mode, a wireframe grid is provided that may be pulled in any direction to alter the flow of pixels in the image.

The *DigiMarc* plug-in is used to place a digital watermark in an image. The watermark may be used to identify the image as belonging to you, if you ever need to prove ownership of the image. Note: Although a fairly strong level of security can be offered for print images, it's still difficult to create tamper-resistant security for Web images because of their lower resolution and the ease with which they can be altered by almost anyone with a computer. You can sign up for a free Digimarc identification number by visiting **http://www.digimarc.com**.

Corel's *Julia Set Explorer* and *Terrazzo* plug-ins provide a unique set of tools for creating abstract images and patterns. KPT fans may recognize the Julia Set Explorer, as shown in Figure 24-11. It originally appeared as the Fractal Explorer in version 2 of Kai's Power Tools and is still a favorite among many designers when creating fractals. The plug-in offers dozens of preset fractal patterns created by programmer/artist Kai Krause and by Corel's engineers, and hundreds of gradient color schemes that may be applied to the fractals. An infinite variety of new fractals can be found by zooming in on your current fractal and by moving your cursor along the *Mandelbrot Map* (named for IBM mathematician Benoit Mandelbrot, the discoverer of fractal energy patterns).

The Corel Terrazzo plug-in expands on the concept of combining math and art to create digital images. Terrazzo uses some of the same fractal geometry concepts found in the Julia Set Explorer to create completely abstract patterns and tiles. In Figure 24-12, a fractal created in the Julia Set Explorer is manipulated in the Terrazzo plug-in to create a new seamlessly tiled pattern. You can learn more about fractals from IBM's fractal science homepage: **http://www.research.ibm.com/ research/fractaltop.html**.

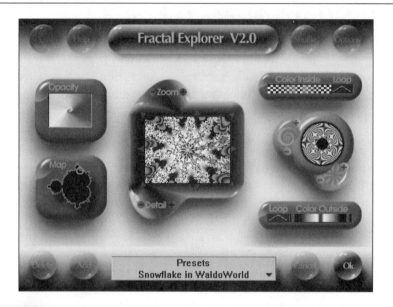

FIGURE 24-11 Corel's Julia Set Explorer

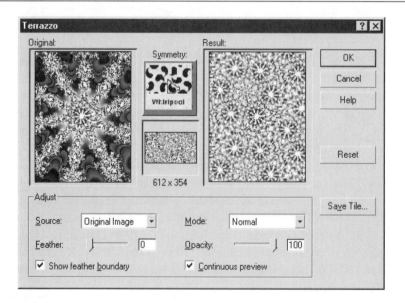

FIGURE 24-12 Manipulating a Julia Set fractal in the Corel Terrazzo plug-in

24

The three KPT filters that ship with CorelDRAW are from KPT version 5, which (along with most of the KPT product line) was recently acquired by Corel. The *Shape Shifter* filter is used to alter color flow in bitmaps with 3D lighting, shadows, and a set of geometrically shaped bump maps. The *Smoothie* filter is used to smooth out rough edges, particularly those that can occur because of aliasing and low-resolution image scans. The *FraxFlame* filter is a new fractal-based filter (see Figure 24-13) that expands on the technology found in the Julia Set Explorer. A main fractal flame image is displayed in the Mutation window, while the 12 images surrounding the center image display mutated versions of the fractal. You may click any of the mutations to make it the new center image, and a new set of mutations is immediately created. In the main window, to the right of the Mutations window, you can pan and zoom in on the fractal, which is updated interactively as you continue the zooming and panning process. The FraxFlame filter provides a highly interactive (and enjoyable) method of exploring the art and science of fractal imaging.

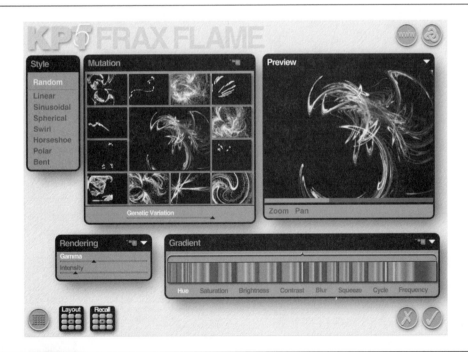

FIGURE 24-13   Creating a fractal with the KPT 5 FraxFlame plug-in

PART VII

Beyond the Basics

CHAPTER 25

Under the Hood of the Print Engine

CorelDRAW 10's print engine contains the tools you need to satisfy almost any printing requirement in our modern computerized age. It will help you accomplish a simple printing task or a highly complex printing operation. With it, you can go from clicking a button and printing a simple document to preparing a multipart signature and merge to printing a complete database. You will learn to print with confidence as this chapter takes you under the hood of CorelDRAW's print engine.

CorelDRAW's printing capabilities have always been more sophisticated than those of most other programs. Unfortunately, along with sophistication comes a certain degree of complexity. CorelDRAW 10 features the largest number of user-definable features ever, but to simplify this process, the print engine has been organized to satisfy all users needs easily, from beginners to experts.

Printing a Document

When designing, you may want to print to a desktop printer to see how a layout will look on paper. Printing options are normally set to default settings, and a single composite page is printed for each page in your document. If you're printing to a laser printer, any color applied to your design will be converted to grayscale, but if you have a color printer, you'll see your design printed in full color according to the color process associated with your printer and/or Corel Color Manager.

Here's how to print a document according to CorelDRAW 10's default printing options:

1. Select File | Print (CTRL+P), or click the Print button on the Standard Toolbar, to open the Print dialog (Figure 25-1).

2. Select the printer you are going to use from the Name drop-down list. If you've previously set up a default printer, its name will appear automatically here.

3. Click Properties and set the printer properties according to your specific requirements, such as page size, paper orientation, and printing resolution.

4. Choose the page or page range you want to print in the Print Range area.

5. Set the number of copies you require in the Number of Copies box.

6. Click the Print button.

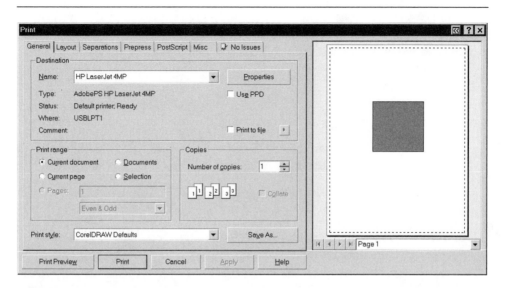

FIGURE 25-1 In CorelDRAW 10's main Print dialog, you can select the most common printing options.

Choosing a Printer

If you use more than one printer, you may find that each has different printable areas, and some may not print all areas in a page. CorelDRAW is set to use the printer that you have selected in Windows as the default printer. To be sure that the printer you are going to use will print the entire area you are designing, the printer should be set as follows:

1. Select File | Print Setup to see the Print Setup dialog.

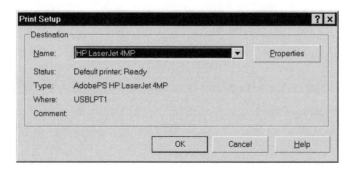

2. Choose the printer you will be using from the Name drop-down list. The selected printer's information will be updated, and the information will be reflected in the Status, Type, Where, and Comment text fields.

- **Status**   Reports on whether the printer is ready to print.

- **Type**   Displays what driver the printer is using. (Windows installs the appropriate drivers automatically when you install a new printer.)

- **Where**   Shows printer port destination, such as LPT1, USP, File, or any other selected port.

- **Comment**   Reflects any notes the driver manufacturer may have added when it was built.

3. Click the Properties button to access the printer properties, such as page size, page orientation, and resolution.

4. Click OK to close the Print Setup dialog.

5. To preview the printable area, select View | Show | Printable Area, and a double marquee will display it in your page.

 If the selected printer in Print Setup is not associated with the document, you may need to set it up again when you reopen the document.

Previewing and Printing Your Document

The Print Preview feature makes CorelDRAW 10's already powerful print engine a super printing tool. With Print Preview, you can see a detailed view of your printed document before you print. You can use several methods to open Print Preview from your document page. You can select File | Print Preview from the command menus; you can place a customized Print Preview button in your workspace and click it when you need to access it; or you may select File | Print (CTRL+P) or click the Print button in the Property Bar, and then click the Print Preview button in the Print dialog.

Anatomy of the Preview Application Window

While Print Preview is open, CorelDRAW10 is still open in the background, along with your document. Print Preview's title bar, menus, Standard Toolbar, Toolbox, Property Bar, and Status Bar operate just like those in CorelDRAW. They provide access to the tools you need to prepare your document for printing while you are previewing your document (Figure 25-2).

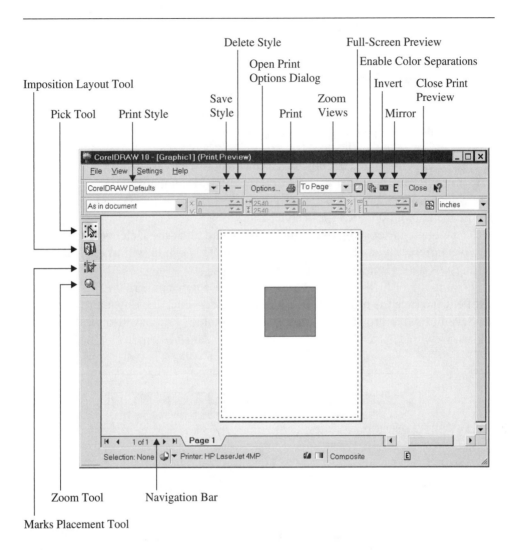

FIGURE 25-2   The Print Preview main window includes title bar, menus, Standard Toolbar, Toolbox, Property Bar, Status Bar, and previewing states.

Using Print Preview Toolbars

The Print Preview Toolbars contain tools and options to help you prepare, preview, and print your documents. Tools like Pick, Imposition, Marks Placement, and Zoom trigger their own set of options in their Property Bars. These tools are used for selecting, moving, arranging, and organizing pages and objects in your previewed, printed document, as well as creating signatures, placing printers marks, scaling, and zooming.

Standard Toolbars   The Standard Toolbars contain a set of buttons and fields that facilitate quick access to different actions. If you place your mouse pointer over any icon or field, a tip box will tell you what this component does.

The Print Style list contains a set of preset print styles that you can select, save, delete, or modify. This tool lets you quickly select a set of styles that will be applied to your printed document. To select a preset style, click the Print Style drop-down list and choose a style. If a preset style does not appear in the list and is on your hard disk or elsewhere, select Browse from the drop-down list and then choose the appropriate PRS (print style) file.

To delete a preset style, highlight the style and click the Delete (–) button. To save a preset style, click the Add (+) button. This action will trigger the Save Settings As dialog shown in Figure 25-3.

Point to the PRS file you want to save, or type a new name in the File Name text field. To save the print style in a different folder, click the down arrow in the Save In field to browse to the folder. In this dialog, you may also create new folders, view folders, and select files as in any browser style windows. Corel's PRS

FIGURE 25-3   You can make various settings, name a file, and select a folder in the Save Settings As dialog.

file format is the only format available in the Save As Type drop-down list. The Settings To Include box displays all the saved print options, and check marks indicate your chosen selections. You can include or exclude options by checking or unchecking them here. Click the plus sign next to a setting to view more options, such as these:

- **Print Options**   Triggers the Print Options tabbed dialog, explained in detail later in this chapter.

- **Print Button**   Sends your document to the Windows spooler using selected print driver options and print style.

- **Zoom**   Lets you select predefined zoom levels from a drop-down list. Click the list and choose.

- **Full Screen**   Opens a full-screen preview window.

- **Enable Color Separation**   Enables color separation according to selected settings in the Separations tab of the Print Options dialog, explained later in this chapter.

- **Invert**   Inverts the previewed and printed image. Used to produce a negative film, which when transposed to a printing plate, changes to the positive state used to print.

- **Mirror**   Flips the printed document horizontally. Films have two sides, and one of them is covered with an emulsion. The image should be printed with the emulsion side down to transpose correctly to the printing plate.

> **TIP**   *Ask your service bureau or print shop about Negative and Emulsion Down options. Generally, imagesetters are set to flip and invert the image. If you select Invert and Mirror options in CorelDRAW and they are set in the imagesetter as well, your film will print positive and emulsion up, and therefore will not transpose correctly to the printing plate. Documents printed on paper that will be photographed to produce a film should not be inverted or mirrored.*

- **Close**   Closes the Print Preview and returns to CorelDRAW's main window.

- **What's This? Help**   Adds a question mark to the mouse pointer, and when you click over a Windows element, it triggers the help file associated with the element.

You can access some of the preceding options by right-clicking in the page and selecting them from the pop-up menu.

Property Bar   The Property Bar is a context-sensitive bar that changes according to which tool in the Toolbox is selected. Elements in Property Bars let you quickly select and apply properties to the active tool. If you place your mouse pointer over any icon or field, a tip box will display what this component does.

Anatomy of the Status Bar

The Status Bar displays general information and options and lets you quickly identify and correct them as necessary.

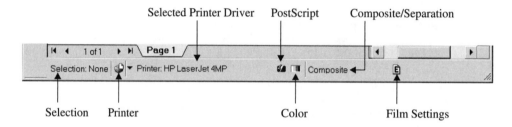

- **Selection**   Indicates whether a page is selected in your preview.

- **Printer**   Provides quick access to available printer drivers and their properties. To change drivers, choose from the displayed list. To access selected driver properties, click Printer Properties.

- **Selected Printer Driver**   Displays the selected printer driver's name.

- **PostScript**   Lets you know whether the selected driver is PostScript.

- **Color**   Tells you whether the selected printer will print in color or grayscale.

- **Composite/Separation**   Reports whether the document will be printed as a composite or separated.

- **Film Settings**   Lets you quickly change your document's invert and mirror states.

Navigating Page Previews

Across the bottom of the Print Preview window is a set of tabs that correspond to each printed page; these tabs provide an easy way for you to navigate among pages and identify them. You can also use the Navigation Bar to move to a particular page in the printed document (see Figure 25-2).

- To activate the viewed page, click the corresponding tab.

- To move to the next page, click the Next button in the Navigation Bar.

- To move to the previous page, click the Back button of the Navigation Bar.

- To move to the document's first page, click the First Page button of the Navigation Bar.

- To move to the document's last page, click the Last Page button of the Navigation Bar.

25

TIP	*You may want to view your printed document in a full window mode without toolbars, menus, and options. To access a full view, click the Full Screen button or press F9. To return to normal view, press F9 or the SPACEBAR.*

Controlling Print Preview's Display

Print Preview provides View menu options that control how your document is previewed. You can choose options according to your system capacity and your viewing needs.

Show Image

Under certain circumstances, you may prefer not to preview images—your images or file may be huge, for example. In these cases, you can turn off image preview in the Print Preview window by selecting View | Show Image. When Show Image is not checked, your document displays as a box, reducing the system resources needed by Print Preview to preview your document.

Preview Colors

By default, Print Preview is set to Auto Simulate Output, but if your selected printer driver does not print in color, your image will show as a grayscale image. To let you preview it in color as it is designed, Print Preview lets you switch between Auto Simulate Output, Color, and Grayscale, whether or not the printer driver is capable of reproducing color. To switch between preview color states, select View | Preview Color and choose the option you require from the flyout, or right-click on your page and select the preview option from the pop-up menu.

Preview Separations

When the Separation option is selected to indicate that you require color separations, Print Preview displays different colors in separated plates. The plates display as grayscale by default because Print Preview is autosimulating output. If you need to view your document as a composite without changing your separation options, select View | Preview Separations and choose an option from the flyout, or right-click on the page and select an option from the pop-up menu.

Choosing Print Parameter States

Print Preview lets you choose between previewing or not previewing some parameter states, such as printable area, how PostScript fill will print, and page tiles, when you are printing oversized documents as tiles. These options are also found on the View menu.

Printable Area

Because each printer has its own printable areas and margins, you could be designing in some areas that your printer may not be able to print. By default, Print Preview lets you view a selected printer's printable area and margins. If you need to turn off this option, click View | Printable Area. When Printable Area is unchecked, the printable area doesn't display.

Rendering PostScript Fills

PostScript fills require complex rendering operations that absorb system resources, and by default this feature is turned off. But if your system is capable, you can turn on this option to view your document as it will print with a PostScript fill. Select View | Render PostScript Fills. When this option is checked, Print Preview displays PostScript-filled objects.

Page Tiles

When your design exceeds the printer's page size capability, you can still print it by using CorelDRAW 10's Page Tile feature. Page Tiles view is turned on by default, but if you need to turn it off to easily resize or move page objects, click View | Show Current Tile.

> **TIP** *Click and hold the left mouse button when the pointer is over the page, or move it outside the page to disable tiling view. To view overlapping pages, move the mouse pointer from tile to tile.*

Using the Preview Toolbox and Property Bar

The Print Preview Toolbox on the left edge of the Print Preview window contains four valuable tools you can use to perform complex printing operations interactively. When you select the Pick Tool, Imposition Layout Tool, Marks Placement Tool, or Zoom Tool, a set of the tool's properties displays in the context-sensitive Property Bar.

Pick Tool

You can select, move, and resize document objects interactively with the Pick Tool. Click the Pick Tool and then click on the object to select it, click on the object and drag to move it, click on the selected object's corner handles and drag to resize it proportionally, or click on the middle handles to resize it vertically or horizontally.

The Pick Tool Property Bar, shown next, lets you move and resize document objects numerically. To move objects to a precise position in the printed document, type a number or click the Increase/Decrease buttons in the vertical and horizontal areas of the Upper Left Corner Position field. To resize an object numerically, type a number or click the Increase/Decrease buttons in Width/Height and/or set the percentage in the Scale Factor fields. To maintain aspect ratio while numerically resizing, click the Maintain Aspect Ratio button. When active, this button appears to be pressed down and the padlock is locked.

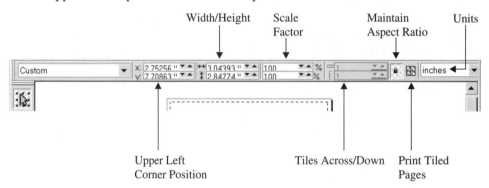

The Pick Tool Property Bar also provides tools to help you set printing options for tiled pages. Click the Print Tiled Pages button to activate this feature and then type or click the Increase/Decrease buttons in the Tiles Across/Down field to set the number of tiles required to print your oversized objects.

The Units drop-down list in the Pick Tool Property Bar lets you choose preset measurement units. The selected unit will be used in the Upper Left Corner Position and Width/Height fields, as well as on the Ruler.

Imposition Layout Tool

The Imposition Layout Tool is one of the greatest features in CorelDRAW 10. This tool lets you prepare complex signatures used in printing multipage documents. In addition, when a multipage document is printed, the Imposition Layout Tool helps organize pages to facilitate printing and binding the publication. When you design a four-page booklet, for example, you work in four individual pages sequentially. The Imposition Layout Tool helps you create a signature, where the first and last pages are printed together on the front of a piece of paper, and the second and third pages are printed on the back of the same sheet.

When the Imposition Layout Tool is selected, its properties display in the Print Preview context-sensitive Property Bar. These features let you prepare your layout signature interactively, as shown here:

Current Imposition Layout   What to Edit

As shown in the illustration, the Property Bar contains the Current Imposition Layout drop-down list, which is a long list of signatures commonly used in the printing industry. You can compose a complex signature by clicking a preset type of signature on the list. Print Preview sets it for you automatically. When you create a custom signature, you can save it by clicking on the plus sign button; then type your template name in the Save As text field in the Save Imposition Layout dialog. The name of a built-in style cannot be changed. To delete a style, select it and click the minus sign button.

The Imposition Layout Tool Property Bar is itself context sensitive. The Edit Basic Settings, Edit Page Placement, Edit Gutters & Finishing, and Edit Margins options trigger their own properties while they are individually active. These sets of tools are grouped in the "What to Edit" drop-down field. (In previous versions of CorelDRAW, these were a set of buttons.)

Edit Basic Settings Property Bar   Use the options on this Property Bar to preview, organize, and group pages in almost endless ways.

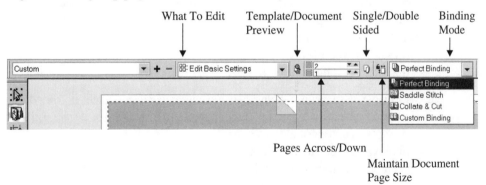

What To Edit   Template/Document   Single/Double   Binding
                Preview   Sided   Mode

Pages Across/Down

Maintain Document
Page Size

- ■ **Template/Document Preview**   Activates document preview while composing a signature. It is active when it appears pressed.

- ■ **Pages Across/Down**   Sets the number of pages per rows and columns imposed in a signature. You could change it by typing a number in the field or by clicking the up or down arrow button.

- **Single/Double Sided**   Organizes pages that are printed on the front and back of the same piece of paper. It is active when it appears to be pressed down.

- **Maintain Document Page Size**   Maintains the original document page size when it is part of a signature. If this feature is not active, the Imposition Layout Tool adjusts document pages to fit the selected printer driver's page size and selected Imposition options. It is active when it appears to be pressed down.

- **Binding Mode**   Contains a selection of tools to set bindings. Perfect Binding, Saddle Stitch, and Collate & Cut are the most common binding styles, as discussed next. If you require a special binding type, a Custom Binding option is available.

  - **Perfect Binding**   In this method, a publication's pages are glued at the spine. This book is an example of perfect binding. Signatures for perfect binding are trimmed at least 1/8 inch on the four sides of the page, and you should consider this when you design and prepare the imposition.

  - **Saddle Stitch**   This method inserts folded sheets of paper one into another, similar to saddling a horse. Magazines are a good example of saddle binding. The gutter is very important when this method is used, because sheets of paper will gradually become smaller from outside to inside after they are assembled and trimmed. Thus to avoid incorrect trimming, the signature gutter should gradually become smaller, too. This is called *creep*, and unfortunately, creep is not supported in the software. Be careful when you use Saddle Stitch binding to prepare signatures in long publications.

  - **Collate & Cut**   This method is used when a printed sheet is folded in one of several ways to produce signatures of 8, 12, 16, 24, 32, or 48 pages that are collated to place the pages in the proper order. The spine will be the final fold, and these signatures are sewed and glued together. When the process is finished, the book is trimmed.

  - **Custom Binding**   This method triggers the Number of Signatures field. It provides almost endless possibilities for composing pages and creating complex signatures. To increase or decrease the number of signatures, type a number or click the up and down buttons in the Number of Signatures field.

> **TIP**   *It is important to consult your printing service before you build signatures. It's important that you use signatures appropriate for the printing service's printing presses. At print time, build a signature and layouts according to your printing service's instructions.*

Edit Page Placements Property Bar   Use these options to set page ordering and rotation. In addition, you may set how many pages will form a signature here.

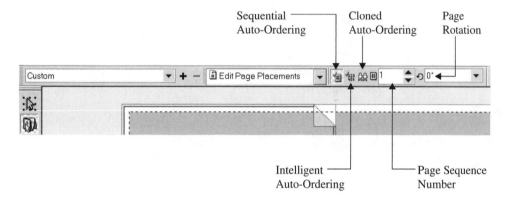

- **Intelligent Auto-Ordering**   Arranges the order of pages in a signature automatically. If you want the Imposition Layout Tool to arrange pages for you, enable this option by clicking the Intelligent Auto-Ordering button. It is active when it appears to be pressed down.

- **Sequential Auto-Ordering**   Arranges pages in a sequential order left to right and top to bottom.

- **Cloned Auto-Ordering**   Lets you place the working page in every frame of a signature. You should use this option when printing step and repeat method will be used. For example, if you are printing 1,000 business cards, you can clone the card ten times in the same 8.5 x 11-inch signature. Your service bureau will print 100 sheets of paper to produce 1,000 cards. This option will help you a great deal in in-house production using your desktop printer.

- **Page Sequence Number**   Changes the sequence number. You should select a signature frame page to change the page number by typing or clicking the up or down arrow in this field. You can also change it by highlighting the page number in the board and typing the desired number directly in the page. Notice that the mouse pointer changes to an I-beam pointer when placed over the page number in the board.

| TIP | *If you're having trouble understanding the Page Sequence Number feature, here's an example. Suppose a client orders two different business cards, but she wants 1,000 prints of one card and 500 prints of the other card. You could prepare a 3-up signature. Change the Page Sequence Number in two cards to 1 and to 2 for the third. This way you can print all the cards in one 500-print run.* |

- **Page Rotation**   Rotates printed pages 0 degrees or 180 degrees. The Collate & Cut binding method requires a row of pages up and a row of pages down, and you should use the Page Rotation feature to prepare the signatures. You can rotate pages directly by clicking on the arrow symbol on the page. Notice that the mouse pointer changes to a rotation pointer when placed over the arrow.

Edit Gutters & Finishing Property Bar   Use these options to change space between pages (gutter) and place fold and trim marks in a signature.

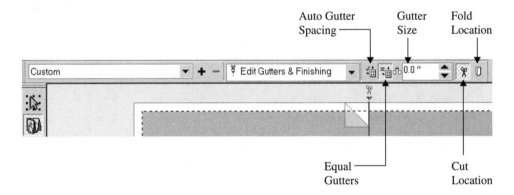

- **Auto Gutter Spacing**   Resizes gutters automatically to accommodate pages in a signature.
- **Equal Gutters**   Triggers the Gutter Size field and sets gutters equally according to the size typed or selected by clicking the up/down arrows in the Gutter Size field. You should select a horizontal Cut or Fold Location mark to set horizontal gutters, or a vertical location mark to set vertical gutters.

- **Cut Location**   Marks where the printed document should be cut. To set a cut mark, select a gutter line and click the Cut Location button, or click slightly outside any end of the gutter line repeatedly until the cut mark displays on the printed document.

- **Fold Location**   Marks where the printed document should be folded. To set a fold mark, select a gutter line and click the Fold Location button, or click repeatedly slightly outside any end of the gutter line until the fold mark displays on the printed document.

Edit Margins Property Bar   Use these options to set imposition margins. Top, Bottom, Right, and Left Margins can be customized independently or automatically.

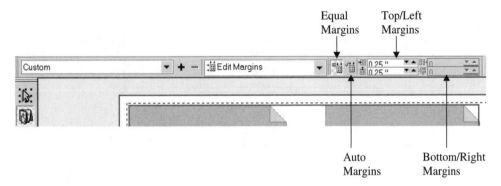

- **Equal Margins**   Activates Top/Left and Bottom/Right Margins fields. There, you can type or select your imposition margins individually.

- **Auto Margins**   Activates Top/Left and Bottom/Right Margins fields. When clicked, it automatically sets the margins.

Marks Placement Tool

Now let's return to the Print Preview Toolbox to look at the Marks Placement Tool. This tool provides options to let you control position, display, and information on crop, fold, registration marks, calibration bars, and density scales. These marks are important in the printing process because they are used as guides, from stripping to final trim.

When the Marks Placement Tool is selected, it activates the Marks Placement Property Bar.

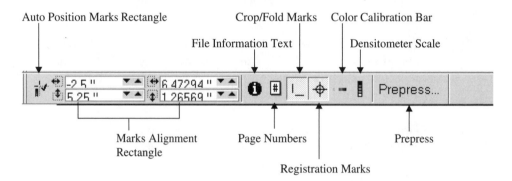

Auto Position Marks Rectangle   Crop/Fold Marks   Color Calibration Bar

File Information Text   Densitometer Scale

Marks Alignment Rectangle   Page Numbers   Prepress

Registration Marks

- **Auto Position Marks Rectangle**   Instructs Print Preview to position the rectangle used to guide marks automatically in the printed document. The rectangle is represented by a red dashed line. When this rectangle coincides with the page size, the marks can't be previewed because they are positioned outside the printing page. In this case, you should select a bigger page in your printer driver or reposition the Marks Rectangle. You have two ways to accomplish this task: interactively or numerically.

  When you place your mouse pointer over the Marks Rectangle, the mouse pointer icon changes to a double-arrow icon. You may click, hold, drag, and drop to a desired position to reposition your marks interactively. When you perform this action, the Auto Position Marks Rectangle feature is automatically disabled. To reposition the Marks Rectangle numerically, disable Auto Position Marks Rectangle, if active, by clicking the Auto Position Marks Rectangle button, and type a numeric location or click the up/down arrows to the appropriate location.

TIP   *When the selected page in the printer driver coincides with the document page size, marks are not visible. If the printer is limited to a required page size, and/or you can't change your document page size due to layout requirements, and you need to print a separation, you can reposition Registration Marks inside your page. These marks are used in the stripping process to position the separation, and they are erased when the plate is burned.*

■ **Marks Alignment Rectangle**   Sets the Marks Rectangle position. Each of these four numeric fields corresponds to a rectangle corner position. You can control the exact position of a Rectangle Marks corner in the printed page by setting these numeric fields.

■ **File Information Text**   Places text information in your printed document. This information guides the printing process. Filename and date information tell your service bureau or print shop that it is the correct document to be used in the process; in case an error is found, they can tell you what document to change and where it is saved in your system. If a color separation is printed, each plate is numbered and identified in a set of plates. In addition, the color profile used, screen frequency and angle printed, inks, and print method information are displayed by this feature in your printed document.

■ **Page Numbers**   Prints the page number in your printed document. This is vital information in a multipage document.

■ **Crop/Fold Marks**   Activates marks that instruct the printer where to crop or fold a printed document. A dashed line is commonly recognized in the printing industry as a fold mark.

■ **Registration Marks**   Enables marks used to register plates conforming to a color separation. These marks are critical to the stripping and printing process. See the preceding Tip about setting registration marks when page and printer size coincide.

■ **Color Calibration Bar**   Prints a set of color marks used by the printer to increase or decrease ink during the printing process.

■ **Densitometer Scale**   Prints a scale of swatches with different grayscale values. These values are read by a densitometer from the printed document in paper or film to establish ink densities. This feature is used to determine dot gain on the filming or printing process, and it is used by the press operator to increase or decrease ink density in the press.

25

| TIP | *It is easier for the press operator to increase ink than to decrease it. You should take this into consideration when you compose a color or when you generate a black plate converting to CMYK. Generally, it is a good practice to use a light GCR generation during CMYK conversion. You should use a color profile in separation, which generates light GCR Black plate in CorelDRAW. It uses the profile in separation to convert to CMYK, and it uses the same profile while printing RGB or Lab images. GCR, Gray Component Replacement, is the percentage of black ink that is going to replace CMY in darker areas. It is easier for the press operator to increase black than to decrease it if necessary; this is why a light GCR is more convenient.* |

- **Prepress** Triggers the Prepress tab in the Print Options dialog, discussed later in this chapter in the "Setting Print Options" section.

Zoom Tool

The final tool in the Print Preview Toolbox, the Zoom Tool lets you preview particular areas in your document by zooming your view in these areas. The Zoom Tool activates a Zoom Tool Property Bar that contains buttons that let you quickly access preset zoom actions.

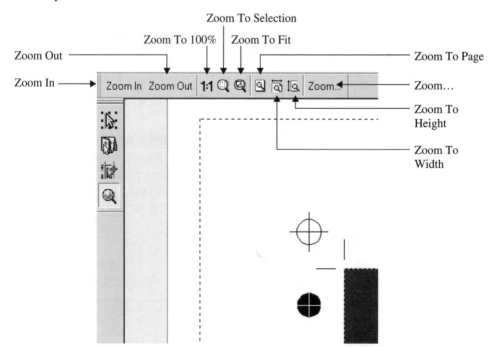

When the Zoom Tool is selected, the mouse pointer changes to a loop icon with a plus sign in it. You can zoom in by clicking in the printed document or by clicking and dragging a marquee in a desired area. To zoom out, press and hold SHIFT while clicking in the printed document.

TIP *If you use a mouse with a wheel, you can move the wheel to zoom in and out faster.*

- **Zoom In/Out**   These buttons are self-explanatory. Click them repeatedly if you want to zoom in or out to predefined zoom levels.

- **Zoom to 100%**   If your zoom is set to a particular area, this area will be zoomed to 100 percent. This is useful for previewing objects at printed size.

- **Zoom to Selection**   Use this button to preview the selected object area.

- **Zoom to Fit**   Use this button to preview all the elements in the printed document, including marks if they are active.

- **Zoom to Page, Zoom to Width, Zoom to Height**   Use these buttons to set zoom level to the active page size, width, or height, respectively.

- **Zoom...**   Use this button to display the Zoom dialog (Figure 25-4), which contains a set of preset zoom levels and a numeric percentage zoom field. You can select preset options by clicking on the check mark radio buttons, or you can type a number or click the up/down arrows in the Percent field. This dialog displays Times New Roman, 10-point fonts in the selected zoom level.

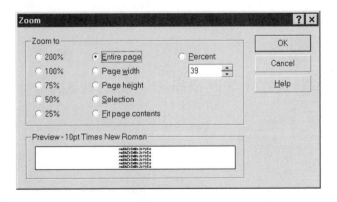

FIGURE 25-4   Select options for zooming in this dialog.

Viewing and Printing Your Document Job Information

CorelDRAW 10 records information related to the document. This information can be provided to your service bureau or print shop, and used to check whether your document opens and prints correctly.

Select File | Document Information to access the active document's information. The Document Information dialog, shown in Figure 25-5, displays the information. The information is organized by topics, which you can add or delete by clicking and unclicking the check boxes.

The Document Information dialog contains buttons to print the information or to save it to a file. Clicking the Print button triggers a Print dialog in which you can select a printer driver and properties. The Save As button lets you browse and save a text file containing the selected document information.

Setting Print Preferences

Print Preview provides options to set your print preferences, giving you further control over printing variables. To access this feature, select Settings | Printing Preferences from Print Preview's main menu to open the Printing Preferences dialog, shown in Figure 25-6. You can access this dialog from CorelDRAW by pressing CTRL+J and moving into Global/Printing in the Options dialog.

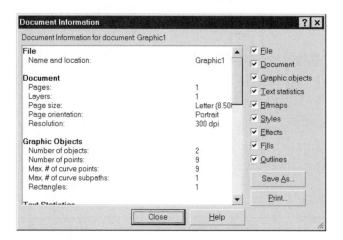

FIGURE 25-5   Access information about the active document in this dialog.

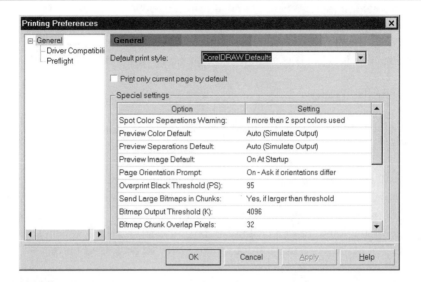

FIGURE 25-6   The Printing Preferences dialog lets you specify special and default settings.

General Options

The Printing Preferences dialog opens to the General options page. Select the printing style for which you want to change printing preferences in the Default Print Style drop-down list. You can employ many customized printing styles according to your printing requirements. If you want only the current page printed, for example, check the box next to Print Only Current Page by Default.

Spot Color Separations Warning   Four different warnings can be set to advise you when you print spot colors (Pantone Matching System colors). By default, this option is set to warn you if more than two spot colors are used, but by clicking this option, a drop-down list displays, in which you can choose to receive a warning if any, or more than one, two, or three spot colors are used.

Preview Color Default   This option controls how your printed document colors display in Print Preview. You can choose from Auto (Simulate Output), Color, or Grayscale. The Auto options simulate selected printer driver color settings.

Preview Separations Default   You can preview your separations as composite or as they will print. Choose Auto (Simulate Output) or Composite to change the Preview Separations default.

Preview Image Default   When you open Print Preview, by default it previews your document. Sometimes you may want to turn off this option, to accelerate preview redraws and free system resources. If your file is big and complicated, turning Preview Image off is a good option. Choose from On or Off At Startup.

Page Orientation Prompt   Print Preview warns you if the printer driver page orientation doesn't match your document page orientation. You can set this warning on or off by default. Choose from Off-Always Match Orientation, On-Ask If Orientation Differs, or Off-Don't Change Orientation.

Overprint Black Threshold (PS)   During overprint functions, Draw sets a default value for overprinting black objects only if they contain a uniform fill of 95 percent of black or more. The Overprint Black Threshold setting may be changed with this option, allowing you to further customize the global overprinting function. You may set the threshold limit to a range from 1 percent to 100 percent of black.

> **TIP** *You should change this option to 85 percent if you are printing to a newspaper.*

Send Large Bitmaps in Chunks   This option works in combination with the Bitmap Output Threshold setting, and may be set to the default Yes, If Larger Than Threshold (referring to the Bitmap Threshold value), or No.

Bitmap Output Threshold (K)   When printing to a non-PostScript printer, you can use this option to set the bitmap size sent to the printing device. CorelDRAW 10 sets this value to the maximum by default. You should set a specific value from 0 to 4096.

Bitmap Chunk Overlap Pixels   This option controls the amount of overlapping pixels when you are printing to a non-PostScript device. You can set a number from 0 to 48 pixels; it is set to 32 pixels by default.

Bitmap Font Limit   This option controls the number of fonts stored in a PostScript printer's internal memory when font sizes below the Bitmap Font Size Threshold preference are converted to bitmaps. You will save printing time by setting this option accordingly. The default is 8, but you may set it from 0 to 100. The default is good for typical documents.

25

Bitmap Font Size Threshold (PS)   CorelDRAW 10 converts small sizes of text to bitmap format when printing to PostScript devices. This option enables you to control at which point conversion occurs based on font size. This option works directly with the Bitmap Font Limit option. The default is 75 pixels, but you may set it anywhere from 0 to 1,000 pixels. The actual point size converted to bitmap varies according to the amount of resolution used when printing a document. The threshold limit will determine exactly which font sizes are affected. The equivalent font size of 75 pixels when printing to a printer resolution of 300 dpi equals approximately an 18-point font size, whereas at 600 dpi, 75 pixels equals a 9-point type, and so on. The higher the resolution, the lower the point size affected. Whether the font has been scaled and/or skewed, Envelope effect, fountain or texture fills had applied, Print scaling options determine whether this control applies. This is available in PostScript devices only.

Small Fonts (Preflight)   You can set the point size at which the preflight will warn you that a small font is present.

Image Resolution Too Low (Preflight)   This option lets you set a preflight warning to alert when a bitmap resolution is too low. You can select the option from the drop-down list or type in the bitmap resolution required for a warning.

Composite Crop Marks (PS)   You can choose to print crop marks in black or in Composite CMYK. This option allows printing crop marks on every plate during a process-color separation printing.

PostScript 2 Stroke Adjust (PS)   This option controls the pixel placement of strokes that straddle pixel boundaries. PostScript automatic stroke adjustments are set by default to PostScript Level 2. If you prefer to output outlines as PostScript Level 1, disable this option.

Many Fonts (Preflight)   This option enables you to initiate the font warning alert if the document you are printing features more than the selected amount of fonts. The default amount is 10 fonts, but you can set this option from 1 to 50 fonts by selecting from the drop-down list.

NT Double Download Workaround   There is a bug in Windows NT in which fonts downloaded using the *"downloadface"* escape are placed into the PostScript stream twice. This option evokes a routine to avoid such a bug.

NT Bookman Download Workaround   There is a bug in Windows NT that causes the always-PS-resident font Bookman to be downloaded, which is never necessary. This option evokes a routine to avoid such a bug.

Render to Bitmap Resolution   This option instructs Corel's print engine to rasterize special effects as transparencies and drop shadows. It renders to bitmap resolution while printing, and does not affect the original bitmap resolution.

Driver Compatibility Options

The Driver Compatibility option is dimmed if you are using a PostScript driver. When you are using a non-PostScript printer, you may encounter driver compatibility problems, and these options (Figure 25-7) help to overcome compatibility problems.

All Text As Graphics   Non-PostScript printers sometimes have problems with printing text. It can be incorrectly printed over by graphics. Select this option to send text as graphics and not as fonts to your non-PostScript printer.

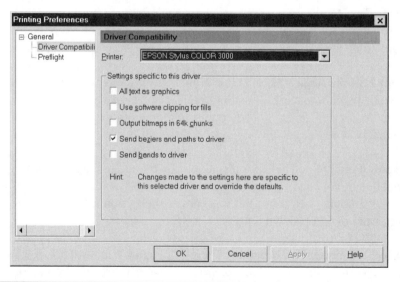

FIGURE 25-7   Set driver options in this dialog.

25

Use Software Clipping for Fills   If you encounter problems printing non-uniform fills, enable this option to let the software control clipping. When you print a fill other than uniform fills, clipping is required when an object is not rectangular, because fills are sent to printing devices as bitmaps, and they are rectangular. Software clipping removes those areas that should not be visible. Usually, this option will make your printing process slower, but will help you to print certain fills correctly to a non-PostScript device.

Output Bitmaps in 64K Chunks   When your bitmaps do not print as expected, this option will help you to send them to the non-PostScript printer in small blocks (64K) named *chunks*. It could help to print your document correctly.

Send Beziérs and Paths to Driver   Generally, non-PostScript printing devices cannot hold a full page in memory, and they may encounter problems printing beziérs and paths. If this is the case, you should send them to the driver by choosing this option.

Send Bands to Driver   When a non-PostScript printer prints slowly or you encounter problems, this option could help you to split your printed document into bands before it is sent to the printer. These printers cannot hold a full page in memory and they print the document in multiple passes called *bands*. Splitting the bands in the driver and not in the printer may accelerate the printing process and/or solve some printing problems.

Choosing Preflight Rules

Preflight is a terrific feature of Print Preview. It checks the document you are printing and advises you about possible printing problems and solutions. You can customize aspects of the Preflight checks and reports. It is especially useful before you send your document to a service bureau. Preflight will warn you about possible problems your service bureau could encounter, and you can fix them before the film is processed, saving you time and money. Figure 25-8 shows the Preflight dialog.

Many Spot Plates   When a printed document with color separations has many spot color plates, this warning will advise you. It is especially useful when your printed document contains Pantone inks and you are going to print CMYK. In this case, you can change the affected object's color space, or you can set CorelDRAW 10 to print spot colors as CMYK.

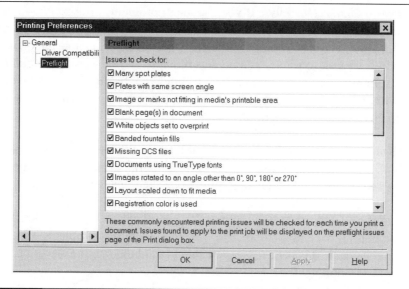

FIGURE 25-8   Set preflight options to warn you about possible problems before you go to the printer.

Plates with Same Screen Angle   While printing, inks should have different printing angles, and by default spot colors are set to a 45-degree angle. You should assign different angles to every plate. This warning reminds you, before you print, to set the screen frequency angles of spot colors.

Image or Marks Not Fitting in Media's Printable Area   If you don't select the accurate paper size in the printer driver, and your design or printing marks do not fit in the printer's printable area, this warning will advise you before you print.

Blank Page(s) in Document   When you print, you may or may not prefer to print blank pages in a multipage document. This option notifies you if blank pages are present in your printed document.

White Objects Set to Overprint   If a white object is set to overprint, this option lets you know that there is a problem present.

Banded Fountain Fills   This option warns you if gradient filled objects are not set to print the proper number of steps.

Missing DCS Files   You are warned if a linked DCS file is not found in your system.

Documents Using True Type Fonts   True Type fonts may cause problems while printing to PostScript devices. When they are present in your printed document, Preflight alerts you.

Images Rotated to an Angle Other Than 0, 90, 180 or 270 Degrees   Rotated images other than right angles may cause printing problems. This option advises you when images are rotated to other angles.

Layout Scaled Down to Fit Media   Sometimes you may set your printed documents to fit a selected printer's paper size for proofing, but when you set them to print to the correct size, you may forget to change the Fit to Page option. In this case, this warning alerts you to a possible printing problem.

Registration Color Is Used   When an object is filled or outlined with a Registration color, it will print to every separated plate. This warning notifies you about the presence of Registration color in your printed document.

Convert Spot Not Applied to Placed EPS Files   EPS files retain Pantone Matching System inks. If your document contains a placed EPS file, and you select to print spot colors as CMYK, this option warns you, because Pantone inks in the EPS will not be converted to CMYK.

Many Fonts to Be Downloaded to a PostScript Printer   Fonts are downloaded to PostScript printers. This option warns you when many fonts will be downloaded.

Text with Texture Fills (PS Level 1 Only)   Text filled with textures can cause problems while printing to PostScript Level 1 devices. This option advises you when texture-filled text shows problems.

Bitmaps in Complex Clipping Paths (PS Level 1 Only)   EPS files with complex clipped paths or complex PowerClips could present problems printing to PostScript Level 1 devices. This option will notify you when these types of problems are present in your printed document.

Texture Fills in Complex Objects (PS Level 1 Only)   Sometimes complex objects filled with texture fills can cause problems when you print to PostScript Level 1 devices. This option warns about possible problems.

Complex Clipping Regions (PS Level 1 Only) PostScript Level 1 devices may not print complex clipping regions. This option will call your attention to a problem in your design.

Objects with Outlines Having Many Nodes (PS Level 1 Only) PostScript Level 1 is limited to print objects with 500 nodes. If any object in your design exceeds the limit, this option will warn you.

Objects with Outlines and Fill Having Many Nodes (PS Level 1 Only) PostScript fills and outlines can contain more than 500 nodes, but PostScript level 1 will not print them. This option will notify you when the limit is exceeded in your printed documents.

Similarly Named Spot Colors You could be using Draw color palettes, colors imported from another application, or custom colors you create in CorelDRAW that have inks with similar names that will print to separate plates. This option notifies you when inks with similar names are present in your prints.

Color Correction Enabled for Non-PostScript Output Non-PostScript printers can output color bitmaps only as RGB. They also may have their own color management system, and using Corel color correction at print time may produce color switches. This warning notifies you about possible problems using color profiles while printing to a non-PostScript printer.

Device Independent PostScript with PostScript Level 2 or PostScript Level 3 PostScript Levels 2 and 3 are not available in certain prepress workflow. If you select a device-independent driver as your printer, this option will advise you to consider using these PostScript levels if you are not sure how your document will be processed by a third party.

Setting Print Options

As you've already seen, CorelDRAW 10 features a huge number of printing options that you can use to control how your documents are going to be printed. These options are organized into a multipage dialog. Each page is labeled with a tab that you click to activate the corresponding page of options. However, some of these tabbed pages are dependent on the selected printing driver, and if the driver is not compatible, the tab does not display in the Print Options multipage dialog.

This is why you should select your printer driver before setting any options. Print options are organized according to purpose and availability as follows: General, Layout, Separations, Miscellaneous, and Preflight. To access the Print Options dialog, press CTRL+P, select File | Print in the CorelDRAW main menu, or click the Print Options button in the Print Preview toolbar.

Setting General Options

The options contained in the General dialog are related to printing devices. Print Destination, Print Range, Copies, and Print Style form the major groups of options (see Figure 25-9). It is wise to select the printer driver first; this is going to allow access to all options the printer is capable of handling. When you click the arrow on the Name drop-down list, a list of printer drivers available in your system displays, and you should select a printing device by clicking its name. The Properties button triggers selected device properties, such as page size, page orientation, printing resolution, and so on. If you are using the Corel Color Manager to print, you should disable printer driver color management in the driver properties. You should use only one Color Manager. The Type text field displays the type of printing device you

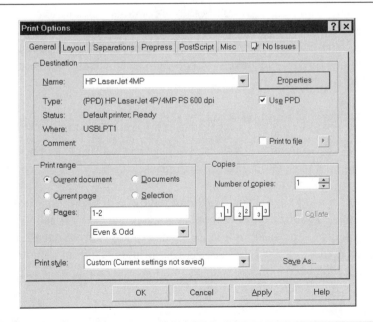

FIGURE 25-9   The General dialog provides options for setting your printing device.

selected. This field tells you if it is a PostScript device. The Status text field informs you if the printer is ready to print. The Where text field provides information about how the print engine will communicate with the device, what port the printer is connected to, or if the device is set to print to a file. If the device driver contains any special comments, this information displays in the Comment text field.

Choosing a PPD

The PostScript Printer Description (PPD) file describes the capabilities and features of your PostScript device. If you check the Use PPD field, Corel's print engine uses all the PostScript capabilities available in the selected printing device. If this option is not selected, Windows generates some of the PostScript. Note that this may cause printing problems on output.

If your selected printer driver is not a PPD driver, you should ask your printer manufacturer for the file. You may need the Adobe PS Setup utility to install and manage PPD files. You can download the utility at **www.adobe.com**.

Setting Print Range Options

When printing a multipage document, you may need to print only certain pages at some point. The Print Range group of options contains fields to select what pages you want to print. When a document is set to a Facing Page layout, at some point you may need to print right or left pages separately. Print Range options contain a field in which you can select even- or odd-numbered pages to print. Click this button and select accordingly.

Current Document   This option prints the active document completely.

Current Page   This option prints the active page in CorelDRAW. For example, if you are working in page 4, only page 4 will print.

Pages   Select this option to print a range of pages. When selected, the range of pages contained in your active document displays. First and last page numbers are separated by a dash. The dash represents a range of pages from page X to page Y, and all pages in this range will be successively printed. To print nonconsecutive pages, separate the page numbers with commas. For example, to print pages 1, 5, 7, and 10, you type **1,5,7,10** in the Pages field.

Documents   You may have several documents open in Draw and need to print all of them. In this case, click Documents. When selected, a box displays containing the documents names preceded by a check box. Check the document names you wish to print, and all the pages in those documents will be printed.

Selection   CorelDRAW can print objects in a page without printing the page completely. If you want to print objects at some point, select the objects in CorelDRAW, and the Selection option will become active. If this option is active, only selected objects will be printed.

Printing Multiple Copies

Print options under Copies let you print several copies and several sets of copies. Set the number of copies you require by typing or selecting the number in the Number of Copies field. This action will print the selected number of copies in sequence. For example, if you type or select five copies in a multipage document, five copies of page 1 will be printed, followed by five copies of each page. If you are preparing a set of the printed document, you can avoid manually sorting the pages by checking the Collate option. This will print the selected number of sets in page sequence.

Choosing/Saving a Print Style

The options you set in the Print Options dialog can be saved as a print style. Print styles are not associated with a document, but you can easily recall a print style, and all the saved options will be activated immediately when you reopen a document to print or when you are going to print a document with similar printing characteristics.

   To select a print style, click the arrow on the Print Style drop-down list and select your preferred style. You can also select a print style if you are in Print Preview by clicking on the Print Style field in the Property Bar.

   You can save a print style by clicking the Save As button on the General tab or by clicking the plus sign button in the Print Style field of the Print Preview Property Bar. Both methods trigger the Save Settings As dialog box (see Figure 25-10).

   The Save Settings As dialog contains a Windows browser that lets you choose where in your system you will be saving your style. It is a good practice to save styles in the default directory because you will have all your print styles in the same folder. You can overwrite print styles by typing or selecting an existing style name.

   If you did not select your printing settings, you can select them from the Settings to Include options box. Click the plus sign to display more settings under the main categories and check the desired options.

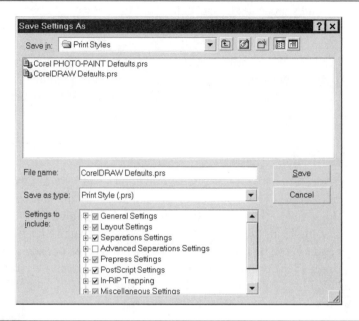

FIGURE 25-10 You can select and save printing settings in this dialog box.

Creating a Print File

Returning to the Print Options dialog, your final option is the Print to File check box. Checking this box activates the button next to it, which accesses several Print to File options. You can print document pages or separated plates to different files by selecting the corresponding option in this menu (see the following illustration). When the document prints, the Print to File dialog will display options for selecting the folder and the filename under which the print will be saved. If you are going to import the generated file into an application, or if you are going to produce a PDF file, you should select PS as the filename extension. Some applications require a file extension to identify the file when opening or importing it.

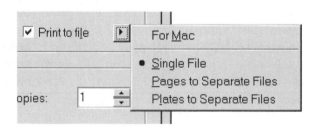

For Mac   When your print file will be output in a Macintosh system, you should select this option. It will add some control characters required by the operating system.

Single File   Select this option if you want to include all pages or plates in a single file.

Pages to Separate Files   When you select this option, a print file for each page will be created, and CorelDRAW automatically adds a sequential number to the filename.

Plates to Separate Files   Frequently, when you produce separations, the generated print file can be huge. You can generate a print file for each plate by selecting this option, and a sequential number will be added to the filename.

Choosing a Print Layout

The document layout may differ from the print layout. The printing page is defined by the paper size selected in the active printing device driver properties. CorelDRAW automatically asks if you want to change device driver page orientation to accommodate your document layout. The Layout dialog contains options to lay out your document in the printing material. Open the dialog by clicking the Layout tab in the Print Options dialog (see Figure 25-11).

Setting Image Position and Size Options

Image Position and Size options control the position of objects on your printed page as a whole. The term refers to the width and depth occupied by your document page objects. If you decide to print your document at the same size, you should click As in Document. This action ensures that your document will not be resized by the print engine.

When you need to enlarge or reduce your page size according to the selected printing device driver page size, the Fit to Page option automatically resizes your document to fit inside the selected printing page. You should be sure that bitmaps in your document have enough resolution to print correctly when they are enlarged.

The Reposition Images To drop-down list contains preset options to position your objects in the printing page. This option activates fields to customize the position and size of the page. When you select a preset option from the list, a bitmap field displays the object's position in the printing page.

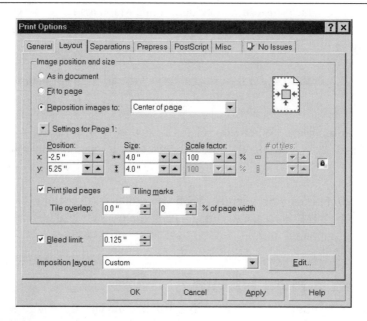

Under typical printing circumstances, you may not need to change these options from their default settings.

Changing Settings for Different Pages/Documents

When you are printing a multipage document, you may require different layout settings for every page. In this case, you should click the Settings for Page arrow button and select the page number you want to change.

Defining Specific Print Parameters

You can define specific printing parameters in your layout by selecting the Reposition Images To field. This action activates the Position, Size, and Scale Factor fields.

Position   Use these fields to precisely position your objects on the printing page. Type, or select by clicking the up/down arrow buttons, the X and Y coordinates where you want to place the objects in the printed document. Position coordinates are directly related to Print Preview's Ruler position and scale. Print Preview's Ruler works independently of CorelDRAW's Ruler, but the selected measure will display in the Print Preview Ruler also.

Size Type, or click the up/down arrow buttons, in the width/height Size fields to change the object's size when printed. The Lock button (on the far right) maintains width/height aspect ratio when it appears to be pressed.

Scale Factor You can resize your objects by typing, or clicking the up/down arrow buttons, in the Scale Factor fields. The percentage selected corresponds to a percentage of the printed object's size. The Lock button maintains width/height aspect ratio when it appears to be pressed.

25

Tiling Your Printed Document

CorelDRAW 10's print features provide options to print oversized documents at their original size. You can divide your documents into tiles and glue them together after they are printed. Tile size corresponds to the selected paper size in the active printing device driver. You can let the Corel print engine automatically set and organize the tiling, or you can customize it yourself.

When you check the Print Tiled Pages option, related options are activated, and tiles are automatically set to accommodate the printing document. You can preview tile layout in Print Preview. To preview overlapping, pass your mouse pointer over the tiles, but be sure that View | Show Current Tile is enabled.

> **TIP** *Using the Pick Tool, select and move your objects in the tiled preview to cause retiling. It may reduce the number of tiles needed to reproduce your document.*

# of Tiles You can set the number of tiles across or down by typing, or clicking the up/down arrow buttons, in the # of Tiles field, but the print engine automatically adds the necessary number of tiles on opposite sides.

Tiling Marks When you are pasting printed tiles together, you may need registration marks to guide you. Select the Tiling Marks option to print registration marks in your printed tiles.

Tile Overlap You may need to overlap tiles when pasting them together. It will help to position the tiles and glue them in a way that the junction marks will not be perceived by the viewer. Type, or click the up/down arrow buttons, to set the overlapping width in the Tile Overlap numeric field. Measures in this field are directly related to the selected measure in Print Preview's Ruler.

% of Page Width   You can set the tile overlap related to a percentage of the page. Type, or click the up/down arrow buttons, to set the overlapping width.

Bleed Limit

When the background in your design touches the page borders, it is a good practice to extend it outside the design page borders. This is called *bleeding* in the printing industry. Setting a bleed area ensures that no white lines display in the page border after they are guillotined. You can control the bleed limit by activating this option and typing, or clicking the up/down arrow buttons, in the Bleed Limit field. Generally, the default setting is satisfactory for common cuts.

Printing Separations

The Separations tab in the Print Options dialog contains all the options you may require to prepare separated ink plates for printing (see Figure 25-12).

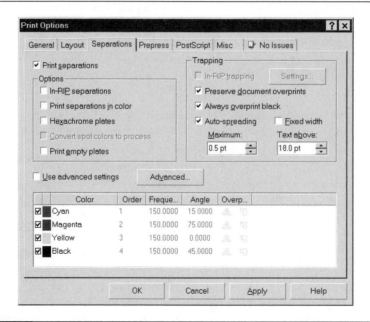

FIGURE 25-12   Choosing separation options causes all the colors in your design to print to separated ink plates.

What Are Separations?

Colors are printed with different inks or a combination of process inks. Printing presses print inks individually, which is why objects in your design should be separated to different printing plates according to the inks that compose them. Years ago printers used a set of filters and a camera to separate the colors. In our time, this operation is performed in computers using sophisticated applications such as CorelDRAW, and lately the responsibility of this operation is passing to the computer artist. That is why it is very important that you learn how to produce separations efficiently and correctly.

Choosing Separation Options

To print separations and activate separation options, check the Print Separations box in the Print Options Separations tab, or click the Enable Color Separations button in the Print Preview Standard Toolbar. Separation options are related to ink presence and selected printing device driver capabilities. If the selected driver does not have the capabilities, related options will appear grayed out.

The Separations tab in the Print Options dialog contains a set of options to control the condition of the printed, color-separated output.

Print Separations in Color When printing to presses, which print one or two inks at the same time, the pressman requires a Color Kit. This is a set of transparencies simulating the color separation that the press will print. Some printers can print transparencies in color, and those transparencies could be used to generate a Color Kit. If you require printing separations in color, select this option.

Hexachrome Plates Hexachrome printing is a relatively new technique. CMYK process inks don't print strong reds and greens, and to improve full-color printing, two special inks have been added to obtain better shades of these colors. Pantone Hexachrome Orange and Green together with Hexachrome CMYK inks are the components of hexachrome printing. Corel's print engine can separate full-color documents to be printed using this technique. You should consult your printing place before you use this option.

Convert Spot Colors to Process Sometimes, when you are designing, you fill objects using a Pantone Matching System (PMS) color (also called spot colors), and when you are processing your color separations, you notice that a separated plate will be generated for the spot colors present in your design. You can select this option to convert spot colors to CMYK colors when printing. Be aware that

Pantone inks are special inks, and sometimes the conversion to CMYK does not produce the desired color.

Print Empty Plates   When a page is empty in a multipage document, or when an ink is not present in a CMYK color, Corel's print engine does not generate separations for this page or ink. On those occasions when you need to print them, select this option to print empty plates.

Selecting Separation Colors and Options

At the bottom of the Separations tab, you can see a box containing process inks (CMYK) and any other ink present in your printed document. Each of these inks represents a separation. You can choose to print all separations or any separation in particular. Checked separations will print; you should uncheck those that you do not want to print. Each separation displays the screen frequency, screen angle, and the overprint status at which they will print. Corel's print engine can print separations to a non-PostScript printer, but Advanced options are allowed only for PostScript printing devices. Enable Use Advanced Settings to access the settings in the Separations tab, or click the Advanced button to open the Advanced Separations Settings dialog, shown in Figure 25-13.

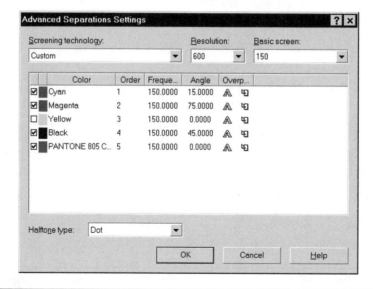

FIGURE 25-13   Advanced options are allowed only for PostScript printing devices.

> *If your ink color names are too long to view in the Color column of the window at the bottom of the Separations tab, you may adjust the width of the columns by clicking your mouse pointer on the divider bar between the labels at the top of each of the columns and dragging left or right.*

Setting Screen Frequency   Screen frequency, also called screen ruling, halftone frequency, and LPI, is a measure of a halftone screen in lines per inch. PostScript devices are the only devices capable of printing at different screen frequencies. Paper quality and printing press capabilities regulate the screen frequency used to print a particular job. You should consult your printing place before you set this option.

You can change screen frequency directly in the box on the Separations tab or in the Advanced Separations Settings dialog. Click the particular frequency, and type the desired lines per inch.

Setting Screen Angles   If inks are not printed at different angles, an undesirable moiré pattern will be printed. Screen angle between inks should have a difference of 30 degrees. Generally, in a full-color print, yellow and cyan inks have a screen angle of 15 degrees apart. This is because yellow is a weak ink and does not create problems with screen frequency. When printing hexachrome separations, orange and green inks are printed at cyan and magenta screen angles, respectively, because they are weak inks. With special inks such as Pantone, Dic, Toyo, and so on, screen angles are set by default to 45 degrees. You should change them, and you should use the 30 degree rule to set their screen angles. It is a good practice to use the same screen frequency used by CMYK, which is, by default, Cyan 15, Magenta 75, Yellow 0, and Black 45. If you run out of angles, remember that you can set weak inks to the same screen frequency assigned to strong inks.

You can change the angles directly in the box on the Separations tab or in the Advanced Separations Settings dialog by clicking the angle and typing the new one.

Setting Ink Overprinting Options   Overprint is a method of color trapping, and it helps to avoid white gaps between adjoining colors caused by bad alignment while printing in a press. When inks are set to overprint, the underlying object will also print. You should set inks to overprint when they are much darker and the combination with the underlying printed color will not produce a noticeable color switch.

Click the text or graphic icons in the Overprint column to change the options. When Overprint is active, the icon display is filled with a gray color. You can change it directly in the box on the Separations tab or in the Advanced Separations Settings dialog.

Using Options on the Advanced Separations Settings Dialog

The Advanced Separations Settings dialog that you see when you click the Advanced button in the Separations tab contains additional options. You should consult your print shop about these before you use them.

Screening Technology   During the digital era, imagesetter manufacturers have been developing proprietary screening technologies. The Screening Technology drop-down list provides access to names of imagesetters and their respective screen technology. Select according to your service bureau's or print shop's instructions.

Resolution   Output resolution is the number of dots per inch (dpi) that an output device produces. Select the resolution you want to print at from the Resolution drop-down list.

Basic Screen   The Basic Screen drop-down list contains available screen frequency presets. Select according to your service bureau's or print shop's instructions.

Halftone Type   In today's printing industry several types of halftones are available, but the round and diamond-shaped halftone types are most commonly used. The Halftone Type drop-down list displays a preset list of halftone types. You should consult your printing place and select accordingly.

Setting Trapping Options

When printing at high speeds, it is difficult to keep the printed inks aligned, because each ink is laid down separately. When two colors that do not have much in common touch each other, gaps or color shifts could appear between the objects. To solve these problems, different methods are used to create tiny overlaps, called *traps*, between printed colors. Corel's print engine provides common and advanced trapping options to compensate for misregistrations.

In-RIP Trapping and Settings

If the output device supports it, In-RIP Trapping can be set to create traps automatically during the RIP process. You do not have to spend time creating traps manually, and it is a great tool for producing excellent separations. In-RIP can create traps between text and underlying colors, between colors within imported graphics, and abutting objects and text. In-RIP traps based in contrasting colored edges can generate traps based on the neutral density of abutting colors, in most cases spreading lighter color into adjacent darker colors. For CMYK colors, it creates the trap color based on CMYK values in the lighter color that are higher than those in the abutting color. For CMYK or spot color next to a spot color, it overprints the lighter color on the darker color in the trap.

You should have a PostScript Level 3 driver active to access In-RIP Trapping settings. Select PostScript Level 3 in the Print Options PostScript tab, and then in the Separation tab, disable Print Separations if it is enabled, and select In-RIP Trapping. These actions activate the Settings button, which triggers the In-RIP Trapping Settings dialog (see Figure 25-14). If you do not have a PostScript printer, you can select the Device Independent PostScript File driver available in the General tab's Destination field.

In-RIP Trapping Settings Columnar Box   You can set Color, Order, Neutral Density, and Type directly in this box.

- ■ **Color**   Displays the ink name.

- ■ **Order**   The order in which inks are trapped. To change the process order, click in the column of the ink you want to change, and select from the drop-down list.

- ■ **Neutral Density (ND)**   A value based on a reading of process ink swatches that conform to the industry standards (for process colors), and for spot colors, ND values are based on the color's CMYK equivalents. ND values range from 0.001 to 10.000.Click the setting under Neutral Density of an ink, and type the new value if you want to change it. For spot colors, you should use their equivalent in CMYK. For example, for PMS 300 (blue), you should type the same ND value as Cyan. For some light inks, such as pastel colors, you should reduce the ND value so the lighter color spreads into the darker one.

- ■ **Type**   The type of ink—Neutral Density, Transparent, Opaque, and Opaque Ignore. You should choose Neutral Density for CMYK ink and most spot inks. Transparent type is used for varnishes and other types of clear inks to ensure trapping in underlying objects. Opaque should be used for heavy nontransparent inks, such as metallic inks, to prevent trapping of underlying colors but allow trapping along the ink's edges. Opaque Ignore is used for heavy nontransparent inks to prevent trapping of underlying color and along the ink's edges.

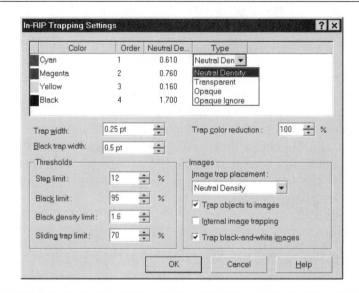

In-RIP trapping generates traps automatically, saving time and increasing productivity.

Trap Width   This field regulates the width of the overlap. You can change this value to increase or decrease overlap width.

Black Trap Width   This field regulates the distance that inks spread into solid black or the distance between black ink edges and underlying inks. This setting is used when the amount of black ink reaches the percentage specified in the Black Limit field.

Trap Color Reduction   Use this feature to prevent certain abutting colors from creating a trap that is darker than either color. Values smaller than 100 percent lighten the color of the trap.

Step Limit   This field controls the degree to which components of abutting color must vary before the trap is created. You should use values from 8 percent to 20 percent. Lower percentages increase sensitivity to color differences and create more traps.

Black Limit   This field regulates the minimum amount of black ink required before the setting in the Black Trap Width field is applied. You should not use a value

25

lower than 70 percent. When tints of black are used in high percentages to produce solid black areas, you should reduce the percentage of Black Limit field to match the tint value, which results in treatment of solid black areas as black. For example, if black areas are tinted at 85 percent of Black ink, set the Black Limit field to 85 percent.

Black Density Limit   This field indicates the neutral density value at or above which In-RIP considers it black. If you want to treat a dark spot color as black, type its neutral density value in this field.

Sliding Trap Limit   This field regulates the percentage difference between the ND of abutting colors at which the trap is moved from the darker side of the color edge toward the center line. You should use this option when colors have similar NDs, because neither color defines the edge. For example, it prevents abrupt shifts in trap placement along a gradient edge.

Image Trap Placement   This field controls where the trap falls when trapping vector objects to bitmap objects. You can choose Neutral Density, Spread, Choke, or Centerline. Neutral Density applies the same trapping rules used elsewhere in the printed document. Using this option to trap a vector to a bitmap can cause uneven edges, because the trap moves from one side of the edge to the other. Spread produces a trap in which the bitmap overlaps the abutting object. Choke causes vectors to overlap the abutting bitmap. Centerline creates a trap that straddles the edge between vectors and bitmaps.

Trap Objects to Images   When this box is checked, trapping between vectors and bitmaps is turned on.

Internal Image Trapping   When this box is checked, trapping for the interior of a bitmap is turned on. You should use this option only when very high contrast images are present.

Trap Black-and-White Images   When this box is checked, trapping between vectors and black-and-white bitmaps is turned on.

Preserve Document Overprints

Overprint is a trap method whereby the underlying object will print when a separation is produced. You can set objects to overprint in Draw by right-clicking an object and selecting Overprint Fill or Overprint Outline. You should check the Preserve Document Overprints option to instruct the separation engine to respect those overprints you created in Draw. If this option is not checked, the separation engine will apply ink overprint options to the objects to which you applied overprint in Draw. In CorelDRAW 10, the separation engine applies overprinting in the following order:

1. It examines the objects for any fill and/or outline overprint assignments. Applying overprint properties directly to an object in your drawing takes precedence over any other overprint operation.

2. It examines the ink overprinting options. If an ink color is set to overprint, and no object fill or outline overprint properties are applied, the ink color overprints underlying objects.

3. It examines the trapping options you have chosen in the Separations tab of the Print Options dialog or in In-RIP Trapping settings.

| TIP | *You can preview objects set to overprint by selecting the Show Overprint option in the CorelDRAW Options dialog. To access this dialog, from the main menu select Tools | Options and then select Workspace/General in the Options dialog. When this option is enabled, you can toggle Overprint view by choosing View | Show | Overprinted Objects from the main menu.* |

Setting Object Fill Overprinting   It is easy to set objects to overprint in Draw. Select the object and right-click it; then click the Overprint Fill option in the pop-up menu.

Setting Object Outline Overprinting   To overprint the outline of an object, select the object, right-click it, and select Overprint Outline from the pop-up menu.

Always Overprint Black

Overprinting black is very important in the separation and printing process. Black ink is very dark, and it can cover underlying inks. Overprinting black is an excellent trapping technique. It is a good practice to fill small text with black ink because small text is difficult to align during the printing process. When you use overprinting, the underlying object or background will print, and the text will overprint it, ensuring good-quality printing, whether or not the press aligns the black plate with the other inks. You should select this option to overprint black ink over 95 percent of black.

Using Auto-Spreading

The Corel separation engine's automatic trapping works well in most common situations. The Auto-Spreading feature creates an outline the same color as the object's fill and overprints this outline over the underlying object. It is created for every object that does not have an outline, is filled with a uniform fill, and is not set to overprint. You should check Auto-Spreading to activate automatic trapping.

The Maximum field regulates the maximum width in points that the spread outline can have. If the color is lighter, Corel's separation engine increases the trap width, but always below the maximum amount selected. If the color is darker, the trap width will be smaller. You should type, or select by clicking the up/down arrow buttons, the amount in points of spread you want to set as the maximum.

In some situations, it may be wise to use a fixed-spread trap. For this, you should check the Fixed Width box. When this option is active, the Maximum field changes to the Width field. Type, or select by clicking the up/down arrow buttons, the amount in points of fixed spread you want to apply.

If you apply Auto-Spreading to small text, the outline it creates can result in illegible text. The Text Above field regulates the text point size that will limit Auto-Spreading applied to text. You could apply Auto-Spreading to text under the 18-point default size, but you should analyze the text construction before you decide to lower the limit. It is preferable that you fill small text with black ink and overprint it.

Setting Prepress Options

These days, prepress operations have been passed to the artist, and CorelDRAW 10's Prepress tab in the Print Options dialog contains a group of options to help you accomplish prepress requirements (see Figure 25-15). Paper/film settings, information required in the printing process, crop/fold/registration marks, calibration bars, and densitometer scales are among them. When you activate the separation engine, many of these marks are automatically set to print with the document, but you can manually activate them in the Prepress tab. Some of these options can also be set by clicking buttons available in the Print Preview Standard Toolbar, and in the Mark Placement Property Bar when you select the Mark Placement Tool.

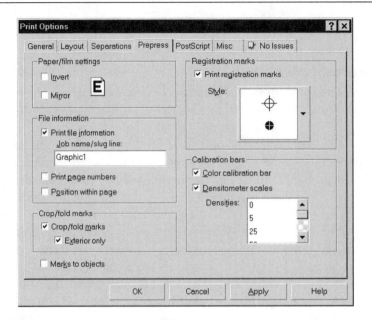

FIGURE 25-15 CorelDRAW 10 provides options to customize prepress marks and other required settings.

Paper/Film Settings

When a film is produced for printing, it is a negative of the printed document, and the film emulsion should be down. To accomplish this task, you use the Invert and Mirror check boxes in the Prepress tab. You should check the Invert field to invert your printed document image to produce a negative image. By checking the Mirror box, you will flip the image to print the film emulsion down.

You should consult your service bureau or print shop before you set these options. Generally, imagesetters are set to invert the image and mirror it. If you set it in CorelDRAW and it is set in the imagesetter as well, the film will be positive and cannot be used in a printing press process.

Printing File Information

To ensure a smooth workflow in the printing process, it helps to include some necessary information in your printed documents. Check the Print File Information box in the Prepress dialog to print the job name in the Job Name/Slug Line field. By default, the active filename is placed here, but sometimes your print shop will know the job by a different name than the one you use to save your file. It is a good practice to name files with the job name that will be used during the printing process.

You should check the Print Page Numbers field when processing multipage documents; it helps to identify what plates correspond to a specific page.

You may encounter a situation in which you need to place the information inside the printed area. In this case, check Position Within Page.

Setting Crop and Fold Mark Printing

Documents are printed in presses using sheets of paper that are bigger than the printed document. These sheets are cropped by a guillotine and sometimes folded by a folder machine. The personnel operating the equipment need instructions to crop and fold the job, and special marks are printed with the document to instruct them where and how to crop and fold the printed document.

Choosing Registration Marks and Styles

During the printing process, inks are printed separately, and to align inks, special registration marks are used. CorelDRAW 10 provides several sets of registration marks that you can use according to printers' preferences.

To activate registration marks, check Print Registration Marks. You can change the registration marks style by clicking in the Style drop-down list and selecting preferred registration marks.

Calibration Bars

Calibration bars and densitometer scales are used in the printing process to calibrate colors and read ink density in printing and films. When printing in a press, the pressman uses the calibration bars as a guide to see if the printed ink matches the required color. They are especially important when inks are printed individually and/or when an ink density reader device is not available. The pressman is constantly comparing the printed document with the calibration bars in the Color Kit. To print calibration bars in your document, check the Color Calibration Bar box.

Densitometer scales are used to check the ink and film density. Swatches printed by the densitometer scale are read by a densitometer, and the densitometer value lecture is compared to the densitometer scale values printed. A service bureau uses the densitometer reading of the film to check that the imagesetter is printing the film with the required density. In the print shop, the densitometer reading is a guide to increase or decrease ink in the press during the printing process. Those readings also provide information to calculate dot gain.

You can print densitometer scales by checking the Densitometer Scales box in the Prepress tab. To change the Densities values in the scale, click the value in the field and type a value or select one by clicking the up/down arrow buttons.

Crop/Fold Marks

You can set crop and fold marks by checking the Crop/Fold Marks box in the Prepress tab. To place those marks in the exterior of the printing area, you should check the Exterior Only box.

Marks to Objects

You may frequently want to place prepress marks around objects but not outside the page layout. If you encounter this situation, you should check the Marks to Objects field, and Corel's print engine will place the marks around the objects in your printed document.

Choosing PostScript Options

The PostScript tab in the Print Options dialog displays when the selected printing device is a PostScript device. This collection of PostScript options controls how Corel's print engine prepares the PostScript page description of your printed document (see Figure 25-16).

 If your printer is non-PostScript, you can convert it to PostScript by installing software or hardware if your printer supports it. With a little research, you may be able to increase your printer's capabilities.

Compatibility

The Compatibility drop-down list lets you select which PostScript level your printing device will use to print. There are three levels, and you should find out what level is compatible with the selected printing device.

Conform to DSC

The Document Structuring Convention (DSC) is a special file format for PostScript documents, and it includes a number of comments. These comments

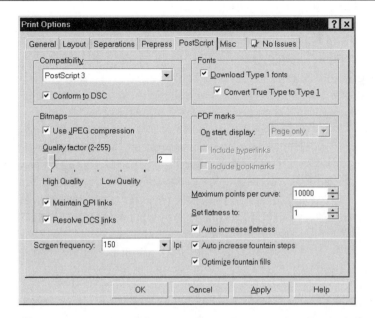

FIGURE 25-16   When you have a PostScript driver active, the Print Options dialog
displays this tab, where you can control PostScript options.

provide information for postprocessors, which work with the document.
Postprocessors can shuffle the pages, print two or more pages on a side, and
so on. If you are going to send your printed file to a service bureau or print shop,
this option enables you to ensure that the printed file conforms to the Document
Structuring Convention.

Printing Bitmap Images

Bitmaps are a very important part of printing, and they generate a huge amount of
information. The PostScript language provides ways to manage and print bitmaps
efficiently using different methods and formats. Corel's print engine gives you
options to optimize bitmap printing.

JPEG Compression   JPEG is a standardized image compression mechanism. Its
name stands for Joint Photographic Expert Group, the name of the committee that
wrote the standard. JPEG is designed for compressing image files, but it is a *lossy*
format, meaning that the compressed image is not the same as the original when it

is decompressed. You should take this into consideration when you use the Use JPEG Compression option in the Print Options PostScript tab.

When this option is enabled, you can print huge images faster, but you can lose quality. Use this option according to your printing objective. For example, if you are printing some proofs, it could help you to accelerate the process. You can move the Quality Factor slide to increase or decrease the compression factor. Higher numbers mean lower image quality, but faster printing.

OPI Links   OPI stands for Open Prepress Interface. It is used by some service bureaus in their servers. The service bureau can scan your image with a high-quality scanner, and they will send you a low-resolution version of your image. You import this image linked into CorelDRAW, and when you send your printed file to the service bureau, their server, through OPI, will replace the low-resolution image with the corresponding high-resolution version.

You should check the Maintain OPI Links option if you are working with your service bureau and using the Open Prepress Interface method.

Resolving DCS   DCS stands for Desktop Color Separation. It is a file format for images that can save images separated by inks or channels. This means that a DCS file can contain files attached to the main file, and each file corresponds to a separated color in the image. For example, a CMYK image saved to DCS format contains five files, one representing the image and the others containing Cyan, Magenta, Yellow, and Black information separately. DCS accelerates the prepress processing time, because the separation is already done. DCS2 holds spot ink information. You can also save nonseparated bitmaps to DCS format.

Adobe Acrobat Distiller does not support the Desktop Color Separation file format. You should save your DCS file as an Encapsulated PostScript(EPS) file if you are intending to distill to PDF a CorelDRAW print files containing images in DCS format. If your document contains linked DCS images and you want to include your original image in the printed document, you should check Resolve DCS Links. If you do not enable this option, the service bureau should replace the low-resolution image linked in your CDR print file with the high-resolution one when printing to the imagesetter.

Screen Frequency

Documents printed by a PostScript printer or a press are printed using tiny dots that simulate a continuous tone print when viewed from a certain distance. Before computers, those tiny dots were formed by imposing a screen over the original document. Corel's print engine re-creates those screens by means of complex algorithms and prepares your documents for printing.

The paper you use, the press/printer capabilities, and the job objective regulate how many of those tiny dots are necessary to print your document at the desired level of quality. Screen frequency is measured in lines per inch (lpi).

You should ask the print shop how many lines per inch they are going to use to print your document before you set this option. To set the screen frequency, type a number or select from the preset list in the Screen Frequency list.

Setting Font Handling

PostScript printing devices can print Type 1 (PostScript fonts) and True Type fonts. They work better using Type 1 because the fonts are written in the PostScript language. CorelDRAW's options let you manage how the fonts are going to be used while printing. It is best to download the fonts to the printing device, as it accelerates the printing process and produces better-looking fonts. To enable this feature, check Download Type 1 Fonts in the PostScript tab. If this option is disabled, fonts are printed as curves or bitmaps.

When you select the Download Type 1 Fonts option, the Convert True Type to Type1 option is also selected by default. This will produce better results when printing to a PostScript device because these fonts are downloaded to the PostScript printing device.

Setup Options for PDF

Corel's PostScript print engine can prepare printed documents to be distilled to PDF format in order to preview and manipulate them in Adobe Acrobat. A set of options in the PostScript tab lets you control how the distilled PDF will display when it is opened by Acrobat. You can also include in the printed document any hyperlinks and bookmarks that you created in CorelDRAW.

On Start, Display   This drop-down list contains preset options to manage how the document will display when it opens in Acrobat. To display the current page, select the Page Only option. The Full Screen option instructs Acrobat to display your document in a full-screen viewing mode. You should select the Thumbnails option to display small panes representing each page of your multipage document.

Include Hyperlinks   Enable this option to include the hyperlinks you create in CorelDRAW in your printed document file. Those hyperlinks will function in Acrobat as you conceived them in CorelDRAW.

Include Bookmarks   You can create bookmarks in CorelDRAW and then include those bookmarks in the printed document file that will be distilled to a PDF file format. CorelDRAW bookmarks will work in Acrobat as you created them in CorelDRAW.

If Your Objects Are Complex

Sometimes your documents may contain very complex objects that can create problems during the printing process for certain devices, especially when you are printing in PostScript Level 1. Corel's print engine offers options to simplify construction of those objects while printing to a PostScript printing device. Check the Preflight tab to see if there are any warnings about complexity of your objects, and adjust settings in the PostScript tab to eliminate the problem.

Curve Maximum   The maximum number of control points that CorelDRAW allows in a curve is 10,000. Some objects could cause problems while printing because they are too complex. You can reduce the number in the Maximum Control Points per Curve field to make it easier for the printing device to process the document.

Controlling Flatness Options   Curve flatness refers to how smooth a curve appears when printed. Increasing flatness reduces smoothness, and the curve appears to be a conjunction of connected straight lines. If you use the flatness controls wisely, you can reduce curve complexity and increase printing efficiency.

The value in the Set Flatness To field plus 10, defines the maximum flatness used by the Auto Increase Flatness feature. Enable this feature by checking the box.

When fountain fills are present in your document, it is a good practice to enable Auto Increase Fountain Steps by checking it. This feature automatically analyzes the file and the print settings; then, if necessary, it increases the number of steps used to render fountain fills to avoid banding. This feature may increase printing time, but it will give you the best results with your fountain fills.

Another option to improve fountain fills is Optimize Fountain Fills. By enabling it, Corel's PostScript engine will analyze your document and the print settings. If the number of steps in your fountain fill is higher than your printing device's capability, the number will be reduced automatically while printing.

> **TIP**   *If your printer is not capable of printing fountain fills correctly and your printout displays banding, you should convert your objects with fountain fills to bitmaps and then apply the Add Noise effect with a setting of 2 to 4 pixels, depending on bitmap resolution. This action reduces banding in your printouts.*

Miscellaneous Printing Options

Corel's print engine provides other important options that are grouped in the Miscellaneous (Misc) tab. To access those options, click the Print Options dialog's Misc tab (see Figure 25-17).

Choosing a Color Profile

Color profiles are files containing specific color data. This data is used to reproduce colors approximately as viewed in your monitor. The Apply ICC Profile option lets you enable Corel's Color Manager while printing. Be aware that you should use one color management system only. If the color manager in the printing device is active, you should disable this option. CMYK objects automatically discard this feature, and no color corrections are performed on them while printing.

When the selected printing device is not color capable and you are printing a composite, this option appears grayed out, but if you are printing separations and the Print Separations option is enabled, this option is available and displays the selected separation profile in Corel's Color Manager. If the selected printing

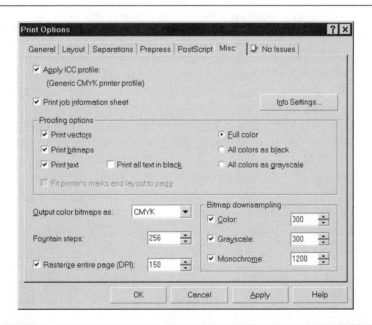

FIGURE 25-17   Important options to control your printouts are available in the Misc tab.

device is color capable and separations are not enabled, then the profile displayed in this field is the profile selected in Corel's Color Manager Composite profile.

Printing an Information Sheet

You can print important information related to your printed documents either on paper or in a file. This information will guide your service bureau or print shop during the printing process. Information about CorelDRAW10, the driver you used to print, the print job, separations, In-RIP trapping, fonts, and links is available when you check the Print Job Information Sheet box.

To change the information you want to print, click the Info Settings button to access the Print Job Information dialog (see Figure 25-18). When you check the boxes on the right side of the dialog to enable them, the related information instantly displays in the main Job Information box.

You can send the information to a printer and/or file by checking the Send to Text File and Send to Printer check boxes. Then select the specific text file or printer by clicking the Select File or Select Printer button.

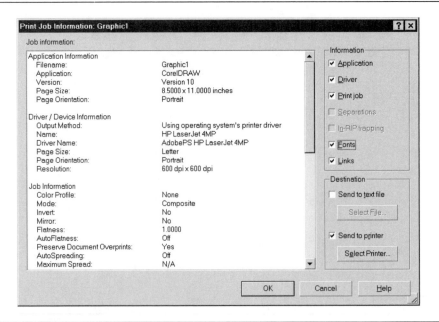

FIGURE 25-18   Select the information that you want to print and/or save by enabling the corresponding information option in this dialog.

Setting Proofing Options

When printing proofs, you may need to print individual parts of your documents as text, bitmaps, or vectors. The Proofing Options group allows you to control what to print, and it will save you precious time. Enable or disable the check boxes according to your needs. If you want all your text printed in black ink only, enable Print All Text in Black.

Fit Printer's Marks and Layout to Page will automatically resize your document and selected printer's marks to fit in the selected page size. This feature is excellent for proofing print marks and imposition layouts.

You may or may not require printing your proof in colors; you can control it by enabling Full Color, All Colors as Black, or All Colors as Grayscale. Enabling one option automatically disables the others. If you will be faxing your proofs, selecting All Colors as Black can help.

Controlling Bitmap Color Space

Corel's print engine lets you change your bitmap's color space when printing without altering the original image. It is useful for printing proofs or outputting CMYK images in printers that convert CMYK to RGB before they print. If you enable Output Color Bitmaps as RGB, the CMYK-to-RGB conversion will be controlled by Corel's Color Manager before it reaches the RGB printer. This action can result in a more predictable color printing. Select your preferred printing color space for your document bitmaps from the Output Color Bitmap As drop-down list.

Fountain Steps and Rasterizing

The Fountain Steps field lets you increase or decrease the steps the printing device will use to print fountain filled objects. Increasing the steps can result in softer color transitions, and reducing them can reduce printing time while printing proofs.

Sometimes, when you encounter printing problems, enabling the Rasterize Entire Page option can provide a good printing workaround. It can be used to produce a bitmap printed file that can be processed in an image editor application. You can produce a rasterized page with low resolution to accelerate printing of proofs. To increase or reduce the rasterized page resolution, type or select the desired dots per inch in the numeric field.

Reducing Bitmap Resolution

The Bitmap Downsampling group provides three options to control output bitmap resolution without altering the original bitmaps. You should enable Color, Grayscale, and/or Monochrome options to increase or reduce output bitmap resolutions in your printed documents, and type or select the desired resolution in the corresponding numeric field.

Analyzing CorelDRAW's Printing Issues Report

Whether you choose to use it or not, CorelDRAW 10's Preflight feature is extremely efficient. Preflight warnings advise you about printing problems present in your printed document and selected settings before you print. Preflight also suggests possible solutions. When a printing problem is detected, the Preflight tab in the Print Options dialog displays a warning, and you can click this tab to read the Preflight observations and suggestions for solving the problem before you print. This features saves you a lot of time and money. Preflight also warns you and offers solutions for problems present in documents that are going to be exported to Flash movies and published to PDF or the Web (see Figure 25-19).

The Preflight For drop-down list displays a set of Preflight options according to printing purpose. You can select a preset option, or you can customize and save your own presets by clicking the Settings button. This action triggers the Preflight Settings dialog, in which you can enable and disable preferred warning options by

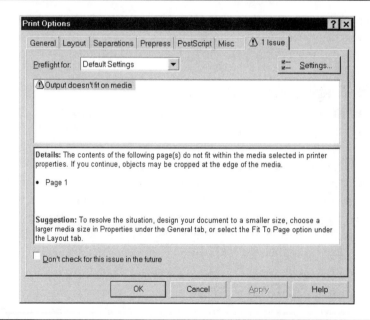

FIGURE 25-19   The Preflight warnings offer a way to troubleshoot printing before expensive problems have a chance to occur.

clicking on each option's check box. To save your customized options, type a new name in the Preflight For text field and click the OK button. To modify current Preflight options after modifying your warning options, click the plus sign button. To delete a Preflight preset, select it and click the minus sign button.

The Preflight dialog shows two panes—the top pane displays current problems, and the bottom pane displays problem information and possible solutions. Highlighting the problem by clicking it allows you to read about individual problems and solutions. You can instruct Preflight not to display a particular problem anymore by enabling the Don't Check for This Issue in the Future option.

Corel's Double-Sided Printing Wizard

You can create booklets and other double-sided printed documents on your desktop printer using CorelDRAW 10's Double-Sided Printing Wizard. To access this feature, select Settings | Duplexing Setup Wizard on the Print Preview main menu. You can also access the Double-Sided Printing Wizard without starting CorelDRAW by selecting Start | Programs | CorelDRAW 10 | Productivity Tools | Duplexing Wizard. If you do not find it there, insert your CorelDRAW 10 CD #1, and perform a custom install. You should select Duplexing Wizard from the CorelDRAW 10 components list.

This wizard is self-explanatory and easy to follow. You have to run it only one time to set any printing device driver installed in your system. When a driver is set to use the duplex printing feature, the Manual Double-Sided Printing dialog displays at the moment Draw's print engine starts to print, asking whether you want to print on both sides of a printed page. You can select to use it or not at this point. If you don't remember how to reinsert the paper in your printer to print the other side, there is an option that will print an instruction sheet to show you which way you should reinsert the sheet of paper after printing the first side.

If you don't want the Manual Double-Sided Printing dialog to display when you print, disable the duplex printing feature by running the Duplexing Setup Wizard and selecting Disable when asked. To access the Disable option, you must run the wizard by selecting Start | Programs | CorelDRAW 10 | Productivity Tools | Duplexing Wizard. This option is not available when you run the wizard from Print Preview.

Prepare for Service Bureau Wizard

Frequently, you will find yourself sending your documents to a service bureau or print shop, or carrying them to another system. CorelDRAW 10 provides a wizard that collects all the information, fonts, and files required to properly display and print your documents in another system. You should be sure that CorelDRAW 10 is installed in the system that will open your files before you run the Prepare for Service Bureau Wizard.

Corel Corporation has a service bureau affiliate program, and service bureaus approved by Corel can provide you with a profile to prepare your document with the Service Bureau Wizard. This profile may contain special instructions that your service bureau may require you to follow before sending your files to them. You should ask your service bureau if it is a Corel Approved Service Bureau (CASB).

You may find a service bureau that does not support CorelDRAW, and in this case you should ask if they can print separations from Adobe Acrobat. To produce separations from PDF files, a special Acrobat plug-in or a third-party application is required. CorelDRAW 10's Prepare for Service Bureau Wizard provides an option to create a PDF file that can be used for professional prepress purposes.

From CorelDRAW's main menu, select File | Prepare For Service Bureau to access the Prepare for Service Bureau Wizard. The first dialog prompts you to select from Gather All Files Associated with This Document or Choose a Profile Provided by Your Service Bureau. The first option collects all the files, fonts, and information associated with the open document. The second option instructs the wizard to use a CSP profile provided by your service bureau.

When you select the Gather All Files option and you click the Next button, a dialog displays a list of fonts present in your document. These fonts can be copied and used by your service bureau when outputting your document. To copy fonts, check the Copy Fonts option. The next dialog asks if you want to create a PDF file. The PDF file could be used by your service bureau as a soft proof, or it can be used to print separations, if the service bureau is allowed to separate from PDF files. You should check the Generate PDF File option if you want to create a PDF file from your CDR document. Click the Next button to continue or the Back button if you want to return to the previous dialog.

In the next dialog, you type the folder location to which you want to save the collected files, or you can click the Browse button and point to a location. The next dialog displays a list of all the collected and created documents that you will send to your service bureau. If they require a hard copy of your document, you should print it from CorelDRAW to your desktop printer. At this point, the process is finished. Click the Finish button to end the wizard and the Prepare for Service Bureau process.

| TIP | *If you are sending your CDR file to a system where it will be opened in a previous version of CorelDRAW, you should select the Save As option, and select the version you require from the Version field. Point to the folder in which the Prepare for Service Bureau Wizard saved your collected documents and overwrite the CDR file produced by the wizard, which has been saved as a current version document.* |

In certain situations your service bureau may send you a Prepare for Service Bureau profile. This profile is a special CSP file that contains settings and print styles required by your service bureau to print your document. This is a great feature because you do not have to set options to print your document properly for this particular service bureau.

When you select the Prepare for Service Bureau option, the first dialog has a radio button to select Choose a Profile Provided by Your Service Bureau. If you have a profile, check this option, and click the Next button. The next dialog displays a box containing available profiles. If you have not used the profile sent by your service bureau before, click the Browse button and point to the folder where you saved it. Select the CPS file and click OK. The profile name displays in the Profile list box; click the Next button to continue. There is also an option to download the profile from the Internet. When this option is selected, your browser connects you with the Corel Web site, where you can access CPS profiles from Corel-approved service bureaus.

TIP	*If you run or work at a service bureau, you might want to contact Corel to become a Corel Approved Service Bureau.*

The next dialog displays special information and/or instructions provided by your service bureau. Follow their instructions and click the Next button. The next dialog displays a list of fonts present in your document and an option to copy them in order to provide your original fonts to the service bureau for use in outputting your document. If your service bureau has the fonts, you may not need to select this option. Click Next to continue.

The displayed dialog contains fields for you to fill in your personal information that is included in the print job information file; this information allows the service bureau to identify your documents and job specifications easily. You should type the required information and click the Next button to continue.

The next dialog contains a field in which you should type the folder location where the wizard will collect all the required files for your service bureau to print your job. If the folder is already created, click the Browse button and point to the selected folder. If the selected folder contains files, a dialog will display advising you about it when you click the Next button.

The next dialog lets you access CorelDRAW 10's Print Preview, in which you can review the printing settings. Be aware that any change you may perform will apply to the printed PostScript file. Click the Next button when you are ready to continue.

At this point a dialog displays a list of all the files produced that will be sent to the service bureau, including a CDR and a PRN file, any of which can be used by your service bureau to produce your document. If any of the required files cannot be collected by the wizard, it will display the filenames presenting problems. If your service bureau requires a hard copy of your printed document, you should print it from Draw to your desktop printer. Click the Finish button to end the Prepare for Service Bureau Wizard process.

When you finish the process, it is a good idea to make a copy of the folder containing the required files that the Prepare for Service Bureau Wizard collected and put it on a removable disk. You should also print out a hard copy of your document.

Print Merge

The new Print Merge feature in CorelDRAW 10 goes farther than any previous version. It allows merging information from databases into CorelDRAW documents at print time. You can create merging fields in CorelDRAW, which are substituted with information contained in the selected database when you print them. The merged information adopts merging fields properties, such as color, font, and so on. This feature lets you personalize printed documents, and its uses are endless. You can use existing databases or create your own database. It also allows using ODBC Data Source to connect databases with CorelDRAW 10's Print Merge feature. ODBC is a programming interface that enables applications to access data in database management systems that use Structured Query Language (SQL) as a data access standard.

You can access CorelDRAW 10's Print Merge feature by selecting File | Print Merge in the main menu. This action triggers a flyout that contains the following three options:

The Create/Load Merge Fields option triggers the Print Merge Wizard, and a dialog displays in which you can choose to create a database from scratch or choose a created database. Click the radio button according to your choice.

When you choose the Create from Scratch option, the next dialog lets you create the fields that will compose your custom database (see Figure 25-20). Type a unique name for each field in the Name a Field text box, and click the Add→

button. Every newly created field displays in the Fields Used in Merge list box. You can move any field from its position in the list by highlighting the name and clicking the Move Up or Move Down button. Click the Rename button to rename a field after selecting it, or you can delete it by clicking the Delete button. This dialog contains the Incremental Field Data option, which you should check if you want to fill the selected field with numbers automatically. This option saves time if you are typing sequential numbers in a database. When this option is active, new fields display, letting you control what numbers will fill your data, and how they will be formatted.

In the Start field, either type or select by clicking the up/down arrow buttons, the first number to be placed in the sequence that will fill the selected field in the database. The numbers will be automatically incremented if you check the Auto Increment option. If you know the last number in the sequence, type or select it in the End field. In the Format drop-down list select a preset format for your number sequence by clicking the arrow button and selecting from the preset list. When you finish reviewing and setting your fields and options, click the Next button.

In the next dialog you see a table with headings containing the names of the fields you created in the preceding dialog. The first column contains the record number, which is automatically assigned by the Print Merge Wizard. The second column contains check mark fields. If a record is checked, it will be used at print time; if not, it will be discarded. You should type the information corresponding

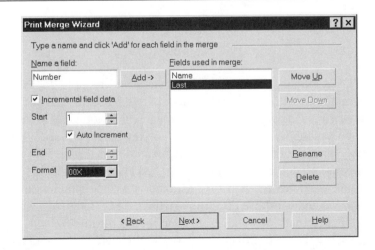

FIGURE 25-20   In this dialog, you create your database fields to merge while printing.

to each record and field. Click the New button to add a new record. You can delete a record by selecting it and clicking the Delete button.

You can switch the table layout's structure from multiple records to a single record structure by clicking on the corresponding button. You can move the table pointer from record to record by using the navigator buttons. You can move the pointer to a specific record by clicking the Find Record button. This action activates the Find dialog, where you can type or select your desired record number, and the table pointer will move to the record automatically after you click OK in the Find dialog.

The next dialog presents an option to save your created database. When saved, you can reuse it in different Print Merge situations, or you can import the information into another database. You can save it to three file formats: text (TXT), comma separated (CSV), or rich text format (RTF).

Inserting Print Merge Fields in the Layout

When the wizard is finished, a Print Merge Property Bar displays in CorelDRAW 10. It contains the tools to insert your created merge fields into your document, as shown in the following illustration:

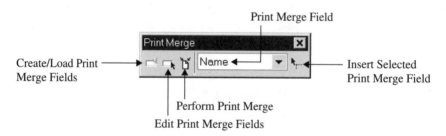

You can insert a field by selecting it from the Print Merge Field drop-down list and clicking on the Insert Selected Print Merge Field button to activate the Insert Tool. Move your mouse pointer to the position at which you want to insert the field in your document page layout and click your mouse. You can select another field and insert it in the document without deactivating the Insert Tool. To deactivate the Insert Tool, click the Insert Selected Print Merge Field button again.

The print merge fields are Artistic Text, and you can change their properties the same way you change those of normal Artistic Text. The field name will be changed by the information contained in each record for this field at print time, but it will preserve the field properties. You should calculate how much space the record with more characters will need to print correctly in a field.

Click the Perform Print button to start printing. You can also access this feature by selecting File | Print Merge | Perform Merge.

Editing Print Merge Fields and Records

You can edit print merge fields and records any time by clicking on the Edit Print Merge Fields button or by selecting File | Print Merge | Edit Merge Fields. This action triggers the Print Merge Wizard, in which you can modify your existing fields and records.

25

Using Existing Databases

When you select the Existing Database option in the Print Merge Wizard and you click the Next button, the dialog that displays lets you choose from Data File, Address Book, or ODBC Data Source.

The Data File option lets you access an existing data file containing the information you are going to merge. You could select TXT, CSV, or RTF files saved in your hard disk, network, or removable media. Click the Open button and point to the file desired. If you create print merge data from scratch and you saved it, you can reuse the data in different CDR documents using this option.

The Address Book option lets you merge data storage in address books with your CDR document. This drop-down list contains the names of address books in your system. Select the address book containing the data you want to merge.

The ODBC Data Source option lets you choose from existing data sources or create a new data source. The Select ODBC Data Source button triggers the Select Data Source dialog, shown in Figure 25-21.

Troubleshooting Document Printing

Troubleshooting printed documents can be a time-consuming and frustrating experience. The new technologies being created almost daily by the software and hardware industries provoke many unexpected incompatibility problems. CorelDRAW 10 is an advanced application using advanced software technology, and it generates complex printing data that some printing devices cannot process correctly, especially if you create complex documents.

To avoid problems, you should simplify your document as much as possible before printing. Be sure to use CorelDRAW 10's Preflight feature, because it advises about possible printing problems present in your document.

FIGURE 25-21 Choose a data source to which you want to connect.

When you encounter a printing problem, ask yourself the following question: What is causing the problem—the printing device, the operating system, or CorelDRAW 10? You can find the answer by isolating the problem.

Isolating a Printing Problem

Your printing device driver uses the Windows spooler to store the printed information before it is sent to the printing device. Windows spooler uses the free space in your hard disk to store the printed information. If there is not enough space, you will encounter a printing problem. It is a good practice to keep 300MB of free space in your hard disk after your document is open. To corroborate this information, double-click My Computer in your Windows desktop. Then right-click your hard disk icon and select Properties. A window displays information about your hard disk, including how much free space is available. If you do not have enough free space, close all your open applications, including CorelDRAW 10, and then access Windows Explorer by right-clicking the Start button and selecting Explorer or pressing the Windows logo plus the E key.

Now open the Windows/Temp folder and delete all files there. Windows writes temporary files to this folder, and several of them are left behind from previous operations. Don't be afraid to delete files and folders in the Windows/Temp folder when all applications are closed. You may encounter a file that Windows won't let you delete; in this case, skip the file and keep deleting.

If you do not have enough free space in the hard disk where Windows is installed and you have another hard disk, it is a good practice to point to this secondary hard disk as the primary swap disk in CorelDRAW 10's Memory option. This way CorelDRAW 10 will write temporary files to the hard disk where Windows is not installed, and Windows can use the free space in the hard disk where it resides to store the printing spooler.

At this point, let's say you found out that you do have enough free space in your hard disk, but your CorelDRAW 10 document still is not printing. Try printing from another application to see if you have problems in your printing device. If you have a problem printing from another application, uninstall your printing device driver and reinstall it. Also check your connection to the printing device. It is a good practice to keep your printing device driver updated to the latest version. An updated version can be found at your printer manufacturer's Web site.

If your printer device is a PostScript printer, you should install the Adobe PS Utility and download from Adobe's Web site (**www.adobe.com**), or from your printer manufacturer's Web site, the PPD (PostScript Printer Description) file corresponding to your printer device. When you use PPD by installing and selecting it in the General tab of the Print Options dialog, CorelDRAW 10's print engine uses all the capabilities available in your printer device, which helps to print especially complex documents correctly.

Now you are sure that your printing device prints well from another application, and you have enough free space in your hard disk. The printing problem is pointing to CorelDRAW 10 and/or settings you selected in your printing device and/or printing options. Try printing another CorelDRAW 10 document with the same printing settings, to be sure that the problem is related to your present printed document. If another document prints well, you have isolated the problem—it is associated with the current document, and the next step should be to simplify your printed document.

Simplifying a Document to Print

CorelDRAW 10 provides several sophisticated tools that produce complex mathematical algorithms and, as a result, complex printing documents. You should simplify those documents to help your printing process. Before you start this process, save your CDR document with another name so that you keep a version you can modify in the future if necessary.

What are these tools and effects, and how do you simplify them?

- CorelTRACE produces complex objects, and sometimes your printing device refuses to print them. CorelDRAW 10's Shape Tool (CTRL-F10) lets you access object nodes. In its Property Bar you'll find the Select All Nodes button, which lets you select all nodes in the object at once. Beside this button you'll find the Curve Smoothness numeric field and slide. You can reduce the number of nodes in your object by typing a number or by moving the slide. This operation may not reduce the number of nodes enough, and it may deform the object's shape. If you are not satisfied with the smoothness, you should convert the object to a bitmap by selecting Bitmaps | Convert to Bitmap from CorelDRAW 10's main menu.

- CorelDRAW 10's Interactive Transparency Tool produces transparency in the selected object, which can cause printing problems. Objects that have transparencies applied should be converted to bitmaps. Be aware that you should select the underlying object together with the transparency lens and convert both of them to a bitmap at once.

- CorelDRAW 10's Drop Shadow feature could be another source of printing problems in certain printers. It is a good practice to separate the shadow from the object by selecting the shadow and clicking Arrange | Break Drop Shadow Group Apart. You can apply the Gaussian Blur effect to the shadow to smooth its borders by selecting the shadow and clicking Bitmaps | Blur | Gaussian Blur or clicking the Edit Bitmap button and applying an Object | Feather Effect (CTRL+SHIFT+F) in Corel PhotoPaint. If a bitmap is underlying the shadow, it is smart to select both of them and convert both to a bitmap together. It simplifies printing and reduces printing time.

- Complex fills can be another source of problems. If you encounter problems while printing complex fills, you should convert these objects to bitmaps. You can encounter banding problems when printing gradient fill objects to laser printers. Laser printers generally cannot reproduce 256 levels of gray, and they can produce banding while printing gradient fills. You can improve the printing by converting them to bitmaps and applying two to four pixels of noise, depending on bitmap resolution. To accomplish this, select the object and convert it to a bitmap; then click Bitmaps | Noise | Add Noise and apply noise accordingly.

■ Fonts can cause problems in your printed document. You should be sure that the font in question is correctly installed and active. Some applications, such as Adobe Type Manager Deluxe and Bitstream Font Navigator, let you activate fonts automatically, and when this fails, the font displays in CorelDRAW 10's Font List with an asterisk beside its name. In this case, you should check the font in the font administrator to activate it manually.

True Type fonts can cause problems while printing to PostScript devices. In this case, you should check the Convert True Type to Type 1 option in the PostScript tab of the Print Options dialog. If this action does not solve the problem, you should install a Type 1 version of the problematic font if possible, or you should convert the text to a curve, by selecting the text and clicking Arrange | Convert to Curve (CTRL+Q). Sometimes the font problem can be caused by a corruption of the font file; in this case, you should uninstall the font completely and reinstall it.

Avoid using many font families in your document. A rule of design says that you should not use more than two font families in the same design—in exceptional cases three. If you apply this rule, you will not only improve your designs, but also avoid printing problems related to fonts.

■ Frequently, image resolution is incorrectly associated with printing quality. You may think that more dots per inch in your image will produce better printing and unnecessarily use huge images, complicating the printing process. Images with 200 dpi to 300 dpi are good enough to print on inkjet desktop printers. Images printing to a press should have between 1.5 to 2 times the lines per inches (lpi) that the pressman will use to print your documents. For example, an image that is going to be printed in a newspaper at 85 lpi needs a resolution of only 170 dpi. It is a good practice to ask how many lines per inch your pressman will use to print your document.

Decoding PostScript Errors

PostScript printers can inform you about printing problems. Select the Print PostScript Error Information option for the PostScript printing device driver. When a related error is present, your PostScript printer will print a document with information about the error. This information is based on codes that you will need a printer manual or information from the printer manufacturer to interpret.

The following common printing errors can help you identify and solve those problems:

- **Limitcheck. Offending Command=Nametype: EOCLIP** This message prints when the printer is unable to complete the rendering of an object because of the complexity of the fill. You should change the object fill or convert the object to a bitmap. If you are printing a color separation, you can try printing separations individually.

- **Limitchek. Offending Command=Nametype: EOFILL** This message is related to object fills and the complexity of the object path. You should reduce the object nodes, convert the object to a bitmap or lower the Maximum Point per Curves value in the PostScript tab of the Print Options dialog.

- **Limitcheck. Offending Command-Nametype: LINETO or CURVETO** This message is triggered when too many nodes are present in the curve. In this case, select the complex object and reduce the number of nodes in the object using the Curve Smoothness feature on the Shape Tool Property Bar or convert the object to a bitmap.

- **Stack Overflow** This is an indication of embedded encapsulated PostScript files, overly complex objects, or fill patterns exceeding printer stack limits. Try changing the object fill or converting the object to a bitmap. If you are printing a color separation, try printing separations individually.

- **Invalid Font** This message prints when a corrupted font is present. Try changing the font family, uninstalling and reinstalling the corrupted font, or converting the text to a curve.

CHAPTER 26

Import and Export Filters

As you become accustomed to using CorelDRAW 10—and as you're probably already aware of if you're an experienced CorelDRAW user—at times, you might want to use CorelDRAW along with other programs, such as bitmap editors, word processors, and presentation editors. Also, you might experience situations in which CorelDRAW's default file format isn't the correct format for the medium that you ultimately plan on publishing your work, such as when you create images for the Internet or for video.

This is where CorelDRAW's Import and Export filters play their key roles. Perhaps you have a CorelDRAW file that you want to edit in an advanced bitmap editor, such as Corel PHOTO-PAINT 10 (which ships with CorelDRAW 10) or another application. In situations such as these, you'll find CorelDRAW 10 contains one of the most complete and powerful sets of Import and Export filters available in any graphic design package for preparing your drawing files in other forms.

How Do Filters Work?

Think of *filters* as translators for files created in other applications. *Import filters* take the data from other applications and translate that data into information that can be viewed and edited from within CorelDRAW. Depending on the type of file you import, you're often provided with additional options for fine-tuning the import, so you bring into CorelDRAW exactly what you need to continue your work most efficiently.

Export filters take data from your CorelDRAW document and convert it into data that "speaks the language" of another program or type of publishing medium. As with Import filters, Export filters frequently contain dialogs that enable you to export the precise data you need for the target application or publishing medium.

TIP   *When you export a file, the new file format may not support all the features that CorelDRAW's native file format (CDR) supports. For this reason, even when exporting work, you should always save a copy of your work in CorelDRAW's native file format.*

How to Import a File

Importing a file is accomplished by clicking the File menu and then clicking Import, or by pressing CTRL+I. This opens the main Import dialog. You may type the drive, pathname, and filename of the file you want to import; or if you're already in the correct drive and path, simply type the filename. You may also search for the file by clicking in the File Type drop-down list box and selecting the file extension your file type uses (such as PSD for Adobe Photoshop or CPT for Corel PHOTO-PAINT). Several options are provided in the File Import dialog (see Figure 26-1).

■ The Link Bitmap Externally option is used to link to your imported file (instead of including the bitmap as part of your imported file). When you

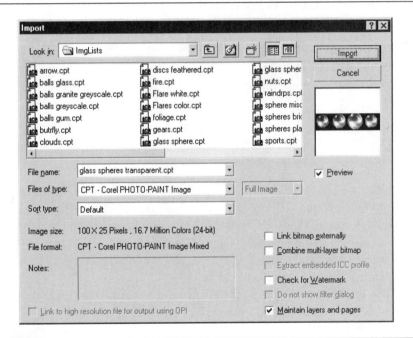

FIGURE 26-1 The File Import dialog

save a CDR file with a linked bitmap, the file size is smaller because the bitmap is stored separately. After you close your CorelDRAW file, you may still access your linked bitmaps separately, and they may still be edited in Corel PHOTO-PAINT, Adobe Photoshop, and other bitmap editing programs.

- The Combine Multilayer Bitmap option is used to open multiple-layer bitmaps as a single flattened (merged) layer in CorelDRAW.

- When imported files contain embedded International Color Consortium (ICC) profiles, you may use the Extract ICC Profile option to extract the ICC profile and save it to a disk drive.

- The Check For Watermark option is used to check a file to see if the image contains encoded DigiMarc watermark code. DigiMarc is used to "sign" images digitally, so they may be identified as belonging to the person who created them. (Note: DigiMarc isn't 100 percent effective, particularly in tightly compressed formats such as GIF and JPG.)

- The Do Not Show Filter Dialog option is used to import the item using default settings. In most cases, you probably want to leave this option unchecked, unless you're certain the default settings are the settings you prefer.

- The Maintain Layers And Pages option is used to maintain the file's original layer and/or page structure when importing a document saved using layers and/or pages (such as Adobe Acrobat files).

- At the bottom of the dialog, you'll find the Link To High Resolution File For Output Using OPI option, which is available when working with TIFF bitmaps and SCITEX CT bitmaps. This option replaces the high-resolution images with low-resolution placeholders when your file is seen onscreen. The high-resolution images are kept, however, and used when printing the document (a concept referred to as FPO or For Printing Only). Because TIFF and CT (particularly CT) images can sometimes be extremely large, this option enables you to work on the surrounding elements of the document (such as text) without having to devote computer resources to the TIFF or CT image.

- On the right side of the dialog, you can see an option to preview the image before opening it. Note, when previewing large images that don't save preview thumbnails, the preview may take some time to be rendered.

- Also on the right side of the dialog is the option to import a full, cropped, or resampled image. If you plan to crop or resample an image immediately on importing it, using this option enables immediate access to a crop or resample dialog. Cropping or resampling an image as part of the import process is faster than importing the image, and then performing the crop or resample.

> **TIP** *You can import multiple files if they are stored in the same folder. Click one of the files you want to open, and then hold down the CTRL key while clicking additional files. You may open an entire folder's contents by clicking the first file, and then holding down the SHIFT key while clicking the last file in the folder.*

> **NOTE** *The OPI option flags an image as a low-resolution OPI image. The high-resolution image doesn't even have to be on your computer. When you print the file, OPI comments get injected into the PostScript stream. The high/low resolution swap happens at the OPI server.*

How to Export a File

Exporting a file is also accomplished via the File menu by clicking File and then clicking Export, or by pressing CTRL+E. This opens the main file export dialog. Folder navigation is handled in the same way as it is handled in the file import dialog. The compression drop-down list box becomes available if the file type you're exporting to supports two or more types of compression, so you may choose the type of compression you want to use. The following options are available (see Figure 26-2):

- The Selected Only option is used to export only your currently selected object (instead of your entire canvas).

- If you're saving a file that's eventually going to be displayed on a Web site, you may want to check the Web_Safe_Filenames option. This automatically fills any spaces in your filename with the _ underscore character. The option is referred to as Web Safe because most Web servers don't support spaces in filenames.

- The Do Not Show Filter Dialog option exports your file using default options, instead of asking you to select options. This is only available when exporting to file types that support multiple export options.

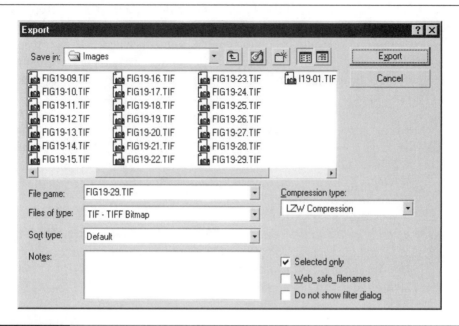

FIGURE 26-2   The File Export dialog

Selecting an object and choosing Selected Only results in a faster export and a smaller exported file size.

Understanding Color Bits and Color Count

Much of what may be imported and exported using CorelDRAW is determined by the Color Bit depth of the file format being used. Color Bits are a way of describing how much disk space the image's format is permitted to occupy. When more bit space is available to define color, the format being discussed has a higher maximum color count. You'll find the following Color Bit depths (and their corresponding maximum color counts) referred to frequently in this chapter:

Bit Depths	Colors
1-Bit Color	Black and White
4-Bit Color	16 Colors
8-Bit Color	256 Colors

Bit Depths	Colors
16-Bit Color	65,536 Colors
24-Bit Color	16,777,216 Colors
32-Bit Color	4,294,967,296 Colors
48-Bit Color	281,474,976,710,656 Colors

NOTE *The term 8-bit may be used to describe both 256 grayscale colors and 256 colors chosen from the full spectrum of available color. Web Safe, Paletted, and Uniform are all common examples of 8-bit color. RGB is the most common example of 24-bit color, and CMYK is the most common example of 32-bit color. For more information, see CD-ROM 6.*

26

TIP *To find the maximum number of colors supported by any bit depth, multiply the number 2 to the power of the bit depth. As an example, consider 4-bit color: The number 2 to the fourth power = 16 total colors.*

Which Files Will Import, and Which Files Will Export?

CorelDRAW 10 contains one of the largest selections of Import/Export filter collections in the graphics industry. Corel's own product line is well supported and includes filters for Corel PHOTO-PAINT, Corel PAINTER, Corel PRESENTATIONS, and Corel WORDPERFECT. File types owned by other software and hardware vendors are also well supported, including those for Adobe Illustrator, Photoshop, and Acrobat; Kodak FlashPix and PhotoCD; Macromedia Flash; Microsoft Word; PostScript's printing language; and Scitex's scanning language.

In addition to these formats, CorelDRAW 10 also includes support for standard graphics industry file types, such as the bitmap formats BMP (Windows and OS/2), GIF (still and animated), JPG, PNG, TGA, and TIFF. Filters are also included for standard vector file types, such as CGM, EMF, and WMF. Standard text types such as RTF and TXT are also supported.

TIP *If you installed CorelDRAW using the Typical option, most Import and Export filters should be available. If you installed using the Compact option, some filters won't be available. If you installed using the Custom option, the available filters will depend on the selections you made during the install process. You may add any missing filters at any time by running the install application again. For more information on installation issues, see Chapter 1.*

Specific Application Filters

Some file formats, such as PSD and CPT, are used to import files from and to export files to specific applications (PSD is Adobe Photoshop's default file format; CPT is Corel PHOTO-PAINT's default file format). Others, such as EMF and TIFF, are not application specific but, instead, are used in many graphics programs. The following application-specific file formats are supported by CorelDRAW 10.

> **TIP** *A difference exists between a filter being installed in CorelDRAW and a filter's file type being associated with CorelDRAW. The fact that a filter is installed means it's available for use by CorelDRAW. When a filter's file type (such as BMP for bitmap) is associated with CorelDRAW, this means CorelDRAW is to be used as the default program for opening the file.*

Adobe Illustrator

CorelDRAW imports and exports files in Adobe Illustrator's default file format, AI. CorelDRAW supplies support for Illustrator releases, including Illustrator 88 and Illustrator versions 1.1, 3.x, 4.x, 5.x, 6.0, 7.0, and 9.0. In addition, support is provided for both the Windows and Macintosh versions of Illustrator.

CorelDRAW's wide-ranging support for the AI format includes the capability to import CMYK fills, Pantone fills, nested groups, filled open paths, locked objects, locked object groups, Photoshop paths, Illustrator paths, and Illustrator text. When importing Illustrator 6.0 (and higher) files, which may contain bitmaps, the bitmaps are imported as long as they're actually part of the AI file (bitmaps that are linked to the AI file cannot be imported).

When CorelDRAW is used to export a file to the AI format, support is available for features, including process colors, multiple fonts, and nested groups (see Figure 26-3). Support for the following features is available only for Adobe Illustrator version 6.0 and higher: inline bitmaps, cropped bitmaps, PowerClip object bitmaps, bitmap pattern fills, and texture fills. These limitations are because of Illustrator's inability to handle bitmap-based data before version 6.0.

Note that Adobe Illustrator and CorelDRAW control paths and fills differently. So, when curves with multiple subpaths are exported to the AI format, it may be useful to check Simulate Complex Filled Curves in the Export to AI dialog.

FIGURE 26-3   Export support is available for these features.

Adobe Photoshop

CorelDRAW also imports and exports files in the PSD format, the native file format of Adobe Photoshop. The PSD format is a variation on the traditional Windows bitmap format, with support for Photoshop's layers, masking/selection data, multiple color models, and Run Length Encoding (RLE) compression.

Adobe PSD files from Photoshop versions 2.5 through 6.0 may be imported into CorelDRAW, but only Photoshop versions 4.0 and higher accept files exported from CorelDRAW. The following color models may be imported and exported using CorelDRAW and the PSD file type: black and white, grayscale, Paletted RGB, and CMYK.

Note that because Photoshop doesn't support object bitmaps, these objects are converted to layers in Photoshop.

Adobe Acrobat

Adobe Acrobat uses the Portable Document Format (*PDF*) format. The PDF format is useful for transmitting complex documents, such as books, across multiple computer platforms (including Windows, Macintosh, and UNIX). CorelDRAW includes full-import support for Adobe Acrobat documents through Acrobat version 4.0. You may also publish PDF documents to print or to the Internet using CorelDRAW 10. For details, see Chapter 25.

AMI Professional

This filter imports and exports text for use with the Ami Pro Word Processor. The Ami Professional format handles text well, but it should not be used to export CorelDRAW graphics to the Ami Professional word processor. Graphics files should be exported based upon the way that they'll be printed. When using a PostScript printer with Ami Professional, use the EPS file format. When using any other printer, use the WMF file format.

AutoCAD Drawings

AutoCAD is one of the graphics industry's more popular CAD programs. *CAD* is an acronym for Computer Aided Design, a type of vector design that's most popular in industrial fields, such automotive design, building construction, and engineering. CorelDRAW 10 supports AutoCAD's DXF file format for both importing and exporting.

The DXF file format is primarily vector based, although it also supports the 3D objects used in CAD design. Note, when saving an AutoCAD image for use in CorelDRAW, it should be saved with the view you plan to use in CorelDRAW. Also, when exporting AutoCAD files, remember that only an object's outline is exported because AutoCAD doesn't support CorelDRAW's fills.

Corel PHOTO-PAINT

As you may know, Corel PHOTO-PAINT is the high-end bitmap editor that ships with CorelDRAW. Because CorelDRAW is a vector application and Corel PHOTO-PAINT is a bitmap application, files imported from Corel PHOTO-PAINT are placed in your CorelDRAW document as bitmaps, and files exported from CorelDRAW to Corel PHOTO-PAINT must first be converted to bitmaps.

When exporting to Corel PHOTO-PAINT's CPT format (and all other bitmap-based formats, such as GIF, JPG, and TIFF), the main CorelDRAW export dialog, upon closing, automatically opens a secondary dialog called the Convert To Bitmap dialog. This dialog contains several options (see Figure 26-4).

Color This option is used to determine the Color mode to be used when exporting your bitmap. The options are black and white, 8-bit grayscale, 8-bit paletted (which may contain up to 256 colors), 24-bit RGB (up to 16.7 million colors), and 32-bit CMYK (up to 4.3 billion colors). Exporting your image using the 24-bit RGB or 32-bit CMYK color counts is usually best because additional color reduction, if desired, can always be performed from within Corel PHOTO-PAINT. The 24-bit RGB selection is best for images to be displayed on computer monitors, such as images designed for use on Web sites. The 32-bit CMYK selection is best for images that are to be printed eventually, because CMYK is the color model most commonly used by printers.

Conversions to the color count selected are performed automatically, with the exception of conversions to 8-bit paletted. When this selection is chosen, after the Convert to Bitmap dialog closes, a third dialog opens, enabling you to select *which* 256 colors are to be used in your exported image. For more information on using this dialog, see the section "Bitmap Filters," later in this chapter.

Anti-Aliasing This is the process of delicately blending the borders of bitmapped objects into their backgrounds. In virtually all cases, you want to apply anti-aliasing to your image to avoid rough or jagged edges around your objects.

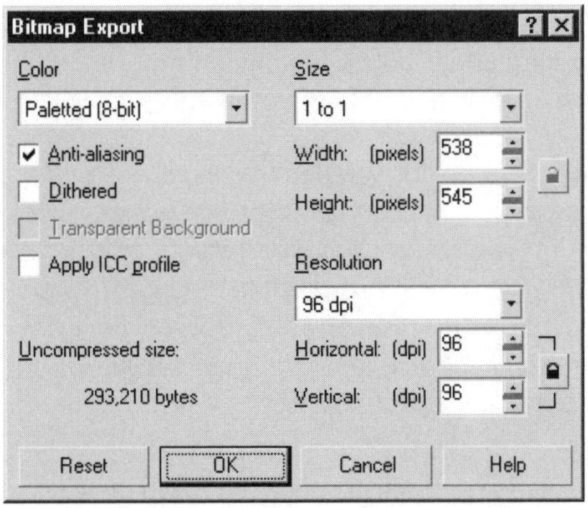

FIGURE 26-4 The Convert To Bitmap dialog controls the conversion from Vector Image to Bitmap Image.

Dithered   This option is available when you select black and white mode or 8-bit paletted mode. Dithering is used in low-color palettes to simulate the presence of additional colors. This is accomplished by placing two base colors very close together so, when viewed, the colors appear to combine and form a third color.

Although dithering can convincingly simulate the existence of additional colors, it can also cause a somewhat grainy appearance in an image. Furthermore, in images that use LZW compression (such as GIF and many TIFF images), dithering increases file size, sometimes dramatically. For these reasons, apply dithering only if needed.

Transparent Background   Both CorelDRAW and Corel PHOTO-PAINT offer full support for transparent backgrounds. Check this box to use a transparent background in your exported image. Note that although Corel's file formats offer full transparency support, some bitmap formats offer limited or no support for transparency. For example, the GIF file format only allows for a single transparent color, while the BMP and JPG formats don't allow transparencies at all.

Use Color Profile   This option enables you to use ICC color profiles to help ensure correct color matching as your image moves from program to program.

Size   The Size drop-down list box enables you to keep the image's current size (the "1 to 1" option) and to switch to one of three common monitor sizes: 640 × 480, 800 × 600, and 1024 × 768. You may also select Custom and enter a size manually in the text boxes under the Size box. Clicking the lock button forces your image to maintain its current proportion of height to width.

> **TIP**   *If your image is to be displayed on a computer monitor, it's particularly important to keep your intended audience in mind when choosing an image size. Although professional designers commonly use a large monitor set at a high- or ultra-high resolution, the typical computer user has resolution set to 800 × 600. Also, in almost every case, a larger image results in a larger file size, something to remember if your images are to be transferred over the Internet.*

Resolution   The resolution you select should be based on whether your image is intended for print or for the Web. Microsoft defines the resolution of 16-bit and higher monitors as 96 dpi, and Apple uses a similar definition for Macintosh monitors. For this reason, 96 dpi is usually the logical choice for images to be displayed on the Web. Printers typically accept much higher resolutions (and thus allow for more detailed images). For images to be printed on typical computer printers, a resolution of 150 to 300 dpi is a common choice, although some high-end printers can print at much higher resolutions. When in doubt, refer to your printer's documentation (or your service bureau) for the ideal resolution setting.

Corel Presentations

Corel Presentations files use the SHW file extension. The format was originally developed by Corel to make exchanging files easy among Corel applications, but it's now the default file format for Corel Presentations images. Corel Presentations is used to create traditional image slides and slide shows for display on computer monitors.

Corel Presentations Compressed

As its name implies, the Corel Presentations Compressed format is a compressed version of the standard Corel Presentations format. Corel Presentations Compressed uses the CPX file extension. When you open a CPX file in CorelDRAW, an uncompressed version of the file, using the filename cmxuncom.tmp, opens in your Windows temporary files folder (usually C:\Windows\Temp\). If you need to import and use the uncompressed version for any reason, change the file extension from TMP to CMX and import it into CorelDRAW.

Corel WordPerfect

WPG is the default file format for graphics used in Corel's popular word processor WordPerfect. The format is vector based but can also contain bitmap data and Encapsulated PostScript (EPS) data.

The WPG format can contain 16 colors (primarily used for compatibility with older versions of WordPerfect) or 256 colors. When using the 256-color option, you may choose which 256 colors are used from a palette of over a million colors.

In addition to using the WPG format for graphics, Corel WordPerfect uses another format, WPD, for storing text. WPD files may be imported to and exported from CorelDRAW 10. Note that the WPD format supports only text—images will not be imported or exported. Use the WPG format for transferring images to and from CorelDRAW 10 and Corel WordPerfect.

CorelDRAW

This is CorelDRAW's native CDR file format, which is capable of storing anything you can create in CorelDRAW. The advantage of importing a file (versus just opening it) is imported files may be added to the document on which you're currently working. When you open a file using the Toolbar Open button or the File Open command, the CDR file opens as a new document.

Kodak FlashPix Image

Kodak developed this file format for storing photographs. As such, it's exclusively a bitmap format. When importing FlashPix images, the secondary dialog enables the adjustment of a variety of bitmap data, including brightness, contrast, saturation, and color channel information.

Kodak FlashPix images may be imported and exported with color depths of 8-bit grayscale (256 shades of gray) and 24-bit RGB (16 million colors). The Kodak FlashPix extension uses the FPX file format and stores images with no compression or with one of four compression types: Single Color, JPEG Standard, JPEG Unspecified, and JPEG By Quality.

Kodak PhotoCD Image

This is another bitmap format developed by Kodak, which is now used as the standard format for its high-quality photo CD collections. As with the FlashPix format, the PhotoCD format also enables you to perform brightness, contrast, saturation, and color channel corrections during the import process (see Figure 26-5).

Kodak PhotoCD images support three color depths: 8-bit grayscale, 8-bit color, and 24-bit color. The format is unique because it stores bitmaps at up to six different resolutions, all within the same compressed PhotoCD file. During the import process, you have the option of choosing from the following resolutions:

- **Thumbnail**   96 × 64 pixels
- **Wallet**   192 × 128 pixels
- **Snapshot**   384 × 256 pixels
- **Standard**   768 × 512 pixels
- **Large**   1536 × 1024 pixels
- **Poster**   3072 × 2048 pixels

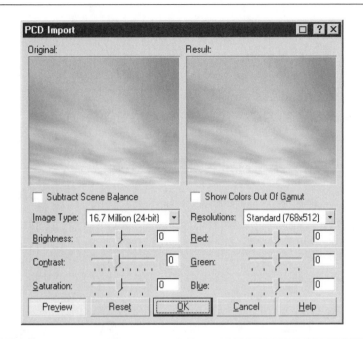

FIGURE 26-5 You can adjust brightness, contrast, saturation, and color channel during the import process.

MacPaint Bitmap

The MacPaint format is a bitmap format used by the Macintosh operating system, mainly for the storage of 1-bit (black and white) images. The format uses the MAC extension and only supports 1-bit import and export.

Macromedia Flash

Macromedia Flash is Macromedia's vector animation format, which is becoming increasing popular on the Web. Although Flash is primarily a vector format, it also supports bitmaps and even audio (note that adding bitmaps or audio increases file size, often significantly).

Flash works as a plug-in for browsers such as Microsoft Internet Explorer and Netscape Navigator. Unlike many other Web plug-ins that disappeared into oblivion shortly after release, Macromedia's Flash was an almost immediate success and continues to rise in popularity. The addition of Flash export capability

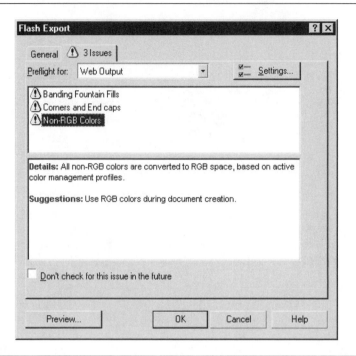

The Flash Export dialog checks your Flash exports for problems and offers suggestions on reaching a solution.

to CorelDRAW 10 (see Figure 26-6) enables designers to use the familiar interface and powerful features of CorelDRAW 10 to create Flash animations, see Chapter 27 for more information.

Micrografx Designer

This format was developed by Micrografx for use in Micrografx Designer. The format, which uses the DRW extension, can contain vector and bitmap images. The DRW filter is used to import and export files from Micrografx Designer 2.x or 3.x. Note: Micrografx's gradient fills cannot be imported.

Microsoft Word

The Microsoft Word format is frequently used for creating and printing text documents. This filter enables you to import formatted text from Microsoft Word and export formatted text to Microsoft Word. The format uses the DOC file extension. When importing or exporting, be certain to choose the DOC filter that matches your version of Microsoft Word.

PC PaintBrush

The PC PaintBrush file format, which uses the PCX extension, is a bitmap format used by the PC PaintBrush program, and sometimes is used to transfer bitmaps between Windows and Macintosh computers. 1-bit (black and white), 4-bit (16 colors), 8-bit (both grayscale and color), and 24-bit (16 million colors) are supported for both import and export.

Picture Publisher

The PP4 and PP5 file formats were developed for use in Micrografx's Picture *Publisher* versions 4 and 5. The filter is used for imports and supports a wide variety of color depths, from 1-bit (black and white) to 48-bit RGB. Version 4 of this format supports a maximum file size of 65,535 by 65,535 pixels, while version 5 supports up to 4.3 billion by 4.3 billion pixels.

WordStar

This file format is used to export formatted text files to the WordStar word processing system.

Combination Vector and Bitmap Filters

The following file types contain combinations of both vector and bitmap data. When the two data types are combined in a single file format, it's often done to make the file's contents available to both vector and bitmap editors. These two data types may also be combined for technical reasons. Image data such as lines, shapes, fills, outlines, and text can be stored most efficiently in vector format, while bitmaps require a format that can save color information and coordinates for every pixel in an image.

Encapsulated PostScript

Although invented by Adobe for use with Illustrator, the Encapsulated PostScript (EPS) file format is popular with a variety of image editing programs because of its capability to print to high-end PostScript printers. CorelDRAW can import and export using Grayscale, RGB, and CMYK color modes. Encapsulated PostScript imports a bitmapped representation of the file.

PS Interpreted

PS Interpreted actually uses three file format extensions: EPS, PRN, and PS. This PS filter may be used to import printer files (the PRN extension) and to import Illustrator EPS files as an editable group of objects.

 If you want to import a PS file for bitmap editing, it's best to import the non-bitmapped EPS Interpreted, and convert the image to a bitmap by clicking Bitmap and then Convert to Bitmap. The bitmapped representation stored in an EPS file is limited in terms of color, which can reduce overall bitmap quality.

Windows Metafile

Windows Metafile, which uses the WMF file extension, is one of the most popular methods of storing vector images for display in editing tools or viewers that may not be vector oriented. The format accomplishes this by storing true vector information along with a set of instructions for converting that information into a bitmap, in case the file is opened in a nonvector viewer or editor. Despite being one of the most popular cross-application vector formats available, WMF files are limited in one major area: They store a maximum of 16 bits of color data (a maximum of 65,536 colors).

Enhanced Metafile

The Enhanced Metafile format was created by Microsoft as a 32-bit successor to the WMF format. It has full support for the newest Windows drawing commands, plus full support for 32-bit color (about 4.3 billion colors). As you may suspect, it also has one problem: The Enhanced Metafile format doesn't work with 16-bit windows applications. Clip-art vendors have often avoided the EMF format because it would be unusable by customers using 16-bit windows (Windows 3.11 or earlier) and/or 16-bit graphics programs. As Windows and 16-bit graphics applications have become more and more scarce, however, EMF has begun to replace WMF as the standard Windows vector format.

Macintosh PICT

The Macintosh PICT format is similar to the EMF format, but it was designed by Apple for use on Macintosh operating systems. PICT files may contain vector, bitmap, and text data. The text in a PICT file imports as editable text, with a substitute if the original font isn't available.

Computer Graphics Metafile

The Computer Graphics Metafile (CGM) file type also supports vector and bitmap images, but is generally used for either one or the other (usually vector). The CGM format is commonly used by desktop publishing applications. Note that when importing CGM files, many bitmaps, PostScript, and texture fills aren't supported. PostScript textures are converted to solid gray fills.

Strictly Vector Filters

Most vector filters offer some compatibility with bitmaps because bitmapping is still the best way to do certain things (such as photo editing). One exception to this rule is supported in CorelDRAW 10, HPGL Plotter Files.

HPGL Plotter Files

Hewlett-Packard Graphics Language (HPGL) plotter files, which use the PLT extension, are used in CAD programs for printing drawings on plotters. This format doesn't use color data in the traditional sense but, instead, uses a set of 256 pen numbers, each of which is assigned a color during the import process. If you're not pleased with the default color assignments, you may change them to custom RGB colors.

The file format can be used for both import and export; but because it's transferring data between two different types of programs, only limited options are supported. Text, outlines, and some fills are imported, and the text is editable, but the font is replaced with a default font on import. On export, only outlines are supported.

Text Filters

CorelDRAW 10 ships with extensive support for word processing, including spelling, grammar, and thesaurus libraries. When the need to import or export text arises, the product-specific filters—such as the Microsoft Word and Corel WordPerfect filters—are usually the first choice. However, because every software package that uses text cannot possibly be supported, CorelDRAW provides two generic text filters, which can share text with any program.

Rich Text Format

Rich Text Format (RTF), which uses the RTF file extension, is supported across all versions of Windows and most Macintosh platforms. The format includes support for basic formatting needs, such as bold, italicized, and underlined text; left, center, and right paragraph alignment; font and font size selection; and 16 text foreground colors. Rich Text Format is used as the default format for the Windows Wordpad text editor (referred to as the Write text editor in early versions of Windows).

ANSI Text

ANSI is a text standard created by the American National Standards Institute. This standard defines text characters, such as uppercase and lowercase letters, numbers, and punctuation marks. ANSI text is text in its simplest form, with support only for identifying actual text characters, and no support for formatting. The format is best used on text that contains no formatting or when no filter is available for the text formatting being used. In this standard, formatting is lost on import or export, but the actual text characters remain intact.

Bitmap Filters

Bitmap filters convert all vector, text, and bitmaps in an image into a single bitmap. The disadvantage to using these pure bitmap formats is some editing capability is lost. For example, you can no longer edit a fill or zoom in on an object quite as easily as you can when you use a vector format. Text also loses its text characteristics and becomes just another part of the stream of pixels in the bitmap.

Of course, bitmap images also have clear advantages. They can contain detail that isn't seen in any other format because every pixel is accounted for and defined with its own color value. The capability to handle detail, along with the capability to handle high color depths (some bitmap formats support as many as 218 trillion colors), make bitmaps ideal for certain types of imaging, such as photography. Bitmaps have also traditionally been the only format supported on the Web (GIF and JPG are both bitmap formats). This is changing, though, particularly with the increasing popularity of the Flash file format, for more see Chapter 27.

JPEG

Along with the GIF format, Joint Photographic Experts Group (JPEG) files are one of the standard file formats used on the Web. JPEG compresses far better than other bitmap formats, but it does so at a price: The JPEG format cannot save a perfect reproduction of your image, even when using the highest quality settings. For this reason, saving a copy of your image in CorelDRAW's default CDR format is particularly important, so you may reexport the image with different compression settings, should the need arise. After converting your image to a bitmap, the JPEG Export dialog opens with several options (see Figure 26-7).

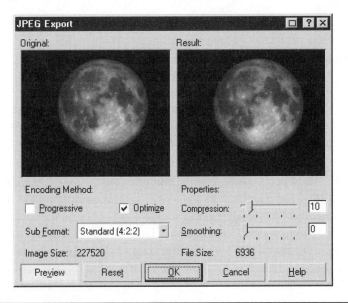

FIGURE 26-7   The JPEG Export dialog offers several options for encoding, compression, and smoothing.

Encoding Method   Three JPEG encoding methods are available: Standard, Optimized, and Progressive. Leaving both encoding boxes unchecked forces the image to be saved with the standard method. Checking the Optimized box enables optimized encoding, which can often shave a few percentage points off your image's final file size. Checking the Progressive box enables Progressive encoding and can also shave a few points off file size and causes your file to come into focus gradually as it's being opened.

No disadvantages exist to using the Optimized encoding method because it's supported equally as well as the standard method and because it doesn't affect image quality in any way. The Progressive method is more widely supported than ever and it also doesn't affect image quality, but some issues should still be considered when you use this method. Older Web browsers, such as Netscape Navigator 2.0 and Microsoft Internet Explorer 2.0, cannot display progressive JPEG images. Internet Explorer 3.*x* and 4.*x* can display Progressive JPEGs, but they don't implement the gradual opening effect. Also, some older e-mail programs cannot display progressive JPEGs received in e-mail, and some older HTML editors cannot display previews of Progressive JPEGS (although the images still display normally when viewed in a Web browser that supports the Progressive format). Considering all the variables, Optimized encoding is often the best selection.

Subformat   Two subformats are available: Standard 4:2:2 and Optional 4:4:4. The standard format results in a slightly smaller file size than the Optional format, so it's usually your best choice.

When exporting an image that contains text, try using the Optional 4:4:4 subformat. Although Standard 4:2:2 compresses files better, it can cause blurring and other artifacts to occur along the sharp edges of text.

Compression   The Compression control enables you to apply a compression setting of 0 to 100. The 0 setting results in the highest quality and the largest file size, while the 100 setting results in the smallest file size and the lowest quality image. The ideal compression setting varies from image to image. However, settings below 10 dramatically increase file size, so they should be used with considerable caution. The ideal Compression setting will usually fall between 10 and 30. Settings above 40 will often result in too much loss of quality.

Smoothing   Smoothing is similar to applying a blur filter to an image. A setting of 0 applies no smoothing, while a setting of 100 applies the maximum smoothing effect. Smoothing a JPG can help reduce file size because a smooth flow of color compresses better than a noisy image, but you may find the benefits of smoothing seldom outweigh the loss of image sharpness.

The terms "JPEG" and "JPG" are identical in meaning and may be used interchangeably.

CompuServe GIF

The Graphics Interchange Format (GIF) was invented by CompuServe in 1987 to provide members with a compact file format for use on the Internet. GIF has several advantages over JPEG when exporting lower color images, because it compresses up to 256 colors with absolutely no loss of quality. When images contain over 256 colors, the compression formula replaces the additional colors with one of the 256 colors defined in the image's palette. GIF also has limited support for transparent background (it supports a single transparent color) and support for animation. After converting your image to a bitmap, the Convert to Paletted dialog opens, with the following options (see Figure 26-8).

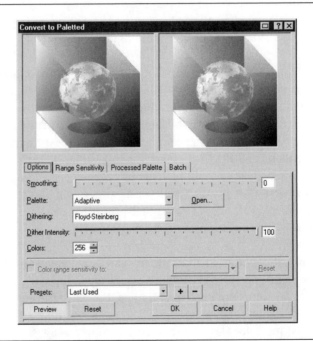

FIGURE 26-8   The Convert to Paletted dialog converts RGB and CMYK images to Paletted images.

Smoothing   This setting works as a blur filter, with options from 0 (no smoothing) to 100 (maximum smoothing). As with JPEGs, no smoothing will probably be your most frequently used selection. Smoothing is only available with the optimized and adaptive palettes because the remaining palettes don't contain enough color variables to apply the smoothing effect.

Palette   The selection of a palette type continues to be one of the more hotly debated topics of Web design. Some designers insist you must always use a Web Safe palette, meaning the Internet Explorer or Netscape Palette. The advantage to using these palettes is that you always know what an image is going to look like, even when seen by a user with a 256-color display, because the colors are chosen from a predefined palette.

   The other school of thought on palette selection says that Web Safe palettes have outlived their usefulness. When using the Optimized or Adaptive palettes, the 256 colors the GIF contains are automatically selected by the Export filter based on the colors in the image, instead of being based on a predefined palette. As a result, the GIF can contain any 256 colors chosen from the 16-million color RGB color model. Obviously, Optimized and Adaptive palettes offer much better color reproduction than the Web Safe palettes. With only 2 to 3 percent of Web surfers still using 256 color displays at press time (November 2000), the need for Web Safe palettes in Web design is certainly highly questionable.

Dithering   As it does when used in the Convert to Bitmap dialog, dithering simulates the existence of additional palette colors by placing two base colors in nearby pixels. For example, the color orange can be simulated by placing red in even-numbered pixels and yellow in odd-numbered pixels. This odd-even pattern is referred to as Ordered dithering. The other options in the dithering drop-down list box (Jarvis, Stucki, and Floyd-Steinberg) apply dithering with more random patterns and can often create a more realistic effect than ordered dithering. Below the dithering drop-down list box is the dithering slider, which is used to set the intensity of the dithering effect. A setting of 1 uses the least intense dithering, and a setting of 100 provides the strongest dithering effect.

Colors   The amount of colors in a GIF image can be set anywhere between 2 and 256. Each color that's added to a GIF palette adds an additional 3 bytes to the file size. Thus, if all 256 colors are used in an image, the palette is 768 bytes, or just under 1K. Of course, other factors affect file size, such as dimensions of the image and smoothness of the color flow (as with JPEGs, noisy images don't compress as well as softer images). But with a 256-color palette adding so little to the file size

(768 bytes download in under one second even on a slow connection), using all 256 colors in your GIF images usually makes sense.

As with most rules of thumb, an exception exists to this rule: If you're creating an animated GIF in Corel R.A.V.E. or Corel PHOTO-PAINT, and you choose the Local Palettes option in the Animation Export dialog, you add a 768-byte palette to *each frame* in the animation file. This means a 20-frame animation contains an extra 15,360K just to handle color palettes! When creating animations, reducing color can become a useful means of reducing file size.

Color Range Sensitivity   When using the Optimized Palette, this option becomes available. It enables you to define a color CorelDRAW favors when creating an optimized palette. For example, if your image contains a large blue sky background with a small amount of black text, you may want CorelDRAW to emphasize the color blue when creating your Optimized palette. This tool enables you to tell CorelDRAW exactly what type of color fine-tuning you want applied to your palette.

| TIP | *Animated GIF files cannot be viewed from within CorelDRAW. When you import animated GIF files, link to the file externally during the import process and view the animation in your Web browser.* |

Portable Network Graphic

As previously mentioned, GIF was created in 1987. Animation was added to the format in 1989 and, since then, absolutely no enhancements have taken place because of legal concerns regarding the patented LZW compression scheme used in GIF. In addition to legal issues, technical issues have also had a negative impact on GIF. The format allows for only a single transparent color, not enough for creating traditional effects, such as delicate drop shadows that can be viewed against any background. And then, there's the 256-color limit. In 1987, this made sense; but, as time went on, and monitors and videos cards became more powerful and less expensive, designers began looking for a more powerful Internet-imaging format.

This is where Portable Network Graphic (PNG) enters the picture. PNG was created by a group of programming volunteers who set out to design a format that could be used as an alternative to GIF. The result is the PNG format, which support color depths of 8 bits (256 colors), 24 bits (16 million colors), and 48 bits (218 trillion colors). When compared to GIFs, 256-color PNGs usually compress about 10 percent smaller with no change in quality. PNG also includes full transparency support, with 256 levels of transparency available in both 8-bit and 24-bit mode, and 65,536 levels of transparency available in 48-bit mode. Perhaps most important, PNG is free of patent restrictions, the problem that originally held GIF back. PNG developers are now working on MNG, a format that will allow for animated PNGs to be created in a fraction of the file space required for animated GIFs.

CorelDRAW 10 doesn't yet support 48-bit PNG images, mainly because the files would be too large for use on the Internet. As broadband technology becomes more commonplace, 48-bit images are expected to become more popular. When exporting 8-bit PNGs, you can choose from a set of palette options that resemble GIF's palette options (see Figure 26-5). There's no need to select a palette when exporting to the 24-bit PNG format, since this format supports all 16 million colors found in the 24-bit RGB color mode.

Both Netscape and Internet Explorer have implemented buggy versions of PNG transparency. When using PNGs with transparency, always test the images in at least *one version of each browser.*

Windows Bitmap

Windows Bitmap is the standard graphics format of the Windows operating system. In fact, whenever you look at a vector image in CorelDRAW, what you're actually seeing is the CorelDRAW vector image rendered to a bitmap for display on your monitor screen. Although the image still exists in vector form in CorelDRAW, a copy of it must be converted to a bitmap for display purposes.

Windows bitmap files are usually 24-bit (16-million colors), although the format also handles lower color depths, including 8-bit (256 colors), 4-bit (16 colors), and 1-bit (black and white).

Tagged Image File Format

Tagged Image File Format (TIF or TIFF), is one of the most widely used bitmap formats in the graphics industry. TIFF is supported by virtually every graphics program on the market, and may even be used as a reliable method of transferring files between Windows and Macintosh computers. TIFF is also frequently used as the default format for hardware devices such as scanners and digital cameras.

TIFF import supports every color depth commonly in use, including 1-bit (black and white), 4-bit (16 colors), 8-bit (256 shades of gray and 256 colors), 16-bit grayscale (65,536 shades of gray), 24-bit RGB and 24-bit LAB (both 16 million colors), 32-bit CMYK (4.3 billion colors), and 48-bit RGB (218 trillion colors). TIFF export also supports all the previous formats, although the 16-bit Grayscale and 48-bit RGB are only supported via export from Corel PHOTO-PAINT because no practical use exists for these color depths in vector imaging. High color depths such as these are used in Photo Editing for the purpose of creating

Gray, Red, Green, or Blue color channels, each capable of displaying 65,536 different shades of their respective color.

TIFF also supports compression, via six different compression methods (see the following illustration). Although you may experiment with different compression options to see which you find most efficient, LZW is generally considered the best for use when moving TIFF files between different programs or operating systems. In addition to high color depths, TIFF also handles large image sizes with support for images of up to 4.3 billion by 4.3 billion pixels.

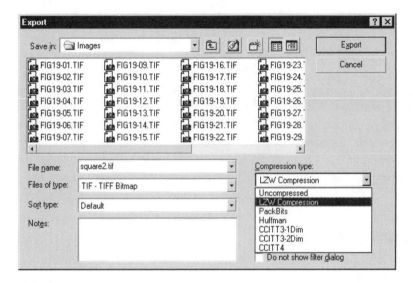

26

Targa Bitmap

The Targa format is similar to the TIFF format because it's generally useful across different programs and different operating systems. Targa, which uses the file extension TGA, imports and exports color depths of 8-bit (256 shades of gray and 256 colors) and 24-bit (16 million colors).

Scitex CT Bitmap

Most bitmap file formats support either RGB or a combination of RGB and CMYK color modes. *Scitex* bitmaps are unusual because they exclusively use either 256 shades of gray or 32-bit (4.3 billion color) CMYK mode. The format was invented by Scitex for use with its high-end color scanners. CorelDRAW supports import and export of Scitex images in both the 8-bit grayscale and 32-bit CMYK color depths.

OS/2 Bitmap

Over the years, Microsoft and IBM haven't agreed on much, and the correct way to store bitmaps is no exception. Microsoft stores Windows bitmaps with data starting at the top of the image and ending at the bottom of the image. IBM stores OS/2 bitmaps in the opposite order, with the bottom of the bitmap contained at the beginning of the file, and the top of the bitmap contained at the end of the file.

IBM's OS/2 operating system has mainly found itself being used as a server platform and has seldom been used for graphics, particularly because Microsoft moved Windows from a 16-bit platform to a 32-bit platform with the release of Windows 95. If you need to work with OS/2 images, however, the OS/2 bitmap is likely to be the ideal file format.

CALS Compressed Bitmap

CALS images support only the 1-bit (black and white) color depth. An advantage exists over other formats, however, because CALS images have no limit to the width and height they can support. CALS is used primarily in industrial fields such as CAD design. The format supports compression during both import and export.

Specialized Files

Desktop Color Separations don't fall into any of the previous categories: They're unique low-resolution files used as placeholders for high-resolution files. This is done as a way of saving resources because bitmap files, particularly those with high color depths and large dimensions, can require an enormous amount of resources.

Desktop Color Separations

Before sending your files to a service bureau, you should confirm whether they resolve DCS links to the original image or whether you should do this beforehand. To resolve DCS links yourself, click File | Print, and then click the PostScript tab. Check the box labeled Maintain OPI Links. If your service bureau handles resolving the DCS links, click File | Print, click the PostScript tab, and then uncheck Resolve DCS Links.

CHAPTER 27

CorelDRAW 10's Web Resources: Introducing Corel R.A.V.E.

Corel has a long-standing custom of enhancing new versions of CorelDRAW with the tools needed to create images for every type of popular media, and CorelDRAW 10 certainly upholds this tradition. Corel has updated its graphics suite with a wide variety of powerful tools for creating still and animated Web graphics, and even complete Web pages.

Perhaps the most significant of the changes in CorelDRAW 10 is the introduction of Corel *R.A.V.E.* (*Real Animated Vector Effects*), a robust new tool for creating and exporting animation files, including Macromedia Flash movies. Using Corel R.A.V.E., you can design your Flash movies from within the comfortable and powerful CorelDRAW interface. In this chapter, you learn more about Corel R.A.V.E. and the other Web features of CorelDRAW 10.

Using the Web Connector Docker

CorelDRAW 10 introduces a new docker window, called the Web Connector Docker, which acts as a miniature Web browser built right into CorelDRAW. You may use the Web Connector Docker to access free CorelDRAW add-ons, learning resources, services (such as free Web space and instant messaging), and Corel Technical Support. To open Web Connector Docker, click Window | Dockers | Web Connector Docker. The docker is available from within both CorelDRAW and Corel R.A.V.E and is also accessible from the Corel Online button on the Standard Toolbar.

Anatomy of the Web Connector Docker

The Web Connector Docker is designed to work in the same way Web browsers work. A series of buttons on the top of the docker are used for controlling the docker window (see Figure 27-1).

The two arrow icons on the left of the docker provide backward and forward navigation. The large *X* icon is used to stop the current page from downloading, and the circular arrow icon is used to refresh the current page. The home icon takes you to the Web Connector home page, the bookmark icon is used for adding and accessing favorites, and the printer icon is used for printing the current page.

FIGURE 27-1   The Corel Web Connector Docker

Browsing the Web

You may browse the Web from the docker in the same way you would from a typical Web browser. Your options include typing an address in the drop-down list box and beginning at the Web Connector Docker homepage. You may also visit previously viewed Web pages by clicking the Favorites button (the fifth button from the left) and by navigating with the Back and Forward arrow buttons. You may drag the left side of the docker to the far left of the CorelDRAW workspace to create a larger viewing area.

Creating Web Objects in CorelDRAW 10 and Corel R.A.V.E.

In addition to navigation, CorelDRAW 10 provides the tools needed for creating Web Objects, such as Rollover buttons, hyperlinks, and image maps. Interactivity can be added to objects such as Rollover buttons without having to write any

27

JavaScript code. Web Objects are created in the same way any other object is created in CorelDRAW. What sets Web Objects apart from other objects is the additional Web features added via the Internet Toolbar and saved via the Publish To The Web dialog. To begin creating a Web Object, first click the object you want to edit, right-click any Toolbar, and then click Internet. This opens the Internet Toolbar, shown next:

Although the process of creating Web Objects is described here as being performed from within CorelDRAW, Corel R.A.V.E. may also be used. Both programs share a common interface and common strengths. When you create Web buttons in CorelDRAW, the Publish To The Web feature exports your buttons as GIF or JPEG images and creates and exports Java script to control the your button's interactivity. When you create a Web button in Corel R.A.V.E., the Publish To The Web feature exports both your buttons and the Flash code that controls their interactivity as a single Flash file.

Creating Rollover Buttons

CorelDRAW and Corel R.A.V.E.'s Rollover buttons may be made from rectangles, ellipses, arrows, text, or any other object you want to use for navigation on your Web page. Making any of these objects into a Rollover button empowers you to have CorelDRAW or Corel R.A.V.E. create code that enables the button to respond to user events (such as running the mouse cursor over the button or clicking the button).

To create a Rollover button, create your object, access the Internet Toolbar, and follow these steps:

1. Click the first icon on the far left of the Internet Toolbar to convert your object into a Rollover button.

2. Click the second icon to begin editing the Rollover button.

3. Click the drop-down list box to access the various button states. You may also use the tabs at the bottom of the screen to move from state to state. CorelDRAW and Corel R.A.V.E. use three states:

> **Normal**   The button as it appears when the Web page opens and when the user isn't hovering over or clicking the button.

> **Over**   Changes that occur in the look of the button when the user's cursor hovers over the button.

> **Down**   The button as it appears when the user clicks the button.

4. When you access a button state (such as Over), make any changes to the button's appearance you want to occur when your Web page viewer is in the selected state.

5. When you finish designing the Rollover button's appearance for each state, click the fourth Toolbar icon to lock your changes into place.

To test the Rollover button, click the fifth Toolbar icon. This causes CorelDRAW and Corel R.A.V.E. to behave in the same way a Web browser behaves, enabling you to see how the button reacts in various states.

When you design objects for a Web page, consider using the default RGB palette instead of the default CMYK palette. The default CMYK palette uses the CMYK color model, which is intended for print documents. The default RGB palette uses the RGB color model, which is the same color model used by the computer monitors that display your Web page. For more information on color models, please see CD-ROM 6.

Editing a Rollover Button

Once you create a Rollover button, you can make changes to it at any time by selecting and clicking the second icon on the Internet Toolbar. When creating various button states, it's better to change color than to change the size or position. An image's size and position are locked into place by Web browsers when the

Web page is initially loaded. Making changes in size or position can produce unpredictable results.

Extracting Rollover Button Contents

Clicking the third icon on the Internet Toolbar extracts the button's Web contents. This means each of the button's various states are removed, and the object returns to being a traditional object. The various states you created aren't deleted from memory; however, they're simply hidden as layers underneath the button. This enables you to reuse them if needed.

Duplicating States

The Duplicate States icon appears just to the right of the Active Rollover State drop-down list box. The button is used to create two or more identical states quickly. For example, you may want your Rollover button to appear the same way in the Over state (when your user is no longer hovering over the button) as it did in its original Normal state. Duplicate state is usable *only* in Normal mode (not when editing) *and* only if the next state is empty/deleted. For example, delete the Over state; then with Normal selected, Duplicate states will be available.

> **TIP** *In addition to setting Rollover button options from the Internet Toolbar, you may set them from the Object Properties Docker—choose Window | Dockers | Properties. Internet properties are set by clicking the spider web icon in the docker window.*

Using the Rollover Buttons Properties Page

The Object Properties Docker has an Internet Properties Page that may be used to specify Rollover button options, as shown next. The Web icon selects the Internet Properties Page. In the Behavior drop-down menu, set an URL, Sound, or Bookmark to activate during the Rollover. In the URL drop-down, type the actual URL or the location of the Sound or Bookmark file. You may select an optional Target frame and type an optional ALT comment. The Define Hotspot Using drop-down enables you to choose an object's shape or its bounding box to act as an image map hotspot. You may select a cross-hatch and background color to identify an object as a hotspot in CorelDRAW. Click the Apply or Lock button to update your Internet Properties.

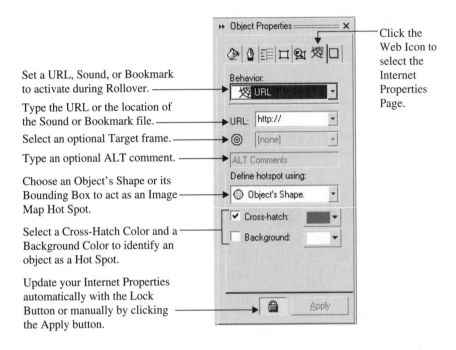

Set a URL, Sound, or Bookmark to activate during Rollover.

Type the URL or the location of the Sound or Bookmark file.

Select an optional Target frame.

Type an optional ALT comment.

Choose an Object's Shape or its Bounding Box to act as an Image Map Hot Spot.

Select a Cross-Hatch Color and a Background Color to identify an object as a Hot Spot.

Update your Internet Properties automatically with the Lock Button or manually by clicking the Apply button.

Click the Web Icon to select the Internet Properties Page.

27

Specifying a URL

Once you finish editing the various states for your Rollover button, you may add hyperlinks to respond to the states. For example, you may want your users to move to another Web page while in the Down state (when the user clicks the button).

As you may already know, each Web page is defined with a URL (Universal Resource Locator). For example, Corel's URL is **http://www.corel.com**. To link a URL to a button state, click the state (such as Down), make sure URL is selected in the behavior drop-down list box, and type the URL in the Internet Address drop-down list box.

All Internet addresses must be preceded with the correct Internet protocol (such as http://) or the link won't open correctly. For example, if you're linking to **www.corel.com,** be sure to use **http://www.corel.com** as the URL. To link to an e-mail address, use the mailto: protocol, such as *mailto:someone@domain-name.com*.

Specifying a Target Frame

If your Web page is going to make use of frames, you may specify the target frame in which you want the URL to open. Several options are available:

None   Use the (none) option when you aren't using frames.

Self   The _self option opens the new URL in the same frame in which the Rollover button is located.

Top   The _top option opens the new URL on top of all currently loaded frames, so all frames are replaced with a single frame containing the new document.

Blank   The _blank option opens a new Web browser containing the new document.

Parent   The _parent option opens the new document in the current frame's Parent frameset. You may also enter custom frame names by typing them in the target frame combo box.

Labeling ALT Text Comments

You may click the ALT Comments button to add ALT text to your Rollover button. ALT text is a text description of the button that's visible until the button downloads and opens on the Web page. Although ALT text isn't required, using ALT text is a good idea for at least two reasons:

1. Some users with extremely slow connections use text-only browsers (which don't display images). Thus, your image won't ever be seen by these users. ALT text provides a viewable replacement that enables text-only Web surfers to navigate your page.

2. Web surfers with visual impairments often take advantage of text-to-speech programs that "read" Web pages in a simulated voice. Providing ALT text can assist these users in navigating your Web page because the ALT text will be read by the text-to-speech program.

> **TIP**   *Windows users with health issues that interfere with their computer use can find a wealth of resources at **http://www.microsoft.com/enable**.*

Setting Bookmark Labels

Assigning a bookmark label to text or to an image within your Web page means the text or image can be directly accessed by a URL. For example, if you have an important graphic near the bottom of a long Web page, you may want users to be able to jump directly to the graphic from the top of the page or from other pages, without having to scroll through the entire page to reach the graphic. When text or images are assigned a bookmark label, they can be accessed in this way.

To set a bookmark label, click the behavior drop-down list box and select bookmark. Then enter a name for the bookmark in the Bookmark text box. To keep things organized, it's usually best to enter a descriptive name (such as pie_chart or bottom_of_page), but this isn't a requirement. Once you create a bookmark, the bookmark's complete URL (both the page name and the bookmark's name) are available from the URL drop-down list box. You may then access the bookmark just as you would access any other URL.

Bookmarks take the form of the Web page's filename, followed by a pound sign, and then followed by the bookmark name. For example, a Web page named index.html with a bookmark named picture will appear as index.html#picture.

Defining Hotspot Shape

Hotspots are used to identify where bookmarks are placed within your Web page and to create image maps. When using an image map, a single image may link to multiple URLs, by clicking different areas of the image map. Each area of the image map that links to a URL is called a hotspot.

Object Shape   You may use an object's exact shape as a hot spot (even if the shape is irregular, as would likely be the case with a Bézier curve).

Bounding Box of Object   You may also use an object's bounding box as a hot spot. The *bounding box* is a box that invisibly surrounds every object and defines the object's outermost dimensions.

Adding Sound to Button States

When using Corel R.A.V.E. to create a Flash button, in addition to changing the appearance of your image for each button state, you can also add sound effects. To specify a sound for a button state, select Sound in the behavior drop-down list box and type the URL for the sound in the Add Behavior text box. You can add a different sound for the Over and Down button states. First, select the desired state, then select sound in the behaviors drop-down list box, and then enter the sound's URL in the add behavior box.

> *The CorelDRAW 10 content CD contains uncompressed WAV files that you can use for sound effects. You may even include MP3 sound in your Flash file, since the Flash plug-in is capable of decoding and playing MP3 files. Of course, you should always be careful not to add unnecessarily large sound files, since this will increase file size and significantly add to the time it takes to download your Web page.*

Enabling Rollover Buttons

As previously mentioned, you can test your Rollover buttons after clicking the Live Preview button in the Internet Toolbar or Object Properties Docker. You can also test your Rollover buttons by clicking the View menu and then clicking Enable Rollover. Note that this is used exclusively for previewing the Rollover effect. To preview sounds and test URLs, you must preview your file in a Web browser. You can do this when exporting your file by clicking the Preview button near the bottom left corner of the Flash Export dialog box.

> *Your Rollover buttons cannot be edited while the Enable Rollover option is enabled. To edit any button, first disable this option. You can enable it again when you finish editing the button.*

Internet Objects

CorelDRAW 10 contains a set of tools called Internet Objects that fall into the somewhat broader category of being types of Web Objects. Internet Objects are Web Objects such as text boxes and list boxes that are used when creating Web page forms.

CorelDRAW 10 enables you to add these Internet Object to your page with ease. To access Internet Objects, click Edit | Insert Internet Object. You may change the properties of any Internet Object in the Property Bar or by right clicking the object and clicking properties.

Inserting a *Java Applet* or an *Embedded File Internet Object* requires that you have the applet or file available to upload to your server. All other Internet Objects require *scripting*, a type of programming, in order to transfer data from your Web page to your Web server. You should contact your Web page host to learn more about the scripts that they allow to operate on their server. You Web host may also be able to assist you in locating free scripts for use in your Web pages. Once you locate an acceptable script for use with your objects, you may enter its Internet location via the Object Properties dialog.

Creating Animated Graphics

Corel has added a powerful new vector animation tool to the CorelDRAW 10 suite with the addition of Corel R.A.V.E. (Real Animated Vector Effects). With Corel R.A.V.E., you can create vector animation by using the familiar CorelDRAW tools and interface.

Converting your images into bitmaps so you can animate them is no longer necessary. Corel R.A.V.E. can export your vector animations using the extremely popular Macromedia Flash vector animation format, which is currently supported by over 90 percent of the world's Web browsers.

In addition to all the previous, Corel responded to user requests for a more productive method of creating bitmap animations by adding GIF, AVI, and QuickTime MOV export features to Corel R.A.V.E. Using Corel R.A.V.E., you can create GIF animations, QuickTime movies, and AVI videos in much less time than was previously possible.

Launching Corel R.A.V.E.

You can launch Corel R.A.V.E. from with CorelDRAW by clicking the application launcher icon. You can also launch Corel R.A.V.E. from the Corel folder located in your Programs menu (click Start | Programs | CorelDRAW 10 | Corel R.A.V.E.).

How Corel R.A.V.E. Differs from CorelDRAW

If you're familiar with the CorelDRAW interface, you should find the Corel R.A.V.E. interface to be quite familiar, see Figure 27-2. This is intentional, because even the most experienced CorelDRAW users are new to Corel R.A.V.E. By using the same basic interface and tools in Corel DRAW and Corel R.A.V.E., users can shorten the learning curve and pick up on using the powerful new features in Corel R.A.V.E. almost immediately.

The main difference you should notice between the two programs is the use of a timeline in Corel R.A.V.E. The purpose of the timeline is to enable you to specify when changes occur in an animation. You may already be familiar with the timeline concept if you use HTML editors, such as Dreamweaver or FrontPage, or if you've

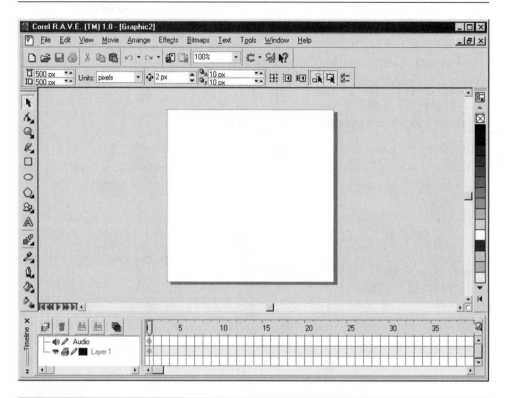

FIGURE 27-2   The Corel R.A.V.E. user interface

worked with Video editing. Fortunately, even if you've never worked with timelines before, the concepts involved are straightforward.

Viewing the Timeline

By default, the timeline opens when you start Corel R.A.V.E. You can collapse the timeline similar to the way you collapse a docker, by clicking the two small arrows at the lower-left corner of the timeline. You can expand the timeline by clicking the two small arrows again or clicking the timeline tab. The arrows point down when the timeline is expanded, and they point up when the timeline is collapsed.

When the timeline is expanded, you may close it by clicking the X in the upper-left corner of the timeline. When the timeline is collapsed, you can close it by right-clicking the timeline tab and then clicking close. To reopen the timeline, click Movie | Timeline.

You can also undock the timeline from the bottom of the screen by clicking the gray area between the timeline's icons (near the top-left side of the timeline), dragging the timeline, and dropping it in another area of the workspace. Once the timeline is undocked, you can collapse it into a CorelDRAW 8 styled rollup by clicking the arrow near the upper-right corner of the timeline.

When using 800 × 600 (or lower) display resolution, you might find some of the toolbox's tools are hidden by the timeline when the timeline is expanded. If this happens, you can drag the toolbox and dock it to the top or bottom of the display, or you can drop it anywhere in the workspace where it won't be in your way. When you do this, the toolbox changes its shape from vertical to horizontal, allowing plenty of room to display all the tools.

Anatomy of the Timeline

At the upper-left corner of the timeline, you see a set of five icons. The first of the five icons is used to add new layers to your animation. The second of the icons is used to delete layers from your document. Layers can be made visible or invisible, just as in CorelDRAW. The third icon is used to add keyframes to your animation, and the fourth icon is used to remove keyframes. The fifth icon is used to turn on Onion Skin mode.

In Onion Skin mode, you can view multiple frames of animation at the same time. This can be useful, for example, when aligning the placement of an object over time. When creating movement, it can be helpful to see exactly where an object will be located a few frames before and after it reaches the current frame. Creating an object that smoothly moves from one frame to the next is essential in avoiding the jittering or jumping movement that is sometimes inadvertently added to an animation.

Underneath the icons, you can find the same Object Manager Docker you may be accustomed to using in CorelDRAW. This is one of the features in Corel R.A.V.E. that Corel DRAW users will appreciate: the similarity of the CorelDRAW and Corel R.A.V.E. interfaces.

To the right of the icons, at the top of timeline, you see the frame indicator. Underneath the frame indicator is the timeline for each object and layer in your movie. This is where you set the keyframes that control the appearance of the objects, layers, and effects.

Keyframes are the essential component of vector animation. In a bitmap animation (such as a GIF animation), you must design a unique image for each frame of the animation. In vector animation, you only need to design the first and last keyframes. Corel R.A.V.E. designs the in between frames. This process, called *tweening,* can make vector animation a major timesaver compared to the bitmap animation process.

As an example of the tweening process, picture a simple ten-frame animation in which a square transforms itself into a circle. If you where designing a GIF animation, you would have to create the square, create the circle, and create the eight steps in between, in which the shape slowly changes from a square to a circle. Using tweening, this is a much faster process. All that's necessary is to create the square in frame one and set this as a keyframe, change the frame to a circle in frame ten and set that as a keyframe, and then you're done. Corel R.A.V.E. creates the eight frames in between the keyframes. Of course, you can add additional objects and additional keyframes to create more complex animations.

Navigating the Timeline

Navigating the timeline is an uncomplicated process. To move to objects, layers, or effects that are above or below what is currently displayed in the Object Manager, use the scrollbar located on the right side of the timeline. To move back and forth to frames that exist earlier or later in the animation, use the scrollbar located at the bottom of the timeline.

The magnifying glass icon at the right of the frame indicator is used to display more or less frames in the same amount of space by squeezing the frames closer together or by spreading them further apart. This doesn't affect playback of your movie. It's simply used as a convenience to make a larger or smaller group of frames available for editing.

The top of the timeline can be dragged up or down to make more objects, layers, or effects available in the timeline workspace. You may also drag the vertical line in between the frames workspace and the Object Manager workspace to make more or less of either workspace visible.

Selecting Objects, Layers, and Effects in the Timeline

Items in the timeline are selected by clicking them in the Object Manager portion of the timeline. You can also select items by clicking their corresponding row in the frames display portion of the workspace. Each object, layer, or effect in the Object Manager corresponds with the row directly to its right in the frame display.

Setting Frame Rate

Frame rate is set in frames per second and it controls how slowly or quickly your animation is played. You can set frame rate by clicking Movie | Movie Setup. You can also change frame rate while setting other options from within the Tools | Options dialog. On the left side of the dialog, click Document | Movie Setup. A higher frame rate results in a shorter movie, while a lower frame rate results in a longer movie. The default frame rate is 12 frames per second.

Setting Sequence Duration

The duration of your movie is determined by its number of frames and the frame rate. Although a movie with many frames may appear longer than a movie with only a few frames, this isn't always the case because the rate at which the frames are played is also a factor.

This concept is similar to GIF animation. Adding more frames doesn't necessarily makes a GIF animation longer because the speed at which the frames are displayed is also a factor in determining the length of the animation.

Movie Setup Options

The fundamental options for your animation are set by clicking Movie | Movie Setup. These options, see Figure 27-3, can also be set from within the Tools | Options dialog by clicking Document | Movie Setup. Default width, height, resolution, and frame rate are all set in this way. Width and height can also be adjusted by clicking the Object Picker Tool, and adjusting the width and height on the far left side of the Property Bar.

Resolution doesn't work the same way on monitors as it does in print. When working with print, moving from a lower resolution to a higher resolution creates a more detailed image because the dots of ink can essentially be squeezed closer together. This effect doesn't occur in monitors because monitors can't squeeze dots closer together. Thus, the amount of pixels your monitor can display in an inch of space cannot be changed. The only effect of changing the resolution of

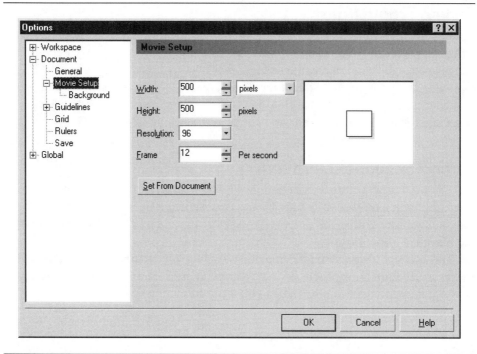

FIGURE 27-3 The Movie Setup options determine the basic characteristics of your animation, such as width and height.

your animation is to change its dimensions, because monitors display the additional dots by increasing your image's dimensions.

For the sake of having a constant frame of reference, it's generally best to keep resolution set to 72 dpi, since this is the resolution used by Flash. By keeping your dpi set to 72, you can make changes to your movie's width and height, knowing that these factors will be represented accurately by the Flash browser plug-in.

Creating Animated Sequences Automatically

Corel R.A.V.E. enables you to creates animation sequences quickly from Blends and Groups. These sequences can then be used on their own or as part of a larger, more complex animation.

From Blends

To create an animated sequence from a blend, first create a blend with the Interactive Blend Tool or the Blend Docker (see Chapter 15). Next, select the blend and click Movie | Create Sequence From Blend.

Create Sequence from Blends can be used as an efficient method of creating scrolling text messages. To do this, create two identical artistic text objects. Position one object where you want the scroll to start and the other where you want the scroll to end. Blend the two text objects using the Interactive Blend Tool or the Blend Docker (click Window | Dockers | Blends to access the Blends Docker).

Next, click Movie | Create Sequence From Blends. The text scroll is instantly created and may be incorporated into more complex animations or exported as is to create a Flash animation. To add color changes to the scroll, fill the two artistic text objects with different colors.

From Groups

To create an animated sequence from a group, first create and select two or more objects, right-click one and create a group (for more information on groups, see Chapter 13). Next, select the group and click Movie | Create Sequence from Groups.

Create Sequence from Groups can be used to create the effect of building an illustration by adding each individual object, one at a time, until the completed illustration is created. To create this effect, first create your illustration or use an illustration from the CorelDRAW 10 Clipart CD (CorelDRAW files can be opened in Corel R.A.V.E.). Then, click Movie | Create Sequence from Group (see Figure 27-4). In the resulting animation, each object in the group appears onscreen for a moment.

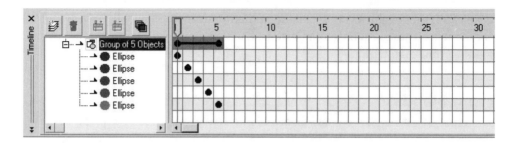

FIGURE 27-4   The Timeline immediately after creating a Sequence from a Group

Next, use the timeline to extend the amount of time each object is displayed, as shown in Figure 27-5. The result may then be incorporated into more complex animations, or exported as is, to create a Flash animation.

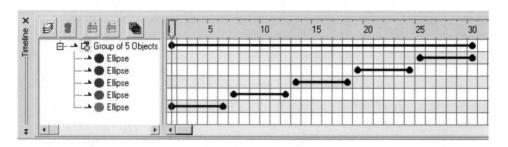

FIGURE 27-5   Extending the amount of time that each Object in the Group is displayed in the animation

Controlling Movie Playback

The onscreen playback of movies is controlled via the set of small blue buttons located on the left of the screen on top of the timeline. You may also control playback by clicking Movie | Control, as shown in the following illustration.

27

Saving an Animation Sequence

You should always save your animation using Corel R.A.V.E.'s CLK file format. In addition to the information normally saved in a CorelDRAW CDR file, the CLK format also saves timeline information. Just as you should always save exported bitmaps as CorelDRAW files—so they can be edited later—you should also always save exported animations as Corel R.A.V.E. files, in case you decide to edit the file in the future.

Once you finish creating your animation, you're ready to export it as a Flash file, QuickTime Movie, GIF animation, or AVI Video. To export the file, click File | Export and select the file type you want to use for exporting.

A powerful additional option exists for exporting Flash animations. Instead of using File | Export, click File and then Publish to the Web. In addition to exporting the Flash animation, this also enables you to export the HTML code for placing the file in a Web page.

You may have noticed the terms "animation," "movie," and "video" being used often and you may wonder what differences exist. There's really no difference between an animation and a movie. And, although the term "video" is usually used to describe real-life action (such as a video of a sporting event), it can also be used to describe computer-generated animation.

It's simply customary to refer to GIFs as animations, QuickTime files as movies, and AVI files as videos. Flash files are often referred to as any (or all) of the previous.

Controlling Web-Specific Properties

Corel R.A.V.E. enables complete control over your animation's Web-specific properties. Web properties are set via the Bookmark and Web Page Dockers. Of course, the information you provide in dockers can also be edited when creating your Web page, but the dockers provide a convenient method of adding this information beforehand. In addition, if you're unfamiliar with HTML editing, you'll find the dockers particularly useful.

Using the Bookmark Manager Docker

The Bookmark Manager Docker is used to organize and make changes to the bookmarks in your Web page. To access the docker, click Window | Dockers | Internet Bookmark Manager. This docker isn't available in R.A.V.E.; it's available only in CorelDRAW.

Linking to a Bookmark

You can use the Bookmark Manager as a convenient method of hyperlinking text or an image to a bookmark. First, select the text or image you want to link. Next, select the bookmark by clicking it in the Bookmark Manager. Click the Link button (located in the lower-left corner of the docker) to create the link.

Changing Bookmarks

Bookmarks may be added or renamed via the Internet Toolbar or the Web page of the Object Properties Docker.

Controlling Web Page Properties

You may control the properties of your Web page via the Object Properties Docker: click Window | Dockers | Properties, see Figure 27-6. From the docker, you enter information such as the page's title and filename, and information used by search engines such as keywords and a description of your page.

FIGURE 27-6   The Object Properties Docker with the Web Page Properties tab selected

Giving Your Document Page a Title

This text box is used to add a title to your Web page. The title is seen in the upper-left corner of the Web page when viewed in Microsoft Internet Explorer or Netscape Navigator. If you're using frames, only the title of the main frames page is seen in Web browsers, although you may title other pages for your own reference. Note, the title of a Web page is merely a user-friendly description, it's not used to control any aspect of your Web page's display. Thus, the title needn't be the same as its filename or any other aspect of the page.

Giving Your Document Page an HTML (.HTM) Filename

As with any document, your Web page must have a filename, which is entered in the Name text box. The filename must end with an extension of HTM or HTML to be recognized by both your computer and other computers as a Web page. The difference between HTM and HTML is nothing more than personal preference. There's no difference in the way computers handle the two file extensions.

Entering Page Information

The Web Page Properties Tab on the Object Properties Docker provides a convenient location for entering page information.

Author

Use the Author label to identify yourself in your Web page's HTML code. You may also include information about yourself such as your e-mail address, but keep in mind that this information is only viewable to those looking for it in your HTML code and does not appear when your Web page is viewed in a Web browser.

Description

The description portion of a Web page is the summary seen by your viewers when they locate your page via a search engine. Entire Web sites and chapters of books have been devoted to writing good descriptions (or description metatags, as they're sometimes called).

One of the most important things to remember when writing your description is to keep it relatively brief (a two-sentence maximum is a good idea). Anyone who has used a search engine has seen descriptions that cut off in mid paragraph. The reason for this is that each search engine only allows a predetermined amount of space for description metatags. Once you go over the search engine's allotted space, the remainder of your description tag is simply ignored.

Keywords

*Keyword*s are the words used to match your page to words entered in a search engine. When a search engine goes through its database of Web pages, those pages containing keywords that match the words being searched for are displayed in the search results. If you were building a Web page about CorelDRAW, for example, you would want to include such terms as Corel, Draw, and CorelDRAW in your keywords. Including concept keywords such as illustrate, vector, art, and image would also be a good idea.

When designing a Web page for a local business, using the city, county, and state the business serves as keywords is also important. An old trick to baiting search engines to Web pages was to overload a Web page with repeated keywords (such as using the term illustrate three or four times). Although this was once an effective technique, it should now be avoided, because most search engines notice repetitive keywords and react either by placing the Web page at the bottom of the list of pages it finds or by not listing the Web page at all. One old trick (assuming such a thing as an old trick exists in the relatively new art of Web design) that still works is to misspell some keywords intentionally because misspelling is common when people use a search engine. For example, if you use the keywords "illustrate" and "ilustrate", good spellers and bad spellers can all find your Web page.

Using CorelDRAW's New Flash Filter

CorelDRAW 10's new Flash export filter is the driving force behind Corel R.A.V.E. since it gives CorelDRAW users the power to create Flash animations, without having to buy the Flash software and learn the somewhat awkward Flash interface.

CorelDRAW is a more powerful vector editor than Flash and contains productivity tools that simply aren't available in Flash. However, the power and productivity of CorelDRAW are fully available within Corel R.A.V.E. With the addition of the timeline and movie menu in Corel R.A.V.E., the CorelDRAW package has become a powerful tool for creating and exporting Flash animations.

27

Saving Your Document as a Web Page

Web design is often thought of as a medium that requires the designer to use multiple programs. This school of thought tells us, at the very least, there's the need to purchase and learn four programs: an HTML layout editor, a vector editor, a photo editor, and a Web editor (see Figure 27-7).

Corel has shed new light on this multiple program concept by making HTML layout, vector editing, bitmap photo-editing filters, and Web export all available from within CorelDRAW.

To create a Web page in CorelDRAW 10, begin by setting the dimensions of your page in the Object Picker's Property Bar or the Options dialog. The width is the only dimension that must be decided on ahead of time because your Web page can scroll to any length you want. The decision of which Web page width to use is of particular importance because, while Web viewers expect to have to scroll up and down to see an entire page, they don't also expect to have to scroll left and right to read your page. Unfortunately, left and right scrolling is exactly what you force on your users if you create a Web page that's too wide.

Currently, a width of 800 pixels is the standard because this can be viewed without left and right scrolling by about 85 percent of users. If you want to play it safe, a width of 640 pixels ensures that your page is viewable without left and right scrolling by about 95 percent of users. However, this does give you less room to work with in terms of page layout. Note that the page may appear smaller than its actual dimensions in CorelDRAW because it will be squeezed into CorelDRAW's available workspace. You may zoom in on your page for greater detail.

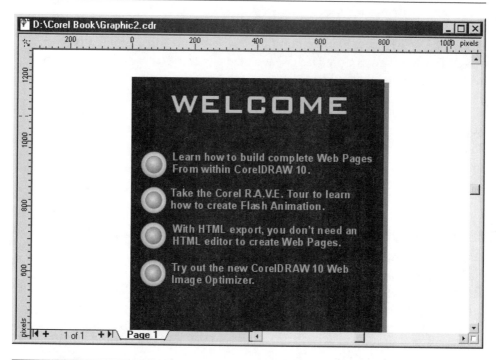

D:\Corel Book\Graphic2.cdr

WELCOME

Learn how to build complete Web Pages From within CorelDRAW 10.

Take the Corel R.A.V.E. Tour to learn how to create Flash Animation.

With HTML export, you don't need an HTML editor to create Web Pages.

Try out the new CorelDRAW 10 Web Image Optimizer.

FIGURE 27-7 The same page layout tools you're accustomed to using in CorelDRAW may now be used for creating Web pages.

Some professionals have been known to use outrageously wide pages, sometimes as wide as 1,600 pixels. Because these pages can only be viewed without left-to-right scrolling by under 5 percent of all users (probably including the Web designer and his or her 22" inch monitor), the use of these extremely wide dimensions seems, at best, self-serving. To keep your Web pages viewable for your entire audience—not just Web designers with huge, high-end monitors—consider using a width such as 640 or 800 pixels.

Once you set your page's dimensions, the task of creating the graphics and text is essentially the same as creating graphics and text for use in any other page layout task. The most important differences between traditional design and Web design to remember are image sizes and choice of font.

Images with unusually large dimensions generally don't compress as well as smaller images, so don't make images unnecessarily large. Fonts are an issue because most users can only view text using the fonts already on their machine. If the font you used isn't available, it will be substituted, often with unpredictable results. For this reason, consider using commonly installed fonts, such as Arial, Times New Roman, and Courier New. If you require a particular font for a specific task such as logo creation, use artistic text, so CorelDRAW will export the text as an image, instead of as traditional text.

Once you create your Web page and save a copy in CorelDRAW's CDR format, you can begin the process of exporting for use on the Web; see Figure 27-8.

The Publish To The Web Command

The *Publish to the Web* command is used to export your Web page. To access this command, click File | Publish to the Web | HTML. Note that if you're exporting an image instead of an entire page, you can click File | Publish to the Web | Web Image Optimizer (see Chapter 26 for more information on Internet image formats). You can also export your Web page with an embedded Flash animation by clicking File | Publish to the Web | Flash embedded in HTML.

Although there is a Flash export filter in Corel DRAW, Flash is best created and exported from Corel R.A.V.E. because Corel R.A.V.E. contains additional

27

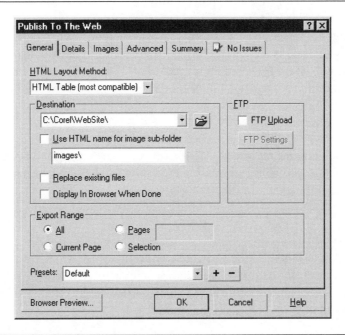

FIGURE 27-8   The Publish To The Web dialog enables you to export your entire document as a Web page.

tools for animation creation, such as the Movie menu and the Timeline Docker. Once created in R.A.V.E., you can click File | Publish to the Web | Flash embedded in HTML to export your Flash file with accompanying HTML code. To export only a Flash file (with no HTML) from Corel R.A.V.E., click File | Export, and select Flash as the File type.

When you click File | Publish to the Web | HTML in CorelDRAW, you're taken to the Publish To The Web dialog, see Figure 27-8. This dialog contains everything you need to save your Web page and images and can even be used to upload your page and images to your Web server.

General

The General tab, as its name suggests, is used to set general export options, such as the folder to which you want to save your Web site on your hard drive. Destination options control where your Web pages are to be saved on your hard drive. You may specify a separate subfolder for your graphics or remove the default subfolder name (images\) to have the graphics saved in the same folder as your HTML document. To give the graphics subfolder the same name as the HTML document, check Use HTML name for Image subfolder.

Regarding the selection of an HTML Layout method, the best choice for the vast majority of users is the default: HTML Table (most compatible) method. If you're using the export filter only to export the HTML code for an image map (rather than an entire Web page), you should select Single Image With Image Map.

Details Tab

The Details tab doesn't require any action on your part, other than reviewing it for accuracy. This tab provides information regarding exactly what you selected for export and what the exported file(s) will be named.

Images Tab

The Images tab is similar to the Details tab, except it deals strictly with images. This tab provides information on the images being exported and the file format to be used for exporting. If you want to change the default setting used to export images, click the Options button.

The Options dialog enables selection of an export format for GIFs, JPEGs, and PNGs. These Web file formats, and recommendation regarding how to best use them, can be found in Chapter 26. The Options dialog also contains antialiasing and image map options. You'll want to leave antialiasing checked, to help ensure that your images don't have rough, jagged edges. "Client" is the best choice for image maps, since Client image maps provide faster interaction with your user than that provided by server image maps.

Advanced Tab

The Advanced tab enables the selection of options for JavaScript, cascading style sheets, and font embedding. If you're using Rollover buttons (buttons that react to mouse states, such as mouse over and mouse down) be certain to check the JavaScript option.

Although it sounds appealing, *Font embedding* comes with both technical and legal risks. The technical risk is that many browsers still don't support font embedding, and many end users don't allow fonts to be downloaded even if their browsers do support it. The legal risk involves copyright ownership: you must be certain you have the legal right to distribute a font before you embed the font. Having a font legally exist on your machine doesn't always mean you have the right to distribute the font file. When in doubt, always check with a font's copyright holder before distributing the font.

TIP	*If you need to adjust your page's background options, you can do so from the Advanced tab by clicking the Options button and then Page Background.*

Summary Tab

This tab provides information on the total size of your Web page and how long it will take users to download your page at various modem speeds. The information is then itemized for each HTML page and image, so you can see if something in particular (such as a large image) might cause an unnecessarily long download time.

Issues Tab

The Issues tab tells you about any preflight issues that may have arisen in the export of your Web page (such as the use of a print color model instead of a Web color model) and, most important, offers suggestions for correcting any potential problems.

Controlling Web Publishing Preferences

CorelDRAW 10 gives you complete control over your personal Web publishing preferences via the Publish to Web options. These options are used to control Publish to the Web File export, which is described earlier. To access these options, click Tools | Options and then double-click both Document and Publish to the Web.

Image Handling

Image handling options are accessed from the Images dialog. This is the same dialog that you can access from the Images tab when publishing to the Web. You can select the default file format for images as either GIF or JPEG and set additional options, such as JPEG compression amount and GIF palette selection. Of course, no perfect file format exists for the Internet: some images are better off saved as JPEGs, while others should be saved as GIFs. The most important factor in making this decision is the number of colors in the image.

An intelligent new feature in CorelDRAW 10 enables you to allow CorelDRAW to decide whether an image should be published as a GIF or a JPEG, based on the image's color count. CorelDRAW counts the colors, and then exports to the appropriate format, using your default compression options for JPEGs or default palette selection for GIFs.

Text Handling

Clicking Tools | Options | Document | Publish to the Web | Text accesses text handling options. Three options are available:

■ **Export HTML Compatible Text As Text**   CorelDRAW makes an intelligent decision as to what text should remain text, and what text would be better exported as an image. When using this option, CorelDRAW exports your text as HTML text if HTML can be used to reproduce the text properly. If the text contains something HTML cannot reproduce, such as a texture fill, then CorelDRAW converts the text to an image and saves it according to your image handling guidelines (see "Image Handling").

■ **Export All Text As Images**   This option should be used with caution because it converts all your text to images. Although this allows for perfect text reproduction, it also adds significantly to download time. In addition, people who use Text to Speech converters to have Web pages read to them won't be able to use your page, because these converters cannot interpret text that's been converted to images.

■ **Export HTML-Compatible Text Using True Doc Technology**   This exports your HTML-compatible text using embedded fonts technology. Because not all browsers can use this technology and because legal issues are involved in exporting font files to the Internet, this is another option to use with caution.

HTML Link Colors

Clicking Tools | Options | Document | Publish to the Web | Links, accesses HTML hyperlink options. The first option is used to tell CorelDRAW whether hyperlinks should be underlined. The next three options are used to set the colors for your links. The Normal Link color is the color of a link before the user has visited the associated Web page. Active Link is the color of a link while your user is clicking on the link. Visited Link is the color of a link for a Web page present in your user's history file (meaning the user has recently visited the Web page).

Web Preflight Rules

You can set your default options for Web preflight review by clicking File | Publish to the Web | HTML | Issues. In this dialog, select Web Output in the Preflight Issues drop-down list box. Click the Settings button and scroll down to Web Publishing. You may use these options to tell CorelDRAW which potential issues you want it to check for and which you want it to ignore.

By default, CorelDRAW looks for problems with all preflight issues. Some issues may exist, however, that you don't want CorelDRAW to review. For example, CorelDRAW Web preflight can tell you if you used any colors in your document that aren't Web safe. Because many Web designers no longer consider Web-safe colors to be an issue in Web design, you may want to uncheck this option, so CorelDRAW doesn't report Web-safe color issues. For more information on Web-safe colors, please see CD-ROM Chapter 6 and Chapter 26.

Using the Web Image Optimizer

The Web Image Optimizer, shown in Figure 27-9, is a new tool used for fine-tuning Web image export. The Web Image Optimizer differs from the GIF, JPEG, and PNG export by enabling up to four live preview images simultaneously. You can set each preview window to use the same file format with different options, or you can set each preview window to use a different file format.

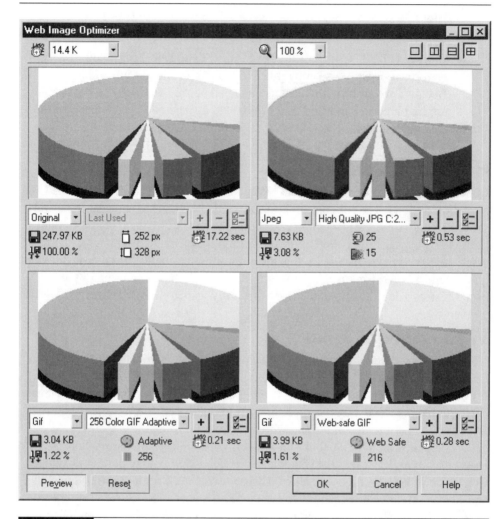

FIGURE 27-9   The Web Image Optimizer with the original image, a JPEG, and two GIF export previews (note the loss of color in the Web-safe image).

Changing Settings in the Web Image Optimizer

A row of controls located across the top of the Web Image Optimizer controls general preview settings. These settings affect the entire Web Image Optimizer dialog. An additional set of controls is available inside each preview window.

These controls affect only the individual window pane you're working in, which enables you to customize the options for each window pane.

> **TIP** *If the preview window panes aren't updating when you change compression settings, press the Preview button, located near the lower-left corner.*

General Settings

The drop-down list box located near the upper-left corner of the Web Image Optimizer dialog enables you to set a modem speed for use in estimating file download time. For example, setting this to 56K causes each of the preview window panes to display an estimated download time for your image for users with standard 56K dial-up connections.

Setting this control to 33.6K gives you the most reliable download time estimates. Few users remain connected at a full 56K because of the amount of traffic on the Internet. Faster estimates, such as those for ISDN and cable, should only be used if you're building a site specifically designed for users with broadband connections.

The magnifying glass icon is used to set the size of the preview image. The amount and type of preview window panes is set using the four buttons on the far-right side. The first button sets a single preview window. The second button sets two vertical preview windows. The third button also sets two preview windows, but with a horizontal, instead of a vertical, orientation. The fourth button is used to set four preview windows.

Individual Window Pane Settings

The drop-down list box in the left side of each preview window is used to determine the file format the preview window pane uses when it previews compression settings. You can choose Original (no compression), GIF, JPEG, PNG (8 bit), and PNG (24 bit). Original is for reference only, and cannot be saved (OK will be disabled if the Original pane is active). The next drop-down list box is used to select a compression preset (such as palette type and color count for GIF, and compression and smoothing levels for JPEG). The plus (+) and minus (−) icons are used to add new presets or to remove presets. The last icon is used to select your own GIF, JPEG, or PNG settings, which can then be used only on the image you're previewing, or be added to the preset list by clicking the plus (+) icon. For more information on how each GIF, JPEG, and PNG setting works, please see Chapter 26.

Preview Display   As you adjust preview settings in any preview window pane, a set of five icons located below the preview image will display a summary of your selections. The icons on the far left always display file size (top) and compression ratio (bottom), and the icon on the far right always displays estimated download time. The icons in the middle differ in what they display, depending on the type of image that you're previewing (except that GIF and PNG 8 both use identical icons, even in the middle, since they both use 8 bit color palettes).

If you're curious as to the source of the image used in the preview windows in Figure 27-10, it's a KPT (Kai's Power Tools) Fractal Flame. The KPT FraxFlame bitmap effects filter ships with the CorelDRAW 10 graphics suite (see Chapter 24 for more information).

Saving Your Image

Clicking on any preview window pane selects the settings used in that window pane as your export settings. The selected window pane is indicated by the rectangle drawn around the settings (see Figure 27-10). Clicking OK exports the image.

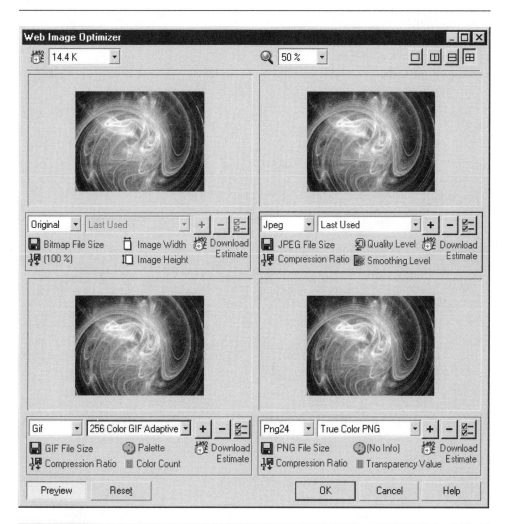

FIGURE 27-10   Clicking on any preview pane selects those settings as your export settings.

CHAPTER 28

Take Control Through Customization

Many loyal CorelDRAW users love their program for what it enables them to create, but they also have their own way of actually *being creative*, which often translates into preferences for how they use their software to accomplish their everyday work. If you're one of those users, you will probably want to tailor your own CorelDRAW 10 application either to suit the way you draw or to maximize your productivity (or both). When it comes to customization, few other applications enable you to accomplish this feat.

CorelDRAW 10's customization features have undergone extensive reengineering from past versions—even from version 9. You may customize virtually anything in CorelDRAW 10, ranging from secondary mouse button actions to command menus and toolbars. In fact, the list is so extensive that even the act of customizing becomes a challenge in itself.

In this chapter, you'll discover how to customize at both the application and document levels, and learn how to create custom toolbars, change command menus, assign and change shortcut keys, and save your entire customization state for specific types of tasks.

Top Customization Tips

Before you plunge headlong into the depths of CorelDRAW 10's customizing features, it may help right away to learn some of the most common and useful customization tasks you can perform. The following sections describe a few of the most common customization operations.

Moving Toolbars

If the docked location of your command menus, Toolbox, toolbars, Status Bar, or Onscreen Color Palette isn't to your liking, you can change any of them to be either undocked or docked to a different side of your application window. Click-dragging the Toolbox, toolbars (such as the Standard Toolbar and Property Bar) from the double-line indicator at the top or left of each of these interface components enables you to reposition them to any side of your CorelDRAW 10 application window (see Figure 28-1).

As you experiment with repositioning the command bars and toolbars, you're either going to discover that new and more useful locations work much better for

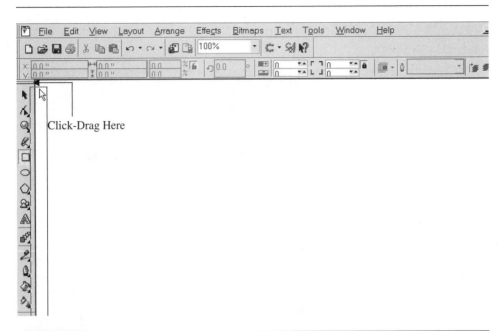

FIGURE 28-1   Click-drag the double-line indicator to undock any toolbar or drag it to a new interface location.

you, or that their default locations work best. Needless to say, you may completely dismantle CorelDRAW 10 and its familiar interface components and create some fairly different workspace situations (see Figure 28-2).

TIP   *If you become hopelessly entangled in interface customization, you may quickly reset your CorelDRAW 10 application to default workspace settings by holding the F8 key immediately after launching the application. This includes launching either from your Windows taskbar, the desktop, or the Start menu. Doing so opens an alert dialog that asks you to confirm the action.*

You may also resize or reproportion most undocked toolbars in CorelDRAW 10, including the Toolbox and the Onscreen Color Palette. To reproportion one of these interface components, hold your cursor at the corner or edge of the undocked toolbar and click-drag either vertically or horizontally to change its proportions.

Onscreen Property   Command   Status   Standard   Toolbox
Color   Bar   Menus   Bar   Toolbar
Palette

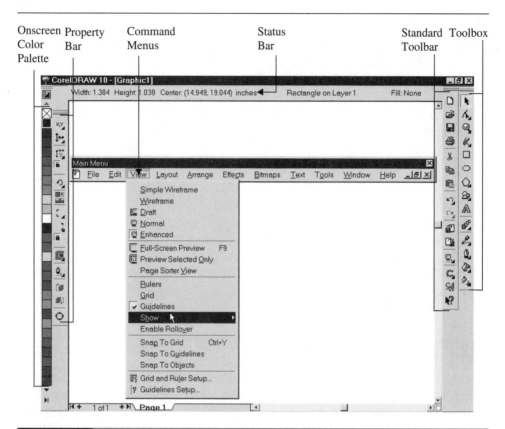

FIGURE 28-2	This workspace has been completely reorganized, with virtually every familiar interface component altered.

 To redock an undocked toolbar quickly and return it to its last docked location, double-click its title bar or use a click-drag action to drag it to a new location.

Moving Toolbar Buttons

A new capability for CorelDRAW 10's customization features enables you to move or copy any toolbar option or Toolbox Tool between toolbars, or delete an unused option or tool altogether. With this new capability, you can interactively customize your current workspace without the need to open dialogs. For example, if you'd like to have access to interactive effects tools while the Toolbox is not in view, you may move the Interactive Tool flyout to either the Standard Toolbar or to a specific Property Bar. Here, the Pick Tool has been copied to the Standard Toolbar:

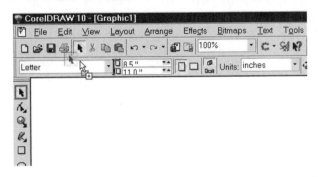

28

The following procedures enable you to move or copy tools and options between toolbars and delete tools:

- **Move Tools/Options**   To move a tool or option from one visible toolbar to another, hold ALT while dragging the tool or option from its current toolbar to the new toolbar location. As you drag the tool or option, your cursor will be accompanied by a symbol indicating the eligibility of the new location, and an I-beam cursor will appear at the new location indicating the insertion point for the item being moved.

- **Copy Tools/Options**   To copy a tool or option from one visible toolbar to another, hold CTRL+ALT as the two modifier keys while dragging between toolbar locations. Again, as you drag the tool or option, a symbol will appear indicating the eligibility of the new location, and an I-beam cursor will appear at the new location indicating the insertion point for the item being moved.

- **Delete Tools/Options**   To delete a tool or option completely from a specific toolbar, hold ALT while dragging the tool onto your document window and away from any existing interface components. As you drag the tool off of its current toolbar and into your document window, an X symbol will appear beside your cursor indicating that your mouse release action will delete the current tool. Deleted tools or options are not permanently removed from toolbars; they are merely removed from the toolbar in the current workspace.

TIP   *For more information on restoring, saving, importing, and exporting saved workspaces, see "Creating and Loading Workspaces," later in this chapter.*

Assigning or Changing Keyboard Shortcuts

Knowing your keyboard shortcuts is perhaps the best way to become productive. But with new software versions such as CorelDRAW 10, shortcut keys often change slightly to accommodate new tools, features, or functionality. Changing existing keyboard shortcuts is a relatively quick operation, but does require opening the somewhat complex customization dialog shown in Figure 28-3. Later in this chapter, you'll discover plenty of things this dialog enables you to accomplish. For now, though, let's zero in on shortcut key assignments.

To assign a new shortcut to a command menu item, follow these steps:

1. Regardless of which command, option, tool, or function you wish to assign to a hot key or shortcut key, you'll need to get to the Options dialog. For commands, click to view the menu item in the specific command menu, and right-click an available command while the command menu is visible to open the pop-up menu.

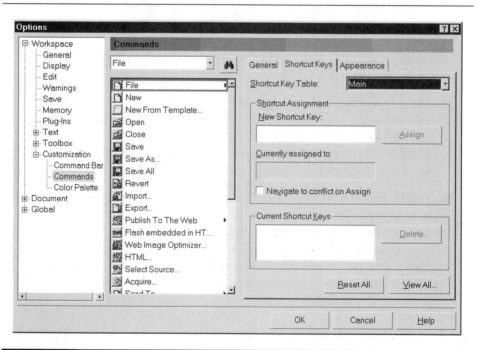

FIGURE 28-3   All shortcut key assigning is done in the Commands page of the Options dialog while the Shortcut Keys tab is in view.

2. Choose Customize | Menu Item | Properties to open the Customization Commands page in the Options dialog, and click the Shortcut Keys tab on the upper-right side of the dialog to view the Shortcut Key options. Specify your new shortcut in the Shortcut Key box by clicking your cursor in the box and pressing your keyboard shortcut. For example, if you wish the new shortcut to be CTRL and 1, press the CTRL key together with the 1 key while your cursor is in this box.

3. If the shortcut you specified is already assigned to a different command, this will appear in the Currently Assigned To box—in which case you'll need to specify something else, or change the existing shortcut. If no other command is assigned, click OK to close the dialog and apply your new shortcut.

To assign a new shortcut to a toolbar or Toolbox item, follow these steps:

1. For Toolbox or toolbar items, the operation is only slightly different. Right-click the option or tool to open the pop-up menu, and choose Customize | Toolbar Item | Properties. The Options dialog opens to the Commands page.

2. Click the Shortcut Keys tab at the upper right of the dialog to view the available options, and specify your new shortcut in the Shortcut Key box by clicking your cursor in the box and pressing your keyboard shortcut. For example, if you wish the new shortcut to be a character or keyboard combination, press the actual key or keys while your cursor is in this box.

3. Again, if the shortcut you specified is already assigned to a different tool or toolbar item, this will appear in the Currently Assigned To box, in which case you'll need to change it. If not, click OK to close the dialog and apply your new shortcut.

Setting Defaults for Text and Graphics

By default, all new graphical objects are created using a Fill of None and a Black Outline Pen color set to Hairline. All new Artistic and Paragraph Text objects are created using a Black Fill color with the Outline Pen properties set to None. If you're creating new text or graphical objects using tools, and these default Fill and Outline Pen properties are not what you require, you can change the defaults to avoid constantly changing these properties after creating your objects. These defaults may be changed to virtually anything you wish.

Changing default fills is a slightly different operation from changing default Outline Pen properties, though, so you'll want to pay close attention to these procedures. To change the default Fill properties for all new objects, follow these steps:

1. With *no objects* selected in your document, click the Interactive Fill Tool in the main Toolbox.

2. Using Property Bar options, specify a Uniform, Fountain, Pattern, or Texture fill using the Fill Type menu. As soon as you do this, a dialog will appear to warn you that you are about to change defaults. In the dialog shown next, you may specify the default to apply to Graphic, Artistic Text, and/or Paragraph Text objects. Make your selection, and click OK to close the dialog.

3. Once the Fill Type is selected, use the remaining Property Bar options to customize the fill as you wish. Each time you change your default Fill properties, the dialog will appear. Click OK to confirm your action and continue setting your default Fill options. From this point on, the default fills you specified will be applied to any Graphic and Text objects you create.

Changing the default Outline Pen properties is slightly less involved and can be done in a single dialog. To do so, follow these steps:

28

1. With *no objects* selected in your document, press F12—the shortcut for opening the Outline Pen dialog. But instead of the Outline Pen dialog opening immediately as it usually does, a dialog similar to the previous dialog appears and warns you that you are about to change your defaults (see the following illustration). As before, you can specify which type of objects you wish to change and click OK to proceed.

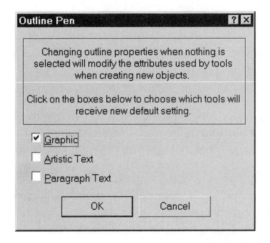

2. In the Outline Pen dialog, choose the properties for your new defaults, including line color, width, style, and arrowheads. Click OK to close the dialog and apply your new defaults. The default Outline Pen properties that you selected will be applied to any new Graphic and Text objects you create.

TIP *To quickly change the default Uniform Fill or Outline Colors for new objects, deselect any objects in your document and right-click (for the outline) or left-click (for the fill) a corresponding color well in the Onscreen Color Palette. As soon as you click a color well, the default alert dialog will appear to let you know you are about to change defaults. Choose your Graphic or Text object options and click OK to apply the new default Outline Pen or Fill color.*

Setting Defaults for New Documents

Whenever a new document is created, CorelDRAW 10 automatically sets the document to the default workspace that is currently selected. If you find yourself spending a few extra moments tailoring the workspace options to your liking each time you create a new document, it might be wise to change your application or document defaults. Changing your document default settings enables you to control general settings such as display modes and unit measurements, as well as Grid and Ruler setup, Page options, Guideline options, Styles, Save options, and Web Publish settings.

To set your document defaults, follow these steps:

1. Open a document that is already set up to suit the way you work, or open a new document and choose your most typical working settings, such as Ruler options, unit measurements, page size, and display mode.

2. Open the Options dialog by choosing Tools | Options (CTRL+J), and click the Document heading in the tree directory on the left side of the dialog to show the Document page options on the right side of the dialog.

3. Click Save Options as Defaults for New Documents. Once selected, this option enables you to select or deselect which document settings you wish to make your defaults (see Figure 28-4). Make your selections and click OK to close the dialog and apply the default settings.

4. Open a new document by choosing File | New (CTRL+N). Notice that your default settings are now exactly the way they were when saved.

Creating Custom Toolbars

By default, all typical toolbars in CorelDRAW 10 provide access to nearly all available commands and options—depending, of course, on which tool you are using and which type of object is currently selected. Although it's convenient to have access to all these resources most of the time, there may be situations when it's more efficient for you to streamline what's available by creating your own toolbar.

Creating your own custom toolbar is an efficient way of assembling your most commonly accessed tools for performing only specific tasks or when you want to have only those you use most often available. It is a relatively straightforward task

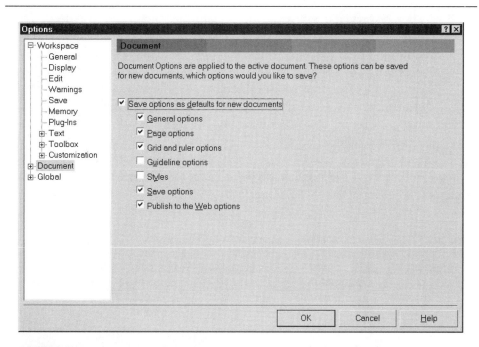

FIGURE 28-4   To control all settings associated with newly created documents, save your Document default options using the Options dialog.

to create and add your own tools and options to custom toolbars. To do so, follow these steps:

1. Open the Options dialog by choosing Tools | Options (CTRL+J).

2. On the left side of the dialog, click to expand the tree directory under Customization, and click Command Bars to view the available toolbars. Check boxes beside each of theses toolbars enable you to make them visible or not.

3. Below this list, click the New button (Figure 28-5). A new toolbar named New ToolBar 1 by default appears in the list. Its check box is selected, making it visible. Enter a name for your new toolbar; choose any Size, Appearance, or Title Bar options you wish to use; and click OK to close the Options dialog and return to your document.

4. By default, new toolbars appear undocked and empty, so you'll need to add your own options and tools to make them available. You may copy any visible options or tools that you want from either the Standard Toolbar, Property Bar, or Toolbox by holding CTRL+ALT and click-dragging from the current toolbar onto your new toolbar. As you drag, your cursor will appear with a small "+" symbol to indicate a copy is being made. As your cursor moves to your new toolbar, an I-beam cursor will appear, indicating the insertion point.

After adding tools and options to your custom toolbar, it will behave like any other toolbar in CorelDRAW 10's interface.

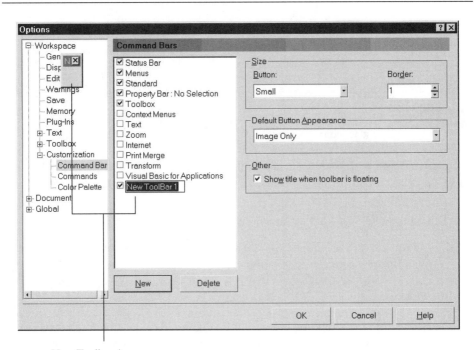

New Toolbar Appears

FIGURE 28-5 To create a new empty toolbar, click the New button in the Command Bars page of the Options dialog.

> **TIP**
>
> *To create a new custom toolbar quickly, hold CTRL+ALT while dragging any option or tool toward the center of your document window. The new toolbar will automatically feature the option or tool you dragged as the only tool, but you may copy and add more by using CTRL+ALT to drag additional tools or options onto the new toolbar. To fully customize the appearance of the new toolbar, right-click it and choose Customize | [New Toolbar 1] Toolbar | Properties to open the Command Bars page of the Options dialog.*

Copying Tools or Options Between Flyouts

To create new toolbar flyouts and copy tools or options from *other* flyouts onto them, you will need to use a slightly higher level of customization mechanics. Let's set a few ground rules for this by calling the new toolbar and flyout that you'll be copying *to* "the target" and the toolbar and flyout you'll be copying *from* "the source."

Right-click the target toolbar and choose Customize | [*toolbar name*] Toolbar | Add New Flyout. With the new flyout added, click the source flyout to open it so you can see the source tool or option you wish to copy. Hold CTRL+ALT while dragging from the source flyout until your cursor is over the target flyout. Before releasing, you'll see the target flyout open. After it opens, move your cursor onto it—then release the mouse (see the illustration). Using this technique, you may copy any tool or option from an existing flyout onto a new flyout on another toolbar.

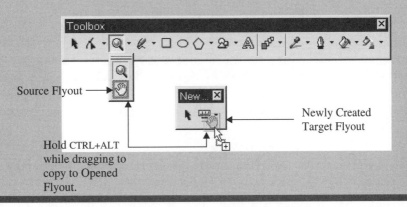

Source Flyout

Newly Created Target Flyout

Hold CTRL+ALT while dragging to copy to Opened Flyout.

Color Palette Appearance

Controlling the appearance of your Onscreen Color Palette is another relatively straightforward customization operation. Your Onscreen Color Palette may be set to display in a very brief or very verbose state, enabling you to view only a limited number of colors or the complete range in the selected palette.

Like any other toolbar, the onscreen palette may be docked or undocked. To undock the palette, simply drag it away from its docked position by clicking an edge or blank portion. To redock the palette, drag it back again or double-click its title bar. An undocked palette will display as many colors as possible according to its current proportions. Where not all colors are visible, scroll bars appear, enabling you to navigate the colors, as shown here:

Title Bar While Undocked

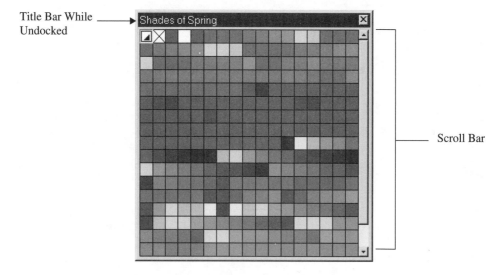

Scroll Bar

You may also customize the appearance of the onscreen palette, set the number of palette rows that are displayed, and set color well and border size using the Color Palette page of the Options dialog (Figure 28-6). To access this dialog quickly, right-click the edge of the Onscreen Color Palette and choose Customize.

Controlling the Status Bar Information Display

The Status Bar is an interface element in CorelDRAW that has long been an anchor for getting information about the objects you have selected, such as node, selection, grouping, position, and transformation. If you're a longtime user of

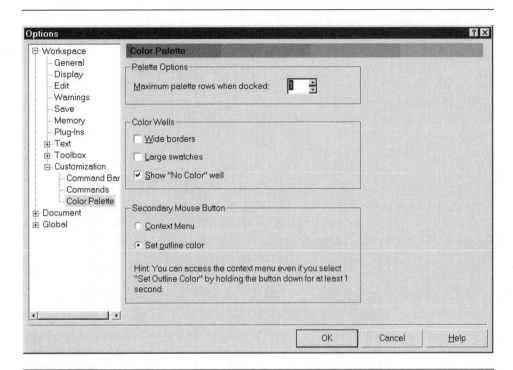

FIGURE 28-6   Customize the Color Palette display using the Options dialog.

CorelDRAW, you may find that constantly glancing at the Status Bar as you work is almost second nature. But certain information provided by the Status Bar is now redundant with other interface elements (such as the Property Bar); and, by default, it does occupy a full two lines of space on your screen—so this may also be a candidate for customization.

You may quickly change the size or position of the Status Bar using click-drag and right-click actions. Click-drag the top edge of the Status Bar up or down to toggle between the default two-line state and the slimmer one-line state. Position the Status Bar either at the top of your page or the bottom by right-clicking it and choosing Status Bar | Customize | Position | Top (or Bottom) from the pop-up menu. Use this same method to reset the Status Bar to defaults by choosing Status Bar | Reset Status Bar.

You may also change the proportions of the cells containing the display information. By default, the Status Bar is divided into three horizontal columns and two vertical rows, totaling six cells that display selected types of information.

To customize their position within the Status Bar, hold ALT while using a click-drag action on the cells, as shown here:

To customize Status Bar cell proportions or change the information each cell displays, right-click a specific cell and choose Customize | Status Item | Properties. You'll see the General tab on the Status Bar page of the Options dialog (see Figure 28-7). While this dialog is open, you may change the mouse position,

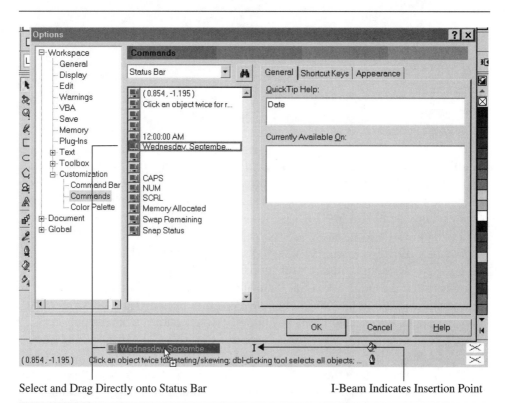

FIGURE 28-7 Change the information provided by the Status Bar using the Options dialog.

object information, time, date, outline, fill, keyboard settings, snap status, and memory status. To assign a specific display property to a cell, drag directly from the list onto the Status Bar, which remains visible while the dialog is open. Clicking a specific cell will automatically indicate the currently selected option in the dialog.

> **TIP** *To quickly control which toolbars are currently visible, right-click any toolbar and select or deselect the check box beside each of the toolbars in the list. Check marks indicate that toolbars are currently visible.*

Using CorelDRAW's Workspace Resources

28

The appearance and behavior of virtually everything in your CorelDRAW 10 application is controlled by your *workspace*, which is essentially an enormous collection of settings. These Workspace settings may be given unique names and saved independently of your CorelDRAW application. You may create new workspaces to best suit the tasks you perform or even emulate the behavior of other applications.

Workspace options are categorized into General, Display, Edit, Warnings, VBA, Save, Memory, Plug-ins, Text, Toolbox, and Customization, each of which may be controlled using pages in the Options dialog organized in the tree directory under Workspace (see Figure 28-8). However, while the Workspace page itself is selected, you may change, create, delete, import, export, and generally manage your workspaces from a bird's-eye view.

Creating and Loading Workspaces

By default, CorelDRAW 10 uses the _default workspace when first installed. But Corel often supplies additional workspaces to emulate certain tasks or application environments. As you'll discover, these resources are relatively straightforward to use.

To load an existing workspace, follow these steps:

1. If you haven't already done so, open a document and choose Tools | Options to open the Options dialog, and then click Workspace in the tree directory on the left of the dialog. By default, the Options dialog automatically shows the Workspace page.

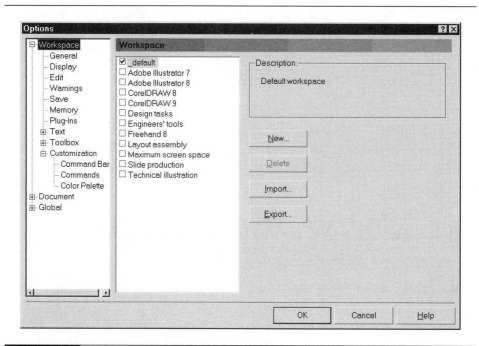

FIGURE 28-8   Use options in the Workspace page to apply all Workspace commands.

2. In this dialog page, you'll notice a listing of available workspaces. If you're using this feature for the first time, the _default workspace will likely be the one selected, indicated by a check mark beside it in the list.

3. To select a different workspace from the list, click the corresponding check box to select it and click OK to close the dialog. When you return to your CorelDRAW application window, the settings for your selected workspace will be applied. In certain instances, this could radically change the appearance of CorelDRAW's interface and the way tools, options, shortcuts, and toolbars appear and are used. To restore the default workspace, or select a different workspace, repeat the previous steps.

To create a new workspace based on your current workspace settings, follow these steps:

1. Open the Options dialog to the Workspace page by choosing Tools | Options (CTRL+J).

2. To the right of the listing of available workspaces, notice the four command buttons. Click the New button. The New Workspace dialog opens, as shown here:

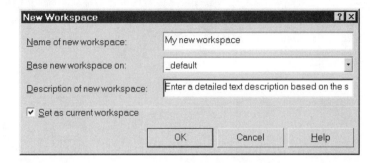

3. In this dialog, enter a name for your new workspace in the first available box. If you like, you may base your new workspace on any of the available workspaces in the list by clicking the Base New Workspace On drop-down menu, or simply base it on your currently selected workspace.

4. Enter an optional description for your new workspace. Although this is optional, if the workspace you're creating is geared toward a specific purpose or task, it may help a great deal to add a few details here. This will not only help jog your memory when you decide to reload the workspace, but will also help others grasp its purpose.

5. To have this new workspace become your current workspace, click Set as Current Workspace in the dialog (which is already selected by default).

6. Click OK to save the workspace and add it to your available list.

Importing and Exporting Workspaces

One of the new features of CorelDRAW 10 is the ability to easily use workspaces from other sources, or save your workspaces to exchange with other users. This functionality comes by way of Import and Export commands selected within the Workspace page of the Options dialog.

To import a workspace from an external source, follow these steps:

1. In the Workspace page of the Options dialog, click the Import button to the right of the list of available workspaces. This opens the Import Workspace

dialog, which is set up in a wizard style, enabling you to choose options and navigate through a progression of steps. Step 1 of the wizard is shown here:

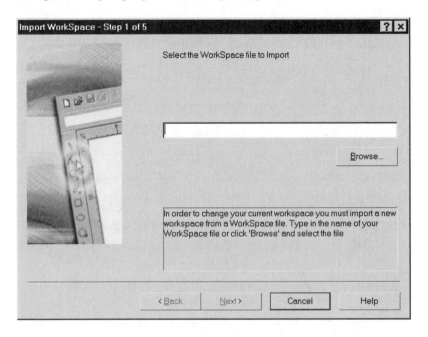

2. Click the Browse button, which causes the Open dialog to appear, and locate any previously exported workspace.

3. With your workspace file selected, click Open to specify the workspace in the Import Workspace wizard dialog and click Next to proceed to Step 2.

4. In Step 2 of the wizard, shown in the following illustration, you may choose all or any properties of the selected workspace to import into your CorelDRAW application. These include all aspects of workspace settings—toolbars, zoom settings, defaults for text and graphics objects, print styles, and so on. To see the changes to your workspace caused by your selection, click the Preview button, or click Next to proceed to the next dialog.

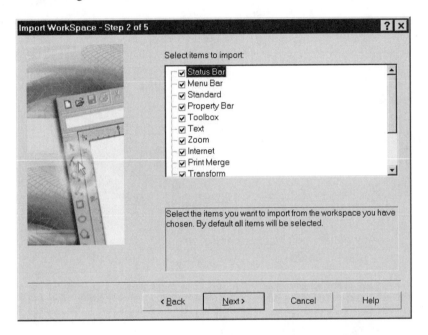

5. In Step 3 of the wizard, shown in the next illustration, choosing Current Workspace (the default) and clicking the Next button will overwrite your current workspace settings with those of the workspace you've chosen to import. Choosing this option will skip Step 4 of the wizard and navigate you immediately to the final dialog.

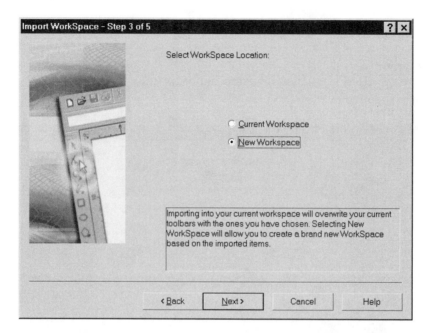

6. Choosing New Workspace in Step 3 enables you to enter a name and description for your imported workspace in Step 4 of the wizard:

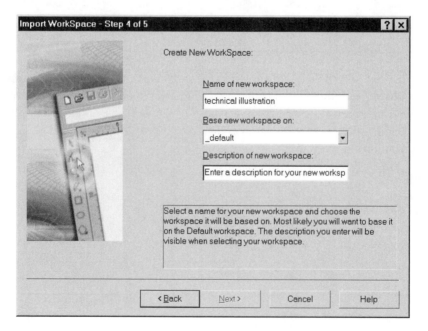

7. Clicking Next displays the final page, shown next, where a summary of your workspace name and selected items is displayed. You may click Finish to save and apply the new workspace and return to the Options dialog, or click the Back button to review or make changes to your selection and repeat the process.

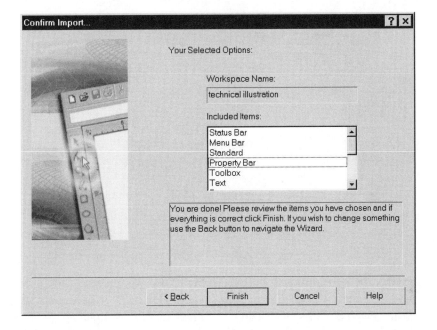

8. Once your imported workspace has been saved, it appears in your current workspace list. Clicking OK closes the Options dialog and returns you to CorelDRAW 10.

Exporting a workspace makes it available for others to import using the previous steps. When exporting a workspace, you may merely save the workspace or you may send it to others via e-mail, provided your system is equipped to do so. To export a workspace for either purpose, follow these steps:

1. If you haven't already done so, open the Options dialog to the Workspace page by choosing Tools | Options.

2. Select the workspace you would like to export by clicking the check box beside it in the list.

3. With your workspace selected, click the Export button to the right of the list to open the Export Workspace dialog shown in the following illustration. Here, you may choose which properties of your current workspace you wish to export by making selections in the tree directory under Toolbars, Menus, and Status Bar. Click to select which properties you wish to include and proceed to the next step.

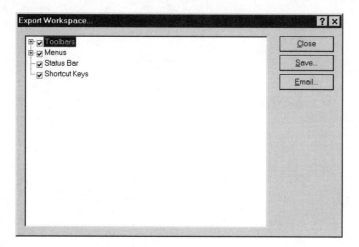

4. Notice the two command buttons in the Export Workspace dialog: Save and (if e-mail is available on your system) Email. To immediately save your selected workspace as an e-mail attachment and open your available e-mail application to a new blank e-mail note window, click Email. To proceed with exporting your workspace to a unique file, click Save.

5. Clicking Save opens the Save As dialog where you can enter a unique filename and specify a location for the exported workspace file. By default, workspace files are given the three-letter file extension .CWF. Clicking Save in this dialog immediately saves your exported workspace and returns you to the Export Workspace dialog.

6. Click Close to return to the Options dialog, reset your current workspace if necessary, and click OK to return to CorelDRAW.

 To quickly access workspace Import and Export dialogs, right-click any toolbar in your CorelDRAW 10 application window and choose Customize | Workspace | Import Workspace, or Customize | Workspace | Export Workspace.

CHAPTER 29

Adventures with Scripts and VBA

CorelDRAW has been scriptable since version 6—that is, the user has been able to control certain aspects of CorelDRAW using scripts in the form of CorelScript. Corel first licensed Microsoft's Visual Basic for Applications (VBA) for CorelDRAW 9 and included both it and CorelScript. The Corel designers have taken the next logical step in version 10, and CorelScript has been dropped. Now all scripting must be done using either VBA or a third-party programming language.

This chapter focuses on VBA, as it is assumed that you don't have access to further tools, although other tools are mentioned at the end. The chapter will give you an introduction to programming in VBA and controlling CorelDRAW 10 with it.

An application in its own right, VBA could fill its own book, let alone its own chapter, and CorelDRAW's object model is not a small topic either. Due to the constraints of this book, this chapter gives the new programmer enough information to get started and guidance on where to go for more information.

What's Possible with VBA

VBA, or more precisely CorelDRAW's Object Model, enables programmers to control most aspects of CorelDRAW through programmed code. Using VBA, you can write small, ten-line programs that perform a simple task, and you can assign that program, or macro, to a button, menu, or shortcut key in CorelDRAW so that it is always accessible, helping you streamline your workflow. Alternatively, you can build mini-applications for performing complex tasks that are otherwise difficult—even impossible—or time consuming.

The simplest example might be the ubiquitous (in programmer circles, anyway) "Hello World" example. However, an even simpler example would be to create a rectangle or an ellipse shape, and then advance to creating text. Other simple examples would be to move and resize objects on the page, change colors, rotate, extrude, and do almost anything you would normally do in CorelDRAW. Also, you can manage all those Backup_of_ files, templates, and much more.

One very important aspect of VBA is that it allows you, the programmer, to fix those bits of CorelDRAW that you feel don't work properly. For example, while the Transformations Docker provides intimate control over objects' sizes, rotations, positions, and skews, any transformation is applied to the *selection* as a whole, and you cannot do it automatically to *each* selected object, one at a time relative to itself. Or, when you paste anything into a document, it is always pasted either in the dead center of the page—or double-page spread—or it is pasted at the exact position it was copied from. Why can't it always be pasted in the dead center of the *current window*, i.e., right in front of you? These, and many other examples, are described in this chapter.

You can assign VBA macros to Toolbar buttons, menus, and shortcut keys in CorelDRAW. This brings your macros right into the interface, where they can really work for you and make your workflow much more efficient and streamlined.

Some Words and Phrases Defined

Programming is much less an art and much more a science. The English language is often ambiguous in meaning, so we need to lay down some syntactical ground rules from this point on. Some of the following definitions are subtle, but they will make life easier later on.

Shape   A *shape* is a drawing shape in a CorelDRAW document. People often call shapes "objects," but that word has a different meaning here. VBA calls anything that you draw in a document a shape, so that is what we will call them.

Object   Objects are nothing to do with CorelDRAW and everything to do with VBA. An *object* in VBA is the general name for any section of CorelDRAW that can be named and programmed, such as Shape, Layer, Page, or Document. It does not mean a shape that you draw in CorelDRAW.

Member   Objects are very useful for breaking larger objects into smaller ones and organizing them. A large object may consist of several things that you can access, generally called *members*: sub-objects, properties and methods. Sub-objects are just the smaller objects that make up this object. For example, a car is an object, but it has an engine and four wheels that are sub-objects—objects in their own right, but in this instance part of a greater thing.

Property   One aspect of objects is that they have properties. A *property* is a characteristic of an object, such as color. For example, you might ask "What color are you?," and the object replies "Cerise." Typical properties are Name, Size, and Position, and you can ask objects for these properties, or tell them what they are ("your name is square").

Method   A *method* is something that the object can "do" when you tell it to: "Move one inch to the right!," "Rotate 10 degrees!," "Group with the other shapes!," or "Delete yourself!." Methods are often called *member functions*, because they are functional, and they are members of the object.

Macro, Sub, Function, and Procedure   All these mean broadly the same thing: a block of code that has a clearly defined start point and end point. We use the word *macro* as a general term for sub, function, or program. A *sub*, or subroutine, is a piece of code that does something and then returns control to the object that called it.

A *function* is a piece of code that does something and then gives a value back to the object that called it. You can see that subs and functions are basically the same, but a function returns a value (a number or text), and a sub does not.

_ (Underscore Character)   When you are writing code, often one line can be hundreds of characters long and much too wide for your screen. This isn't important as far as VBA is concerned, but it does make the code harder to read. You can break a line into several shorter ones by adding a space followed by an underscore and a line break at the point you want the line to wrap. VBA treats the code on the next line as a continuation from the current line. You can break a line as many times as you want, but you cannot split words in two, and you have to be careful when breaking quoted text. The underscore character is used where necessary in this book, because the pages are too narrow to display enough characters in some instances.

Installing VBA and the Samples from the CD-ROM

Before you start working through this chapter, you must make sure that VBA is installed and configured, and that you have installed the sample macros from the book's CD-ROM. These modules contain all of the more advanced samples and freebies.

Installing VBA

VBA is *not* installed by default. One reason is that it takes up quite a lot of room on your hard disk (about 50MB), so it is not installed in order to keep the default CorelDRAW installation size down.

To install VBA, run Setup from the CD and choose Custom Install. In the CorelDRAW 10 Components tree, expand Productivity Tools, and then put a check mark in the box next to Visual Basic for Applications 6.0 and IE5. Clear all the other check marks in the setup tree (this does not uninstall those other components, it just does not reinstall them). Click Next and follow the rest of the instructions to the end, clearing the check boxes at each stage. This will *add* VBA to the existing CorelDRAW installation, without deleting anything. Next time you start CorelDRAW, it will have VBA ready for you.

The IE5 component required by VBA is for programs that have been digitally signed by the author to enable you to determine their trustworthiness. VBA on its own cannot process digital signatures, and it uses IE5 to do it over the Internet with the Trust Authority—a private, trusted company (not Corel or Microsoft). If you don't need digital signatures, or you don't want Internet Explorer on your system, deselect Digital Signatures using Internet Explorer 5 in the Components tree; however, you may be unable to use any third-party VBA programs that are digitally signed.

Installing the Sample Code from the CD-ROM

The sample code has been put together to make it as simple to use as possible. To install the code, first you need to create a target directory, which is not optional:

1. Close CorelDRAW.

2. In Windows Explorer, navigate to the c:\Program Files\Corel\Graphics10\ Draw\ folder.

3. If it does not exist already, create a new folder in the Draw folder called GMS. This name is not optional!

4. Now copy all the .GMS files from the folder d:\Tutorials\Chapter 29\Sample Code\ from the CD into the new folder GMS on your hard drive.

5. Select all the .GMS files in the GMS folder on your hard drive, and right-click and choose Properties from the pop-up menu; or choose File | Properties. Clear the check mark in the Read Only check box, and click OK. This has to be done when copying files from any CD-ROM, because CD is a read-only medium.

6. Restart CorelDRAW.

The code is all stored in .GMS files. These are defined by Corel as "Global Macro Storage." Global macros are macros that can be accessed at all times in CorelDRAW. Some macros can be saved as part of a .CDR file, and can only be accessed when that file is open in CorelDRAW; hence, those macros are no longer global, but local.

Using Old CorelScript Files

Corel has now officially dropped CorelScript in favor of VBA. However, that doesn't mean you can't still use your old CSC and CSB files. You can, but only in a limited way.

To run a .CSC or .CSB file in CorelDRAW 10, you can use only the Tools | Run Script command, or use the Corel Scripts Manager Docker (from the Window | Docker menu).

However, you must make some simple changes to the scripts. The first thing you will notice is that there isn't a CorelScript Editor anymore. You must either use the editor supplied with CorelDRAW 9, or you can simply use Windows' NotePad, which is more than adequate for the following change.

29

Upgrading CorelDRAW 9 Scripts to 10

To get your CorelDRAW 9 scripts to work properly with CorelDRAW 10, simply change the lines `WithObject "CorelDRAW.Automation.9"` to `WithObject "CorelDRAW.Automation.10"`. The rest of the code should be the same, as the CorelScript object has not been modified much.

If you are upgrading CorelDRAW 8 scripts, there are quite a few more changes between it and CorelDRAW 10. At this point, you should seriously consider biting the bullet and rewriting the entire script as VBA macros.

Upgrading Scripts to VBA

To upgrade a Script to VBA can be quite a long task. However, there is a quick, simple method, although its results are variable.

To upgrade, copy the script's contents into a new, empty module in the VBA Editor (which is described later in the chapter). Then, wherever you see

```
WithObject "CorelDRAW.Automation.9"
```

change it to

```
With CorelScript
```

and change the `End WithObject` line to `End With`.

This simple change will convert about 70 percent of your previous hard work in Script to something that the VBA Editor can run. However, such script-macros will not run efficiently at all, and you are positively encouraged to rewrite them as real VBA macros and to use the CorelScript object as little as possible. But as a stop-gap translation, this will get you by for now.

Recording and Playing Macros

The quickest way for any new programmer to learn how to program CorelDRAW, or any VBA-enabled application, is to record a few actions in CorelDRAW using the VBA Recorder. While it is recording, the VBA Recorder converts your actions into logical VBA code. You won't always get the result you were expecting, but that in itself is a good lesson to learn.

Experienced programmers also benefit from recording macros occasionally: CorelDRAW is a big beast, and finding the exact keyword to do whatever it is you are trying to do can be difficult. Old hands often record the action they need to program and then look at the keywords that the Recorder creates, which tells them what they need to know. They delete the recorded macro but use that keyword in their own custom macro or program.

Perhaps it should be mentioned before you start: The VBA Recorder records what it sees you doing. However, it often interprets your actions in roundabout ways. For example, if you create a shape and then fill it, the recorder does not realize that the shape in each action is the same shape; so it adds extra, unnecessary code that does the job, but not as efficiently as if you had hand-coded it. Also, there are some commands that, for various reasons, cannot be recorded, including text commands and node-editing commands. Instead, VBA adds a remark into the code to warn you.

Recording Macros Using the VBA Recorder

There are several ways to invoke the VBA Recorder. The simplest way is from CorelDRAW's Tools | Visual Basic menu. Click the Record command, shown here:

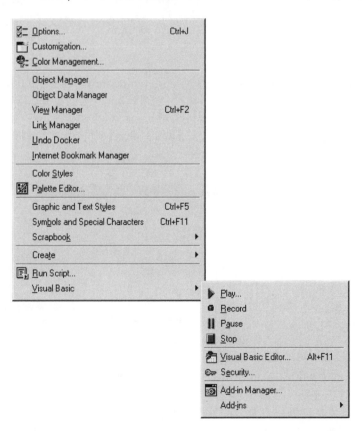

29

A better way is to make the Visual Basic for Applications Toolbar visible: Right-click any Toolbar area and choose Visual Basic for Applications from the pop-up toolbars list. The VBA Toolbar has six buttons, as shown here:

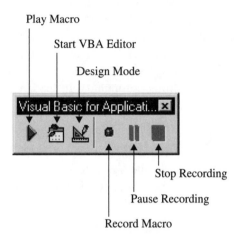

Play Macro

Start VBA Editor

Design Mode

Stop Recording

Pause Recording

Record Macro

To record a macro, click one of the Record commands—either the button on the Toolbar or the menu command. This opens the Save Macro dialog, shown in the next illustration. Give the macro a logical name, such as "DrawRectangle"— but don't use any spaces or punctuation. The name must start with a letter and can *only* contain the characters A–Z, a–z, 0–9, and _ (underscore).

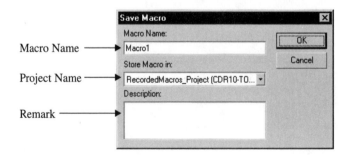

Macro Name

Project Name

Remark

Choose a VBA project to save the macro in. By default, the macro will be stored in the active document, which means that it will only be available when that document is open. If you want it to be accessible at all times—that is, globally— store it in a .GMS project file. The filename is given in parentheses after the project name in the list.

Give the macro a brief description if you want, and it will be stored as a remark in the code. Click OK and VBA will now record each subsequent action you perform in CorelDRAW. Valid actions include creating shapes, moving shapes, and changing shape properties. When you have finished, click Stop.

When you start recording, the Record button on the Toolbar and the Record menu command are disabled, and the Pause and Stop buttons are enabled. If you have the Toolbar open, this gives you a good indication of the recording status.

If you want to pause a recording, so that you can perform some intermediate actions in CorelDRAW that you don't want to record, click the Pause button. Click Pause again to resume.

You should be very careful to do the bare minimum of actions necessary in CorelDRAW when recording. If you undo actions, the Undo is not recorded, but the undone actions are not deleted from the VBA recording, either. Some actions are not recorded, including changing the zoom and pan settings of the document. Other actions cannot be recorded, such as editing text or drawing extra line segments with the Freehand Tool. These nonrecorded actions can be programmed manually, though.

Saving Undo Lists as VBA Macros

A new feature in CorelDRAW 10 is the Undo Docker, from which you can save the Undo list as a VBA macro. The docker is next. To open the Undo Docker, select it from the Tools menu or from the Window | Dockers menu.

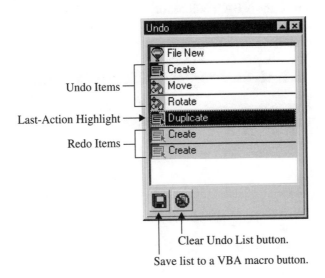

The list that you see contains the available actions that you can undo or redo using Undo and Redo from the Edit menu for the active document. The last-action highlight indicates the last action you did, which is also the action that will be undone if you choose Undo from the Edit menu. If you choose Edit | Repeat, the highlighted item will be repeated, if repeatable.

The first item in the list is always File New; and if you click it, all of the actions in the list will be undone. If the number of actions you have done since the document was opened or created is greater than the Maximum Undo Levels in Options | Workspace | General, the first items in the list will be discarded and the new actions will be added to the bottom of the list. You can only undo back to File New; any discarded items cannot be undone.

If you click the Save List button, the list of commands starting at—but not including—File New, right up to the selected command, will be saved to a VBA macro. Clicking the Save List button opens the Save Macro dialog. Choose a suitable name, project, and description as before, and click OK.

The Clear Undo List button removes all of the Undo and Redo items in the list. If you clear the list, you will not be able to undo anything already done in CorelDRAW. However, if you want to save an undo list as a macro, clearing the list before you perform your actions is a good thing, because it removes all the other actions that you don't want in your macro.

Playing Back Recorded or Saved Macros

To play back a recorded macro, or any valid macro that you have written yourself, click the Play button on the VBA Toolbar, or choose the Play command from the Tools | Visual Basic menu. You will be presented with the VBA Macros dialog, where you can choose the macro you want to run, as shown here:

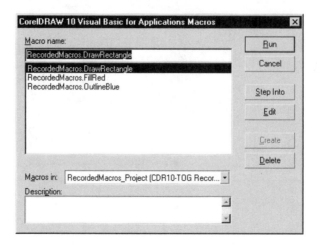

Choose the correct project in the Macros In list, and then click the macro you want to run in the macro list. Then click the Run button.

Assigning Macros to Buttons, Menus, and Shortcut Keys

If you record or write macros that you use regularly, the best way to use them is to assign them to a Toolbar button, a menu, or a shortcut key in CorelDRAW. This puts the macro right at your fingertips, and this is where you can use macros to optimize your workflow, saving you time and, ultimately, money.

To customize your workspace and assign macros to buttons, menus, or shortcuts, refer to Chapter 31, "A Primer in Using CorelDRAW 10's Interface." The VBA macros are all listed under VBA Macros near the bottom of the command groups list. Each macro is listed as a member of its project, for example, RecordedMacros.DrawRectangle, where the macro DrawRectangle is a member of the project RecordedMacros. The macros are listed in the order they were created within the project.

29

Let's Record a Few Macros

If you are at the beginning of the learning curve for programming CorelDRAW, a very useful exercise is to record a few macros and see how they work.

Before we start to program in VBA properly, first let's see what a VBA macro looks like. The word *macro* in this context means "a series of text commands that imitate the user's actions." A macro can be run, or executed, any number of times, and the results will be the same every time.

Drawing a Rectangle

We are going to record something very simple: creating a rectangle. The size is not too important, but it should be about two inches wide by one inch high.

1. Select Record Macro from the VBA Toolbar, or from the Tools | Visual Basic menu.

2. Give the macro the logical name DrawRectangle. Remember, don't use any spaces or punctuation; the name must start with a letter and can *only* contain the characters A–Z, a–z, 0–9, and _ (underscore).

3. Click the drop-down arrow of the Store Macro list and choose RecordedMacros_Project, which you copied from the CD earlier, or GlobalMacros if you haven't installed the .GMS files from the CD.

4. Give a brief description, such as "Tutorial: recording a rectangle."

5. Click OK. Don't be fooled by the lack of activity: VBA will record every action that you do from here.

6. Select the Rectangle Tool (F6), and draw a two-inch-by-one-inch rectangle in the approximate center of the page. The rectangle does not have to be precise.

7. Now, click Tools | Visual Basic | Stop.

And that's it, you have recorded your first VBA macro. You can now play the macro back to create a new rectangle at the same position as the original.

Recording an Ellipse

Another straightforward example is recording an ellipse. Repeat the procedure for creating the rectangle, but use the Ellipse Tool instead of the Rectangle Tool, and name the macro DrawEllipse.

Again, playback instantaneously produces an ellipse exactly where the old one was created.

Recording Fills and Outlines

With the ellipse from the preceding section selected, record the application of a 3-point–thick blue outline and a uniform red fill; call this macro RedFill_BlueOutline. Stop recording. Now, select a different shape and run this macro. The red fill and blue outline are applied to this new shape, not to the one that was recorded with. This is similar to using styles, except that you don't have to worry about accidentally ruining the style sheet when you import other graphics into the open one.

 At the time of this writing, a run-time error occurs when running the RedFill_BlueOutline macro to apply the blue outline. Before running this macro, the VBA code must be manually edited. This is likely to be modified in a future Service Pack from Corel.

This illustrates how easy it is to perform several operations in one macro and how to work around some of CorelDRAW's foibles.

Recording Transformations

Select a shape in CorelDRAW and record the application of several different transformations: Scale the shape, move it, skew it, and rotate it. Name this macro ScaleMoveSkewRotate. Stop recording. Now apply this macro to a different shape and you will see that it is performed exactly as before.

By now you should begin to see a pattern: Most of us do something in every drawing the same way. Wherever those actions take more than one mouse-click or menu, we should be able to add all of the user-interactions into a quicker macro—assign it to a button bar and you have saved yourself time in every illustration you do. This affects some people more than others, but using such optimizations can save more than 50 percent of your time!

Introducing the VBA Editor

The Visual Basic for Applications Editor is written by Microsoft and licensed to Corel for inclusion in CorelDRAW. This means that while the CorelDRAW Object Model—the commands that CorelDRAW exposes to VBA—are the responsibility of Corel, the Editor is solely Microsoft's. The big advantage here is that the Visual Basic Editor is mature, refined, and first class, as it derives so much from Microsoft's long line of software development tools.

The VBA Editor includes many features designed to assist the programmer, including

- **Syntax Check**   This feature checks each line as you type it and immediately identifies any problems it finds.

- **Auto List Members**   A list of all valid members of an object pops up, from which you can choose one, or you can just type it yourself.

- **Auto Indenting and Formatting**   The Editor tidies up your code and automatically inserts tabs as you are working to maintain a uniform look, which makes the code easier to read and easier to debug, although it has no effect on performance.

- **Color Coding**   Your code is colored according to whether the words are reserved keywords, remarks, errors, or normal code.

- **Form Designer**   You can quickly design custom forms that are powerful and interactive. You can even place other people's ActiveX controls onto your forms to add various super features, such as Internet browsing or CorelDRAW documents.

29

There are many other useful features of the VBA Editor, but you will discover these for yourself once you start using it.

The VBA Editor Layout

The VBA Editor has three main areas: menus and toolbars, dockers, and code and form-designer windows. These are shown in Figure 29-1.

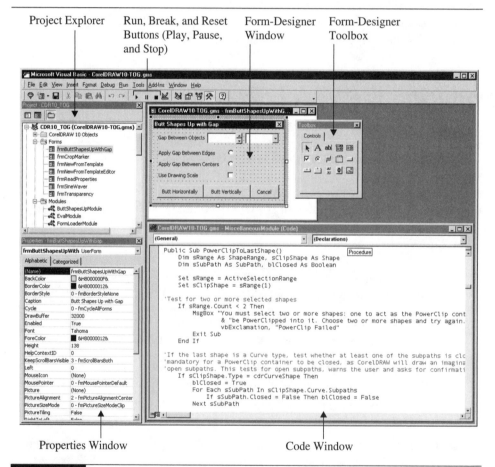

Layout of the VBA Editor

The most important window is the code window, as this is where you do most of your hands-on programming. It is where your code is listed and where you enter new code and edit existing code. The next most important window is the Project Explorer, as this enables you to quickly navigate between all the modules and components of all of your open projects. The Properties window is important, particularly if you are editing forms.

The final powerful feature of the VBA Editor is the Object Explorer. This is a fundamental tool for when you decide to start programming by hand, rather than just recording macros.

The Project Explorer

The Project Explorer can be switched on from the View menu or by pressing CTRL+R, and is shown in Figure 29-1. This lists all of the loaded projects (GMS files) and all of the modules, forms, and class modules that they contain. This is very much like Windows Explorer, and you can think of the projects as folders that contain other files—namely, the modules and forms. With this paradigm in mind, you can see that it is very simple to use the Project Explorer to keep your VBA code organized.

You can perform various filing operations within the Project Explorer, including creating new modules, importing and exporting modules, and deleting modules. These are explained next.

Opening Modules and Forms   You can open a module or form simply by double-clicking it in the Project Explorer, or right-clicking and choosing View Code. Forms have two parts—the visual form and the code. Double-clicking displays the form; right-clicking and choosing View Code displays the code. Or you can press F7 to open the selected module or form.

Creating New Modules and Forms   Right-click anywhere inside the project you want to add a module or form to, and choose Insert | Module or Insert | Form. The new module or form will be added to the appropriate subfolder. You can name the module or form in the Properties window, but the naming convention is the same as for naming macros (no spaces or special characters).

Exporting   Right-click the module or form that you want to export and choose Export File from the pop-up menu. This is a simple way to share small parts of your work with other people.

Importing   Click anywhere within the project you want to import a module or form into, and choose Import File from the pop-up menu.

Deleting Modules   You can delete a module or form by right-clicking it and choosing Remove from the pop-up menu. This actually removes the module from the project file; so if you do want to keep a copy of it, you *must* export it first. VBA asks you whether you want to export the module to a file before removing.

The Code Window

The typical VBA Editor code window has several features: the main code pane, the Object List, the Procedure List, and the Procedure View and Full Module View buttons—as shown next. The code window shows the code from a single module, class module, or form, although you can have as many code windows as you like open at the same time.

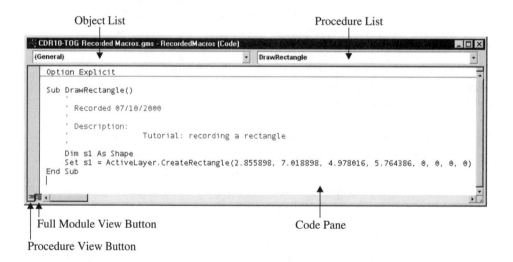

Object List   Procedure List

Full Module View Button   Code Pane

Procedure View Button

The code pane is where all of your hard work is put in. This is the text area of the window where you edit the code.

The Objects List gives the available objects for that module. If a module is displayed, there is only one object, the "(General)" object. If a form's code window is open, as well as General, all of the form's controls (buttons, labels, text boxes, list boxes, and so on) will be listed. The Procedures List gives the names of the available procedures for the selected object. For most modules, this is merely a list of all the subs and functions (VBA records macros as subroutines, which it identifies with the keyword Sub). Basically, these two lists give you a table of contents for zooming around large modules. Some modules can grow to several hundred lines in length, so assistance is often very welcome. However, for small modules, you probably won't need the lists.

The View buttons swap between seeing all of the procedures listed one after the other, to seeing just one and forcing you to use the Object and Procedure Lists. If your module is full of large procedures, Procedure View may be useful; whereas if your module is full of short procedures, Full Module View is better.

The Object Browser

The Object Browser is the key to programming the CorelDRAW Application object. The Object Browser shows you how every object, member function, and property within CorelDRAW fits together. And it shows you the exact syntax you must use (the exact words and variables). To start the Object Browser, select it from the View menu, or press F2. It is shown next. When you have a look at it, you will see just how large the Object Model for CorelDRAW really is!

The left-hand list is the list of object types, or classes, that exist within CorelDRAW. Each class may exist as a sub-object of the main CorelDRAW Application object, or it may be a sub-object of a sub-object. The right-hand pane lists the members of that class, including all of its properties, methods (procedures, or subs and functions), and events (not many). The bottom pane lists the member's definition, including its parameters.

You can click any green words in the bottom pane, and you will be taken straight to that class's member list.

The Object Browser is a powerful tool, but you won't need to use it until you have practiced recording lots of macros first. Indeed, once you are familiar with using VBA, it is quicker to use the Object Browser to find the definition you are looking for than to record a macro and analyze its recorded code.

There is a search function within the Object Browser to help you locate the definition you are looking for—another helpful feature.

Auto Syntax Check

Syntax Check occurs every time you leave one line of code and move to a different line. When you do, the VBA editor reads the line you just left and checks the *syntax*, or the words you have typed. If any obvious errors are there—maybe you missed a parenthesis, or the word "Then" from an If statement—that line will be highlighted in red.

Also, in its default state, the VBA Editor will tell you there is an error and will prevent you from leaving that first line until you have corrected the mistake. There is an option under Tools | Options that allows you to disable Auto Syntax Check. The line will still be highlighted in red, but you won't get a message; and you will be able to go unobstructed to another line before correcting the error on the first line, such as to copy some text.

As you are beginning, it is a good idea to leave Auto Syntax Check enabled, since the messages provide you with information on the exact problem. However, as you get more fluent, you will find that the messages don't tell you anything that you don't already know and they are just intrusive and disruptive, so you may want to disable them.

Auto List Members

Each object in VBA has a set of associated members—properties and functions that the object "owns." With Auto List Members enabled, when you type a dot or period (.) after a valid object name, that object's member properties and functions will pop up in a scrolling list. You can choose one of the properties from the list by scrolling down to it and double-clicking it, or selecting it and pressing TAB.

This feature is extremely helpful for beginners and experienced coders alike. It allows you to use less brain power for remembering exact syntax and spelling. Instead, you can think "it's something like . . ." and pick the right one from the list. However, this list only appears when you enter a valid object name first.

If you want to use this feature on a new line, right-click and choose List Properties/Methods. You will be given a list that comprises all of the possible objects, variables, functions, and subs within that part of the module. The list is very long, so it isn't quite so useful, as it is much harder to find what you are looking for. But it's there, and you can use it.

Form Designer

The Form Designer is used for designing objects called *forms*: every dialog box consists of a form. A form is a blank, gray piece of screen that you can place buttons, check boxes, text boxes, lists, groups, labels, and other ActiveX controls on. You can choose whether it has its own titlebar or not.

29

To design a good, easy-to-use form takes practice. Since this chapter only introduces the basics of VBA, and since forms are usually used only in complex macros and applications, designing forms is not covered here. However, should you need to design a form, keep the following points in mind:

Keep It Simple   There's nothing worse than a form that is so intricate or over-clever that it would just be quicker to do the job by hand in CorelDRAW and not have to use that macro. Keep your forms *simple*. Only use the controls you actually need to use.

Make It Useable   The best thing to do when designing any form or application is to use it when you are doing a real job, and have other people use it. You will quickly see what does and doesn't work. If you make the form illogical and difficult to use, your user base will be unhappy and unimpressed. A clean, logical layout is important.

It's Been Done Before   People have been designing forms for over a decade in Windows and you can learn a lot from professional applications. Look at what makes a good form and what makes a bad one! Learn from the professionals.

Pay Attention to Detail   When you have finished designing the layout of a form, pay careful attention to the detail. Make sure every control has an Accelerator Key. At least the most important controls should have ControlTipTexts. Make sure that the TabIndex order is logical and straightforward. Ensure that controls are neatly arranged and pixel perfect, since this assists the user's eye to scan the form quickly.

Setting Up VBA for First-Time Use—Options

There are a number of very useful options to set up right from the start to ensure that you learn how to program effectively. The most important is to check the VBA Security settings. The next is to set up one or two of VBA's more helpful features.

Setting Up VBA's Security

Just like any application that includes VBA, there is a security issue that you need to know about. You can store macros inside CDR files, so that when you send that file to somebody else, they can use that macro. A typical macro may be one that remembers the selected shapes when you close a document and then reselects those shapes when somebody else opens the document.

It doesn't take a genius to see that this can be a very useful feature, but that it can also be a risky one. It is not hard to write a small macro that deletes the user's hard disk when he or she opens a .CDR file. However, you can set up CorelDRAW so that it is *not* possible to run a document-macro without your consent, which is what we are going to do.

The first thing to do is to open the VBA Editor by choosing Tools | Visual Basic | Visual Basic Editor, or pressing ALT+F11. And close it again! This loads VBA into CorelDRAW—it is only loaded into memory when you first use it in that session, to keep your RAM clear. Now, in CorelDRAW, open the Options dialog at the VBA page, by choosing Tools | Options | Workspace | VBA, shown here:

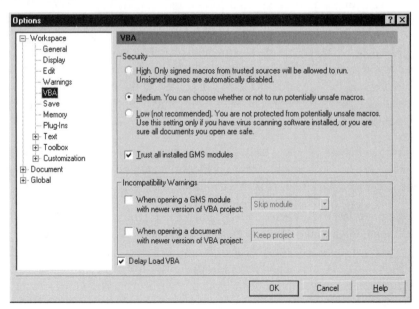

There are three sections: Security, Compatibility, and Loading. Whenever you try to open a CorelDRAW file that contains a macro, you will be asked specifically whether you want to load that macro into VBA, even if you created the macro. If you know what the macros are and who wrote them, and you *trust* them, click Enable Macros. However, if there is *any* question over the macros, you should disable them. If the macros are digitally signed by the author, you can examine the trustworthiness certificate, which is like a public declaration of trustworthiness, and includes the name and address of the signer. If you do trust them, you can enable the macros; if not, then disable them.

We work on the basic assumption that nothing will install into the \Draw\ GMS\ folder without our permission, so we give trust to those .GMS files that we install ourselves. If you clear the Trust All Installed GMS Modules check box, every time VBA is loaded, you will be asked whether you trust each .GMS file in the GMS folder. The only .GMS file not to be queried is the Draw\ CorelDRAW10.gms file, which is the default file.

Compatibility is about opening newer versions of installed macros. By default, the installed macros take precedence over any newer versions. This discourages newer modules from "hijacking" older ones and usurping your own code. Leave these as they are set in this safe state; you probably won't encounter these conditions in real life—but if you do, you will be safe.

VBA is another program and requires its own RAM and resources to run. To start VBA takes time. The Delay Load option enables you to set when VBA loads, which affects both how quickly CorelDRAW starts and whether your workflow will be interrupted by a few seconds. When Delay Load is checked, VBA will *not* be loaded into memory until you first use a VBA feature or run a macro. When the option is cleared, VBA will be loaded when CorelDRAW starts. If you know that you use VBA every time you start CorelDRAW, you might as well clear this check box; otherwise, leave it checked.

Setting Up the VBA Editor

There is just one thing to do to set up the VBA Editor: Go to Tools | Options; and on the Editor page only, put a check mark next to everything and set the tab size to 4. Leave the other Options pages alone, although you can change the Editor's font on the Editor Format page.

Developing Advanced Macros from Recordings

You can write macros from the ground up, or you can record approximately what you require and modify it later. The former method is for experienced programmers only, but results in a better program. The latter method is what we are going to look at here, as it requires far less knowledge beforehand.

First, we are going to look through the code that we recorded a few sections ago. Then we are going to optimize the RedFill_BlueOutline macro. Finally, we are going to create an advanced macro, using the optimized RedFill_BlueOutline as a basis. This advanced macro will apply the fill and outline to the selected objects. However, it will only apply the fill to those objects that have a fill already, and the outline to those objects that have an outline. This will demonstrate where programming really does have the power above either styles, or Find and Replace in CorelDRAW.

Analyzing DrawRectangle

In the VBA Editor, open the Project Explorer and navigate to the module RecordedMacros in the project RecordedMacros_Project. Double-click the module to open it. You should be presented with the following code. (Note that the underscore character is used to break the penultimate line to fit within this book's width, and this is valid in Visual Basic also.)

```
Option Explicit
Sub DrawRectangle()
    '
    ' Recorded 07/10/2000
    '
    ' Description:
    '                Tutorial: Recording a rectangle
    '
    Dim s1 As Shape
    Set s1 = ActiveLayer.CreateRectangle(2.855898, 7.018898, _
        4.978016, 5.764386, 0, 0, 0, 0)
End Sub
```

The various lines have the following meanings:

- **Option Explicit** Don't worry about this—just leave it wherever you see it.

- **Sub DrawRectangle()**   Do you recognize this? That's the name that you gave your macro. The word `Sub` tells VBA that this is the beginning of a subroutine, colloquially called a macro. The parentheses here are empty, but sometimes they have stuff inside.

- **'**   That's right—an apostrophe! Wherever you put an apostrophe, VBA completely ignores the rest of the text on the line after the apostrophe. The apostrophe is an abbreviation for `REM`, which is the BASIC statement for Remark, or comment. All that green stuff is just commentary.

- **Dim s1 As Shape**   `Dim` is short for dimension; and it reserves enough space in memory for the variable called `s1`, which is of type `Shape`. *Variables* are containers for something that is not known until the program is running. For example, if you ask the user his or her name, you won't know the result until the program is run and asks the question, and you store the answer in a *string* or text variable. Your program then handles the variable's contents as if they were hard-coded into the program.

- Variables of type `Shape` are not shapes in themselves; they are a reference to a shape. Think of it like a shortcut in Windows to the CorelDRAW .EXE file: You can have many shortcuts (references) to the same .EXE file, but they are all forward links. The CorelDRAW .EXE file knows nothing of the shortcuts until one of them passes a command along the reference. `Shape` variables are the same: The shape that `s1` later refers to is not bound to `s1`; `s1` is merely a forward reference to that shape.

- **Set s1 = ActiveLayer.CreateRectangle...**   This is the interesting part—this creates the rectangle. The first four parameters are the left, top, right, and bottom coordinates of the rectangle, in inches from the bottom-left corner of the page. The last four parameters are the corner roundness of the four corners. You use `Set` each time the reference is changed from one shape to a different shape.

- **End Sub**   This closes the sub again and control passes back to the object that called the sub, which could be VBA, CorelDRAW, or another sub or function. It basically tells VBA, to "stop here." It is mandatory to end something that you have started, including subs and functions.

29

Words in blue are *reserved keywords*, which are special to VBA; you cannot use these words as variable or procedure names. Words in green are comments or remarks; VBA ignores these completely. Words in red are lines with syntax errors—VBA hasn't got a clue what you are talking about! All other words are in black.

The important things to note are as follows:

- Recorded macros are created as enclosed subs, starting with a Sub statement and ending with an End Sub statement.

- Variables are dimensioned before you use them.

- You use Set to set a variable to reference that object. If the variable is a simple variable—that is, it just holds a number or a string (text) and not a reference to another object—you do not need the Set statement.

Analyzing DrawEllipse

The DrawEllipse macro looks very similar to the DrawRectangle macro:

```
Sub DrawEllipse()
    '
    ' Recorded 07/10/2000
    '
    ' Description:
    '                 Tutorial: Recording an ellipse
    '
    Dim s2 As Shape
    Set s2 = ActiveLayer.CreateEllipse(2.543516, 7.829476, _
        4.683606, 5.689386, 90#, 90#, False)
End Sub
```

Apart from the .CreateEllipse method, this is identical to DrawRectangle. Just like the DrawRectangle method, the first four parameters define the left, top, right, and bottom edges of the ellipse, in inches from the bottom-left corner of the page. The next two parameters are the start angle and the end angle of the ellipse— for creating pies or arcs. The hash symbol tells VBA that even though 90 is an integer, it must be thought of as a floating-point number (90.0). The last parameter is Boolean (either true or false). It tells CorelDRAW whether the ellipse is to be drawn as a pie (True) or an arc (False).

If you right-click CreateEllipse and select Quick Info, the definition for the CreateEllipse method is displayed, and you can see from the parameter names the meanings of each parameter.

If you have a look at the Layer class in the Object Browser, you will see that there are quite a few members of Layer that start with "Create." These are the basic VBA shape-creation procedures; so if you wanted a polygon, you would use .CreatePolygon, or some text, .CreateArtisticText. You could even offer users the option of what type of object they wanted to create.

Analyzing RedFill_BlueOutline

For this macro we recorded two distinct actions. Thus, the code is going to be longer and have more parts to it:

```
Sub RedFill_BlueOutline()
    '
    ' Recorded 08/10/2000
    '
    ' Description:
    '                   Tutorial: Applying a fill and outline
    '
    Dim ss3 As Shape
    Set ss3 = ActiveSelection.Shapes(1)
    ss3.Fill.UniformColor.RGBAssign 255, 0, 0
    ss3.Outline.SetProperties 0.041665, OutlineStyles(0), _
        CreateRGBColor(0, 0, 255), ArrowHeads(0), _
        ArrowHeads(0), False, False, cdrOutlineButtLineCaps, _
        cdrOutlineMiterLineJoin, 0#, 100
End Sub
```

That .Outline line is a very long one and I have used VBA's break-line character to make it all fit on the page.

NOTE *At the time of this writing, the CorelDRAW Type disallows OutlineStyles(0). When you run this code, you will get the error "Value is out of range." If you change it to OutlineStyles(1), the error goes away; but the outline is now a short-dash style. This is likely to be modified in a future Service Pack from Corel. This workaround enables you to use this common command. The simplified version of this line—later in this section—specifies the procedure.*

In the previous examples, a reference has been set to the created object, but it has not been used. In this example, the reference is set to the object ActiveSelection, which is the selected object in the active window. But it's more than that: One member of ActiveSelection is the shapes that are selected. There may be no objects selected, or there may be 100. The last shape selected is always number one, or ActiveSelection.Shapes(1). The first-selected is always (in shorthand notation) .Shapes(.Shapes.Count).

Anyway, the two important lines in the preceding code are the Fill and Outline lines. Since a fill is a property of a shape, as is an outline, we reference both the fill and the outline by using dot notation. For the fill, first we reference the shape ss3's fill as ss3.Fill. Then we reference the fill's own member .UniformColor, and its member function .RGBAssign. This cascade of member references is written in one line: ss3.Fill.UniformColor.RGBAssign, and the parameters at the end are used by the .RGBAssign function (in RGB terms, 100 percent Red (0–255) and no Green or Blue).

On the other hand, to set the outline, we not only have to set the outline color, we also have to set the width. The member that the VBA Recorder chose to use is long. It chose this because the Outline dialog was used to set the outline. If the Property Bar and color palette had been used, there would have been an extra line setting the color first and then the same long-winded .Outline.SetProperties member.

It is an unfortunate aspect of the VBA Recorder that it is not very efficient, as seen with the large outline member. We only want to change the width, but the VBA Recorder recorded us changing everything about the outline. Consider if we had recorded several outline changes on the Property Bar, where each change would be recorded as a separate action—all of the outline properties could be set three or four times over. If we did this for tens or hundreds of objects, CorelDRAW would take quite some time to apply the settings. This is where it is much more efficient to write code by hand. A much more efficient version of RedFill_ BlueOutline could be as follows:

```
Sub RedFill_BlueOutline()
    Dim ss3 As Shape
    Set ss3 = ActiveSelection.Shapes(1)
    ss3.Fill.UniformColor.RGBAssign 255, 0, 0
    ss3.Outline.Color.RGBAssign 0, 0, 255
    ss3.Outline.Width = 0.041665
End Sub
```

This is far simpler to read and is quicker for VBA and CorelDRAW to execute. The next problem, though, is that the outline width is given in inches, despite our specifying points. This is because CorelDRAW's default document units in

VBA are inches. To set the units to points, you have to insert the following line before setting the outline width:

```
ActiveDocument.Unit = cdrPoint
```

and follow that with

```
ss3.Outline.Width = 3.0
```

But be careful if you are also drawing shapes that were recorded in inches—or they will be much smaller than you were expecting (1/72). Note that the decimal 3.0 is different in VBA from an integer 3: When VBA sees 3.0 it will type-cast it as a floating-point or decimal number, called a Double. If you had just put 3, VBA would cast it as an integer-number type, probably a Long. Since Width is measured as a floating-point number, passing a Long-type number to it will generate an error. You could also have written: 3#, or CDbl(3), which both explicitly force the number to be cast as a Double type.

CorelDRAW supports lots of different units, including feet, millimeters, centimeters, meters, points, pixels, and pica. When you type the line in the preceding code into VBA, as soon as you type the equal sign, a pop-up list will appear populated with all the available units. Click one, or select it with the arrow keys, and then press TAB or SPACE.

Extending RedFill_BlueOutline

We are going to take our basic RedFill_BlueOutline procedure and add some extra code so that the fill is applied to the selected shapes that already have fills, and the outline is applied to the selected shapes that already have outlines. In order to do this, we have to introduce two fundamental programming methods: the loop and the decision.

But first, we have to introduce a very powerful feature in VBA: the Collection.

Collections

VBA provides the programmer with a strong method of handling many similar objects as one object, and it's called a Collection. Let's say that you have ten shapes selected in CorelDRAW and you run a script that starts like this:

```
Dim sShapes as Shapes
Set sShapes = ActiveSelection.Shapes
```

We have dimensioned the variable Shapes as type Shapes. It just so happens that the Shapes type is a type of collection of shapes. Think of it as a container that can hold many references to similar objects. Now, the type Shape (singular) basically means anything drawn in CorelDRAW, so the collection of Shapes contains lots of references to shape—that is, to things drawn in CorelDRAW.

This may seem pointless, but the beauty of it is this: Once we have set a reference to a collection of shapes, we can reference each shape in the collection individually using a loop, which is what we will do next. The other big advantage is that you do *not* need to know the size of the collection at any time; VBA does all of that for you. If the user doesn't select anything, you will just get a collection whose members number zero. And if the user selects a thousand objects, you will get one selection of a thousand shapes. The rather tiresome chore of always having to know exactly how many shapes are selected has been taken over by VBA, and you can get on with some clever coding.

Looping

A loop is a piece of code that is run, and run again, and rerun until a condition is met, or a counter runs out (which is the same thing). The most useful loop to us is the For-Next loop, of which there are two types: basic For-Next and For-Each-Next.

The basic For-Next loop could look something like this:

```
Dim lCount as long
For lCount = 1 To 10
    MsgBox "Number" & lCount
Next lCount
```

This just counts from one to ten, displaying a message box for each number.

The For-Each-Next loop comes into its own when dealing with collections, though. The purpose of a collection is to allow us to reference the collection without really knowing what's inside. Thus, to step through all the shapes in the collection, the following code is used.

 NOTE *This loop code is a fundamental algorithm when programming CorelDRAW. It is strongly recommended that you become very familiar with it, because you will doubtless need to use it often.*

```
Dim sShapes as Shapes, sShape as Shape
Set sShapes = ActiveSelection.Shapes
For Each sShape in sShapes
    ' We will add our own code into this loop
Next sShape
```

Note the `Dim` line: You can dimension more than one variable on a single line by separating them with a comma. With large modules that have tens of variables, this helps to keep the module length down.

This code simply loops through all of the shapes in the collection, and we can replace the remark line with our own code—as many lines as we need. Each time the For line is executed, `sShape` is set to the next shape in the collection. We can then access that shape's members within the loop by referencing `sShape`:

```
Dim sShapes as Shapes, sShape as Shape
Set sShapes = ActiveSelection.Shapes
For Each sShape in sShapes
    sShape.SizeWidth = 2
Next sShape
```

This now sets each shape's width to two inches, one at a time. This means that the size will be set with reference to only that shape, and not to the selection, so each shape will now be two inches wide; but the selection's width will still be approximately the same.

If we really wanted to, we could use the old, longhand version, which looks like this:

```
Dim sShapes As Shapes, sShape As Shape, lCount As Long
Set sShapes = ActiveSelection.Shapes
For lCount = 1 To sShapes.Count
    Set sShape = sShapes(lCount)
    sShape.SizeWidth = 2
Next lCountsShape
```

It's not much extra work, but it isn't as simple. Sometimes, however, the extra control offered by this harder method is necessary, but not often.

Now we are going to come to grips with making decisions, and then we are going to put loops and decisions together.

Decision Making—Conditionals

Decision making is what really sets programming apart from macros. Macros in their original sense are little pieces of "dumb code." Macros do not make decisions; they just perform a series of actions—originally keystrokes—without any understanding of what they are doing. As soon as you introduce decision making, the macro has turned into a program.

Decisions in VBA are made using the If-Then-Else construction: "If (something) is true Then do (this), Else do (that)." The conditional statement—the "something"—must be able to give the answer "true" or "false," but VBA is quite tolerant. For example, you could write

```
If MsgBox("Yes or No.", vbYesNo) = vbYes Then Beep
```

And as long as the Yes button is clicked, you will hear a beep. In this case, the conditional statement was true or false: The button clicked either *was* the Yes button, or else it was *not* the Yes button.

You don't have to have the statement all on one line, and usually you would not do so. Instead, you might present it more like this:

```
If sShape.Type = cdrEllipseShape Then
    MsgBox "Ellipse"
Else
    MsgBox "Something Else"
Endif
```

Just like most things in VBA—what is opened must be closed, so, don't forget to put in an Endif statement. If you do start to get strange errors, such as "Next without For," check that you have an Endif statement for all your If statements, unless the complete If statement is on a single line.

You can also string If statements together, and you can nest them too:

```
If sShape.Type = cdrEllipseShape Then
    MsgBox "Ellipse"
ElseIf sShape.Type = cdrRectangleShape Then
    MsgBox "Rectangle"
ElseIf sShape.Type = cdrTextShape Then
    If sShape.Text.Type = cdrArtisticText Or _
            sShape.Text.Type = cdrArtisticFittedText Then
        MsgBox "Artistic Text"
    Else
        MsgBox "Paragraph Text"
    End If
Else
    MsgBox "Something Else"
End If
```

VBA works through each If statement, starting at the first one. If it evaluates to True, the statement's instructions are carried out; otherwise, control passes to the next If statement. If one does evaluate to True, once its instructions are completed, control passes to the line after that If's Endif, and all the lines stepped over are ignored. The final Else is a catchall: It catches everything that doesn't fit elsewhere. You don't have to supply one if it's not necessary, but it is a good programming technique.

Notice also that you can use Boolean operators, such as And, Or, Not, and XOr, to combine results from two or more conditional statements. In the example in the preceding code, if the type is either Artistic Text or Fitted Artistic Text, the result will be true. The only other possible values for Text.Type are Paragraph Text and Fitted Paragraph Text.

Conditional Loops—Putting It All Together

Now, we know how to assign an outline and a fill (RedFill_BlueOutline), and we have looked at looping through collections (For-Each-Next). We also have a fairly good idea about decision making (If-Then-Else). The trick is to put all of this together so that we apply the fill and the outline based on whether each object already has a fill or not, or an outline or not.

Most of the code already exists for us in the previous code. The only missing part is a reliable decision-making routine for this particular instance. What we need to determine for each shape is

- **Does it have a fill?** If it does, then apply the new fill; else do nothing.

- **Does it have an outline?** If it does, apply the new outline; else do nothing.

Fortunately, determining an object's outline is simple: The Shape.Outline.Type property returns either cdrOutline or cdrNoOutline. All we have to do is ask whether the outline type is cdrOutline.

Determining whether a shape has a fill is slightly trickier: There are ten different fill types, including uniform, fountain, PostScript, pattern, and so on. So instead of asking, "does the shape have a fill?," and having to ask it for all the different types, it is easier to ask, "does the shape *not* have a fill?," and invert the answer, as in "is the shape's fill *not* of type cdrNoFill?" For this we use the greater-than and less-than symbols together, which means, "not equal to" in VBA.

29

Put all this together and here is what we get:

```
Sub Apply_RedFill_BlueOutline()
    Dim dDoc as Document
    Dim sShapes As Shapes, sShape As Shape
    Set dDoc = ActiveDocument
    dDoc.BeginCommandGroup "Apply Red Fill & Blue Outline"
    dDoc.Unit = cdrPoint
    Set sShapes = ActiveSelection.Shapes
    For Each sShape In sShapes
        If sShape.Fill.Type <> cdrNoFill Then
            sShape.Fill.UniformColor.RGBAssign 255, 0, 0
        End If
        If sShape.Outline.Type = cdrOutline Then
            sShape.Outline.Color.RGBAssign 0, 0, 255
            sShape.Outline.Width = 3
        End If
    Next sShape
    dDoc.EndCommandGroup
End Sub
```

This code steps through the collection of selected shapes, one at a time. It first asks, "Does shape have a fill type that is not cdrNoFill?" and applies the new fill if the condition is true. Then it asks "Does shape have an outline" and applies the new outline if it does.

I have added a little gem that crept into CorelDRAW 9: CommandGroup. The .BeginCommandGroup and .EndCommandGroup pair group all of the commands together into a single Undo statement in CorelDRAW, with the name that you specify. This is such a simple, professional touch that I could not resist introducing you to it now: If you select Undo after using this routine, even if it was applied to a thousand shapes, CorelDRAW will go right back to the state it was in before you ran it, in a single step. However, be warned: You must have an .EndCommandGroup. If you don't, you will be forced to close the document and open it before you can use Undo properly again, although you will be able to save before closing.

Alternatively, To Apply to All in One Go

There will be times when you don't need to apply formatting to each object in turn depending on that object's existing properties. You might want to unilaterally apply the new properties. For this, we need to go back and have a closer look at ActiveSelection:

1. Open the VBA Editor.

2. Launch the Object Browser.

3. Click the Application in the Classes pane.

4. Click the ActiveSelection in the Members pane.

5. Look at the definition in the bottom pane.

   The definition of ActiveSelection is given as

   ```
   Property ActiveSelection As Shape
   ```

   This means that ActiveSelection is a property of Application, and that its type is Shape. Now, look at the members of the Shape class.

6. Click the green Shape in the bottom pane.

7. Scroll through the members of Shape.

You should notice that Shape has all sorts of interesting members, including Fill and Outline. And we know that ActiveSelection is of type Shape, so it follows that ActiveSelection also has two properties—Fill and Outline. And it does. This makes it very simple to apply the fill and outline to all of the selected shapes in one easy go:

```
Sub Apply_RedFill_BlueOutline2()
    Dim dDoc as Document
    Dim Shape As Shape
    Set dDoc = ActiveDocument
    dDoc.BeginCommandGroup "Apply Red Fill & Blue Outline"
    dDoc.Unit = cdrPoint
    For Each sShape In ActiveSelection.Shapes
        sSelsShape.Fill.UniformColor.RGBAssign 255, 0, 0
        sSelsShape.Outline.Color.RGBAssign 0, 0, 255
        sSelsShape.Outline.Width = 3
    Next sShape
    dDoc.EndCommandGroup
End Sub
```

The preceding code is just a simple example of what can be done. You could easily modify the code to do something else, depending on what you are trying to do. The most important thing to understand is the process by which we got from a couple of very basic recorded macros to a very effective looped decision-making routine that adds intelligence to the macro to create a program.

Distributing Your Own VBA Macros

When you become confident in programming CorelDRAW with VBA, you will soon be asked to give or to sell your macros to other people. At this point you must consider how you actually go about distributing them.

There are a couple of methods for distributing macros. The only way you could do it in CorelDRAW 9 was to put the distribution macros into one or two modules, export those modules to your hard disk, and then instruct the user on how to import them into their own installation of CorelDRAW. This is because CorelDRAW 9's VBA only recognized a single .GMS ("Global Macros Storage") file. This still works in 10, but there is now a better way.

In CorelDRAW 10, it is possible to use more than one .GMS file. If you have installed the sample .GMS files from the accompanying CD-ROM, you will already know this. But it follows that you can use these .GMS files to organize your macros: Maybe you have a mini-application that consists of three or four forms, several modules, and a couple of class modules. You could place all of those into their own .GMS file and distribute just the one file, making it much simpler to install on another computer.

Creating New .GMS Files

The only method to create a new .GMS file is to copy a different one and remove all of the forms and modules from it. There isn't a New .GMS File command in CorelDRAW's VBA Editor.

The default CorelDRAW 10 installation has just one .GMS file—in the \Corel\Graphics10\Draw program folder there is a file called coreldraw10.gms. This is the basic .GMS file—*do not delete it or move it!* You can copy this file, though, and it can be the basis for any new .GMS files, if you wish.

All other .GMS files exist only in the \Corel\Graphics10\Draw\GMS folder. You can copy the coreldraw10.gms file into this folder and rename it. When you restart CorelDRAW, the .GMS project file will appear in the Project Explorer in the VBA Editor. Before doing anything else, in the Properties window, give the GMS project a new name! This will help you distinguish between .GMS files, although the filename is also given in parentheses after the project name.

You can remove all of the forms and modules from the copied .GMS file now, resulting in a blank, new .GMS file.

To help you, there is a blank .GMS file on the CD: It is called Empty GMS File.gms and has the project name Empty_GMS_File. Just copy this into the GMS folder, and rename it and give it a new project name in the Project Explorer. Now you can add your own code to it.

> **NOTE** *Every .GMS file must have a unique* project name, *as well as a unique* filename.

Installing .GMS Files

Distributing .GMS files is now a simple case of copying the .GMS file to another computer's \Corel\Graphics10\Draw\GMS folder and restarting CorelDRAW on that computer. When it starts up, VBA will recognize and load the new .GMS file. It's that simple!

To go one step further, if you have customized your workspace to add new toolbars and buttons with icons to access your macros, you can export those toolbars from your computer and import them onto your client's computer so that they can share your interface experience.

> **NOTE** *The more GMS projects that VBA has to manage, the slower it gets and the more resources it uses. However, the performance loss is tiny on today's computers and you won't notice much difference until you start installing 20 or more .GMS files on one computer. Just don't create too many, and you will be okay.*

Example Macros

If you installed all the .GMS project files from the CD-ROM, you should have one called CDR10_TOG (CorelDRAW10-TOG.gms). If you expand the project in the Project Explorer, you will see that there are six or seven forms (dialogs), eight or nine modules, and a class module.

Open the module called MiscellaneousModule. In it you will find quite a few small and large macros that you might find useful. You are free to use them yourself, but you are not allowed to distribute them. But they also help to illustrate how to use VBA to do different things in CorelDRAW, and you should see them as an opportunity to discover and learn. All of the code is fully commented, so you can read through the code and understand what is going on.

One topic that has not been covered in this chapter is that of designing interfaces or forms (dialog boxes). This is because forms are a VBA topic, not a CorelDRAW one. However, you will find that many of the examples in this .GMS file do have their own forms, and you can use these as guidance on how to go

29

about constructing your own. As for designing forms: Look at the forms in this project, as well as software from other companies, and then see if you can do something similar.

One of the things you should see in most of the macros is that they each solve a particular problem with CorelDRAW. Some of the problems are minor, others are omissions, and others are bug fixes. The important thing to realize is that VBA is powerful enough to enable individuals to provide themselves with solutions instead of waiting for Corel's own bug fixes to come down through the system.

SetPageBgColor( )

SetPageBgColor( ) simply changes the background color of all the pages in the document. It is very simple: It uses the Document.BeginCommandGroup and .EndCommandGroup methods to set the Undo string. After running this macro, have a look at the Edit menu in CorelDRAW, and you will see that it reads "Set Page Background Color." This is a very useful method to remember. If you do a hundred things in your macro, but it's all in a CommandGroup, selecting Undo in CorelDRAW will undo all one hundred actions in one go! This simplifies the user experience, and your users will be very impressed.

The actual page-color command is straightforward and almost self-explanatory: The color is changed to CMYK 15 percent yellow—a color that is useful when creating black-and-white line art, although not much else. But you could change this to whatever you wanted. And, in case you were wondering, the page background color doesn't print unless you specifically tell it to, so it acts as an onscreen aid.

This is a workaround to compensate for CorelDRAW, because the new-document template for CorelDRAW does not store the background color. Normally, if the users want to apply a background color to each document, they must go into the Options dialog and set a color there. This takes at least seven mouse clicks, plus users must select the color each time, which is slow. In addition, there's often the risk of selecting a similar color, but not the exact one that was required.

SetPageBgColor( ) can be assigned to a Toolbar in CorelDRAW, so that one click will change the page color to the exact one required with no time-consuming interaction with color lists. This was not possible in CorelDRAW 9, and it's a welcome addition.

CycleViewQuality( )

CycleViewQuality( ) cycles the screen view quality from Enhanced to Draft to Wireframe and back to Enhanced. A problem with CorelDRAW is trying to get the Toggle View command to toggle between the correct views, and then saving that setting for next time. With CycleViewQuality( ), you can choose the view qualities and choose how many of them to cycle through.

CycleViewQuality( ) uses the ActiveWindow.ActiveView object first to determine the current view quality and then, using an If-Then-Else construction, applies the next view quality in the sequence. If one of the noncycling view qualities is manually chosen, this will jump back to Enhanced before continuing with the cycle.

CreateInchCircle( )

CreateInchCircle( ) is a simple macro that demonstrates a very useful method with VBA: doing things at the center of the *screen* instead of the center of the *page*. The necessary properties, ActiveWindow.ActiveView.OriginX and .OriginY are new to CorelDRAW 10.

CreateInchCircle( ) creates a one-inch circle at the center of the screen. It uses the new .CreateEllipse2 member function, which creates an ellipse based on its center point and its radii (or just a single radius if it's a circle). The center point coordinates are set the same as the window view, so the circle is created right in front of you. This means you don't have to start scrolling around the drawing, trying to find the shape you just created.

PasteCenterWindow( )

Also by using the ActiveWindow.ActiveView.OriginX and .OriginY properties, PasteCenterWindow( ) simply pastes whatever is on the Clipboard at the center of the window, instead of the center of the page. This means that you won't have to go hunting for whatever you pasted somewhere else in the drawing when you are zoomed right in on the page.

Look closely at how the center-to-window routine works: The .Paste member function returns a shape to the calling object, and you can reference that shape directly by tagging the .SetPosition command onto the end.

PowerClipToLastShape( )

PowerClipToLastShape( ) is an exercise in using ShapeRange objects. A *shape range* is a collection of shapes that you control. Unlike a Selection-type shape, a shape range does not select the objects in CorelDRAW. Instead, you can create a collection of shapes, step through them, and manipulate them without changing the ActiveSelection. The two big advantages of this are that you can provide users with unique levels of control because you can do things for them without losing their selections, and it is much quicker to process a large shape range than it is to process a large Selection object.

PasteIntoPowerClip( )

The only reason PasteIntoPowerClip( ) is here is that I remember back to when I used to use a Macintosh. With the Mac, the normal method of pasting objects into other objects, known as PowerClipping in CorelDRAW, is to copy the shapes that are going inside to the Clipboard, select the shape that is to contain them, and then "Paste Inside." This code emulates that functionality.

Basically, this code is the same as the one before, but the content's shapes are selected in a different manner. This demonstrates how to use Layer.Paste.

DummyText( )

DummyText( ) will fill the currently selected Paragraph Frame and fill it with dummy, or fake, text. Two different texts are used, the classic "Lorem Ipsum" text beloved of desktop publishing applications, and "Corporate Mumbo Jumbo." This macro is extremely useful when creating a template design. You fill your text blocks with dummy text, and then you can set up the text styles and content layout before you have to use it with real text.

This routine demonstrates how to handle text. Unfortunately, though, the text object is not as advanced as some, so it's not a very fast routine or as clever as it could be.

> **NOTE** *There is a bug in the VBA Object Model somewhere, and any text block longer than about 1,600 characters will cause an error—so only use this routine on small text blocks!*

CenterAlign( )

If you are familiar with customizing CorelDRAW, you should check the available Alignment commands. There are quite a lot of them, but the one that is missing is AlignToCenters. This is a very simple macro that does just that: aligns the selected shapes to the center of the last-selected shape.

To add a little twist to the code, I added a call to one of a group of useful functions in the project, GetShiftState( ), which returns true or false depending on whether the SHIFT key is pressed. If SHIFT is not pressed, the code aligns the shapes to the center of the last-selected shape. If SHIFT *is* pressed, the shapes are aligned to the center of the page.

The Align commands used in this code are members of CorelScript. CorelScript is steadily being deprecated in favor of the newer Object Model derived from Application.Document. However, there are no comparable methods in the new Object Model, so the old CorelScript ones still have to be used.

CenterAlignWindow( )

This is a twist on the earlier macro, but this time, the selected shapes are centered on the active *window*, not the *page*. Press SHIFT at the same time and the window is centered on the *selection*, much like Zoom to Selection, except Pan to Selection instead.

DrawBézierHulls( )

This draws the hulls that define a Bézier curve. If you draw a curve with the Freehand Tool and then edit it with the Shape Tool, each curved segment between two nodes is defined by four points: two end nodes and two control points. The three straight lines that connect these four points are collectively called a *hull*. Think of it as a bounding path for a curve. Sometimes it is useful to be able to see this hull, and it can be used for extracting the precise node information for writing other macros.

DrawBézierNodeControlLines( )

This macro is a twist on DrawBézierHulls( ) in that, instead of drawing complete hulls as a single curve, it places a straight line at each curve-type node that goes from end to end of the control handle, stopping at the node in the middle. Again, it is useful for getting precise control-point information from a curve. This only creates control lines for the *selected* nodes.

CreateWebSafeColorTable( ) and CreateWebSafeColorPalette( )

These two routines create Web-safe color tables. One draws a table in the active document, and the other creates a new palette. They both use the same basic nested-loop code to create the colors. The table is created as 216 swatches of color. The palette is created as a single palette of 216 colors.

Web-safe colors are those RGB colors that are reliably rendered by all Web browsers, even in 256-color mode. For this reason, they are known as "safe."

Unfortunately, the Color.Name property is read-only, so the code is not able to name all the colors with the correct HTML name—maybe in CorelDRAW 11, but not yet.

29

Example Programs

There are a couple of quite complex programs—by VBA standards—on the CD-ROM, which you will have installed if you copied all of the .GMS files to your hard disk. These demonstrate many aspects of programming in VBA, as well as controlling CorelDRAW.

These are all real programs, some of them developed especially for this book. Some of them are more useful than others, and some people will get more from some than others, depending on what you use CorelDRAW for.

When you are stuck on how to do something, you should have a careful look through these examples. See if there is anything similar, and learn how to do it before going back and applying it to your own code.

Relative Transformer

A common complaint from CorelDRAW users is that whenever you apply a transformation to a selection of objects, the transformation is applied to the selection as if it were a group. There is no option to apply the transformation to each shape about its own center point, or bottom-left corner, or whatever. This is where Relative Transformer steps in.

The whole of Relative Transformer is contained in its own project, called Relative Transformer. To start Relative Transformer, run the sub RelativeTransformer( ) in the module LaunchModule within the project. This will launch Relative Transformer as a modeless or nonmodal window—while it is open you will still be able to select shapes and do other things in CorelDRAW. The Relative Transformer form is shown here:

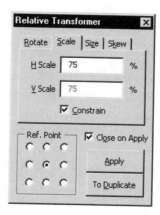

Relative Transformer is an excellent example of what is required of consumer software: a good, simple interface; "remembered" settings; and usability. Subtle features are included, such as, if you click the units labels, they toggle between inches and millimeters. Most of the controls in the dialog have ToolTips, which explain their function.

When browsing through the code, pay particular attention to the Initialize and SaveSettings procedures. All of the settings are stored in an INI file that is stored with the user's workspaces.

> **NOTE** *Relative Transformer is completely encapsulated within the RelativeTransformer.gms project file.*

Backup Killer

Backup Killer is a usable fix for those "Backup_of_" backup .CDR files that litter your hard disk. This program will move or rename those backup files so that your hard disk is organized, but you still have the backup files to go back to.

Backup Killer relies on events to work. In VBA, certain CorelDRAW events can be used to run procedures. The events used here are called AfterSave and AfterSaveAs. Every time you save a CorelDRAW document, VBA will look in all the project files in the ThisDocument module and will run any procedures that match the event—in this case, GlobalDocument_AfterSave( ) and GlobalDocument_AfterSaveAs( ).

The parameter for these procedures contains the path and name of the file being saved. Backup Killer then checks in the same folder for a file with the same name, but with "Backup_of_" prefixed to it. If it finds such a file, it renames or moves the file.

The user can configure Backup Killer by running the BackupKiller_Options( ) sub. All of the settings for Backup Killer are stored in the Registry using VBA's SaveSetting( ) and GetSetting( ) functions.

> **NOTE** *Backup Killer is entirely encapsulated in the BackupKiller10.gms project file.*

Crop Marker

One thing that CorelDRAW doesn't have built in is a method for adding crop marks to specific shapes on the page. Crop Marker solves that problem. You can select a shape or many shapes in CorelDRAW and add crop marks to each of

29

them, or to the selection as a whole. You can set the width, length, and standoff of the crop marks, as well as a margin distance—even negative values in order to provide a bleed area. The user can include or exclude center marks, useful for folding, and registration marks. Crop Marker, shown next, is a very usable tool.

Crop Marker stores its settings in an .INI file. It uses the class module clsINIFile to access the .INI file, and this module is available for you to use as well.

 Crop Marker is stored in the CorelDRAW10_TOG.gms project file. To launch Crop Marker, run the CropMarker( ) sub in FormLoaderModule.

Butt Shapes Up

Butt Shapes Up provides a function that should be built into CorelDRAW's Align and Distribute dialog—the ability to place objects edge to edge either horizontally or vertically. Furthermore, Butt Shapes Up can also be used to position shapes' centers, or edges, a certain distance apart.

To butt shapes up to each other horizontally, run the ButtShapesUpHorizontally( ) procedure in the ButtShapesUpModule in the CDR10_TOG project. To butt vertically, use ButtShapesUpVertically( ). Either type of butt only works in one direction; so if you apply a horizontal butt, the vertical positions of the shapes will not be changed, only their horizontal positions—and vice versa.

To apply a spacing to the butt, run ButtShapesUpWithGap( ), which opens the following dialog:

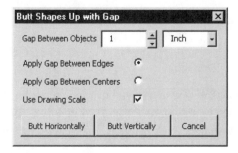

All three operations use the same core code, which includes a simple sort routine, as well as some good examples of arrays of variables in action.

New From Template

The New From Template command is much improved in CorelDRAW 10. However, it still relies on either the fixed folders designated by Corel, or on a single other folder that you can navigate to. While this is only a small problem, in that you may have to browse through a few folders to find the exact template you were looking for, it is still worthy of an alternative, such as this.

New From Template must be configured for the particular templates you use regularly. When you launch New From Template for the first time, you are faced with the New-From-Template Editor, as shown here:

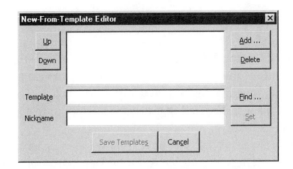

Click the Add button to add your own templates to the list. Give the template a nickname, which will appear in the lists, and click Set to save it to the list. When you have chosen all your templates, click Save Templates to save the list to the .INI file. This will take you to the New From Template dialog:

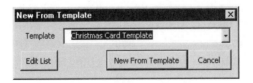

Now that the list is populated, each time you start New From Template, you will only see the dialog, not the editor. Thus, if you are spending a week creating drawings from just one template, you need only select that template on day one, and each subsequent time you start New From Template, you only need to press ENTER to create another new document from that template.

29

New From Template is stored in the CDR10_TOG GMS project. To launch it, run the NewFrameTemplateNewFromTemplate( ) sub in the FormLoaderModule.

Sine Waver

CorelDRAW cannot draw mathematical curves on its own; it needs a bit of assistance. Also, you cannot use a simple Bézier curve to model a sine wave, so you must use short lines to approximate a sine curve. This macro asks for the dimensions of the curve and the number of cycles before creating it.

To run the code, run SineWaver( ) from the FormLoaderModule in the CDR10_GMS project.

Where to Next?

As already mentioned, using VBA and CorelDRAW is a huge topic that extends well outside the limits of this book. You should already have a good understanding of how to record your own macros and how to play them back. That in itself should be quite useful. But also understand that there is a lot more that you can do than just record a few keystrokes.

There are two main areas that you have to develop in order to become a master of programming CorelDRAW with VBA: on the one hand CorelDRAW's Object Model, and on the other VBA. I have only touched upon the topic of VBA here. You will find a lot of information about all of the VBA Editor and command syntax in the VBA help files. Likewise, CorelDRAW's help files contain plenty of help, and the Object Browser is also a great place to go.

The basics of extending a macro have been covered: The most useful two programming fundamentals to enhancing a macro for CorelDRAW are the loop and the decision. Yes, there is much I could say about lots of other interesting and powerful algorithms, but they are less about CorelDRAW and more about VBA. If you want more information about these, it's time to seek external help.

Newsgroups

Corel runs a large number of support newsgroups for their products. You can find details of the newsgroups at on their Web site at **http://www.corel.com**. Navigate to the Support area and follow the instructions for getting access to the newsgroups.

One newsgroup, or maybe two by the time you read this, is dedicated to programming CorelDRAW. It is called corelsupport.draw-script. You can seek help freely on the newsgroups and there are always plenty of people, both Corel employees and private users, ready to assist in any way they can.

Corel Web Sites

Corel has several different Web sites. The most useful for articles on programming CorelDRAW is Designer.com at **http://www.designer.com**. Besides articles on programming, there are free macros and code samples, and lots of other information about CorelDRAW.

Visual Basic Web Sites

There are many excellent Web sites with information on how to program with Visual Basic, and some to do with Visual Basic for Applications. Since VBA is a cut-down version of Visual Basic, you can use the Visual Basic Web sites as an excellent learning resource, bearing in mind that some of the more advanced programming features are not available to you, but everything else is.

To find good Web sites, use an Internet search engine to locate a few VB sites and browse them. Check the links pages of the better sites, and you will immediately be browsing through some of the best VB material out there: The best Web sites only link to other good sites, so find a good one and stick with it.

29

PART VIII

Appendix

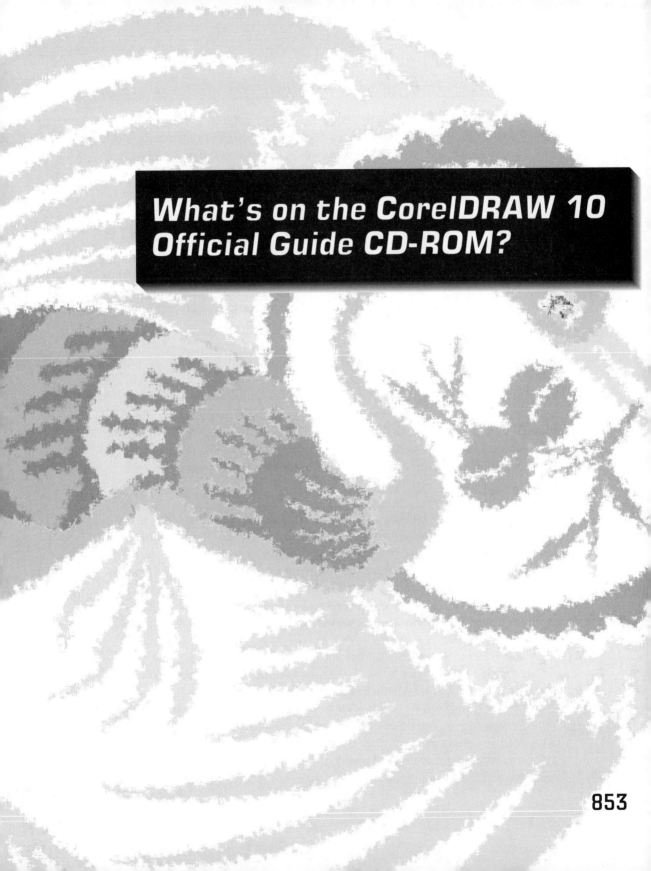

What's on the CorelDRAW 10 Official Guide CD-ROM?

The CD-ROM accompanying this book includes a wealth of CorelDRAW 10–related resources and software aimed at extending your learning experience with the application and providing support for certain chapters. You'll discover everything from images to special electronic document chapters.

CorelDRAW 10: The Official Guide Resources

The CD-ROM includes an enormous collection of learning resources for use with your CorelDRAW 10 application. You'll find bitmap frames, clip art, digital photos, animated GIFs, custom brushes and spray lists, and preformatted document templates to help you on your way as you work through the chapters and refine your CorelDRAW design and illustration skills.

Resources

Inside the Resources folder are seven individual folders containing a variety of resources courtesy of Corel and Designer.com, which regularly offer CorelDRAW-related resources free for the downloading. In addition to the following resource files, check out Designer.com either from the link within your CorelDRAW 10 Welcome Screen while online or on the Web (**www.designer.com**). In the meantime, take advantage of these excellent learning resources as follows.

Brushes   In the Brushes folder, you'll find a collection of images stored in CMX format and designed to be used as brushes in combination with CorelDRAW 10's Artistic Media tool. For these images to be available as brushes in your CorelDRAW 10 application, copy the files from this folder into your *Drive Letter*:Program Files\Corel\Graphics10\Draw\CustomMediaStrokes folder (where *Drive Letter* represents your local hard drive). After copying, these brushes will be available from the Brush List selector while Brush is selected as your Artistic Media Tool mode.

Spray Lists   In the Spray Lists folder, you'll find a collection of images stored in CDR format and designed to be used as Sprayer images in combination with CorelDRAW 10's Artistic Media Tool. For these images to be available as Sprayer styles in your CorelDRAW 10 application, copy the files from this folder into your *Drive Letter*:Program Files\Corel\Graphics10\Draw\CustomMediaStrokes folder (where *Drive Letter* represents your local hard drive). After copying, these Sprayer styles will be available from the Spray List selector when Sprayer is selected as your Artistic Media Tool mode.

Templates   In the Templates folder, you'll find a collection of document styles stored in CorelDRAW Template (CDT) format and designed to be used with or without their content as document templates. To open a document template in this folder from CorelDRAW 10, choose File | New From Template to open the New From Template dialog, and click the Browse tab. Use the Browse features in this tab to navigate to this folder, and click to select a file. When a file is selected, the dialog preview window displays a representation of the template.

Bitmap Frames   This folder contains an assortment of bitmap frames in Corel PHOTO-PAINT (CPT) file format. Bitmap frames are designed to be used specifically with Corel PHOTO-PAINT. To use the bitmap frames in this folder with your Corel PHOTO-PAINT 10 application, copy the files to your Program Files\Corel\Graphics10\Custom\Frames folder. Once copied, the effects of these custom bitmap frames may be applied using the Effects | Creative | Frames command to open the Frame dialog. Double-click the next available frame box in the Select Frame list to open the Load Frame File dialog, click to select a bitmap frame image, and click OK to close the dialog. Once selected, you may use dialog options to customize the frame effect or click OK to accept the settings and close the dialog.

Clip Art   In this folder, you'll find a range of clip art stored in both CorelDRAW native file format (CDR) and Corel Presentation format (CMX). Either file type may be opened (choose File | Open) or imported (choose File | Import), either as new documents or into existing documents, respectively.

Photos   An assortment of digital images stored in JPG file format is available in this folder. Use the File | Import command to import the files directly into CorelDRAW 10, or use the File | Open command to view the files in Corel PHOTO-PAINT 10.

Animated GIFs   A brief collection of animated GIF images is available in this folder. Animated GIFs may be imported using the File | Import command from CorelDRAW 10 or viewed in Corel PHOTO-PAINT 10 using the File | Open command.

A

Chapter Examples

Specifically for when working in chapters, the Examples folder contains resources from three chapters depicting layering, transparency and lens effects, and VBA macros.

- ■ **Chapter 12**   In this folder, you'll find a CorelDRAW file containing an aircraft illustration saved with a layering structure using features available in the Object Manager. This image is used in Chapter 12 to illustrate the use of structuring an illustration in layers.

- ■ **Chapter 16**   This folder contains 12 CorelDRAW files to support Chapter 16, with each file illustrating specific effects. These images, depicted in the chapter itself, appear on pages 1 to 7 of the color section of this book. To view the effects, use the File | Open command from CorelDRAW 10 to open each of the files.

- ■ **Chapter 29**   This folder contains VBA macros in support of Chapter 29. For instructions on installing macros, see the section "Example Macros" in Chapter 29.

Electronic Document Chapters

Six additional chapters are only available on the CD-ROM. They have been prepared in Adobe Portable Document Format (PDF), providing detailed reference information on working with text and applying color fills and outlines. To view the files, you'll need to have Adobe Acrobat 4 installed on your system. The most recent version of Adobe Acrobat Reader for Windows 98 is provided in the folder Adobe Acrobat Reader 4. If you require a different or more specific version, you may download the software free of charge from Adobe's Web site (**www.adobe.com/products/acrobat**). Electronic document chapters are as follows:

- ■ CD-ROM 1: Mastering Text Properties
- ■ CD-ROM 2: Linking Text to Objects
- ■ CD-ROM 3: Resources for Perfect Writing
- ■ CD-ROM 4: Mastering Object Outline Properties
- ■ CD-ROM 5: Filling Objects with Color
- ■ CD-ROM 6: CorelDRAW 10's World of Color

IsoCalc

The IsoCalc folder contains trial evaluation software that may be used in combination with CorelDRAW 10, courtesy of our script master Nick Wilkinson. IsoCalc 3 is a plug-in-type application. With IsoCalc and CorelDRAW 10 you may create precise, complex, three-dimensional isometric illustrations for technical documentation or Web sites (or just for fun). Instead of using VBA, IsoCalc is written in full Visual Basic. This means that it's actually a stand-alone application, not strictly a plug-in, and it works with several versions of CorelDRAW at the same time. However, it uses all the same commands that you would use in VBA and demonstrates what's possible with a little application and a lot of math!

To install IsoCalc 3 from the CD, double-click the file isocalc306setup.exe. Follow the instructions given by the installer to choose a folder for installing IsoCalc. When installation is complete, the installer will close. To use IsoCalc 3 for the first time, launch it from the Windows Start Button menu, where it will be in \Programs\ IsoCalc.com folder. You will be asked which version of CorelDRAW you want to use IsoCalc with, and you should choose the version you are going to use. You can change versions later in IsoCalc's Options.

Tutorials for getting you started quickly in IsoCalc 3 and CorelDRAW 10 are available from the Help menu under Quick Start. You're well advised to work through at least the simple tutorials in order to familiarize yourself with IsoCalc, which is a complex illustration tool.

A

Index

859

How to Use This CD-ROM

The CD-ROM accompanying this book contains a wealth of CorelDRAW 10 resources organized into folders according to file type and subject matter.

To access these files, insert the CD-ROM into your CD drive. Refer to the Appendix earlier in the book for information about the folder contents and procedures that detail installation instructions for using the resource files with CorelDRAW 10. You'll also find instructions on installing trial software and accessing software for viewing the six additional chapters contained *only* on the CD-ROM and prepared in Adobe Acrobat portable document format (PDF).

WARNING: BEFORE OPENING THE DISC PACKAGE, CAREFULLY READ THE TERMS AND CONDITIONS OF THE FOLLOWING COPYRIGHT STATEMENT AND LIMITED CD-ROM WARRANTY.

Copyright Statement

This software is protected by both United States copyright law and international copyright treaty provision. Except as noted in the contents of the CD-ROM, you must treat this software just like a book. However, you may copy it into a computer to be used and you may make archival copies of the software for the sole purpose of backing up the software and protecting your investment from loss. By saying, "just like a book," The McGraw-Hill Companies, Inc. ("Osborne/McGraw-Hill") means, for example, that this software may be used by any number of people and may be freely moved from one computer location to another, so long as there is no possibility of its being used at one location or on one computer while it is being used at another. Just as a book cannot be read by two different people in two different places at the same time, neither can the software be used by two different people in two different places at the same time.

Limited Warranty

Osborne/McGraw-Hill warrants the physical compact disc enclosed herein to be free of defects in materials and workmanship for a period of sixty days from the purchase date. If the CD included in your book has defects in materials or workmanship, please call McGraw-Hill at 1-800-217-0059, 9am to 5pm, Monday through Friday, Eastern Standard Time, and McGraw-Hill will replace the defective disc.

The entire and exclusive liability and remedy for breach of this Limited Warranty shall be limited to replacement of the defective disc, and shall not include or extend to any claim for or right to cover any other damages, including but not limited to, loss of profit, data, or use of the software, or special incidental, or consequential damages or other similar claims, even if Osborne/McGraw-Hill has been specifically advised of the possibility of such damages. In no event will Osborne/McGraw-Hill's liability for any damages to you or any other person ever exceed the lower of the suggested list price or actual price paid for the license to use the software, regardless of any form of the claim.

OSBORNE/McGRAW-HILL SPECIFICALLY DISCLAIMS ALL OTHER WARRANTIES, EXPRESS OR IMPLIED, INCLUDING BUT NOT LIMITED TO, ANY IMPLIED WARRANTY OF MERCHANTABILITY OR FITNESS FOR A PARTICULAR PURPOSE. Specifically, Osborne/McGraw-Hill makes no representation or warranty that the software is fit for any particular purpose, and any implied warranty of merchantability is limited to the sixty-day duration of the Limited Warranty covering the physical disc only (and not the software), and is otherwise expressly and specifically disclaimed.

This limited warranty gives you specific legal rights; you may have others which may vary from state to state. Some states do not allow the exclusion of incidental or consequential damages, or the limitation on how long an implied warranty lasts, so some of the above may not apply to you.

This agreement constitutes the entire agreement between the parties relating to use of the Product. The terms of any purchase order shall have no effect on the terms of this Agreement. Failure of Osborne/McGraw-Hill to insist at any time on strict compliance with this Agreement shall not constitute a waiver of any rights under this Agreement. This Agreement shall be construed and governed in accordance with the laws of New York. If any provision of this Agreement is held to be contrary to law, that provision will be enforced to the maximum extent permissible, and the remaining provisions will remain in force and effect.

NO TECHNICAL SUPPORT IS PROVIDED WITH THIS CD-ROM.